APPLIED SOCIAL PSYCHOLOGY

A GLOBAL PERSPECTIVE

APPLIED SOCIAL PSYCHOLOGY

A GLOBAL PERSPECTIVE

V.K. Kool
Rita Agrawal

Published by

ATLANTIC

PUBLISHERS & DISTRIBUTORS (P) LTD

7/22, Ansari Road, Darya Ganj, New Delhi-110002
Phones : +91-11-40775252, 40775214, 23273880, 23275880
Fax : +91-11-23285873
Web : www.atlanticbooks.com
E-mail : orders@atlanticbooks.com

Printed & bound in India by Atlantic Print Services

PREFACE

While books on social psychology are available in plenty, there are unusually few that deal exclusively with the applied aspects of social psychology. One reason for this could be that even though the quest for developing hard-boiled, laboratory-based experiments has grown appreciably in the current literature, social psychology as applied to problems in the everyday world has not developed as fast. This unsavory situation poses a peculiar dilemma for social psychology, especially since many of its theories were evolved to explain the social dimensions of real world phenomena. We draw our readers' attention to the words of the famous social psychologist, Lewin, who advocated that a theory is not a good theory unless it has sensible applications. In short, a theory and its application must go arm-in-arm. Thus, knowledge regarding how social psychology can be applied has as much relevance as that on the basic principles of social psychology. In the following paragraphs, we would like to present to our readers, an overview of what encouraged us to write this book and how our book attempts to offer a different perspective from those written by others.

Firstly, a survey of textbooks that are available reveals that they seem to adopt a very myopic viewpoint, either focusing exclusively on Western situations and models, or tending to analyze only the regional perspective, and thereby confining themselves to the researches conducted on predominantly Western or regional samples only. A major goal of the present work is to collate the findings from both the East and the West and to seek interventions that helped in one culture, but were not necessarily applied to, or were applicable to, other cultures. It is hoped that in this sense at least, the readers will find the material in the present textbook not only unique, but also aimed at the global approach that social psychology must adopt, thereby demonstrating why its theories succeed or fail with variation in the socio-cultural context.

Secondly, if social psychology were the study of behavior, a book on Applied Social Psychology would not be considered complete without examining the impact of powerful sources that influence our social behavior. Let us take the two of the most dominant forces that influence our behavior: religion and technology. Regretfully, both areas are rarely mentioned in the textbooks on social psychology. The ways in which terrorism and other forms of violence are making an impact on our lives has also been ignored in many textbooks.

Moreover, reference to non-violence is almost completely missing in many books. This becomes more important when one realizes that violence and non-violence have different roots and meaning in the Eastern and Western societies.

Thirdly, most recent books on Applied Social Psychology seem to focus on conventional social domains, such as social psychology of environment, social psychology of physical health, social psychology of consumer behavior, etc. In our endeavor, we followed the same topics but added additional areas, such as those of technology, non-violence/aggression and religion, that have hitherto remained neglected in other similar books. We have attempted to relate material from one topic to another whenever it was possible and especially when making comparisons across regions or societies.

Finally, most available books fail to take into account recent international developments and issues. For example, how do we learn more about euthanasia in a global perspective? Issues concerning cloning, gene banks, selective breeding, etc. have global concerns, and their implications are not merely confined to the Western societies. Social change makes it imperative to continuously update and to envision problems in the years to come. As changes in technology occur, corresponding changes in attitudes and behavior lag behind, resulting in enormous behavioral issues that need to be studied, analyzed and intervened.

Overall, this book covers extensively and intensively, at least nine important areas of application: physical health, mental health, environment, law, consumer behavior, technology, religion, education, and aggression and non-violence. In each chapter, we have made an attempt to incorporate research from both the West and the East, so as to increase the level of universal applicability and thereby its appeal to readers around the globe. It is expected that besides undergraduate and postgraduate students who might use it as a textbook, researchers, and even practitioners, will find much of the material useful. It is also envisioned that when a book covers many spheres of life, both professionals and non-professionals from various walks of life would become interested in it.

In order to facilitate the assimilation of information and knowledge, various tools have been incorporated. Thus, there are small side boxes that point out new concepts and ideas. There are larger full and half page boxes providing supplementary material for those who want greater in-depth information. These boxes have also been used to provide examples for many of the concepts and principles explained in the text. The chapters also introduce the reader to a variety of psychometric measures for the concepts under consideration. Wherever possible, sample items have been provided so that the reader gets a more complete idea regarding the nature of the items used. Additionally, the key concepts covered in the text have been listed at the end of every chapter. For the interested reader, each chapter also ends with some suggestions for further reading.

The challenge that writers face, especially on topics of a global nature, is that access to material and its understanding may limit the coverage of the subject area and in some way even raise questions regarding the interpretation of facts. Consistent with Baumeister's statement that in social sciences while talk is cheap, the facts are few, we endorse this statement and hope that the reader will not view our writings from the "talk" side only—and rightfully so, as we tended to validate the material in the text with available research findings. However, if the facts available from the research studies are perceived as questionable, we do not intend to hold on to our views dogmatically and offer our sincere apologies in advance. After all said and done, it is also a bitter truth to swallow that our understanding of different cultures and societies is limited. The scenario humbles us even more when we find that besides differences between cultures and societies, each culture also varies over a period of time. Therefore, a uniform and tacit formulation from the available material, say, some belonging to a relatively older period of time and some not so old, becomes a challenging task. Generalizations, in such cases, are prone to misperception or even misjudgment. We request our readers to offer their feedback on such gray areas to enable us to make improvements in our future endeavors.

For the preparation of this book, we would like to thank all our colleagues and friends who read portions of this book and offered their comments. In particular, we would like to thank the students at the State University of New York, Institute of Technology, Utica, USA, who, while studying a course on Applied Social Psychology offered by one of us (V.K. Kool), submitted their critical comments, thereby improving the text in more ways than one. Last but not the least, we also thank Dr. K.R. Gupta, Chairman of Atlantic Publishers and Distributors (P) Ltd., for keeping his promise to bring out the book in a brilliant form and in record time.

V.K. Kool
Rita Agrawal

CONTENTS

AN INTRODUCTION TO APPLIED SOCIAL PSYCHOLOGY

1

Chapter Outline

- Social psychology as the study of social influence
  - Functions of social influence
- Social psychology as distinct from other social sciences
- Social psychology in its applied form
  - Towards a definition of applied social psychology : Major characteristics
  - Salient features of applied social psychology
- The global perspective of applied social psychology
- Applied social psychology, ethics and society
- The historical perspective of social psychology in the context of its applications
- Theoretical perspectives of social psychology
  - The social learning perspective
  - The phenomenological perspective
  - The social-cognitive perspective
  - The evolutionary perspective
- Evaluation research, interventions and social psychology
- Areas of applications of applied social psychology
  - Social psychology and physical health
  - Social psychology and mental health
  - Social psychology as applied to legal issues
  - Social psychology and religion
  - Social psychology of technology
  - Social psychology and environment
  - Social psychology and consumer behavior
  - Social psychology of aggression and non-violence
  - Social psychology of education

SOCIAL PSYCHOLOGY AS THE STUDY OF SOCIAL INFLUENCE

Let us begin by trying to understand what social psychology is. We normally think of social psychology as the scientific study of understanding and explaining how our behavior, feelings, emotions, thought processes, and beliefs are influenced by the presence of other people. Have you noticed how your behavior changes with the situation? While in your office, you may be sitting in an informal, casual way in the absence of your boss, but with his/her arrival in front of you, your posture changes. No wonder the physical distance between President Kennedy and his close associates increased with the announcement of the result of the Presidential election. Individuals as well as situations tend to influence our behavior, cognitions and feelings. This influence may or may not be necessarily caused by real people. This influence could be imaginary. Persuading people to buy merchandize is an example of real influence. On the other hand, children's behavior in fantasy is a good example of imaginary influence. After watching a violent character in a movie shown in a laboratory setting, young children, began to imitate the violent character when put into a free play situation (Bandura, Ross & Ross, 1961).

A study of the **influence mechanism**, a focal area of study in social psychology, is not an easy task. If you stand at a street corner and fix your gaze at the top of a tall building, people may react to you in several ways. Some may ignore you. Some others may ask you if they can join you in watching something unique in the building. Still others may ask you if you need any help. Does that not leave you wondering that though you had been minding your own business, and had not the least intention of influencing anyone, your behavior was influencing others? Not surprisingly, you find that your neighbors often have more information (with dates and time) about the visitors at your home than what you can recall about them! Whether you like it or not, people may become influenced by you even when there is absolutely no intention to influence them. At other times, you may be wanting to influence someone, but to no avail. Whether others are influenced or not, depends not just on the influencer, but also on who is being influenced. The late Professor Stanley Milgram (1974) conducted several interesting studies on the mechanism of influence both in real life and laboratory settings. A sample of his work is described in Box 1.1

BOX 1.1

How influence can lead to aggression in the laboratory:
Milgram's classic study on obedience to authority

In a classic, albeit controversial, experiment, Milgram (1964) clearly demonstrated the extent to which people can be influenced. This was done through a study on the effects of obedience to an authority figure. The participants (that is, the subjects) were told that this was an experiment on the study of the effect of punishment on learning. They were instructed that they would play the role of a teacher in the experiment and in this capacity, they were expected to teach a "student" (actually a confederate of the experimenter) a list of word pairs. Further, each subject was told that he must teach the "student" the words, by punishing him with increasing levels of electric shock, each time the learner gave a wrong answer. This "teacher" subject had before him a panel of switches ranging from 15 to 450 volts, the switches being labelled, "slight shock," "very strong shock," "danger," "severe shock," etc. With each wrong answer, the experimenter told the "teacher" to move to one higher level of shock. In reality, the learner (the confederate) did not receive any shock, and his pleas and the grunting, as a consequence of shocks, actually came from an attached tape recorder. But the "teacher" subject was made to believe that the shocks were actually being delivered to the learner.

Milgram described the above experiment to 110 psychiatrists, college students and middle class adults. People in all the three groups felt that they would disobey by about 135 volts, and none expected to go beyond 300 volts. But when Milgram conducted the same experiment with 40 men, 25 clearly went beyond 450 volts. In other words, 63% complied with the experimenter's command and stopped only after the experimenter actually called the experiment to a stop. Even when the learner's pleas were increased, it had seemingly no effect on compliance by the "teacher": of the 40 participants, a majority of the subjects fully complied with the experimenter.

Why did the subjects comply? Among the reasons offered by the subjects, one was, that the experiment was being run by an eminent professor at a top-notch university. How does one disobey so eminent a person? Milgram found that a number of other variables were related to obedience to the request from the experimenter. For example, the level of shocks were higher, when the experimenter was physically present in the same room as the "teacher" subject. In other words, how does one not comply when the person demanding obedience is in the very same room.

Milgram also reported that a few of his subjects (less than 2%) refused to deliver shocks. Taking a cue from Milgram's work, Kool and Sen (1984) devised a test of non-violence (NVT) in India and requested the subjects, scoring high and low on non-violence on the NVT, to administer shocks to their victim in a laboratory setting. Because of the influence of religion (For example, Buddhism and Jainism) and Gandhian philosophy in India, many subjects, scoring high on non-violence, either declined to deliver shocks or kept its intensity very low. Ironically, the level of obedience, in general and as a social phenomenon, is reported to be very high in the Indian society (Kool, 1983). It seems that a cultural feature in the form of non-violence tends to obscure the demands on being obedient if it leads to an antagonistic behavior—violence. Although Milgram's experiment has been replicated with success in many countries, cultural and social factors tend to set limits to the interpretation of the results of a Milgram-type experiment.

So what can we conclude? Authority does influence people, but personal authority can be overridden by the authority exercised by cultural, social or religious norms. But all the same, it is the factor of influence at work, both in the Milgram experiment and in the Kool and Sen experiment. The only difference is in the source of the influence.

Functions of social influence

Social influence: To provide us knowledge about the environment

Why do we get influenced? Are there any motives behind direct or indirect, real or imaginary influence? The most important **function** of influence is to **enhance the survival value** of an individual. It helps a person to understand his/her surroundings and to devise strategies for adjustment. If I see suspicious characters in my neighborhood but I have nothing to do with them, an obvious precaution I will take is to become careful in my movements and avoid being alone. The presence of others influences us in more ways than what we can imagine or calculate. One important function it serves is to make us **knowledgeable** about, or realistic in, our dealings with the environment.

Social influence can affect our feelings

Our past affiliation or identity with a group or community may also influence our behavior. This type of influence may **nurture our feelings and emotions**. Several years ago one of the authors of this book was teaching at the University of Wisconsin at Eau Claire, USA and he had virtually lost all contact with the people at the campus and the town. While driving at the Beverly Hills in California he saw a bus with a plate displaying "Eau Claire, Wisconsin." Obviously, he believed that the travelers were from Wisconsin. His first reaction after seeing the bus was to stop his car and say "hello" to the visitors. He felt a sense of affiliation with the people of a community in which he had lived several years ago. This is a simple example of how we identify even with those people who we do not know or with whom we have no existing interaction or relationship.

BOX 1.2

Social influence in the lives of people with visual impairment

You would be well aware of the difficulties that people with visual impairment, or for that matter, any form of impairment, face in a world fashioned for people with unimpaired faculties. When we analyze models of stress, they suggest that people with visual impairment should be more stressful than their sighted counterparts. In her work, Agrawal (1999) discussed various models of stress and their implications for people with visual impairment. More specifically, Agrawal hypothesized that the visually impaired would be more stressful than their sighted counterparts.

In her research, consisting of 163 people with visual impairment from various residential schools for the blind in Northern India, Agrawal administered various psychological measures including those that measured stress, adjustment, locus of control, personality, and intelligence.

What did she find? Contrary to the expectation, the visually impaired were not characterized by higher levels of stress than the sighted. Although blind girls were more stressful than blind boys, they too were less stressful than their sighted counterparts.

Surprising though this may seem, a more detailed analysis of Agrawal's results led to the understanding of the coping mechanism for stress among people with blindness. The most important source of their lowered stress was social support. Staying as they were, in the residential schools for the blind, they were sheltered from the ravages of the larger world, which the sighted were forced to face. This study also revealed how gender-based role typing influenced stress levels of boys and girls. Since the ideal sex role for boys in India is in terms of extraversion, independence, radicalism and dynamism, the boy who fails to fit into this picture would be more vulnerable to stress. Girls, on the contrary, are actually expected to be weak, submissive and conservative. Girls who developed opposite traits became social outcasts. In short, as the discrepancy in sex role typing increased, so did the stress levels of both sexes.

We can therefore conclude that these people were influenced by the institute and its social support. They were also influenced by the prevailing sex role norms in India.

Can guide our behavior

In addition to knowledge and identity functions, influence may be seen in the form of **social support** (Box 1.2). Children learn that they can get support from parents when they show obedience and respect to them. Similarly, misery loves company. Strangers communicate and support each other during distress. This is the reason why groups such as the Alcoholics Anonymous are very effective in helping alcoholics to overcome their problem.

Social influence affects all three facets of mental life: Cognition, feelings and action

The examples above show that the presence of others can (1) be a primary source for broadening our knowledge database; (2) act as a stimulus to serve our needs of identity and affiliation; and (3) help in enhancing social support. Broadly speaking, the impact of the presence of others is related to all the three functions of our mental life—cognition, feelings and action. Thus,

The odd behavior of strangers → gaining new knowledge → COGNITION:

Meeting unknown people from a native area → a feeling of identity/ affiliation → FEELINGS:

Seeing strangers in misery → helping behavior → ACTION

To sum up, all areas of psychology, including social psychology, study the following **three** facets of our mental life:

- **How we know (cognition)?**
- **How we feel (affect)?**
- **How we act (action)?**

Social psychologists, like other psychologists, find that our knowledge, feelings and behavior may not be congruent with each other. People continue smoking cigarettes owing to peer pressure (action), and even later enjoy smoking (feelings), though they know that smoking might cause cancer (cognition). When attempts are made to understand this kind of **incongruent behavior** in terms of individual personality, needs, etc., it is the **psychologist** who is in the driver's seat. However, in attempting an explanation in terms of the situation in which the individual is placed, it is the social psychologist who is at work. More specifically, **social psychologists**, unlike other psychologists, explore how knowledge, feelings, and action become congruent or incongruent because of the **presence of other people**. A person who smokes a cigarette may also believe that he would not suffer from cancer because not every one who smoked suffered from cancer (Box 1.3).

SOCIAL PSYCHOLOGY AS DISTINCT FROM OTHER SOCIAL SCIENCES

A very ironical aspect of our mental life is that if you ask your friend why he behaved the way he did, he may not be able to offer you an explanation. Very often we are not aware of the origins of our own behavior. An important question before us is: what do social psychologists do to understand behavior under such circumstances?

There are two ways to examine the context of an action. **First,** social scientists make an attempt to study the **characteristics of a social environment**, for example, how a culture shapes the behavior of its individuals. This type of approach in the study of behavior is pursued by cultural anthropologists and sociologists. **Second,** social scientists may investigate **how people are influenced by the inferences** they make about their social environment. This is the arena of

BOX 1.3

What we believe versus **what we do**

Suppose you buy an expensive car far beyond your means. This car also consumes a lot of fuel and it is very costly as far as repairs are concerned. What will happen if you continue to drive it? Most likely you will believe (and say) that, after all, it is not a bad car, as you had been first told. According to Festinger (1957), we tend to reduce our dissonance and seek consonance. It is a human tendency to resolve conflicts in beliefs; otherwise mental life could become very strenuous. In a classic experiment, Festinger demonstrated that when subjects were paid $20 to perform a very repetitive, boring task, they believed that the task was indeed very boring. However, when they were paid only $1 for doing the same task, they felt that the task was not after all so boring. The low payment for doing a monotonous work offered them a justification to reduce their dissonance, but the unusually high payment for a boring task could not. The lesson we learn from such experiments in social psychology is that we avoid, or minimize the impact of situations that continue to cause dissonance.

Saudi Women and Schizophrenia:
Dr. Khaled M. Batarfi's column in *Arab News*, August 3, 2003

"When I wrote here about our schizophrenia two weeks ago, the first example I gave was about how we behave in different environments in different ways. We get into planes to travel abroad and by the time we get off a plane in another country, we have become different people. Many women, discarding their abayas, change into tight and revealing clothes, while some men seem to forget many of their important traditions and religious regulations."

"Many women thought that I was targeting their freedom to dress as they wish."....."What I really truly wanted to say is: We have to synchronize our beliefs, behavior and attitude. If we believe in our religion and culture, then Allah is everywhere. We cannot pray five times a day in Saudi Arabia, and then skip even Friday prayers abroad. We shouldn't cover hands and toes at home, and wear shorts when we are away."

To the reader: Did you notice Dr. Batarfi's words, "We have to synchronize our beliefs, behavior and attitude." Cognitive dissonance will remain until beliefs, behavior and attitudes are not synchronized!

the social psychologist. The issue of objective reality is less important to social psychologists in comparison to the issue of how people interpret or perceive reality. If a tiny lighted dot (static) in a dark room is perceived as moving by an individual, his/her observation constitutes the reality of his/her perception. However, social psychologists would be interested in this (false) interpretation of movement if it was caused by the presence of some high status people who, acting as a confederate of a researcher, reported that the "static" light was indeed "moving". The important point here is not what the high status people had said but how it was understood or interpreted by an individual. In other words, social psychologists focus on the **construction of reality** rather than reality *per se*. Going back to the Milgram experiment cited earlier, the subjects delivered shocks because they were perceiving that there was a "real" student receiving the shocks.

Take another example. Whereas sociologists and cultural anthropologists are interested in showing how authoritarianism, a fascist view to dictate and control behavior of others, causes an increase in the obedience levels of the members of a culture, social psychologists are interested in demonstrating how an individual's own needs and personality lead to the acceptance of authoritarianism. The latter explanation focuses on the inner dynamics of an individual and explores how situations cause change in the internal states of the mind. On the other hand, sociologists and cultural anthropologists are more interested in the way institutions in a culture or society support the authoritarian forms of behavior.

Social psychology deals with micro aspects; **Sociology** deals with macro aspects

For example, in an Eastern society like India, obedience and respect are considered more important virtues than in the West (Kool, 1983). This is due to the significance attached to such forms of behavior in that society. However, authoritarian behavior, as demonstrated by Adorno and co-workers (1950), may be guided by the personality needs of individuals to gain control and power, an area in which social psychologists are more interested than their counterparts in sociology and cultural anthropology.

A simple way to understand how social psychologists differ from other social scientists in their attempt to study behavior is by examining the way different disciplines approach a subject. Social psychologists pursue a **micro** level of analysis, that is, how a particular psychological process relates to the behavior of an individual. A social psychologist will demonstrate how frustration may or may not lead to aggression. On the other hand, a sociologist, who prefers a **macro** approach, will focus on how social conditions that cause frustration vary from one society to another.

Within the divisions of psychology, the boundaries between social psychology and personality psychology are often very fuzzy. Personality psychology studies the consistency and the uniqueness of behavior of individuals. For example, why are some people more outgoing (extraverts) than others? If behavior is steady across the situations, an obvious conclusion will be to link it to a trait of an individual. Whereas personality psychologists show how behavior does not vary across situations, social psychologists show how behavior varies when an individual interacts with his/her environment. Needless to say that both personality psychology and social psychology share a lot of common ground but both differ in their focus of analysis.

In the foregoing paragraphs we have described what social psychology is and what it is not. In addition, we have mentioned that social psychology focuses on the behavior of individuals in interaction with people and situations. If we remove the situation aspect from the analysis, social psychology will merge with personality psychology. Similarly, social psychology will lose its independent identity from sociology if the focus shifts from the person to the situation alone.

Are there two social psychologies, one dealing primarily with the person and the other dealing mainly with the situation? Is it true that the focus of analysis between a person and a situation derives from one source and spills to another? Simply stated, is it common among social psychologists to show a preference for the social environment over the person or *vice versa*? You will find the answer to these questions if you open textbooks written on social psychology for students in psychology and sociology. A textbook adopted for students in a psychology program will focus on topics like social perception, cognition, attitudes, and interpersonal attraction, but a textbook of social psychology in a sociology program will have a different set of chapters, for example, work environment, cultures, social institutions, subcultures, and so on. As mentioned earlier, the topics are more molar in nature in a sociology program in comparison to those in a psychology program.

The difference in the approaches to study social psychology is reflected in the language social psychologists use in addressing the concepts. When one of the authors (Kool) began his research in the area of aggression several years ago, he noticed that sociologists used the word "violence" more often than psychologists to describe behavior designed to harm other people. War is a collective action to harm adversaries. It does not focus on an individual's behavior because the concept is molar in nature. Like sociologists, psychologists too study behavior involving harm to other people, but they are more concerned with how individuals are influenced under such conditions. Groebel and Hinde (1989) concluded that this difference between the approaches of psychologists and other social scientists has an important bearing in understanding social issues. Psychologists, according to them, have not done enough to demonstrate the implications of their work in molar settings. In other words, when social psychologists make an attempt to stretch their findings from molecular to molar settings, they face an inherent disadvantage, because the purpose and language of their discipline is not geared to address a broad social context. More specifically, when psychologists stretch their findings on individual aggression to explain collective violence such as war, they leave behind many unanswered questions. As a result, psychologists have a weaker say on social policy matters as compared to other fellow social scientists.

The approach adopted by Eidelson and Eidelson (2003) in identifying domains with respect to individual and group categories may be helpful in bridging the two. They have argued that the core beliefs of individuals and the groups they belong to need to be understood and parallels be drawn to highlight the nature of the discrepancy. For example, to study horrors of violence, they suggested the following classification based on five domains (Table 1.1).

TABLE 1.1

Identification of domains with reference to the individual and the group (*Source*: Eidelson & Eidelson, 2003)

Domain	Individual	Group
Superiority	Social rules are irrelevant	Ethnocentrism
Injustice	Perceived mistrust	Legitimate grievances
Vulnerability	Living in harm's way	Fear about future
Distrust	Malign intentions of others	Perception of outgroup
Helplessness	Actions will fail	Mindset of powerlessness

SOCIAL PSYCHOLOGY IN ITS APPLIED FORM

The goal of any science is to explain the occurrence of an event. For this purpose, research is conducted to explore the event in several ways. After a broad general understanding of a phenomenon, an attempt is made to integrate the findings into a generalized form so that predictions can be made to explain the occurrence of the event in future. In other words, all sciences develop theories to explain their subject matter and make predictions about the occurrence of events. This is the **basic nature of a science.**

The **goal of social psychology** is to present a set of integrated concepts to explain and predict how individuals are influenced by others. For this purpose social psychologists formulate hypotheses, conduct research and develop theories not only to explain present behavior but also to make predictions about such behavior. Basic research deals with establishing a cause-effect relationship. For example, does prolonged exposure to violence on mass media increase the likelihood of aggression? Does frustration cause aggression? Social psychologists are concerned with these and similar issues; they develop appropriate research methods and procedures to investigate the problem, collect data, and, provide explanations of present behavior.

BOX 1.4

The accuracy of an eyewitness testimony: Bad memories can cause a havoc

An extremely critical issue in a court judgment is whether a person is guilty of a crime or not. Such decisions are often based on the testimony of an eyewitness. It is risky business using eyewitnesses for testimony because memories undergo both forgetting and changes over a period of time. In her well known research, Loftus (1979) found that the nature of the question itself might change the overall testimony provided by the eyewitness. For example, after viewing a movie, a group of students were asked whether they had seen a stop sign or a yield sign. It was found that their memory-based judgment anchored the subsequent report that led to a false conclusion: those who reported seeing the stop sign gave a different report from those recalling a yield sign. In this context, it is important to note that children as eyewitnesses are most vulnerable because they are highly suggestible. Obviously, eyewitness testimony is a risky phenomenon (Roper & Shewan, 2002). It is estimated that thousands of innocent people were sent to prison simply because of false eyewitness testimony. Recently, the Governor of the State of Illinois in the USA freed several criminals and one key factor in his decision was the use of unreliable eyewitness testimony while sentencing the people.

Given the above background regarding the nature of basic social psychology, it is natural to ask: what does social psychology have to offer in order to improve human conditions, for example, in a legal setting? If we know that eyewitnesses are susceptible to errors owing to misleading and suggestive questions, how do we improve the quality and the accuracy of eyewitness reports? Under such circumstances we need to devise ways to put to use our knowledge of behavior in a social context. This is what various researchers have done. Davids and Bottoms (2002) have demonstrated how children could be helped to resist suggestions while giving testimony. Similarly, Parker and Myers (2001) have established empirically that children's eyewitness reports improve through practice. However, they caution that while girls increased their correct identification, boys tended to show an increase in their false rejections, that is, calling a person not guilty when indeed such a person was guilty. These studies are good examples of **how social psychological research can be applied to solve real life problems.** Thus, Box 1.4 shows how basic research on eyewitness reports in the laboratory have implications for the acceptance of eyewitness reports in real life crime.

Towards a definition of applied social psychology: Major characteristics

Applied social psychology: A discipline concerned with development, and implementation of interventions based on social psychological principles

Applied social psychology is therefore concerned with the development and implementation of intervention programs based on social-psychological principles so as to improve the quality of behavior. So, first and foremost, applied social psychology uses **theories and principles derived from social psychology**. These theories are then utilised **to formulate intervention programs**, the purpose of which is to **solve problems**. What are the types of problems amenable to social psychological interventions? The range of such problems is extremely wide, from the effects of TV on childhood aggression patterns, to the development of pro-environmental attitudes, to getting people to use safe sex methods, etc. Moreover, applied social psychology does not stop with the mere study of social problems. An extremely important realm of applied social psychology is to **develop interventions** to solve the problems in our lives. An **intervention** is a planned effort that directly influences behavior. Let us take the example of the effect of watching violence on television in increasing the aggressive tendencies of children. Parents who enjoy watching violent programs on television may act as models for their children and thereby reinforce their children's viewing of violent programs. An intervention program would involve the use of a psychological theory, such as reinforcement theory or social learning theory, to design an action plan to help parents understand how their own behavior can reinforce their child's behavior and what they should do to deal with the situation.

Salient features of applied social psychology

1. Firmly rooted in theory

Applied social psychology has three major features

Firmly rooted in theory

Use of any knowledge without a theory is likely to make applications less effective or even counter-productive. A theory serves **three important functions** in the design and application of an intervention program. **Firstly**, a theory defines the nature and focus of an intervention program. Let's take the case of two popular theories of learning. First, the social learning theory that explains how children learn behavior by imitating others and how such behavior may grow stronger with continuous reward (Bandura,1977). On the other hand, Skinner's theory (1938), based on operant learning, focuses on reinforcement that involves contingencies for changing a child's behavior. While both theories agree that learning is an acquired phenomenon, they both disagree on the role of reinforcement in learning. For Skinner, reinforcement is a key element in learning, but for Bandura it is important but not essential. Intervention programs could be developed following either or both theories, but the nature of the theory will define and limit the operation of the intervention program. Moreover, a popular theory is easily accepted by experts and laypersons alike, and, any intervention program based on such a popular theory is smoothly implemented and accepted in a community.

In designing intervention programs, social psychologists often face a conflict in their preference for one theory over another. Such a conflict is not unusual in a discipline. Physicians and lawyers often differ in their treatment or litigation approaches. There may be wide differences between the physician trained in allopathy to another trained in homeopathy. No wonder, the applied social psychologists, too, face a similar dilemma in their preference for one theory over another in seeking solutions of a psychological nature.

Secondly, a theory can help monitor the implementation and success of an intervention program. A good theory makes sound predictions. If parents stop their viewing of violent programs on television and notice that a change in their behavior has an impact on their child's behavior, this success of the intervention program can be tested at various intervals. Similarly, the failure of a program can be also tested if a theory is weak or its application unrealistic. In short, a theory can help us monitor the steps involved in an intervention program and explain the level of success of such a program at various stages.

Finally, a theory is useful in trouble-shooting. No theory is perfect. According to Popper (1959), a good theory is one that keeps room for improvement. There are no absolute theories. A theory is vulnerable if it cannot be disproved even if it is wrong. Knowledge is space; it is not a boundary. As new knowledge is acquired, a theory is modified or dismantled. If we develop a theory that all behavior is instinctive in nature (for example, that war is inherent in human nature) and state it at a level of omniscience to explain the relationship between the viewing of violent programs on television and aggressive behavior of children, we will be offering an absolute explanation of behavior. Such an explanation will provide very little use as an intervention program that is geared to control the aggressive behavior of children. On the contrary, if we fieldtest interventions based on different theories and learn how improvements in behavior can be achieved, we can then develop effective intervention programs to solve real life problems.

2. Focus on applications

Focus on applications

When Lewin (1951) made the historical comment, "there is nothing so practical as a good theory," a historical landmark was created for the applications of psychology. Most social scientists believe that a good theory leads to effective application and view the relationship between theory and practice as a one-way traffic. Indeed, this was the state of affairs when social psychology, as a young science, was developing its scientific roots and had not demonstrated sufficient applications in the real world. The perspective of this relationship has now changed as aptly presented by a French psychologist, "There is nothing so theoretical as a good application" (Levy-Leboyer, 1988). Let's take the example of the Head Start program, the most elaborate and expensive intervention program ever undertaken in the USA to enhance the cognitive abilities of young children (Refer to the Chapter on Education). The expectation in the Head Start program was that it would cause at least a ten-point gain in the IQ of its participants. While this gain of ten points remained, by and large, elusive, the operation of the program itself helped researchers to better understand the nature of cognitive development in children and the limits of their own endeavors in formulating an unrealistic program for enhancing the IQ levels (Hernstein & Murray 1994). Please refer to Chapter 10 on Education.

Sometimes it is difficult to draw a fine line separating the relationship between a theory and its practice. A major task in theory building is to gain knowledge and to explain and predict a phenomenon. Using such knowledge, applied social psychology makes an attempt to actually solve a problem in real life. According to Weyant (1986), the **practical applications of social psychology** may be viewed in the following three categories:

- Basic
- Applicable
- Applied

As stated earlier, **basic research** deals with the development of theory and the refinement of concepts. A lot of basic research is aimed at developing an understanding for putting knowledge to practical applications. While psychologists and educationists believed that a ten-point gain in IQ was possible in the Head Start program, they learned real life limitations in sharpening cognitive skills. Understanding a problem, according to Weyant, is the first step in solving a problem.

The **applicable** aspect of social psychology, according to Weyant, is the potential for practical application. Consider the Head Start program again. Psychologists were optimistic that a ten point gain in IQ was possible in the program, that is, there was a potential for the use of our knowledge of psychological measurement and cognitive development.

3. The goal of applied social psychology is intervention

Goal is intervention

The third issue in the application of social psychology, mentioned by Weyant, deals with solution of real life problems, that is applied social psychology. When social interventions are field-tested and used as tools to solve problems, the nature of social psychology becomes **applied**. In its applied form social psychology deals with a wide variety of topics ranging from the effects of school segregation to managing stress. The concepts of social psychology have been used very effectively to develop interventions and to find solutions in the areas of education, health, law, consumer behavior, environment and many more. Bearing in mind the relevance of certain issues, we have focused on a few selected areas in this book at the end of this chapter and in the remaining part of this book.

The three-tier approach, as suggested by Weyant, in understanding the nature of practical applications of social psychology needs to be supplemented by the issue of applicability of intervention, that is, to what extent a program is desirable and whether it is acceptable to the community. Take the issue of euthanasia. A patient who is not only terminally ill but also suffering from unbearable pain and finds that there is no point in prolonging life, requests for medical assistance in ending his life. This patient wants to decide the future of his life, but the society does not grant him this right. If a physician assists him, like Dr. Kovorkian of Michigan did, he will be charged with murdering his patient. In this example, we find that the issue is our knowledge that the patient cannot be cured. The applicable aspect of the problem is concerned with our ability to develop an intervention program such that patients can die without any additional suffering to what they have already had. And finally, the applied nature of the intervention consists of a positive demonstration that such assisted suicide is possible. One issue that remains important is that of applicability, that is, the desirability of an intervention program and its acceptance. Given the religious concerns about sanctity of life and other legal issues that vary from one culture or society to another, the issue of euthanasia has become very contentious. While it has been resolved in Holland, within the USA it is hotly debated and the individual states differ in their approach for dealing with this issue.

The rationale considering applicability may also take an ugly form. Hitler believed that one "good" intervention program for improving race was to exterminate Jews. For this purpose, (false) basic research was conducted, samples of the behavior of Jews were highlighted through mass media (applicable), and finally, a program of eugenics was implemented (applied). However, one important question remained unanswered: Was this social intervention desirable? Hitler believed that he was right. And so did several German social scientists. What about other social scientists? Should they remain silent? In fact, many instantly became critical of what was done by Hitler. In short, social psychologists cannot separate themselves from social issues because their findings have social implications. Some further examples of Weyant's three tiered approach, along with the aspect of applicability, are presented in Boxes 1.5 and 1.6.

BOX 1.5

Example of the four-tiered approach as used in the social psychology of law: Can we depend on a child's testimony in a criminal case?

- **Basic research:** Children under 10 are very suggestible and their testimony cannot be considered reliable.
- **Applicable:** Not applicable: Laws prohibit their testimony as supportive evidence.
- **Applied:** Social psychologists must define the limits of the use of children's testimony based on basic research, for example, with good practice children improve their accuracy levels (Roper & Shewan, 2002).
- **Applicability:** Lawyers may cause emotional damage to children in cross-examination; Children can offer some clue as to the nature of the crime.

BOX 1.6

Example of the four-tiered approach as used in the social psychology of consumer behavior: Advertising and pathological behavior of consumers

- **Basic research:** Advertising of goods results in increase in consumer spending.
- **Applicable:** Consumer goods are allowed to be advertised.
- **Applied:** Social psychologists must demonstrate the impact of advertising. For example, how intense advertising is resulting in pathological consumer behavior of living beyond their means in the Third World countries. Are their virtues in altruistic marketing, that is, teaching consumers the use, abuse and misuse of advertised products? Please see chapter on consumer behavior.
- **Applicability:** Should the advertisers warn consumers about their consumption habits as in case of cigarettes?

An increasing number of social psychologists are now concerned with the moral, ethical and pragmatic issues of an intervention program so that another black-page in the history of human race, as in the case of Hitler supporting eugenics leading to the killing of Jews, is not added to our shame. Unfortunately, in their efforts to develop a science of social behavior, social psychologists have ignored social policy issues for a long time. Such policy issues range from abortion to implications of gene selection and from homelessness to child abuse. Even stalwarts such as Sigmund Freud and Albert Einstein refused to comment on the destruction caused by war, though both were deeply involved with the problem. While Einstein invented the ingredients of atomic power, Freud analyzed the death instinct residing in the human mind. Given this scenario, do we expect social psychologists to remain silent on social policy issues after they have conducted basic research, found an applicable intervention, and demonstrated its use in an applied setting? After all is said and done, they should be accountable for what they have initiated. The issue of applicability, though not as concrete as that of the applicable and the applied side of social psychology, raises broader issues of a philosophical nature, including the types of social behavior that needs to be changed by social psychologists. Because the applicability issue involves taking sides on ethical and moral grounds, the scientific creed of social psychologists, in seeking applied solutions, seems to be compromised.

THE GLOBAL PERSPECTIVE OF APPLIED SOCIAL PSYCHOLOGY

Applied social psychology and the global perspective

The application of the principles of social psychology is immense. Unfortunately, practitioners and professionals are often balked by a model that is working extremely well in one situation, but may be totally ineffective in another. This seems to be true for areas as diverse as the marketing of products (for example, consumer behavior), perception of safe sex and leading a healthy life, or the management of environmental wastes and conservation of environmental resources. Thus, people may have pro-environmental attitudes but behave in ways opposite to such a belief. They buy gas-guzzling cars and vans, and yet favor minimizing air pollution. A few minutes ago one of the authors saw on TV the CEO of a global company, EMCOR, being interviewed by the CNBC. Based on his experience, this CEO categorically stated that the facilities management of his company did not work similarly even in the two developed countries—the USA and the UK—leave alone other developing or undeveloped countries.

Need to internation-alize social psychology

We believe that the immediate task of social psychologists is to globalize or **internationalize social psychology** because of the fast changing world, thanks to the advances in global communication. For example, the recent World Health Organization (2001) report shows that the mental health problems are rising at an alarming rate in the developing countries. It will be almost impossible to understand the nature of mental health problems if we do not study how individuals interact and cope with the changes in such societies. The classification of clinical diseases, such as schizophrenia, is well understood in the Western societies, but it may take a different meaning in an exotic cultural context. A common symptom of schizophrenia is the withdrawal from reality. But, how about the withdrawal from reality for spiritual reasons? For example, should

Hindus and Buddhists, who learn to detach from the material world and hence exhibit a split in their thought processes, be classified as schizophrenics?

Interventions are not equally effective across different cultures

Let us take another example, of faith healing, a commonly used method in almost all cultures for dealing with stress and illness. The Texas Department of Health in the USA supports faith based initiatives in health care (Pattilo & co-workers, 2002) because it fits in with the local culture. In Pakistan, according to Frogget (2001), typical Western methods of treatment are considered inadequate unless such methods are routed through the traditional healing conventions leading to psychic integration. In sharp contrast to such individual beliefs and the institutional support that is offered to nurturing such beliefs, is a recent study in the UK that compared the effects of spiritual healing on those who received it and those who did not. The results showed that there was no difference between the subjects undergoing spiritual healing and their control counterparts (Abbot & co-workers, 2001). The purpose of citing the above examples here is to make the reader understand that when people's beliefs are tested empirically, the results might not show any causal and consistent relationship between their beliefs and healing. Owing to their extreme religious beliefs, a couple in the State of Arizona in the USA recently refused medical treatment for their child. It is contended here that an intervention program will work smoothly in a culture if it is routed through the traditions of that culture and does not create dissonance in the belief system of its members.

Etic: Behavior common across cultures

Emic: Behavior unique to a culture

Realizing the need for a global perspective in social psychology, Moghaddam (1998) emphasized that social psychology must discover behavior that is common among individuals (**etic**). But, in addition, we must also explore the exotic nature of behavior, behavior that is unique in a culture (**emic**). Unfortunately, the scientific literature in social psychology is vastly North American. According to Smith and Bond (1999), a survey of books on social psychology revealed that non-American citations were extremely rare in the popular books on social psychology. Behavior is not the property of one nation or culture. It is a universal phenomenon and it must be studied in its varied forms and styles. As behavior is the core issue for psychologists, they must search both its consistencies and its uniqueness. Inter- and intra-cultural differences help us understand such consistencies and uniqueness of behavior.

Hofstede: How cultures differ

In order to explore the global perspective that is meaningful for applied social psychology, it is suggested that we enrich our understanding of behavior with studies across different cultures. Such studies provide an analysis of the salient characteristics of a group of people in a culture and offer an insight into the ways in which its members behave similarly or differently as compared to members of other cultures. In a landmark work consisting of data collected on over 1,00,000 people from 40 countries, **Hofstede** (1980) emphasized that each culture becomes unique or similar, depending on what its values are. After subjecting the data to factor analysis, a statistical technique that seeks inter-relationships between variables and common structures, **four important consequences** of a culture were identified: **power distance, individualism versus collectivism, masculinity versus femininity,** and **uncertainty avoidance.** Let us take the example of the individualism-collectivism dimension.

Individualism v. Collectivism

Research studies clearly conclude that Americans attribute success to individual factors such as hard work and motivation (individualism) as compared to the Japanese, who attribute their success to support offered by their group, that is, collectivism (Smith & Bond, 1999). The later chapters of this book will show how useful the Hofstede dimensions are for understanding differences in behavior across cultures.

The independent self v. **The inter-related self**

Information about ourselves comes through two sources: how we perceive ourselves and the information we get from other people. Both tend to define the nature of the self, a core issue in the study of personality. When our own view of the self (for example, I am hardworking and I do not care about what others say) becomes autonomous and is guided less by how others view us, the **independent construal** of the self emerges. According to Markus and Kitiyama (1991), this type of self is commonly seen in Western people who emphasize autonomy and independence. This is in sharp contrast to the people in the East who value **inter-relatedness of the self.** For example, Asians often attach importance to the opinion of family members in the selection of their mate.

Implicit theories of the self: Based on lay descriptions of how people construe behavior

The above stated explanation based on the analysis of the self has yielded limited success in the understanding of human behavior. People tend to change their behavior as they interact with their environment and therefore in many conditions it is almost impossible to know the real nature of the self. Having said this, it is easy for us to understand why people behave in one way on one occasion but entirely differently in another situation. More recently, personality research has focused on specific situations in which the occurrence of behavior could be predicted. Thus, in a critical situation, as in the game of baseball when the bases are loaded, or, as in cricket, when only one ball is left to score a run, even the best of the best batsman will feel nervous. **Implicit theories** of personality offer explanations for such variations in behavior and account for the widespread instances in which behavior could be given a different label. As stated above, the emic explanations of behavior with a focus on culture-specific consequences, would offer insight to social psychologists in deciding which interventions would work in a culture (Dweck, Chiu & Hong, 1995). It is not surprising that a few Hindus, who refrain from eating beef but not other varieties of meat, privately told one of the authors that the mad cow disease is the result of disrespect to and the killing of cows in the West. It is widely known that cultures generate stereotypes (the Jews are thrifty; the Americans enjoy violence; and the Japanese are secretive, etc.), but the speed with which such stereotypes fuel human thinking in a given direction is of significance to the social psychologist. Now the reader is invited to decide the relationship between the mad cow disease and the belief of Hindus. As a science, applied social psychology does not take sides, but simply guides the policy maker and the implementer as to what type of, and to which extent, an intervention will work in a community. Therefore, we may conclude that while applied social psychology is not a normative science, it will gain from the understanding of behavior in different cultural contexts.

APPLIED SOCIAL PSYCHOLOGY, ETHICS AND SOCIETY

Earlier in this chapter we mentioned that social psychology is mainly concerned with how people interpret social situations, but not with the objective assessment of that situation *per se*. This construal nature of social psychology raises several **ethical questions**. What right do social psychologists or others have to change the interpretation made by an individual? Are our interpretations superior to those of others? At what critical point should social psychologists intervene? There are no easy answers to such questions, but it is a fact, that today there is greater awareness of this problem among social psychologists than ever before.

According to Saranson (1981), psychologists do not easily deviate from the existing beliefs and practices prevalent in the modern society. People in power tend to exert influence and ordinary people accept their influence unquestionably. In the article, *Psychology and the Status Quo*, Prilleltensky (1989) examined the relationship between psychology and society in two ways. The **first** issue is the **epistemic nature** of the relationship, involving attempts by a scientist to select one critical explanation out of several explanations. In doing so, the scientist may operate from a framework preferred by him or her. The **second** issue, called **non-epistemic**, is based upon existing socio-cultural and political beliefs. This latter approach is mostly regulated by institutional support and tends to endorse predominant ideology. According to Prilleltensky, whether we involve the epistemic or the non-epistemic approach, it is impossible to escape the values that influence our scientific practice.

Kipnis (1994) has also lashed out at social psychologists by stating that they ignore the ethical issues. If social psychology is to be involved in the task of changing the behavior of people, its existing framework, devoid of values, is very inadequate. According to Kipnis, there is also an inherent danger in using social psychology for behavior control. If non-epistemic values are adopted, influential and rich people will control the lives of ordinary citizens.

Prilleltensky's (1989) statement that "it is unlikely that we, as psychologists, merely describe what appears to be, without at the same time subtly prescribing what we regard as desirable" (p. 797) makes a lot of sense. The question psychologists frequently ask is not whether values influence scientific practice, but how values define the range and scope of scientific practice. Gergen (1973) has echoed the same problem by stating that it is virtually impossible to achieve professional ends in the total absence of value commitments.

What is the role of social psychology in addressing **social issues**? Is contemporary social psychology facing a dilemma by distancing itself from ethical issues? It is true that social psychology has a long history of avoiding such issues, but it has also faced and tried to address vital issues. The use of **informed consent, debriefing,** and **evaluation of ethics of procedures** are good examples that show how social psychology addressed ethical issues whenever it was considered desirable. To what extent applied social psychology has been carried to the extent of social empowerment and amelioration, critics argue, is a matter of controversy and we find inadequate answers for several important questions.

Borrowing from Freire's work (1975), Prilleltensky (1989) has argued that there are at least **two ways** in which the issue of **ethical considerations** can be addressed. **First,** psychologists should not hesitate to face social responsibility by educating people to focus on obstacles that prevent perception of reality. This process of conscientization involves understanding the nature of the confusion on a social issue and eliminating myths that confuse people. For example, if psychologists help women who fight for their self-esteem, psychology will not become a weak science. The **second** step is annunciation that involves replacing the current system and developing an alternate arrangement. If no such effort is made by psychologists there are chances that the applications of social psychology will not proceed beyond the level of conscientization. If it is important to treat women for "battered women's syndrome" (symptoms that are caused by the battering) so that they regain self-esteem, it is also necessary that social psychologists indulge in activities that sustain women's self-esteem in future.

Weissberg, Kumpfer and Seligman (2003) stated that the **changing context** in which psychological problems, for example, mental health, are studied make it difficult to seek solutions to the psychological problems. They reported that the essence of applications, the preventive program, might be in conflict with the conceptualization in treatment. For example, they argued that the prevention framework of mental health consisting of primary (decrease new cases), secondary (early identification of the problem) and tertiary (rehabilitation to reduce severity) is not acceptable to many. The Institute of Medicine preferred to deal with prevention differently by creating separate categories: universal prevention (focus on general public); selective prevention (focus on specific target); and indicated prevention (high risk people with symptoms). Most preventive programs require cooperation between different professionals, including psychological, medical, social and others. Now the question is: whose approach would you adopt? In other words, the dilemmas faced by the applied social psychologists are both intense and multiple.

G

The history of scientific psychology is not very old. And the history of modern social psychology is definitely much less old. It is not easy to describe systematically the theories that have made an impact on the history of social psychology in general and applied social psychology in particular. Most social psychologists would agree with Roger Brown (1965), of Harvard University, that it is difficult to isolate a common denominator in social psychology. Therefore in this section, we will refer to the growth of applied social psychology in terms of its theoretical development and subsequent applications.

Wundt is given the credit for establishing the first laboratory of psychology at Leipzig, Germany. His work in the area of social psychology, known as folk psychology, remained unknown for a long time partly because of problems in its English translation and partly due to Wundt's support to Germany during the First World War. In fact, his work in both areas—group mind and language—became popular topics of study in later years.

However, it was **Triplett** (1897) who is believed to have conducted the first study on applied social psychology approximately a century ago to investigate why behavior was different when people moved or worked together. For example, the speed of biking or reel winding after fishing was different in group settings as compared to when individuals were working alone. For example, he found that the bicycle riders tended to move faster in a group than when bicycling alone. He did not have any specific theory to account for his results, but relied on his commonsense explanation that the presence of others affected the performance of an individual. Subsequent research by **Allport** (1924) and others called this positive effect of the presence of others, social facilitation. A major psychological research on this topic was conducted by **Zajonc** (1965) who demonstrated that the presence of others tended to cause arousal and hence the differential performance. In short, the reader will notice that a topic like social facilitation that had no theoretical basis to begin with, remained a hot subject of study for more than five decades.

Contrary to the results obtained in **social facilitation** studies, research also demonstrated a phenomenon known as **social loafing**. This effect is characterized by the tendency to contribute less than one's optimum performance while working in the company of others. **Ringelmann**, a French engineer, found out in the 1880s that when people were asked to pull a rope in the game, they tended to put in less effort. Also, you might notice that in the company of others, people in general, shout less louder as compared to a similar situation in which they are left alone. A leader of a group often requests the audience to clap louder to thank the artist who had just finished her presentation.

Later studies on the positive and negative effect of the presence of others showed the limits of social psychological research. For example, through a series of studies, sport psychologists demonstrated that the mere presence of others might not be important. The critical variable is the interaction of the audience that may result in the facilitation or the inhibition of performance. The interactive audience often facilitates the behavior of its athletes and results in "home court" advantage. No wonder, athletes perform better in their own country or playground as did the Boston Celtics at Boston Gardens with a record of 94 wins out of the 97 games played.

A landmark study in social psychology was conducted by **Sherif** (1937) on the **autokinetic phenomenon** in which the subjects experienced a spot of light as moving (though actually static) because others had already confirmed its movement. Sherif, who was testing the Columbia students, reported that a group norm emerged when assessments of the moving light were varied on successive trials. At that time, he offered a commonsense explanation of suggestibility to account for his results. Further research by Jacobs and Campbell (1961) demonstrated that the autokinetic phenomenon could transmit from one set of subjects to another. By replacing carefully one confederate by a real subject in a series of experiments, they found that the enduring nature of suggestibility can be passed on to the successive "generations."

Perhaps the most pervasive experiment to demonstrate the effect of group pressure was reported by **Solomon Asch** (1955). He showed a standard line and asked his subjects to match it with the correct one in a set of three comparison lines. When two or more confederates consistently gave wrong answers, the responses of real subjects conformed to those given by the confederates. Such is the power of group pressure! **Milgram's** work on obedience to authority was reported earlier in this chapter. Applications of studies on conformity and compliance amply showed how other people influence our behavior.

It was not until the 1940s when **Kurt Lewin**, known as the **founding father** of applications of social psychology, systematically demonstrated the need for and the existence of applied social psychology. He believed that theory and practice must go arm-in-arm and that each should benefit from the other. During World War II when there was an acute shortage of meat, Lewin made an attempt to persuade people to consume visceral meat that was not favored by most people. He followed a conventional approach to change the habits, that is, a group of homemakers participated in a lecture session. The other group participated in a discussion session in which a leader was involved and each participant had the time and opportunity to ask questions. Surprisingly, there was 32% change in favor of visceral meat in the active participation group in comparison to only 3% in the conventional group.

The most critical concept in Lewin's theory is **life space**, a psychological field in which a person moved. Thus, if a boy wants to become a physician, his goal is to be a physician, and the intermediary steps for this purpose are passing the entrance examination for admission in a medical college, complete the internship, and set up one's practice. Lewin identified how changes in aspiration and motivation levels would influence the movement of this young man in the psychological space. Although he offered several mathematical concepts to garnish his theory, he was basically concerned with the practical applications of his concept, which he did with his thoughtful experiments.

A major influence of Lewin's work was in the field of cooperation and competition. Research that followed, especially that by **Morton Deutsch** (1985, 1994) showed its applications in the field of conflict resolution—to cooperate or to compete. In his research, he asked his subjects to imagine a situation in which they were asked to make one of the two choices: Player A had the option to select X or Y; Player B also had the option to select X or Y. Thus, their choices would result in either of the following combinations (a 2 × 2 matrix): XA, XB, YA, and YB. If both X and Y opted for the same gain, they would be locked in a competitive situation such that only one would win. However, if both cooperate, they would both gain, but with a smaller amount. Several variations of this **Prisoner's Dilemma game** appeared in which two suspected criminals could vary their strategy, cooperatively or competitively, to change the outcome of their punishment.

A variation of the above game was the **Acme-Bolt Trucking game** that received an award from the American Association for the Advancement of Science. In this experiment, two truck drivers were asked to reach their destination through either separate but exceptionally longer route or a shorter route but with only one truck moving to pass at a time after some distance. The latter choice required cooperation by both truckers to reach their destination. Would the two truckers compete or cooperate with each other when placed in a situation of maximizing their gain? The results of this study clearly showed that when players made threats to each other, the outcomes were most harmful to both parties. The applications of research in this field were extended to train executives, diplomats and politicians in the resolution of conflicts.

The surge of research that dominated social psychology for three decades was due to the exceptionally brilliant work of **Festinger** (1957) on **cognitive dissonance**. He was a student and colleague of Lewin and was obviously influenced by his work. In his work, Festinger demonstrated that people have an enormous capacity to keep to their beliefs even though they have clear evidence that the beliefs were false. In other words, he was interested in finding out how people could hold inconsistent beliefs and live with them. Knowing that smoking causes cancer, people still continue to smoke. Why? According to dissonance theory, such inconsistency may change our belief system such that we may say, "Not everyone who smokes dies of cancer". Keeping opposite beliefs increases tension and hence people tend to generate harmony within their conflicting mental states.

The development of dissonance theory has an interesting history. A small town housewife of Minnesota proclaimed that she was receiving messages from supernatural powers. She announced that a great flood would take place and most people in that area would perish. The researchers visited this area and met with the followers of this belief. When the flood did not take place, the researchers asked the followers the reasons for the flood not taking place. The believers responded that the God became merciful at the last moment. Ironically, the followers now became more trustful of the cult than ever before. The wide range of applications of the dissonance theory will be described later in several chapters of this book.

An alternate explanation to solving dissonance was offered by **Bem** (1972) in his theory of **self perception**. Since we are uncertain about our beliefs in a dissonant condition, we tend to look at our own behavior and seek a conclusion. For example, when we keep on smoking even after knowing that smoking causes cancer, we look at our own behavior that has not resulted in the onset of cancer. This theory of self-perception has been successfully applied in many domains of social psychology such as health and gender roles.

Perhaps the most significant development in social psychology is in the field of **attribution,** that is, the analysis of causes of behavior. **Heider's research** (1957) demonstrated that we tend to respond on the basis of inferences that we draw from our experience, and not necessarily by the stimulus presented to us. For instance, if our neighbor is unemployed, we might say that he is lazy, but, if I do not have a job, I would blame the harsh economic situation. Such internal (being lazy) and external (economic situation) causes are very commonly used in our daily lives. Consider the attributions of two tennis players. If one tennis player makes a great serve, an ace, he might think that it was the result of his ability (internal), but the opponent might describe his success as a mere fluke (external). A few examples of internal and external attributions in sport are given in the Box 1.7 below.

BOX 1.7

Examples of internal and external attributions

INTERNAL	EXTERNAL
We are no good	The umpires are biased
I did not give my best	Their teamwork was superb
I was distracted by the crowd	No luck for me today

The internal and external attributions were further analyzed in terms of stable and unstable causes and can be best stated in a 2 × 2 matrix below (Weiner, 1974).

	INTERNAL	EXTERNAL
STABLE	Ability	Task difficulty
UNSTABLE	Effort	Luck

Heider believed that we often act like an intuitive scientist, thanks to the constant use of attributions. Why do we do it? Attributions tend to enhance the predictability of events and of human behavior because attributions lead us to find the cause: why something is happening the way it is happening. In this sense, when the interest in the field of cognitive dissonance was waning, research in attributions in the 1970s bridged the gap between the two unconnected concepts of social psychology. Researchers began to reinterpret the concept of cognitive dissonance as self-attributions, that is, when a conflict in our belief occurred, we attributed the cause to our own doing. At this point, we refer the reader back to Roger Brown's statement that the growth of social psychology remained fragmented for a long time and it was never easy to find a common, cohesive framework to describe modern social psychology.

Latane and Darley (1970) were concerned with the inaction on the part of people when they simply watched a gruesome murder or some other pathetic event. More specifically, their studies were triggered by the passiveness with which many bystanders watched the **Kitty Genovese's** murder in New York City's Borough of Queens. Based on their research in which they created an emergency situation such as a fire in a corner of the laboratory, they concluded that help was delayed when more than one person was witnessing the event. Their research opened a vista of studies for understanding altruistic behavior and perspective taking, the topics that were hitherto not explored in the field of social psychology.

The above research findings on bystander intervention, attributions, cognitive dissonance and norm formation have been woven into the common fabric of our mental phenomenon, popularly known as "**social cognition**" or "cognition of social psychology." It is an area of research of social psychology that deals with the way people think about a social issue. On the other hand, "social psychology of cognition" deals with the broader social issues in the context of culture that tends to influence the mode of thought of individuals. For instance, how subgroups of violence in a culture tend to increase the aggression levels of its members. In short, the former deals with behavior at a micro level, that is, analyzing the thought processes, while the latter draws inference at the macro level as to how social conditions shaped the thought processes.

It is true that psychology, let alone social psychology, does not have a long history. Since psychology, as a very young science, has not offered robust theories, the applications that it has offered to its sub-fields, including social psychology, are not very firm and conclusive. Lewin was a rare social psychologist who understood the dilemma of social psychology and felt that a lot of applied work in social psychology would also lend support to improvised theory construction. Therefore, unlike other social psychologists, he argued for a two-way traffic in the relationship between theory and practice, both getting help from each other.

Another concern for social psychology is that it grew out of its very narrow, opportunistic segment consisting of available subjects who were mostly college students. Understanding real social issues requires real effort with real people. The narrow band of samples employed by social psychologists at times did hurt rather than help the cause of the discipline. When Kohlberg (1976) offered his theory of moral development, he based his conclusions mostly on the males that he studied. On the contrary, Gilligan (1982), using young females in her research, showed how females prefer caring over justice, a conclusion that could have never been reached using the approach of Kohlberg.

The most scathing criticism of the development of social psychology came from Gergen (1990) who believed that social psychology should not be treated as a science because it merely accounts for the behavior as a matter of a time slice; it offers explanations for a particular sample or cultures, rather than engaging in construction of universal principles of behavior. As such, social psychology is more a part of history than science. For example, whereas people in the West may find cognitive dissonance as discomforting, people in the East may find it positive for their growth. Kabir, a saint in India with a large following, remarked that if you are not being surrounded by several critics, you may not grow as a healthy person. Gergen argued that social psychology indulges in social constructivism, that is, it simply creates an explanation based on prior experiences of social issues in a time-bound frame.

THEORETICAL PERSPECTIVES OF SOCIAL PSYCHOLOGY

Broadly speaking, there are five major theoretical perspectives that are offered in the study of social psychology: socio-cultural, evolutionary, social learning, phenomenological, and social cognition. These perspectives are briefly described below.

The social learning perspective

Traditional learning theories provide classical and operant conditioning explanations of social behavior. Classical conditioning shows how people respond consistently to a neutral stimulus if it is paired in time and space with another stimulus. Pavlov's classic experiment on dog's salivation (1927) applies well on us, too, when the sound of the favorite Ben and Jerry ice cream makes our mouth watery. A siren during war triggers escape behavior. Classical conditioning explains social behavior on the premise that people become conditioned to some specific aspect of their environment.

The operant learning theory of Skinner (1938) constitutes perhaps the most significant influence in the study of behavior. The core concept in operant conditioning is reinforcement, defined as a probability of occurrence of a response. This is determined by the consequence of a response. If we open our refrigerator and find food we will continue to do so (consequence) but will stop doing so if it remains empty all the time. Praise in the form of a social reward continues to elicit praiseworthy behavior. If we get rewards based on time or frequencies of behavior, schedules of reinforcement are established and social behavior can be controlled by developing appropriate contingencies. In his book, *Beyond Freedom and Dignity*, Skinner (1971) made an attempt to design a culture and the underlying basis for this creation was his notion of reinforcement. In his article written a few years before his death, Skinner (1987) went to the extent of accounting for the unselfish behavior of a prominent leader of non-violence, Mohandas Gandhi. He wrote, "When Gandhi was asked, What are we to do?" he is said to have replied, 'Think of the poorest man you have ever met and then ask if what you are doing is of any benefit to him'.... Action is the problem and contingencies the solution" (p. 785).

The **social learning theory** of Bandura (1977) grew out of the limitations of the concept of reinforcement and emphasized that learning can take place by observing or imitating others and without any reinforcement or behavior contingencies. He proposed a concept named **"vicarious reinforcement"** which means that learning can be reinforced positively or negatively depending on whether a model has been rewarded or punished. A waitress learns her work by observing how her supervisor is serving the guests. In other words, observation of consequences of others' work may serve as reinforcement for one's own behavior. Bandura's explanation based on the cognitive components of learning had a major impact on studies of an applied nature.

The phenomenological perspective

This perspective was highlighted by **Lewin** who believed that social behavior is guided by the way an individual moves in his **psychological space**, that is, how he/she interprets events in the real world. In doing so, Lewin did not deny objective reality, but instead encouraged scientific studies on how an individual interacts with his environment. Pessimistic as it is, **Gergen's** (1990) view on **social constructivism**, as stated above, falls in this category as well. The issue that we raised in identifying the goals of applied social psychology—theory, applications, applicability and applied—are embedded in the phenomenological perspective. For example, while we might believe that a gain of 6 points in IQ in a Head Start program will be helpful, the administrators could decide otherwise. Whose reality and belief do we accept? Commenting on psychology's inability to open the closed doors of their laboratory, Gergen remarked, "Theoretical accounts of the world are not mirror reflections of the world but discursive actions within the community. In effect, theory is itself a form of practice" .... "Even biological universals like pain have been studied in the context of culture" (p. 811).

The social-cognitive perspective

The central theme of the social cognitive perspective is the role of society or group at large in shaping the behavior of its members: for example, the role of nationalism, culture-specific factors, values, social class/institutions and social norms. A reference to these factors was made under the macro components that influence our social behavior. Psychologists focus less on this perspective as compared to the sociologists.

The evolutionary perspective

Although McDougal's (1908) concept of instincts, known as innate patterns of behavior, was deterministic and fell out of favor with the vast impact of behaviorism, the **role of biological factors** gained popularity in the 1960s with the studies on ethology, the study of behavior in a natural setting (Lorenz, 1976). Since social behaviors, such as selection of mate, courtship, men's attraction to beautiful and healthy women or conversely, women's attraction to resourceful and healthy male, needs for affiliation and recognition, etc. are instruments for the survival of many species, the evolutionary perspectives have deviated from the traditional explanations of the role of biological factors in understanding social behavior. Seeking support from Darwin's theory of the survival of fittest and the ability of genes to change themselves to enhance adaptation, social psychologists began to understand the role of biological factors in explaining human behavior. Consider the following examples that are not easily and fully accounted by other perspectives: our feelings of love for and keeping safe the new born baby; long term relationships and bonds; dislike for asymmetrical faces; the role of gazing in love, etc. Are such evolutionary explanations of behavior useful in applied settings? The answer is not at all easy. In this regard, the reader is referred to the work of Richins (1996) in the chapter on consumer behavior. Richins has categorically demonstrated that the biological explanations of emotions were inadequate for developing an insight in understanding consumer emotions.

In retrospect, when we look at the growth of social psychology in general and applied social psychology in particular, we find that unfortunately, Lewin's contribution could not motivate a significantly large number of social psychologists for a long time to engage in applied research. Rodin (1992) concluded that the poor growth of applied social psychology has been due to the preoccupation of social psychologists to prove the scientific credibility of their discipline. Moreover, they have been unsure regarding extending the findings of their laboratory studies and applying them to real life situations. A typical example is the work of Milgram (1974) who believed that the results of his obedience study could be a valuable tool for explaining the behavior of Hitler's followers who did not hesitate in executing Jews. Milgram went on to argue that what happened in Germany would probably never be repeated in the history of mankind but he could demonstrate through his laboratory experiments how his subjects delivered dangerously high levels of electric shocks under instructions from the experimenter. The reaction to such a broad claim by Milgram resulted in a strong rebuttal by other social psychologists. Baumrind (1964), for example, challenged the findings of Milgram's experiment and concluded that the baseline for obedience in a Milgram type of experiment was higher than what would be found in everyday life. She also questioned the ethics of Milgram's experiment because a number of Milgram's subjects suffered from feelings of guilt after the experiment.

More recently, researchers in the field of social psychology have started perceiving the poor impact of psychology on social issues. They have come to realize that **laboratory studies have limitations** of their own and it would be virtually impossible to extend most of them to everyday life. As a result, they have developed, like Lewin, a distaste for pure basic research. Second, without testing the results of laboratory studies in natural settings, doubts were commonly raised regarding generalizations from narrow experimental studies. Baumrind's criticism of Milgram's work, as stated earlier, is a typical example of such a doubt. And finally, there was a realization that the modern social psychology was not involved in the service of society to a level it should have been decades ago. Self-realization is the key for progress in any aspect of life. With the dawn of such a realization surged a new wave of a wide variety of applications of social psychology in the field of education, health, law, environment and consumer behavior. The list is long and the applications are numerous. Sensing such an impact of applications of psychology, Koch and Leary (1985) have described our time as a "psychological century." Only time will tell if the turmoil in social psychology is healthy or not. The problem in social psychology is not unique, for other sciences have gone through rough periods in their growth as well. As opposed to the pessimistic contention of Gergen, are scholars like Schlenker (1974 T, cf. Gergen, 1990) who argue that the physical sciences too had difficult periods and suffered from contradictory observations, but they survived as their subject matter matured and the inconsistencies harmonized.

EVALUATION RESEARCH, INTERVENTIONS AND SOCIAL PSYCHOLOGY

As stated earlier, applied social psychology is concerned with the development and implementation of interventions. From alcoholics to spouse abusers, and from gender bias in classrooms to racial tension in a community, we need interventions in the form of programs to deal with the problems. When social psychologists develop interventions, they have an **obligation to evaluate the success (or failure) of a program** in collaboration with other specialists. If social psychologists do not use a good theory or provide input in the implementation of a program, something may go wrong. If anything will go wrong, it will, states Murphy's Law. Failure to follow details, inadequate data collection procedures and poorly trained staff are very common reasons for the failure of even well-designed programs.

Social psychologists, therefore, work closely with evaluation researchers to monitor the operation of programs and initiate corrective measures at critical intervals.

Evaluation research attempts to study the **effect of an intervention.** It operates on the premise that each intervention has an intended goal and that the expected outcomes of an intervention can be measured (Posvac & Carey, 2003; Rossi, Lipsey & Freeman, 2004). This type of research is **descriptive** and highly **global** in nature in comparison to experimental research. For example, the Head Start program was designed for the overall cognitive growth of children and it was expected that it would lead to a ten point gain in the IQ of the participants.

Evaluation research: Study of effect of intervention

The following paradigm shows how basic research, social interventions and evaluation research are interrelated:

Basic Research (For example, Psychology of Development and Cognition) →
→ Social Intervention (Head Start Program) →
→ Social Policy/Implementation (Funding, staffing, etc.) →
→ Evaluation Research (Assessment and report)

Evaluation research is a **practical approach** to understand the application of a project. Very often it involves a **cost-benefit analysis.** If a new intervention program is extremely costly, evaluation research may help social psychologists to come out of their utopian research endeavors and suggest a viable intervention that does not drain the resources of a community. Due to the expensive nature of many intervention programs, applications of social psychology are not even considered by the members of the community in the Third World.

In the USA, it is now federally mandated that each social service program must be evaluated. Because of its effective nature and utility, evaluation research has been called "**growth industry**" (Guttentag, 1977).

If social psychology is offering a product in the form of an intervention to solve some real life problems, for example, reduction of drug use, healthy eating habits, etc., it must design a system of its operation and define its goals and objectives. Evaluation research examines the purpose of an intervention and helps social psychologists to understand the real value of their work, that is, what, when, where, and how they can contribute effectively and economically to the members of a society.

The interrelationship and difference between basic research, social psychology and evaluation research are summarized in the Table 1.2.

TABLE 1.2

Interrelationship between research, social psychology and evaluation research

Category	Purpose	Operation
Science	Theory building	Seek cause-effect relationship
Psychology	Theory of behavior	Seek IV-DV relationship
Social Psychology	Theory of social behavior	Seek IV-DV relationship
Applied Social Psy.	Design real life solutions	Use interventions
Evaluation research	Assessment	Means-end relationship

IV = Independent Variable; DV = Dependent Variable

Evaluation research has an advantage over scientific research in the sense that it aims at correcting the relationship between the means and the end. If a ten point gain in the IQ of the participants was not possible in the Head Start program, the evaluation researcher will ask, was the program totally ineffective? Were the goals of the Head Start program unrealistic? Did the program help unintended targets like parents who are also learning to become better parents? In other words, evaluation research examines the goals and objectives involved in an intervention and establishes bi-directional causality, that is, unlike experimental research in which simply a cause-effect relationship is established, evaluation research focuses on how an outcome in the form of some gain and loss in a program takes the shape of an independent variable and, in turn, helps modify the intervention program, that is, the original independent variable itself. Owing to this applied nature of evaluation research, the results of interventions based on social psychological principles can become effective and practical.

AREAS OF APPLICATIONS OF APPLIED SOCIAL PSYCHOLOGY

In the past three decades social psychologists have shown how their discipline could be useful for solving real life problems. Borrowing from natural sciences such as biology at the one end and several social sciences at the other end, social psychology has made tremendous progress in showing how our own behavior is responsible for damaging our immune system, enhancing our stress level, and reducing our subjective sense of well-being. Religion has influenced our behavior for centuries and technology has radically altered our life style. Needless to say, both religion and technology have had a tremendous impact on our lives. Environmental issues have had a global impact. It is the behavior of human beings that is disturbing the eco-system without realizing its long-term effects. The sudden surge in consumerism is depleting the limited natural resources on earth. In short, there are several areas of concern in our lives in which social psychology has already demonstrated, or is likely to show, its usefulness. While the issues in our lives may be addressed in various forms and with different titles, the authors have identified here some areas of prime significance. These have been discussed in this book. The areas included are as follows: Technology, Religion, Physical Health, Mental Health, Environment, Law, Consumer Behavior, Education, and Non-violence. Our intent in preferring these areas is solely guided by our everyday experience of forces that control our lives.

In the remaining part of this chapter, we will describe briefly the above-mentioned areas of applications of social psychology with a view to make the reader familiar with the material that follows in this book in the form of an individual chapter on each area.

Social psychology and physical health

An extremely important aspect of our life is health—whether it is mental or physical. One may wonder how physical health could come under the purview of social psychology. Well, there is enough in the literature today to show that while health is primarily the concern of medical practitioners, one cannot ignore social factors in the prevention or prognosis of diseases such as HIV AIDS, cancer, etc. Maintenance of good physical health and its promotion are as much of a social phenomenon as a medical problem. The third chapter on **Social Psychology of Physical Health** is divided into two parts. The first part focuses on the effects of stress on the well-being of individuals. Research studies in areas such as optimism, social support and learned helplessness have been reviewed to show how they are related to health and its management. Recent research in the field of Psychoneuroimmunology (PNI), an interface between the brain, the immune system and behavior, has also been introduced to highlight how physical health issues are related to psychological factors.

The second part of the chapter focuses on the role of social psychology in the understanding and control of health-endangering behavior. It is estimated that approximately 50% people suffer from physical health problems as a consequence of their own behavior, for example, eating too much but exercising less, indulging in sex to feel macho but not using condoms, etc. Only recently has the world started understanding the cultural aspects of dealing with such behavior. For example, in a recent interview with the UNAIDS Executive Director, Peter Piot (*The Times of India*, July 3rd, 2002), some of the ramifications for aids control in different parts of the world have been discussed. In this section, the applications of social psychology have been described in the field of HIV AIDS, weight control, anorexia nervosa and bulimia, cancer and smoking.

Social psychology and mental health

If physical health is influenced by social factors, as stated above, it is not difficult to understand how and why mental health could be affected by the social environment around us. The interpretation of what constitutes normal and abnormal behavior shows wide variations around the world, as also do therapies and their efficacy in various cultures. The range of such therapies is huge as it varies from Taoism in China to the Freudian psychoanalysis in the West.

The chapter on **Social Psychology of Mental Health** (Chapter # 2) begins with an understanding of the limitations of the biological factors in explaining mental health issues. An attempt has been made to present a social psychological framework for the understanding of mental health. Borrowing from the findings in the field of developmental psychology, this chapter explains how mental health problems among children are different from those of adults. Some critical aspects of the patient-therapist relationship have also been examined in the light of empirical research on the self-fulfilling prophecy, the role of priming and the preference of intuitive judgment over statistical information.

The next section of the chapter focuses on what has been called the common cold of mental illness, that is, depression, and the social psychological issues related to it. In the last section of this chapter, we have discussed the contribution of a relatively new approach in social psychology, that is, positive psychology, and how it is helpful in the promotion of mental health.

Social psychology as applied to legal issues

The chapter, **Social Psychology as applied to legal issues** (Chapter # 4), deals with two major issues that are used in court to prove the guilt or the innocence of a defender. The first is eyewitness reports. The role of social factors such as suggestion, misleading questions, etc. have been highlighted to demonstrate how such factors influence the recall of events. Research on acquisition, storage and retrieval from memory has been applied to lineups and the identification of the suspect. Further, problems with the eyewitness testimony of young children have been discussed.

The second part of the chapter deals with the role of the jury in the legal process, and ways in which bias can creep into judgment by the jury. Cultural factors, effects of race, and class have been discussed, as also the effect of size of the jury. Many countries do not have the jury system, but if they do, as in Pakistan and India at the village level, they are plagued by corruption, religious biases and other cultural factors. In this context we kept our focus narrow to help understand what role social psychology can play in understanding legal issues.

BOX 1.8

Some Cheer for Gloomy Juvenile Homes (*The Times of India*, July 8, 2002)

Social Psychology at work in delinquency homes of India:

The UN convention on the Rights of the Child categorically stated that institutionalization should be the last option for child rehabilitation. A better way to promote the psychological growth of the child is envisaged through children homes under the supervision of the Juvenile Welfare Board. The government has also joined hands with several non-governmental agencies to ensure quality care for these children. It will also promote alternatives such as adoption, foster care and sponsorship of the children.

The rationale behind the entire program is to bring child care to international standards and to see that these children grow up with a sense of positive self esteem rather than one of inferiority.

Social psychology and religion

The relationship between psychology and religion has had a great past, has a lukewarm present but will hopefully have a vibrant future. It was decided to include a chapter on religion simply because religion has a powerful influence in the lives of many persons. Yet, we do not find chapters devoted to it even in the most comprehensive of publications on social psychology, such as *The Handbook of Social Psychology* (Lindzey & Aronson, 1969). The chapter, **Social Psychology of Religion** (Chapter # 5), begins with a review of the contributions of prominent psychologists to the study of religion, for example, the works of William James, Freud, Hall, Skinner and Maslow. Subsequently, a number of variables related to religious behavior have been examined.

The second part of the chapter deals with the issues of measurement of religious attitudes, beliefs and behavior. Several scales have been critically examined. The difference between religiosity and spirituality has also been analyzed. The chapter ends with a review of recent research on and issues concerning the role of religion in influencing the mental health of people. Research from various parts of the globe have been presented, ranging from Taoism to other forms of faith healing in European countries such as Finland.

Social psychology of technology

There is no doubt that technology has a dominant effect on our lives. And yet, the adaptation of technology, its use and abuse, and the resistance to technological advances has not been properly understood in the absence of psychological research. After describing some of the popular expressions that are used in defining the effects of technology on people, the chapter, **Social Psychology of Technology** (Chapter # 6), focuses on the role of technology in the lives of individuals. Is excessive use of computers pathological? One mother felt guilty because for two years she had been so obsessed with computers that she fed her children fast food and rarely cooked for her three children. Specific aspects of technology that are discussed in the chapter include the effect of computers—especially its effects on children; the effects of the World Wide Web; and the differences between face-to-face interaction and virtual interaction. Also included in the discussion is the role of office automation and its implications for the employees, methods of communication and its influence on the globalization of business.

BOX 1.9

Automation in the Army

A recent article in *The Times of India*, July 2, 2002, writes about the plans for greater automation in the army of the United Kingdom. Britain's soldiers are to be turned into high-tech robot soldiers in a 1 billion pound project to create one of the most technologically advanced armies. Rather than being strapped with traditional helmets, uniforms and rifles, the soldiers will have gadgets that include a gun capable of shooting around corners, a computerized helmet that can download maps and a whisper sensitive radio implanted into the ear. The first of such kits will be introduced from 2008, with the whole army modernized by 2012.

Yes, UK soldiers will bristle with state of the art equipment. But will they be psychologically ready for it? Both theory and practice have shown that technology is effective only when it is preceded by training, not only in how to use the gadgetry, but more importantly, to change the mindset.

The effects of automation have also been discussed with special reference to job satisfaction of workers. Box 1.9 describes how the British Army plans to get highly automated. What will be the effect of such changes on their job satisfaction? What sort of interventions can be planned for such problems? The cross-cultural issues related to the effects of technology such as use of equipment and conflict with cultural beliefs have been examined. A dedicated Muslim, who wants to pray five times a day, will find it impossible in orienting himself toward Mecca while traveling in a revolving space ship. Further, how technology has differently influenced the perception and the behavior of people in the developing, developed and underdeveloped countries has also been brought to the fore.

Social psychology and environment

What are we doing to our Mother Earth? Needless to say, our own behavior is leading to its destruction. We have an obligation to help protect and conserve it. Social psychological studies show clearly that while we hold pro-environmental attitudes, pro-environment behavior is much less common. How can social psychology help understand the difference between pro-environmental attitudes and behavior, and more importantly, how can we, as psychologists, promote pro-environmental behavior? The chapter, **Social Psychology of the Environment** (Chapter # 7), deals with behavioral issues related to energy conservation, water conservation, litter control and recycling.

The next section of the chapter deals with the following issues: environmental stressors and its effect on the social-psychological well being of people; the effects of crowding, and especially the perception of crowding, personal space, and proximity; and the effects of urbanization. A number of examples have been cited from countries in Southeast Asia, the Americas and Europe to understand behavior that is anti-environmental. The last part of the chapter deals with special environments such as the isolated confined environment and the field of ecopsychology.

o ial s olo an ons er e avior

This chapter, **Social Psychology of Consumer Behavior** (Chapter # 8), begins with an analysis of attitudes people hold towards money. After all, the advertisement industry of over 70 billion dollars in the USA thrives on the assumption that advertisement alone can lure people to buy the advertised products. No wonder, with the introduction of Joe Camel, the sale of Camel cigarettes increased by 13% and most of this increase was among the teenagers. In this section of the chapter, variables like need for social identification and enhancement of self-image have been discussed to show how they lead to changes in consumer behavior. Further, the chapter deals with the mechanism of persuasion that involves an understanding of routes of information analysis. As can be seen from the Box 1.10 on credit cards in India (below), people across different cultures may perceive the same product in various ways. What has become part of routine life in the West may not be accepted in a more conservative culture such as India. Applied social psychology can help us not only understand such problems but also to offer suggestions to companies for persuading recalcitrant consumers.

BOX 1.10

Credit remains a dirty word in the Indian psyche
(*The Times of India*, July 3, 2002)

How do Indians perceive credit cards? A recent survey by ORG-Marg, a marketing research company, found that most Indians are still wary of plastic money and still prefer to pay with good old currency notes. The study concluded that Indians prefer the currency notes over plastic money because the majority feel that credit cards lead to overspending, impulse purchases, self-indulgence and above all, it fuels desire which is an absolute no-no from the religious-cultural standpoint. Indians continue to lay emphasis on saving up for unknown exigencies. Credit card users also have a cultural barrier against going into debt. Saving is seen as a sign of respect for one's income. This finding on Indians is in sharp contrast to many North Americans who fall behind in their credit card payments and remain in debt.

The remaining part of the chapter is focused on the effects of viewing television. Research shows that such effects could be both intentional and non-intentional. The chapter focuses particularly on the effects of television violence on children. Also discussed in this chapter are issues related to altruistic marketing, that is, warning consumers regarding the use, misuse and abuse of buying products and what causes pathological behavior among consumers. Also examined are the effects of the newest method of marketing—the Internet. Finally, the cross-cultural aspects of consumer behavior, such as gifting, buying behavior, etc. are also presented.

BOX 1.11

An industry driven by sexual instinct will always thrive (*The Economist*, May 24, 2003)

The emerging area of evolutionary psychology seeks to study the relationship between genes, nervous system, behavior and ecology. Babies as young as few months old tend to respond to what is beautiful. They look at faces that are symmetrical, but avoid those that are not. Obviously, distorted faces are considered ugly. After analyzing the mating preferences of 10,000 people in 37 cultures, David Buss concluded that physical attractiveness was on top or near on top of the list of every man. No wonder that efforts to look beautiful have created a global industry worth 160 billion US dollars. Annually, Americans spend more on beauty than on their education.

Besides the advantage in mating, beauty offers several social advantages as well. Attractive people earn more, receive lighter punishment from jury, are judged more intelligent, and are considered better in the bed. Is this the age of "Survival of the Prettiest"?

Social psychology of aggression and non-violence

Social psychologists have neglected the area of non-violence for a long time. Whereas the work of William James, the founding father of modern American psychology, is well known in the areas of emotion and memory, his contribution to the field of non-violence remained unknown (Kool, 1993). On the other hand, so great has been our preoccupation with aggression and violence, that while typing out this manuscript, one of the authors herself unwittingly typed "aggression and violence" as the heading of the chapter. The chapter on **Social Psychology of Aggression and Non-violence** (Chapter # 9) has been divided into three parts. Following a brief description of aggression and its types, the first part deals with the control of aggression. Various techniques based on social psychological principles have been discussed. The second part of the chapter focuses the management of conflicts. Is social

BOX 1.12

On justifying invasion of Iraq

On May 31, 2003, *The Economist* wrote the following, describing how the President of the USA, George Bush, would justify attack on Iraq even if no weapons of mass destruction were found: "Even those who said that the war should not have been fought must see that the removal of Mr. Hussain has had useful consequences, including some for Palestine. It has left America on a position to bring new pressure on potential spoilers such as Syria and Iran, and the rejectionist guerillas they succor. By removing a threat to Israel and a source of support for the Intefada, it has made it safer for Israelis to compromise and harder for Palestinians to believe that they will achieve their aims by violence" (p. 11).

Mann (1993), through his empirical research, showed how his subjects changed the nature of their attributions when they were asked what would be fair in war if they were viewing their country as opposed to the enemy. As expected, the rules of war changed when the subjects evaluated the atrocities perpetuated by their own people versus those by the enemy.

psychology helpful in reducing violence at the workplace and at home? Instead of cataloging the volume of research that has been conducted to show the contributions of social psychology, we chose to focus on a few sample areas where knowledge of social psychology has yielded some results. The issues concerning violence in schools will be discussed in the Chapter on Social Psychology of Education.

The third part of the chapter is devoted to the role of social psychologists in the promotion of peace and non-violence. In this context, it is argued that the control of violence does not mean the presence of non-violence because the forces that promote non-violence are opposed to that of violence. By suppressing the behavior of people we cannot achieve peace, for peace involves sustained efforts in building trust and goodwill. The chapter ends with some reflections on the contributions of psychology of peace in resolving international and community disputes and the developing of communities of peace.

Social psychology of education

The behavior of children at school and social psychology bear a very special relationship. Outside the home, the schools are not only the first places where the child normally spends a lot of time, they are also important as agencies of socialization. In a group setting such as a school, social psychological principles apply very clearly. For example, there is a plethora of research to demonstrate how attitudes and behavior of teachers influence the performance of children in the classrooms. Students, too, have expectations from their teachers and research data show that these expectations also have an impact on the behavior of teachers. In short, teachers and students are involved in an interactional situation in a school where both tend to continually influence each other (Brophy, 1986).

This chapter, **Social Psychology of Education** (Chapter # 10), also deals with the social psychology of the classroom. For example, how do seating arrangements influence the learning of children? Ways of changing the traditional classroom have also been discussed in the light of research on the Jigsaw technique, peer tutoring, and other forms of cooperative learning. Issues concerning teacher effectiveness are also presented. Drawing lessons from the Head Start program, the limits of the applications of psychology are reported. Other topics dealt with in this chapter refer to the issues concerning testing, stress among children and learning styles. Recent research studies on learning styles based on cultural characteristics, for example, Confucian versus Socratic, show that those students who were used to learning in a particular style found it hard to learn when transplanted into a new system of education (Kool & Misra, 2003; Tweed & Lehman, 2002).

In conclusion, we believe that the applications of the knowledge of social psychology are vast and they cover practically all aspects of our lives. As mentioned earlier, we have been selective in terms of the significance of the above areas.

BOX 1.13

Applied social psychology in the news

Why does applied social psychology need to have a global perspective?

A recent interview with the Executive Director, UNAIDS, published in *The Times of India*, 3, July, 2002, helps us to understand the need for a global perspective. The emphasis of the Executive Director was not just on how things have changed in the Indian scenario, but also on the lessons learnt from other countries, and how these can be put to use in India. The interview is being excerpted below:

Q: "You have been to India over the years. Do you see any difference in the approach towards HIV/AIDS?"

A: "Yes, compared to two years ago I see an enormous difference. The states are doing a lot more, there is a national policy now, ..."

Q: "Is that enough?"

A: "It is one part, society has to be involved in the fight. But there has to be political leadership, look at the Brazil example. We need a multi-sectoral approach, this is not a matter for the health ministry alone."

Q: "Have you seen an innovation worth mentioning?"

A: "Yes, the involvement of railway employees is one. Millions of people use the Indian Railways every year. This is a good opportunity to spread information and awareness, we can replicate this in other sectors, notably the education sector........"

Q: "Can you give some examples where the clergy has played a positive role?"

A: "Yes, across the world, Imams have used their sermons and quotations from the Quran to create awareness of HIV/AIDS. In Uganda, it has worked. In Senegal, the Friday prayers focus on themes like HIV/AIDS. In Manipur, the church has been involved in the battle. In Thailand, Buddhist monasteries have done a great deal to disseminate information and even provide care and treatment to patients."

Q: "Do you feel that generational icons can play a greater role?"

A: "..........Magic Johnson did more to break the silence around the disease than all the publicity campaigns at that time."

Q: "An international AIDS vaccine trial is on the cards in India. Do you think this will raise ethical issues?"

A: "We definitely need a vaccine. But we in UNAIDS have published a booklet on ethical guidelines........there can be no testing without involving the community as a whole in the full awareness of their rights."

Q: "So the prevention route is what you recommend?"

A: "Yes, the impact of preventive strategies can be seen in Cambodia, Zambia, Tanzania where young pople were targeted. It is showing positive results."

Q: "Do you see a sense of denial in India on this issue?"

A: "While I do see greater activity on this front, yes, there is not enough of a sense of urgency. Sex is a fundamental part of life and there is no point denying it. No one is above contracting HIV. After all, four million people in India did not get infected from transfusions alone. This is not a problem for poor people, it affects everyone, the middle class must involve itself more actively in this campaign."

The excerpts from the interview are relevant to the domain of applied social psychology. First and foremost, the UN realizes that lessons learnt elsewhere in the world could help in developing a strategy for India. One strong argument in favor of any global perspective is that, by using such a perspective, we can learn not only from our successes but also from our failures. Similar countries may demand similar interventions. Even if they do not, this similarity across cultures can act as the starting point for the development of an intervention program.

Summary

The chapter starts out with what social psychology is and attempts to define it, especially in the ways in which it is different from sociology or personality psychology. We then go on to define applied social psychology and delineate its salient features, with a special focus on the need for social psychology from the global perspective, and its role as a normative science. The contributions of applied social psychology cannot be understood without reference to the history of social psychology. Similarly, it would be difficult for the reader to grasp the intricacies of the applications without some idea of the major theoretical underpinnings of the discipline. After a brief description of the social learning, the phenomenological, the social-cognitive and evolutionary perspectives, the chief characteristics and the importance of evaluation research for applied social psychology have been discussed. The chapter ends with the outline for the rest of the book in terms of the specific areas of application to be focused upon.

Some Key Terms

Applied social psychology
Emic
Etic
Implicit theory
Independent construal of self
Individualist *v.* Collectivist cultures
Interdependent construal of self
Social influence

SOCIAL PSYCHOLOGY OF MENTAL HEALTH

2

Chapter Outline

- An introduction to social psychology of mental health
  - The burden of disease due to mental illness
- On the limitations of a biological model of mental health
- The cross-cultural aspect of mental health
- Insights from developmental psychology
- Social psychology of clinical psychology
  - When the therapist gets the expected information
  - When a thought process is activated
  - When we expect two events to be related
  - When information arrives after the fact
  - When to rely on clinical prediction
  - When to correct inferential errors
- The common cold of mental health: Depression
  - Cross-cultural aspects of depression
- Some social psychological theories and clinical intervention
  - Bandura's social learning theory
  - Social comparison theory
  - Social psychology and attribution therapy
  - Social exchange theory and clinical psychology
  - Social psychology, mental health and the layperson
- From mental illness to mental health
  - Positive psychology
  - Positive psychology at the individual level
  - Positive psychology at the subjective level: Subjecting Well Being (SWB)
  - The concept of SWB
  - Positive psychology at the group level
- Role of SWB in life and at work
  - SWB at work
  - SWB in old age
  - SWB across cultures
- Social psychology and therapy
  - Spirituality in mental health
  - Community based mental health care

"...the burden of psychiatric conditions has been heavily underestimated..."
(National Institute of Mental Health, USA, 2001)

Even half a decade after our entry into the 21st century, we are being made to realize that the challenges for mental and physical health are far more complex and numerous than those faced at the end of the 20th century. Migration, automation, nuclear power, and changes in political, religious and cultural institutions, at a remarkable speed around the globe, have contributed to not only numerous but also new concerns for mental and physical health. The number of working-women has increased phenomenally during the past 30 years alone, but men have not learned how to share the burden equally at home. Also, both men and women have not kept pace with the changes at the technological and cultural levels. As a result, people feel stress, anxiety, and depression—not because they are not "normal" people—but because they do not know how to prepare themselves for the avalanching changes in their environment. There are other costs too. In view of the rising incidence of mental illness in Canada, Statscan, an agency that conducts population surveys started questioning 30,000 Canadians on their mental health in May, 2002. Estimates of cost to economy are placed at $13.4 billion a year through lost productivity and sick days alone (Monchuk, 2001). Similar is the case with other developed countries. Suicides in Japan hit a record in the year 2003 with the figures topping 34,000 deaths (*Canadian Press*, 2004). And, we know that one of the major causes of suicide is depression. In Afghanistan, ravaged by war for twenty-three years, one of the most prevalent reasons for people to visit the health center is fear. Women in particular are badly affected. In Kabul alone, an estimated 60,000 widows are forced to subsist without the traditional family support (*WHO Special Report*, 2001). In Kerala, a southern state in India, the suicide rate has increased to one every hour.

AN INTRODUCTION TO SOCIAL PSYCHOLOGY OF MENTAL HEALTH

The burden of disease due to mental illness

The **burden of mental illness** on health and economy has long been underestimated. On the basis of a massive project, the Global Burden of Disease study undertaken jointly by the World Health Organization, the World Bank and Harvard University, there are data to show that mental illness, including suicides accounts for over 15% of the burden of disease in established market economies, such as the USA. This is more than the disease burden due to all cancers taken together (NIMH, 2001). As an index to the burden of disease, the **DALY**, that is, **Disability Adjusted Life Years index** was developed. This index measures lost years whether due to disability or due to premature death.

DALY: Disability Adjusted Life Years: an index to measure the burden of disease

The projections show that with the aging of the world population and the conquest of infectious diseases, psychiatric and neurological conditions could increase their share of the total global disease burden by almost half, from 10.5% of the total burden to almost 15% in 2020.

And yet, mental health is being neglected the world over. One of 4 people will be affected by mental illness, but few will seek help. As many as 40% of countries have no mental health policy and two thirds of the countries spend 1% or less of their health budget on mental health (Nullis, 2001).

This is where **social psychology** can step in, not only in making people more **aware of mental health and illness**, but also by helping to **remove the stigma** attached to mental illness, a major deterrent to the seeking of professional help. It is commonly known that 80% of schizophrenics could be helped by antipsychotic drugs; about 60% of the depressives could recover; and, 70% of epileptics could be seizure free (Nullis, 2001).

In this regard, recent work by the American Psychological Association is commendable. According to Dr. Henry Tomes (2003), American Psychological Association's, Executive Director for Public Interest, mental health has been neglected for a long time. The Surgeon General's Office (USA) also raised national awareness through a report entitled, *Mental health: a report of the Surgeon General.* The purpose of the report was to educate the public regarding research, prevention and treatment of various categories of mental disorders. What is of greater importance to us as social psychologists is the supplement to the report *Mental health: Culture, Race and Ethnicity.* The most recent development in the mental health arena is the New Freedom Commission on Mental Health, created by the White House in 2002. With the formation of this commission, it is hoped that mental health will receive the due attention from various quarters.

It is clear today that mental health issues, whether viewed from the angle of dysfunction or optimal functioning, are related to a wide range of conditions, including the social environment. Obviously, social psychology should have played a leading role in the understanding of mental health issues. Unfortunately, the applications of social psychology in mental health have been demonstrated only very recently. According to Ruble, Costanzo and Higgins (1992), important research in social psychology, unlike medicine, is abstract in nature and does not demonstrate a tangible influence of a fixed quantity. As a result both the policy makers and the public have less faith in social psychological findings as compared to a "medical pill."

Mental health and physical health are interrelated because both interact and affect each other. It is not intended here to disjoint them while describing the contribution of social psychology in two separate chapters on mental and physical health, that is, in the present chapter and the next chapter 3. Rather, this plan is considered useful so as to allow us to focus on issues that are primarily physical or mental in nature. Moreover, there are issues that are uniquely related to psychotherapy. For instance, how do we judge that the depressive patients perceive reality better than the normal people? Do we teach them to deny reality? Such issues are posing problems to so-called "normal people" because they themselves show self-serving biases. As we mentioned in chapter 1, scientists, including social and clinical psychologists, tend to accept current social beliefs and practices and shape their interventions based on the judgments of normal people.

It would probably be wise to leave the issue of "who is normal?" to pundits in clinical and abnormal psychology, instead. It is more relevant to discuss how social psychologists can address the issues of mental health in their domain and offer solutions to everyday problems. There are **two ways** to look at **the issue of mental health. First,** according to Kazdin (1993), is "the absence of dysfunction in psychological, emotional behavioral, and social spheres" (p. 128).

In terms of psychiatric analysis, such disorders are related to schizophrenia, depression and anxiety. However, all problems need not be classified into diagnostic categories. They may result from the environmental conditions to which an individual belongs. At the second level, Kazdin views mental health as "optimal functioning or well being in psychological and social domains. Well being is not merely the absence of impairment; rather it refers to the presence of personal and interpersonal strengths that promote optimal functioning" (p. 128). Typical examples of such behavior are sharing and caring, dealing with adversity, maintaining social competence, and focusing on positive goals.

Another reason for the delayed application of social psychology in the realm of mental health is the very ability of psychologists to seek dynamic applications in the real life of people. Social psychologists do not provide a framework for the application of their work beyond the laboratory setting. Both the above reasons have left a big gap between the proverbial lip and a cup of tea. In many instances, the claims of social psychology have been considered either too small or too tall or have remained misunderstood. At the same time, a purely biological analysis of mental health does not seem to suffice.

ON THE LIMITATIONS OF A BIOLOGICAL MODEL OF MENTAL HEALTH

Biological and medical experts have held the popular notion that physical and mental problems can be diagnosed and treated using identical approaches. It has been argued that if there is a mental problem, there will be some neurological basis for it. Recent work in neurology, developmental biology, genetics and bioengineering shows that mental problems are linked to some form of degeneration within the body. While such researches are undoubtedly important, so are social psychological findings that emphasize a return to abnormality if the interventions are not implemented. A physician can treat an ulcer with the help of a medicine but he/she cannot change the stressful environment that could cause the ulcer again. At this point we are reminded of our colleague who died of liver problems ten years ago. When his physician first noted his symptoms, he advised the colleague to avoid fried food. His instant reply to the physician was: "If I don't eat such stuff with my friends and at parties, I am going to die anyway. Doctor, you do your job and let me eat what I enjoy. And the rest I leave in the hands of God!" Not surprisingly, our colleague did not survive for long because he ate what he craved for.

Martin Seligman, a key figure in the field of depression and President of the American Psychological Association, 1997, recalled in an interview that when he faced opposition from the committee members in the MacArthur Foundation for funds to continue his research on depression, Jonas Salk, a celebrity on polio cure, came to his rescue and remarked: "Marty, if I were a young scientist today, I would do immunization, but I'd do it your way: psychologically, not biologically" (p. 33, DeAngelis, 1996). This conversation between a renowned physician and an expert in designing intervention programs for depression shows that biologists, too, are beginning to understand the limitations of their own work and now desire to have psychologists as their partners.

THE CROSS-CULTURAL ASPECT OF MENTAL HEALTH

Researches **across cultures** also show the **inadequacy of medical explanations** for treating mental disorders. In contrast to **China,** where the somatic aspect of depression is more acceptable, within the **USA** the affective diagnosis is quite common (Kleinman, 1988). Further, **men** seem to manifest bodily or behavioral symptoms in depression more than **women** who tend to manifest dysphoria. Marsella (1980) concluded that one difference between the objective and the subjective culture is related to symptoms in depression. Individuals belonging to a **subjective culture** tend to view themselves and evaluate their life. On the other hand, indicators like time spent in schooling, climatic conditions, etc. characterize **objective culture**. According to Marsella, people from objective cultures manifest affective and cognitive forms of depression in contrast to those from subjective cultures in whom somatic forms are dominant.

Landrine and Klonoft (1992) concluded that **White Americans** tend to have a different notion about health than many people belonging to **ethnic minority groups**. While an average white individual believes that a disease can be described and treated without reference to the family or community, the members of many ethnic groups view illness as an interpersonal matter that has its roots in changing relationships and problems within the family. Is this not reminiscent of the Holmes and Rahe readjustment concept of stressors? It certainly is? Therefore the schema of health among white and nonwhite people differs; the former regard it as a micro level problem but the latter consider it as a macro level problem. For example, Haitians regard AIDS as a curse for those who violate social and behavioral taboos.

Murphy (1982) reported that the rate of hospitalization for treatment of schizophrenia was higher among Irish Catholics than among others. He attributed this rate mainly to reduced clarity of information, a major factor contributing to schizophrenia. Murphy further argued that a culture could provide a unique view of a disorder in terms of several parameters, for example, definition, acceptance, and recognition of a disorder. **Cross-cultural studies** clearly point out that the **behavior through which a symptom is expressed** need not be the same in all cultures. A World Health Organization study (1979) clearly shows the extent to which **profiles of symptoms in nine countries (Columbia, Czechoslovakia, Denmark, India, Nigeria, Taiwan, UK, USA and USSR)** differed for patients who were all diagnosed as schizophrenics. For example, the Nigerian sample scored differently on hallucinations and insight. At the same time, such cross-cultural studies do not deny the existence of a common profile of symptoms associated with a mental disorder. There could be cross-cultural differences in health-seeking behavior too. A survey of health-seeking behavior among various ethnic groups of **Bangladesh** clarified that while some ethnic groups preferred paraprofessionals, unqualified allopaths were consulted by another group, and, qualified allopaths by a third ethnic group. In fact, sex, types of illness, ethnicity, household head's education and household's landholding were significant predictors of treatment-seeking behavior (Ahmed, 2001). Information such as this should be useful in the designing of health interventions in the future.

If behavior is so different in different cultures for the diagnosis of an identical disorder, a major task of social psychology is to help the therapist to understand what forms of such behavior are **local** and **exotic** in nature in comparison to others that are classified as **universal** and form the core of a disorder. Understanding how people in a culture perceive, interpret and categorize information and react to social influence is a prerequisite for delivering any kind of psychotherapy to the members of that culture. The statement that all politics is local (late Tip

O'Neil, Speaker of the House, USA) can be used for psychotherapy as well: All psychotherapy is local, too.

The idea that **all psychotherapy is local** is no more clearly evidenced than in the indigenous cultures of various countries. Two cases are discussed below. In both the cases it has been shown that culture should be treated as a resource and not as a diversity problem that requires a solution. The first case is of the National Indian Child Welfare Association, USA. Terry Cross (2003) has given us various examples of how we can enhance positive emotions such as joy, interest, contentment and optimism through the music, dance, festivals and other celebrations of the culture. In fact, he makes it clear that the local culture acts as a resource for theories that can help one to understand human behavior; as a resource for healing; as a resource for clinical practice and as a resource for mental health and wellness. Social psychology can be of help by explicitly trying to encourage people to participate in such events. Similar is the case of the aborigines of Australia. The indigenous people of Australia have their own understandings of mental health on the basis of which indigenous mental health care can be planned (Brown, 2001).

Several myths surround mental illness

Kleinman and Cohen (1997) concluded that there still persist several **myths** concerning mental illness. **First,** that mental illness is similar everywhere. **Second**, that some part of mental illness is biological but its experience is culture specific. **Third,** that certain exotic places show culture specific disorders outside the West. And **fourth**, that there is not much that can be done to treat mental illness. A major task of social psychology is to dispel such false beliefs. As expressed by the Director General, World Health Organization,

> "Mental health is not a personal failure....It is to be found in the way we have responded to people with mental and brain disorders", Brundtland (WHO, 2001).

Why don't people seek professional help? Often because of shame. This shows that there is still a stigma attached to mental illness and it is only after this **stigma** is removed that a sufficient number of people will start benefiting from the current scientific knowledge regarding the prevention and treatment of mental illness.

From the World Health Organization report (1995) it is clear that the general health care physicians fail to diagnose mental health problems in almost 50% of the cases. Or, when they diagnose it correctly, they often prescribe drugs that are improper for the treatment. Moreover, the market for psychiatric drugs is growing around 12% annually and it has an effect on lifestyle disorders that are rising and are likely to rise still further in the coming years.

People are living longer now than ever before. As the life expectancy is increasing from the forties to the sixties in age, in the third world countries the physical well being of individuals is becoming associated with an increase in mental health problems. According to psychiatrist Murugesh Vaishnav, depression and anxiety is the third largest illness in India, after infections and cardiac diseases (Chavda, 2002). Schizophrenia, too, is rising at an alarming rate in low income societies. It is expected that given a base rate of 1985, it will rise 45% by the beginning of the 21st century.

INSIGHTS FROM DEVELOPMENTAL PSYCHOLOGY

After examining the limitations of the biological explanation of mental health, the obvious question before us is, "is it possible for social psychology to develop a set of generalized rules to deal with mental health issues and to offer standardized guidelines to the concerned mental health professionals? Unfortunately, this is not the case. For a long time social psychology simply did not engage in research to show how the social influence mechanism works differently for people at different age levels. Rather, it focused on a general set of principles that could account for social behavior universally at all age groups.

Problems of children's mental health different from those of adults

Commenting on the issue of understanding **children's mental health**, Saxe, Cross and Silverman (1988) wrote, "It is widely recognized that children's mental health problems differ from those of adults and that failure to treat such problems leads to later difficulties. Given this knowledge, it is puzzling, then, that a more effective system to treat children's mental health problem has not developed" (p. 800). In another article published slightly later, Kazdin (1993) argued that research on the mental health of both children and adolescents has been neglected for a long time and that social psychologists were slow to understand and use the insights gained from developmental psychology. Kazdin further remarked that between the two groups, adolescents were less explored for mental health problems than children.

Three reasons for poor contribution of psychology in understanding adolescent mental health

According to Kazdin, there are **three reasons** that account for the poor contribution of psychology to the understanding of the adolescent's mental health. **First,** the period of adolescence has been generally viewed as a time of transition from childhood to adulthood and therefore researchers have not viewed it as a stable period. **Second**, because the problems of adolescence subside over a period of time, a unified explanation for ongoing changes in the behavior during this period was ignored. This stage of development was dismissed as a period of maturational unfolding and little attention was paid to the situation-person relationship. And **finally,** this period also poses several methodological problems because of biological (for example, height, weight, etc.) and psychological changes.

It is estimated that approximately five million adolescents in the United States suffer from mental health problems. Some of their problems are carried over from their childhood but a number of emotional and behavioral problems are unique for this age. Commenting on the disorders during adolescence, Kazdin (1993) remarked, "In community samples as well, there is a sharp rise in report of symptoms of depression from childhood to adolescence. In addition, in adolescence gender differences in prevalence emerge" (p. 131). Girls show higher levels of depression than boys.

Mental health problems of children different from those of adolescents

Research on the **mental health of children** shows that their problems are not similar to those of **adolescents.** For example, owing to children's high dependence on others, they are highly vulnerable. Changes in the family environment—say, divorce or poverty—may exacerbate their disorder. It is estimated that approximately 11% children, that is, 6-8 million, are in need of mental health treatment in the United States. Further, unlike adolescence, the disorders during childhood that need intervention are autism, conduct disorders and attention deficit. Third, children show self-destructive behavior, such as suicide, less often as compared to adolescents. It is estimated that approximately 14% adolescents attempt suicide and 0.1 per cent actually commit it.

Some recent investigations on the mental health of children and adolescents provide further insights. One important issue in this context is the **well-being** of children in the face of **traumatic experiences.** The recent war in Bosnia Herzegovina provided social scientists the opportunity. A gender balanced sample of 40 adolescents was selected on the basis of the Harvard Trauma Checklist and the Hopkins Symptoms Checklist to include an equal number of high and low scorers. After a year of participant observation of these children, in-depth interviews were conducted to explore into their understanding of the war and their own well being. The results show that the degree to which the adolescents attempted to understand the war led to feelings of insecurity with lower happiness as the end result. In contrast, those who did not think too much about the war were happier (Jones, 2002).

A number of studies (for example, Ben-Zur, 2003) have provided evidence for a strong relationship between the **happiness of children** and the level of **well-being of their parents.** The study based on data from 121 Israeli 15-19 year olds, clarified that there was a positive relationship between the parents' and the adolescents' subjective well being. Moreover, adolescent mastery and optimism were also related to positive relationships with parents (Ben-Zur, 2003). Parental warmth was found to be a significant predictor for the subjective well being of school children from Hong Kong too (Chang, McBride & others, 2003).

In the developing as well as the developed world, there is a need for ethical guidelines to address potential abuse of psychopharmacological medications in children. We also need to consider that children placed in difficult circumstances such as war, drought, famine, etc. need to be differentiated from the more stable disorders such as autism. Then there is the need to consider the degree of disability associated with a diagnosis.

In short, the **contribution of social psychology in the area of mental health** can be best understood in **two ways. First,** an approach based on a medical intervention alone will not go far because most mental health problems are related to environmental conditions. The partnership between medical and psychological approaches must be acknowledged. **Second,** both medical and psychological approaches are bound to fail in the absence of lack of sensitivity to cultural and developmental factors that are related to the understanding of mental health.

It is clear from the above discussion that social psychology needs to link antecedent conditions and behavioral outcomes indicating mental health problems. With a view to encompassing the contribution of social psychology, Ruble, Costanzo and Higgins (1992) have proposed **a process-oriented model** to account for the mediating role that social psychology can play in dealing with mental health issues (Figure 2.1).

Figure 2.1: Social psychological mechanisms as mediators in the study of mental health issues (adapted from Ruble, Constanzo and Higgins,1992).

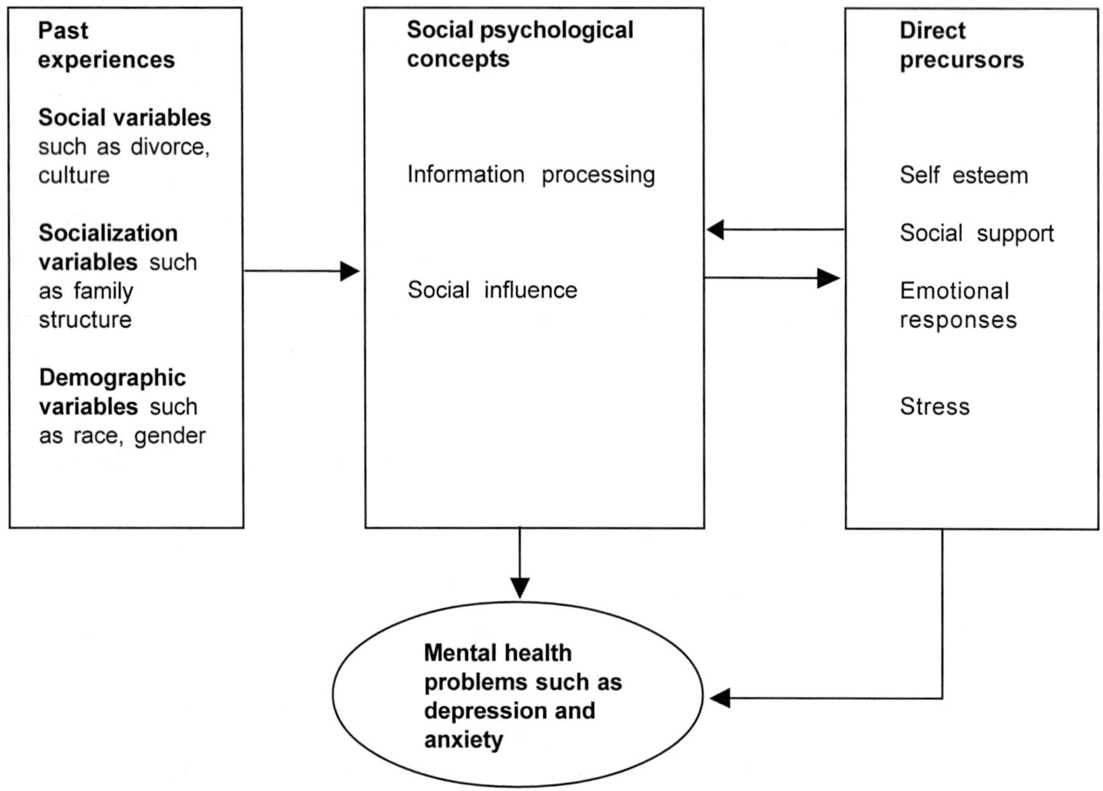

Fig. 2.1 shows that the beginning of the understanding of mental health issues is rooted in the **antecedent conditions** comprising,

- **The social context, for example, divorce, poverty, etc.**
- **The socialization process, for example, parental attitudes, family structure, etc.**
- **The demographic factors, for example, age, race, gender, etc.**

The above factor/s, operating **through social psychological mechanisms,** may result in direct precursors such as **self esteem and stress.** According to this model, mental health problems may be linked either directly to these precursors or to a combined influence of antecedent conditions and direct precursors operating through social psychological mechanisms such as social influence, cognitive consistency and social comparison.

The above model has a very distinct **advantage.** It aims directly at the place where the social psychological processes play a pivotal role in a very complex study of mental health problems. Generally speaking, whereas sociologists and other social scientists will focus on the antecedent conditions, on the one hand, and physiologists on the consequential bodily changes, on the other hand, in their quest for studying mental health problems, social psychologists "mediate the relation between precursors, such as self esteem, and mental health outcomes (paths c and d)" (*ibid*, p. 12).

Mental health issues are **interdisciplinary** in nature and the above model provides a general description to help us understand how social psychology mediates in **combining various perspectives** on mental health. Please note that for the most part, a model provides a simple analogy to explain the nature of processes without necessarily testing each process independently or even conjointly. Moreover, as agreed by Ruble, Costanzo and Higgins (*ibid*), processes similar to those described in their model may be studied differently under different labels in different contexts. For example, in order to study how people attain mastery or control, social psychological approaches have varied from how people learn to show helplessness (learned helplessness) to what they do to achieve self efficacy, a concept that involves narrowing the gap between their belief and action.

While proliferation of knowledge through various models and approaches is a healthy sign for any discipline, it is important, at the same time, that we understand the role that social psychology has to play in solving everyday problems related to behavior. Based on some key research findings in the field of social psychology that have bearings on mental health issues, the next section of the chapter will be devoted to certain insights that social psychology can offer to clinical judgments.

SOCIAL PSYCHOLOGY OF CLINICAL PSYCHOLOGY

Clinical psychology involves assessment and treatment of people having mental problems. The interaction between a patient and a therapist creates a situation in which both may have similar or dissimilar perception and judgment of a problem. The task of a therapist is to help the patient to understand his problem and to deal with it to regain his health.

Studies in human cognition have shown that we develop **schemas** for objects and people. For example, elderly people and professors are considered "absentminded." Schemas help us classify people and objects and provide economy in our thinking. Additionally, a schema for a person develops an expectation within us for a particular behavior in others and this expectation may lead to eliciting that behavior in others through our own behavior. When teachers expect good performance from some students, they give signals to students through praise and other means. In other words, their action makes students work hard to get good grades and to fulfil their own expectations. When people's expectations take the shape of reality, it is called **self-fulfilling prophecy.**

> **Schemas:** The ways in which we classify incoming information

From the above example it is clear that our classification of other people guides our expectation and behavior. It is likely that our action in certain conditions may actually elicit that behavior from others. The implication of this and other similar studies bears a strong influence in judging behavior in a clinical setting.

In the following discussion, a few selected issues reflecting on the relevance of social psychology in the clinical setting will examined.

> **Self-fulfilling prophecy:** When reality tends to parallel expectations from others

1. When the therapist gets the expected information

Remember, in a therapist-patient situation the therapist leads the process by asking questions and the patient answering. In this type of scenario, a patient may, and in fact they do, provide information as per the expectation of their therapist.

Through a number of simple experiments, social psychologists have shown that people tend to ask those questions that are **consistent with their schema.** For example, in a study by Snyder and Swann (1978) subjects were asked to interview a partner regarding her personality traits. The subjects were divided into two groups. While the task of one group was to determine whether the partner was an extravert, the task of the other group was to determine if she was an introvert. Each subject was given a list of questions that contained three types of questions: extravert-oriented, introvert-oriented and neutral. You can guess how the two groups selected their questions. Those in the extravert group selected more questions from the extravert category and the opposite was true for the introvert group. In other words, when we attempt to diagnose a problem, we tend to show our bias in determining the course of our curiosity. This tendency is exhibited by laypersons as well as by experts, for example, by physicians, sports commentators, lawyers, historians and others.

2. When a thought process is activated

In the Snyder and Swann experiment, subjects were clearly instructed to look for introversion or extraversion features in their partners. Because their schemas for the two personality characteristics were different they looked for specific features in their partners. Let us take another example. As we have dissimilar schemas for a traditional restaurant and a fast-food restaurant, nobody waits to be seated at a Wendy or at a MacDonald. Because children do not have independent schemas for the two types of restaurants, they often run to grab a seat or food even in a formal restaurant.

Priming: When a schema is activated by a recent event

A recent experience has the potential for activating a schema. This phenomenon is known as **priming.** While watching a horror movie at home, the noise from our refrigerator may lead us to think of an intruder. In the O.J. Simpson trial a witness recalled that he suspected an intruder after he heard a dog barking continuously. An experimental proof on priming was presented in an experiment by Higgins, Rhodes and Jones (1977) who showed that when subjects were asked to evaluate ambiguous behavior, their negative or positive evaluations depended on how they had organized their experience and what was accessible to them. For example, those subjects who were instructed to memorize words such as independent, self-confident, etc. described the character as a likeable fellow in contrast to those who had learned negative words.

Priming effects are very useful in our daily lives, albeit they connect us to negative or biased information on several occasions. Observation of violence on mass media can trigger a negative schema and provide impetus for violent behavior. Berkowitz and LePage (1967) demonstrated how the presence of weapons had resulted in the elevation of aggression levels of their subjects. Josephson (1987) demonstrated that aggressive and non-aggressive behavior of boys in a game was associated with exposure to a violent or to a non-violent script.

It is well known that depressed people are negative in their thinking. Once this negative thinking begins, it sets off a chain of associations leading to depressed moods. William James, known as the founding father of modern psychology in America, defined priming as the wakening of associations. In a clinical setting, priming influences the retrieval of information in several ways. First, patients, such as average individuals, have a tendency to recall events effectively if questions refer to life events of patients rather than deriving information from events in the life of other people and then constructing their own. This phenomenon, called, **self-reference**, is well documented in memory. Self-related information, writes Loftus and others (1994) is "apparently more affect-laden, more familiar..." (p. 115). Further, patients seem to recall the events regarding their health on the basis of landmarks or salient events that improve a patient's ability to retrieve events from the past.

Self-reference: The extent to which events refer to the experiences of the person

Another impact of priming is related to **telescoping** in memory. If an event takes place several months prior (say, 20 months) to a landmark, it is reduced to a few months. This phenomenon, called forward telescoping, has been observed in patients' recall protocols (Loftus & co-workers, 1994). Knowingly or unknowingly, a therapist is likely to prime schema regarding the health of a patient but ignore the bias in the accessibility of patient's schema regarding the temporal events in his/her health problems. If forward telescoping takes place repeatedly in the recall protocol of a patient, it is likely that two unrelated health issues will be associated and result in a misdiagnosis of a problem.

Telescoping: Reduction of time gap between the event and present recall

3. When we expect two events to be related

An important contribution of social psychology in the clinical setting has emerged from studies on **illusory correlation**. This is defined as the relationship between two variables when in actual practice no such relationship exists. Such relationships are the products of our preconceptions. For example, crime is associated with certain groups of people. How do illusory correlations affect us? Consider the following:

Illusory correlation: Perceived relationship between two variables where none in fact exists

> When told about hypothetical positive or negative personality traits of members of an ethnic, racial or occupational group, people will later remember having observed far more stereotype-confirming behaviors in group members than actually occurred. This stereotype distorts their memory to create an illusory correlation between group membership and the frequency of behaviors. Research has shown that by overestimating the frequency of stereotype-confirming behaviors, illusory correlation helps to maintain stereotypic belief. In essence, believing is seeing (p. 482, *NAMHC Report*, 1996).

How do judgments of co-variations apply in clinical settings? Despite the fact that the validity of several clinical tests have shown to be invalid, clinical experts use them in making their judgments (Chapman,1967; Chapman & Chapman, 1967). One example of such a false, albeit popular, test is the example of Draw-a-Person-Test. In this test, a subject is requested to draw a human figure, and, based on the lines and appearance, the expert makes judgments about the personality of the subject. If a subject draws a face with big eyes, it is considered as a sign of paranoia. A false assumption filters in the judgments of a therapist if he believes that a subject is likely to draw big eyes in a state of paranoid than in a non-paranoid condition. Such a false co-variation in clinical settings explains how illusory correlations dominate clinical decisions.

4. When information arrives after the fact

If your friend filed for bankruptcy soon after buying a Ferrari, you might comment, "I knew it would happen sooner or later." Therapists are known to make similar remarks in their practice. Consider the following: After a patient suffers a heart stroke, the physician remarks, "well, he did not watch his diet and the consequence is there."

A lot of the above type of remarks is based on hindsight. A well known study by Rosenhan (1973) illustrates this point very well. When normal subjects faked their complaint regarding "hearing voices," they were admitted in the hospital for diagnosis and treatment. However, they reported their life histories and emotional states honestly. Guess, what was the diagnosis? Most subjects were diagnosed as having schizophrenia. In his subsequent study, Rosenhan told the staff of the hospital that during the next three months at least one or more normal person may fake and attempt to get admission in the hospital. Out of approximately 200 patients admitted during the period of three months, none was fake but the staff suspected that at least 41 genuine patients were phoney.

One of the most devastating effects of "after-the-fact-diagnosis" is the feeling of guilt suffered by the patient's family, significant others and physician. While this may not be very important for minor problems but in case of suicide or life-threatening conditions, the amount of guilt caused by the loss of a person is very significant.

5. When to rely on clinical prediction

Consider the following situation. A teacher predicts the performance of a student at the beginning of a semester (intuitive assessment). However, his/her prediction is contrary to the information based on the relationship between the obtained SAT and GPA scores (statistical prediction). Similarly, a therapist also faces a conflict when he/she has to use either intuition or statistical information. After inspecting my neuro-imaging report (MRI), my surgeon concluded that I was suffering from corporal tunnel syndrome but he also added that the chances of any serious problem in future were not seen in patients like me. Knowing my habit of using the computer for my writing work, he made a prediction that my neck would bother me a lot. In other words, clinicians rely on both statistical and intuitive information in making their judgments.

Robin Dawes (1994) has shown that when faced with a choice, most clinicians show preference for intuitive judgments. On the other hand, although statistical predictions are unreliable, they fair better than human predictions. The question before us is: why do clinicians prefer to use intuitive judgments when data are presented to them? It seems that clinician, like any other average person, is an unyielding theorist who sticks with his schema even though contrary information is given. Mental health professionals, parole board members, educationists and social workers are known to show this type of bias in their decisions.

6. When to correct inferential errors

Heider (1957) remarked that we have a tremendous capacity to attribute (Chapter 1). Although research has shown that people prefer internal explanations (personality features) over external explanations in judging others, a phenomenon known as the **fundamental attribution error**, people generally respond to their favorable schema. Errors in judgment take place when people are not involved in a situation or know little about it. Studies have shown that unless people are not motivated enough, they do not make complex judgments. In a study by Harkness, DeBono and Borgida (1985), female subjects were asked to comment on a man who was dating several

> **Fundamental attribution error:** Use of external attributions for own behavior as contrasted to internal attributions for behavior of others

women. In making their judgments, the female subjects used simple strategies. However, when the female subjects were asked to comment on this man if they were to date with him, most subjects used complex strategies. In other words, when the reference point changed to the individual herself, the strategy also changed, and became more complex.

Over-confidence barrier: Overlooking of important information because of overconfidence

In a clinical setting, the therapist is involved at a deeper level in his/her interaction with the patient. Any decision making has got to be complex in almost all cases. But, as it has been mentioned before, the therapist, like any other person, also makes errors of judgment and needs to balance his decisions. In particular, he may think that his reasoning is correct in the present form and hence continues to process information according to set notions. Social psychological studies aimed at inviting subjects to consider the opposite point of view have helped therapists to understand the other side of the issue and thereby make fewer errors in their judgment (Lord, Lepper & Preston, 1984). When people have overconfidence in making their judgments, they tend to overlook some useful information. This phenomenon is known as **overconfidence barrier**.

Another way to help people to reason correctly is through formal training. Nisbett and others (1987) have shown how students in psychology and medicine scored higher than their counterparts in law and chemistry after a formal training in statistical reasoning. Psychiatrists, clinical psychologists, school psychologists and psychiatric social workers are required to take continuing education courses in many states and learn not only about new developments in their field but also about new techniques to improve their practice.

To sum up, results based on several social psychological studies show that there are many useful lessons to learn from the social psychology of clinical psychology. Physicians, nurses, social workers, psychotherapists and hospital administrators are humans who make errors in their judgments. Applications of social psychology will help them to minimize their rate of errors.

THE COMMON COLD OF MENTAL HEALTH: DEPRESSION

BOX 2.1

The invisible disease: Depression (NIMH, 2001)

Why does National Institute of Mental Health call depression an invisible disease? The outstanding characteristic about depression is that in most cases there may not be any overt characteristic at all. People suffering from depression may go around with their daily life routine in such a way that onlookers may not even realize that this person is suffering. Compare this to some of the other mental disorders. Schizophrenia, for example, has clear overt symptoms such as the withdrawal from reality or the "word salad." Even manic-depressives manifest clear signs: the phasic fits of depression and mania—extreme quietness only to be followed by extreme activity. In contrast to both of these, the depressive is a silent killer. Yet, when we look at the global statistics for depression, we certainly cannot ignore the problem.

- **Major depression is the leading cause of disability in the US and the world over.**
- **Depression disorders affect an estimated 9.5% people in the age group 18+, or about 18.8 million people in the year 1998 alone.**
- **Nearly twice as many women (12%) as men (7%) are affected by depression every year.**

We all undergo periods of sadness or negative thinking. When such feelings become pervasive and dominate our daily functioning, we reach a stage of clinical depression. Generally speaking, depression is best described in terms of the following three symptoms. **First,** it is accompanied by a sad mood and other **emotional changes** such as anger and anxiety. **Second,** a number of **physical changes** are associated with depression such as loss of appetite, weight and energy. **Finally,** at the **behavioral** level, it shows symptoms of helplessness and low self-esteem. When depression becomes psychopathological, a clinician finds the symptoms occurring together at a rate higher than the chance level.

BOX 2.2

Some current data on depression

Treatment for depression in the US soared over a period of 10 years. The number of Americans treated for depression between 1987-1997 soared from 1.7 million to 6.3 million. During the same period, people who used antidepressants rose from 37% to nearly 75%. At the same time, people who received psychotherapy declined from 71% to 60% (Tanner, 2002).

Even in Canada, visits to the doctor for depression reached an all time high in the year 2001: the number of prescriptions for depression in the year 2000 rose by 50% from 1996. It is believed that over 3 million people may be suffering from depression, but only 1/3 of these seek help.

The 9/11 crisis led to a large number of cases of depression requiring long-term treatment (Schmidt, 2001).

The **attributional style** of depressed people is found to be distinctively negative in three ways (Seligman & co-workers, 1984). First, their internal attributions relate to personal inadequacies rather than to situational factors. Second, they show stable attributions that are relatively enduring in nature (for example, related to personality effects). And third, depressed people suffer from global attributions for negative experiences. They believe that some general aspect of their personality is responsible for their problems instead of some particular weakness that can be easily corrected.

Research on depression has raised some critical issues that are of major significance to both clinical and social psychologists. Those suffering from mild depression seem to make more realistic judgments than those who claim to be in a normal condition. This phenomenon, called **depressive realism,** has been explored to point out that it is the normal person who exaggerates control over his/her environment. Depressed people take responsibility for their action and are more realistic in their approach to the future than their normal counterparts (Taylor, 1989).

Depressive people show a pattern of explaining life events that is different from that of normal people. They feel that their failures are caused by their own actions, are long-lasting and will affect a large segment of their life. Such attributions are in sharp contrast to the self-serving illusions of normal people. When normal people exaggerate their success, it causes in them a feeling of happiness and self-worth. They become less self-preoccupied.

Depressive realism: Negative coping style that has its own reward for the depressed person

Raleigh (2002) concluded that women with mild depression live longer. Raleigh's report is based on the work of Blazer, a Duke University professor of psychiatry and behavioral science, in which 2401 women and 1269 men were divided into three categories: depressed, mildly depressed and not depressed. Women in the mild depression category were found to live longer, though the degree of depression was not related to mortality in men. After all, it seems that mental problems too have adaptive purposes, unless, of course, they are linked to our optimal functioning.

Findings reported above and elsewhere point out that depression may be an **adaptive mechanism**, allowing people to cope with their problems in a more realistic fashion and to remove themselves from dangerous and harmful situations. It seems to help people to move away from the unachievable and so they do not waste time on things that they won't do or will not be able to do.

What is the role of a therapist in dealing with depression of a patient? Should the therapist impose the self-serving illusions of normal people on the realistic assessment of depressive people? Is there a lesson for normal people to learn from the "blues" of their own and those observed at a greater magnitude among the severely depressed people?

There should be no disagreement that the effect of depression that leads to a negative style of attribution should be treated by a therapist so that an optimistic attributional style develops. However, it should be noted that the realism of a depressive person is achieved at a substantial cost.

In their article, *The Illusion of Mental Health,* Shedler, Mayman and Manis (1993) reported that just as depressive people use a negative attributional style, among the so-called normal people the illusion of control phenomenon may be exhibited by two groups of people: one, the **defensive deniers**, who have a tendency to distort, and two, **healthy people who do not distort** much. In their judgment, "the presence of defensive deniers would account for the paradoxical finding that "normal" subjects distort more than depressive subjects. In short, positive illusion findings may be nothing but artifacts, due to researchers' inability to access mental health in any meaningful way" (p. 1128, 1993). They further argued that the normal people who are prone to distort reality also give distorted information on psychological tests.

From the above discussion it is clear that the concept of "depressive realism" among mildly depressive people is **a negative coping style** that has its own rewards for a depressive person. Similarly, "defensive deniers" among the normal population represent illusory thinking that promotes optimism. And *real* "realism" lies somewhere in between the two, a demarcation that defines the mental make-up of a real healthy person.

While psychotherapy provides interventions for behavior and emotional problems associated with depression, a social psychological approach will focus on interventions designed to reduce at-risk behaviors and dysfunctions. The **task of social psychology** in the area of depression will begin with the **etiological factors** contributing to depression in a **community.** For example, the incidence of depression has been doubling every ten years in many industrial countries. Suicide is the third leading cause of death among adolescents in the USA. Social isolation has increased in the family because one in every four families consists of only one member. On the other hand, the Old Order Amish, who lead a simple life, have depression rates 80% lower than residents in nearby Baltimore (Robert Wright, *Time*, August 28, 1995).

Is there a message in the enormous popularity of Cheers, a TV show? Probably yes. We all want to be at a familiar place where we can talk about ourselves and others and settle issues informally without violence. Do we have enough support groups to induct at-risk people, especially adolescents, to make them understand the virtues of a healthy life? Seligman and his colleagues have been helping young teenagers to cope up with their mild depression. Here is an excerpt from Tori DeAngelis' (1996) report on the intervention technique used by Seligman:

BOX 2.3

Seligman: Optimism can be a vaccination

"Seligman's latest research has produced the first data on preventing mental illness using psychological techniques," Seligman said at a Master Lecture at APA's 1996 Annual Convention. Specifically, the team is using cognitive therapy techniques with children at risk for depression to help them unlearn their pessimistic thinking, according to Seligman's earlier research. Seligman and his graduate students are now "vaccinating" 10- and 12-year-olds through research-intervention projects with four populations: suburban children; inner-city youth; children and their parents, and teachers, who then train children in the techniques. The team chose youngsters based on two risk factors shown to foster later depression: suffering mild depression and having parents who are in regular conflict."

"At the convention, Seligman presented data from the study on the suburban youngsters. Those who learned such skills such as disputing their negative thoughts and negotiating with peers showed less moderate depression than control children."

"And 'over time, that effect gets bigger and bigger': As the youngsters entered their early teens, 44 per cent who were moderately depressed became even more depressed, compared to 20 per cent of those who received treatment, the team is finding."

"The theory and application of 'learned depression' are themselves optimistic, Seligman believes."

"Unlike intelligence, IQ or your waistline, pessimism is one of those characteristics that is imminently changeable," he emphasized (p. 33, *American Psychological Association Monitor*, October 1996).

Cross-cultural aspects of depression

Does **depression** mean the same thing across nations **or across cultures**? A cross-national study of **28 countries** recently examined this question. On the basis of the Beck Depression Inventory (a scale commonly used for the measurement of depression) the authors found that the same correlates were obtained across countries. This provides evidence for a cross-cultural equivalence of the concept of depression (Van Hemmert, Van de Vijver & Poortinga, 2002). In another study, women from **South Wales, the UK and Ghana** were interviewed regarding their health. Talking about what distresses them, the women spoke of issues that were very similar and were mainly related to material deprivation and gender relations (Stoppard & McMullen, 2003).

In the context of cultural orientations, an understanding of the attributional style used by **Buddhist** monks is an eye opener. Unlike the concept of the self in Western theory and practice, the self in Buddhism is considered an obstacle, something that hinders happiness. According to Rude, (cf Dingfelder, 2003), "a depressed person may make himself feel worse by interpreting his suffering as meaning he has failed in some way" (p. 48). A trained Buddhist monk, on the other hand, regards suffering as an inevitable part of life. This acceptance of mental suffering as an inevitable part of life, rather than as a personal failing, helps monks face sadness with equanimity. Psychologists such as Rude and Davidson agree that Buddhism can teach people with depression to reconceptualise their ideas about the self in such a way as to promote mental health (Dingfelder, 2003).

SOME SOCIAL PSYCHOLOGICAL THEORIES AND CLINICAL INTERVENTION

Bandura's social learning theory

Bandura (1986) has argued that a theory of learning based on reinforcement alone is inadequate for explaining behavior. By adding a cognitive component of **observational learning**, a state in which no reinforcement is provided to the observer, he advocated a social psychological origin of learning.

Observational learning: Learning based on observing

According to Bandura, the following four processes influence learning:

- **Attentional process,** that is, a model must be attended to.
- **Retentional process,** that is, information gained must be retained.
- **Behavioral production process:** translation of learning into performance.
- **Motivational process:** reinforcement must create an expectation in the observer and provide an incentive for translating learning into performance.

Clinical psychologists have made extensive use of Bandura's theory in reducing phobia and socially inappropriate behavior. A technique, called **vicarious extinction,** makes use of Bandura's concepts in reducing avoidance of feared objects. When subjects watch a model who continuously interacts with a feared object and yet suffers no harm, the observer experiences vicariously the behavior of the model. Bandura, Grusec and Menlove's study (1967) was designed to reduce or eliminate fear of children from dogs. Participating children were divided into several groups. In one group, a fearless model, also a young child, played freely with a dog in a party. There were other groups with the variation of context, for example, no model present or no party situation. When a behavioral avoidance test was conducted after a month, children in the model group scored highest in their approach to a dog. In another study by Bandura and Menlove (1968) in which the live model was replaced by a film model, the effects of modelling were obtained again, although live model effects were found to be more effective than the film model.

Vicarious extinction: Reduction in response frequency because of watching model

In another study, Bandura, Blanchard and Ritter (1969) compared the effects of **modelling** with participation, symbolic modelling and desensitization in treating snake phobia. In the desensitization group the subjects were asked to imagine anxiety-provoking scenes with snakes. Although all the three treatment methods were successful in reducing the fear of snakes, the results of the modelling participation method were the most effective.

Modelling: Observing, imitating a person who is being reinforced

The vicarious extinction technique has also been used in the treatment of withdrawal behavior in children. O'Connor (1969) randomly assigned socially-withdrawn children into modelling and control groups. After they were exposed to a film showing how children engaged in social activity, a model joined their activity and reinforced children's behavior of smiling and holding a conversation. Subsequently, observers who were unaware of the group to which these children belonged assessed the behavior of the children. The results of the study clearly showed that social isolates interacted at the same level as their social counterparts did, after they were exposed to both film and model together.

Social comparison theory

The applications of the social comparison theory are very significant in addressing the issues of health. Generally speaking, the social comparison process leads to self-evaluation, self-improvement and self-enhancement (Wood, 1989). When patients begin to compare themselves with others having similar problems they may compare themselves with others who are alike, worse or better off than themselves. Generally speaking, individuals tend to compare themselves with those like themselves for self-knowledge. When they compare themselves with those who are worse off, they indulge in self-protective and self-enhancing behavior known as **downward social comparison.** Cancer patients often make this type of comparison (Taylor, Lichtman & Wood, 1984). On the other hand, **upward social comparison** involves comparison with those who are highly accomplished. This type of comparison leads to self-improvement. Research by Sun and Croyle (1995) shows that the level of perceived threat in a situation acts as a moderator variable in the comparison process. In their research, participants were led to believe that they had a cholesterol level that was either high or low. Some participants believed that their cholesterol level was controllable and others thought that it was not. The results showed that the perception of threat (control of cholesterol) was the key factor in determining the direction of the upward or downward comparison. When subjects indulged in upward comparison, they showed stronger effects, that is, self improvement, than when they reported downward comparison. Sun and Croyle's study also reported that breast cancer patients show a significantly high rate of downward comparison.

Downward social comparison: Comparison with people who are worse off than the person making the comparison

Upward social comparison: Comparison with those who are highly accomplished in any realm

Social psychology and attribution therapy

In chapter 1 and the present chapter, the **relevance of attributions** was explained. Research on attributions shows how people **explain causes of behavior.** When attributions are directed toward our own behavior, they can be self-enhancing or self-defeating. As described earlier, negative attributions in depression may cause psychological disorders if they are maintained for a long time.

Psychotherapy involving attributions helps people to change the style of their attributions, especially their **habitual style of self-attribution**. For instance, when people have difficulty falling asleep, they make self attributions by thinking that something is wrong with them. With a view to exploring this issue further, Storms and Nisbett (1970) conducted a study to find out if elevated autonomic activity was related to insomnia in their subjects. They recruited college students who were suffering from problems in falling asleep. The participating students were then divided into two groups: (a) those who took a pill with the information that it would increase arousal, and (b) those who took a pill with the information that it would decrease arousal. Actually, the pill was a placebo in both cases. As predicted, those who believed that the pill would increase arousal slept earlier than their previous baseline, while those who believed that the pill would cause lower arousal, took more time to sleep in comparison to their previous baseline. In other words, when the subjects attributed sleep to an external source, that is, to the pill given to them, they felt comfortable and slept faster than their counterparts who were unable to seek such an attribution.

Although the above study by Storms and Nisbett has many shortcomings (Kellogg & Baron, 1975), given the nature of this and other similar studies, a serious question arises concerning the deception and ethical considerations involved in such studies. Is it fair to deceive a patient regarding the actual effects of a pill? What if a non-perjorative effect of pill escalates to some other emotional disorder? What would happen to subjects who would expect acceleration in their heart rate, etc. after knowing that the pill would cause such effect but eventually it did not? Such a therapy would raise many more questions than it would answer. The point here is not what therapy was used in the past or is being currently in use; rather, the focus is on the intervention by a social psychologist who can help a therapist to understand that a good therapy is one that cures the present problem and has no side effects.

Social exchange theory and clinical psychology

When the patient approaches a therapist she encounters a situation involving a **social interaction** in which certain **rewards and costs** are involved. The patient expects rewards in terms of treatment, approval and understanding of her problem by the therapist. The costs that are involved in this relationship are:

- **The pressures caused by the therapist in accepting treatment.**
- **The time and money spent by the client.**

Social exchange theory: Interactions based on a cost-benefit analysis

In this relationship both the client and the therapist should feel that they are having a **beneficial exchange**. If the patient feels that the therapy is not worth the efforts and the money, the patient has two options—either to stay in the relationship or to quit treatment. Why do patients who have little faith in being cured continue with a therapy? When patients perceive that there was no better deal available to them, they continue with the same therapist. The situation here is very similar to a spouse who is unhappy in a marriage but she continues to stay in the relationship because of fear of loneliness or unanticipated problems in another relationship. More specifically, social exchange theories help us to understand why people stay in a relationship and how our understanding of interpersonal relationships can help improve the patient-therapist relationship in a therapeutic situation.

Social psychology, mental health and the layperson

For a layperson, mental health issues start from her knowledge of unhappiness and dissatisfaction. I remember noticing a sticker on a car that read: 'My boss is like a diaper. No matter how many times I provide service, it is going to stink again.' I felt like telling the owner of the car that instead of facing the stinky boss, it would be better to change your job. But if there is some merit in the Peter's principle that people rise to the level of their incompetence, all of us really have no choice but to tolerate a stinky boss, who has risen to the level of incompetence. Anyway, most of us are unhappy somewhere: in the family, at work, or in material gains. And we begin to believe that our mental health has been either damaged or is at risk, to say the least.

We have reached a point where parents and teachers have difficulty in figuring out how to discipline children. Equally confusing are the rules imposed on children. A child is disciplined for coloring his hair like Dennis Rodman or for bringing a knife to school to cut his apple. And for all such problems we need counselors, psychotherapists and psychiatric social workers. Our claim of an advanced modern society pushes us to the level of scrutiny that no problem is too small and that any dissatisfaction or unhappiness may have the potential for a catastrophic effect.

Pop-psychology and recent popular therapies offer fulfilments that are gratifying to the client. A counter question, then, emerges: Is there a psychotherapy that teaches us how to live with suffering? Are there lessons to learn from stoicism? When is individual happiness less important than sacrifices are? Unfortunately, there are no easy answers that comprehensively view mental health as understood by a layperson. While for a layperson, some unhappiness and dissatisfaction is a genuine cost of operation in daily lives, "in the therapeutic culture," writes Wendy Kaminer (1996), "being healthy equals being saved" (p. 22). Given this cleavage in the understanding of mental health, Kaminer punches a final blow to modern psychotherapy by stating:

> The culture of therapy is insensible to the virtues of stoicism, which is mistakenly identified with denial or emotional repression—just as passivity in the face of tyranny is associated with political repression. Stoicism, however, doesn't imply the denial of pain so much as a capacity to tolerate it. Should someone endure unhappiness without complaining? All you can say is, "It depends," remembering the tragedy, by definition, is what can only be endured. (Los Angeles *Times Magazine*, p. 22, 1996).

The task of applied social psychology becomes burdensome in the light of the above criticism of psychotherapy. If there are doubts about the culture of psychotherapy in the minds of people, social psychology has to take a lead in determining what is pragmatic for a community. There is nothing great about a therapy if it is not acceptable to the clients of a community. Needless to say, some applications of social psychology in the field of mental health will be seen in the form of its ombudsmanship.

FROM MENTAL ILLNESS TO MENTAL HEALTH

Positive psychology

From the very beginnings of psychology, there has been a greater emphasis on the pathologies of human behavior than on the salutogenic factors. The last few years have witnessed a paradigmatic shift—one from the pathologizing of human experience as in the DSM, to its antithesis—**positive psychology** (Maddux, 2002). For a long while, we have focused on the pathologies of behavior. There has been a greater effort to identify abnormalities in behavior and then to look for the antecedent factors. While Freud focused heavily on the pathologies of behavior, even Bandura, decades later,

> **Positive psychology**: The branch of psychology that focuses on positive experiences and effects rather than on the negative

developed his theory of social learning to understand how children learn violence from watching aggression over the TV, rather than to understand how children learn altruistic behavior.

As Martin Seligman (2003), the psychologist famous for introducing the concept of learned helplessness, puts it,

> .... "relieving the states that make life miserable has relegated building the states that make life worth living to the distant back seat. There has been a profound obstacle to a science and practice of positive traits and positive states: the belief that virtue and happiness are inauthentic, epiphenomenal, parasitic upon or reducible to the negative traits and states" (p. 126).

According to Seligman, positive psychology is about **happiness**, and rests on three desirable states of happiness: the **pleasant life**, the **good life** and the **meaningful life.** So positive psychology is all about deploying our strengths and virtues in all major realms of life: work, parenting, love, etc.

The 3 states of happiness: The pleasant life, the good life and the meaningful life

One result of the shift towards the exploration of positive mental health has been the introduction of the Eastern practice of meditation into Western scientific study. Not only do we see the inclusion of meditation in scientific research, we also see meditation being applied widely in the corporate world even in the West. The chapter on the social psychology of physical health gives further examples of the use of meditation by corporate houses. For further information, the reader is referred to Agrawal's book, *Stress in Life and at Work* (2001).

Positive psychology can be seen to operate at **three levels**: the first level is the **subjective experience** (that is, well being, satisfaction, joy, happiness, optimism, hope and faith). The second is the **individual level**, which is all about positive personal traits (that is, the capacity to love, courage, interpersonal skills, perseverance, forgiveness, high talent, vision and wisdom). And the third is the **group level** (that is, about civic virtues, and the institutions that move individuals towards better citizenship: such as responsibility, nurturance, altruism, civility, moderation, tolerance and work ethic). However, it is important to note that positive psychologists do not say that every individual who is happy will experience all or even most of these positive emotions and gratifications. (Emmons & others, 2002).

Levels of operation of positive psychology: The subjective experience, the individual the and group level

Positive psychology at the individual level

What are some of the individual strengths that can make life happy? **Emotional intelligence** is one such positive strength. "Emotional intelligence represents the ability to perceive, appraise and express emotion accurately and adaptively...emotional intelligence refers to the ability to process emotion-laden information competently and to use it to guide cognitive activities like problem-solving and to focus energy on required behavior" (Salovey, Mayer & Caruso, 2002, p. 830). This is fairly easy to comprehend. If you are feeling anger, and show that anger through violent behavior, you do no good to yourself or to the victim of your anger. However, if you realize that your blood pressure is

Emotional intelligence: The ability to perceive and express emotions accurately and appropriately

rising, and then try to cool down consciously, you will have done a good deed to yourself and to the world around you. By consciously cooling down, you have helped the homeostatic functions of your body to once again regain balance; by not showing your anger, you have stopped yourself from hurting something or someone. And what is the end result: the quicker you cool down, the easier it will be for you to concentrate on the need of the hour, maybe to put something straight. Some of the other individual traits are **forgiveness** (McCullough & Witvliet, 2002), **humility** (Tangney, 2002), **compassion** (Cassell, 2002) and **optimism** (Peterson, 2000).

Optimism: Positive expectations about the future

Optimism has been defined as "a mood or attitude associated with an expectation about the social or material future—one which the evaluator regards as socially desirable to his/her advantage or pleasures (Tiger, 1979, p.18). Cognitive approaches treat optimism as a cognitive characteristic, that is, as a goal or an expectation. Seligman and his colleagues have termed it an individual's characteristic explanatory style: how he or she explains the causes of bad events, based on attribution styles and the concept of learned helplessness (Buchanan & Seligman, 1995).

Positive psychology at the subjective level: Subjective Well Being (SWB)

Subjective Well Being: A sense of happiness

How can we define Subjective Well Being (hereby abbreviated as SWB)? Can we say that it is the antithesis of mental illness? Or, is it the flip side of poor physical health? Though SWB has a lot to do with both mental and physical health, it certainly cannot be said to either of the above. Instead, we find it defined as "**a sense of happiness,**" reminding us of Maslow's work on self actualization. When we express our ability to its fullest extent, we reach this stage of self-actualization contributing to the sense of happiness.

Unlike the pathological aspects of behavior that need to be defined by others (no psychotic or even neurotic person will say that she is abnormal), there is no manual (such as *the DSM*) regarding SWB. If I am feeling happy, I can be said to be characterized by SWB. I may be in poor physical health, I may even be suffering from a terminal illness, I may know that I have only a few more years, or even few more months to live, but, if I am happy, I am satisfied, I am experiencing positive mental states and affect, I have high SWB. However, the same cannot be said for many forms of mental illness. Thus, if I am suffering from depression, I will not be experiencing positive mental states, and therefore, I will not be said to have high SWB. Dr. Francis Crick, who along with Dr. James Watson, was famous for his discovery of the double helix structure of DNA passed away on the 28th July, 2004. Remembering him, Watson remarked that Crick would always say, 'don't be disappointed. Look at me, I am suffering from colon cancer, but I have never accepted defeat.' And, according to Watson, Crick never accepted defeat even till the day of his death (Watson, 2004). The famous scientist, Stephen Hawking would be another such example. Confined to a wheel chair, with an artificial pace maker and artificial voice box in place, suffering from various physical problems, continues to lecture far and wide. Though he has not been assessed for SWB, we are sure that he too would be classed as being high on SWB.

SWB is at the core of positive psychology, and as psychologists, especially those dealing with positive psychology are turning their focus to such positive states, we are learning more about SWB. For example, what are the other characteristics (such as personality, cognitive, social, etc.) of people who experience SWB? What are the effects of SWB? Can we counsel, teach people to experience greater SWB? What are the correlates of SWB? And what is the developmental trajectory identifiable for SWB? The answers provided by research on SWB help us to understand not only the concept, but also why a social psychologist should be interested in the concept.

The concept of SWB

SWB is defined as a **person's cognitive and affective evaluations of his or her life** (Diener, Lucas & Oishi, 2002). Recent researchers have differentiated between **Subjective Well Being** and **Psychological Well Being** (for example, see Keyes, Shmotkin & Ryff 2002), and substantiate the conceptualization by data which shows that these two concepts relate differently to socio-demographics and personality, with high SWB and high Psychological Well Being (PWB) being the optimal. They define SWB as evaluation of life in terms of satisfaction and balance between positive and negative emotions. PWB, on the other hand, is the perception of the extent to which the individual engages with the existential challenges of life. How does one move towards SWB? According to Langer (2002), a move towards **mindfulness** rather than mindlessness is very helpful. Mindfulness is an attribute of consciousness long believed to promote well being (Brown & Ryan, 2003). Considering the importance of the role of mindfulness in promoting SWB, the authors have developed a scale, the MAAS, to measure the construct. In their recent research, they have described not only the psychometric properties of the scale, but have also provided us with correlational, quasi-experimental and laboratory data that prove the independence of the construct of mindfulness from other related well being concepts. Finally, they also describe a clinical intervention study that demonstrates that mindfulness is related to decrease in mood disturbances and stress in cancer patients (Brown & Ryan, 2003).

> **Subjective Well Being:** Evaluation of life in terms of balance between positive and negative emotions

> **Psychological Well Being:** The extent to which the person feels meaningfulness in life

Positive psychology at the group level

At the group level, we have already mentioned that positive psychology focuses on **civic virtues**. One such civic virtue is **positive ethics**. When we speak of ethics, we are normally referring to negative ethics, that is, ethics that helps us to refrain from doing acts that would cause harm to others. So society develops a norm for conduct, deviation from which leads to ostracization and it is this fear of ostracization that stops many of us from doing wrong acts. Positive ethics, in contrast, focuses on the joy one gets from conducting oneself in a morally correct manner, untainted by a fear of punishment (Handelsman, Knapp & Gottlieb, 2002).

ROLE OF SWB IN LIFE AND AT WORK

SWB at work

With the rise of violence and stress at the work place, organizations have turned their focus to what has been called **Quality of Work Life** (QWL). This is a term used to denote a **combination of both physical and psychological well being at work**, and has as its antecedent factors, a whole host of work-related variables.

> **Quality of Work Life (QWL):** A joint index of physical and psychological well being at work

The need to focus on QWL is becoming increasingly important when one considers the data on workplace depression and stress. It has been found, for example, that today, Canadian workers are far more stressed and depressed and are less loyal to their employers than they were a decade ago. The frustration seems to cut across all demographic categories as shown by a study on 6,500 people from 40 organizations in 2001. Only 45% were highly satisfied with their jobs, as against 62% in 1991. The trends are the same in a larger study funded by Heath Canada that surveyed 31,800 people (Monchuk, 2001).

Talking of positive psychology at work, Turner, Barling and Zacharatos (2002) argue that it is important to concentrate on research on **"healthy" work,** not simply because it provides a foundation for studying the determinants of healthy work, but more because work experiences have both direct and indirect effects on other aspects of an adult's life. In other words, they are of the view that healthy work experiences would promote SWB. Positive psychology at work has also focused on positive groups. Some of the characteristics that have been attributed to positive groups include the ability to handle workplace diversity, the adoption of a win-win attitude towards negotiation and conflict resolution. According to Henry (2003), this has already been tried out in various small and mid-sized organizations, though its efficacy in large organizations is still open to question.

SWB in old age

Social support is a key concept in social gerontology, the world over. It is commonly felt that individuals experience a decline in health status during old age. Paradoxically, they could continue to be in a state of good SWB. The moderating factor is sometimes **social support.** There are other older adults who start feeling a cumulative effect of health related chronic life strains and show lower SWB. Thus, the older old in Germany were found lower on SWB than the younger old (Smith, Borchelt, Maier & Jopp, 2002).

It is not just the numbers but also the **quality of the social support system** that is important. Evidence for such an association comes from a variety of studies. For example, Fernandez-Ballesteros, (2002) have found a relationship between quantity and quality of social support and health indicators, SWB and Quality of Life among the aged in Spain. Conversely, SWB was negatively associated to negative social support among older adults (mean age 77 years) in the USA (Kim & Nesselroade (2003). Lower social support is anticipated among childless couples. The empirical data however show that the parent-child relationship is linked to worse outcomes for both mothers and fathers in terms of loneliness and depression (Koropeckyj-Cox, 2002). The explanation could be that childless couples become resigned to not having children and seek other sources of social support. Couples with children, on the other hand, thinking that they already possess a strong support system, may not seek other forms of social support, and, in the process end up feeling lonely and depressed. In the chapter on physical health, the role of social support has been further highlighted, especially concerning its positive effect on well being and recovery from illness.

SWB across cultures

Even with people of other age groups, social support forms an extremely potent resource for coping with calamities. Residents of **Uzbekistan** were surveyed after the Aral Sea disaster. While they

Behavioral congruence: Behavior that is consistent with one's self

displayed somatic symptoms related to long-term stress, their SWB was better compared to that in **Russia**, due to the high level of informal social support (Meer, Small & colleagues, 2002).

One noteworthy finding is that variables often correlate differently with life satisfaction in different cultures. **Individualistic cultures** stress importance of the individual and happiness is often correlated with personal goal fulfilment in such cultures. **Collectivistic cultures**, on the other hand, focus on social responsibility and are willing to sacrifice personal goals for the greater good. Thus self-esteem correlates more highly with SWB in individualistic cultures than in collectivistic cultures (Diener & Diener 1995). Studies, however, show that this relationship is culture bound. Similarly, congruence, that is, acting in consistency with one's self predicts life satisfaction to a much greater degree in the **US** than in **Korea** (Suh, 2002). However, when two ethnic groups within the US (that is, **Asian Americans** and **European Americans**) were compared, self-esteem was found to be an important predictor for both groups (Benet-Martinez & Karakitapoglu-Ayguen, 2003).

BOX 2.4

Turning happiness into economic power (Kersting, 2003)

Noted psychologist and Nobel Prize winner, Daniel Kahneman, remarked:

"There's a need for a measure of well being that goes beyond power and wealth, for which countries can be valued...there's a need for the concept of well being account (Kersting, p. 26)." If psychologists are truly interested in improving public health and happiness, they will need to join hands with economists. Economists are already on their way to study the extent to which external factors predict people's happiness (Oswald, 2003).

In order to achieve what Kahneman recommends, we will require a new genre of leaders: positive leaders. Describing the qualities of a positive leader, psychologist Robert Hogan remarked that they should be imbued with self-control, the ability to work well in a team, and business skills. Over and above these attributes, they will require integrity, decisiveness, overall competence and the ability to devise and communicate an overall vision.

Positive leaders also succeed by making the most of what has been called psychological capital (Csikszentmihaliyi, cf Kersten, 2003). The idea behind this novel concept is based on the idea of financial capital, that is, it is the saving of resources for future use in more important situations. Just as we save financial capital, we can withhold psychological resources too, that is, save them for future returns. What is the primary psychological resource? It is attention to topics of present and future value. One such personality trait is Concientiousness, that is, the degree to which one has impulse control, responsibility, orderliness, achievement and conventionality (as described by the proponents of the Big Five personality theory (Costa & Mcrae, 1985). High levels of this trait are seen to correlate with higher activity levels, better diets, less alcohol, and drug use, less risky driving behavior, less risk of suicide and fewer instances of violence. Some further evidence for the important role of conscientiousness is provided by regression analysis results, revealing that it is a variable relevant for the understanding of SWB (Hayes & Joseph, 2003).

Thus why not invest mental effort for such a huge psychological resource that can be capitalized in the future.

Research has also shown that the SWB of people in **rich countries** is higher than that of people in **poor countries**. One reason could be that wealth leads to happiness through greater fulfilment of basic needs. The paradox however is that when people within the country are compared, there is no relationship between income and SWB. The poor nations in the World Values Survey (*World Values Study Group*, 1994), for example, Nigeria and China did not show the extremely low SWB levels as one would expect. Diener, Oishi & Lucas, (2003), too, found that happiness does not increase in the nations where there had been a dramatic increase in income. Ahuvia (2002) proposes that economic development leads to higher levels of SWB not by increasing consumption but by making the culture more individualistic. As a result, the culture starts encouraging people to pursue personal happiness over the pursuit of social obligations. **Personality variables** could be playing an important moderating role in SWB.

With the burgeoning research findings on SWB, a natural corollary would be to ask, is SWB really good and important for the individual, and even more so for the society? Most of the findings, though correlational, do show that happy people participate more in community organizations, are more likely to be liked by others, perform better at work, tend to live slightly longer, are less likely to get divorced and earn higher incomes (Diener, 2000). Though we do not as yet know why happy people exhibit such desirable characteristics, it seems clear that they are the ones who are more productive and sociable. Most of all, there is no evidence to date to suggest that SWB is harmful for either the person or the society.

SOCIAL PSYCHOLOGY AND THERAPY

BOX 2.5

Hypotherapy: an unconventional therapy for a conventional disorder (Szczupal, 2004)

A recent issue of the Annuntiatus, (*The Bulletin of the International Association for Special Education*) showcased a very interesting intervention initiative for a multi-profile improvement of children with motoric dysfunction, autism, intellectual deficit or infantile cerebral palsy.

Hypotherapy, that is, therapy through horse-riding and other activities with a horse can take various forms:

- **Therapeutic horse-riding: Seating the child on the back of a walking horse helps in making the handicapped child feel as if he is really walking, and sometimes for the first time.**
- **Horse rehabilitation: Doing exercises on horseback.**
- **Horse contact therapy: Mere emotional contact of the child with the horse has a therapeutic effect. The child does not even need to mount the horse.**
- **Educational and therapeutic horseback performance: Athletic acrobatics on horseback. This is a combination of a close horse contact and athletic exercises.**

Hypotherapy can be used once a week after the child is three years of age, and takes at the most 10 30 minutes.

Spirituality in mental health

As one practicing psychologist, William Hathaway, puts it "just being sensitive to a possible **role of religion** in a client's life can broaden your evaluation and provide different solutions. Being able to help a person connect with a variable of spirituality in their lives can be beneficial and important therapeutic accommodation" (Hathaway, cf Kersting, 2003, p. 40).

With the rise in interest in positive psychology in the 1960s, one result was towards exploring the role of **Eastern meditation** in Western scientific study (Shapiro & co-workers, 2002). Spiritual healing is probably the oldest known treatment practiced in virtually every culture of the world throughout history. It may be done by **shamans** or medicine men, by the clergy or through **distance healing** in the form of prayer or meditation (Benor, 2002). As far as the Indian experience of healing is concerned, we have the example of a Hindu temple in south India, where a reduction of 20% was observed in psychiatric symptoms. This is comparable to what is generally observed when psychotropic drugs are used (Raghuram & co-workers, 2002). For an extensive section on faith healing, the reader is requested to consult the chapter on physical health.

Shamans: Medicine men in traditional cultures

How does the effect of religion, or for that matter, spirituality work? According to Oman and Thoresen (2002), there are **four ways** in which the mechanism may operate. **Religion may causally influence health** by

- **Any mechanism, including social support and improved health behavior.**
- **Additional mechanisms, such as enhanced positive psychological states (faith, hope, inner peace) acting through the psychoneuroimmunology or psycho-endocrinological pathways.**
- **Offering psychological strength for acquiring and maintaining positive health behavior.**
- **Causally influencing health by distant health or prayer.**

Looking at the far-reaching implications of spirituality on mental health as also on physical health, there seems to be a critical need for change in health care systems the world over. Struve (2001) proposes a **faith based community** at the core of the health care model, the core teaching being to define what it means to be human and healthy. Within this context, a variety of concerns could be addressed, ranging from health information, education, prayer, care and support for most chronic illnesses, to life style change and end of life concerns (Struve, 2001). In fact we have faith healing communities in Africa organized by two ministers in two regions of Africa. They have incorporated hope-generated healing processes in their practice and have found gains in helping the people cope with the conditions there (Nyoye, 2002). For more information on this topic, the reader is referred to the chapter on the social psychology of religion.

Faith based community: Use of spirituality in the therapy process

Using **religion or spirituality in therapy** however has its pitfalls when used incorrectly. Some of the **precautions** that can be observed are:

- **Ensuring proper supervision for those learning to use religious tools.**
- **Psychologists need to be particularly careful of their personal ideas regarding religion.**
- **They need to be careful of counter-transference problems.**

- The practice as a whole needs to be based more on scientific evidence instead of on anecdotal treatment strategies (Kersting, 2003).

Community based mental health care

Community based mental health care: Mental health care provided in the community of the patient and with the interactive help of other community members

Wilson and Hayes (2003) trace the development in the field. Of special importance is the community mental health movement and the delivery of mental health services. Giving impetus to the **community model of mental health care** was the message delivered by the World Health Organization on World Health Day, 2001.

What are community mental health services like? An example of a community based intervention program in the Box 2.6 illustrates the idea.

A major reason for the greater effectiveness of community based mental health programs is that the patients and their families are able to override the **stigmatising effects of institutionalization**. Moreover, allowing them to stay in the community keeps intact the **social support systems**, so important for the maintenance of sound mental health. And institution of course, when one looks at the **cost to the economy** it is much less as compared to institution based therapy. There would be fewer

BOX 2.6

A community based intervention program for low-income older adults (Shapiro & Taylor, 2002)

Using a waiting list for community-based services, 105 moderately at risk community dwelling older adults were recruited. 40 of these were randomly assigned to receive the intervention while the remainder did not receive any intervention. All subjects were interviewed every three months for 18 months. What were the dependent variables? These were:

- **Depression**
- **Satisfaction with social relationships**
- **Environmental mastery**
- **Life satisfaction**
- **Permanent institutionalization**
- **Mortality**

What were the results?

- **Base line data indicated that there were no significant differences between the groups on socio-demographic or health characteristics.**
- **Yet, those who received the intervention had significantly higher SWB and were less likely to be institutionalized across the 18 month period.**

The findings thus provide support to the idea that community based interventions can prove to be extremely effective for older adults. Moreover, not only are such interventions effective in terms of psychological effects, they are also cost-effective.

institutions to be maintained. The **penetration of mental health services** would also increase because of the many people who do not seek professional help for fear of stigma. One group that could benefit from community based mental health programs is **women in rural communities**. A study from Canada reports that many of the rural women face a multitude of barriers when it comes to seeking help for depression. These barriers include lack of services, inability to access services for financial reasons and social stigma. The communities were also characterized by other factors that could serve as deterrents, for example, economic instability, geographic isolation and traditional attitudes about the role of women. (Scattolon, 2003). The WHO, Regional office for South East Asia's initiative delineates the **advantages: availability, accessibility, acceptability, affordability and assessment—the 5 As** on which any community based program can be based (WHO, 2001). Countries (for example, Brazil and Sri Lanka) have already started remodeling their mental health programs along the WHO guidelines. Time will tell us how effective they have been.

Summary

The rate at which this world is changing has an enormous impact on our mental health. While clinical psychologists focus on the treatment of mental disorders, social psychologists are concerned with the well being of individuals in the absence of impairment and the promotion of optimal functioning. This chapter began with the analysis of the limitations of mental health explanations based on biological factors alone. Cross-cultural studies clearly show that the perception and the etiology of mental illnesses are different in different cultures. Further, an understanding of mental health problems of children and adolescents is guided by factors that are radically different from those of adults.

A mental health model presented by Ruble, Constanzo and Higins (1992) demonstrates the pivotal role of social psychology in addressing mental health issues.

Several domains concerning expectations and biases were examined in the portrayal of a patient-therapist relationship. Self-fulfilling prophecy, role of priming, illusory correlations and preference of intuitive judgment over statistical information were discussed in the context of the patient-therapist interaction. The next section of the chapter addressed issues concerning a social psychological analysis of depression. In the analysis of perception of reality, studies suggest that those who suffer from mild depression show negative coping style but on the contrary they also distort reality less than the normal people.

The applications of three major social theories were also discussed in this chapter: Bandura's social learning theory, social comparison theory and social exchange theory. The strengths and breadth of each theory demonstrates the far-reaching applications of social psychological approaches in the field of mental health. This section ended with a question from the layperson's point of view: at what point of our problems or unhappiness do we need therapy? In a pragmatic way, the answer lies in the ability to deal with suffering and maintain stoicism.

From mental illness, we then moved to mental health. A recent upsurge of interest in what promotes mental health has led to the growth of positive psychology. The chapter discusses the concept, its scope and utility in the present day scenario. Special emphasis has been given to the concept of subjective well being and how it relates to life, work, old age and culture. The chapter then goes on to delineate how religion and spirituality can guide therapy for mental disorders. It ends with a focus on the role of the community in mental health care and the establishment of community mental health care services.

Suggestions for Further Reading

Diener, E., Oishi, S. & Lucas, R.E. (2003). Personality, culture and subjective well being: Emotional and cognitive evaluations of life. *Annual Review of Psychology*, 54, 403-425.

Lopez, S.J., Prosser, E.C. & others (2002). Putting positive psychology in a multicultural context. In C.R. Snyder & S.J. Lopez (Eds) *Handbook of Positive Psychology*, London: Oxford University Press, 700-714.

Loftus, E.F., Smith, K.D. *et al* (1994). Memory and mismemory for health events. In J.M. Tanner (Ed) *Questions about Questions*. NY: Russell Sage Foundation.

Some Key Terms

Behavioral congruence
Community based interventions
DALY
Depressive realism
Downward social comparison
Emotional intelligence
Faith based communities
Fundamental attribution error
Illusory correlation
Modelling
Optimism
Positive psychology
Psychological Well Being
Quality of Work Life
Schema
Self-fulfilling prophecy
Shamans
Social exchange theory
Subjective Well Being
Telescoping
Upward social comparison
Vicarious extinction

SOCIAL PSYCHOLOGY OF PHYSICAL HEALTH

3

Chapter Outline

- An Introduction to Social Psychology of Physical Health
  - Differences between mental and physical health
  - Physical health myths
- Stress
  - Psychological factors in stress
    1. Significance of perceived control
    2. Learned helplessness
    3. Hardiness and optimism
    4. Social events
    5. Social support
- Psychoneuroimmunology (PNI) and Stress
  - The multiple functions of PNI
- Health Endangering Behavior: The Role of Social Psychology
  - Acquired Immune Deficiency Syndrome (AIDS)
  - HIV AIDS stigma
  - Understanding HIV-AIDS associated risk behavior
  - Aids prevention
  - Interventions with people with AIDS
  - AIDS and women
  - AIDS and substance abuse
  - AIDS and the Lazarus effect
  - Cancer
  - Cancer: A global perspective
  - Smoking
  - Intervention
  - Intervention programs: A global perspective
- Weight Control and Eating Disorders
  - Interventions
  - Eating disorders
  - Role of familial factors in the etiology and treatment of ED
  - Eating disorders: The global perspective
- Expectations from the Therapist
- Limits to Social Psychology of Physical Health

AN INTRODUCTION TO SOCIAL PSYCHOLOGY OF PHYSICAL HEALTH

Think of the habits of an average citizen and you will find that most people work hard to realize their dream, enjoy life in parties in which they consume alcohol and smoke cigarettes, and relish fast food in restaurants, which, at the same time, is also very convenient. While people may think that life is good and that they can't complain, physical health may take a downturn if stress from work and consumption of alcohol, cigarettes and calories is not controlled. Unfortunately, in order to succeed in a competitive society, a number of people, burnt-out from work, find it convenient to collect food from a fast food restaurant, and to overindulge in drinking and smoking.

All these problems are the result of our own behavior—the amount of time we work, the alcohol we take in, the cigarettes we smoke, or the beefy burgers we gorge on. The Center for Disease Control (CDC) estimated that approximately half of the deaths in the US seem to be related to some problems of our own behavior. To add to the above, the sexual behavior of people around the globe has caused a great deal of concern during the past two decades due to the epidemic of AIDS.

Social psychology helps us to understand both functional and dysfunctional physical health

In our discussion of mental health in Chapter 2, the issue of "normal versus abnormal" was addressed from the point of view of dysfunctional and optimal functioning of an individual. By employing the same criteria for physical health, we can say that the applications of social psychology are significant for those physically ill patients who are **terminally ill** (dysfunctional) as well as for those who are functional at present, but are **at risk** (for example, chronic smokers or drug abusers). The applications of social psychology are easier to comprehend in this area as compared to that of mental health because improvement in physical health can be easily recognized through tangible indicators such as blood pressure tests, etc., but such parameters are not easily identifiable in case of mental health.

Differences between mental and physical health

Role schema: Set of expectations related to a particular illness

A patient who reports a physical illness displays a **role schema** consisting of conforming symptoms and precautions. People attach a set of expectations related to a disease and anticipate changes in the behavior of a patient according to those expectations. After the diagnosis, if the patient does not show changes in behavior for any reason, others doubt if she is really ill. If you come to know that your friend has been diagnosed with a liver problem but continues to eat hamburgers and French fries, will you really believe the seriousness of his complaint? In other words, after the diagnosis of a disease, we expect people to show certain changes in their behavior. Unlike changes in behavior due to mental illness, this type of change in behavior due to physical illness can be easily recognized, measured and interpreted.

Schema for physical illness more concrete than that for mental illness

In a study conducted by Rosenhan (1973), several normal people were asked to approach hospitals for certain psychological problems (such as hearing voices and so on). When normal people faked illness and were admitted to the local mental hospitals for treatment, even very normal behavior (like watching television, etc.) was linked to symptoms of schizophrenia. Studies in social psychology have clearly demonstrated that once people develop a schema for a particular person or situation, it is extremely difficult for them to keep unrelated information separate and not allow it to integrate into their existing schema.

In short, the **schema for a physical illness** appears to be more **concrete** than that for mental illness. As a result, people do not weigh consequences of mental and physical health equally. As stated in the chapter on mental health, mental health issues are either ignored or not given due priority, especially in the Third World countries, often because of poor knowledge of the conception and consequences of mental health.

There is another important difference in our cognitive assessment of mental and physical health. In the case of chronic illness such as arthritis and cancer, people know that the chances of cure are very low. On the other hand, several chronic mental health problems result from the complex interactions involved in certain situations such that significant improvement in the condition of the patient is possible by simply taking her out of that situation or helping her to reinterpret the conditions. Moreover, while a chronic physical health condition symbolizes deterioration leading to death, chronic mental health conditions do not signal the possible end of life in the near future. In short, behavior associated with the role schema of physical and mental health problems are not similar and weigh differently on our minds.

Physical health myths

There is another reason for examining the applications of social psychology in the area of physical health. Many people, especially adolescents, believe that the effects of drugs are within their tolerance limits. They begin to believe that their body has the capacity to absorb the negative effects of the drug. Such a false belief can be dangerous and self-defeating. To measure the effects of such false beliefs, Sussman, Dent and Stacy (1996) developed a measure of **myths related to drug use**. Based on the results of their study on a sample of 502 adolescents, they concluded that **self-defeating myths** concerning the intake of drugs very often resulted in the overuse of drugs and misinterpretations of the effects of drugs. When such myths continue to guide behavior of people at risk, the success of an intervention program weakens significantly.

Drug Myths: Belief that body has capacity to absorb negative impact of drugs

TABLE 3.1

Some sample items from the Drug Use Myth Scale
(*Source*: Sussman *et. al.*, 1996)

1. What happens when a person "gets used" to a drug?
   (a) One has learned how to enjoy using the drug to control its effects.
   (b) Body warning signals are giving up and addiction is beginning.
2. When one gets into trouble with the authorities because of drugs.
   (a) The authorities are usually picking on someone they don't like.
   (b) The authorities are trying to protect people from harm.

This chapter will focus on two major issues of health that are of interest to social psychology. First, it is important to understand how people **deal with stress and stay healthy**. Based on several studies, it is now well known that stress can damage our immune system, and that social support can help us combat the effects of stress. Research evidence is now available to show that even the common cold is related to stress (Cohen Tyrell & Smith, 1993). The other issue is related to **health endangering behaviors that cause illness.** In this context the epidemic of AIDS, smoking and eating disorders will be discussed in detail. While the prognosis for victims of AIDS is uncertain due to the lack of suitable medication, several AIDS patients have been known to bounce back in their lives (for example, Irvin Johnson and David Brudnoy in the USA). In other words, a related but significant issue facing social psychology is to study how people get back to their lives after they have successfully fought the disease. The present chapter will focus on these and related issues that concern the social psychology of physical health. Accordingly, the chapter has been divided into **two sections**, the first dealing with **stress** and its effect on physical stress, and the second with **health endangering behavior** and physical health.

Two major issues regarding social psychology of physical health: Stress and health endangering behavior

STRESS

It is estimated that 70% visits to doctor's office are directly or indirectly related to stress (Agrawal, 2001). Blood pressure and heart rate are easily impaired by prolonged stress. Imagine the plight of residents of the Three Mile Island who lived in constant fear of radioactive material contamination. Baum (1990), after analyzing pre- and post-accident blood pressure data of residents from previous visits to doctors in the Three Mile Island area of the USA, concluded that both systolic and diastolic blood pressure of people residing near the nuclear facility had increased. Thus, prolonged stress had altered the health of the residents. And, it is not blood pressure alone that gets altered with stress. Stress is known to precipitate a variety of physical health problems, ranging from mild insomnia to sexual impotency and even to the entire gamut of what has been called psychosomatic disorders (asthma, ulcers, skin disorders, allergies, etc.).

After noticing that a wide variety of toxins caused some identical effects, **Selye** (1956) offered a biological approach to study stress. According to him, stress is a response to a harmful agent and its effect takes place in three stages. It begins with an **alarm reaction.** In the second stage the person shows **resistance.** Finally, the person shows signs of **exhaustion.** Although Selye's theory, called **General Adaptation Syndrome** or GAS, remained very popular for a long time, it failed to answer a major psychological question: why does the same stimulus cause stress to one person but not to another? Realizing the limitations of biological explanations of stress, **Lazarus** (1966) offered a **cognitive approach** to show how stress is related to the way in which a person appraises a given situation. If the incoming threat is perceived as being harmless, it is dismissed by individuals at their **primary appraisal** level. However, when individuals expect a damage or loss, they become involved in a threat appraisal. At the end, individuals make a **secondary appraisal** to cope with the challenge.

Selye: General Adaptation Syndrome (GAS): Based on adaptation to stressor

Lazarus: cognitive appraisal of event: Stress depends on how we perceive the stressor

Both biological and psychological explanations have been further advanced and refined since the pioneering work of Selye and Lazarus. For a useful review of work in the field of stress, the reader is referred to (Agrawal, 2001). From the point of view of social psychology and its applications, psychological and social factors related to stress will be examined in this chapter.

Perceived control: Degree to which we think we are the master over events

Psychological factors in stress

1. Significance of perceived control

Two types of perceived control: Internal v. External locus of control

How would you feel if you perceive that you are in command of your daily routine than when you are not? The very fact that you know that you are in control of a situation makes a lot of difference in coping with your stress. As stated in Chapter 2, normal people believe that they are in control of situations and feel optimistic, compared to depressed people who are pessimistic but, ironically, more realistic.

Are there people who have a stronger belief in control than others? If there are such people, do they believe that their own action determines the outcome of events? Rotter (1966) believed that people tend to perceive the outcome of events in either of two ways. First, there are those who believe that luck or chance determines the fate of events and they have little control over them. On the other hand, there are people who believe that they are responsible for the outcome in a situation. Having this dichotomy in mind, **Rotter** constructed a scale of **Locus of Control**. Three items from this scale are reproduced in the Table 3.2 below:

TABLE 3.2

Three items from Rotter's Scale of Locus of Control
(*Source*: Rotter, 1966)

1 a. Many of the unhappy things in people's lives are partly due to bad luck.
   b. People's misfortunes result from the mistakes they make.

2 a. One of the major reasons why we have wars is because people don't take interest in politics.
   b. There will always be wars, no matter how hard people try to prevent them.

3 a. In the long run people get the respect they deserve in this world.
   b. Unfortunately, an individual's worth often passes unrecognized no matter how hard he tries.

External items are underlined.

Rotter's scale has also been tailored to examine locus of control on health issues (Wallston & co-workers, 1978). For instance, an item like, "I am directly responsible for my health," refers to an internal locus of control. Research has consistently shown that subjects scoring high on internal locus of control cope effectively when faced with health problems.

Perceived control leads to under-estimation of risk of illness

A very interesting social psychological finding showing how **perceived control** is linked to an underestimation of risk was reported by Greening and Chandler (1997). In their study, people were presented with aversive risk situations such as being involved in a car accident, a pet's illness and so on. Then, they were made aware of the base rate for each incident. In their study, the base rate was perceived to be the amount of risk taken by an average person. As compared to other people, the subjects reported themselves as better than the average person in a given scenario presented by the experimenter. After comparing themselves as a part of the entire group for which a given base rate was available, the subjects perceived themselves, and then adjusted their risk factor for a scenario. For example, a risk factor in a car accident could be adjusted in an optimistic direction if a person perceived herself as being a more skilled driver than the "average person."

Perceived control is a factor in health counselling

It is clear from Greening and Chandler's study that perceived control is causally related to our **understanding of risk.** This bias may lead to several consequences of vital significance in our lives. For instance, a person's indifference to buying health insurance could be due to his belief that he is in better than average health condition. This tendency to make comparisons with others and the existing level of perceived control helps to predict **risk underestimation or overestimation behavior.** In general people are biased towards risk underestimation. This bias can be corrected if people begin to examine how information about themselves interacts with the base rate to predict one's risk. For instance, if people compare themselves with both better and worse off patients, they may become more realistic about themselves.

The effects of perceived control have been found to be **vital in health counselling.** After collecting data from 72 genetic counsellors in Israel, Shiloh *et al.* (1997) reported that the clients used either of the two commonly seen coping strategies in dealing with threat from a genetic disorder. First, some used problem focused coping, that is, individuals used the counselor's knowledge directly to understand what the problem was and what needed to be done. Second, others used emotion-focused coping, that is, clients learnt to control their emotional responses when they failed to control the outcome of a genetic defect. The key element in counselling was perceived personal control because through perceived knowledge, the counsellors could help clients control their behavior.

We should have a realistic appraisal of our health problems

Janis (1958) found that college students who reported moderate fear and understanding of postoperative procedures had smoother recovery compared to their counterparts who were either more relaxed or more fearful before the surgery. Realistic results and optimistic views of patients regarding their own health have their own rewards. When patients are unrealistically optimistic, they tend to suffer a great deal (Scheier & Carver, 1993). Taylor (1995) analyzed the illusions concerning health and found that those who had an exaggerated sense of control over their health problems suffered from unrealistic illusions.

In short when people perceive control over an outcome, they **mobilize their resources to deal with the problem.** Given the knowledge that they are better than average can give them a sense of control. Failing to perceive their potential can lead to helplessness.

2. Learned helplessness

BOX 3.1

The youngest in class face stress: A case for low control over the environment
(*The Times of India*, August 30, 2003)

A survey of over 10,000 children in Britain between the ages of five and fifteen showed that regardless of when their school year began, if they were the youngest in the class, they faced greater stress. The leader of the team, Robert Goodman, from the Dept. of Child and Adolescent Psychiatry at Kings College, London, concluded that though it is moderate stress, it affects a sizable proportion of children and should therefore be taken seriously. Goodman points out that other studies have also found that the younger in the school class tend to have lower levels of university entrance.

Could it be that these younger children had a lowered sense of perceived control over their social and therefore their physical environment?

How do we respond to situations in which we feel helpless, especially when we have tried several times but have failed? Seligman (1975) began to study this issue by conducting a series of experiments on dogs, who, after learning how to avoid electric shocks, failed to avoid them even though they were responding in exactly the same way that had earlier saved them from these shocks. After the dogs were transferred to a new situation, Seligman found that those dogs who had been unable to control the shocks simply endured the shocks and did nothing to escape them, in comparison to another group of dogs who had learned to escape from them successfully.

Learned helplessness: A feeling of incompetence learned through failure

The implications of this work have been extended in the context of attribution theory, that is, learned helplessness is observed when people attribute stable features such as their incompetence as being the cause of their failure (Abramson, Seligman & Teasdale, 1978).

Learned helplessness explains how people undergo **motivational and cognitive deficits in chronic illness** because they believe that they have no control over their condition. Studies on cancer patients and elderly people have shown how we can benefit from our knowledge of the mechanism of learned helplessness. Taylor, Lichtman and Wood (1984) found that women with breast cancer, who had scored high on internal locus of control, showed better coping skills than their counterparts who scored low on internal locus of control. The former group also reported better adjustment and lower depression.

Learned helplessness has an important role to play in physical illness

Elderly people who are admitted to a nursing home feel that they do not have much control over their daily lives. Once in a nursing facility, they are required to follow routine patterns and rules of the facility. With a view to examining the effect of loss of perceived control, Langer and Rodin (1976) conducted a study in which the residents in a nursing facility were given some responsibility in controlling their lives. For instance, they selected the day to see a movie and how to tend their plant. In contrast, all the instructions for taking responsibility were deleted in a comparison group. The results of this study showed that the residents in the responsibility group became more happy and active than their counterparts in the control group. Another study on elderly people in a nursing home was conducted by Schulz (1976) to determine if increased control by the residents would have a positive effect on them. He recruited undergraduate students for volunteer work in the residential facility. While one group of residents was free to decide the schedule, including the duration of visits of students, the other group had no such privilege. After two months the two groups were compared for their level of happiness, health and fitness. In line with the results of Langer and Rodin, Schultz found dramatic positive effects on those elderly people who could control their lives.

3. Hardiness and optimism

If we examine the other side of loss of perceived control, the following questions emerge: Are there people who are able to negotiate stress well? Do people find bliss despite adversity? Do people enjoy change and commitment? Do people perceive hopefulness rather than helplessness?

The hardy personality: People who perceive strong sense of control

Based on a series of studies, Suzanne Kobasa (1982, 1979) concluded that there are people who demonstrate a personal sense of control rather than a loss

The 3 Cs of personality hardiness: Control, commitment and challenge

of control. Such individuals are able to effectively mobilize the resources available to them and to positively deal with stress. The mission and life styles of Gandhi, King, Tutu and Mandela are glowing examples of a **"hardy personality,"** a concept proposed by Kobasa that explains how a sense of personal **control, commitment and challenge**, together, can help people to find meaning in the face of adversity. In her research, Kobasa used the following tests to measure the three components of hardy personality: Rotter's scale for control; an alienation scale for commitment; and a need for security scale for challenge. Those who scored high on stress and low on hardiness were found to have more health problems than those who scored low on stress and high on hardiness.

Recent research studies have shown several problems in Kobasa's conceptual and methodological work. Wiebe and Williams (1992) have effectively argued that the hardiness effects are inconsistent and those who do show hardiness need social support. Others have suggested that challenge need not be an integral part of the hardy personality (Williams & co-workers, 1992). In short, the work on the hardy personality, both in terms of its conceptual and practical value, has been criticized. Several popular textbooks of social psychology have not included any reference to Kobasa's work (Sabini, 1995; Myers, 1996; Aronson & co-workers, 1994).

While recent textbooks may not have included a section on the hardy personality, it does not mean that recent research on the concept is not there. A brief review of research on personality hardiness during the years 2001-2004 reveals that the concept is still useful for our understanding of stress and its effects. While some questions have been raised regarding its direct effects, the role of personality hardiness as a moderating variable in the stress-illness relationship is clear. Thus personality hardiness has been found to have a buffering effect on the long-term effects of stress among POWs in Israel (Zakin, Solomon & Neria, 2003; Waysman, Schwartzwald & Solomon, 2001). The interesting aspect about these studies was the finding that personality hardiness and attachment work in a mutually compensatory manner and were inversely related to Post Traumatic Stress Syndrome (PTSD) and psychiatric symptomatology. Even among young people (aged only 17 years), who were candidates for the defense services in Israel, personality hardiness was positively related to a secure attachment style, and was negatively related to an avoidant or ambivalent attachment style. When the data were subjected to regression analysis, the results suggested that both attachment and personality hardiness were predictors of mental health in real life stress (Yuval & co-workers, 2001). Personality hardiness has also been found to be positively related to the use of constructive coping strategies in a variety of populations: Slovakian secondary school students (Baumgartner, 2002); Australian university students (Beasley, Thompson & Davidson, 2003); geriatric samples of age 60-95 years in the USA (Wallace, Bisconti & Bergeman, 2001); university lecturers in Czechoslovakia (Paulic, 2001); and prospective teachers in Hong Kong and China (Chan, 2003). As far as the workplace is concerned, people who are high on personality hardiness tend to engage in more of what has been called organizational citizenship behavior in the USA (Turnipseed, 2003), and have enhanced stress tolerance levels, as seen in a study in Japan (Lambert, Lambert & Yamase, 2003), and to find greater meaningfulness in their work (Britt, Adler & Bartone, 2001). So pervasive can be the effects of personality hardiness that it has been found to produce differences in the number of Natural Killer cells, so important for the immune response (Dolbier & co-workers, 2001).

BOX 3.2

Weathering the storm of peri-natal bereavement via hardiness

A recent article by Lang, Goulet and their colleagues in the September, 2001, issue of the journal *Death Studies*, provides a very succinct account of the effects of personality hardiness.

The article has been abstracted as follows:

....."hardiness is a personal resource that can potentially diminish negative effects of life stress. To increase understanding of the role that it can have on the health protection and promotion of bereaved parents following a perinatal loss, this article uses the J. Wilson's 1969 method of concept analysis of hardiness. It is maintained that this analysis provides not only a fresh perspective for understanding the experience of perinatal loss but has also induced the development of a hardiness instrument. The authors argue that knowledge development in this area is paramount for professionals interested in enabling bereaved parents to draw on and develop their hardiness, not only to transcend the experience but ultimately to gain a sense of personal growth following their loss."

Optimism: Expectation of success

Social psychologists are also focusing on the concept of **optimism** and especially on the level of optimism people demonstrate in dealing with their stress. Optimism, according to Scheier and Carver (1985), involves **expectation of success and positive events.** It grows out of social support and a sense of efficacy that may include hardiness. Having such a view on optimism, Scheier and Carver (1985) constructed a scale, **Life Orientation Test (LOT)**, to find out if people experience stress as a sign of growth. Consider the following item from the LOT:

"In unusual times I usually expect the best."

Those who believe in optimism translate their belief into action and actively seek social support to complete their mission. On the other hand, pessimists feel the negative consequences of stress. Not surprisingly, Scheier and Carver found their optimist subjects reporting greater happiness and well being than their pessimist counterparts. See chapter on social psychology of mental health, section on Positive Psychology for further details.

4. Social events

Life events can cause stress and require readjustment

How do people adjust when several members die in a car accident or when they lose a decent job? What happens to people when several tragedies occur in a short time? Obviously, one needs to change his/her life style to make a readjustment. In other words, the greater the degree of readjustment, the greater the amount of stress.

Believing that certain stressful events precede illness in several patients, Holmes and Rahe (1967) prepared a list of 43 events and asked their subjects to rate the extent of readjustment they had to make for these events.

TABLE 3.3

The first ten items from the Holmes and Rahe's Social Readjustment Rating Scale (*Source*: Holmes and Rahe, 1967)

Rank	Life event	Mean value
1.	Death of spouse	100
2.	Divorce	73
3.	Marital separation from mate	65
4.	Detention in jail or other institution	63
5.	Death of a close family member	63
6.	Major personal injuries or illness	53
7.	Marriage	50
8.	Being fired from job	47
9.	Marital reconciliation with mate	45
10.	Retirement from work	45

Holmes and Rahe's work contributed to **two major developments. First**, any event is not equally stressful to all individuals. Remember, in an earlier chapter, we gave an example of our colleague who told his physician, after being diagnosed for liver problems, that the job of a physician was to give medicine but that he was going to enjoy the gift of life by eating all sorts of food. While our colleague did not care about his acute liver problems and showed little stress, others often become upset with a minor headache.

Secondly, Holmes and Rahe's work led to the construction of more specific and refined scales to measure life experiences as related to stress. For instance, Crandall and co-workers (1992) developed a Stress Questionnaire for undergraduate students. The average student on this scale checks 18 items and beyond this point they are reported to have above-average stress (Table 3.4 below).

TABLE 3.4

Sample items from Undergraduate Stress Questionnaire (*Source*: Crandall *et al.* (1992)

Item	Rated severity of stress
Death (family member or friend)	3.97
Had a lot of tests	3.62
It's finals week	3.62
Applying to graduate school	3.59
Victim of a crime	3.59
Breaking up with boy/girl friend	3.45

For those who become upset with minor life events, known as **daily hassles**, scales have been prepared to find out the relationship between simple things, such as misplacing objects frequently or having too many things to do, and physical health. Not only was the relationship between the two variables significant, that is, between physical health and Hassles Scale scores, but, to the surprise of the researchers, this relationship was also stronger than the correlation between physical health and Life Events Questionnaire.

Daily hassles: Minor irritants in day-to-day living

TABLE 3.5

Some typical items for the assessment of daily hassles

Misplacing or losing things
Troublesome neighbors
Social obligations
Inconsiderate smokers
Health of a family member
Concerns about owing money

5. Social support

Social support is an important factor in reducing stress. Wallston *et al.* (1983) defined social support as "the comfort, assistance, and/or information one receives through formal or informal contacts with individuals or groups" (p. 369). Such a comfort or assistance may be considered as resource managed directly or indirectly by people in caring for the needy person. Cohen and McKay (1984) analyzed **three forms of support:**

Social support: Comfort derived from social contacts

- **Tangible support: for example, help in meeting daily needs.**
- **Cognitive support: for example, knowledge about a condition.**
- **Emotional support: for example, loving and caring.**

Two models account for the impact of social support on our health. The **main effect model** of social support explains how patients learn health enhancing behavior through models and reinforcement. Social support can enhance self esteem and well being. However, this model lacks consistent empirical support (Kaplan & Toshima 1990).

Social support affects health in two ways

The other model contends that social support tends to **moderate** the effects of stress by influencing the relationship between variables. Prokop, *et al.* (1991) contended that "social support acts as a **buffer** when a person experiences a stressful life event" (p. 115). For instance, women experienced less pain during child birth when their husbands were present. Serum cholesterol levels were found higher in those blue-collar workers who lost their job as a result of factory closings and felt unsupported than those who felt supported by family members and friends (Gore, 1978). An earlier study by Kraus and Lilienfield (1959) showed that young widows who had positive social relationships reported fewer health problems within one year of their husband's death as compared to those who had negative social relationships. Men who were cared for by their wives after heart surgery recovered faster than men who lacked social support from their

Learning of health enhancing behavior through social reinforcement

Social support as buffer to stressful events

wives. Encouraged by these results, researchers have proposed a **stress buffering hypothesis** to show that social support protects an individual from the negative effects of a stressful situation (Coob, 1976). It seems that social support influences the primary appraisal of an individual because it tends to reduce the impact of a threat in a stressful situation. Thus, social support has an important role to play in coping with cancer, as has been identified by Holland and Holahan (2003).

Too much social support has a negative impact on health

At the same time, many studies have shown the **negative effects of social support**. For instance, when families provide too much of protection, adjustment or return to a normal level is affected. In a study (Lewis, 1966), it was found that men with heart problems did not return to work if they perceived their families to be protective. Emotional reactions may be precipitated by social support because such a type of support is a constant reminder of a person's illness. Due to this reason, family members and friends generally avoid a prolonged discussion with a patient concerning his/her illness.

Quality of relationship more important than number of relationships

In accounting for the relationship between social support and stress, it is important to understand that the **quality and type of social support** play a significant role in reducing stress. Burman and Margolin (1992) found that the rate of mortality was lower in married people than unmarried people, but this finding is related to the quality of the relationship maintained by the couple. After the death of a spouse, a partner becomes lonely, distressed and less supportive. In general, men suffer more than women after the loss because women have broader and richer social networks than men. However, if women have negative social relationships, then the difference between the male and female spouse could vanish.

Social support can be **ineffective** even if it is well meaning. For example, Dakof and Taylor (1990) found that cancer patients reported lack of emotional support because their casual visitors were unable to provide such support. On the other hand, patients suffering from less chronic diseases like headaches found support from casual visitors very helpful.

Agrawal (2001) provides useful **tips for providing social support** to people with terminal illness. While we want to help our friends in distress, we fail in many ways. Sometimes we are over enthusiastic, while at other times we adopt an attitude of pity. Therefore, according to Agrawal: learn to listen; provide a shoulder to lean on; be perceptive of what might hurt the feelings of the ill person or his family members; respect the person's privacy, and do not overstep the level of intimacy.

Social support can be measured in three ways

There are **three ways** in which social support can be measured. **Epidemiological studies** investigate a pattern of disease in large populations. Such studies use **broad measures** of social support (for example, "Are you married?"). **Self-report** studies focus on an individual's social support in terms of its degree, kind and duration. And finally, **social network measures** rely on information concerning the number and interconnectedness of social supports. In a study conducted in Alameda County, California, it was found that among those men and women who had most social ties, the death rate was lowest, as against men and women who had the fewest social ties (Berkman & Syme, 1979). Although this study is primarily an epidemiological study, it also blends with self-report and social network methods.

BOX 3.3

When social support becomes sour

"Shame and Silence in Rexburg," is a front page report in the *Los Angeles Times*, November 25, 1996. This report is about Dr. LaVar Withers, a competent physician, who provided a very efficient service for three decades to a small community of 15,000 people in Idaho. However, his female patients had problems with him and were reluctant to speak publicly. The *Los Angeles Times* reported: "For three decades, women had whispered about Withers' conduct in examining rooms. Those who didn't have their own stories to tell about the friendly physician fondling breasts and genitals knew someone else who did. The 'booby doctor,' they called him."

"Some had come to him with colds or the flu, others with sinus infection, broken ankles.... All told much the same story. Withers' groping wasn't the least subtle or ambiguous. At times his gloveless fingers moved into their vaginas."

The *Los Angeles Times* reported further the experience of a 16 year old female patient: "He had me lay down on the examining table. There was no gown, no nurse, no explaining what he was doing. He lifted up my skirt. He was feeling my stomach area, abdomen. Then he unzipped my pants. He started feeling lower and lower. Pretty much as low as you can get. I don't know what he was doing down there. I'm thinking, 'Why is this idiot playing with me.' I'm thinking, 'He's a dirty blink.' Then he went under my skirt, started playing around there."

PSYCHONEUROIMMUNOLOGY (PNI) AND STRESS

PNI: Science studying the interplay between psycho-social factors and human immunity

It has been clearly established today that stress can affect the immune system. However, the mechanism through which stress operates on the immune system is less clear. A new interdisciplinary area of research, known as **psychoneuroimmunology (PNI)**, has emerged recently, helping us to understand the mechanism that relates behavior, the immune system and the nervous system. This newer approach, that is, PNI, emanates from the belief that the relationship between the above-mentioned three aspects does not work autonomously. The researchers believe that there exists a **bidirectional communication** between the immune system and the central nervous system (CNS) and both tend to influence each other. Where do psychological components come into the picture? "Of course," write Maier, Watkins and Fleshner (1994), "the existence of neural-immune interactions permits behavioral-psychological events to enter the matrix; if neural processes regulate immune processes, then there is a pathway by which psychological factors could impact immunity. Conversely, if immune processes alter neural functions, then they can also potentially impact on behavior, emotion and thought. PNI, then, is the study of these complex interactions between neural, immune, and behavioral processes" (p. 1005).

PNI can be traced to the ancient scriptures

The **history and development of the field** of PNI transcends many cultures and began several millennia before R. Ader first coined the term in 1975. Ancient mystics, philosophers and healers have focused on the impact of one's mental state on physical health and *vice versa* (Solomon, 2002), and one can find elements of PNI in the religious traditions of Buddhism, Hinduism Taoism, Confucianism, and Shinto (Griffiths, 2002). Rapid cultural and economic changes have however devastated many a cultural group's natural immunity. Thus, results of a study on Samoan adolescents (McDade, 2001) indicate that an inconsistency between the household's natural style of living and its SES led to a reduction in the cell mediated immunity of the group as a whole.

PNI tackles two major issues

According to Stowell *et al.*, (2003), the field of PNI addresses the following issues:

- **How psychological factors influence the immune system through neural and endocrinological pathways.**
- **How these relationships are relevant to immunologically mediated health problems such as infectious diseases, cancer, autoimmunity, allergy, wound healing, etc.**

BOX 3.4

The PNI mechanism (Koenig & Cohen, 2002)

In their book, "Psychological Stress and Autoimmune Disease" Koenig and Cohen (2002) have devoted a chapter to the link between PNI and the faith factor. In this chapter, they have also very succinctly discussed the operation of the PNI mechanism. According to them, the brain and the immune system work in tandem with each other, that is, the chemicals from the immune system signal the brain, and then, the chemicals from the brain signal the immune system. We all know that the brain can suppress the activity of the immune system in times of stress. It is also clear that the brain can also increase the functioning of the immune system. However, when this regulatory function is disturbed, it can lead to increased immune activity that could in turn make the body more vulnerable to disease.

In the same volume, Herberman (2002) has contributed a chapter on stress, natural killer cells and cancer. Pointing to the knowledge regarding the ways in which an individual copes with stress and its effect on the development and progression of disease such as cancer, he goes on to describe the process by which immunological mechanisms could mediate the influences of the nervous system on natural killer cells of the body.

If mental states are important precursors of physical health, any condition impacting mental states should have an impact on physical health too. This could be why **prayer has a healing value.** In fact, Kaye (2002) has discussed the implications of **spirituality** and **religious practice**, and how health care workers utilize the power of religion for the care of their patients. Rather than reintegrating religion back into medical practice, Kaye proposes that research on PNI and faith may result in the "**medicalization of religion,**" and not the "spiritualization of medicine." Thus religion can be practiced essentially for its therapeutic benefits and one can develop a "therapeutic" attitude towards religion. Though such therapeutic aspects are generally ignored in Western religious traditions (Brown, 2002), if "God is presumed to be a supernatural person who hears, cares about and responds to prayer, then it is possible that praying to God could engage interpersonal processes known to enhance the immune function" (for example, social support, benefits of disclosure and other positive consequences of interpersonal contact).

The multiple functions of PNI

As we have mentioned earlier, stress can influence the immune system by down regulating it, that is, by causing physiological changes consisting of alterations in levels of hormones and neuropeptides. In their review of the **relationship between stress and immunity**, Maier and co-workers (*ibid*) have cited studies on the effects of examination, battle task vigilance, and sleep deprivation on the immune system. Depressed people have been found to show dysfunction in their immune system (Irwin & co-workers, 1987). So do people when they are angry and feeling anxious (Fleshner & co-workers, 1993).

Stress has an effect on the immune system

Glaser & Kiecolt-Glaser (1994) found a link between quality of life and the immune system among **cancer patients**. Alzheimer's disease caregivers who showed depression and lack of social support showed significantly poorer functioning of their immune system than noncaregivers. Cohen and Williamson (1991) have shown how stress and common cold and infections are directly related.

Unfortunately, the relationship between stress and the immune system cannot be traced directly. Summarizing the current status of research in his area, Maier, *et al.*, commented: "It should be emphasized that the study of the psychological modulation of immunity has only scratched the surface of the relationships that probably exist. Obviously, psychological factors cannot directly contact white blood cells and are capable of altering immunity because they modulate autonomic information and the release of peripheral hormones that modulate immunity." (p. 1009, 1994).

So pervasive is the role of PNI that it has provided a framework for the study of **behavioral factors in stress and disease**. The real value of these psychological factors can be seen for diseases for which there is neither a cure nor a vaccine (AIDS is one example). Some of the questions to which researchers (reviewed by Ironson and co-workers, 2002) have tried to seek answers are:

- Can stress increase susceptibility to diseases?
- Does stress affect the effectiveness of vaccines?
- Can stress, disease and coping alter the course of infectious disease progression?
- Can stress influence reactivation of latent virus and thereby promote disease development?
- Can stress management affect disease progression?
- Can health psychologists help prevent and treat infectious diseases (that is, by helping patients change sexual behavior, adhere to medical regimes, etc.).

Let's take each of the above questions posed by Ironson. Firstly, can stress increase **susceptibility to disease**? Stress is normally associated with three emotional consequences: anxiety, depression and anger. There is empirical evidence (for example, that by Kiecolt-Glaser & co-workers, 2002) that depression can directly stimulate the production of substances that influence a wide spectrum of conditions such as aging, coronary heart disease, diabetes, certain cancers, functional decline, etc. At the same time, depression also has indirect effects by down-regulating the immune responses. Together, these pose the greatest risk for older adults. Thus aging interacts

Stress can increase susceptibility to disease

with depression to enhance risk to disease. This means that if people who are aging, are also depressed for some reason, they will be at a higher risk for certain diseases. In other words, psychological interventions for depression among such people could enhance their health and their longevity. Coe (1999) and Guttman (1998) have reached similar conclusions. It is also interesting to note that every individual who is depressed does not succumb to disease. Studies by Marsland and co-workers (2002) reveal that there are many intra-individual factors that mediate the effect of stress on the immune system. Some of these intra-individual factors are variables such as gender, financial hardship, low education, vulnerability to stress (Halim & co-workers, 2000) and personality hardiness (Dolbier & co-workers, 2001). Factors that act as buffers to stress, for example, social support have also been found to have a direct effect on natural killer cell numbers (Miyazaki & co-workers, 2003).

Similar to the effects of depression on the immune system, is the effect of anxiety, (Song, 2001). Stress has also been found to delay wound healing (Kiecolt Glaser & co-workers, 1998), while PNI interventions have been seen to mitigate general asthma symptoms (Freeman, 1998) and to even help nurses to intervene to prevent premature childbirth (Ruiz & co-workers, 1999).

We can also find research on the third question raised by Ironson, that is, can stress and coping alter the course of the disease? Yes, it is possible. It has been found to alter the course of cervical cancer (Visser & co-workers, 2000).

Can stress management affect disease progression? Meta analysis of studies on the effects of hypnosis, conditioning, disclosure and stress management, relaxation reveal that the effects are modest, being greater for hypnosis and conditioning than for the others (Miller & co-workers, 2001). Hypnosis is also seen to reduce susceptibility to colds, influenza and viral infections, especially during stress periods such as examinations (Gruzelier & co-workers, 2001).

Are PNI studies delivering a message to social psychology? Or, what advantage can social psychology draw from PNI studies for applications in everyday life? Of course, PNI studies have opened several doors for applied work. For a group of cancer patients, relaxation training and social support intervention had a positive effect on their quality of life which, in turn, improved their immune system functioning (Kiecolt-Glaser & Glaser, 1992). Other interventions that have worked successfully are: information about disease and treatment, focused interventions for disease-specific problems, and behavior-coping strategies. Recent practice in the field of stress and the prevention of disease as the end result, has examined the role of humor in enhancing not only healthy coping styles but also immune system functioning. There is considerable evidence today that humor and laughter can do much to alleviate stress (Lefcourt & co-workers, 1998).

HEALTH ENDANGERING BEHAVIOR: THE ROLE OF SOCIAL PSYCHOLOGY

Acquired Immune Deficiency Syndrome (AIDS)

HIV: Human Immuno-deficiency Virus

AIDS is caused by a virus, the **human immunodeficiency virus or HIV**, that attacks the **immune system**, specifically the T helper cells. The disease **spreads** by sexual contact, infected blood, or blood products. Except for some success by using a cocktail of AIDS pills (AZT, Crixivan and 3TC), there appears to be no cure for this killer disease. Fifteen years ago, not many people, including physicians, had heard about AIDS. Currently, more than 5,00,000 Americans are suffering from AIDS and many have died or will die soon. This disease is continuing to spread by an extraordinarily alarming rate among both men and women, especially among Hispanic and Afro-American groups (*Newsweek*, December 2, 1996). It is estimated that over 22 million people are suffering from AIDS throughout the world (*Los Angeles Times*, December 27, 1996 quoting UN AIDS data). China too is witnessing a crisis, with increasing epidemics of AIDS and other sexually transmitted diseases, the main reason appearing to be the lack of knowledge regarding the disease, its mode of transmission and prevention (Grusky *et al.*, 2002).

AIDS is frequently transmitted through unsafe sexual behavior

AIDS is frequently **transmitted** through unsafe sexual behaviors. Findings from Senegal too clarify that males who were from the lower end of the social scale and who either frequented brothels or had occasional sex, without the use of condoms were more likely to contract HIV AIDS (Gomes de Espirito & co-workers, 2003). Therefore, an important step in developing an intervention program for prevention of this disease will consist of understanding why people indulge in unsafe sex with high risk and what needs to be done to control or modify their behavior.

At the Kinsey Institute, Reinisch and co-workers (1988) analyzed the sexual behavior of white people and projected that 37% of husbands and 29% wives had at least one additional sexual partner in their marriage. Approximately 33% men had sex with a prostitute. This study also found that a significant number of women had sex during their visit to one of the ten high HIV-prevalence cities.

Although sexual risk taking can be minimized through the use of condoms, people seem to be reluctant to use them. Out of the 60% white male and females who have sexual intercourse by age 18 and 19, respectively, only 50% used a contraception the first time (Brooks-Gunn, Boyer & Hein, 1988). According to a report (cited by DeAngelis, 1995) from the University of California, San Francisco, "...only 5% of unmarried heterosexuals in committed relationships use condoms, regardless of how many other sex partners they have or had. That figure rises to only 15% for unmarried singles who are not in committed relationships but are sexually active" (p. 43, *APA Monitor*). Obviously, it is not difficult to imagine the magnitude of risk involved in spreading HIV.

Ways of getting people to adopt safe sexual practices: Creating awareness and changing group norms

Psychologists have been actively involved in the prevention of AIDS since 1983 (Morin, 1988). Taking lead from a market research study, a pioneering work was undertaken to help San Francisco's gay and bisexual men. The action plan involved a number of efforts ranging from safer sexual practices to town meetings, workshops and stress reduction. As a result the city reported fewer new cases of HIV infections. It is believed that two factors contributed to the success of this program: first, information about how the disease spreads, and second, an organized effort to change group norms. "This success," writes Morin (1988), "gives public health officials new hope that prevention efforts designed to facilitate behavior change can control the spread of HIV" (p. 838). The most striking effect of the intervention program was that in some high incidence areas, such as, San Francisco, approximately 49% gay men approached for psychological help.

Michael Antony (cited by DeAngelis, *APA Monitor*, October, 1995) reported the success of his intervention program during the mini convention of the American Psychological Association, New York, 1995. Two groups of HIV-infected people—one in the stress management group and the other in the waiting list—were studied. The treatment group not only suffered reduced isolation and loneliness but also showed improvement in warding off the virus, as compared to those in the waiting list. In short, such intervention studies suggest that prevention not only helps reduce the incidence of a problem but that it also accelerates mental and bodily recovery.

Dissemination of information regarding the disease is even more important when we consider the **global perspective**. One of the principal reasons for the spread of AIDS in developing and underdeveloped countries is the lack of awareness regarding the causes, prevention, transmission and treatment of AIDS. Some data are available regarding the effects of providing information to people in the **Third World countries**, for example, in **Thailand** (Mullany & co-workers, 2003), and to prison inmates in **India** (Chowdhury & co-workers, 2002). Positive results were noted in all these and other surveys (Visconti & co-workers, 2002).

Feelings of helplessness, social withdrawal, increased anxiety, depression, and reactive prejudicial attitudes/feelings are commonly linked to AIDS. The problem with AIDS is that it is so different from other diseases. It is hidden in our body and its unseen agent can attack us any time. The HIV-infected person feels out of control, and his judgments to cope with the new situation are made under anxiety.

Homophobia: Fear of homosexuals

Social rejection of AIDS patients is very common. The belief that it is a "homosexual" disease leads to homophobia (rejection and fear of homosexuals). Cohn and Swift (1992) found that when their female subjects interviewed an AIDS victim, they set chairs at a farther distance than when they interviewed someone with other life threatening diseases such as cancer. McKusick (1988) has classified three potential reactions to AIDS:

(a) those pertaining to disease and death.

(b) those pertaining to sexuality and intimacy.

(c) those pertaining to the notion of caretaking or being taken care of (p. 935).

Tables 3.6 and 3.7 report the issues and reactions related to AIDS.

TABLE 3.6

A comparison of possible reactions to positive and negative HIV antibody status (*Source*: McKusick, 1988)

Aspect	Positive HIV Status	Negative HIV Status
Disease and death	Anxiety, depression	Relief
	Fatalism	Lower stress
	Alienation	Refocusing on other life concerns
	Psychosomatic symptoms	
	Shopping for treatments	
	Increased spirituality	

Aspect	Positive HIV Status	Negative HIV Status
Sex & sexual relationships	Sexual dysfunction	Sexual repression
	Psychological and social distancing	Fear of intimacy
	Feelings of guilt over previous sexual behavior	Fear of sex and people with high levels of sexuality
Caretaking	Feelings of dependency	Greater interest in volunteer groups for HIV people
	Fear of stigma in interpersonal contact	Phobia about being touched
	Change in attitudes towards caregivers	
	Change in attitude towards medical and paramedical personnel	

TABLE 3.7

Some effects of not being tested for HIV antibodies (*Source*: McKusick, 1988)

Aspect	Suspected positive	Suspected negative
Disease and death	Denial and avoidance of medical care	Feeling that death could be caused by other diseases
	Death anxiety	
Sex & sexual relationships	Anger, denial, guilt	Fear of contact
	Fear of stigma	
Caretaking	Distrust	Involvement in health care programs related to HIV

An interesting observation made by McKusick concerns the "survivor guilt" of some gay community members: "Why did I escape? This feeling was especially pervasive when the bonds between the two partners were strong.

HIV AIDS stigma

Social stigma: Prejudice against certain abnormalities

Stigma towards people with AIDS is seen in various forms and has important repercussions for all aspects of the disease. Thus AIDS stigma in Ghana is manifested by the immense need for secrecy, which in turn affects the woman's access to treatment and to financial and emotional support from the family (Mill, 2003). Stigma produces a strange **ambivalence**: families want to care for the infected person, feel close to the person, and yet may remain distant or almost invisible. This is the experience of HIV affected families in a developed country like Switzerland (Spirig, 2002). Stigma has also been observed in the US, causing AIDS infected people to live in "closed" support groups. Yep *et al.* (2003) observed it in an ethnic minority group—Asian Americans. But fear of social isolation is seen even in the general **work situation**, with managers being wary of sharing AIDS-related information with co-workers of an AIDS-infected worker (Vest & co-workers, 2003).

Among the many attempts to remove AIDS stigma is the use of theatre and roadside drama. A cheap and effective method used in many Third World countries, including India, is the use of **community theatre** specialists. Such a method has been documented in Tanzania. Young theatre specialists trained young community members in participatory research theatre, who then engaged in research and encouraged community members to discuss and evaluate the factors in HIV transmission. Through such theatre groups, it was found that economic, social and health problems facilitated the spread of HIV. The discussions and evaluations caused a considerable breakdown of silence and stigma barriers. More importantly, condom demand rose in all the districts (Mabala & co-workers, 2002).

A large scale review of 22 studies testing a variety of interventions to reduce AIDS stigma in both developing and developed countries has been reported by Brown and co-workers (2003). The results suggest that though some of the interventions were effective in combating AIDS stigma, at least on a small scale or for a short term period, many gaps remain. Kalichman & co-workers (cf. Bechtel & Churchman, 2002) noted that the benefit of AIDS awareness programs is better achieved with **home access to information**, that is, where the person can get the information in the privacy of his home. Using this as the cue, maybe one way of bypassing stigma could be by providing information through the Internet. Here we see a good example of how technology can be of service to the solution of health related issues.

Understanding HIV AIDS associated risk behavior

The applications of social psychology in understanding risk behavior that leads to AIDS have been drawn from **three** different viewpoints. First, **a psychosocial model** focuses on psychological and social factors that are related to high-risk behavior. Second, **cognitive models** within psychology, that emphasize the role of attitudes, beliefs and perception of others. And, finally, there is **a social learning theory,** in which modelling effects are combined with self-efficacy and perceived efficacy. Unfortunately, most of these theories were developed long before we knew anything about AIDS. As a result the above approaches to combat the problem of AIDS have limited value. Some of the applications of the above theories have been described below.

Kirby and others (1994) found that the **social learning model** was highly successful in a **school setting.** Flora and Thoresen (1988) suggested a variety of methods for reducing the risk of AIDS in adolescents: safe and protected sex, abstaining from sexual activity, safe practice in IV drug use, and safety in the use of devices. They suggested a model AIDS prevention curricula based on social learning theory. Such a type of intervention combines: (1) information on health endangering behavior; (2) recognizing high risk environment; (3) reasons to engage in high sex behavior; and (4) behavior participation. The intervention approach, according to Flora and Thoreson, should encompass cognitive, environmental and behavioral components. They have also stated that the success of any intervention program will depend on social marketing, a concept similar to business marketing, which includes consumer-oriented programs, audience need analysis, formative pre-testing, and a "marketing mix" consisting of targeting specific groups.

TABLE 3.8

A Comparison of some Educational Approaches for Primary and Secondary Prevention of AIDS among Adolescents (*Source*: Flora & Thoresen, 1988)

Theoretical approach	Educational approach	Primary prevention	Secondary prevention
Cognitive/emotional	Providing knowledge	Regarding avoidance of certain behaviors	Regarding safer sex practice
	Self talk	"I don't have to have sex"	"It is OK to use condoms"
	Self efficacy	Perceived ability to resist sex	Perceived ability to use condoms
Behavioral	Behavior outcomes	"Avoiding too much alcohol increases my control over sex behavior"	"I can talk to my partner to use condoms"
	Social skills	Resisting peer pressure for sex	Negotiating with partner for safe sex
Societal	Social support systems	Peer encouragement for avoiding sex	Peer encouragement for safer sex
	Incentives	Getting social rewards for avoiding sex	Increased intimacy permitted if partner agrees to limit sex
	Vicarious learning	Training older peers to demonstrate avoidance of sex	Modeling of safer sex practices

The **sexual orientation** and HIV status of educators play an important role in changing the perception of risk linked to AIDS (Evers, Bishop Gerhan & Weisse, 1997). They employed a 2 × 2 factorial design in which subjects were presented four videotapes with varying information concerning sexual orientation and HIV status of the educator. The results of this study show that the intention to get tested for HIV increased among subjects when they learned that the model shown to them was HIV positive than when it was not. In another study, David and Cindy Struckman-Johnson (1996) found **fear arousing appeals** to be effective in AIDS prevention. They suggested use of public service announcements related to intentions to use condoms (for example, men and women buying, carrying and preparing for use of condoms). According to them, even symbolic modelling is helpful in the prevention of AIDS.

AIDS prevention

Sex education is helpful in controlling unsafe sexual practices

It is said that prevention is better than cure. One of the major initiatives the world over is through sex education in general and education regarding AIDS specifically. An evaluation of one such **educational program** for AIDS was conducted for a student-teacher training course in Zimbabwe (Chifunyise & co-workers, 2002). The parameters of evaluation were: (a) changes in student-teacher's level of knowledge about AIDS in general; (b) their attitudes towards AIDS patients; (c) their sensitivity to the impact of the epidemic; and, (d) their sensitivity to teaching about each of the above. Results showed positive changes on all four indices. The study also helped analyze some of the ingredients necessary for an effective program. These included mandatory course attendance, curriculum updating, use of peer educators, and participatory techniques for the internalization of attitudes and behavior, and the need to address the lack of female empowerment in making decisions regarding safer sex. The impact of peer education programs in raising community awareness and in decreasing infection-related practices has been documented in Zambia too (Hughes-d'Aeth, 2002). Similarly in Columbia, **mass education** by a combination of **school-based peer education** and **classroom teaching sessions** has been found to be an effective **primary prevention strategy** (Perez & co-workers, 2003). Can we explain the success of peer induced prevention programs through social psychological theory? How about the principles of social learning and the greater advantage of reinforcement on the basis of modelling?

Primary prevention becomes somewhat more difficult in **migrated groups**, for example, in refugees and immigrant populations. Soskolne & co-workers (2002) observed that as far as the prevention of AIDS is concerned there are both macro level factors (such as social and cultural deterrents) and micro level factors (such as individual factors) at work. The social-cultural deterrents include lower SES, limited social capital and cultural norms. These tend to interact with individual level factors such as new stressors related to the migration of families; depleted psychosocial resources, change in or loss of cultural beliefs and the low use of health services (Soskolne & co-workers, 2002).

Interventions with people with AIDS

What happens when preventive methods fail or are not adhered to? People fall victim to the HIV virus and then the intervention strategies are very different from those used for primary prevention purposes. In most countries, a combination of medical treatment and behavioral intervention has been successful. In a survey by Kamali & others (2003), an attempt was made to assess the effects of such an intervention in rural Uganda. All adults living in 18 communities in rural Uganda were randomly assigned to 3 conditions:

A: To receive behavioral intervention alone (N = 6918).

B: To receive both behavioral intervention and treatment of sexually transmitted diseases (N = 6856).

C: To receive routine government health service and community development activities (N = 6742).

Outcome indices were HIV incidence and incidence of STI (Sexually Transmitted Infections). The results showed that while the interventions were insufficient to reduce HIV incidence, they certainly decreased the incidence of STI.

Community based programs are successful

A major intervention initiative was the development of the **International Harm Reduction Development Program.** The program was established for the express purpose of promoting HIV prevention and health promotion among drug users in Central and Eastern Europe, the former Soviet Union and Central Asia. According to Coffin (2002), the program was established in 1995, and has been funding a large number of programs since 1998. Because of its success, it was granted 3 years of continued operation, though it was supposed to close down in 2001.

Practitioners the world over and even caregivers of AIDS victims have vouched for the effectiveness of **social support.** One way of providing social support is through community based intervention programs. One such program has been outlined in the box below (Demarco & co-workers, 2003). Another interesting intervention is the formation of buddy programs with volunteers providing social support to HIV patients (Burrage & co-workers, 2003).

Despite major efforts, intervention strategies sometimes fail. For instance, the reasons for the **failure** of a Texas-based program included the following: Community providers were not able or willing to follow the evaluation protocol; mail back response were too low; and rapport formation and trust development were extremely difficult. Initial increases in pro HIV prevention behavior often reached a plateau, because of boredom, or loss of interest because of dissatisfaction with the efficacy and adequacy of programs, for example, in Hong Kong, during 1994-2000 (Lau & co-workers, 2002). Adherence to drug regimens sometimes becomes low. This may be because of lack of social support and difficulties of treatments with injections (Carrieri & co-workers, 2003). Another example of ineffective intervention is given below (Tambashe & co-workers, 2003).

Efforts were made to assess the impact of a family health and AIDS program in the Ivory Coast in Africa. The program was a **mass media campaign** in Burkina Faso on the truckers' likelihood of talking with colleagues about HIV AIDS, using condoms with an occasional sex partner and intentions to use condoms in the future.

BOX 3.5

An effective community based intervention program

It has often been seen that intervention programs for not only HIV AIDS but also for smoking and alcoholism is successful when people who have actually been smokers or alcoholic and have now turned over a new leaf partner intervention programs. In line with this fact, one program was started in 1998 for women with HIV AIDS.

How was the program run? It was an interdisciplinary team that attempted to take action in communities. The program was run with the collaboration of a medical center, a community based HIV AIDS service organization, a university school of nursing and women living with AIDS in an inner city community.

For whom was the program designed? It provided programs for not only the victims of AIDS but also for their family, friends and caregivers, the focus being on providing insights into the disease. Since they would be meeting other women who were living with AIDS, it was felt that the program would get better acceptance.

What was the nature of the program? It was a series of educational programs, focused on self care and empowerment so that the patients would be able to take control of their wellness and health care while still continuing to live in the community.

What were the results? First and foremost, the collaborative nature of the program engendered trust between all partners in the program: the academicians, the clinical and community service givers, the professional caregivers and the recipients of their care. But even more significant was the new-found confidence in the women who had been living with the deadly virus. They found their experiences in this program so satisfying for themselves and the recipients of the program, that "they turned their health and life experiences into action by planning a research project that will test the efficacy of an intergenerational HIV prevention program for adolescent women of color in their community in the future" (Demarco & Johnson, 2003).

Firstly, baseline interviews were conducted on a particular trucking route with 764 drivers (aged 15-49 years). Thereafter, 1032 truckers were interviewed regarding the same points. The results show that though the truckers' exposure to the campaign had been high, and that the main message had been understood, the campaign failed to have direct behavioral impacts. Moreover, while exposure to radio spots and participation in group discussions were found to be significantly associated with truckers discussing AIDS with their colleagues or reporting intentions of using condoms in the future, exposure to TV messages and billboards were not found to be significantly associated with either discussions with colleagues or with future intentions of condom usage (Tamashe, Speizer, Amouzou & Djangone, 2003).

What does the above initiative show? That unless and until there is **direct participation** in such programs, mere seeing of messages over the TV or on billboards does not seem to have any favorable effect. Since this has been found in the West coast of Africa, we do however need to consider the cultural and socio-economic differences before making any generalizations for the world over.

Interactive participation is more effective than billboards and TV programs

What happens when all fails? Will mandatory compliance help? Law-makers are contemplating mandatory HIV testing and restrictions on people who knowingly have unsafe sex. Still personal responsibility, not public policy, remains the greatest hope for stopping AIDS (Kalichman 2003). Yet, how can this be achieved when even the UN committees fight shy of including sex education in their documents. In May 2002, delegates from 180 countries debated on whether the final declaration of the summit should contain words such as "abortion," "counseling for adolescents," or "sex education" or "reproductive health services". So, rather than the summit focusing on the plight of young children infected by HIV, they focused on whether the final document should have any reference to abortion and what would be the objection from the clergy or the mullah to any reference to sex education in the document. Can we fight the scourge due to this dreaded disease if even world bodies such as the UN refuse to accept the reality?

AIDS and Women

The Center for Disease Control (1994) has reported that the cases of AIDS among women are on the rise, albeit their current number is less than 1,00,000. From 1981-82 to 1993-94, their proportion has jumped from 4% to 16.7%. From the behavioral standpoint, the difference between men and women infected with AIDS is that whereas in men it is mainly transmitted through sexual contact between gay men, among women it is transmitted through heterosexual transfer or injection drug use (Amaro, 1995). Only 3% cases among men suffer from AIDS through heterosexual transmission.

The above statistics points out that "male-to-female transmission of HIV is more probable than female-to-male transmission. ....the odds of male-to-female transmission are 12 times greater than of female-to-male transmission" (p. 438, Amaro, 1995).

Is there a **gender dynamics** in the issue related to AIDS? Given the socialized passivity of women, unequal power and gender-related attitudes, there is a growing sense that psychological research in particular should be sensitive to recognizing and identifying gender issues related to AIDS. Here is an excerpt from Amaro's article (1995), "Love, Sex and Power":

Gender dynamics is an important issue

> "...in most studies, sexual risk behaviors (*e.g.*, not using a condom) in both women and men are seen as the same behavior. In fact, these are distinctly different behaviors. For men, the behavior is wearing a condom; for women, the behavior is persuading the male partner to wear a condom or in some cases, deciding not to have sex when the male partner refuses to wear a condom" (p. 440).

A study by Pleck and co-workers (1993) supports the above conclusion. Boys who had a traditional sense of masculinity were found to have a negative attitude toward condom use and, in fact, used condoms less frequently. Gomez and Martin (1993) also reported that anticipated fear in the request for use of a condom is a critical factor among Latinos.

AIDS and substance abuse

Does **substance abuse** make a person vulnerable to sexual risk taking behavior? Alcohol and drug abuse have long been viewed to interfere with decision making capacities of an individual. Not surprisingly, their use in combination with sexual activity would increase chances of risky behavior. However, given the nature of the complex relationship between substance abuse, sexual activity and risk factor, empirical work showing a cause-effect relationship is very difficult to establish.

In a careful study, Leigh and Stall (1993) attempted to study the relationship between **substance abuse and high-risk sex.**

In their analysis, Leigh and Stall cited evidence to show that drinking habits are correlated with liberal sexual behavior; use of substance is related to risky sexual activity; and use of alcohol is related to non-use of contraception. They concluded that 'interventions designed to prevent risky sex include a component of substance use prevention" (p. 1040). The importance of tackling substance use along with interventions for preventing risky sex, is corroborated by findings in China too. Wang and Lin (2003) report that HIV related risk behavior is common among female heroin users in China. Wang *et al.* also provide the reason for this nexus: female heroin users in China were found to exchange sex for drugs or for money to buy drugs.

BOX 3.6

I have learned to hope: David Brodnoy, Boston Talk Show Host (*Newsweek*, December 2, 1996)

"Fear. Denial. Acceptance. Hope. That has been the trajectory of my life with AIDS during the past two years. Let me explain. In 1988, pushed to get the AIDS antibody test by a friend who thought that my pallor and rundown health were suggestive of something beyond a lingering cold, I found that you don't have to practice anal sex or trade dirty HIV needles or undergo blood transfusions or even engage in your garden variety heterosexual sex with infected partners to get "it". A lesson learned: oral sex, albeit rare as the entrance route for HIV, is not an impossible method of transmission"....

"Denial. The greatest performance of my life was my self-delusion. I pretty much convinced others of what my denial had convinced me: that I merely had a lousy flu"....

"I live with AIDS, realizing that the experience has been not only phenomenally instructive but also, oddly enough, enlightening, enriching, life enhancing and liberating."

The scenario becomes worse for women who have substance abuser husbands habitually indulging in sexual relationship with multiple partners. Dolcini (cited by DeAngelis, *The APA Monitor*, Sept. 1995) conducted a study on 209 women who were in such a relationship but because of their economic condition and conservative values, were unable to leave their husbands. She concluded that it would be very difficult to offer a psychological intervention program to such women. In short, as variables such as gender, substance abuse and ethnic groups interact, the creation of a viable psychological intervention program for AIDS becomes more difficult.

AIDS and the Lazarus Effect

As new drugs for the treatment of AIDS are flooding the market, the victims of AIDS have found some hope for a longer life. This hope has been called "**the Lazarus Effect.**" A combination of drugs has particularly helped those who could afford or have afforded such a cocktail. David Brudnoy (see Box 3.7) felt that he had lost his battle with his life but somehow bounced back. Earvin Johnson, known as Magic to basketball fans, remarked, "I am going to go on and I'm going to beat it." Such hardy personalities who could combine their psychological make-up with proper medication have survived so far from the fatal effects of AIDS.

The Lazarus Effect: Ability to bounce back to life through medication combined with optimism

The question before such survivors is: What do I do now? How do I get back to normal business in life? They are living in a hope that is combined with fear. For them, to return to normal life and its risk behavior will be worse, for if they infect their partner, there is little hope for this new HIV patient on whom the drug will be less effective. It is well known that the virus becomes resistant after use of a drug. Such survivors need intervention programs tailored to their needs. The lesson: Watch out, folks. One shot intervention programs may not be good enough!

Cancer

Cancer is one of the leading causes of death in the USA. It accounts for 23% of all mortality. Although the link between behavioral factors and cancer is not well known, research on patterns of coping with cancer have shown **five features** that have clear social psychological implications:

1. Cognitive escape—avoidance—expecting a miracle.
2. Behavioral escape avoidance—effort to improve.
3. Distancing—downplaying the effect.
4. Becoming positive.
5. Joining social support.

A surprising finding regarding cancer patients is that those who express unhappiness and become combative live longer than those who are non-aggressive and polite (Levy, 1990). Terminally ill cancer patients tend to have problems in communicating with others. While significant others provide support to the patient, they tend to avoid talking. While there are stories about heroic cancer patients who battled very hard to fight this fatal disease, there is scant research evidence to show how they succeeded (Doan & Gray, 1992).

Some of this evidence is regarding the **effects of positive emotions on the immune function**. For example, Berk and colleagues (1989) were able to demonstrate that a few minutes of laughter while viewing a humorous film is able to lower the epinephrine and cortisol levels of the subjects. In an interesting study on students, the effects of **emotional expression** on the immune function were clarified. Students were asked to write about traumatic events in their lives or about emotionally neutral events every day for four days. Six months later, it was found that those who had expressed themselves about their traumas were happier and less depressed than their counterparts who had written about neutral events in their lives. The former also manifested better lymphocyte activity, suggesting better immune function than their colleagues (Keller & co-workers, 1994).

With reference to cancer specifically, the investigation conducted by Spiegel, Bloom, Kramer and Gottheil (1989) is relevant. Women who had been showing a recurrent breast cancer underwent group psychotherapy every week for one year. Not only did the participants of the study survive longer than those who were given medical care alone, but they also showed strong personal bonds and learned to express their emotions freely, even negative ones to other members of their group. While this study shows a strong association between social relationships, emotional status and health, the mechanism mediating this relationship is not as yet very clear. However, we can leave that for the medical researchers to ruminate over, while we, as social psychologists, ponder over the significant effects that social interaction can have on the prognosis of cancer.

Figure 3.1: A bio-behavioral model of disease progression in cancer (adapted from Kiecolt-Glaser & Glaser, 1994).

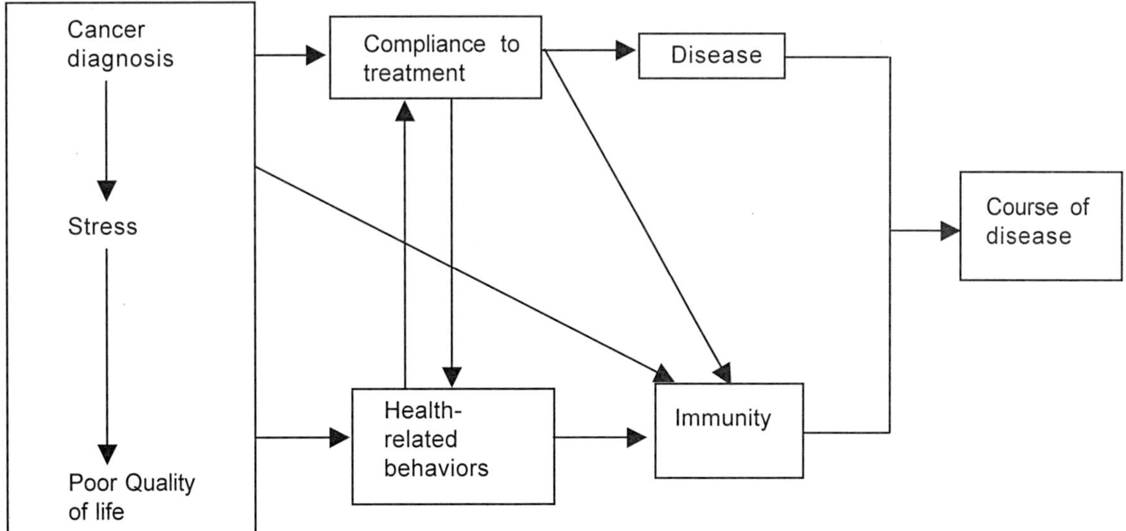

Based on the results of several empirical studies, Anderson Kiecolt-Glaser (1996) concluded that people suffering from cancer show appetite disturbances, sleep problems and non-compliance for treatment due to discouragement. Additionally, sensory changes tend to occur during radiation therapy. In short, the researchers suggested that sufficient direct evidence exists linking health behavior and immunity. Based on their own research and available data, they proposed a bio-behavioral model (Fig 3.1). Two important conclusions can be drawn from such studies. First, immune changes that occur due to stress in cancer do not habituate. Second, over a period of time, low social support was associated with a weakened immune system.

Cancer: A global perspective

Social factors are an impediment to cancer diagnosis and treatment

An assessment of cancer prevention and treatment around the world points to the role of a variety of **psycho-social factors.** One such would be **socio-economic status** (SES) and the **ethnic group** to which the person belongs. Women from low SES or ethnic groups in **Spain** failed to have the necessary information regarding diagnosis, risk factors and prognosis (Estape & co-workers, 2003). In **China,** the problem involves both the uncertainty of disease detection (usually followed by shock, disbelief and fear of death) and treatment choices because of **social stigma** and **exclusion** (Lam & co-workers, 2003). Even in the highly developed **Swedish** society, the principal barrier to mammography was "getting no respect" from either the society or the health care system (Johansson & co-workers, 2003). Other reasons for **inadequate use of mammography** were obtained for **African Americans** (Russell & co-workers, 2003). In **Japan,** the situation is apparently different. Sadler and others (2003) report that though less than half of the women in the sample felt that they had enough knowledge about breast cancer, there was high adherence to mammography screening guidelines. In rural areas of **Australia,** the problem was that of **financial assistance** for travelling to cancer treatment facilities (Davis & co-workers, 2003). The lack of knowledge, cultural factors and concern for children were the major themes emerging for **Asian Americans,** making them move towards spiritualism (Ashing & co-workers, 2003).

Lack of awareness is another impediment

Thus, the recurrent theme from around the world, and especially for people from rural, low SES and ethnic minority groups, is the **lack of sufficient information or financial help.** Breast cancer still seems to be associated with **stigmatization,** becoming a major barrier to diagnosis or treatment, leaving the women with few options beyond seeking spiritual solace. It also seems to explain the **turn to meditation** and other complementary therapies by cancer patients (Canales & Geller, 2003; Tacon, 2003; Lee & co-workers, 2002). This is where social psychology can help—in the **removal of prejudice** towards people with curable forms of cancer. Knowledge about, or the provision of medical facilities, does not ensure its usage *per se.* A number of psycho-social factors are called into play. Studies on the role of social support (Holland & Holahan, 2003) and support groups for patients and their families (Roberts & co-workers, 2002) provide further justification. Some of this stigmatization effects can be overcome by people using Internet sites for information (Fogel & co-workers, 2003) and cyber support (Sullivan, 2003), but considerably more needs to be done.

Smoking

Nearly 50% men in the world and approximately one-third of the people in the U.S. smoke cigarettes. Although this figure is down by approximately 20% since the early fifties in the U.S., much of the two to three per cent drop per year during the last decade was not visible in the recent years. Cigar sales are up and consumption of cigarettes is holding steady,

BOX 3.7

Prevalence of smoking around the world

An effort was made by the authors to compile data from various surveys to help the reader understand the magnitude of the problem from the global perspective.

Jordan: The prevalence of smoking was found to be 28.6% among university students, with friends being the main source of first smoking, generally after 15 years of age. Females preferred to smoke in the bathroom but males smoked in public. The main advantage reported by male smokers was help in calming down, while for females it marked a show of independence. (Haddad & Malak, 2002).

Iran: A survey of 501 university students found 47% of the males and 14% of the females reporting tobacco use. Opium and hashish were also used by the students (Ahmadi & Yazdanfar, 2002).

Australia: A survey of smoking among 4217 aboriginal people of eastern Australia (over 15 years of age) revealed the following figures for the year 1999:

	Kava	Alcohol	Tobacco	Cannabis
Males	46%	53%	68%	31%
Females	18%	12%	65%	8%

The study also reports that there is a recent rise in the use of cannabis, especially among the females, a decline in kava use among the males and a change in tobacco use patterns among the females (Clough & co-workers, 2002).

India: A survey on the health status of the elderly in India is of interest because one of the issues was tobacco usage among the elderly. The survey based on 2253 persons aged 60 years and above from 5 Indian states revealed among other problems a prominent use of tobacco (Rajan, Mishra & Sarma, 2001).

Cape Town, South Africa: A survey of 2930 high school students clarified that 27% engaged in smoking cigarettes, 31% used alcohol and 7% smoked cannabis. The rates were lower for black females. A significant finding was that not being raised by both parents was associated with cigarette smoking (Flisher & co-workers, 2003).

The USA: Survey findings for a large scale 3 year cross-sectional survey of students from 6th to 8th grade in an urban setting reported a disparity in the prevalence rates between African Americans, Whites and Hispanic youth. It is important to note that although weak in 6th grade, by 8th grade, White and Hispanic students are smoking 2-4 times the rates of the African American classmates (Kelder & co-workers, 2003). A study in urban Philadelphia too confirmed differences in the rate of smoking between ethnic/racial groups. The authors found that social sources were the most often cited source for starting to smoke, and that the rate of smoking was exceptionally high with 50% of the students ever having smoked and 15% smoking daily (Ma & coworkers, 2003). In New Jersey, cigar smoking was even higher among middle and high school adolescents than among adults (Delnevo & co-workers, 2002).

contributing to boost a solid 487 billion dollar industry. In several developing countries too, like China, the consumption of cigarettes has increased very significantly (Chandler, 1988).

More boys smoke than girls; first smoke often due to peer pressure in adolescence

What can we conclude from the information given in the box above? Data from around the world show that more boys than girls engage in smoking, and that they often start smoking during adolescence. While the first smoke is often due to peer pressure, smoking later on is more related to attempts to get away from boredom or from stress.

It would be interesting to note whether knowledge regarding smoking and its health hazards affects attitudes towards smoking. A survey of medical, nursing and pharmacy students in Hungary revealed that there was a high acceptance of smoking among all three groups with smoking being the most frequent among the nursing and the medical students and least among the pharmacy students. If this is the case of health care professionals, that they themselves are unable to cope with avoiding the hazards of smoking, how will they work in their responsibility as medical personnel of reducing smoking? (Piko, 2002).

BOX 3.8

An international comparison of tobacco smoking, beliefs and risk awareness in university students from 23 countries (Steptoe & co-workers, 2002)

Countries sampled: Belgium, Bulgaria, Colombo, France, Germany, Greece, Hungary, Iceland, Ireland, Italy, Japan, Korea, Netherlands, Poland, Portugal, Romania, South Africa, Spain, Thailand, England, the US, Venezuela and Slovakia.

Thus you can see from the sample of countries, that all three classes of developed, developing and underdeveloped countries had been included in the sample.

The sample: Consisted of 19, 298 university students aged 17-30 years, both males and females studying courses unrelated to health.

Measures: Standardized measures of smoking, wish to stop smoking, ratings of beliefs in the importance of not smoking for health and awareness of influence of smoking on lung cancer and heart disease.

Prevalence rate varied widely, highest in the South European countries and lowest in developing countries, that is, Thailand and South Africa. Awareness of health risk was variable, lowest for Asian, South American and other developing country samples. As we know from research on attitudes and beliefs, inconsistencies between attitudes, beliefs and consequent behavior are often found. An inconsistency between the awareness regarding the risks of smoking and actual behavior was evident in the analysis.

While the debate over the effects of smoking are being fought at social, political and legal levels, it is very clear that the incidence of cancer is ten times higher in smokers than non-smokers. Smoking has been found to be related to coronary heart disease and, among pregnant women, it has an adverse effect during pregnancy. Those who smoke also endanger the health of others through the effect of what has been called **passive smoking.**

From the standpoint of social psychology, two important issues are of major concern. **First**, given the knowledge that smoking is likely to cause cancer, why do people smoke? The **second issue** is: do people who smoke estimate accurately the health hazards linked to smoking?

Smoking manifests itself in four stages

To the first question, the answer is obvious: most people become addicted to nicotine much like coffee or tea drinkers; for some others, it is associated with power or a sense of "growing up" as among adolescents; and, for still others, it may be linked to social pressure. For Freud, who had to undergo jaw surgery, cigar intensified his capacity to work. For Mark Twain, it was asking for a "light." People do not easily give up smoking even after the first detrimental signs begin to appear. Like any other strong habit, it is very resistant to extinction. According to Leventhal and Cleary (1980), smokers manifest four stages in their smoking behavior. **First, the preparation stage,** in which the smokers try a cigarette and form an image of a smoker. **Second,** as peers and significant others urge someone to smoke, the smoker enters **the initiation stage.** If the smoker consumes a number of cigarettes consistently at this stage, he is likely to become a regular smoker. **Third,** within two years, **the habit of smoking** is formed and the smoker can tolerate the effects of smoking. And, during the **fourth** stage, **smoking is maintained** as it satisfies both physiological and psychological needs.

Social psychological theories are able to account for the behavior of smokers very well. For **social learning theory**, the explanation lies in observation of behavior of other smokers who have led a healthy life. An explanation based on **cognitive theory** will account for the mismatch between the attitudes and the behavior of people. We may believe that smoking causes cancer, but we also know that not all people who smoked had cancer. Therefore, they continue to smoke hoping that they would not be victims of cancer.

Concerning the second issue, that is how people estimate health hazards linked to smokers report an almost 50-50 chance of dying due to smoking (Lamb, 1995). On the contrary, 90% of those who smoke do not die of smoking related illness. In other words, denial of health hazards is not a critical factor in the behavior of smokers; it is their inability to foresee the impact of smoking. Because the effects of smoking do not show up instantly, it is a deferred risk.

BOX 3.9

Life with a cigarette

For smokers, cigarettes are a seductive mistress, at once a spiteful and delectable. They break the tedium of the day into manageable units of pleasurable anticipation. Like a friend, they are there in moments of reverie and depression. And with the tiny "hit" produced by each puff costing a penny or two, they are—whatever the ultimate costs—our cheapest, most accessible opiate, quieting uneasiness, soothing stress, dulling pain, honing focus, both sedating and exciting, depending on the intensity of and number of inhalations" (David Lamb, *Los Angeles Times*, November 5, 1995, p. A 11).

Intervention

Although 70% smokers said that they would like to quit smoking, and, few would encourage their children to smoke (Lamb, *Los Angeles Times* survey, November 5, 1995), most of them do not give up smoking.

Smoking can be reduced by behavioral interventions

At least two behavioral treatments of smoking have been tried. First, **aversive procedures** consist of rapid smoking, say, every six second inhaling, until the craving stops. Negative reinforcements, such as electric shock, is associated with this procedure.

The **self-management technique** involves monitoring the number of cigarette consumption and record-keeping. A behavioral technique called **contingency contracting** involves setting up a goal to reduce cigarette consumption in consultation with a therapist who will accept a deposit from the client for this purpose. If the client meets the goal, the deposit will be returned to the client. However, this technique showed only temporary effects because the long-term effects of this method were rarely visible (Lando, 1993). It is generally combined with the **nicotine fading method** that encourages the smoker to consume cigarettes with lower nicotine.

Three behavioral techniques: Self-management technique, contingency contracting, nicotine fading method

In the treatment of smoking, behavior therapies are used in combination with counseling and chemical methods. On the whole, the effect of such efforts have been mixed.

Role playing has shown some promising results in changing the behavior of smokers. In an earlier study, Janis and Mann (1965) used emotional role playing to help smokers to quit smoking. In this method, participating subjects played a distressing role in several scenarios. Other participants simply listened to a tape conversation. The main idea behind such an intervention was to demonstrate that people do not change their behavior simply by participating as a member of the audience (tape group) but by actively engaging in a real life scenario. The results of this study showed clearly that role players showed greater change in their attitudes than those in the tape group. A follow-up study after 18 months again showed that cigarette consumption was significantly reduced in the role playing subjects in comparison to the subjects in the tape group.

Role playing leads to greater attitude change than mere passive watching

A key finding of the above study was that a simple analysis of attitude change through the study of characteristics of the audience, the message and the source (the well known Yale group findings) is not enough. Attitude changes can be demonstrated through active participation, personal involvement, empathy and fear as a motivational variable.

Suedfeld and Ekard (1974) investigated the effects of **sensory deprivation** on smoking. Sensory deprivation was created by reducing light and sound and by confining the subject in a small room. A dramatic effect of this study was that smoking reduced among all the groups of sensory deprived subjects irrespective of whether they received messages for reducing smoking or not. Is sensory deprivation therapeutic? While there is no scientific evidence, there seems to be a lesson in curtailing external pleasures. Another problem with such studies is that most of the information is collected through self-reports. The reliability of results based on this method alone is not always trustworthy. It is also likely that subjects in

Sensory deprivation: Reducing light, sound and confining person in small room

the control group who were not given any antismoking messages were sensitized at the time they were prepared for the sensory deprivation.

Consumption of cigarettes among teenagers has been a major concern for all communities. Using McGuire's theory of **attitude inoculation**—a concept analogous to that in the medical sciences that people become resistant to medicine with weak doses. Evans (1976) conducted a study in which he integrated social learning theory with inoculation on high school students. He exposed teenagers to a video show in which teenagers at their level smoked because of peer pressure or parental models. However, they also saw in films on how they could resist such pressure. Further, they were shown the immediate effect of smoking, for example, accumulation of toxins in the body. The results were dramatic. A significant number of students quit smoking.

Attitude inoculation: Showing of negative effects of smoking

Public commitment to non-smoking increases chances of quitting of smoking

Evans developed an intervention strategy to reduce smoking on the ground that if social pressures can increase smoking, they can also be used to reduce the incidence of smoking. Subsequently, the social influence program not only retained what was learned from social learning and inoculation studies but also added two more dimensions: **public commitment and role playing.**

Social psychological research has consistently shown that once people make public commitments, they tend to behave consistently better than when they hold private beliefs (Keishler, 1971). In one study when students were requested to announce their intention to quit smoking in the classroom, they did reduce their smoking (McAlister & co-workers, 1980). Further, the effects of role playing were also positive in reducing smoking because role playing not only provides opportunity to receive information concerning the unhealthy behavior but also provides an opportunity to practice skills to cope with the new situation. In short, an intervention program to reduce smoking may require a multipronged effort consisting of role playing, public commitment and lessons from social learning and inoculation.

Intervention programs: A global perspective

In this section we will show you how intervention programs were applied in different countries. An innovative attempt was made in a **German school**, where a smoke-free class competition was held. Results showed that students who had participated in the competition not only had a lower increase in smoking habit, but the baseline prevalence rate also showed a downturn (Wiborg & co-workers, 2002).

The hospital setting provides an opportune venue for the implementation of smoking cessation programs. The social psychological relationship between the health service provider and the health service seeker affords a necessary platform. The success of such **hospital-based programs** is seen from a program conducted in the **Netherlands**, where midwives effectively implemented the smoking cessation program for their patients (Bakker & co-workers, 2003). When **doctors in Canada** were contacted, it was found that only 10.5% provided thorough counseling to stop smoking (O'Laughlin & co-workers, 2001). At the same time, 54% of **Canadian addiction programs** offered smoking cessation services (Currie & co-workers, 2003). Another missed opportunity occurred in a large **London teaching hospital**

Hospital setting provides ideal ground for smoking cessation programs

where at least 23% of the patients were categorized as current smokers. The majority of these would like to quit, but this was not part of the hospital services offered (Hunt & co-workers, 2003).

Extra-curricular activities can be designed for reducing smoking among teenagers

Within the **USA, Project 4-Health,** a research based program to prevent tobacco use among youth enrolled in 4-H clubs, showed moderate short-term effects, but long-term effects were conspicuous by their absence (D'Onofrio & co-workers, 2002). Greater effectiveness was obtained for a **Canadian program** based on **extra-curricular activities** developed by the teachers and students to reduce smoking. The success of the intervention program can be seen from the reduction in the number of male regular smoking 10th graders and increase in the number of male never smoked category in the 8th grade (Brown & co-workers, 2002). A program in **India,** based on the dissemination of posters, booklets, classroom activity, debates, signature campaign and home-based activities, showed a significant reduction in tobacco and alcohol usage among the adolescents (Reddy & co-workers, 2002). Awofeso (2003) reported effective smoking cessation programs implemented to help **prisoners in Australia.**

What motivates adolescents to stop smoking? The most common reason appears to be future health (73%), followed by physical appearance (59%), cost (52%) and athletic performance (51%) (Riedel, *et al.*, 2002). What stops adolescents from quitting? Riedel *et al.* concluded that the most important withdrawal effect was the strong need to smoke (60%) followed by irritability (51%) and difficulty concentrating (41%). Moreover, significant ethnic differences were obtained with Caucasians reporting greater withdrawal effects than African Americans (Riedel & co-workers, 2003).

WEIGHT CONTROL AND EATING DISORDERS

Failure to control weight is considered to be a major cause of death, second only to smoking, in the US Approximately one-third of males and 50% women feel that they are overweight. Actually, 31% females and 24% males in the US are obese. In medical terms, people are considered obese when they have 20% to 40% excess of body fat; moderately obese with 41% to 100% fat; and overweight with over 100% fat. Obesity is linked to several health problems: cardiovascular problems, diabetes, hypertension, kidney stones and can be a threat to longevity.

At the psychological level, obese people are victims of prejudice and discrimination. People think that they lack willpower and self-control. Fat people face problems at their work and in getting a job or admission in school (Canning & Mayer, 1966), airline seats, and renting an apartment. Here are some excerpts from a report:

> "One researcher asked a group of college students who they would be least inclined to marry. The obese ranked near the bottom, with the students preferring to wed embezzlers, ex-mental patients, cocaine users or shoplifters"..... "As for fat people themselves, many regard their condition as the worst curse imaginable. ....Collen Rand, a University of Florida obesity researcher, asked formerly obese people whether they would rather be fat again or suffer some disability. 91% said they would rather have a leg amputated, while 89% said they would rather be blind" (*Los Angeles Times* E-4, December 27, 1994).

In addition to biological researches based on set point and identification of a gene that triggers obesity, psychological origins of obesity are generally linked to unmet needs of nurturance and emotional distress. Obese people tend to eat more rapidly with larger bites. Their craving for food is triggered off by external factors, such as the site of food, in contrast to normal people who are guided by internal signals, such as hunger pangs.

Interventions

In general a weight loss program consists of **four** elements (Prokop & co-workers, 1991):

A typical weight loss program consists of four elements of eating and its effects

1. **Making people understand their eating pattern.**
2. **Understanding what precedes eating.**
3. **Becoming aware of the eating process.**
4. **Program incentives to reduce weight.**

Three specific techniques can help in a weight loss program. **First,** cognitive restructuring helps people to think differently about the segments of behavior that are related to eating. **Second,** people need to understand the value of regular exercise. And **third,** some kind of empowerment is needed to help fat people understand that they are not alone in their fight. Groups, such as TOPS (Take off Pounds Sensibly), provide social support to obese people.

In a very stimulating article, *The Dieting Maelstrom,* Brownell and Rodin (1994) noted that 24% men and 40% women are dieting currently in sharp contrast to 7% men and 14% women who were dieting between 1950 through 1966. This statistics tells us that people are more conscious about their fitness now than they were two decades ago. They argue that those who come to clinics for treatment of obesity are mostly binge eaters but their number is small compared to the 5% obese in the general population. The majority of people having eating problems take their own decisions for reducing fat.

Eating disorders

With people realizing that **eating disorders** (ED) are not totally biological, and with sufficient research to back such a conjecture, the category of eating disorders has now been included in the **DSM IV**. The current DSM IV includes **two eating disorder syndromes: anorexia nervosa** (AN) and **bulimia nervosa** (BN). While the first leads to an obsession with thinness and dieting so as to lose weight, the other is characterized by an obsession with eating, and therefore leads to excessive obesity. The clinical classification of disorders as contained in the DSM IV also includes a provisional third category, that is, **binge eating.** These are people who go into uncontrolled fits of excessive eating, or eating binges.

3 types of eating disorders: Anorexia nervosa, bulimia nervosa and binge eating

Generally, eating disorders are seen more commonly among females, but that does not mean that it is non-existent among males. We do find males with eating disorders, though the prevalence is much lower than that for females (Robb & Dadson, 2002). Another fact about the prevalence of eating disorders is that it is more commonly seen among young adults. There are childhood cases too, and their numbers are growing. It is imperative that we focus on childhood ED: at its origin, maintenance and treatment (Watkins & Lask, 2002).

Eating disorders more common among females

BOX 3.10

Boys too are victims of eating disorders (Times News Network, *The Times of India*, June 4, 2002)

Professor and Head of the Psychiatry Department at PGI, Chandigarh, India, Dr Savita Malhotra, reported that it is for the first time that she has diagnosed two teenage boys suffering form AN. Interestingly, both were obsessed with the body image of a well known cine star.

The phenomenon could also be linked to globalization and the constant exposure to thinness, which has been a trend in the Western world. This is the opinion of Dr Helmut Remschmidt, President of the International Association for Child and Adolescent Psychiatry. According to him, he did not observe any case of ED during his first visit to China but was surprised to see a number of cases on his next visit. He felt that while some of the ED might have a genetic background, the greater part could be duc to environmental influences.

What **causes** such eating disorders? Is there anything that would be of interest to us as social psychologists? Can social psychology be applied to understand ED? Research data and practice definitely seem to point to the important role that social psychology can play. Rather than excessive weight or excessive thinness being the cause, studies on people with AN or BN show that ED is linked to **biological, psychological and social factors** (Steiner & co-workers, 2003 for a good review of causative factors of ED). While in recent years, new biotechnologies have led to a greater interest in genetic factors as the cause of ED, the role of genetic factors is still far from clear. Thus, while some recent literature shows a substantial heritability component (for example, Bulik & co-workers, 2003), a Romanian sample showed a very low heritability component (Grigoroiu-Serbaneseu & co-workers, 2003). In fact, the challenge now seems to be to understand the complex ways in which biological factors interact with psycho-social factors to produce the disorder (Schmidt, 2003).

BOX 3.11

Does environment matter?

In what ways do children within the same family differ regarding whether they develop an eating disorder or not? Klump and others (2002) believe that the difference might be understood in the context of the non-shared environment for siblings. What is non-shared environment? Even when twins are reared in the same family, siblings do not face exactly the same environment. What are the critical differences? This review of studies clarifies the role of factors such as differential paternal relationships, body weight teasing, peer group experiences, and life events, causing the ED to develop in one sibling but not in the other. We can clearly identify that all of these aspects have relevance in a social context.

According to Klump and associates, 17 – 46% of the variance in both AN and BN could be accounted for by such non-shared environmental factors (from Klump, Wonderlich Lehoux & co-workers, 2002).

Role of familial factors in the etiology and treatment of ED

Attitudes of the family towards eating is an important antecedant factor of ED

Have you ever thought that the cause of extreme thinness or even extreme obesity, or that an obsession with eating could be due to the **family** of the person? Well, this apparently is one of the most important factors. How important this variable can be is brought out in a study of 345 undergraduate women with bulimic symptoms. Even after the contribution of all other non-familial factors was controlled, negative family communication, external control of food intake and rules relating to family meal times remained as significant predictors in the regression analysis. (Crowther, Kicher, Shewood & Kuhnert, 2002). Not only is the family important for the development of such disorders, but also for the recovery from the disorder. When 69 female adult subjects were extensively interviewed regarding the cause of their AN or BN, the most commonly perceived factors were dysfunctional family environment along with other personal factors such as stress. Moreover, **supportive interpersonal non-family relationships** contributed as much to their recovery as the therapy (Tozzi & co-workers, 2003). Other important family aspects appear to be cohesiveness within the family, how expressive the members are and the degree of encouragement provided by the family (Latzer & co-workers, 2002), and a general dysfunctional family environment (McDermott & co-workers, 2002).

Multifamily therapy: Where groups of patients with their families are counseled simultaneously

The family may unwittingly cause ED by **excessive pressure for achievement, overprotection or control.** When children of such parents start having difficulties in expressing their emotions, or start suffering from low self esteem, ED often results (Schwartz, 2002). The high premature dropout from interventions (as high as 50%) is also, to a very great extent, due to family and other social factors (Eivors & co-workers, 2003). Often people with ED, and especially children, join ED health care services only to back out later. One reason is stress resulting from the strict dietary regime on which they are put. To help people cope with this stress and stop the dropout, Maudsley hospital in London, UK, has developed what has been called the **Maudsley approach.** The approach focuses on the family as a resource for recovery. Parents are counseled on the need to provide motivation, and made to understand the significance of a supportive milieu, to help the child cope with stress and prevent a relapse (Lock, 2002). It is not only the ED patient who gains from the **family therapy,** it also benefits the family members. In Sweden, for example, the families were found to become more cohesive, and even show a higher degree of competency and adaptability (Wallin & Kronvall, 2002). While family therapy is very effective for the reduction of ED (Kanas, 2002), a combination of individual and family therapy is also fruitful (Patel & co-workers, 2003). A variant of the family therapy is **multifamily therapy**. Here we find that groups of patients, with their families, are provided counseling simultaneously. A large London-based national health service hospital tried this variant and the feedback questionnaires verified that the family members did find this approach to be useful (Colahan & Robinson, 2002).

Eating disorders: The global perspective

Studies from around the globe provide interesting insights regarding prevalence rates, causes, treatment and prevention of ED. For one thing it is clear that ED is not just another American phenomenon. Studies conducted in **Pakistan, Romania, Israel, Spain, Japan,**

ED is prevalent almost all over the world, but more so in Westernized countries

Hong Kong, Australia, England, France, Oman, Germany, Italy and Sweden, provide new perspectives on the syndrome. Research on ED confirms a pattern of **seasonal variation.** Yamatsuji and his colleagues (2003) saw that there was a seasonal variation in the disease among **Japanese** patients, with seasonal variation being highest for the BN subtype, though lower than that found in the **US** samples. Does it help us to know that there is seasonal variation? The authors use their findings to suggest that light therapy could be used for the control of the BN subtype at least. Another common finding is that in the **West, drug use disorders** are commonly seen among those with eating disorders. However when the same was studied in **Japan,** it was found that drug use disorders (DUD) are not as common among Japanese people with eating disorders, as was found among Western samples with eating disorders (Nagata & co-workers, 2002). Does this not tell us that while there may be a common core of impulsivity running through both ED and DUD, the two disorders do seem to have a different etiology. Talking of etiology, an Israeli group of health care providers at the Kaplan Hospital in **Israel** have recommended a new **bio-psycho-social approach** for understanding the emergence and maintenance of AN and (Blank & co-workers, 2002).

BOX 3.12

Treatment: A bio-social model (Blank & co-workers, 2002)

On the basis of extensive literature review and their own personal clinical experience, the authors have developed what they call a bio-psycho-social model of the emergence and maintenance of AN and BN. The very name of the model tells us what the focus is and the belief of the authors that ED is caused and maintained through a host of factors interacting with each other.

After developing the model, they then set out to demonstrate its effectiveness by applying it for the treatment of people with ED. Therapeutic guidelines were drawn from the theoretical model and applied on 97 AN and BN patients from the eating disorders unit at Kaplan Hospital in Israel. Out of the 97 boys and girls on whom the treatment was tried, 37 were hospitalized while 60 were being treated by the out patients department.

What were the results of the therapy? After one year, 74 patients were doing well in all respects. Fourteen, however, still needed a lot of supervision in eating. Five were still hospitalized and four were lost during follow up.

What do we learn from the above? According to the authors,

> The proposed model proves to be more than just another theory in that it is successfully applied in treatment. Short systemic treatment is very effective. The longer the delay in drastic, aggressive treatment, the worse the prognosis. Extended hospitalization periods worsen the prognosis. Weakness of the parental unit is a strong indication for in-patient care. The longer the experience in treating ED, the shorter the hospitalization and number of interventions (Blank & co-workers, 2002).

A common measure for the **assessment** of ED is the Eating Attitudes Test (**EAT-26**). Not only is the test used in the Western World, it has been tried out in other parts of the world too. We have an **Arabic** version of EAT-26 found valid for identifying people with ED in

Muscat, Oman (Al-Adawi & co-workers, 2002). While EAT 26 is normally quite an effective assessment tool, there does seem to be some cultural variation. For **Chinese** people in Hong Kong, it has been seen to underestimate the number of people with ED (Lee & co-workers, 2002), though it has been successfully used in **Pakistan** (Suhail & Nisa, 2002), enabling the authors to isolate the causes of high prevalence of ED in Pakistan. In the same study multiple regression analysis shows that greater exposure to the Western culture and dissatisfaction with body shape are important predictors for ED in Pakistan. Such a dissatisfaction with one's looks is often caused by an unconditional acceptance of society's norms for beauty. Also, the more women accept society's emphasis on thinness and youthfulness, the more importance they place on their own appearance (Sicalides, 2002). While some degree of **body dissatisfaction** is apparent the world over, there are cultural differences in the intensity of such a dissatisfaction. When a series of 10 silhouettes were shown to 1751 medical and nursing students from 12 countries, the most extreme degree of body dissatisfaction was found in northern Mediterranean countries, followed by northern European countries, countries undergoing westernization and non western countries, respectively, with the last showing very low level of dissatisfaction (Jaeger & co-workers, 2002). What increases our understanding regarding the psycho-social aspects of the disorder is that the same sample clarified that body dissatisfaction is not a direct function of the body mass index (a parameter which shows whether your weight is proportional to your age, sex, height, etc.).

EATS-26: A common tool used for the assessment of eating disorders

Some recent studies could also be located regarding **therapy** of ED from various regions of the world. As had been noted for other samples, an **Australian** sample from Sydney showed that while the effects of individual cognitive-behavioral therapy seemed to be superior to group therapy, this effect was only short-term and did not continue through the 3-6 month follow-up period (Chen & co-workers, 2003). Another outcome study of **Swedish** teenagers over a ten year period showed that those who had poor overall outcome had had life long problems with social interaction and had been showing obsessive-compulsive behavior (Rastam, Gilberg & Wentz, 2003). Temperamental differences were also noted in a **Spanish** sample, with the BN group preferring avoidance coping while the AN group looked more for social support and constructive coping measures (Valdes-Diaz & co-workers, 2002). Temperamental differences have also been noted in a **Japanese** study, with the AN group showing novelty seeking behavior but not the BN group (Nagata & co-workers, 2003). Temperamental differences have also been noted in an **Italian** sample (Fassino & co-workers, 2002). Stress and problematic coping behavior seems to be another cause of ED, as seen among **Dutch** (Bekker and Boselie, 2002) and **Spanish** women (Valdez-Diaz & co-workers, 2002), while **French** women with ED showed high levels of anxiety disorders (Godart & co-workers, 2003).

Group therapy more effective than individual therapy

EXPECTATIONS FROM THE THERAPIST

A patient's therapist is a key player in the process of treatment. Naturally, patients rely on their therapist's judgment and feel close to them. **Two common complaints** against therapists are: they do not have enough time, and they use a lot of jargon (that is, technical) language. Due to these reasons, the relationship between a patient and therapist can become ambivalent.

Therapists, on the other hand, often complain that their patients tend to ignore instructions and do not take their medicine regularly. They also face difficulty when they communicate with people from diverse cultural backgrounds and socio-economic strata.

In general, **trust** is an important resource in any relationship, and when one's life is at stake, as in surgery, the relationship becomes a critical factor in the therapeutic process. The relationship between a patient and a physician involves building a partnership. In this relationship, speech maintenance, that is, the normal and familiar way of conversation, is a critical factor. Borrowing from the work on communication research, social psychologists became interested in the study of physician-patient communication, with reference to the use of the common or the technical language. Bourhis, Roth and MacQueen (1989) reported that although physicians felt that they spoke to the patients in a non-technical language, both the patients and the nurses disagreed with the perceptions of the physicians. In order to understand this gap, it is important to analyze what they expect from each other. It is estimated that a visit to a medical clinic lasts less than 20 minutes and out of this period, only a few minutes are spent with the physician. The interest of the physician in meeting the patient is to diagnose a problem by asking a few structured questions. On the other hand, the patient is expected to describe her problem using simple language. This dialogue is followed by treatment, prognosis, etc. Studies show that the nonverbal behavior of a doctor plays a significant role in determining the confidence level of a patient. Maintaining eye contact, touching when appropriate, and controlling facial expression and voice are small things but count a lot in determining the level of social support from the therapist (DiMatteo, 1985).

DiMatteo and DiNicola (1982) found that although many patients followed the instructions of their physicians, there were a significant number of patients who showed **non-compliant behavior**. Surprisingly, physicians tended to underestimate the non-compliant behavior of their patients. Such non-compliance was significant among patients who were expected to adopt changes in their lifestyle (for example, change in diet and smoking). Non-compliance was also high among patients suffering from high blood pressure. Because drugs for this condition caused sexual dysfunction and drowsiness, patients avoided medication. When there is a reason to avoid recommended medication or therapy, patients tended to show noncompliance.

Additionally, female physicians have been reported to spend more time with their patients than their male counterparts. Moreover, female physicians talk more to their female patients than to their male patients. In short, communication, gender, and compliance are some of the key issues in physician-patient interaction.

In this chapter, we have made an effort to show that the onset, treatment and prognosis of physical illness are far from being caused by purely physiological factors acting in a linear fashion. Given below (Fig 3.2) is a diagrammatic representation of the traditional model of illness—what has generally been christened the **bio-medical model of illness**. The model illustrates a pathogenic agent such as an infection or a cancer acting on an otherwise normally functioning person. The therapy or therapies applied have known curative powers and are given to the patient in the hope that the health of the person will be restored. However, as the diagram shows—any one of the three possibilities are there: the disease is cured, the disease is maintained in the chronic state or death could result. The key feature of the model is that the cure works with or without the assistance or even knowledge of the individual to whom it is being administered. The cure is, furthermore, purely physical, and is not affected by the psychological conditions of the person being treated.

Figure 3.2: The traditional medical model for disease (adapted from Lovallo, 1997, p. 14).

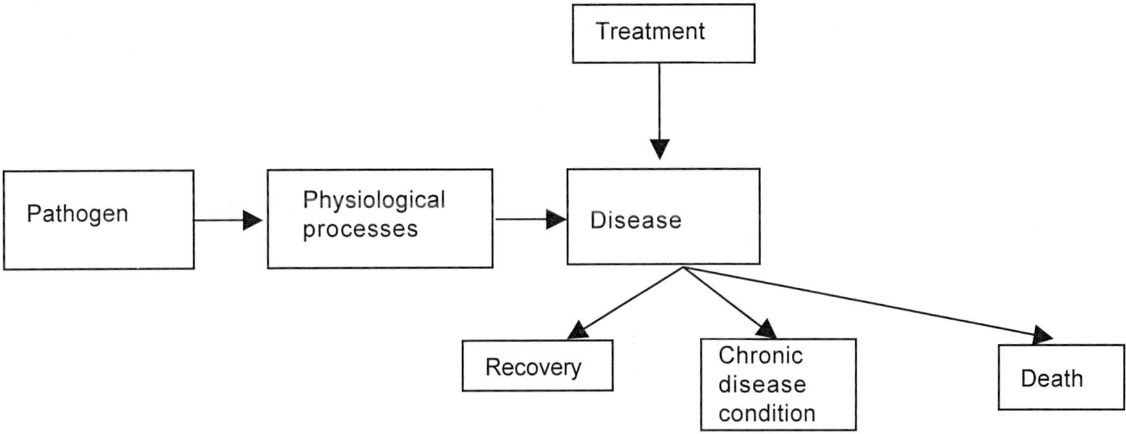

Today, however, even medical practitioners are aware of the fact that the psychological condition and thoughts of the patient have to be factored into the prognosis of the disease. Lovallo (1997) presents a more contemporary **bio-behavioral model** of physical health and illness. He attempts to include all the varied inputs required for a thorough understanding of the etiological and concurrent conditions of a disease. A special emphasis must be laid on the person's learned history and his socio-cultural environment. The chief axioms of the bio-behavioral model posited by Lovallo are illustrated below:

1. The person's thoughts, emotions and spoken words and the informational interchange between the person and her socio-cultural environment regarding the disease and its cure can affect the outcome of the illness.
2. There is a two way interaction between the pathogen and the immune system, the actions of the immune system also altering the pathogen.
3. Thus, while the treatment will still have an effect on the disease, the outcome will depend on the interaction between the treatment, the patient, the pathogen, the social environment and the psycho-social functioning of the individual.

Lovallo further suggests that an expanded definition of disease should look as follows:

> "...a disorder of body functions or systems arising from malfunctioning at the level of physiological, psycho-physiological or socio-cultural functioning" (p. 14).

In other words, a biological analysis of behavior must incorporate social and psychological explanations for fully understanding the range and breadth of diagnosis and treatment of patients.

LIMITS TO SOCIAL PSYCHOLOGY OF PHYSICAL HEALTH

The potential for social psychological research as applied to physical health is vast but its impact is weak. Raising the issue, "why don't people do what is good for them", Winett

(1995) emphasized that the contribution of social psychology will not be fully appreciated unless it is presented within the broader framework of other scientific explanations. For example, he argued that, in the absence of health promotion programs, people will continue to engage in health endangering behavior. One way to enhance the contribution of social psychology is to join other scientists in identifying the causes and spread of disease, that is, to cooperate in the epidemiological research. Winett suggested a framework for the promotion of health and prevention of disease in which social psychology figures prominently. Further, he showed how psychological research on reinforcement, modelling and communication can be made useful in public education programs.

Another major issue in the applications of social psychology is the usefulness of a known theory or model. For example, recent research on stress and its management shows how social psychological theories have limited application in changing the behavior of people. When individuals struggle hard to control adversity, their efforts can lead to a decrease in stress. Due to this reason, social psychological research should take into account the **critical personal variables** that are associated with control, such as, **behavioral competencies** (skills and ability), **cognitions** (self efficacy and responsibility) and **motivation** (desire to control). Additionally, the significance of these personal variables should be examined in the social context of an individual.

Summary

Approximately 50% of the deaths in the USA are due to the problems caused by our own behavior. Obviously, as a science of behavior, a major role of social psychology is to help health experts not only diagnose problems of people and to suggest how to stay healthy, but also, to assist in the social rehabilitation of patients. This chapter was divided into two parts. The first part dealt with the effect of stress on the well being of individuals. Research on perceived control, learned helplessness, hardiness, optimism and social support was described to show how they are related to stress and its control.

The second part of the chapter described the role of social psychology in the understanding and control of health endangering behavior. In this context, the applications of social psychology in the study and prevention of AIDS was specifically mentioned. How this epidemic affects women and minorities was also examined. The other health endangering topics presented in this chapter were weight control and eating disorders, smoking and cancer.

Suggestions for Further Reading

1. Lovallo W.R. (1997). *Stress and Health: Biological and Psychological Interactions.* Thousand Oaks: Sage.
2. Carlson, L.E., Goodey, E., Bennett, M.H., Taenzer, P., and Koopmans, J. (2002). The addition of social support to a community based large group behavioral smoking

cessation intervention: improved cessation rates and gender differences. *Addictive Behaviors*, 27, 547-559.

3. Ironson, G., Antoni M.H., Schneiderman, N., Chesney, M.A., *et al.* (2002). Coping: Interventions for optimal disease management. In Chesney, M.A. and Antoni, M.H. (Eds). *Innovative Approaches to Health Psychology: Prevention and Treatment Lessons from AIDS.* Washington DC, US: American Psychological Association, xxi, 340, 167-195.
4. Orzolek-Kronner, C. (2002). The effect of attachment theory in the development of eating disorders: Can symptoms be proximity seeking? *Child and Adolescent Social Work Journal*, 19, 421-435.

Some Key Terms

Acquired immunity deficiency syndrome
Anorexia bulimia
Anorexia nervosa
Attitude inoculation
Binge eating
Bio-behavioral model
Bio-medical model
Cognitive appraisal
Daily hassles
Drug myths
Eating disorders
EATS 26
External locus of control
General Adaptation Syndrome
Homophobia
Human immunodeficiency virus
Internal locus of control
Lazarus effect
Learned helplessness
Optimism
Perceived control
Personality hardiness
Psychoneuroimmunology
Role schema
Social stigma

SOCIAL PSYCHOLOGY AS APPLIED TO LEGAL ISSUES

4

Chapter Outline

- An introduction to social psychology as applied to legal issues
- Experts as witnesses
- Eyewitness: Identification and testimony
  - Wrongful conviction
  - A definition of wrongful conviction
  - Memory factors in eyewitness accounts
  - Sources of distortion and error in memory
- Social psychology of lineups
  - The composition and conduction of lineups
  - Factors affecting eyewitness testimony
  - Problems in eyewitness testimony
- On children's testimony
  - Resistance efficacy
- The lie-detector test
- Psychology of the jury
  - The scientific study of juror bias
  - Rape myths and jury bias
  - Authoritarianism and the jury
  - Jury size
  - Physical attractiveness and the jury
- Social psychology and law enforcement
  - Women in law enforcement
- Law and the rights of children
- Victim trauma and the law
  - Classical conditioning theory
  - Crime related psychological trauma
  - Victim expectations
  - Interventions for crime related psychological trauma
  - Post victimization factors
- Juvenile delinquency
  - Predictors of juvenile delinquency

- New frontiers in social psychology as applied to legal issues
  - Restorative Justice
- Limitations to the application of social psychology in law

BOX 4.1

Applied social psychology in the news

There has been a realization of late that juvenile delinquents are often those who have been destitute children or have, for some reason, lived, what Bowlby (Bowlby & Salter-Ainsworth, 1965) once called, an "institutionalized" life. Such children, who later turn to delinquency, require much more than a terminology different from that used for adult criminals, and need to be segregated from adult criminals. While the latter led to the formation of what has been called remand homes, the former led to the coining of a set of terms aimed at reducing the stigma of being accused. This was in furtherance of the dictates of the UN Convention on the Rights of the Child (Saks, 1996), which proposed that 'institutionalization' should be the last option for child rehabilitation.

The impact is being felt in India with the implementation of the Juvenile Justice Act, 2000. An article in the daily, *The Times of India* is an evidence to endorse the change. To start with, remand homes will now be called children's homes, and the Juvenile Welfare Board has been rechristened Child Welfare Committee. The government has also joined hands with non-government organizations such as CRY to ensure quality care for these children. The partnership will also promote alternatives such as adoption, foster care and sponsorship, as has been done in many Western countries.

Why is this necessary? In the state of Maharashtra, in India alone, these measures will be a boon for nearly 26,000 destitute children. While such children have been provided food and shelter, they are offered poor care and personal attention. These children grow up with a sense of inferiority and have difficulty getting into the mainstream. The children had till now been given a badge which had their number on it and they were addressed by these numbers. With new legislation, they will be called by their names, and as Mehta, Chairperson of the Welfare Board, affirms, this will go a long way to raise their self esteem.

This is one way by which attempts are being made to control delinquency. While the article does not specifically refer to psychological research in this context, it definitely is in line with what social psychologists have been advocating: raise the self esteem.

(Adapted from Roli Srivastava, *The Times of India*, July 8, 2002)

AN INTRODUCTION TO SOCIAL PSYCHOLOGY AS APPLIED TO LEGAL ISSUES

The relationship between social psychology and law can be traced to the early part of the last century. According to Monahan and Walker (1988), the use of social science research in courts was first introduced by Louis Brandeis in the first decade of the twentieth century. Around the same time, Whipple published extensively in the first 15 volumes of *Psychological*

Bulletin on everyday issues such as eyewitness (Elizabeth Loftus, 1993). Munsterberg is also known for his efforts to bring psychology in action in everyday life. And yet, even after a century, the relationship between psychology and law remains very fuzzy. Why? There are several reasons that have contributed to the current situation. **Firstly,** experts in the legal system are, by and large, not sufficiently **aware** of the scope and applications of psychology. Most of them simply do not understand what psychology can do to help the legal process.

Secondly, the manner in which psychologists present their findings to legal experts is loaded with jargon and technical information. Even psychologists face problems in understanding the work of their fellow psychologists. Consider the statement of Elizabeth Loftus (1993), a well known researcher in this field, regarding an article written by another famous researcher, Wells (1993), in the same issue of the *American Psychologist*: "The typical police officer, I imagine, would not find Wells's (1993) article easy to read. It contains much terminology that even psychologists who have soaked themselves in terminology for half a lifetime would struggle with (*e.g.*, ecphoric similarity, propitious heterogeneity). I have spent more than 20 years studying these issues and occasionally have found myself asking, "Do we really need a new term here?" (Loftus, 1993).

Thirdly, there is a considerable amount of disagreement among social psychologists regarding the legitimacy of social psychology in providing insight into legal matters. As the reader will notice in the section on eyewitness in this chapter, two distinguished researchers, Wells (1993) and Egeth (1993), have held opposite views on the issue of eyewitness research: the former strongly advocating the use of psychological findings in legal cases, whereas the latter expressing several reservations. In sharp contrast to the title of Wells' article, "What do we know about eyewitness identification?" Egeth chose the title, "What do we *not* know about eyewitness identification?" Such is the magnitude of difference in advocating the role of social psychology in legal matters.

Fourthly, social psychology as a science is neutral; it is not influenced by the position taken by any prosecution or defense team. And yet, there exists a strong bias that psychological findings mostly favor the defendant. Could this be because psychologists are often invited by the defense team to describe the mental state of a defendant tried in a criminal case? Because psychological principles go beyond a particular case and the fact that two legal cases are rarely alike, psychological interpretations are often used, misused or abused in the courts for vindicating a position. An example is given by Fiske and co-workers (1991) who report how arguments concerning gender-based stereotyping were twisted in the Price Waterhouse *v.* Hopkins case.

Finally, what is the role of **ecological validity** or what has sometimes been called mundane realism? Most of the psychological research on issues of concern to legal practice has been conducted on mock jurors, mock lineups, etc., using undergraduate students as subjects. It is felt that even when there is considerable empirical validity, its generalization to real life may still be low, or even questionable (see Box 4.2).

Ecological validity: Validity of studies for prediction of real life events

BOX 4.2

Two examples of how psychologists do research in the psychology of law

We have already pointed out that legal practitioners are sometimes loath to accept psychological findings because they feel that the findings have little relevance to real life. We present below two examples of how psychological research is conducted on issues of legal relevance. The first is a laboratory study while the second is a field study.

Study 1: Compliance and eyewitness testimony: Do eyewitnesses comply with misleading "expert pressure" during investigative interviewing? (Roper & Shewan, 2002).

One of the issues regarding compliance to pressure during interviewing is whether compliance depends upon how eyewitnesses are judged by the interviewer. The authors hypothesized that eyewitnesses alter their responses only when they think that the interviewer sees them as being unobservant and/or unhelpful.

Forty undergraduate university students from the age group 18-31 years acted as subjects for the experiment. Using a before-after, repeated measures design, the subjects were tested for their ability to testify before and after being labelled as good or poor witnesses. They watched a short video clip and were then asked specific questions regarding what they had witnessed. After watching a second video clip that was very similar to the first, they were labelled as either good or poor witnesses. Thereafter they were again submitted to questioning regarding the first video clip.

What were the results? Subjects, who had been labelled as poor witnesses altered their original responses in line with the lead questions. In contrast, those who had been labelled as good witnesses, actually improved their eyewitness observation scores.

Thus, the results clearly show that eyewitnesses may yield to leading questions and pressure from the authority figure, but only if they are negatively assessed by that person.

Study 2: A field study of own race bias in South Africa and England (Wright, Boyd & Tredoux, 2001).

This was a two-country comparison of own race bias conducted in South Africa and England. In order to introduce an element of mundane realism, the prospective participants were visitors to shopping centers in the two countries. Black and White people were approached by either a Black or a White confederate (a confederate is a person who pretends to be no different from the participants, but, is actually party to the experiment and is in league with the experimenter). After that, they were asked to identify the confederate from both sequential and simultaneous photo lineups.

What did the findings show? In both the countries and under both types of lineups, people from the same race as the participant, was better recognized than people from the other race. In other words, Black people were better at correctly identifying Black confederates, while White people were better at identifying White confederates. Thus, even when measured in two such diverse cultures, the own race bias was very vividly validated.

Despite the above difficulties in understanding the elements that bridge the relationship between psychology and law, it seems that both social psychology and law have a lot to offer to each other. Borrowing from Haney's (1980) work, Bartol and Bartol (1994) distinguished three relationships that describe meeting grounds between psychology and law:

1. Psychology **in** law.
2. Psychology **and** law.
3. Psychology **of** law.

Psychology in law

The first form of relationship, **psychology in law,** is most common in legal circles. Psychologists are invited to present their views but the legal experts determine what they will accept and present. In other words, psychology plays a role only when it is needed by a legal authority who also happens to monitor the impact of psychology. For example, psychologists are often consulted in cases of mental disorders and, if necessary, called to testify.

Psychology and law

In the case of **psychology and law**, the relationship between the two is unspecified. Law does not tell people how to behave but if people do misbehave, law is involved. For example, law does not tell parents how to discipline their child but law can identify child abuse based on examples of punishment inflicted by parents. Under such circumstances, research in psychology can (1) support the value of current legal interpretation; (2) criticize the existing legal position; or, (3) forge a new relationship with the legal position. Consider the following two examples that have been featuring in the media, both in television talk shows and newspapers and tabloids:

- A six-year old boy is suspended from school for kissing a girl in his class.
- A new non-citizen immigrant from a middle east country marries a minor Muslim girl of 14 years—illegal in the USA but not in the native country of the new immigrant.

Both incidents invite psychologists and legal experts to focus on the context of moral development: of the boy, in terms of his age and that of the new immigrant, in terms of her native culture. The nature of agreement or disagreement between psychology and law will determine the future course of relationship between them. For example, neither will psychology change its theory of moral development to accommodate law nor will law change—at least for the present—to allow six years olds to kiss another girl openly and freely. The example given in Box 4.1 regarding juvenile delinquents points out to a similar problem between law and society.

Psychology of law

Third, the **psychology of law** deals with how law influences behavior. For example, why do people obey or defy law? Why did Mahatma Gandhi or Martin Luther King indulge in civil disobedience? Are there any limits to law? When would soldiers disobey orders from their superiors? There are no simple answers to the above questions, but because all of these issues deal with behavior with specific reference to obedience and conformity, both psychology and law must learn how to relate to one another.

EXPERTS AS WITNESSES

In specific cases, courts allow experts (non-clinical) to present their views as a part of a defense or prosecution case. Psychologists have been called upon to testify in a variety of cases: battered women syndrome, sexual abuse of children, defective products, misleading advertisements, children's testimony, and so on. According to Walker (1986), three types of research evidence from psychologists are useful for legal purposes:

1. Research concerning empirical assumptions (for example, children's ability to make their own decision), called social authority.
2. Facts related to a case (for example, the comparison of similar products or gender bias in the employment of male and females), called social facts.
3. General conclusions based on social sciences research (for example, children's eyewitness memory.

Generally speaking, there are two issues that concern the role of a psychologist as an expert. First, the expert may act as an advocate such that he presents information to strengthen the arguments of the party that hires him. On the other hand, she may act as a neutral scientist, or serve as an educator, with the genuine intention of helping the concerned parties to reach a fair decision. In practical terms, this role is very difficult to play once the defendant or prosecutor has hired the psychologist to work on a case. Many expert psychologists then face a moral dilemma, since they may be asked to provide information that could hurt the case of their clients.

Expert witness: Professionals who may be called in to provide knowledge not generally known to the layperson

Expert witnesses, such as psychologists, are also used when information is expected to be beyond the scope of what the layman would likely know. At the time of testifying, the expert's training, experience, and special qualifications are normally explained to the jury. These are summarized and outlined in the expert's curriculum vitae. As an expert, one should be prepared to be criticized, or even professionally questioned on these points by the cross-examiner. One may also feel that one lacks the training or the experience of acting as an expert witness, and may face adverse personal consequences because of that (Gutheil & Hilliard, 2001). If the psychologist has been unwittingly thrust into this role, the negative consequences could be even greater. To enhance the functioning of a psychologist in the role of an expert witness, Decaire (2002) has provided specific guidelines for what to expect in the courtroom and for being a witness.

The second role of psychologists is concerning the ultimate issue of testimony. In this role, a psychologist is expected to testify, based on a theory, to show that her client represents an example of the case. As stated earlier, in the case of Price-Waterhouse *v.* Hopkins, Fiske, *et al.* (1991) presented a strong argument in favor of gender discrimination at work and used evidence based on psychological research to represent her client (see Box 4.3).

EYEWITNESS: IDENTIFICATION AND TESTIMONY

Wrongful conviction

Imagine your friend or yourself being accused of a crime and a person testifying (wrongfully) that you were present at the time of the crime. Needless to say, you or your friend will be devastated and life will appear to come to an end. O.J. Simpson, the popular American football player, was acquitted from the criminal charge in October,1995, for killing his wife and a young man. Subsequently, he lost a civil suit for damages caused to the family of the victims. Witnesses for this case described having seen a tall, dark figure and a van (allegedly used by him), but no

Wrongful conviction: Conviction of an innocent person

BOX 4.3

Psychological ideas in two legal cases (adapted from Loftus, 1991)

Probably the first case in the US to use research findings in psychology in court was a well known case of Ann Hopkins versus Price Waterhouse. Ann Hopkins was an extremely competent, hard working and committed person. Despite these qualities she was not allowed to become a partner in the leading accounting company where she had been working. Ann Hopkins went to court and filed a petition against the company. A social psychologist testified on behalf of Hopkins, citing research in stereotyping, its antecedents, indicators and consequences. Taking the research findings into account, the court ruled in Hopkins' favor. Price Waterhouse naturally appealed but again even in the Supreme Court, it was Hopkins who won. Though this was not the first time that research on gender stereotyping had been introduced in court, it was the first time that the Supreme Court had taken cognizance of it, making it a unique case.

Loftus cites another case from Africa. Before 1990, defendants in cases of murder received the death penalty. This was so even for people who had not been directly involved in a murder but had simply been a part of a mob on a mass violence spree. It was in one such case in which people had been sentenced to death simply because they had been part of a mob, that social psychology came to the rescue. Andrew Colman described to court various social psychological processes related to conformity, deindividuation, bystander apathy, and attributional processes. The result of the presentation of such research findings was that a number of people originally convicted were not sentenced to death.

Both these cases show that, if presented in the right perspective, social psychological findings can be applied in court and can come to the rescue of innocent persons.

authentic eyewitness testimony was presented to pinpoint his presence at the site of the murder.

In contrast, Adams, who languished in prison for several years after being falsely convicted of a murder, was not so fortunate, for eyewitnesses reported having seen him before the murder. People remembered his beard and mustache, but not the clean shaved face of the real culprit. By the time the real culprit was found out, a lot of damage had already been done to Adams. There are no statistics that show how many people have suffered like him because of wrong identification. "Analysis of what went wrong in producing more than 1,000 convictions on innocent people," writes Wells (1993), "have revealed that the single largest factor leading to these false convictions was eyewitness error" (p. 553). And we all know that both public and judicial system place a great deal of emphasis on eyewitness identification. Unfortunately, in staged-crime experiments, the rate of false identification has been found to be remarkable (Wells, 1993).

A definition of wrongful conviction

According to Huff Rattner and Sagarin (1996, p. 10 cf. O'Connor, 2001) "Convicted but innocent refers to people who have been arrested on criminal charges, most often armed robbery, rape, or murder, who have either pleaded guilty to the charge or have been tried and found guilty, and who, notwithstanding plea or verdict, are in fact innocent."

O'Connor (2001), however, is of the view that this definition requires further analysis. He therefore writes:

> It is important to understand what this definition includes and excludes. It includes repeat offenders who may have committed many (or related) crimes, but are innocent of the specific charge for which they have been arrested or convicted; innocent people who, faced with overwhelming evidence against them, such as wrongful identification, perjury, or forged documentation, are greatly tempted to accept the plea bargain that their lawyer so strongly recommends. It excludes people who get "lost in the system," or held without trial for long periods of time while being detained in a jail, out on bond, or simply awaiting charges (such cases are more properly termed wrongful imprisonment); those who are factually guilty but are found not guilty by reason of the exclusionary rule, or who have escaped justice because of some loophole, police mishandling of evidence, violation of constitutional rights, or reversal upon appeal (there is a difference between being "legally innocent" and complete exoneration because one is factually innocent).

Though eyewitness misidentification is a common cause of wrongful convictions, they are often the most convincing part of a trial. Yet, we should be wary of the errors that could creep in. These could range from "good faith" errors to those caused by racial prejudice or even the trauma being faced by the eyewitness (O'Connor, 2001).

What is the rate of errors of misidentification? While there have been various attempts to estimate the error rate, there is great variation in the figures provided by the researchers, making it almost impossible to draw any conclusions. Some of the studies cited by O'Connor (2001) point to error rates from a low of 29% to a high of 90%.

BOX 4.4

Some famous examples of wrongful convictions (Adapted from O'Connor, 2001)

- **Captain Alfred Dreyfus** (1894)—the so-called "Dreyfus affair" in which other army officers, motivated by anti-Semitism, manufactured forgeries, fabricated evidence, and used handwriting analysis to wrongfully convict Dreyfus of selling military secrets to the Germans.
- **The Scottsboro Boys** (1927)—an Alabama case involving nine young black males who were riding a freight train with two white females, and the women alleged that they had been raped. Community pressure and racism against blacks resulted in the death penalty for all but the youngest of the boys, but it turned out the girls had only concocted the story to explain why they were riding the train with blacks.
- **The Lindbergh Baby Kidnapping** (1936)—a sensational case in which a German immigrant named Bruno Hauptmann was convicted and executed because Germans at the time in America were convenient scapegoats.
- **Ivan the Terrible** (1987)—Ivan (John) Demjanjuk was the first trial of a Nazi war criminal held in Israel since the trial of Adolf Eichman (1961). Ivan was picked up as a

factory worker in Cleveland and deported from the U.S. as a wanted concentration camp guard. Photographic (through-the-years) evidence and eyewitness testimony of survivors along the lines of "That's Ivan, no doubt about it" characterized the trial. Demjanjuk was acquitted only on the narrowest of margins.

- **Gary Dotson** (1989)—an Illinois case involving the first "DNA exoneration." Dotson had already served 10 of 25 years of a wrongful conviction for rape based on a suggestive police photographic array in which, it turns out, was an entirely fictional description of the rapist by the victim, but Dotson had been in trouble with the law before. First, the victim recanted out of conscience. Then, the Governor of Illinois refused to grant a pardon and decreed the victim's recantation false. Dotson and his lawyers then obtained DNA testing which proved to be the crucial exculpatory evidence.

Memory factors in eyewitness accounts

All three stages of memory involved in eyewitness accounts: acquisition, storage and retrieval

Atkinson and Shiffrin (1968) presented an elaborate and widely accepted model of transactions that take place in memory. In its simple form, any eyewitness account will involve the following three stages:

1. Acquisition of the actual event in memory.
2. Storage of the event in memory.
3. Retrieval of the event.

In the first stage, the person acquires the information

In the **first stage**, an eyewitness perceives and attends to an event. Unfortunately, perceiving and attending events of crime that usually take place within a very short time involve several constraints on the acquisition process when compared to normal day to day events. For instance, lighting conditions, sound of gunshots, masks, are some of the conditions that may cause deviations from normal viewing conditions. Moreover, we do not expect a gunshot or robbery every time, say we enter a bank. As a result, we focus on

Figure 4.1: Based on Atkinson and Shiffrin's (1968) three stage model of memory.

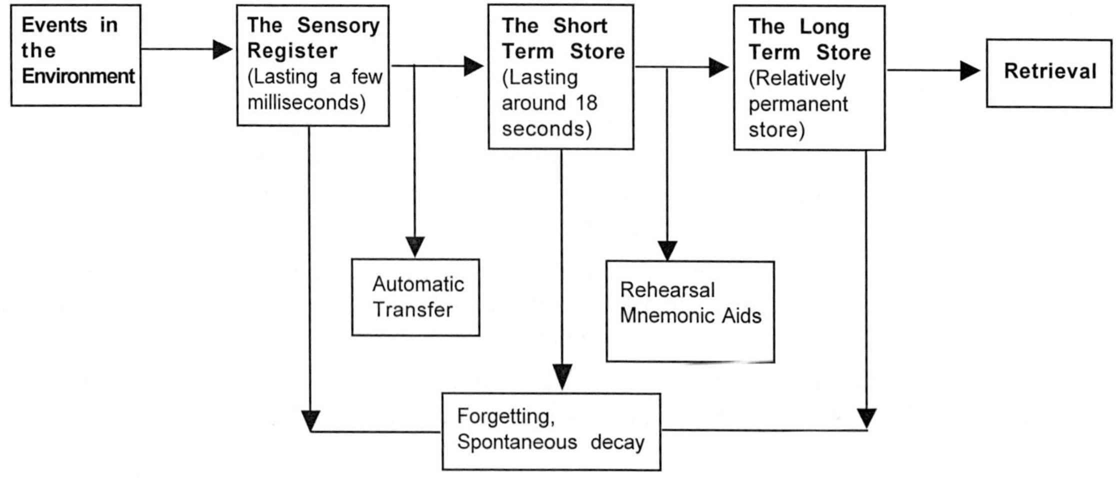

our business and less on the details in the surroundings. When a crime does occur, we normally perceive it and attend to it on the basis of an instant snapshot that sticks in our memory. For instance, a major cause of misidentification of Adams was that he sported a beard and a mustache that was a salient cue in comparison to the common appearance of the real culprit. Psychological researches have consistently shown that information at the sensory level tends to dissipate rapidly (that is, within 2 to 4 seconds), and at the short term memory level that involves attention, but not rehearsal, within 18 seconds.

In the second stage, the person stores the acquired information

During the **second stage**, the witness stores the information. If not properly rehearsed or documented, memory may fade away with the passage of time or reconstruct itself with additional information that is received after the actual event. In one of her researches, Elizabeth Loftus (1979) has shown how changes in memory take place after witnessing an event. In one experiment, she showed pictures of a car stopped either at a stop sign or a "yield" sign. Then she cleverly varied the questions at the time of recall of the information. When asked what they had seen, the subjects were able to identify the correct picture of stop or yield sign in the recall test consisting of two pictures—accurate and inaccurate. However, when the question was varied such that the subjects saw a stop sign but were asked if the other car stopped at the yield sign, their responses became significantly inaccurate (Loftus, Miller & Burns, 1978). In other words, misleading questions can cause changes in memory. It is commonly known that attorneys exploit this weakness in their cross-examination of eyewitness.

In the third stage, the person recalls or retrieves the information

During the **third stage**, an eyewitness retrieves information from the memory store. A very common demonstration of retrieval is seen in police lineups. Wells and Luus (1990) presented an analogy of a lineup as an experiment of social psychology in the following way:

> "....the officer conducting the lineup is like an *experimenter*, the eyewitnesses are the *subjects*, instructions to the eyewitnesses can be likened to an experimenter's *protocol*, the suspect is the *stimulus* and the selection of lineup members and the positioning of the suspect in the lineup are part of the *design*" (Wells & Luus, 1990 p. 106).

Sources of distortion and error in memory

Most people tend to remember their high school grades as being higher than they actually were. Similarly, most people tend to fabricate a story passed on to them. Both are examples of cognitive error, the first one due to an error in **autobiographical memory**, while the second is an error of **recollective memory**. When mistakes are made with memory on the witness stand, such cognitive errors are commonly involved.

Emotions can affect accuracy of recall

A variety of factors affect accuracy and recall. One of these is **emotion**. When the eyewitness is made to recall information regarding emotional high points of the event, both recollective and autobiographical errors may occur. Thus, the eyewitness may distort not only what she saw but also details regarding her own behavior at that time.

Memory is assisted by imagery

Imagery also has an important role to play in recall from memory. If someone is repeatedly shown a fake picture, or, is brainwashed by flooding him with sensory data, false events can be placed in memory. While the events themselves are false, they have as much reality for the individual as actual events.

Besides emotion and imagery, some of the other important factors causing errors in recall are **gender, age and ethnicity**. Gender differences often appear due to mothers socializing girls to remember things more emotionally. Moreover, women tend to be superior in recalling aspects such as height, weight, hair color. Age is important in that during childhood, memory is very suggestible. Ethnic factors tend to work in favor of remembering intra-ethnic details, leaving cross-ethnic memory widely susceptible to distortion. People in the age group of 18 to 29 years tend to make the best identifications of other people.

Gender, age and ethnicity affect memory

It is often noticed that we find it easier to observe differences in people from our own race and from our own age group. The former has been called **own race bias** whereas the latter is known as **own age bias**. This phenomenon of own race bias has been found to cut across geographical boundaries. Thus Wright, Boyd and Tredoux (2001) observed own race bias in both South Africa and in England: countries with very different demographic and cultural characteristics. The effects of own age bias were even more interesting. When tested in culprit absent lineups and culprit present lineups, the own age bias was seen for the latter but not for the former (Wright & Stroud, 2002).

Own race bias: Better observation and recall of people from own race

Stress too can have important effects on memory, though there is considerable controversy regarding whether stress hinders or facilitates memory of an event. But, what does seem clear is that stress acts as a distractor, making the person focus more on the stressor and its effects than on what is happening in the environment.

Stress can affect memory

SOCIAL PSYCHOLOGY OF LINEUPS

A process commonly followed for the identification of culprits is through what is called a police **lineup**. This is a series of people who are brought in front of the eyewitness to the crime and the eyewitness is asked to identify the person whom he remembers as the culprit. There are normally **two ways** of presenting the lineup: **simultaneous** and **sequential.** In the former, all the people in the lineup are brought in front of the eyewitness simultaneously. In the latter, each person chosen for the lineup faces the eye witness one at a time. Lineups can also be presented either through still photographs and video-tapes or by a live presentation of the people forming the lineup. A third way of varying the nature of the lineup is to have the criminal actually present in the lineup or of creating a criminal absent lineup. The people other than the actual criminal who are part of the lineup are called the **foils.**

Lineups: Series of people are brought in front of the witness for identification of the culprit

The composition and conduction of lineups

There is a strong tendency among witnesses to pick up from the lineup an individual who resembles the criminal. In such cases, the question arises: What should be the composition of people in the lineup? Should we have all people resembling the criminal? Or, should we have no person resembling the criminal? Generally speaking, it is advised that all people in the lineup should resemble the suspect and it is not necessary to have the criminal present in the initial lineup.

The size of the lineup is also important. While it may be debated as to how large the lineup should be, lineups of at least size 40 should be used for multiple choice sequential lineups. However, too large a size has also been found to affect the number of mistaken choices, especially in a culprit-absent lineup.

Size of the lineup is important

If the retrieval process is to involve a photographic identification, it is recommended that photos be presented sequentially, and not simultaneously. The advantage in sequential presentation is that a witness cannot compare all the photos at a time to form a judgment.

Wells and Luus (1990) have made the following recommendations for conducting lineups and photo identification:

- Witnesses should be separated as soon as possible.
- At no time should a witness be led to believe that the actual perpetrator is in the set of mugshots.
- The officer conducting the photo spread should not be knowledgeable of whom the police suspect in the case.
- If there is more than one witness, the position of the suspect in the photo spread should be changed for each witness.
- No cues of any kind should be given to the witness concerning whether or not the identified person is the suspect in the case (at least until a statement of certainty is obtained from the witness) (p. 109).

The American Psychology-Law Society (cf. O'Connor, 2001) suggests the following four principles, some of which are very similar to those suggested by Wells and Luus:

- The person conducting the lineup should not know which member of the lineup is the suspect.
- The eyewitness should not be warned that the criminal might not be present.
- The foils should be selected on the basis of the eyewitness's verbal description of the criminal.
- Confidence level of the identification should be recorded at the time of the identification.

Kebbell (2000) observed that these four rules, with minor modifications are satisfied by the way lineups are conducted in England and in Wales. Does this not show that eyewitness identification follows more or less the same principles, be it in the USA, England or in Wales? In short, psychological principles have universal value and their usefulness cannot be undermined.

Conduction of lineups follows a similar procedure across countries

How can we improve eyewitness identification? At least for children, it is seen that practice has important effects. However, there is a word of caution: while girls increased their correct identification, boys tended to show an increase in their false rejections (Parker & Myers, 2001). Seeing the important role played by both verbal and non-verbal behavior of the officer administrating

Lineup identification can be improved

the lineup, it is generally found that blind procedures of creating and administrating lineups reduces the bias. The same has also been advocated by the Canadian court (*Law Times*, June 24, 2002, p. 5).

Scheck, Neufeld, and Dwyer (2001) have made the following recommendations for improving the quality of legal judgment:

- **DNA Testing—pass statutes modelled after New York and Illinois.**
- **Videotaping—all police ID practices, especially confessions.**
- **Snitch Committees—to vet the informant's testimony before being used.**
- **Crime Lab Reviews—to ensure quality control.**
- **Eliminate Junk or Sloppy Science—anything without controls or error rates.**
- **Investigate Misconduct—by prosecutors and police.**
- **Increase Public Defender salaries—and standards, investigative resources.**
- **Victim Assistance—for those who were wrongfully convicted.**
- **Moratorium on Death Penalty—and other death penalty reforms.**

According to Wells, eyewitness identification deals with the following issues:

Eyewitness identification is different from eyewitness testimony

1. System variables, for example, the number of people in the lineup.
2. Function of lineups, for example, uncertainty reduction.
3. Structural features of lineups, for example, presence or absence of the suspect.

Wells (1993) has also applied a signal detection type of analysis in understanding eyewitness identification in single-suspect and all-suspect lineups. In a single-suspect situation, only one person is a suspect and the rest are fillers. In an all-suspect situation, all the members of the lineup are considered suspect. The following description shows that an innocent suspect has chances of being identified as a culprit in an all-suspect lineup but not in a single-suspect lineup. See Fig 4.2.

BOX 4.5

Stricter witness laws sought. Do witnesses change their original statements because of memory factors?

What happens when a witness who had earlier testified decides to change his statement? In the much publicized Bharat Shah (a film financier) case in India, 12 of the 51 witnesses reversed their original statements, causing a setback to the legal proceedings against the accused. Such witnesses who reverse their original testimony are called hostile witnesses. The Supreme Court says that the evidence of a hostile witness should be accepted if it is corroborated during the court proceedings, and that such evidence cannot be wiped out totally. However, in view of the frequent witness hostility, the issue requires a re-examination.

Why do witnesses change their testimony? Criminal lawyers say that it is mainly because of fear. As such it is suggested that the identity of the witness be kept secret. This is what is done in the US, where witnesses are relocated from their residences, provided new identities and protected from the accused until the end of the trial.

Figure 4.2: A signal detection analysis of witness identification in terms of lineup status (Wells, 1993).

Single-suspect lineup

Lineup status	Witness identifies	
	Culprit	**Innocent suspect**
Culprit present	Correct	Cannot occur
Culprit absent	Cannot occur	False identification

All-suspect lineup

Lineup status	Witness identifies	
	Culprit	**Innocent suspect**
Culprit present	Correct	False identification
Culprit absent	Cannot occur	False identification

Hinz and Pezdek (2001), too, are of the view that simply being exposed to an innocent suspect (whether that innocent is identified by the witness or not) increases the possibility of misidentifying the innocent suspect and decreases the probability of correctly identifying the culprit in a subsequent lineup. This has implications for practice for both lineup conduction procedures and for the interpretation of lineup results in the court room.

Factors affecting eyewitness testimony

Testifying is more complex than identifying

Wells (1993) has warned that there is a difference between eye-witness identification and eyewitness testimony and that the two involve separate issues. Eyewitness testimony is a more complex issue than eyewitness identification because testimony involves several players in a legal system, including lawyers, police, social workers, judges, etc. There are a number of factors that affect eyewitness testimony.

Time, face, age and race affect the testimony

Time: It is common knowledge that the accuracy of our recall will increase with the increase in time of looking at a face or an object.

Face: We have an amazing capacity to recall photographs even after a gap of several months. Faces especially can be better recognized if the viewer has a full view of the face. In an evening news program, a videotape of a purse-snatching event was shown to the viewers. The viewers were also told that the culprit may not be in the picture—actually he was present. When the viewers were later asked to identify the culprit from the lineup of six people, only 15% could correctly identify the culprit. It seems that unless ideal conditions are present for viewing, there are problems with eyewitness testimony for face recognition.

Age: Eyewitness testimony of children is usually questioned owing to reasons of competency. Their memory is considered more inaccurate than that of adults, particularly when the age of the witness is below 12 years. Many states in the USA require competency determination prior to using children's testimony as evidence.

The issue of evidence based on children's memory has received favorable support in recent years, especially when cases of childhood trauma including sexual abuse were brought to the attention of courts (Loftus, 1993). The case of George Franklin, Sr. who was charged with murdering an eight year old girl, Susan Kay Nason, was opened more than 20 years later when her own daughter, only eight years old at the time of Susan's murder, testified that she could vividly recall the crime of her father. The concept of **repressed memories** has received support from psychoanalysis on the premise that unpleasant events are repressed in our mind, remain isolated for several years, and surprise us by their sudden emergence on some other day. At the same time, critics question the trustworthiness of repressed memories because they regard this phenomenon as nothing more than a clinical speculation (Holmes, 1990). Ceci and his associates (1994, 1995) have conducted pioneering work regarding the limitations in children's eyewitness testimony.

Own race and cross race effects should be considered at all stages of the investigation

Race: It is generally true that people tend to discriminate the faces of their own race better than those belonging to a different race (differential experience hypothesis). Studies involving white and black subjects who were shown faces of same and/or different race/s clearly showed that both white and black subjects were superior in recalling pictures of the members of their own race (Malpass & Kravitz, 1969; Cross, Cross & Daly, 1971). An important way in which research in social psychology can be applied is the suggestion by Sporer (2001). Based on a large number of studies on the cross race effect in standard face recognition paradigms, the scientists have suggested that consideration of ethnic differences should be considered at all stages of the investigation: from police to eyewitness to the court room. Another application of social psychological research in law is the research by Valentine and co-workers (2003), who found that video technology can produce lineups that are less biased against the suspect than live lineups. Taking the cue, the authors suggest that such a technology can be used as a safeguard against ethnic minority bias.

Unconscious transference: Mis-identification due to having seen the person elsewhere

Unconscious transference: When a witness identifies a person present at the place of crime but had actually seen the person at some other place, it is called **unconscious transference**. Loftus (1979) stated that when one input gets mixed up with another input such that a new integration takes place, it could lead to memory distortion. Sales people and store clerks, for example, are likely to show this type of distortion in identifying customers.

Weapon effect: Daunted by the sight of the weapon and thus not able to focus on other characteristics of the criminal

Weapon's effect: Do we remember equally well all the features at the scene of crime? The answer is in the negative. When we focus on features like gun, blood and sound, our attention is likely to be less on the face, dress and hair of the criminal. Moreover, the scene of the crime involves fear and anxiety that tend to distort our perception. Given this situation, a witness pays less attention to details of the characteristics of the criminal than what he would report under ordinary circumstances.

Expectation: In an interesting study, Shoemaker, South and Lowe (1973) requested their subjects to select facial photographs on the basis of their likelihood of involvement in a murder or robbery. Although all the pictures shown were those of non-criminals, the participants in the experiment tended to categorize faces as criminal and non-criminal. Male subjects were guided by facial stereotypes more than their female counterparts. Researches in cognition have clearly shown how expectations regarding gender and race can affect our judgments. Expectations of lineup administrators can also have an effect on the post identification confidence of the eyewitness. Garrioch, *et al.* (2001) concluded that eyewitness identification confidence is malleable and is a function of the interviewer's beliefs about the criminal's identity.

Rapport: Results obtained by Collins and co-workers (2002) clarify that in a "rapport" interview, participants recalled more correct information but, even more interestingly, the same amount of incorrect information as participants in a "neutral" or "abrupt" interview.

BOX 4.6

A summary of estimator and system variables in eyewitness testimony (Scheck & co-workers, 2001)

Estimator Variables (factors over which the justice system exerts little or no control):

- **Age of witness**—children and the elderly tend to be less accurate than adults.
- **Level of confidence**—this is not strongly correlated with accuracy of identification.
- **Facial distinctiveness**—faces rated highly attractive or highly unattractive are recognized better than other faces.
- **Suspect disguise or changed appearance**—this leads to less accuracy in identification.
- **Target salience**—it is harder to identify a perpetrator if many people were present at the crime scene.
- **Exposure duration**—it is harder to identify a perpetrator if the viewing time is short.
- **Weapon presence**—witnesses tend to focus attention on the weapon.
- **Crime seriousness**—people tend to be less accurate in identification tests if the crime is thought to be less serious.
- **Stress and arousal**—moderate arousal tends to lead to better acquisition of information.
- **Cross-gender bias**—people are more accurate when they identify someone of their own gender.
- **Cross-racial bias**—people are more accurate when they identify someone of their own race.
- **Time delay**—memory declines over time.
- **Changes in experiential context**—it is sometimes difficult to recognize someone if he or she is seen in a different place.
- **Post-event information**—this can distort a person's memory, and can also be a system variable, since this information can come from an interview.

System Variables (factors that are under the control of the justice system):

- **Lineup instruction**—if a witness expects the perpetrator to be present in the lineup, he or she may feel obligated to pick someone, even if the perpetrator is not there. The witness should be told that the culprit is not present is a legitimate answer.
- **Foil bias**—the suspect should not stand out from the innocent distractors (foils, fillers) in a lineup. The people should wear similar clothing, etc.
- **Investigator bias**—the investigator may unintentionally let the witness know which person in the lineup is the suspect.
- **Presentation bias**—a sequential presentation of people in a lineup is better than presenting all people simultaneously.

BOX 4.7

A summary of the effect of factors leading to wrongful conviction (Scheck & co-workers, 2001)

- 81% of time—Mistaken Identification by eyewitnesses.
- 51% of time—Serology Errors (ABO, protein blood typing).
- 50% of time—Police Misconduct.
- 45% of time—Prosecutorial Misconduct.
- 35% of time—Forensic Hair Comparison Errors.
- 34% of time—Junk/Sloppy Science admitted at trial.
- 32% of time—Bad Lawyering.
- 22% of time—False Confessions.
- 20% of time—Deliberately False witness testimony.
- 19% of time—Deliberately False snitching by informants.
- 7% of time—Other Forensic Science errors.
- 1% of time—DNA testing errors.

Race and Mistaken Identification:

- 44% of time—Caucasian misidentifying African American.
- 25% of time—Caucasian misidentifying Caucasian.
- 21% of time—African American misidentifying African American.
- 4% of time—Latino misidentifying Latino.
- 3% of time—Caucasian misidentifying Latino.
- 1% of time—Latino misidentifying African American.

Behrman and Davey (2001) analyzed 271 actual police cases to address issues in eyewitness research literature. The findings of the actual cases upheld many of the research findings. Thus, suspect identification declined significantly over time, same versus cross race conditions, witness type and weapon presence. Suspect identification rates were greater for field show-ups than for photographic lineups: the difference being as large as 76% versus 48%.

Problems in eyewitness testimony

There is no doubt that psychological findings have an important bearing on eyewitness testimony in legal matters. However, it is also true that psychologists show substantial differences in determining what research should be accepted in eyewitness testimony. In other words, given the impreciseness in perceiving, remembering and retrieving information concerning a crime scene, is there a strong agreement on at least some aspects of eyewitness that is considered credible by a majority of psychologists? To answer this question in depth, Kassin, Ellsworth and Smith (1989) conducted a study on the experiences of 63 experts on eyewitness testimony. Initially, the researchers presented 21 eyewitness topics to the experts and evaluated their level of agreement on each topic with the belief that a central criterion of acceptability might emerge. Using 80% agreement on a topic as a criterion, Kassin, Ellsworth and Smith found that only nine out of a list of 21 topics satisfied this criterion:

- **Shows-ups: The use of a one-person show-up instead of a full lineup increases the risk of misidentification.**
- **Lineup instructions: Police instructions can affect an eyewitness's willingness to make an identification.**
- **Exposure time: The less time an eyewitness has to observe an event, the less well he or she will remember it.**
- **Forgetting curve: The rate of memory loss for an event is greatest right after the event, and then levels off over time.**
- **Accuracy-confidence: An eyewitness's confidence is not a good predictor of his or her identification accuracy.**
- **Post event information: Eyewitness testimony about an event often reflects not only what they actually saw but information they obtained later on.**
- **Wording of questions: An eyewitness's testimony about an event can be affected by how the questions put to that witness are worded.**
- **Unconscious transference: Eyewitnesses sometimes identify as a culprit someone they have seen in another situation or context.**
- **Attitudes, expectation: An eyewitness's perception and memory for an event may be affected by his or her attitudes and expectations.**

Kassin, Ellsworth and Smith (1989) also noted that although eyewitness testimony is often influenced by post event information, very few experts "believe that it is common knowledge among jurors" (p. 1097).

ON CHILDREN'S TESTIMONY

As the number of reported child cases has increased substantially in the past few decades, the courts are using children's reports as testimony more than ever before. Twenty per cent of the women and eight per cent of men have reported sexual abuse before the age of 16 years, and approximately 300,000 children are sexually abused every year in the US. A significantly higher number of false allegations of abuse were made by adolescents than by children under six years of age.

In a typical case involving child abuse, children are first presented open-ended questions and they are prompted to recall as much as they can remember. Saywitz, Goodman, Nichols and Moan (1991) reported that most children who visit a pediatrician did not disclose genital contact unless they were asked, "Did the doctor touch you here?" Due to this reason, anatomically detailed dolls are used to assist children in recalling their experiences. However, the use of dolls has raised several questions.

In their research, Ceci and co-workers (1994; Ceci & Bruck, 1995) found that the accuracy of reports by children was influenced by a number of different interviewing techniques. Ceci conducted a series of experiments to demonstrate how reports of young children were used, abused and misused in the legal world. Some of the major research findings are reported below:

Source attribution error: Errors in recalling memories from different sources

1. When we ask parents, teachers, social workers, and researchers if they recognize that children had given them an accurate account of a family outing, visit to a friend's birthday party, and so on, most of them will report in the affirmative. If this is true, then what is wrong with children's description of events in the court?
2. Ceci reported that the analysis of the materials of the day care cases—little rascals, Michaels, country walk and the old cutter, within the USA, revealed that the allegations of children in these centers emerged due to the extremely biased interviews. In fact, the interview techniques were so suggestive that the persistent interviewers created a confirmatory bias.
3. In his research, Ceci found **source attribution error** among children. That is, the children faced problems in separating the sources of their memories. Using a simple procedure in which a child was asked to recall some event repeatedly (for example, "got finger caught in the mousetrap and had to go to hospital to get the trap off") 58% of the children recalled false narratives to one or more of the fictitious events. "What was so surprising to me," wrote Ceci (1994), "was the elaborateness of the children's narratives. They were embellished, describing an eternally coherent account of the context in which their finger got caught in the mouse trap as well as the effect associated with it" (p. 34).
4. In addition, Ceci also showed how the recall of pre-schoolers was biased after creating a stereotype. After a stranger, named Sam Stone, visited the pre-schoolers, the interviewers asked questions regarding his visit, for a period of 10 weeks. Subsequently, a new story was told to these children depicting him a clumsy man. This stereotyping had its effect: 42% of these children responded to the suggestion probes by telling things that Sam Stone had never done (for example, "he soiled the teddy bear," etc.). Poole and Lindsay (1995) also came to similar conclusions with children being interviewed regarding a "Mr. Science."

Summarizing the results of his studies, Ceci (1994) wrote,

Child witnesses are not as suggestive as people suggest

> "The majority of children are neither as hyper-suggestible and coachable as some pro-defense advocates have alleged nor are they resistant to suggestions about their own bodies as some pro-prosecution advocates have claimed. Children can be led to incorporate false suggestions even into their accounts of intimate bodily touching if these suggestions are made by powerful adult authority figures and are delivered repeatedly over prolonged periods. Children can also be amazingly resistant to false suggestions and be able to provide highly detailed and accurate reports of events that transpired weeks or months ago" (p. 44).

Research conducted by Sutherland, Gross and Hayne (1996) showed that the accuracy of children's reports were compromised more by interviewers who had prior information about what had actually happened than by the interviewers who were naïve. In other words, the researchers concluded that any additional information regarding the interpretation of children's testimony might contaminate the evaluation of potential jurors. The old proverb, "ignorance is bliss" seems to work well with the uninformed interviewers. Poole and White (1993) argued that research on children's testimony in particular lacks theoretical cohesion because the available theories of perception and memory are not easily applicable to this field. Additionally, motivational and social factors may also influence reporting of the event. In their research, they found that subjects, six years of age or older, performed consistently on "yes-no" type questions, but they became less consistent with repeated questioning. It is clear from this study, as well from others, that a set of complex variables, ranging from prior knowledge of the incident to the type and frequency of questioning plays a significant role in determining the extent of accuracy of children's reports.

The accounts presented above fit in well with an overview of how children perform when called upon to provide eyewitness accounts about experienced and non-experienced events. Schaff and co-workers (2002) argue that:

- **Children are often, although not always, hesitant to disclose abuse.**
- **Children have the capacity for accurate memories of abusive experiences.**
- **Many children can, to a certain degree, resist suggestive questions about abuse, although some children are more prone to false report, especially in multiple suggestive contexts.**
- **The current focus on false reports and false memory, although clearly important, often overstates the problem of children's suggestibility about abuses and risks disbelief of child witnesses when belief is justified (see Box 4.8).**

Dale, Loftus and Rathbun (1978) found that whether the question was asked in the affirmative-negative, definite-indefinite article, or some-any quantifier definitely affected the answers.

BOX 4.8

How seriously should child testimony be taken in child abuse cases

A recent study at the Cincinatti Children's Hospital and Medical Center, (Daso & Shapiro, 2000 cf. Cincinatti Children's Medical Centre, 2000), revealed some very interesting facts. The concern of the project was whether child testimony should be taken seriously in child sexual abuse cases.

The researches reviewed records of 31 paedophiles (adults who commit sexual abuse against children) who had confessed during the period 1994-1999. All the case files were examined. Out of the 47 children who had been abused, 45 were old enough to provide a history of the event. The testimony provided by these 45 children described 111 acts of sexual abuse by these 31 paedophiles. The confession records revealed that the adults confessed to 101 acts, many being multiple acts. It also revealed that the adults confessed to 68% of the allegations, denying only 6%, these latter being cases of extreme abuse. Thus, the confessions matched to a very great extent with the testimony provided by the children. This finding takes on added importance when we consider the fact that physical examination of sexually abused children often proves to be unreliable.

Dr Shapiro, one of the researchers, was therefore led to conclude:

> We are not saying that children never make things up, but the responsible reaction is to listen carefully to allegations of abuse so that abused children will be identified and false allegations recognized.

Resistance efficacy

Children's perceived self efficacy for resisting interviewers' suggestions can be increased by the interviewer providing social support. Thus, when social support was provided to children, they were able to resist misleading questions to a greater extent than when the misleading questions were asked by a non-supportive person (Davis & Bottoms, 2002).

Resistance efficacy: Ability to resist suggestions by the interviewers

Does the same hold for adults? To what extent do adults comply with misleading 'expert pressure' during the interview? Results obtained by Roper and Shewan (2002), clarify that individuals who are labelled as 'poor' witnesses altered their responses and succumbed to leading questions, whereas 'good' witnesses actually improved their eyewitness observation scores. It therefore shows the power of an authority figure, especially for those eyewitnesses who are low in confidence.

THE LIE-DETECTOR TEST

The **lie-detector machine** is used when it is suspected that a person is making a false statement. The machine consists of a **polygraph** that records physiological responses related to heart, breathing and perspiration. In the case of Anita Hill, who accused judge Thomas on his Supreme Court nomination in the USA, the results of this test revealed that she was telling the truth regarding sexual harassment by judge Thomas. On the other hand, O.J. Simpson failed this test and fought against using the findings in his case.

Lie -detector test: Use of physiological responses to decide whether the person is telling the truth

There is a lot of controversy concerning the use of this test. There is certainly a large group that considers the lie detection test as one of the important contributions that psychology has made to law. However, there is an equally large group that feels that such tests are unethical. Decaire (2001) analyzed some of the issues, and concluded that results of the lie detection test should be used only to get further clues that need to be followed up, and not aimed to get a confession. The test has proved superior to some other detection methods, but it should not be considered to be a sure shot answer to prove the guilt of the accused. At best it predicts under normal circumstances whether a person is telling the truth well over chance level, and it is less prone to false positives. The effects are based on creating a stress situation, for both the guilty and the innocent, and its effectiveness could be challenged in conditions where it is coupled with physical stress, such as increasing the temperature of the room (Decaire, 2001). Except under special circumstances like drug use, a number of American states prohibit the use of a lie-detector test.

PSYCHOLOGY OF THE JURY

Every citizen is guaranteed to have a jury trial under the Sixth Amendment of the U.S. Constitution. In the USA, a pool of jury is generally drawn from those members of a community who have the right to vote or possess a driver's license. This first stage, called **venire**, is followed by **voir dire** (to speak the truth), a stage in which a judge, in consultation with attorneys, decides the fitness of prospective jurors by searching information about them. The main purpose of voir dire is to insure an impartial jury for the trial.

Venire: Selection of jury pool from members of community

Voir dire: Decision by judge regarding fitness of selected jury members

Because the decision of the members of the jury seals the fate of a trial, psychology is interested in finding out:

1. Do personality characteristics of the members of a jury have a bearing on the outcome of a trial?
2. In what ways do the members of a jury influence one another, especially when they arrive at their final decision?
3. Do events before a trial (for example, pretrial publicity) influence jury decision?

If you are an attorney, imagine whom you will like to have as a member of the jury in a murder trial? If a person is a member of a local Quaker group opposed to death penalty, obviously you will prefer to have or reject this person, depending on whom you are representing—prosecution or defense. Very authoritarian and liberal jurors are considered biased and are phased out of the final jury selection. So are rich, high status people. It is assumed that such people not only have a mind-set but they might also influence other members of jury with their strong beliefs.

Scientific jury selection: Process of systematically choosing jurors on the basis of demographic and biographic details

Scientific jury selection, a process involving consideration of the demographic profile of members of a community and biographic information about prospective jurors, became popular since the "Harrisburg Seven" trial in which Vietnam War protesters were tried in a politically conservative city of Pennsylvania—Harrisburg. In this case social scientists used their knowledge for the systematic selection of the jury. Several high profile cases in the past, for example, O.J. Simpson, Rodney King, and Menedez brothers, involved complex jury selection procedures in which social psychological information was used. However, it should be remembered that such cases were expensive and also time-consuming.

The scientific study of Juror Bias

Juror Bias: Tendency of jurors to be prejudiced in their judgments

In order to facilitate the scientific selection of jury members, a number of **Juror Bias scales** have been developed. Recent studies have proved the reliability and the validity of such scales. Using mock jurors, the Juror Bias scale was found to have high predictive validity: it was able to successfully predict the verdict and other related questions in two real life homicide cases. (De La Fuente & co-workers, 2003). A major criticism of jury studies is that because mock jurors (generally undergraduate students) are used, the results so obtained may not be generalizable to real life jury behavior. Lecci and Myers (2002) therefore attempted to validate the Juror Bias scale using 617 juror eligible adults (aged 18-84 years) from the community, across three distinct trial scenarios. The results regarding the factor structure of the scale were very similar to those obtained on college students.

It is true that the attitudes of jurors affect the magnitude of the sentence. If jurors possess strong in-group feelings, they tend to punish a member of the out-group defendant more harshly than a member of their own group (Sweeney & Haney, 1992). It is known that White jurors on an average punish Black defendants more vigorously than members of their own race. Similar conclusions have been reported from studies based on mock trials.

Rape myths and jury bias

Rape myths: Incorrect beliefs regarding rape victims and culprits

Research on victims of rape shows that there are people who firmly believe that rape victims often invite trouble for themselves. In fact, they believe that women unconsciously enjoy rape. Burt's Rape Myths Scale (1980) measures the extent of such false beliefs of people toward rape (Box 4.9). Application of research in this area has shown that those jurors who believe in rape myths are likely to be less harsh to the defendant in a rape crime (Borgida & Brekke, 1985).

BOX 4.9

Sample items from Rape Myths Scale (*Source*: Burt, 1980)

1. A woman who goes to the home or apartment of a man on their first date implies that she is willing to have sex.
2. Any female can get raped.
3. Any healthy women can successfully resist a rapist if she really wants to.
4. Women who get raped while hitch-hiking get what they deserve.

Vrij and Fermin (2001) used this scale to get more clarity regarding the ways in which **physical attractiveness** affects jury behavior. Eighty subjects were exposed to an extract of a victim's story about an alleged rape case. The physical attractiveness of both victim and defendant were systematically varied, and the degree to which the subjects conformed to the rape myth was assessed using the Burt scale. The results were in the expected direction. Subjects who especially endorsed "rape myths" were found to be more favorable towards both victims and defendants who were good-looking. Moreover, females were found to be more favorable towards the victim than males. This gender difference also depended on their scores on the Rape Myth scale.

Can the above finding be applied to real life, especially in the light of findings that members of the jury do show a bias, favoring people who are attractive? The authors of the above study suggest that prospective jury members especially for people who are likely to be confronted with victims of sexual offences should be administered the Rape Myths Acceptance Scale. It is not just prospective members of a jury, whose acceptance of the rape myth would bias judgments.

Authoritarianism and the jury

Authoritarianism: A personality trait known to produce juror bias

Research on authoritarianism (Adorno & co-researchers, 1950) has shown that people with fascist tendencies are intolerant of minorities, homosexuals and lack of obedience. For your consideration, three items from Adorno and co-workers' (1950) scale of Authoritarianism, known as the F scale, are reproduced in Box 4.10. Examine the item on homosexuals. A person who endorses this statement very strongly is likely to be a very prejudiced juror if he/she serves in a jury considering punishment to a homosexual offender. Research in the area of authoritarianism has also shown that it can take many forms. For instance, given the right opportunity, a submissive authoritarian can also behave, contrary to popular belief, at the level of an aggressive authoritarian in displaying his/her fascist tendencies. The effect of authoritarianism can also vary with the race of the victim and the race of the accused, such that the authoritarian person may behave differently with people of different races. This was concluded by Landwehr and co-workers (2002), who found a significant three way interaction between authoritarianism, race of victim, and race of the defendant. The following Table 4.1 describes nine dimensions of the authoritarian personality as explored by the Adorno group.

BOX 4.10

Three items from Fascist Scale (*Source*: Adorno *et al.*, 1950)

1. Obedience and respect for authority are the most important virtues children should learn.
2. Homosexuality is a particularly rotten form of delinquency and ought to be severely punished.
3. People can be divided into two distinct classes: the weak and the strong.

TABLE 4.1

Nine dimensions of the authoritarian personality (*Source*: Kool & Ray, 1983)

1. Conventionalism: Adherence to middle class values.
2. Authoritarian submission: Avoiding rebellion.
3. Authoritarian aggression: Inclination to punish those who violate norms.
4. Anti-interception: Reject subjective approaches.
5. Superstition and stereotypy: Thinking in rigid categories.
6. Power and toughness: Belief in leader-follower, strong-weak categories and exaggerated concern regarding these dimensions.
7. Destructiveness and cynicism: Hostility leading to degradation.
8. Projectivity: Assuming wild and hostile activities.
9. Sex: Over-concern with matters pertaining to sex.

As it has been mentioned earlier, some people have strong convictions against the death penalty. In such cases, it is likely that a criminal will be awarded a lenient punishment by the jurors irrespective of the nature of the crime. Therefore, they are likely to be excluded from the jury in trials involving capital punishment.

A **death penalty** actually involves a trial in **two phases**: the **guilty phase** and the **penalty phase.** During the guilty phase the jurors, by and large, focus on how the victim was tortured (aggravating circumstance) and what was the mental condition of the defendant (mitigating circumstance). Based on our knowledge of the orientation of authoritarian people who support death penalty, it is safe to argue that such people are likely to ignore or undermine a testimony involving mitigating circumstances. It is also likely that blacks and females who are opposed to the death penalty significantly more than others have greater chances of being excluded from the jury, a process that may lead to an unbalanced formation of a jury, that is, fewer blacks and females as jurors.

Jury size

Jury size to be limited to 12 members for cases on capital punishment

Another issue concerning the jury in which the contribution of social psychology has been acknowledged is **jury size.** Traditionally, a jury consisted of 12 members in capital cases, but in other cases the legal system has been operating with considerable flexibility. In many instances, a jury consisting of six members was considered reasonable and not unconstitutional (Williams *v.* Florida case). However, in another case (Ballew *v.* Georgia case), the judge ruled that a jury should consist of at least six members and any number below six would be unconstitutional. To the delight of social psychologists, the judge did seek help from social psychological findings regarding inability of small groups to function accurately and deliberate effectively.

Judges instruct jurors not to punish a defendant until they find a cause beyond reasonable doubt. This type of scenario places jurors in a situation wherein they act like an experimenter who poses a hypothesis and evaluates the chance level at which he/she would be accurate. And like experimenters, jurors also commit **Type I** and **Type II errors**. They commit a Type I error when an innocent person is sentenced. On the other hand, a type II error is made when a guilty person is acquitted. Based on our knowledge of advantages and disadvantages of a small or large jury, Roper (1980) suggested that while a twelve person jury is likely to eliminate Type I error, a six person jury will be useful for avoiding a type II error. Although this type of theoretical analysis sounds remarkable, it has serious problems of applicability, for neither do we know in advance what type of error we will be making nor do we know in advance what is better for us.

A question frequently asked is: Do jurors make **errors** in their judgment? In general, the answer is that they make errors, like any other human beings, in making a decision. For instance, business organizations believe that jury awards against them are usually very high and they sometimes try to overturn the judgment against them. As you know, members of a jury in the US are mostly average citizens who believe that business organizations can afford to pay hefty damages. Wrongful conviction of Randall Adams in the murder case of officer Wood, in the USA, as mentioned in the section of eyewitness, is another example of poor jury verdict.

Physical attractiveness and the jury

Is beautiful innocent? Are jurors influenced by **physical attractiveness** and other features of the defendant? Several researchers (Efran, 1974; Dion, Berscheid & Walster, 1972) have contended that physical attractiveness plays some role, if not a major one, in determining the crime of a suspect. Although well over ninety per cent students in Efran's study (1974) reported that they would not attach any significance to attractiveness as a factor in determining guilt or innocence of a defendant, the students from the same college did in fact rate physically attractive people as less guilty and deserving less harsher punishment than their unattractive counterparts. Stephen and Tully (1977) found that mock jurors tended to give larger monetary awards to attractive plaintiffs. Landy and Aronson (1969) manipulated social attractiveness of the victim and the defendant in their study involving a drunken driving accident to investigate how social attractiveness influenced the jurors' decision. They found that when a **high status person** was killed, the decision of jurors was harsher. On the other hand, they were less harsh to a high status defendant in comparison to a low status person, although both high and low status people were charged with the same crime. When the factor of social status is combined with race, it puts some people in a double bind. Being a celebrity had a distinct advantage for white defendants, whereas, for the black, it was a liability as far as rape accusations are concerned (Knight & co-workers, 2001).

Physical attractiveness of victim, culprit and witnesses can cause juror bias

Researches have shown that people like those who are similar to them. Using this perspective of attitudinal attractiveness as a model, Griffith and Jackson (1973) demonstrated that the greater the degree of similarity between the attitudes of defendants and mock jurors, the less inclined the jurors were to punish the defendants. Because perception of any similarity is considered rewarding (Byrne, 1971), it is not surprising to find jurors responding favorably to attractiveness of defendants.

Attitudes toward attractiveness are brought out very clearly when we look at the findings regarding same race/same sex bias among jury members. When studies are conducted using mock jurors, who are either black or white, and are presented with a simulated case in which a female plaintiff accuses a male defendant of sexual harassment, it has generally been found that mock jurors of both races tend to favor litigants of their own race and their own gender. Moreover, we again see a gender difference appearing, with males showing much greater bias than female subjects (Wuensch, Campbell & co-workers, 2002).

Reverse discrimination: Showing negative biases towards members of own group

However there are times when people become so cautious not to show prejudice that they go to the other extreme. This is an example of what has been called **"reverse discrimination."** Thus, jurors may evaluate black defendants as less responsible in order to appear unprejudiced (Foley & Pigot, 2002). We can explain this on the basis of self-presentation theory, which proposes that individuals are generally concerned with how they are perceived and evaluated. For example, most people want to appear unprejudiced. The study by Foley and Pigot attempted to gain insights into such impression management in a very innovative manner. The experimenters varied the race of both the victim and the accused, and presented a black or a white individual. Jurors were found to attribute much less responsibility to the black defendant when the person was black, but there was no change in attribution when the person was white. The authors suggest that a black person makes race salient, or it makes people aware of the race factor, thus jurors evaluate black defendants as less responsible in order to appear unprejudiced. These mock jurors therefore exhibited reverse discrimination.

Profession of witness and juror bias

Jury members can also be biased in terms of the profession of the witness. Every profession carries with it a certain connotation and a certain status in society. Also to every profession are attached certain stereotypes: so we expect all teachers to behave in one fashion, all doctors to behave in ways that are more similar to others in the same profession, etc. Can jurors separate themselves from their perception of the ideal gender for a profession from testimony of an expert witness representing that profession? Couch and Sigler (2002) concluded that gender, normally an important bias factor, is undermined by occupational stereotypes. Thus, when the gender of the expert witness was systematically varied, their mock jurors were not affected by the gender of the witness, and there was no significant effect of gender on effectiveness of expert witness who was an automotive engineer.

Race-crime congruence: Certain races are associated with certain crimes

Race crime congruence: Certain races are generally associated with certain crimes. Results show that jury bias can depend on whether or not the race of the defendant is congruent with the crime. When crime is perceived to be congruent with the race of the defendant, the verdict and the attributions were found to be more negative, the search was more limited and more confirmatory evidence was sought (Jones & co-workers, 2003).

To be a part of a jury in a criminal case is like watching a murder mystery movie in which pieces of a puzzle appear intermittently with clear, obscure, or false evidences. The difference, of course, is that in a movie, the director provides you the solution but in real life, you, as a juror, put together the pieces of a puzzle to arrive at a conclusion. Do jurors ask themselves (self-talk), "What must have happened?" At least for Pennington and Hastie (1986) the answer was in the affirmative. They believe that jurors construct their own story even before a trial provides enough evidence for guilt or innocence. Such a story model also receives support from Smith's (1991) work that showed how jurors process information based on pre-existing conceptions.

Memory factors affect jury proceedings too

Do **memory factors** come into play even at this **deliberation stage**? The court normally assumes that when the jury retires to deliberate over the proceedings, many memory gaps would be filled in with corroborative facts remembered by jury members. So if one jury member did not remember or had not interpreted facts in the right way, the deliberation process would enable the correction of such errors. Laboratory studies show that there is only a very slight memory improvement after deliberation. And those who were most likely to change their verdict, were not those who had the least accurate memories but those who had least confidence in their memories (Pritchard & Keenan, 2002). When we are unable to explain events on the basis of available facts, we sometimes start thinking of what could have been the other alternative ways in which the event may have occurred. Such a reconstruction of the event has been called **counterfactual thinking.** This is a natural reaction for all of us, and since jury members are humans first, they would be equally susceptible to factors in human nature. Why is it that people who have a lower memory span are more susceptible to such counterfactual thinking? Why are people susceptible to wrong interpretations and subsequent wrongful blaming? One factor could be that whereas counterfactual thinking occurs naturally, one has to suppress it if it is not corroborated by further evidence. This suppression takes conscious effort, and people who are under high memory load may not have the needed attentional resources to perform such conscious processing of the data (Goldinger & co-workers, 2003).

Researches on jury decision making have also shown that **hindsight bias**, a tendency for people to say, after the outcome is known, that this is exactly what they had predicted even before the decision, contaminates the decisions of a juror (Hawkins & Hastie, 1990). This type of hindsight bias is particularly harmful in medical and product liability cases in which a juror is supposed to focus simply on the state of a defendant prior to the damage because most people take remedial steps soon after allegations of damage.

The just-world hypothesis: "as you sow, so shall you reap"

If a juror believes that people in this world get what they deserve because this world is a just place for all practical purposes, such a simplistic understanding may influence the outcome of a decision. Such a belief, called **Just-World Hypothesis** (Lerner, 1980), brings cognitive consistency in our thinking. For example, if a woman wears a very sexy dress and is raped after the party, a juror might think, "Well, she invited trouble and got it."

Bias in decision making based on attractiveness and a concept of a just-world may have something in common—those who are attractive have earned their attractiveness; they deserve better life, too. Not surprisingly, believers in a just-world tend to be lenient to attractive defendants or plaintiffs.

While a lot has been said and done regarding the biases of jury members, we do not know enough about the ways in which defendant lawyers attempt to influence the attitudes of the jury. The scant research that is available does show that lawyers use **impression management techniques** in their opening and closing sentences. Black attorneys addressing a predominantly black jury were found to use stylistic and rhetorics from the African American vernacular English to construct a 'shared identity' (Hobbs, 2003).

SOCIAL PSYCHOLOGY AND LAW ENFORCEMENT

The behavior of law enforcement personnel is an important area of study for social psychologists because such personnel react to stressful situations, collect evidence, and present the entire case. Notwithstanding meager research in this area, interest on this subject has been sparked off in the past few years after the brutal treatment of Rodney King by four police officers and Furman's lying in the O.J. Simpson's case. Another case that has caught public attention was the alleged assault of a private citizen by the Metropolitan Toronto Police in 1984. Loftus and Rosenwald (1995), too, cite the case of an 18 year old Asian inmate of New York prison in 1982, who was assaulted by several prison officers and ended in a mistrial. All these cases often make us wonder, "should police officers be always trusted?"

In the Rodney King case, it was found that police memory was perceived as being more reliable than videotaped evidence. One would expect that anything that has been mechanically recorded would be more reliable for the sole reason that personal biases of the type discussed above, or even memory lapses would not be affecting the evidence. However, just a little bit of thought—the camera can only record to what it is pointed at! This is the reason why Loftus and Rosenwald (1993) also concluded that videotaped evidence should not take precedence over evidence provided by actual people at the site of the crime.

In the section on eyewitness testimony in this chapter, it was mentioned that eyewitnesses have problems recalling the features of a criminal because they tend to look at the weapon and at their own security. Solomon and Horn (1986) reported that police officers also suffer from perceptual distortion during shooting. Common observations of several police officers were: time was slowing down, everything was happening in slow motion, and visual perception was becoming vivid.

Unlike an average citizen, police officers face stress caused by violence almost routinely and adapt to it in several stages (Violanti, 1992, 1996). During the first stage, called the alarm stage, they experience "reality shock" because their average life experiences and training in the academy are different from real life experiences. After five years they enter the disenchantment stage (6-13 years) during which they realize that the demands of work outweigh their abilities. With the onset of the personalization stage (14-20 years), the police officers begin to focus on their personal goals, for example, retirement, pay, etc. During the final phase of their career (20 + years), called the introspective stage, most officers look back on their career. Their activity level reduces and they tend to request an early retirement.

BOX 4.11

Law enforcement made easier through state-of-the-art gadgets

A report from Chicago tells us about the latest gadgets that can help the police and other law enforcers to locate children who are kidnapped or even lost.

For decades, parents have had their children's fingers printed by local law enforcement, so that if the child is lost or kidnapped, they can be identified. However, a recent spate of highly publicized kidnappings across the UK in the year 2002, parents and law enforcers have been on the lookout for more sophisticated means to keep their kids safe.

One product getting a lot of interest today is the GPS Personal Locator for Children. This is a watch like amulet worn on the wrist by the child. Using a satellite based Global Positioning System technology, the gadget can locate the child within minutes. Another similar device is the Safety and Location Monitor. This is a combination clip on watch that can be worn by children and the elderly for emergency medical alert purposes. Other devices include a safety device that goes off when the child wanders beyond a certain distance, say, 30 feet (*The Times of India*, September 3, 2002).

Women in law enforcement

The social psychology of women in law enforcement reveals that their acceptance in the police force suffers particularly because this profession has been dominated by men and that police work *per se* generates a masculine stereotype. While women have been serving in police cadres from the beginning of this century, their role has mostly been viewed as that of a matron. How do policewomen adjust to a male dominated, masculine profession? According to Judie Wexler (1985), most policewomen, realizing their individual and social limits, have either adopted a business-like attitude or have become semi-masculine to function realistically at work. An excellent example of successful women in the police services is that of Ms Kiran Bedi, a high ranking and very respected police officer in the Indian Police Services, who, despite having encountered many problems during her work, has earned great respect.

LAW AND THE RIGHTS OF CHILDREN

Children's rights have been viewed in two different ways (Wrightsman, 1991): nurturant rights and self-determination rights. The former is paternalistic because society decides what is good for its children. On the other hand, self-determining rights permit children to decide what they want. For example, a girl in her teens is free to exercise her abortion rights.

Historically, children had no rights of their own. For example, when a couple divorced over 100 years ago, it was decided to hand the child over to the local animal shelter. Traditionally, fathers had the custody right for their children because children were treated as property. This scene has changed during the past 50 years. Although in most cases children are now assigned to mothers (Reppucci, 1984), both parents have some rights. The most encouraging development in the custody battle between parents has resulted in the recognition of rights of children who can now express their preference for a parent upon divorce.

VICTIM TRAUMA AND THE LAW

Psychological trauma impairs the ability and/or willingness of crime victims to cooperate with the criminal justice system, to such an extent that it can make it almost impossible for the justice system to do its work. There are at least two aspects that require attention:

Victim trauma and classical conditioning: Spread of terror to other non related stimuli

- **Crime related mental health problems of the victim.**
- **Aspects of the criminal justice system process are stressful to victims.**

One way to solve the above-mentioned problems of victims of crime is through effective partnerships between the criminal justice system, victim assistance personnel, and trained mental health professionals.

Why do victims undergo trauma and why do interactions with the criminal justice system prove stressful for the victim. One theory that is immensely relevant for gaining an insight into victim trauma is the **classical conditioning theory.**

A violent criminal victimization can become a real life classical conditioning experience in which being attacked could be an **unconditioned stimulus** that can produce **unconditioned responses** of fear, anxiety, terror, helplessness, pain, and other negative emotions. Any stimuli present during the attack can be paired with the attack and become conditioned stimuli capable of producing conditioned responses of fear, anxiety, terror, helplessness, and other negative emotions. Thus, **characteristics of the assailant** (*e.g.*, age, race, attire, distinctive features), or **characteristics of the setting** (*e.g.*, time of day, where the attack occurred, features of the setting) might become conditioned stimuli.

Avoidance of certain stimuli because of classical conditioning

The most common response to conditioned stimuli is **avoidance behavior.** Thus, there is a natural tendency for crime victims to avoid contact with such conditioned stimuli and to escape from situations that bring them in contact with such stimuli.

Second order conditioning: Pairing of conditioned stimuli with another neutral stimuli

Another classical conditioning mechanism that has important implications for understanding the behavior of crime victims is **second-order conditioning.** This refers to the pairing of a neutral stimulus with a conditioned stimulus such that this neutral stimulus can become a second-order conditioned stimulus. Thus, any stimuli present at the same time as a crime related conditioned stimulus can become a second-order conditioned stimulus, to evoke fear, other negative emotions, and a strong tendency to engage in avoidance behavior. Thus, the police, prosecutors, and victim service providers may become associated as a second-order conditioned stimulus, with the person tending to avoid all of them.

Victim trauma requires community help

So pervasive can be the effect of trauma faced by the victim, that a large number of criminal events have been specifically mentioned in the Diagnostic and Statistical Manual (IVth Edition) as being capable of producing Post

Traumatic Stress Disorder (PTSD). Besides PTSD, victims also show depression, suicidal thoughts, greater alcohol and drug use, etc. They have also been found to experience problems in personal relationships.

Purpose of law for minors is different from that for adults

While victims may expect help from the judicial system, legal professionals are generally not equipped with counseling training. Even if they are not able to acquire counseling skills, they should at least be able to guide the victim regarding where to get such help from. There are other groups also that can be of help to the victim. These include the clergy and nurses with mental health training. One problem has of course been that while there is a plethora of counseling techniques, there is none specifically tailored for use with crime victims. The recovery of the victim from the trauma will also depend on two other factors. One is social support, while the other is the degree and the nature of the exposure to the judicial system.

JUVENILE DELINQUENCY

Why has crime by children been classed differently from those by adults? Why are they tried in juvenile courts rather than in the regular courts and even the sentences are different? To answer these questions, it must be kept in mind that the **purpose** of juvenile courts is **rehabilitation** rather than conviction. As a means to this end, the very terminology used by juvenile courts is different from that used by courts for crimes by adults. Thus, juvenile courts use the term, " take into custody" or "apprehend" rather than the term "arrest;" "delinquent act" instead of "misdemeanor" or "felony;" "supervision" and not "probation." The terms "plea of guilty" and "plea of not guilty" have also been altered. Juvenile courts use the term "admit the petition" for the former and "deny the petition" for the latter. Despite such precautions being taken to reduce the psychological harm to the child, the juvenile may face trauma and the social worker may need help in understanding the child. The parents can play a very important role in helping the child adjust to the juvenile justice system. The parents should therefore be ready to help the social worker to understand the child's emotional and behavioral history and its current mental needs, etc.

While juvenile courts exist and are used extensively, it is felt that today it is easier to impose adult sentences on juveniles (Evans, 2003). But as posed by Evans, "Are they competent to stand trial?" For those found competent by the authorities, the IQ was lower than the "juvenile norms" expectation of competency. This finding questions the use of IQ as the sole determinant of judging the competency of juveniles. Grisso and Associates (2003) too noted that adolescents are incompetent to stand trial.

Predictors of juvenile delinquency

Psychological family patterns and behavior problems are chief predictors of juvenile delinquency

Studies from around the globe reveal a very strong link between psychological family patterns, early childhood behavior problems and juvenile delinquency. A unique multi-site, multi-country investigation, that is, across six sites in three countries (**Canada, New Zealand and the USA**) noted that behavior problems in childhood are the best predictors of juvenile delinquency (Broidy & co-workers, 2003). Among **German** adolescents too, the quality of family relationships coupled with contact with deviant peers was seen to contribute to behavior problems (Werner & co-workers 2003). As recently as the turn of the century, studies in **Australia** (Moore & Ohtsuka, 1999) revealed that Australian youth were evincing a strong interest in gambling, as reflected in participation rates, intentions to gamble and attitudes towards gambling. A study on 505 Australian young adolescents aged 15-17 years, found 60% of them gambling annually, of which 3.5% would be classified as manifesting problem behavior according to the DSM IV-5 (Fisher, 1999). That family patterns are important is also revealed by research on attitudes towards gambling. Attitudes of youth towards gambling were found to be strongly influenced by familial, social and cultural norms. More frequent gambling was correlated with parental and peer gambling and also with pro-gambling attitudes (Delfabbro & co-workers, 2003). We can certainly apply findings such as these for the reduction of gambling tendencies among youth. Delfabbro (*ibid*) also found that adolescents whose parents taught them about the value of money, for example, of budgeting, saving, etc. were less likely to express an interest in gambling. This is an important finding because it tells us that both the promotion and the prevention of vices among adolescents could be due to parental factors and that the parents may require counseling as much as their children who are engaged in gambling.

Youth attitudes towards gambling influenced by family, social and cultural norms

The USA fairs no better. It is one of the most violent countries of the world, if we consider the rate of exposure to violence. For young adults, the exposure rate has been found to range from 76% to 82% for victimization and 93 to 96% for witnessing violence (Scarpa, 2003). The American youth and the American family have been found to constitute a high risk group for substance use, adolescent, pregnancy, youth violence and school dropout (Weissberg & co-workers, 2003). Such a high exposure rate has important repercussions for the psycho-social health of these youngsters. Scarpa (*ibid*) has also concluded that young adults with high levels of exposure to violence report more psychological maladjustment. Along the same lines, a study on 88 male violent offenders (mean age 16.63 years) and a normal control group concluded that the offenders used more immature styles of coping than their control counterparts (Xu & co-workers, 2002). Maybe, one way to reduce violence among youth would be to teach them more constructive and healthy styles of coping.

While there is considerable agreement among lay theories of delinquent behavior (Tyson & co-workers, 2000), the cultural variable has however remained an oft-neglected factor in empirical research. That culture could be an important factor is revealed in a study by Tyson and his colleagues (Tyson & Hubert, 2002). After controlling for SES and other demographic factors, differences were found between Australian adolescents hailing from either collectivistic or individualistic cultural backgrounds, with the individualistic group tending to emphasize more internal oriented attributions for delinquency. Thus the adolescents coming from individualistic cultures tended to attribute their delinquent behavior more to boredom or excitement (both internal factors). Conversely, those coming from collectivistic cultures tended to emphasize the fact that "they copy what they see on TV and elsewhere, *i.e.* external factors."

Personal attribution for delinquency based on collectivistic-individualistic cultural differences

If early behavior problems are so important for the later development of juvenile delinquency, ways have to be found for treating them. Psychologists have commonly advocated two methods. One is the use of group interventions, for example, at the reform schools, where groups of juvenile delinquents can undergo group therapy. The other is family therapy, where the juvenile is retained in the family and the entire family undergoes therapy. Such family therapy has been found to be particularly helpful for the treatment and modification of adolescent problem behavior such as substance use among Hispanics (Santisteban & co-workers, 2003). The authors also draw upon their findings for policy and practice. Though such treatment is normally considered expensive the above study shows that even short-term family therapy can be effective. Moreover, it is sometimes noted that the less expensive group therapy can reinforce rather than reduce delinquent behavior (Dishion & co-workers, 1999). Family therapy would bypass this problem. In fact, there is considerable recent data to show that multi-modal treatment of child and juvenile delinquency is effective (Fago, 2003; Nation & co-workers, 2003; Levant & co-workers, 2002).

Group therapy: Where groups of delinquents can undergo therapy together

Family therapy is extremely effective

Arson, especially that committed by youth, is another problem that plagues the USA, since it causes injuries and deaths, destroys homes, and destabilizes neighborhoods (Maciak, Moore, Leviton & Guinan, 1998). We now describe how this problem was solved in a Detroit community, where there had been a record number of arson fires on Halloween "Devil's night" (many committed by youths). The strategy deployed was the formation of a long-term community coalition between the mayor's office, Detroit neighborhood city halls (nine decentralized city halls), city government departments and agencies, public schools, community based organizations, and the private sector. On the suggestion of this coalition, public safety personnel were redeployed, arson targets were eliminated, volunteers were mobilized and were given training, activities for children and teenagers were thought of, a youth curfew was imposed and there were impositions on the purchase of fuel in portable containers during the Halloween period. Active help of the media was also solicited. Using such a multi pronged intervention strategy, Maciak and associates concluded that there was a decrease in the number of fires in a 10-year period of arson prevention interventions. An inverse relationship between the number of fires and the number of volunteers was also noted, suggesting a causal effect (Wandersman & Florin, 2003).

Community efforts can help solve arson problems

NEW FRONTIERS IN SOCIAL PSYCHOLOGY AS APPLIED TO LEGAL ISSUES

Restorative justice

There are many people who feel that the present justice systems are far too retributive in nature, and challenge the traditional wisdom to resolve crime issues; they believe that it is necessary for the offender to feel the pain of imprisonment.

Justice is not simply about retribution and punishment. It should not be based upon the "eye for eye" principle. Restorative justice, as the nomenclature suggests, is an attempt to restore balance within the community after offences have been committed. The idea is that traditional justice systems create recidivism, and the punished become even more cynical towards society at large.

Restorative justice: Attempts to restore balance within the community after the offence

Restorative justice is used as an alternative to imprisonment, and the focus is on developing a balance between the offender and the victim. This is done by a three-pronged effort that includes

- **The offender.**
- **The victim.**
- **The communities of which both the offender and the victim are residents.**

The important idea is that the victims must be reinstated into the process of justice and must not remain just as witnesses. This can be done by providing them an opportunity for confronting the offenders and for understanding why the crime was committed.

Let us look at some recent experiments on restorative justice. The most advanced experiment is in Belgium, where they have been working on this idea from the mid nineties. Not only are there mediation processes between the offender and the victim, but there is also the supply of information to the victim and their supporters. Attention is also paid to educate the broader community. In a similar manner, the London-based International Center for Prison Studies has partnered with the NGO, "Inside-Out Trust" to run pilot projects in a number of British prisons. It is hoped that prisons will become more restorative by encouraging prisoners to take personal onus for their offence and its consequences, by providing greater opportunities to make amends and by establishing formal channels of mediation between prisoners for resolving conflicts. In South Africa too, efforts are being made to transform prisons on the basis of the recommendations of the Truth and Reconciliation Commissions. Some of these recommendations are described below:

- **Prison officers should receive human rights training so that they are able to show more humane treatment towards the prisoners.**
- **Prison staff should be trained in prison law, their duties and responsibilities, ethics and conflict resolution.**
- **Prison staff should receive training in creative and humane ways of motivating prisoners to regain their human dignity and cooperate with the rehabilitation process in prisons.**

Along similar lines, there are recommendations for prisoners too.

- **Prisoners should receive skills training.**
- **They should receive training in recognizing their basic needs.**
- **They should be given training in human rights and non-violent conflict resolution techniques.**
- **They should have access to literacy classes.**
- **There should be counselors in every prison.**

It is hoped that through such restorative practices, not only will the victim benefit, but also at the same time, the prison would be a better and more humane institution. We should not forget that these offenders in the prisons are also human beings, and that they have the same emotions, needs and motivations as non-offenders. Is someone listening when social psychologists present their views as above? Probably not, though social psychologists hope that someone will in the future.

BOX 4.12

Restorative justice in jails in India

An age old Asian stress management technique is Vipassana. It is a 2,500 year old, self observation and mind purifying technique that originated in India but was later lost. This technique, now being introduced in a number of jails in India, has been shown to produce changes even in hardcore criminals and their jailors. Vipassana is a ten-day course with an objective of studying one's own mind-matter phenomenon by observing one's sensations. It is no miracle. It requires hard work: sleeping on the floor, remaining silent during the 10 day period, following the strictest regimen regarding food, sleep, yoga and meditation. It was implemented in one of the largest jails in India in the capital city of New Delhi and at present at least 15 other jails all around the country organize regular courses for both jailors and the jail-birds. It has been found to help overcome negativities such as anger, greed, emotional insecurity and other deep-rooted complexes (Agrawal, 2001).

LIMITATIONS TO THE APPLICATION OF SOCIAL PSYCHOLOGY IN LAW

Although the contribution of psychologists in legal matters has increased substantially in the past two decades, the evidence presented by them is considered less effective than that presented by the experts in the biological sciences (for example, DNA evidence, etc.). As stated in the beginning of this chapter, the problems with applications of psychology in legal matters emerge from two sources: firstly, contributed by the psychologists themselves; and secondly, referring to the legal experts' indifference and inability to understand and appreciate the impact of psychological evidence. As psychological research becomes more robust and scientific in the near future, the credibility earned by it will lead to its greater acceptance in legal circles. For example, Ceci (1994) has argued that a lot of misunderstanding over children's testimony in cases of child abuse would have been avoided had the experts used alternate hypotheses in testing such children. Ceci has shown that if the children are also encouraged to deny the occurrence of an abuse (rival hypothesis) the results of the investigation will be more trustworthy. Moreover, psychologists need to improve their data collection methods to minimize the effects of suggestibility and confirmatory bias.

The Supreme Court's decision to accept the judgement of a six-member jury but not a five-member jury is not based on any psychological theory of group dynamics. The decision was purely arbitrary. It is based on common sense that the number of people serving a jury should not be too low. In other words, unless psychological evidence is rooted in an impeccable theory that demonstrates why a six-member jury is superior to a five-member jury, the courts will continue to use their own decision. Moreover, courts weigh evidence from other social sciences too, before granting any preference to the evidence based on psychological research only.

In this chapter we have not mentioned several issues connecting psychology to law. For example, body language of witnesses and the defendant, insanity, rights of the mentally retarded, and gender discrimination have not been discussed either because these issues have less scientific material to offer or the topics have been adequately presented by other disciplines. Consider the following instance of subtle gender discrimination as late as in 1980 in New York. When a lady during voir dire was asked to describe the profession of her husband, she refused to answer the question on the grounds that men were not asked to describe the profession of their wives. She was charged with disobeying the court and was sentenced. In the state of Mississippi, it was not until 1970 that it was considered important to have women in the jury. The prejudice against women is a psychological phenomenon rooted in historical and social factors.

Summary

The relationship between social psychology and law can be viewed in the following three ways: psychology in the law, psychology and the law, and psychology of the law. While the nature of the first relationship is commonly known because legal expert call psychologists to present their views, the issue concerning psychology and law envisages a relationship in which both disciplines can benefit each other. Psychology of law deals with how law influences behavior. In short, these three ways of describing the relationship between psychology and law indicate a stronger bond between the two disciplines than was anticipated several decades ago.

This chapter deals with two major issues that describe a significant amount of research in psychology as applied to law: the eyewitness report and the role of the jury. The topic of eyewitness has been described in the classic model of memory research involving acquisition, storage and retrieval of information. Research studies were cited to show how capacity limitation or distortion in memory can cause misidentification of a person. A typical example is the case of a lineup to identify the suspect. After cataloging the critical variables such as race, age, weapon's effect, unconscious transference and face in the eyewitness testimony, a critical appraisal of problems in eyewitness testimony were presented. This section also examined the issues concerning the usefulness of children's testimony. In this context, the description was focused on two issues: reliability of children's report and the problems caused by the interviewer.

The second issue concerning the jury was presented mainly from the point of view of the size of the jury and its composition. The advantages and disadvantages of a large and a small jury were examined in the context of Supreme Court stand approving a six-person jury but not a three-person jury. Other topics discussed in the chapter were psychologists as witnesses, children's rights and the lie detector test. The chapter ends with a brief section on restorative justice.

Suggestions for Further Reading

Roper, R. and Shewan, D. (2002). Compliance and eyewitness testimony: Do eyewitnesses comply with misleading 'expert pressure' during investigative interviewing. *Legal and Criminal Psychology*, 7, 155-163.

Davis, S.L. and Bottoms, B.L. (2002). Effects of social support on children's eyewitness reports: A test of the underlying mechanism. *Law and Human Behavior,* 26, 185-215.

Wright, D.B., Boyd, C.E. and Tredoux, C.G. (2001). A field study of own race bias in South Africa and England. *Psychology, Public Policy and Law,* 7, 119-133.

Some Key Terms

Acquisition
Atkinson and Shiffrin model
Authoritarianism
Classical conditioning
Ecological validity
Expert witness
Eyewitness identification
Eyewitness testimony
Jury bias
Just world hypothesis
Juvenile delinquency
Lie detector test
Lineups
Memory distortion
Memory factors
Mundane realism
Own age bias
Own race bias
Photo lineup
Psychology and law
Psychology in law
Psychology of law
Race crime congruence
Rape myths
Resistance efficacy
Restorative justice
Retrieval
Reverse discrimination
Scientific selection of jury
Second-order conditioning
Sequential lineups
Simultaneous lineups
Source attribution
Storage
Unconscious transference
Venire
Victim trauma
Video lineup
Voir dire
Weapon effect
Wrongful conviction
Yerkes-Dodson Law

SOCIAL PSYCHOLOGY OF RELIGION

5

Chapter Outline

- An introduction to social psychology of religion
- Psychology of religion
  - Concept of religion
  - Measurement of religious behavior and its applications
  - Experimental and non-experimental research on religion
  - Recent issues in the measurement of religion
- Functions of religion/spirituality
  - Religion as social support
  - Religion as attachment
  - Religion as vehicle for social learning
  - Religion as purpose of life
- The development of religiousness
- Psychology and religion
  - Religion and physical health
  - Religion and mental health
  - Gender differences in the religion-health nexus
  - Religion and psychological coping
  - Religion and sexual behavior
- Spiritual healing or faith healing
  - Some traditional forms of faith healing
  - Shamanism
  - Tao
  - Zen
- Spiritual intelligence: An emerging area connecting religion and psychology
- The future of social psychology of religion

AN INTRODUCTION TO SOCIAL PSYCHOLOGY OF RELIGION

The social psychology of religion has had a great past, is warming up very fast at present and will have, hopefully, an extremely promising future. The most comprehensive publication on social psychology, *The Handbook of Social Psychology,* a five volume publication in the mid-sixties (Lindzey & Aronson, 1969), had a chapter on the psychology of religion, but the same book, when revised and up-dated in the mid-eighties had neither a chapter nor a major description concerning religion.

Landmark in early psychology: William James: "The Varieties of Religious Experience"

Approximately a century ago, when psychology had convincingly begun to establish itself as an independent science, religion figured prominently in the writings of its founding fathers. **William James'** *The Varieties of Religious Experience* (1902), is regarded as a landmark in this subject. He believed that the essence of religion is to be found in an individual's experience. Accordingly, he was concerned with personal religion or a **communion with the divine** rather than ritualistic aspects of religion. For him, institutional religion was of little value beyond our efforts to satisfy certain aesthetic needs that were associated with the divine power. Even for personal religion, he showed his disapproval when it was aimed at pleasing a deity by self-torture.

G. Stanley Hall: Religious development in adolescence

At an unusually different level from William James, another key figure in the history of psychology, **G. Stanley Hall** (1904) analyzed the relationship between psychology and religion from a **genetic** point of view. According to him, conversion experiences take place at puberty: a period during which several physiological changes occur. For him, adolescence is the apex of religious development. He collected an enormous amount of data on adolescents' spiritual transformations and their sexual development, and showed how a transition from egocentrism to altruism takes place during this period. The role of religion is to help the adolescent to grow safely.

Freud: Religion viewed as a neurosis

Notwithstanding what the founding fathers of psychology had envisioned, **Freud** (1913) gave a major set-back to the union of psychology and religion. He was notorious for his comments on religion, for he considered religion to be a manifestation of **universal obsessional nuerosis**. The formation of a religion, he believed, was based on **suppression**. The compulsive rituals of neurotics could be traced to the repression of a sexual desire. He laid emphasis on the Oedipal disturbance—a son's ambivalence toward his father—and related it to religious transformation. Even in his personal life, Freud disregarded religious ceremonies at his home.

Behaviorism: Religion as source of conditioning

For **Watson and Skinner**, both legendary figures in founding behaviorism, religion was a **powerful source for conditioning** individuals. According to Skinner (1974), the origin of religious behavior can be traced to the source of reinforcing stimuli. His experiments on **superstitious behavior** in pigeons demonstrate how the birds learned to display such behavior when reinforcement was scheduled without any consideration to their behavior. The behavior of birds under such conditions was peculiar. For example, one bird bowed without touching the floor and another turned round and round in circles. Superstitious behavior established through such adventitious reinforcement has a tendency to persist even under intermittent reinforcing conditions. Think, why do people wear the same dress in which they had been successful in their job interview on a previous occasion? While drawing parallels between animal and human learning, Skinner also believed that human behavior is complex, and that all religious behavior cannot be accounted for by superstition. His radical behaviorism focused on interpreting various facets of religion. Concepts like faith and belief explain the likelihood of occurrence of religious behavior in the same way as we can explain any other form of behavior. Explaining Skinner's position, Wulff (1991) wrote, "Faith....is our customary way of accounting for persistent behavior when we are ignorant of the environmental events that reinforce it" (p. 125).

Maslow: Type Y and Type Z

Revolting against the negative view of human nature offered by Freud and a mechanical explanation presented by the behaviorists, there emerged a third force in psychology, called **humanistic psychology**, based on an optimistic attitude about human nature. **Abraham Maslow** (1954; 1968), a popular leader of this school, contended that during the course of their development, individuals struggle to satisfy their needs that are arranged in a system or hierarchy ranging from deficit to growth needs. At the apex of this system is self-actualization, an embodiment of the expression of one's abilities, leading to the satisfaction of one's growth needs. According to Maslow, while those who experienced only self-actualization were the **type Y**, those who experienced full development at all levels and became priest-like and god-like were the **type Z**. Both could be considered healthy individuals in their own sense, but Maslow found that the number of type Y people in the population was very small and that they were often treated badly, in sharp contrast to the type Z who were considered desirable and virtuous (Tamney, 1992). Because religion tends to affirm self-denial and rejection of one's own needs, adherence to religion is likely to create conditions that might inhibit self-actualization. In fact, Gartner, Larson and Allen (1991) found a negative relationship between self-actualization and religiosity. Like religion, self-actualization also promotes a lifestyle but in modern societies, it is not bound by religion. Having stated this position on self-actualization, Maslow (1968) went on to assert that humanistic psychology is destined to replace religious influence in the near future.

Type Y: Who experience only self-actualization; **Type Z**: Who experience full development and become priest-like

Religion: Derived from **Latin "religio"** meaning greater than human power

As the momentum of scientific psychology began to escalate, the meeting ground of psychology and religion started getting lost. Historically speaking, several factors contributed to **destroy the relationship** between the two disciplines. **First**, the term "religion" does not mean the same thing to different groups of people. Literally, the word is derived from the Latin word "**religio**," which means greater than human power. It may refer to feelings related to such power, ritual acts, a mode of life and so on. In fact, the study of religion is so large that a tangible universal conclusion bound in an algorithm is almost impossible. And what happens when psychologists make an attempt to connect religion and psychology even in such adverse conditions? According to Wulff (1991), "...the application of psychology to religion is carried out by particular individuals, each with a personal history and outlook" (p. viii). Under such circumstances, they will be at odds and there will be chaos among those who try to interpret and explain the relationship between psychology and religion.

A **second** reason for psychologists avoiding religion is that it is not easily possible to trace the source of religious experience. Growth of religion is based on self-conscious reflection, but in terms of cultural practice it is appreciated for a while and then often dispensed with. Children are excited about Santa Claus but as they grow older, they learn that Santa does not exist and that they had grown up in a fictional environment.

Third, the growth of a science depends to a great extent on the beliefs of the scientists who are involved in that discipline. If a scientist does not believe in religion, he will not be interested in studying it. We learn from the history of psychology that Hugo Munsterberg (see chapter on law also), one of the pioneers in the field of applications of psychology at the beginning of this century, was opposed to the study of the relationship between psychology and religion and conveyed his position in no uncertain terms (Starbuck, 1937). As described earlier, Freud openly showed his distaste for religion. George Miller, a distinguished psychologist working at Princeton University, found his Christian beliefs and cognitive psychology at odds (See Tina Adler's *report*, 1991, Box 5.1).

BOX 5.1

George Miller, Christian beliefs, and cognitive psychology

"I was brought up believing that if you thought right—if you had the right thoughts—you could somehow be happy and healthy and successful. And I was also taught...psychology was a sin....So it took me a long time to look at psychology, but when I did, I came to it with a view that perhaps the mind really does have power to influence things."

He gave up being a Christian scientist and became a cognitive scientist and psycholinguist. His grandmother suffered terribly with glaucoma because she wouldn't go to a doctor.

(Excerpts from a report by Tina Adler in *APA Monitor*, December, 1991, p.13).

In an earlier study, Leuba (1934) randomly selected names of scientists listed in *The American Men of Science* and three professional directories and requested them to respond to questions regarding God and personal survival after death. The results of his survey are summarized in Table 5.1. He found that with greater eminence and increased knowledge of a scientist, there was a decline in the belief in God and immortality.

TABLE 5.1

Belief in God and immortality among scientists
(*Source*: Leuba, 1934)

	Lesser Scientists		Greater Scientists	
	1914	1933	1914	1933
(all figures in percentages)				
Belief in God				
Physical scientists	50	43	34	17
Biological scientists	39	31	17	12
Sociologists	29	13	19	13
Psychologists	32	13	13	12
Belief in personal survival after death				
Physical scientists	57	46	40	20
Biological scientists	45	32	25	15
Sociologists	52	31	27	10
Psychologists	27	12	9	2

However, things are changing. An another study (Martin-Causey, 2002) on primarily academic and primarily practicing psychologists shows that the term 'religion' does not seem to have the same negative connotation that it once did. Further, there were no significant differences between the two groups on their level of spirituality.

The **fourth** reason for the poor relationship between psychology and religion is attributed to the way the two disciplines are approached. Are we dealing with "The Psychology of Religion" or "Psychology in Religion" or "Psychology and Religion"? **"The Psychology of religion"** implies that religion will be subjected to a psychological analysis. The domain of this relationship represents an abstract approach to religion as a determinant of behavior (the reader will note that this is similar to the one mentioned in the chapter on law, Bartol & Bartol, 1994). Following this approach, we will be concerned with the way religion alters our behavior, how it promotes altruistic behavior or restraints violent behavior and so on. This approach may lead to an interpretation that religion is subordinate to psychology (Wulff, 1991).

Psychology of religion

"Psychology in religion" implies that religious experts will invite psychological analysis as and when it is required. It is well known that many people prefer psychological help from a clergy to visiting a psychotherapist during their personal crisis. In other words, the role of psychology would be limited as per the determination of its use by religious scholars and leaders.

Psychology in religion

"Psychology and religion" describes a relationship that is dominated by neither psychology nor religion. Both are independent disciplines but both could have several common interests. For example, do religious people require a therapy different from that required by non-religious people? Should we rely on religion when psychotherapy fails? Do we recognize the healing power of prayer? Do religious beliefs tend to reduce substance abuse? Does harsh religion increase substance abuse? And so on. In such cases both disciplines share issues of mutual interest but at the same time maintain their own identity.

Psychology and religion

While the "psychology in religion" approach has not been dealt with, the remaining two approaches, "psychology of religion" and "psychology and religion" have been dealt with in detail in the present chapter.

As a matter of scientific inquiry, applications of the general principles of behavior as applied to the understanding of religious behavior bolsters the essence of existence of psychology as a universal science. Conversely, if the discipline of psychology fails to recognize its limitations and refuses to learn from a source as powerful as religion (that controls a wide range of human behavior), the applications of psychology will suffer, much as what happened during the greater part of the twentieth century. At least three crucial questions have been largely overlooked in recent research on the psychology of religion. Firstly, are we putting too much emphasis on the effects of religion on mental and physical health? Secondly, could negative emotions associated with religion lead to adaptive outcomes in some situations? And thirdly, should we begin to devote greater attention to specific religious beliefs? By attending to issues such as these, research on the psychology of religion could become more meaningful (Exline, 2002).

PSYCHOLOGY OF RELIGION

Why are we interested in the psychology of religion? One reason is that religions do not merely exist in the mind (Snibbe & Markus, 2002). Our minds are cultural products, and the study of religion helps to seek these cultural groundings of psychological findings. It should also be interesting to know more about the psychological processes through which religion affects physical and mental health (Funder, 2002).

Concept of religion

> **Religion:** Institutional, formal, doctrinal experience

While William James (1902), differentiated between a first-hand **experiential religion** and a second-hand **institutional, inherited religion**, typically, religion and spirituality have been measured by **global parameters** such as frequency of church attendance, self-rated religiousness, etc. Hill and Pargament (2003) highlight some of the recent advances regarding the conceptualization of **religion and spirituality**. Lopez and Snyder (2003) too, have discussed the issues in the measurement of religiousness and spirituality and have differentiated between the two. They then go on to use a **hierarchical model** for organizing the scales at two levels: at the **dispositional level** are the scales that assess broad individual differences in people's religiosity and spirituality. At the **operational level**, there are scales that can measure the motivations behind a person's religiosity—the ways in which an individual may use religion in coping and prayer.

> **Spirituality:** Individual, subjective, freeing expression

One is thus witnessing, particularly in the US, a polarization between the terms **religion and spirituality**. While the former is representing **"an institutional, formal, outward, doctrinal, authoritarian, inhibiting experience, the latter representing an individual, subjective, emotional, inward, unsystematic, freeing expression"** (Koenig, *et al.*, 2001). Despite the seemingly heuristic value of such differentiations, they can be dangerous. Thus, religion seems to be bad, while spirituality seems to be good, although research has shown that there are helpful and harmful effects of both (Pargament, 2002). Further, such a bifurcation seems to override the empirical reality that people do not differentiate between the two. Rather, for most people, spirituality is experienced under an organized religious context (Marler & Hadaway, 2002). It thus seems better to think of the two as related rather than independent concepts (Hill *et al.* 2002).

Measurement of religious behavior and its applications

While we are still debating over the role of prayers in our schools, psychologists began to explore its effect more than a century ago. Galton (1869) was interested in finding out whether public prayers increased the longevity of the reigning sovereign. In fact, he found from his data that males in royal houses had the shortest life. Leuba's (1934) work on beliefs of scientists in God or personal survival after death was mentioned earlier in this chapter.

> **Thurstone:** Analysis of religious attitudes

L.L. Thurstone, a prominent University of Chicago scholar, who is famous for his contribution in the field of factor analysis, was interested in a quantitative analysis of religious attitudes. He and Chave (1929) invited a large number of subjects to arrange statements on religion in 11 piles in order of their preference. Another group of subjects were asked the extent to which these statements reflected their own views. In other words, an attempt was made to investigate the relevance of an item for an individual. Following an elaborate procedure, an equal appearing interval scale was constructed. Subsequent work on measurement of religious attitudes led them to construct five forms:

- **Attitude towards God**
- **Belief in reality of God**
- **Ideas of God influencing conduct**
- **Attitude towards Bible** (two forms)

Of all of the above scales, the **Attitude towards Bible scale** has been most widely used in psychological studies. Although Thurstone did not pursue his research on measurement of religious attitudes for long, his impact on this field was felt for several decades.

A number of scholars used the above and other related scales to investigate the factors that were related to religiousness. Thelma Thurstone (1934 cf. Bashaw & Bashaw, 1982), wife of L.L. Thurstone, noted that the Church, Sunday Observance and God scales correlated significantly to form a cluster, an important index in factor analysis to demonstrate how one group of items load on the items of other group/s. Positive attitudes toward birth control and evolution were also found to be related. **Yinger** (1969) developed a seven item scale to measure non-doctrinal religion.

TABLE 5.2

Sample items from Yinger's Non-Doctrinal Religion Scale (*Source:* Yinger, 1969)

Efforts to deal with the human situation by religious means, whatever the content of the beliefs and practices, seem to me to be misplaced, a waste of time and resources
Despite the often chaotic conditions of human life, I believe that there is order and pattern to existence that someday we'll come to understand.

Using Glock's (1962) dimensions of religion, another scale for the measurement of religious attitudes patterned after Guttman's cumulative technique, was developed by **Faulkner and DeJong** (1966). This scale had five subscales:

1. Ideological (belief)
2. Ritualistic (practice)
3. Intellectual (knowledge)
4. Experiential (feeling)
5. Consequential (effects)

Intercorrelations between the subscale items yielded some interesting observations. For example, the values of the relationship between ideological and ritualistic dimensions were higher for women samples than for male samples. Of the above five scales, the Ideological scale or the Orthodoxy scale was the single best measure in many situations.

A major contribution of the effort to measure religiousness emerged in the early finding that religion and prejudice are positively related. In their landmark research detailed in *The Authoritarian Personality,* Adorno *et al.* (1950) concluded that ethnocentric attitudes are shown by conventionally religious people who view religion as a means rather than as an end. For example, such people (**institutionalized type**) join a church with the specific intention of seeking the company of privileged people. On the other hand, several other people (**interiorized type**) join religious institutions with genuine intentions of attaining certain core values. Religiousness among individuals in this latter category do not show any significant relationship to prejudice. Research studies that failed to account for this type of difference among people of different religious orientations contributed to a great deal of misunderstanding and confusion for a long time in accounting for the relationship between religion and prejudice (Shaver, Lenaurer & Sadd, 1980; Wilson, 1973). It is clear from several sources that those who rescued Jews during the holocaust were either highly religious or not religious at all (Oliner & Oliner, 1988). After some painstaking researches by social psychologists, it has generally been agreed that the relationship between religious attitudes and prejudice is curvilinear (Hood, 1976; Hoge & Carroll, 1973). Friedrichs (1959) found that those who attended between 31-60 religious services in a year were more prejudiced than those who attended more than 60 services or no services at all.

Institutionalised type: Who join church for social reasons

Interiorized type: Who join church for certain core values

Seeking an explanation to why religious fundamentalists tend to be prejudiced, a study conducted on university students concluded that fundamentalist students reported receiving strong training in identification with the family religion from a very early age. Such results indicate how early family experiences serve as a template and influence behavior later in life (Altemeyer, 2003).

Perhaps it would be appropriate to say that the credit to keep alive the dying relationship between religion and psychology goes to Gordon Allport (1960) who was primarily interested in the personality profile of the two groups of religious people—institutionalized and interiorized—as identified by the Adorno group. In his analysis, Allport labeled them as people with **extrinsic and intrinsic religious orientations**. In the category of extrinsic orientation are those who view religion as instrumental and utilitarian and providing security and solace. It serves as a means to attain status and self-justification. The intrinsic type are those who find religion

Allport: Extrinsic and intrinsic religious orientation

TABLE 5.3

Sample items from the Allport-Ross Religious Orientation Scale (*Source*: Allport & Ross, 1967)

Items for intrinsic orientation:

My religious beliefs are what really lie behind my whole approach to life.

Religion is especially important to me because it answers many questions about the meaning of life.

Items for extrinsic orientation:

One reason for being a church member is that such membership helps to establish a person in the community.

The primary purpose of prayer is to gain relief and protection.

as a means for attaining genuine experiences, and embrace it as a way of life. In sharp contrast to the extrinsic type, such people orient their self toward religion and devoutly feel this consummation. In its classical sense, the diametrically opposed intrinsic-extrinsic dimension of Allport is widely respected in the academic circles but the psychometric analysis of the test developed by Allport and his associates (1967) has many limitations (Donohue, 1985). At the same time, after a careful analysis of the implications of intrinsic-extrinsic dimension, Feagin (1964) found that the intrinsic and extrinsic items in the Allport-Ross Religious Orientation measure do not correlate significantly. They seem to represent independent factors.

Research that followed using the Allport-Ross measure indicated that individuals with an extrinsic orientation showed a conservative orientation, prejudice, authoritarianism and fear of death (for a useful review, see Wulff, 1991). Those with an intrinsic orientation displayed positive correlation with an internal sense of locus of control and negative correlation with depression. Several other correlates of religious orientation are, however, not as clear.

Batson: Quest orientation: Sensitive to the needs of others

Among other prominent researchers in the field of measurement of religious orientation, **Daniel Batson** stands out as a leading figure. In addition to intrinsic and extrinsic orientations, Batson and his colleagues (1982) developed an **Interactional scale** that measures **Quest Orientation**. From his data, he found out that whereas intrinsically religious people have an internal need to be helpful to others and go beyond the level of help requested by the needy person, people with quest orientation are sensitive to the needs of other people and act out as per needs of the needy person. **Factor analysis** of the Interactional Scale (see Table 5.4) revealed three factors: **identity** (items 1 and 2), **doubt** (items 3 and 4), and **residual** (items 5 and 6). His field studies on the Good Samaritan led to our understanding of the circumstances in which people help others without any reciprocity or self-interest. Unfortunately, because the correlations between the factors of the scale were inconsistent, Batson concluded that the content of the scales measuring religious orientation limits its use.

TABLE 5.4

Factor analysis of Batson's Interactional Scale

Identity factor

1. I have been driven to ask religious questions out of a growing awareness of the tensions in my world and in my relation to my world.
2. My religious development has emerged out of my growing sense of personal identity.

Doubt factor

3. It might be said that I value my religious doubts and uncertainties.
4. Questions are far more central to my religious experience than are answers.

Residual

5. I do not want my religious convictions to change in the next few years.
6. God wasn't very important to me until I began to ask questions about the meaning of my own life.

Note: #5 was reversed in scoring.

Experimental and non-experimental research on religion

Latane and Darley's (1970) famous experiment on the bystander's reluctance to help others in need opened a new vista of research in social psychology. In a study, Darley and Batson (1973) found that the conditions and the style in which help is offered is crucial in understanding **Good Samaritan behavior**. They noticed that when their subjects were in a hurry, the context of a situation led to a decrease in helping behavior. On the other hand, subjects scoring high on the Interactional Scale were tentative in their help in contrast to low scorers who insisted on helping the victim. Their major conclusion was that religiosity of subjects was an important factor in those conditions in which the subjects had decided to provide help to the victim. In a subsequent study by Batson and Gray (1981), it was found that subjects with intrinsic orientation were helpful under both help-wanted and help-not-wanted conditions but those with quest orientation were responsive only to the extent a needy person requested for help.

Bock and Warren (1972) placed their high, moderate and low-scoring subjects on religiousness in a **Milgram-type** experimental condition in which an accomplice often fails at his/her task. They found that relatively higher levels of electric shocks were administered by the moderate group of subjects as compared to those who scored at either extremes on religiousness.

In order to investigate the relationship between religious attitudes and religious behavior, Fishbein and Ajzen (1974) requested subjects to complete questionnaires measuring their religious attitudes and to indicate the frequency with which they engaged in 70 different kinds of religious behavior (for example, attending religious services, donating money, etc.). The data revealed that no single religious behavior correlated significantly with the religious attitudes but when a composite score based on all the 70 behaviors was prepared, the relationship between religious attitudes and behavior became highly significant. Fishbein and Ajzen emphasized that such results tend to support their theory of reasoned action. They proposed that unless attitudes and subjective norms (normative social pressures) are aligned, it is difficult to bridge the gap between belief and action of individuals.

Are religiously committed people involved in helping others more than those who are moderately religious or not at all religious? Benson and co-workers (1980) reported that in contrast to non-religious students, the religiously committed students worked longer as tutors, relief workers, and so on. A comparison of non-attenders and church-attenders showed that the charitable contribution of the latter group was more than double. With increase in the frequency of visits to church from once or twice a month to weekly, the contributions of members again rose sharply (Hodgkinson & Weitzman, 1992). Does religiosity influence political attitudes? Duriez and co-workers (2002) note that even apart from its effect on values, religiosity does provide additional information in predicting attitudes.

It is not intended here to offer an exhaustive review of experimental and non-experimental studies concerning the relationship between psychology and religion. From the few studies mentioned above, it is clear that religion tends to influence behavior ranging from prejudice to altruism, and from volunteering to mental health.

Recent issues in the measurement of religion

Recent advances in the measurement of religion show that religiosity is far from being a uniform process. It is a complex variable, involving cognition, emotion, behavior, interpersonal and physiological dimensions. Today, there are at least 125 scales (Hill & Hood, 1999) that are available, but most go unused by psychologists. The reason for this is that the majority have been published in specialized journals, for example, the *International Journal for the Psychology of Religion* and *The Journal for Scientific Study of Religion*, that are rarely consulted by psychologists and other health workers. This could also be the reason why the area is under-represented in educational curricula (Shafranske & Maloney, 1990), or are not mentioned in textbooks of psychology (Lehr & Spilka, 1989).

This picture is fortunately beginning to change and some of the more promising areas for which scales have been constructed have been cited by Hill and Pargament (2003):

1. Perceived closeness to God.
2. Religion as an orienting motivating force.
3. Religious support.
4. Religious and spiritual struggle.

FUNCTIONS OF RELIGION/SPIRITUALITY

BOX 5.2

Application of spiritualism in life and at work (Venkatesan, *The Times of India*, March 24, 2003)

Today business houses are gradually realizing the importance of the spirituality factor as a big help to their operation and productivity. With the shift from a linear mechanistic way of doing business to a more organic and holistic one, spirituality is seen as offering definite advantages. It is in this context that applied spirituality and eco-systemic perspectives of business are being sought after.

What is applied spiritualism? Applied spirituality is an application of spiritual knowledge in raising inner awareness. The difference between applied spirituality and applied rationality lies in the key term "awareness." The ancient scriptures of India mention that ordinary human beings can rise to a higher level of awareness, where one obtains total awareness of reality. Those who believe that the locus of control is predominantly internal rather than external are able to bring down their stress levels as an increased awareness reveals the futility of impressing others.

One of the major reasons why social psychologists should be interested in studying religion is that religion serves a number of **social functions**. It also helps to clarify that religion is basically a social variable and not something supernatural or divine.

Religion as social support

Religion forms a social support system

Probably the most commonly perceived function of religion/spirituality (RS) is its significance and use as a **social support** variable. The religious congregation is a powerful support system for the members. Using instruments designed to measure the social support function of religion, a national survey of African Americans was carried out. The results indicate that two out of three respondents indicated that they needed the support of their fellow congregational members (Taylor & Chatters, 1988). Religious social support is associated with lower levels of depression and greater life satisfaction (Fiala, Bjork & Gorsuch, 2002) and is probably more helpful in stressful situations (Maton, 1989), such as the Gulf war (Pargament, Koenig & Perez, 2000).

The effects of religious social support are generally more far-reaching and deeper than that of secular social support. Through multiple regression analysis, a powerful tool for statistically determining the predictive power of independent variables, religious social support emerged as a significant predictor of psychological adjustment even after controlling for the effects of general social support (VandeCreek & co-workers, 1999). How deep does it run? It is commonly seen and now even established through research that a congregation's support during personal crises may even include provision of help with children, financial help, meals, emotional support and moral support (Plante & Sherman, 2001). Kahn and Antonucci (1980) liken a religious support system to a "support convoy" that can accompany a person from birth to death. Although people making up the convoy may change, the individual can count on the assistance from a group of like-minded people with similar values and even a similar world-view (Ellison & Levin, 1998). The effect of the support is further strengthened by the belief that others are praying for the individual's welfare. Whether the outcome is in the form of health disadvantage (Zuckerman & co-workers, 1984), minority status disadvantage (Steffen & co-workers, 2001), educational disadvantage (Krause, 1998) or female gender disadvantage (Strawbridge & co-workers, 2000), regular church attendance offers a lifeline of resources. The congregation can also connect the individual to resources to which it may not have access, along with allaying the feelings of isolation, low control and despair (Thoresen & Harris, 2002).

Perhaps what we now need to know is the limiting aspects of religion as social support. Findings show that when people start feeling that God has abandoned them, they may inadvertently subvert the efficacy of the treatment they are undergoing (Powell, Shahabi & Thoresen, 2003). In other words, the impact emanating from religion can fizzle out.

Regular church attendance leads to positive effect

In contrast to the above, wherein the salutary effects of religion are due to the social support provided by the congregation, evidence is also available to show that regular church attendance may be associated with an ongoing experience of positive emotions and not just an absence of negative emotions (Idler & Kasl, 1997). Regular church attendance may encourage meaningful social roles that provide a sense of self-worth and purpose through the act of helping. Those nursing home residents who were given work responsibilities lived longer than those who were not (Langer & Rodin, 1976); helping others also lowers depression and bolsters feelings of personal control (Kraus, Herzog & Baker, 1992), and voluntary work may even reduce mortality (Oman, Thoresen & McMohan, 1999). Such positive emotions may also be induced by the habitual periods of rest on Sabbath (Muller, 1999).

Religion as attachment

Why does perceived closeness to God lead to better health related outcomes? Attachment theorists liken God to an **attachment figure** (Kaufman, 1981; Kirkpatrick, 1995). As children look to parents for support, so do people look to God for support especially in times of grief and other stressful situations, such as transplant surgery (Tix & Frazier, 1998), medical illness

(Koenig & co-workers, 1998) and natural disasters (Smith & co-workers, 2000). As would be predicted on the basis of attachment theory, people who are closer to God perceive less depression and higher self esteem, (Maton, 1989), less loneliness, (Kirkpatrick, Kellas & Shillito, 1993), greater relational maturity (Hall & Edwards, 2002), and psychosocial competence (Pargament & co-workers, 1988). The crucial role played by religion is seen by the fact that results such as these have not been explained by non-religious factors such as general coping, demographic and other variables. Hence the unique role played by religion seems more useful in as much as it contributes to psychological well being (Tix & Frazier, 1998).

God as a significant other: Religion provides an attachment figure

Religion as vehicle for social learning

There are many situations for which we lack role models and even direct experience. A simple example faced by us is how to react when we face a bereavement. Should one remain quiet, should one wail loudly, what should one say, should one comfort the bereaved, and if so, how does one comfort the bereaved, are just some of the many questions that arise. Why talk of bereavement? Even a minor instance of pain, distress or loss of some precious belonging can create maladjustment.

Religion provides social models

It is for situations such as the above, for which **exemplars** are not readily available, that regular church attendance helps. Watching people in the congregation and attempting to understand their behavior in similar circumstances can allay many of the fears one has, and provide answers otherwise unavailable. The church and its members provide opportunities to observe vicariously, yet consistently, people who model a variety of altruistic behaviors. These include positive, hopeful, compassionate and caring behavior (Bandura, cf. Powell *et al.*, 2003).

Religion as purpose of life

Religion serves as an important **orienting** force. In fact, religions around the world encourage their followers to see themselves and the world as something sacred. As early as in 1950, Allport too concluded that religion provides an overarching framework that provides **meaning and purpose** to life. Having such a motive to live has important implications for health. For one, if people consider their lives as being sacred, they are more liable to treat it with respect and care; secondly, even in the midst of trauma, religion can provide a purpose to life (Baumeister, 1991), and can produce coherence in personality when faced by destructive social and cultural forces (Hill & Pargament, 2003). Research findings also corroborate the hypothesis that having a meaning in life leads to better health outcomes. People report less conflict with, derive greater satisfaction from, and invest more time, money and energy into those aspects that they consider sacred (Mahoney & co-workers, 1999; Tarakeshwar & co-workers, 2001). Further, people who report a higher number of spiritual strivings also indicate greater purpose in life and higher levels of well being (Emmons, Cheung & Tehrani, 1998). It has also been associated with better mental health, and family relations, and lower levels of drug use, alcohol use and sexual promiscuity (Payne & co-workers, 1991).

Religion provides life with a purpose

THE DEVELOPMENT OF RELIGIOUSNESS

If religion has such a pervasive effect on our lives, it is but natural to ask what could be some of the factors that heighten or lower one's beliefs in religion or one's religiosity? Little attention seems to have been given to this aspect but at least two studies can be cited. Both are important from the social psychological point of view because they attempt to unravel the role of social influence by primary socialization agencies in the development of religiosity among adolescents and college students.

Family plays important role in development of religious attitude in children

The first study by King and colleagues (2002) attempted to explore the impact of the **family** and the **peers** on adolescents' experience of God. A sample of 413 children from the age group 13-17 years were asked to respond to a questionnaire designed to assess religious importance, religious experience, family religious support and peer religious support. The latter two were assessed on the basis of frequency of talking about religious issues and participation in religious activities. The findings provide very strong evidence for the role played by the family and peers in the development of religiousness. Both these variables were found to be significant predictors of adolescent experience of God and the importance of religion in their lives, showing that social influence from "significant others" is important in the development of religiousness among adolescents.

The second study is by Lee (2002), who attempted to explore into the development of religiousness among college students. The question that he had in mind was whether the **college environment** would influence changes in the religious beliefs of its students. Based on earlier research on student religiosity and theories in social psychology, three hypotheses were developed. These were:

1. Overall, students will experience a decline in religious beliefs and convictions.
2. The characteristics and experience identified in earlier profiles of the disaffiliated would also appear among college students who disaffiliated.
3. Greater involvement in diversity related experiences would be strongly associated with weakened religious beliefs.

Social diversity experiences do not awaken religiousness

The results were indeed very surprising! First, while students tend to show a change in their religious beliefs, more students were found to experience a **strengthening** of religious convictions than those whose faith showed a weakening. Moreover, the study clarified that engaging in diversity related activities does not necessarily lead to the weakening of religious convictions. Another unexpected finding was that institutional affiliation does not affect changes in students' religious beliefs. Elsewhere in the chapter it has been said that psychologists are wary of studying religion because it is felt that the power of religion has decreased in this age of science and rationality. The above findings show that even college students, who could be considered an extremely impressionable group, are vulnerable to changes in values because of institutional identity formation, often remain unchanged as far as their religious affiliation is concerned.

PSYCHOLOGY AND RELIGION

Religion and physical health

In the recent past, a number of researchers have suggested that the investigation of spiritual and/or religious factors in health is clearly warranted and even clinically relevant. However, what needs to be understood is "Does religion cause changes in health?" Oman and Thoresen, (2002) have used causal path diagrams to arrive at four divergent interpretations.

BOX 5.3

Is religion of any interest to scientists?

While we may not still know how scientific religion is, scientists are definitely becoming interested in the ways in which religion works. Evidence for this is a crucial exchange between modern science and Buddhism held at the Dalai Lama's residence at Dharamshala, India, in October, 2002.

The participants were well known scientists: the Nobel laureate physicist, Steven Chu, leader of the human genome project, Eric Lander, chemist Luigi Luisi, geneticist Ursula Goodenough, physicist Arthur Zajonc and biophysicist Michel Bitbol. Together they discussed the nature of matter and life with Buddhist monks led by the Dalai Lama himself. Most scientists knew little about Buddhism, but felt it important to have a dialogue. Chu later explained what had brought him here: "As scientists, I think our sight often becomes too narrow and we are unable to touch the broader humanistic issues that concern us all." Lander too agreed: "Science is posing ethical questions today that need to be answered urgently. For me, this conference is really about posing those questions to Buddhism and looking at the reactions." The origin of life, the testing of fetuses for genetic abnormalities and the use of animals in research were among the topics discussed.

(*The Times of India*, October 7, 2002)

Religion influences health by:

1. Any mechanism, including factors such as social support and improved health behaviors.
2. Additional mechanisms, such as enhanced positive states (faith, hope, inner peace).
3. Offering psychological strength for acquiring and maintaining positive health behavior.
4. Causally influencing health by distant healing and prayer.

The Ironson-Woods Spirituality-Religiousness Index

Whereas health related outcomes, usually positive, have been reported throughout the world, the reason for the health-religion nexus remains a mystery. An example is the oft-supposed relation between religiosity and health outcomes being due to the social support function served by it. Using the **The Ironson-Woods Spirituality-Religiousness Index**, it has been found that the relationship between spirituality, religiousness and important health outcomes for HIV patients was not due to social support (Ironson & co-workers, 2002). If the effects are not due to social support factor, what could be the mechanism through which religion works? Koenig and co-workers (2002) examined the possibility of religion affecting health through known neuro-endocrine and immune mechanisms. It has been suggested that the relation between religion and health could be akin to the effects of psychoneuroimmunology (PNI). We next examine the effects of religion, both direct and indirect, on the course of certain life-taking diseases.

Just as diseases such as tuberculosis and herpes have been found to be prone to the influence of psycho-social factors, so too is the case of **HIV AIDS**. In fact, the case for HIV is even stronger, since HIV is due to a deficiency of the immune system, and any factor that affects the immune system should alter the course of the disease. In particular, the way in which people cope with stressors, their social connections, and their attitudes and beliefs have been found to play a significant role in the course of HIV infection. What is interesting for us is that these coping mechanisms are in turn affected by religious and spiritual beliefs, thereby playing an indirect role in the course of HIV infection as well (Ironson & Schneiderman, 2002). Similarly, Koenig and Cohen (2002) discuss the ways in which religious involvement enhances social support and reduces stress, and in doing so may decide **wound healing** and **post operative recovery**. While the cure for cancer continues to elude us, an emerging area of **psycho-oncology** provides new hope for the understanding of the psycho-social needs of cancer patients. There is evidence to show that psycho-social variables have an impact on both cancer recurrence and survival; further, psycho-social intervention, including religion and spirituality, has a role to play in the support, treatment and prognosis of **cancer patients** (Spiegel & Fawzy, 2002). Religious rituals play an important role in the cancer trajectory (diagnosis, treatment and post treatment) of breast cancer, and are an important resource for coping, meaning and social support even in a traditional culture such as that in Central Appalachia (Simpson, 2001).

While the majority of the research points to positive implications of religion, religion could also be **negatively** implicated. A study on 220 Jewish women completed surveys as part of an ongoing study of breast cancer risk counseling. The results of the study show that intention to follow routine recommendations for mammography, intention to perform monthly breast examination and interest in genetic testing for breast cancer susceptibility was positively related to the cultural identity of the women but inversely related to their religious identity (Bowen & co-workers, 2003). Thoreson and Harris (2002), too, contend that a certain amount of skepticism is in order. While one needs to remain open to the possibility, one also needs to look critically at the empirical evidence. Questions that are in order: do specific religious factors influence health outcomes? What possible mechanisms might explain a relation if one exists? Are there any recommendations for health professionals at this point of time? At present the relation appears far more complex & modest than some realize.

Religion and mental health

Psychologists and for that matter, social scientists in general, have kept their distance from religion/spirituality (RS). Clinicians have little to do with religious leaders and while they seek referrals from religious groups, they rarely make referrals to the clergy. In research too, RS seems to be an understudied factor in health related research in psychology, psychiatry, family practice, gerontology, etc. In fact, Weaver & co-workers, (1998) found that only 2.7% of articles in APA journals between the years 1991 to 1994 included a RS factor. And yet, we all know that religion and mental health have a deep relationship.

What are the reasons for such a neglect in both research and practice? Hill and Pargament (2003) point to at least **three** reasons:

1. RS as concepts are less central and important to psychologists than to people at large.
2. RS are mistakenly assumed as falling outside the purview of scientific study.
3. RS are believed to be far less important in the age of science and rationality.

Even in studies that have included the RS factor, they have been only add-on variables, hardly ever the central focus of studies (Larson & co-workers, 1986). So where demographic variables are being studied, RS is just one more variable added to others such as age, gender, educational qualification, etc. Another problem is that RS has been assessed mostly as single or other global indices, due to which the effect does not appear as strongly as it should (Koenig & co-workers, 2001).

Despite such lacunae, RS has appeared as an extremely robust variable in predicting health related outcomes. A meta analysis of 1,26,000 participants, has shown that people who had higher RS involvement had 29% greater odds for survival (McCullough & co-workers, 2000), suggesting that even simplistic measures of religion predict health outcomes significantly (Koenig & co-workers, 2001). Thus, the recent interest shown by psychologists (for example, see Pargament) is a timely move in addressing the complex social phenomena called religion (Cacioppo, 2002).

Relating religion and mental health involves a double jeopardy, for neither mental health nor religion mean the same things to different people. Batson and Ventis (1982) made an attempt to solve the problem of the conceptualization of religion and by grouping various studies of religion in different interpretations of mental health and then the subsequent emerging valence provided the index of their relationship. The mental health issues were classified under **seven** categories: absence of mental illness, adequacy of social behavior, worry and guilt, self-acceptance/actualization, personal competence/control, open-mindedness, and unification and organization. In terms of the first criteria of absence of mental illness, religion constituted a positive effect. However, using other criteria implied that religion was associated with impaired psychological functioning. Further, while the **extrinsic religious orientation** showed **negative** relationship with mental health, the **intrinsic religious orientation** was **positively** related to all seven criteria of mental health, a finding with which several scholars have disagreed (Schumaker, 1992). Batson and Ventis did not have much to offer on the quest orientation.

The **connection** between religion and physical health also remains largely a mystery. Are these effects owing to supernatural influence of a divine creator? Or might natural mechanisms be invoked to help explain the connection? (Koenig & co-workers, 2002). When we look at the therapeutic functions of **confession** for example, what do we find? There is data from Finland suggesting that a **very natural mechanism**, that of **catharsis**, can be used to explain its effect. Data from Finland on the role of confession clarifies that it is not the form of the confession, but rather its function, that is, giving relief, in line with pastoral counseling and psychotherapy, that plays a significant role. The goal should therefore be not to stimulate confession *per se* but rather to stimulate ways of helping people (Kettunen, 2002). Even in Pakistan, where Sufism is used as a faith healing process, its appeal may probably be best understood in terms of a **quest for recognition** (Frogett, 2001), whereas in a study in the US, it has been concluded that praying about difficult experiences to God acts as **self disclosure** to God (VandeCreek, Janus, Pennebaker & co-workers, 2002).

Gender differences in the religion-health nexus

Historically speaking, religions around the world have not treated men and women equally and fairly. At the global level, women are fighting for their abortion rights; at the local level, they are pleading courts to spare them from genital mutilation (for example, in Egypt) or freedom to discard the veil (Burka) and dress freely. Imagine what impact religion will have on the mental health of Muslim women in the USA. if they are ordered, as per Muslim religious requirement, to wear Burka? After all, not long ago they did not have the right to divorce their husbands or to vote in the elections. Studies on the relationship between religion and mental health of women have yielded mixed results. Shaver, Lenaurer and Sadd (1980) showed high religiosity was associated with improved mental and physical health. Spilka, Hood and Gorsuch (1985) concluded that while religion may be responsible for suppressing mental disorder and free socialization, psychopathology and religion are not positively related. Religion helps in dealing with stress and maintaining self-esteem and self-identity. It is also true that a number of problems of women are rooted in their socialization leading to sex-typing. Higher incidence of depression and poor sense of adequacy in them may be traced to such differential socialization in which religion plays an important role.

One reason for the gender differences in the effectiveness of religion could be in the ways in which **men and women perceive their religiousness**. Using a short self-report measure of religious activity, developed so as to be comparable across religions, people from four different religions (230 Christians, 56 Hindus, 157 Jewish, and 87 Muslims) were asked about their religious activity. Results indicated that women (n=302) described themselves as significantly less active than did men (n=226). Interestingly, this was confined only to the Christian group, indicating that the gender differences could be tempered by cultural and religious affiliation difference (Loewenthal & co-workers, 2002).

Religion and psychological coping

Religion has been seen to afford an extremely strong **coping mechanism**. Thus, when a powerful earthquake took place in the area of Bhuj in **western India,** survivors were found to use their faith in Karma for restoring peace and harmony in their lives (Priya, 2002). Similar were the findings on refugees from **Bosnia** and **Kosova.** A study was conducted on 138, 17-79 year old refugees from Kosova and Bosnia who had recently resettled in the US. A path analysis model demonstrated that optimism was positively related to positive religious coping, while hope was negatively related to negative religious coping (Ai, Peterson, & Huang, 2003). Even in times of peace we find religion helping people to **cope with adversity**. Findings on **African American** women suggest that religion/spirituality help these women in a number of ways. "It helps them to interrogate and accept reality, to gain an insight and courage needed to engage in spiritual surrender, confront and transcend limitations, identify and grapple with existential questions and life lessons, recognize purpose and destiny, define character and act within subjectively meaningful moral principles, achieve growth and trust in the viability of transcendent sources of knowledge and communication" (Mattis, 2002). That religion helps people to **cope with severe psychiatric disorders** is borne out by Reger and Rogers (2002). They found that people with schizophrenia, schizo-affective disorder and bipolar disorder reported using religion for a significantly greater number of years than those with depression. They also found that schizophrenics and those with schizoaffective disorders reported the most benefit from religious coping, and therefore feel that it is imperative that Christians serve and comprehensively treat this population. The role of religion as a **buffer to life stress** is also supported by the finding that religiosity reduces the impact of life stress on initial substance use and also on the rate of growth in substance use over time among adolescents in the US. So much so, that religiosity was inversely related to alcohol, tobacco and marijuana use (Wills, Yaeger & Sandy, 2003).

Religion and sexual behavior

The issue of religion affecting sexual behavior of people around the world has received a great deal of attention. A sexual act that does not lead to procreation has been traditionally condemned by almost all religions. The hostility of Christianity to sex is known for centuries. Although Jesus did not say much about sex, St. Paul regarded celibacy as superior to marriage. Given a long history of the impact of religion on sexual behavior, Patton (1988) stated that Catholicism has caused severe psychological damage to its adherents because they have suffered from shame, anxiety and guilt that is related to sexual behavior. In his famous report, Kinsey & co-workers (1948) concluded that religion had its impact on masturbation among men and women. The more religious they were, the less often they masturbated. As compared to inactive Protestants, among devout Catholics and Jews the frequency of masturbation was lower. Kinsey and co-workers (1953) also showed religious backgrounds of females had a significant impact on their sexual outlets. The rate of oral genital sex and achieving orgasm within a few years of marriage was higher among them as compared to the previous generation.

Sociologists in particular and social scientists in general were concerned about the higher **rate of suicide** among Protestants than Catholics (Pescosolido, 1990). Durkheim (1897) related this phenomenon to the less integrated Protestant system in which an individual does not subordinate to rituals. Because Catholicism provides a strong order and subordination, it brings a sense of purpose in relating with others and respect for group life. Such a framework keeps an individual away from personal troubles that constitute potential causes for suicide. Analysis of religious publication rates by Breault and Barkey (1982) led them to discover that it had a life-saving impact. Steven Stack (1992) concluded that suicide and religiosity are negatively correlated, that is, the higher the religiosity, the lower the suicide rate. Commenting on how religion contributes to lowering suicide rates and **depression,** he argued that an individual's belief in a purpose in suffering and spiritual success may reduce the incidence of suicide and depression.

We now consider issues concerning the **use of religion in psychotherapy**. "The antipathy of contemporary psychology to religion," writes Hood (1992), "is well established in the experimental literature" (p. 110). Such a pessimistic conclusion is now changing, albeit slowly. For example, such a change is seen in one issue of *American Psychological Association Monitor* (August, 1996) which contains an article on "Religion and Psychology Share Ideals and Beliefs" (p. 47). In the same journal, Clay has summarized the views of several psychologists who were participating in the 1996 APA Convention. It is interesting to note that although approximately 75% Americans are guided by some religious beliefs in their lives, only a third of psychologists feel the same impact. Does this discrepancy cause any implication in psychotherapy? How would an **atheist psychotherapist** handle a highly religious patient with an entirely different sets of values? One danger is that consciously or unconsciously, a psychotherapist may subtly inject his own values in a patient that may later cause more harm than good. For many psychologists, psychology has substituted religion in understanding guilt, human values and ethics. Several such issues are of serious concern to psychologists and they are addressed in a publication of American Psychological Association, *Religion and the Clinical Practice of Psychology* (1996).

Available data show that approximately 40% of Americans would prefer to consult a **clergyperson** first for advice concerning their personal problems. This preference for a clergyperson is reported to be very high among Afro-Americans partly due to their lack of faith in psychotherapy and partly due to affordability. The issue at heart in picking up psychotherapy or religion is the fundamental difference between their approaches. While the focus of psychology is individualistic, religion has a communal orientation. A person having roots in a communal environment is bound to find himself/herself at odds with a therapy that would help an individual to focus on his/her own self. Needless to say that if psychologists work with religious leaders without sacrificing their scientific focus, they can achieve a lot by way of community intervention. After all, for centuries religious leaders have been addressing psychological problems of the members of the community. It is time that psychology associates with them to make a stronger base in the community than ever before. No one will disagree that such a merger has its problems but a few will believe, as Ellis (1962) opined, that religion is a major source of neurotic disturbances.

Psychologists interested in religion lack adequate models to conceptualize how religion contributes to positive mental health. If God is viewed as a caring, dependable friend, some extension of attachment theory already available in psychology can be useful. The problem is that when distressed people begin to look at God for help, they are already classified by psychologists as having psychiatric problems. However, such a change in moving toward God may be a sign of restoring the lost balance rather than slipping deeper into trouble. Besides conceptual problems, psychologists have to focus on variables that are reliable in assessing the real contribution of religion in sustaining mental health. Recent research has shown that hard variables (for example, divorce, death, etc.) show positive relationship between religion and mental health but the soft variables like dogmatism and rigidity bear relationships that are questionable (Gartner, 1996 as quoted by Clay at the APA Convention).

In view of the large bulk of findings relating health to religion and other psycho-social factors, it has been suggested that a **multi-disciplinary bio-psychosocial model of health** (with inputs from medicine, psychology, sociology, social work and religion) would be more efficacious than the presently used medical model of health (Zittel & co-workers, 2002). At the same time we should not overemphasize the positive role of religion: it can become addictive, and extremes of any form is not wholesome for the individual. In fact, such an obsession with religion has not only harmful effects for the person but also devastating effects for the family. Taylor (2002) discusses connections between scrupulosity and obsessive-compulsive disorder, and the effects on the addict, the co-dependent spouse and children and even the adult children.

SPIRITUAL HEALING OR FAITH HEALING

Spiritual healing is probably the oldest known form of treatment and it has been practiced in virtually every culture and across recorded history. In traditional cultures it has been administered by shamans and what has been called medicine man, and has been very much a part of the fabric of the culture. A recent volume, *Handbook of Complementary and*

Alternative Therapies in Mental Health, edited by Shannon (2002) has a chapter on "Spiritual Healing" in which a large number of mechanisms and techniques of faith healing have been explained (Benor, 2002). The mechanisms described range from conventional energetic, to mechanical or even chemical interventions. The treatment may be handson treatment, generally lasting for 15-60 minutes on a weekly basis. Distance healing has also been practiced and may be sent as a mental intent, meditation or prayer by a group of healers or by individuals. The length of the treatment and its periodicity would be determined by the severity of the condition, fewer sessions being required for less acute conditions. Some of the specific techniques are therapeutic touch, reiki, qigong, and prayer.

Faith healing in some form or the other is common around the world and cuts across cultural divides. In the Luo culture of **west Kenya,** learning to heal is deeply imbedded in the close relationship between the grandmother and the grandchild. Through shared daily experiences in life, the child gradually develops social skills such as social sense, respect and compassion for people as well as practical skills (Prince & Geissler, 2001). Faith healers in **Pakistan** use techniques of suggestion and cultural psychotherapeutic procedures. One such procedure is based on a mystical aspect of Islam known as Sufism (Frogett, 2001). So great is the impact of such faith healing, that Saeed, Gater, Hussain and Mubbashar (2000) suggest that there should be methods of collaboration that will permit people with mental health problems to access effective and culturally appropriate treatment. (Raghuram & co-workers 2002), describe a Hindu temple in **south India** where people have been known to come for help with serious mental disorders. A study of 31 patients who came and stayed at the temple for 3 months revealed a gain of nearly 20%, a figure matching gains made by many psychotropic drugs. In addition, family care givers too thought that the patients had improved during their stay at the temple.

Faith healing is not just a product of the East. It has also been used in the traditional cultures of the West. In **Finland** a healing ritual based on the ancient Finnish epic Kalevala's poetry is used (Hiltunen, 2001). An in-depth study of cancer patients was conducted by Simpson (2001) in **central Appalachia.** The entire period of diagnosis, treatment and post treatment phases revealed the strong influence of religion at all phases, and the survivors felt that not only did God help them in coping with the disease but it was God only who had healed them. Native teachings important for faith healers have been found in the culture of the **American Indians:** among the Mohawks, the Iroquois and other **Canadian Indians** (Forest, 2000). From down under, we have data on how the Hmong women of **Australia** use a type of shamanism to deal with maternal death at childbirth (Rice, 2000).

While the modern Western society has generally been skeptical of spiritual healing, we do find spiritual healing being used as a **therapy for chronic pain** (Abbot & co-workers, 2001), and for the treatment of **ADDH** children (Bussing & co-workers, 2002). So pervasive is the effect of spiritual healing, that a **faith community nursing network** has been set up in central Texas, based on and emerging out of the growing body of knowledge on parish nursing (Pattilo & co-workers, 2002).

All of the above suggest that there is probably a critical need for change in health management systems the world over. According to Struve (2001), religious organizations can facilitate the change, by not just redefining health but also by shaping primary health services of the future. The model that is proposed is that **faith based communities** become the core health model, the emphasis being to teach what it means to be human and healthy. The goal should be that no illness needs to dominate over the person. Within this context, health information, education, prayer, care and support for most chronic illnesses, life style change and end of life concerns could be addressed (Struve, 2001).

Some traditional forms of faith healing

The helping profession can draw from a variety of spiritual traditions from across the world. Brandon (2001) reported at least **five** such traditions: **Zen, Sufi, Quaker, Tao** and the **Hassidic-Judaistic** tradition. The common denominator for all of these is the concern with living rather than with theological arguments. Moreover, rather than being exclusive, the ancient traditions can complement modern scientific theory, and can play a therapeutic role in the development of a healthy society. One can draw from the "living" myths such as the *Song of Songs, Tao Te Ching, Rig Veda, The New Testament* and the *Ancient Myth* of Hainuvele, to develop a healthy society (Leeming, 2002).

Shamanism

Shamanism: Group of techniques using altered states of consciousness in the priest

Shamanism refers to a group of techniques, using **altered states of consciousness** in the shaman, that is, the priest, who then enters the world of spirits, obtains information and uses that information to heal and to help other people (Krippner, 2000). The efficacy of shamanistic healing is seen in the description of a heavily traumatized child soldier in Mozambique (Igreja & Riedesser, 2002), in counseling clients with alcohol problems (Walters, 2001) and in the prevention of neonatal death, stillbirth and maternal death (Rice, 2000).

The ways in which the global perspective can help advance psychological theory is exemplified by the study of the many analogies that exist between Jungian and shamanistic dream imagery (Elsensohn, 2002). Thus the study of shamanistic practice can help enrich theory and practice of Western Psychoanalyisis (Igreja & Riedesser, 2002).

When one attempts to understand the personal mythology of a shaman, and the ways in which a shaman is called and initiated, there are strong parallels with the native American Indian culture (Terhune-Young, 2001). There is a very telling account of how one individual became a shaman. Elements can be drawn from a variety of matriarchical systems (the Mohawk, the Iroquois, the Canadian Indian, Mongolian and Mayan shamanic spiritual practices), and synthesized to produce a system that can be used to restore the soul and the spirit (Forest, 2000). Another interesting account is provided by a university professor (Kerr, & McAlister, 2000). The experiences as a shamanic apprentice have been narrated in detail, and especially how she found her life transformed in extraordinary ways. We generally think that a person interested in faith healing and especially something as esoteric as shamanism would be engaging in witchcraft and would be leading a life as esoteric as the skills being practiced. This may not necessarily be so and is evidenced by the account of this professor who was able to integrate the shamanic arts with her professional career.

Tao

As we enter the 21st century, we find more and more people turning towards the East, and deriving benefits from Eastern traditions of therapy along with the formal Western psychotherapy. A recent book by Gregson and Efran (2002) on Taoism helps us to understand how to apply Eastern philosophy to enhance recovery from alcohol and drug abuse.

Tao: A Chinese faith healing procedure focusing on the Yin and the Yang

Taoism focuses on the union of two opposites—the **Yin** and the **Yang,** or the body and the mind. One of the essential elements of the Taoist cosmogony is **Ch'I,** or the vital energy. This vital energy is similar to the soul: the mediator between the body and the mind, the yin and the yang. An exploration of Ch'I can provide a new perspective on the relationship between body, mind and spirit (Chee, 2002). The central aspect of Tao is the **metamorphosis** of one's false self into one's true self. Through this transformation, one attains **integrity** (wholeness), and **wisdom** (spiritual knowledge). Does this emphasis on wholeness or integrity not appear familiar? Is not Eriksonian theory based on wholeness and the establishment of personal identity (the identity crises)? Does not Maslow speak of a concept very similar to transformation and reaching the true self (self actualization)? These points show how Taoism is not completely alien to Western psychological theorizing. Even Jung (1957/1967) was familiar with Eastern thought and had introduced it to his Western readers, though he had omitted the in-depth discussion of the Chinese alchemical process. He was aware of Ch'I, but did not associate its transformative properties with the Chinese meditative process (Chee, 2002). Rather it can be very easily and comfortably integrated with the psychologies of Jung, and even the humanists, Erikson and Maslow (Rosen & Crouse, 2000).

Zen

Zen practice is another Eastern tradition, based on **one-ness, emptiness, no self** and **enlightenment,** obtained mainly through **meditation.** Magid (2002) has explored the common ground of Zen and psychotherapy, and attempts to find answers to many questions. Is meditation simply a self-help psychotherapy? Is the relation between the meditation student and his teacher the same as that between the patient and the psychotherapist? How does the use of the depression drug Prozac fit with spiritual practice? And most importantly, how can we make the best of both worlds: how can we learn from both the systems so as to address human problems? Magid has shown how Zen practice, especially when integrated with psychoanalytical principles can be used for the alleviation of mental health problems.

Zen: An Eastern practice based on one-ness and enlightenment

SPIRITUAL INTELLIGENCE: AN EMERGING AREA CONNECTING RELIGION AND PSYCHOLOGY

Another interesting way in which religion may add to psychological theorizing is the emergent construct of **Spiritual Intelligence** (SI). A relatively new area in the history of psychology is that of multiple intelligence. Spiritual Intelligence would be one component of such multiple intelligence systems. According to Noble (2000), SI is an innate capacity that can help people to

Spiritual intelligence: Innate capacity that can help people grow spiritually

BOX 5.4

Zen and the art of corporate productivity
(*The Times of India,* August 6, 2003)

For Dave Jakubowski, Vice President of business development for internet service provider United Online, the job is not what it used to be. Instead of an unlimited expense account and stays at plush Chateau Marmont, the 31 year old now has brown bags lunch and stays at the Hyatt when he is in Los Angeles. He logs 18 hour days to reach sales targets. How does Jakubowski cope with this sort of life? He says that "I am in business and I need results." So what does he do? He recently turned to a mat and 60 minutes of silence. "Its amazing," he says. "I am able to sort through work challenges in this state of calm much faster than trying to fight through it. And I make fewer mistakes."

Increasingly, the overstretched and overburdened have a new answer to work lives of gunning harder for what seems less and less: "don't just do something—sit there." Companies all over the world are turning to meditation to solve some of the stress related problems of their employees, goaded on by researches at the National Institutes of Health, the University of Massachusetts, and the Mind-Body Medical Institute at Harvard University—all big names in the research arena—names whose research findings can certainly not be scoffed at.

There are no hard statistics on how many companies have added meditation benefits, but the anecdotal evidence is mounting, the reason generally being the rising costs due to stress related lowering of productivity. The National Institute for Occupational Safety and Health finds that stress related ailments cost companies about $200 billion a year in terms of increased absenteeism, tardiness and loss of talented workers. Between 70% to 90% of employee hospital visits are linked to stress. And job tension is directly tied to a lack of productivity and loss of competitive edge.

How does meditation help? Meditation quiets the mental chatter, explains coach Trower of New York's Balance Integration Corp, which develops meditation programs for large corporations. Other effects include the laying of foundations for better decision making and communication.

grow in psychological breadth and depth. A detailed analysis of the lives of 9 adults (aged between 25 and 50 years) revealed that spiritual growth occurred in 5 areas:

1. Greater understanding of and ability to endure adversity.
2. Conscious rejection of self destructive attitudes and behavior.
3. New found/renewed ability to recognize and utilize inner resources.
4. An enhanced acuity of feeling and empathy for self and others.
5. Commitment to participate more fully in life.

The importance of the above areas for social psychologists cannot be undermined. Earlier, we noted that there could be a downside to religion or spirituality. People can get so involved in their religiosity that they start finding it difficult to adjust to the real world and to their daily lives. Does it not appear from the above that people who are spiritually inclined and who are spiritually intelligent would be better able to utilize religion or spirituality for the enhancement of their well being? Thus SI could help in the alleviation of this downside and may help in the optimization of use of RS for helping rather than harming the individual.

In a very innovative study, comparisons of the construct of spiritual intelligence was made through a Lexis-Nexis search of the printed media, vis-à-vis that obtained through a discourse analysis of 7 spiritually oriented therapeutic conferences. The study clarified that the concept of SI is based on 5 principles, these are:

1. The key to develop SI is to value diversity.
2. SI defines reality as multidimensional.
3. Consciousness includes multiple ways of knowing.
4. People with SI have a distinctive relationship with the world around them.
5. Rituals are vehicles for SI.

While a special edition of *The International Journal for the Psychology of Religion* has raised many thought provoking comments, there still seem to be some conceptual distinctions that need to be made. According to Edwards (2003), we still need to address at least 3 issues:

1. Is SI autonomous from other forms of intelligence?
2. Does using spirituality to solve problems imply that a set of problems can be specially designated as spiritual ones?
3. Can we distinguish spiritual knowing from knowing about spirituality?

THE FUTURE OF SOCIAL PSYCHOLOGY OF RELIGION

Is RS always in the service of its adherents? Does belief in RS always produce positive gains? Some data has started to appear on questions such as these. Pargament (2002) has drawn our attention to the bitter and the sweet of religiousness. Concluding on the basis of empirical literature, he has drawn five conclusions:

1. Some forms of religion are more helpful than others. Well being is linked positively to religion that is intrinsically oriented and motivated and negatively to a religion, that is, imposed from without.
2. There are advantages to even extreme forms of religion such as fundamentalism.
3. Religion is particularly helpful to marginalized groups.
4. Religion is more helpful during crises situations that force people to push their resources to its limits.
5. The efficacy of religion is tied to the extent to which it is well integrated in the person's life.

Larson and Larson (2003) also point to some of advantages and disadvantages of religion. While the advantages are the same as has been documented in the previous pages, one disadvantage is that the patient's religiousness may serve as a source of conflict linked with poorer health outcomes. They suggest that if trained chaplains are made part of the healthcare team, it would go a long way in alleviating the psychological distress of the patients.

Using scales such as those by Batson and co-workers (1993), both the trials and the tribulations of religious struggle have been delineated. Religious disappointments with the congregation may raise doubts about general trustworthiness of others (Krause & co-workers, 2000); internal religious conflicts can raise self doubt; questions about God's nature may lead to fear, etc. Spiritual struggles have been found associated with a variety of psychological distress parameters, such as anxiety, depression negative moods, panic, etc. (Exline & co-workers, 2000). They have been predictive of poor medical recovery (Fitchett & co-workers, 1999); longer hospital stays (Berg & co-workers, 1995) and greater risk of mortality (Pargament & co-workers, 2001). In short, religious struggle can be extremely distressing for the individual, but this should not make us oblivious to the gains from religious struggle, open-mindedness, self-actualization, lower levels of prejudice (Calhoun & co-workers, 2000) or to draw attention away from what is probably a necessary prelude to spiritual growth (Batson & co-workers, 1993).

It is time for social psychology to learn from sister disciplines in realizing that in many ways religion is not different from other human endeavors. Both sociology and economics have recently employed comprehensively a rational choice view of religion and have identified the costs and benefits associated with it. Church participants know anticipated costs (such as, time and donations) and benefits (such as, social support) and realize that payoffs for participation are enormous. It is no wonder that church attendance has risen from 17% to 60% during the past two centuries (Coughlin, 1996). Pluralism and competition in our society are strengthening the roots of religious participation as it lends support to the psychological needs of identity and affiliation among diversified people. Iannaccone (cited by Coughlin, 1996) is currently developing an economic model of religious behavior to account for the increase and decline of membership in churches in terms of payoffs. Are people reluctant to join the Mormons who prohibit alcohol and caffeine? Are Seventh Day Adventists more popular among vegetarians? In the wake of intense competition, churches are luring people and changing their behavior by giving them benefits without defining the costs.

Are there any lessons for social psychologists? Using the rational choice model, we know that many people prefer to go to a clergy rather than to a psychologist because of low cost and high benefits (no cost, more emotional support, unlimited availability and so on). By developing networks with various agencies in the community—churches included—psychological intervention programs to enhance mental health of fellow members can be designed by social psychologists without causing any conflict. When psychologists such as Eric Erikson analyzed the lives of great people, they discovered that religion was not a hindrance in initiating a social movement; rather, it was the source of creating new choices to guide humanity to attain superior goals. For example, Erikson remarked that when people reached a stage of generativity, they tended to define themselves by whom they cared for in their lives and to what extent. Such generativity might consist of a mere expression (factual reality), or a true action that is felt by the individual (actuality). In other words, religion guided many people in terms of mere expression, but for others, it became a way of life. It seems that the bond between psychology and religion will grow with the understanding of the stage of actuality. When people of various religious denominations will find themselves caring for others effectively, both psychology and religion will not face any conflict. Like individuals who mature and accomplish landmarks in their lives, relationships between disciplines develop to create a new identity. Religion provides meaning and purpose in life to many individuals, and the task of social psychology is to examine how it contributes to their well-being.

Summary

Hardly any book of social psychology devotes much attention to the relationships between psychology and religion. Because religion has a powerful influence on the behavior of many individuals, we decided to include a chapter on the topic. In the first part of this chapter, a review of the work of some prominent psychologists on religion was presented. Among them were William James, Hall, Freud, Skinner and Maslow. Next we examined the nature of the relationship between the two disciplines: psychology and religion, psychology in religion and psychology of religion.

The second part of this chapter dealt with the measurement of religious beliefs and attitudes. In this context, several scales to measure religious attitudes and behavior were described: Thurstone's scales, Yinger's Non-Directional Religious Attitude Scale, Faulkner and DeJong's scales and the Allport-Ross scales. Finally Batson's Interactional scale and his empirical studies were also described.

The next section discussed the functions of religiosity and spirituality and the development of religiosity in the individual. The chapter then went on to the role of religion in physical and mental health and coping with stress. The chapter ended with a section on traditional forms of faith healing, including Shamanism, Tao, and Zen. The last part of the chapter introduced the upcoming topic of spiritual intelligence as one of the multiple intelligence aspects.

Suggestions for Further Reading

Hill, P.C. & Pargament, K.I. (2003). Advances in the conceptualization and measurement of religion and spirituality. *American Psychologist*, 58, 64-74.

Monitor on Psychology : Spirituality and Mental Health, 2003, 34.

Some Key Terms

Depth psychology
Extrinsic religious orientation
Faith healing
Institutionalised type
Interiorized type
Intrinsic religious orientation
Ironson-Woods Spirituality-Religiousness Index
Quest Orientation
Religio
Religion
Shamanism
Spiritual intelligence
Spirituality
Tao
Type Y
Type Z
Zen

SOCIAL PSYCHOLOGY OF TECHNOLOGY

6

Chapter Outline

- An introduction to social psychology of technology
- Technology and the individual
  - The technological fix
  - Technophobia
  - Technophobia among older adults
  - Technostress
  - High tech- high touch
- The acceptance and adoption of technology
  - The digital divide
- Technology and individual control
- Technology in education
- Technology at work
  - Office automation
  - Telecommuting
  - Factory automation
- Technology and health
  - Technology and dissemination of health information
  - Technology and telemedicine
  - Technology and reproductive medicine
  - Technology and therapy
- Technology and communication
  - The social psychology of cyber space
  - Types of communication and organizational position
  - The shared social context in organizational communication
- The limits of social psychology of technology

AN INTRODUCTION TO SOCIAL PSYCHOLOGY OF TECHNOLOGY

Cybersickness: Symptoms very close to those of motion sickness due to participation in tasks of virtual reality

"The future of the human mind lies in the steady, increasing evolution of technology that will make fundamental changes in human abilities. New prosthetic devices will enable the ill and the injured to thrive. New cognitive technologies will make the combination of person + machine even smarter, but make the person even more attached and dependent upon technology...the future of human evolution lies outside of the human; it lies in technology. Today we are at the start of the cognitive revolution in technological artifacts that increase the power of the mind. Although the mind itself can no longer grow because it is limited by biological constraints, especially that of physical size, the power of the mind can expand through the aid of technology."

So wrote Donald A. Norman in a chapter entitled *The Future of the Mind Lies in Technology* (1995, p. 247).

Compare the scenario of work now with what it was 60 years ago when there were no computers. Now, over 50 million workers are using computers. Originally, computers were developed simply for the purpose of computing, but we now use them for a wide variety of other purposes ranging from e-mail to searching for new material. New health problems (for example, Carpal Tunnel Syndrome) are emerging due to repetitive motion. While the good old manual typewriter gave some rest to our fingers when we moved to the next line, our fingers can run nonstop as we continue to type on a modern PC. Those who have participated in virtual reality tasks have experienced "**cybersickness**"—symptoms parallel to motion sickness like dizziness, disorientation and nausea. There is no doubt that technological advancements have tested the limits of human abilities, and in some cases have even caused debilitating effects. Such issues are being addressed to by a growing discipline called human factors engineering or **ergonomics** that deals with the compatibility of the man-machine system.

Ergonomics: Study of compatibility between man and machine

BOX 6.1

Computers and their use across the world

The pace at which computers were disseminated in the final years of the 20th century can be illustrated by the growth in the numbers of computers being used over the period 1985-2000 (Thomas, 2001)

1985	38.1	million computers in use throughout the world
1991	129.4	million computers in use (a growth of 260%)
1995	257.2	million computers
2000	535.9	million computers

The social psychological implications of technology are far deeper than what they appear to be on the surface. New situations create new problems, and we have to find new ways of dealing with these novel situations. Think of a devout Muslim in a space-lab orbiting the earth. A solar day is of only 90 minutes, because of the high speed of the earth orbiting, and it is in these 90 minutes in which the sun rises and sets every 45 minutes. Under such conditions, how can he face Mecca, an integral part of Muslim worship? How will he decide his prayer time to read the religious book? Or, think of a conservative Hindu priest who decides not to worship the moon, one of the seven sacred elements of the universe, simply because a human being had touched its surface and so defiled it. Technology has already changed, and is continuously changing our attitudes and our beliefs. In a simple physical sense, people are found to be sitting in front of their computers for longer periods than they are in libraries, parks and elsewhere.

BOX 6.2

Computer use in a South Asian developing country

It is not just the West that has promoted the use of computers in all spheres of life. The developing countries, especially countries such as India and China, have sensed the scope of computers. Here is some data on how the use of information technology has grown in China. According to Chen, Sullivan and Savanye (2002), China's telecommunication sector grew at an annual rate of 30-50% over the past 10 years, and has today emerged as the second largest information technology market in the world. By the year 2000, 6% of all urban households in the country and 10% of households in China's larger cities owned personal computers; while during the 18 month period between January 2000 and July 2001 the number of Internet users had increased from approximately 9 million to 27 million.

In viewing the **relationship between social psychology and technology**, we will **first** focus on how technology has changed our lives. The **second** part will describe the factors underlying the acceptance and adoption of technology. This will be followed by a section on the role of technology in education, in the work sphere and in health. **Finally,** we will discuss the role of technology in communication and on several issues that need serious consideration when substituting face-to-face interaction by videoconferencing and other technological methods.

TECHNOLOGY AND THE INDIVIDUAL

According to Spacapan and Oskamp (1990), computers, robots and aerospace industries are the three areas of technology that have shown rapid advancement in recent years and each of them have had a major influence on our lives. Technology has become so pervasive that it has even affected our conversation. When we have a business lunch, we call it "networking;" when we are in conflict, we address it as our inability to "interface;" and so on. Spacapan and Oskamp gave four examples to show how technology has overwhelmed us.

1. The technological fix

In our country, people are so dependent on technology that they often wait for a technological solution of a problem instead of changing their own behavior. Our **dependence on technology** is so strong that we prefer to rely on condoms rather than change our sex behavior and would rather install antipollution devices than opt for a carpool.

Technological fix: The continued use of technology to the utter neglect of better options

2. Technophobia

There are a large number of people who have been and still are against the use of technology. Teachers resisted the use of computers in schools. Unions feared that automation would lead to lay-offs. We notice even today that there are some people who continue to resist the use of new technology in schools, at work, and in homes. Conversely, when media interviewed parents of a student who scored 1600/1600 in the SAT (1997), the parents very proudly said that they did not have television in their home.

Technophobia: An intense fear of technology

In an attempt to assess the psychological impact of technology from the global perspective, 3392 students were sampled from 23 countries. The findings clarify that

technophobia was mildly related to **gender** and **age** in less than a quarter of the countries. A more salient variable appeared to be **experience with computers/technology**, which was related negatively to technophobia in most of the countries (Weil & Rosen, 1995). Similar findings regarding the role of experience with computers were obtained on a sample of South African students by Anthony, Clarke and Anderson (2000). Further, the same study revealed that technophobia is related to **personality dimensions.** Using the currently well known **Big Five scale for personality** (NEO—Five factor Inventory), it was found that technophobia was higher among those who obtained a high score on the Neuroticism dimension and those who obtained a low score on the Openness dimension of personality (Anthony, Clarke & Anderson, 2000). This makes sense, since it is expected that a person who is high on openness should manifest openness in all aspects of life, including the use of technology.

e i ive ersonalit a tors
enness
ons ientio sness
troversion
otional sta ilit an
reea leness

That attitudes of people towards computers and to science and technology in general can cover the entire range of attitude valences, is clarified by factor analytical studies. **Three factors** have been obtained. The **first factor** consists of an attribution to the computer of negative effects at the individual level; the **second factor** attributes negative effects to the computer at the social psychological level; while the **third factor** is a positive factor, attributing positive effects at an instrumental and organizational level (Sensales & Greenfield, 1995). Thus, an example of the first would be a negative attitude among individuals that computers are detrimental to health. An example of the second factor would also be a negative attitude but would be manifested in terms of the thinking that computers stop people from socializing. The third factor, in contrast, being a positive factor, would consist of attitudes that show that the person thinks that computers are useful both in life and at work.

e no o ia a on ol er a lts

Despite the fact that it is near impossible to do even the most mundane tasks without the help of technology, there are a large number of people who continue to resist technology and insist on doing things their way, that is, manually. The single largest demographic group among those who resist technology is that of **older adults.** When one tries to understand the reasons for their resistance, we soon realize the **double disadvantage** being faced by old people. For one thing they have hardly any experience with technology, and secondly, they do start showing declines in cognitive and motor function with increasing age. This latter limitation significantly restricts their use of technology.

The ways in which people resist technology even for entertainment was the object of a recent investigation. An empirical comparison of the use of entertainment technology (or what has been termed **infotainment**), by older and younger adults across the USA, Germany and Croatia revealed that though socio-economic status is sometimes an important predictor of technology use, age, gender and culture are by far more important. This is highlighted by the fact that despite economic advancement, the Germans were seen to be less active users of and less familiar with the information technology. The patterns were similar to those found for Croatia, which in turn was found slower than that for the US. Most

n otain ent
e se o in or ation te nolo or entertain ent r oses

importantly, the differences were more pronounced for the older group (Mundorf, Bryant & Brownell, 1997).

Recently, a few psychologists have formed a group for the scientific study of the effects of aging on the use of technology. With the acronym **CREATE** (The Center for Research and Education on Aging and Technology), they will specifically be focusing on issues such as how aging influences the use of technology, which types of technology work best for the aged, and what techniques can be used to best instruct older adults in technology use. The group hopes that they will finally have enough data to help the industry to design products that can be effectively used by older adults (Azar, 2002).

Thus the studies help us to identify what types of people would tend to have a more negative attitude towards computers. Knowing that, we can devise educational programs to overcome such psychological resistance.

4. Technostress

Harmful effects of technology are cited in several studies. Compared to their Western counterparts, Australian clerical workers have more frequently complained about computer-related injuries. Those who work in virtual environments for a long period of time report disorientation, eye-strain, and illusory sensation. It is known that when several objects move past the nose of viewers with varying velocity and direction in a virtual environment, they begin to feel dizzy.

Technostress: Stress resulting from the use of technology

5. High tech-high touch

This concept was first proposed by Naisbitt (1982). It denotes the cost at which we have adopted new technologies and the efforts we are making to compensate for it. Naisbitt noticed that there are three ways in which high tech is related to high touch. **First,** high tech has facilitated high touch, for example, airplanes made face-to-face business meetings possible. **Second,** high tech and high touch have emerged simultaneously due to social changes and the impact of technology, as in the case of the hospice movement and the increased use of life-monitoring equipment. And **third,** high touch has rejected high tech. For example, a number of people think that the automatic payroll and the polygraph test dehumanize them.

High tech-high touch: The cost of adopting the technology and making compensations for it

While it is true that technology has an immense effect on our lives, an extreme view depicting the unidirectional impact of technology on human lives has also been advanced. If technology causes limits to human behavior, its impact should not only be confined to the individual, but to all levels of human organization (Feigenbaum & McCorduck, 1983). Technological determinism is strengthened by the belief that technology has consequences that can be predicted. Spacapan and Oskamp (1990) have illustrated it by quoting the theme of Chicago's World Fair (1933):

Science discovers.
Technology applies.
Man conforms.

There is little doubt that a few changes, at the minimum, are required in introducing a new technology. At the organizational level, these changes could be either cultural or structural or both. Any change that grows out of interactions between individuals, situations and technology is called **"technological emergence."** When such a type of interaction is described in terms of predictable consequences, then it is called **"interactive determinism"** (Spacapan & Oskamp, 1990). While these concepts are of little value to chief executives, they all need to understand that undermining social aspects of technology could lead to disastrous consequences. Commenting on their own position, Spacapan and Oskamp wrote, "Technology does not automatically de-skill (lessen the skill value of) jobs; it can empower people, augment their skills, and create a more varied work environment that allows more input from workers. Neither does it necessarily improve the lot of workers; it can centralize office or shop floor operations and put extreme power in the hands of management" (p. 20).

Technological emergence: Any change that grows out of interactions between individuals, situations and technology

Interactive determinism: Technological emergence that has predictable consequences

THE ACCEPTANCE AND ADOPTION OF TECHNOLOGY

As seen in the section on technophobia, there are individuals who are literally so scared of technology that they can be classed as being phobic. And, it is not just individuals who can be so scared of technology, so can entire countries.

While technologies can be easily transferred, there is a strong likelihood that the people of the receiving country may not accept it. Cross-cultural studies clarify that there are at least **two major factors** that influence the success of the transfer. These are, **firstly,** the **technological characteristics**, and **secondly**, the **societal and cultural differences**. It has already been explained in chapter one, that the Hofstede dimensions are extremely useful for understanding differences in behavior across cultures. The same has been found for attitudes towards technology. Kedia and Bhagat (1988) clarify that such attitudes can be best understood using the Hofstede dimensions of differences across cultures, namely, the dimensions of uncertainty avoidance, power distance, gender, degree of collectivism and abstractive versus associative thinking. Since every innovation brings in its wake a certain amount of risk and uncertainty, it seems understandable that countries that are lower on uncertainty avoidance would show lower negativism towards the technology than those who are higher on uncertainty avoidance. Similar findings on the role of cultural differences have been noted in technology transfer from the West to **Third World countries** (Contractor, Fulk, Monge & Singhal, 1986). In **Turkey** too, technology innovation was seen to be favored only when it was compatible with their social and cultural expectations (Oener, 2000). At the same time, we should take note of the cognitive model of attitudes towards technology transfer, which lays emphasis on cognitive factors such as beliefs of the adopter, compatibility, value addition, perceived benefits and difficulties, over and above the external environmental factors (Au & Enderwick, 2000). Thus, if a person believes that the technology transfer will bring about a change that is compatible with his beliefs and skills, that it will help to increase his value, say, help him to show enhanced performance, then only would he be prone to accept the technology transfer. At the same time, every individual makes a cost-benefit analysis, and only if the benefits seem to override the costs, would the person show any interest in the transferred technology.

The digital divide

Digital divide: The line separating those who have access to computers from those who don't

Technology in all its ramifications has had the misfortune to be unequally accessible to different regions of the world, and to different countries. Most of this inequality stems from economic disparities, since scientific and technological advances require financial inputs. As a result, we can divide the countries of the world, into the "haves" and the "have-nots," based on the extent of technology available to them. It is this which has been named the "**digital divide.**" Warschauer (2003) is of the view that such a digital divide has far reaching social psychological implications, especially in terms of social and economic stratification and inclusion. Taking examples from both developed and developing countries (including Brazil, China, India and the USA), he has cited case studies of how the ability to access, adapt, and create knowledge using information technology is critical for social inclusion. Another factor causing a digital divide is the uneven division of access to digital technology in the rural areas.

As we refer to the digital divide, it is but imperative that we consider ways for removing this divide. The strategies involve more than the mere transfer of technology from the "have" countries to the "have not" countries. Two examples of how the digital divide was addressed in India will illustrate how a developing country can deal with emerging technologies.

Worried by the stark chasm between the "haves" and the "have-nots" of access to digital technology in India, and recognizing that unless some timely steps are taken, the chasm could become worse, both government and non governmental bodies have started initiatives in this direction. Some examples are presented as follows: **WARNA** was the first information technology project started in the state of Maharashtra, India, and it has demonstrated the effectiveness of such technology for accelerating the socio-economic development in the villages. **Bhoomi,** meaning land, is a Karnataka government initiative to maintain computerized land records across the state. The forerunner in the white revolution in India, Anand, in the state of Gujarat, is a cooperative body that has a computerized milk collection system and allows on the spot reading of milk quality and quantity and maintains daily records of milk societies at the village level.

TECHNOLOGY AND INDIVIDUAL CONTROL

Technology can threaten individuals' perception of control over their lives. For instance, astronauts rely on life-support devices and they have virtually no control over their environment. According to Spacapan and Oskamp (1990), research and development personnel expressed a diminished sense of autonomy as working environments became more complex and the dependence on computers increased. If users of technology suffer from a sense of helplessness, there will be no accountability for product quality or management of disasters. It is very important that human operators maintain a great sense of control over the technological devices they use. For example, developing a high sense of perceived control in a space lab will require a fluent communication between the astronauts and the ground control personnel.

According to Gutek and Winter (1990), computers create a new culture to which new users may adjust smoothly or fail miserably. Some people display computer anxiety longer than others, and this state may influence their attitude toward computers in addition to their performance. Given the attitude of people toward computers and how they can adjust to the features of computers, a symbiotic interaction develops between the two—people and computers. During this interaction people may perceive the degree of control they have over the machine. To assess this impact, Gutek and Winter developed a test of measures of control over the computers (Table 6.1).

TABLE 6.1

Measures of control over the computer

Range of Response	
1. The computer uses me.	I use the computer.
2. I cannot choose when to use the computer.	I can choose when to use the computer.
3. The computer controls me.	I control the computer.
4. I am here to use the computer.	The computer is here to assist me.
5. My job is to use the computer to do my work.	The computer is a tool to be used at my convenience.

After compiling a report based on presentations by several psychologists, Tori DeAngelis (1995) examined whether "technology contributes to a sense of isolation by teaching people to focus more attention on the cold glare of a computer or TV screen than on the warmth of a friendly face" (p. 46). DeAngelis reported that while watching TV might make people passive, research on 50 families by Kraut and others (cited by DeAngelis, 1995) show, on the contrary, that those who use the Internet and e-mail did not feel lonelier or more socially isolated than their counterparts. Personality factors and openness to new experiences, however, were critical variables in such experiences.

Failed impulse control: The inability to control one's impulses

During the 1996 American Psychological Convention, Kimberly Young (1996) reported that using any computer network, like the Internet, forms a habit in some people that could be compared to pathological gambling. It involves **"failed impulse control"** without any intoxicant. After watching Internet users for a long time, she developed criteria for assessing one's dependence on the Internet (similar to the one used to classify pathological gambling based on the DSM-IV). Those who were addicted to the Internet often:

- **"Felt preoccupied with the Internet; Felt a need to use the Internet with increasing amounts of time in order to achieve satisfaction; Had an inability to control their Internet use.**
- **Felt restless or irritable when attempting to cut down or stop Internet use.**
- **Used the Internet as a way of escaping from problems or of relieving poor mood.**
- **Lied to family members or friends to conceal the extent of involvement with the Internet.**
- **Jeopardized or risked the loss of a significant relationship, job, educational or career opportunity because of the Internet.**
- **Kept returning even after spending an excessive amount of money for online fees.**

- **Went through withdrawal when offline.**
- **Stayed online longer than originally intended."**

"Participants who did not meet three or more of these criteria over a 12-month period were classified as **nondependent users**. In the study, 396 users (239 females and 157 males), were classified as "**dependent**" and 100 (54 females and 46 males) volunteers are classified as "non-dependent .... Internet use could disrupt academic, social, financial, and occupational life the same way well-documented addictions like pathological gambling disorder for alcoholism can" (p. 277).

TECHNOLOGY IN EDUCATION

Look at what computers have done to children. Their daily lives have changed since the introduction of video games. The Japanese parents complain that their children devote less time to studies since the introduction of television, video games and computers.

Leeper and Gurtner (1989) analyzed the impact of computers on the behavior of children. They reported that the use of computers has helped the traditional learning environment. In a sense, computers have become **tutors** in schools. **Second,** when a standard curriculum fails to serve the needs of students, computers help them in their efforts **at mastering complex skills. Third,** computers can **enhance writing and communication skills**. Additionally, computers facilitate **organization of one's knowledge** through the use of data-base. **Fourth,** computers can be helpful in **promoting cooperation and collaboration** as students share common knowledge. And **finally,** children can **set their own pace of learning** while they work with computers. This situation provides for equality of educational opportunity and no negative teacher effects (Please refer to the chapter on education in this book).

Leeper and Gurtner (1989) pointed out that the use of computer-based technology has several **disadvantages** as well. For example, if children continue to depend on computers in correcting their spellings and grammar, they may never learn several fundamental skills of creative and technical writing. Due to the rapid developments in the field of computers, social psychologists have been unable to keep pace with the advances. Table 6.2 shows the possible positive and negative effects of different forms of educational computer use on learning. In other words, Leeper and Gurtner cautioned against the excessive use of computers in classrooms. They remarked:

> The computer may serve as a tutor, an assistant, a coach, a mentor, or a drill Sargent; it may offer experiential learning opportunities through simulations, microworlds, or hypertext programs; it may also provide tools for word processing, data analysis, music composition, and telecommunications. Moreover, exposure to programs of these different sorts may have varied, and sometimes antithetical, effects on particular aspects of children's cognitive, motivational, or social functioning. A didactic "drill" on chemical formulas and an open-ended simulation of a chemistry laboratory, for example, may have quite different consequences for children's learning of, or interest in, that subject (p. 173).

In the 21st century we have moved from mere computers in education to the use of smart machines, which is bound to revolutionalize education. Forbus and Feltovich (2001) in their edited volume entitled *Smart Machines in Education: the Coming Revolution in Educational*

Technology provide us a gamut of such computer software for the interested teacher. The volume emphasizes how the use of artificial intelligence systems will change the face of education. Of how it will help us to understand how people think, solve problems and learn. Using results from artificial intelligence, scientists can create software with more human-like qualities, so as to enable the student to learn better.

One of the latest uses of information technology in education is the web based conferencing system that allows a multidirectional flow of information from instructor to students, from students to instructors and from students to other students. Thus, we can now study from mentors and teachers from any, where in the globe, without loss of the non-verbal communication since the non-verbal expressions are available through the video-based technology. Cummings and Bonk (2002) describe one method to enhance discussion on web-based education. It is called **virtual debate** and is used to promote critical analysis and personal reflection. The virtual debate comprises the posting of an initial position statement, rebuttal and personal reflection. Such web based conferencing systems have been used for graduate and undergraduate students for the teaching of educational psychology. Both students and instructors have felt that it allows them to discuss important personal issues and to receive advice from peers and mentors around the globe.

Virtual debate: A web-based debate on the Internet

How do students react to the use of technological tools in the learning process? Forty eight undergraduate students who had participated in courses using listservs, e-mail, web based assignments and electronic critique and submission of work were asked to complete questionnaires regarding their experience. The students felt that the electronic tools were very useful, because it gave them adequate opportunity to process course content and expand their discussions outside the classroom. Some of the important advantages: as many as 85% of the students either "agreed" or "strongly agreed" that electronic discussions provided the quieter students an opportunity to speak; and 83% reported broaching subjects that they might not have otherwise brought up in the classroom (Huff & Edwards, 2001). So we see not only enhanced learning but also certain social advantages of using electronic media in education.

How can we enhance the efficacy of web-based learning and instruction? Newlin and Wang (2002) provide 7 principles for the same. These are:

- **Encourage contact between students and faculty.**
- **Develop reciprocity and cooperation among students.**
- **Use active learning techniques.**
- **Give prompt feedback.**
- **Emphasize time on task.**
- **Communicate high expectations.**
- **Respect diverse talents and ways of learning.**

The authors give concrete suggestions on how to use each principle to maximize the potential of web-based technologies and to promote positive learning outcomes in the virtual classroom.

TECHNOLOGY AT WORK

Technology alters the conditions of work in a system. For example, in a space-lab, crew members do not walk in an erect manner; instead, they take a floating position in reaching from one point to another (Wickman, 1990). They do not stay at one block for a long time. They operate with one hand for approximately one third of their time because they have to hold on with their other hand, to avoid floating caused by the lack of gravity. According to Wickman (*ibid*), "Ultimately, applied social psychologists will have to work more intimately with design and engineering professionals from the time of the very first discussions about a design prototype. For this interaction to be effective, social scientists will have to increase their technological literacy, and engineers will have to reciprocate by becoming more literate in such areas as human factors" (p. 277).

In short, with reference to human behavior, the role of technology should be viewed in terms of its effect on an individual (for example, its pathological use) and the new conditions that cause changes in an organization and via this impact on job satisfaction, perceived control, and work design. Some specific issues relating to the applications of social psychology in the area of work will follow.

Over the last 40 years, major changes have taken place in the workplace. Along with globalization, the use of information technology at work has brought in its wake, massive organizational restructuring, changes in work time scheduling (for example, flexitime) and changes in work contracts. All these have produced radical transformations in the nature of work and in the workplace. While such changes impact the bottom line of the organizations (the balance sheet), they also have widespread implications for employee well being. In view of the above, at least **four issues** are of concern to organizations and to the workforce. These are **job insecurity, work hours, control of work and managerial style** (Sparks, Faragher & Cooper, 2001). So pervasive are the changes due to the use of information technology at work, that a whole new range of emerging topics for industrial/organizational psychology is envisaged. These range from the issue of measurement to that of training; from automation to job analysis; from our understanding of group dynamics in organizations to the computer modelling of behavioral events in organizations (Crespin & Austin, 2002). Since technology at work affects management's dependence on their employees, there would also be new ramifications to the issue of management-employee trust (Wells & Kipnis, 2001).

Office automation

When hand-scribing was eliminated by the manual typewriter, people took time to adjust to the new device. Currently, the manual typewriter is being rapidly replaced by computer. However, the intended results in the use of office automation were disappointing, for out of 2,000 US companies surveyed approximately 40% had not achieved their own targets (Turnage, 1990).

There are several reasons for this failure, and in most cases the problems are related to the human side of the organization. **First**, office automation has caused **technostress.** Those who work in offices frequently report headaches, shoulder, neck and back pains, and strain in the eyes. On the other hand, there are people called **techno-centered**, who have successfully

Techno-centered people: People who have successfully adopted technology adopted to, and identify their work with computers. Such people begin to behave like machines and display no emotion (Brod, 1988).

Second, there are people who believe that advancements in technology have taken away their freedom. More than 6 million workers in our country are subject to technological surveillance which results in loss of autonomy and personal dignity (Smith, 1988). A good example of this is the use of surveillance systems during or before a job interview. In a typical case, as you walk across the lobby, a staff member of the opposite sex greets you. Those vital seconds are recorded on digital videotape. By the time you arrive at the interview, the tape has provided the interviewer with a personality profile that reveals your aptitude for the job. If you are a male, it will have gauged how much of a risk taker you are. If you are a female, it has gauged how you react to unknown members of the opposite sex. In both cases, the observers will also have a good idea of whether or not you fancied your greeter. For the first time, science looks as if it has cracked the complex signaling processes that are involved when men and women hit it off. This is the promise of a research project taking place at the Ludwig Boltzmann Institute for Urban Ethology at the University of Vienna, which specializes in studying emotional communication (*The Times of India*, 2001). What the opinion of the prospective employee would be remains a moot point. In fact, the team leader of the project too admits that "the work raises some worrying ethical questions."

Third, office automation does not yield the same satisfaction through videoconferencing or teleconferencing as a face-to-face meeting does. Also, the response to managing work away from the traditional office (teleworking) has not accelerated, although the savings from this type of work are substantially high (Turnage, 1990). In other words, the effects of using technology are limited in several ways.

And **fourth**, as technologies are becoming integrated at a fast pace and are leading to more power by means of linkage between local and long distance networks and reduced cost, the structure of organizations will change. For example, the demand for middle managers will reduce because rather than depending on them, the senior managers will be able to obtain operational data directly from the networks. Additionally, the rapid rate at which technology is changing may also swamp senior managers who will be caught between learning new technologies and concentrating at the same time on the policy matters of their companies. The reduction or elimination of middle managers will also require increasing attention to details (micromanaging) which will not be possible without delegating more responsibility to the lower level workers or altering the organizational structure to achieve a balance between the organizational units.

In short, organizing office work through automation needs to address several issues that have social psychological implications: redesigning workplaces, training in teamwork through integrated electronic networks, and restructuring organizations. These issues become all the more important when one considers the ways in which workforce diversification is taking place. We have more women at work, the number of dual earning couples is increasing as also the number of older workers. The impact of the use of information technology at work could have important repercussions for the well being and occupational health of these new entrants to the workforce and definitely requires due consideration (Sparks, Faragher & Cooper, 2001).

Telecommuting

Telecommuting: Working from locations outside the office, using information technology

In this world of burgeoning organizations, highways packed with vehicles often emitting noxious fumes, parking lots bursting to their seams with cars, what better option can one find than telecommuting. As the name suggests, the employee does commute, but not physically by any vehicle, but connects to the organization through information technology. The concept that does not make it mandatory for the employee to come to the physical office building and permits the employee to work from either his home or any other place that is more convenient to him. The idea of allowing people to work from environments away from the organization is becoming so common, that the search engine, Google, yielded 4,80,000 entries in a matter of just .26 seconds for telecommuting.

Telecommuting is proving to be **advantageous** at all three levels of analysis: for the **individual**, for the **organization** and for the **society**. While everything comes at a cost, the advantages accruing from telecommuting far outweigh the disadvantages. Harpaz (2002) identifies some of the important benefits and costs.

BOX 6.3

Relative advantages and disadvantages of telecommuting (Harpaz, 2002)

Key advantages:

At the individual level: Increased autonomy and flexibility.

At the organizational level: Increased human resource capacity and savings in direct expenditure.

At the societal level: Reduction in environmental damage, solutions for people with special needs, savings in infrastructure and energy.

Key disadvantages:

At the individual level: Possible sense of isolation, lack of seperation between home and work.

At the organizational level: Costs of transition to new work methods, training, damage to committmnt and identification with organization.

At the societal level: Danger of creating detached individuals.

The mammoth **IBM** company took upon itself to compare how three work venues: **traditional office** (n=4316), the **virtual office** (n=767) and the **home office** (n=441) influence various aspects pertaining to the job and personal life of employees. The aspects of the job focused on were **job performance, job motivation, job retention, work load success and career opportunities.** The results indicated that the influence of the virtual office was mostly positive for the job aspects, but somewhat negative for the personal life. In contrast, the influence of the home office was generally positive while that for the traditional office was negative for both the job and for personal life (Hill, Ferris & Martinson, 2003).

But are all managers and all companies ready to allow their employees to opt for teleworking? Part of the answer is related to cultural differences regarding trust and power distance orientations. A study comparing Northern and Southern European countries revealed that the Hofstede dimensions of cultural differences can be used to understand to partly explain why some companies allow their employees to telework while others may not (Peters & den Dulk, 2003). Santana and Rocha (2002) have delineated the factors that determine Portugese companies' (n=97) willingness for implementing teleworking and telecommuting.

One of the advantages pointed out by Harpaz is that it helps the society to provide employment for people with special needs. Anderson and Bricout and West (2001) vouch for the same. In another investigation (Bowe, 2001), it was found that people who are deaf or hard of hearing use instant messaging an e-mail extremely effectively so much so that virtually all of the 884 respondents had e-mail and instant messaging access at home.

All of the above make it extremely clear that the word 'virtual' is today's buzzword for organizations—virtual reality, virtual space, virtual organizations and even virtual teams. With its ability to cut across time space and cultural boundaries, virtual teams have indeed become one of the fastest growing high-tech trends in the office (Johnson, Heimann & O'Neill, 2001). However, understanding and managing what you can't see may mean a totally different thing. It implies many new challenges for the manager of the 21st century. While they do require new approaches to evaluating, informing and training employees, perhaps the greatest challenge lies in the designing of organizations that can sustain such virtual structures (Helms & Raiszadeh, 2002).

Factory automation

Consider a traditional metal work industry in which machine tools like lathes, drill presses, grinders, etc. are used. In order to run this industry, we need trained machinists who are qualified to use each of these machines to complete specific jobs required to finish a product. With the introduction of robots, **computer-aided design** (CAD) and **computer-integrated manufacturing** (CIM), many of these functions allocated to the machinists are taken over by computerized technology. For example, using CIM at an IBM plant can help manufacture several things ranging from keyboards to typewriters simply by reprogramming the software driving the equipment. At the John Deere plant in Iowa, robots are used to do the painting work and they can do many other jobs by simply reprogramming them. Under such conditions, will the organization of a traditional factory change? What will happen to human qualities, such as pride, control and autonomy, that are associated with the completing of a task? Will the trained machinists become deskilled? What will happen to the displaced workers who will lose their jobs as a result of factory automation?

CAD: Design of articles with the help of the computer

CIM: The manufacturing process in which active use is made of the computer at all stages of the manufacturing process

The above questions have posed a whole new set of problems for the applications of social psychology in a modern technology oriented organization. The approach of traditional industrial psychology based on "finding the right people for the right job" or "fit them to the job," does not work because the work is performed in a system that also includes, among other things, equipments, workplace, and the conditions in which the work is transacted. More simply, because automated systems substitute the work traditionally conducted by the human beings, a division of work between the man and the machine must be determined in order to get the best results. Such a task requires suitable adjustments in the structure of a technological organization.

Research in social psychology has shown that alterations in jobs resulting from automation might lead to deterioration in the performance of workers (Nieva, Newman & Bottlik, 1990).

The **first** impact of **factory automation** is the loss of jobs. Approximately one-fifth of the welding jobs were eliminated in the automobile industry as a result of automation (Tornatzky, 1990). The figures in the spray painting jobs are even worse than welding (37%). According to Majchrzak and Davis (1990), factory automation would cause loss of 45% of all jobs in our country. As a result, there is bound to be a change in the workforce despite the claims that a wide variety of new jobs will be created in the future. One solution offered to meet this problem is to retrain the existing employees which, in turn, is causing a number of other problems. While a worker is expected to perform well in his present job, he has to prepare himself to become qualified for the new job at the same time. With the rapid advancement of technology, changes in the use of machines are inevitable, and it will take all the worker's energy to keep up with such changes, with little time left to acquire skills that allow promotion in the company.

Secondly, given the conditions associated with automation, the well-being of the workers is bound to be adversely affected. Many changes ranging from ergonomics to rationales for implementing a new plan will need the involvement of workers in the decision making process. According to Nora and Imada (1988), one solution to minimize such adverse effect is to develop "**participatory ergonomics.**" That is, workers should be involved in decisions that affect their well-being. When workers are involved in the implementation of solutions that are based on ergonomic principles and task analysis, they show greater commitment and interest.

Participatory ergonomics: Developing machines through active discussion with workers who will use those machines

Thirdly, the overall results of factory automation have shown a 50% to 75% failure rate in our country (Turnage, 1990). The USA is not the world leader in the use of robots. Based on these statistics, it is reasonable to ask what is wrong with our country and in our claim to be the world leader in the creation of technology. The gains from technology are realized in a social context of an organization, and if the work habits of the workers and the decision making attitudes of the managers do not change, the new technology may become a liability.

Technology can reduce the autonomy and control of a worker which may lead to disastrous consequences. In this context, Turnage mentioned how the dough-makers and the oven-operators adapted to a new manufacturing technology in contrasting ways in a bakery. The dough-maker's job was adversely affected by automatization (weighing, mixing and adding) because their residual job after automation became less challenging and required lower skill. Consequently, they became bored and careless, and acquired no knowledge to get promoted. On the other hand, the oven-operators continued to use discretion in monitoring and controlling the equipment and received feedback on their performance. They adopted to the automation without any problem. In other words, automation had two opposite effects in the same manufacturing plant. According to Majchrzak and Davis (1990), the failure to assess the skills and motivation of workers by the management and the inability to incorporate changes in the organizational structure will lead to adverse results. The success of automation requires continuous integration, coordination and communication (Majchrzak, 1988).

Fourthly, the nature of work involved in the use of new technologies may lead to stress at different levels. Ettlie (1986) pointed out that the level of stress varied according to the job type and a lapse of time. For example, skilled workers faced stress in the latter phase of implementation of a new technology because they were the ones who were involved in implementing the actual production. They performed well in the beginning because they were thoroughly trained to run the machinery. On the other hand, the supervisors were vulnerable early in the process because they were the last to be trained and had little experience in handling the new situation resulting from automation. Another study showed that the mental workload of operators increased when they worked with the robots (Argote, Goodman & Schkade, 1983). To sum up, both the type of work and periods of work are influenced by factory automation.

Fifthly, we should be able to gauge the relationship between technology development and the meaning of work. This is of special significance in the cross-cultural perspective. Investigating the perceptions of technology change and its subjective impact on 3098 workers in the US, Germany, Sweden, Japan and Israel, the results indicated significant cross-country variation due to both the pace of change and socio-cultural differences. Perceived impact also varied between males and females and between blue collared and white collared workers. Interestingly, while the impact was generally positive, exceptions were the Japanese, who reported greater job related alienation resulting from technology change (Yuchtman-Yaar & Gottlieb, 1985).

And **finally,** after all is said and done, the implementation of successful factory automation will involve a user-oriented approach. That is, unless technical, human resources, and strategic issues are not effectively coordinated to enhance organizational outcomes, there will be little hope for gains (Turnage, 1990). The decision to implement new technologies should not be decided by the senior executives alone; the middle and lower level managers should be also involved in the decision process.

TECHNOLOGY AND HEALTH

Technology and dissemination of health information

One of the major obstacles to the improvement of population, health and the adoption of more healthy practices is the widespread dissemination of information concerning health. Health communication efforts often fail simply because people do not often have the time to read, or watch programs and information of this kind. Even the best-intentioned people often find it difficult to change behavior within the complex contexts of their lives. It is in this direction that e-health communication, that is, communication using computers and other digital technologies seem to have great potential, through unique features such as mass customization, interactivity and convenience. Thus, one may **access online sites** for more **information** on a certain ailment as and when one needs it. One can **interact with experts** from diverse health areas through videoconferencing. And, one may even **interact with peers** facing the same problems, either that of actually suffering from the ailment or as a caregiver. A survey was conducted on 96 men and 51 women living with HIV-AIDS on their experience in using the Internet. What were the results? The respondents were found to use the internet for a wide variety of activities, ranging from searching for health and AIDS-specific information to communicating with service providers. However, the use of the Internet varied as a function of years of education. People who had less than 12 years of education were less likely to have used the Internet. Secondly, Internet usage was greater among those who had Internet access at their homes (Kalichman & colleagues, 2002). This is just one example regarding the scope of e-communication in the field of health. There is considerable initial evidence that e-health communication can improve behavioral outcomes (Neuhauser & Kreps, 2003), but we have yet to learn much regarding whether the technical promise of such communication will be effective within the cross-cultural context.

Technology and telemedicine

Telemedicine: The delivery of medical aid through the use of information technology

Another application of technology in health is in the upcoming field of **telemedicine** and **telehealth**, that is, the use of computer and other digital technologies to provide **online advice** and even **medical aid**, especially in remote areas. Thus, **rural health** would be one customer for such telemedicine, providing help in areas as diverse as direct patient care, training and supervision and consultation, continuing education, and for helping to ameliorate the isolation of rural health systems. Stamm (2003) reviews **four challenges** to the use of telemedicine in rural areas. These are: **establishing effectiveness, reimbursement, licensure** and the **uneven distribution of access to technology**, that is, overcoming the digital divide. Even in the urban areas, technologically advanced methods of medical diagnosis are on their way in. Giving his keynote address on "2003 and beyond—challenges facing research and pharmaceutical industry" Professor Trevor M. Jones, Director General of the British pharmaceutical industry said that we are crossing new frontiers in biodiagnostics and would be soon able to deliver innovative and yet convenient ways of diagnosis. One of the examples provided by him is that you can cough into your mobile phone and your doctor will be able to diagnose the pathogen responsible for it, give the exact drug and dosage which would help the patient to take immediate care without waiting to go to the doctors chamber. It looks like a scene from "Star Wars" when compared to the health facilities in the Third World.

Technology and reproductive medicine

Technology has enabled the crossing of new frontiers in **reproductive medicine.** The foremost among these is **cloning.** Discussing the future of human cloning, Tenant (2002) describes it as an extreme form of artificial selection and speculates on problems of such artificial reproduction as contrasted to natural sexual reproduction. In a very stimulating manner, the author discusses the implications of cloning for "sibling rivalry" the "war between the sexes!" Along a similar vein are the findings regarding attitudes toward **genetic testing.** Invented as a way of reducing the cases of known inheritable forms of disability through abortion, people the world over have had differing views regarding genetic testing ranging from the absolute "no-no"attitude of some religious sects to the "it is all right" attitudes of others. Berth, Dinkel and Balck (2002) conducted a study on 2,076 Germans and their results reveal that overall there is a wide acceptance of genetic testing, with about two thirds holding a positive attitude. While differences for several demographic variables were insignificant, a clear difference emerged for religious affiliation, with subjects who stated that they were members of a religious group consistently indicating a less favorable view of gene tests.

Technology and therapy

When cyber psychology meets clinical psychology, we see the emergence of **e-therapy** for **mental health care.** Thus, as the name suggests, e-therapy refers to the use of information technology for delivering therapy, as contrasted with traditional face-to-face therapy. Clinical psychologists have been wary of the use of e-therapy mainly because a large part of the therapy relies on the verbal and even more on the non-verbal aspects of interpersonal communication. The facial expression of the client and the many nuances of tone of voice add considerably to the understanding of the client's history and to the therapeutic process. While nothing can probably replace face-to-face communication, information technology certainly has a lot to offer. According to Castenuovo, Gaggioli and Riva (2001), some of the **e-therapy modes** are **e-mail counseling, self help therapy** and **self help groups**—all of which help to widen the length and the breadth of coverage of the clinical psychologist. **The tools** would include **e-mail, chat** and **video conferencing.** Another useful tool would be **shared hypermedia,** which enables the simultaneous browsing of the same website by different users and gives them a chance to communicate with each other. An empirical test comparing computer-based versus traditional individual therapy was conducted by Jacobs and colleagues (2001). The results indicate that though traditional clinical therapy outperformed computer-based therapy on some parameters, the results were favorable and comparable in both the conditions.

> **e-therapy:** Therapy given over the Internet

During the last few years we have seen a proliferation of **e-support groups** that enable patients and their care-givers to communicate with health professionals and other patients and their care-givers. In an investigation looking into the advantages of e-support groups, it was found that patients suffering from either ovarian cancer or cancer of the prostate were able to derive support from the Internet (Sullivan, 2003). In another investigation, the potential benefits of Internet use was studied among patients with breast cancer. The findings revealed that the benefits varied with the ethnicity of the patient, with African American and Hispanic American patients being benefited to a greater extent than White patients. The most pervasive of the benefits from Internet was as a source of social support (Fogel, Albert, Schnabel & co-workers, 2003). Such findings have special relevance for health care management of racial/ ethnic minorities.

The impact of technology in the sphere of health can also be seen in the way technology has impacted **physical activity and exercise interventions.** Though technology can be blamed for a secular decline in the physical activity, there have been clear advantages too. It has allowed the proactive recruitment of large audiences, the individualization of interventions on a large scale, the delivery of activity promoting interventions to large audiences via differing channels. (Nigg, 2003). Other useful areas are the use of **interactive TV** and **virtual reality.** The latter has been found to be very useful for many aspects of rehabilitation assessment, treatment and research (Schulteis & Rizzo, 2001). A good example of the use of virtual reality is its use for the reduction of fear of flying, since it produces an environment in which the patient can hear and feel the experience of lying and is yet safe in the therapist's office (Rivera, Arbona, Perpina & Castellano, 2001).

TECHNOLOGY AND COMMUNICATION

The social psychology of cyberspace

Cyberspace: The physical psycho-social and virtual environment of the World Wide Web

Cyberspace is standing out there, waiting to be studied from the psycho-social aspect. While researchers have shown an interest in the phenomenon, what appears to be missing is a truly psycho-social theory. An attempt in this direction has been made by Galimerti and Riva (2001). Focusing on three aspects: the actors, the artifacts and the interrelationship between these two, they have formulated a model for the study of cyber interaction.

Cyberspace has opened up a completely new channel for communication—the **chat room**—a relatively new form of text-based communication that allows individuals to interact with each other over the Internet. Can the social psychological theories of traditional forms of communication explain the behavior of people using this medium? (Markey, Wells & Markey, 2002) report three extremely innovative studies in this context (see Box 6.4 below).

BOX 6.4

Social and personality theory in the chat room

To demonstrate the validity of social and personality theories for understanding the interaction and behavior of people in the chat room, Markey, Wells and Markey (2002) presented three studies. We now describe two of these studies.

Study 1: They observed a sample of 780 individuals in 60 different chat rooms in the US. The behavior observed there suggested that interventions are seen in the virtual world of the chat room too, and that the theoretical framework presented by Latane and Darley for the explanation of bystander intervention can be used to explain and predict intervention in computer mediated interactions too.

Study 2: This was a study on compliance in the chat room. Observations were made on 200 participants. The findings clarify that the "foot-in-the-door technique" (Freedman & Frazer, 1966) is capable of being used in the chat room as much as in the real world.

Taken together, the authors are of the view that psychologists are well-equipped with theories to understand interactions and behavior in the virtual world of the chat room.

Types of communication and organizational position

In an office information is processed, stored and retrieved. The situations and the sources of information in a typical office are depicted in Table 6.2. However, the status of a worker plays an important role in the use of communication (Table 6.3). For example, while face-to-face conversation is mostly used by those in the upper ranks, the staff belonging to the lower ranks use document-based communication. Although technology has revolutionized the work in offices, there are no automated aids to substitute for face-to-face conversation, supervision, counseling, or negotiation. And where it is used, such as videoconferencing and teleconferencing, the results are not always encouraging.

TABLE 6.2

Where office workers go first for information (partial list) (*Source*: Hodges & Angalet, 1968)

Situation	Source	Frequency
No search required	Recall	19.0
	Asked a colleague	14.5
	Searched own collection	13.0
Local work environment	Departmental files	5.5
	Assigned to subordinate	4.5
	Asked supervisor	1.0
External to work environment	Customer	2.0
	External consultant	1.0

TABLE 6.3

Major types of communications in offices (*Source*: Hodges & Angalet, 1968)

Type of Communication	Exec.	Manager	Knowledge worker	Secretary
Face-to-face	53	47	23	Negligible
Document	27	29	42	55
Telephone	16	9	17	20
Other	4	15	18	25

The shared social context in organizational communication

A lot of work in offices is accomplished via informal communications. Such communications are often unplanned and spontaneous. According to Kraut and co-workers (1990), an informal communication eliminates hierarchy, promotes feedback, and interaction. Often there is no planned agenda scheduled in advance. People communicate according to their current interests and modify their statements frequently to make adjustments. Table 6.6 illustrates the difference between formal and informal communication.

TABLE 6.4

The formal dimension of communication (*Source:* Kraut *et al.*, 1990)

	Formal	Informal
•	Scheduled in advance	Unscheduled
•	Arranged participants	Random participants
•	Preset agenda	Unarranged agenda
•	One way	Interactive
•	Impoverished content	Rich content
•	Formal language and speech register	Informal language and speech register

Kraut and co-workers (1990) focused on informal communication in a research and development (R & D) enterprise where most research was collaborative and the product remains uncertain. Under such conditions, opportunistic, work-related conversations were common. After carefully studying the behavior of R & D personnel, Kraut and co-workers found that 85% of the interactions and approximately 50% of the conversations in this R & D facility were unplanned because the participants did not know the purpose of communication. They also found that physical proximity was a strong contributor in such communications, for 87% of the people who communicated shared the same floor in a building. Fifty two per cent of all conversations between people took place among those who worked within the same corridor.

Having the above scenario in mind, Kraut and co-workers conducted a study based on a VideoWindow System which connected two public lounge areas with video channels. This system allowed nearly the entire area to be visible. The system was open 24 hours a day and operated by simply saying "hello" to the person at the other end. The results of this study showed that compared to face-to-face conversations, the VideoWindow conversations were substantially fewer. The researchers commented that even with the life-sized images in their study, people might have reacted uncomfortably and maintained psychological distance with the communicator.

A common social psychological problem in the use of interactive technology is perspective taking. That is, the ability of the speakers to take into account the addressee's characteristics in formulating their message. With the help of perspective taking, both speakers and hearers establish and maintain the level of their communication (Krauss & Fussell, 1991). According to Fussell and Benimoff (1995), perspective taking is influenced by (1) the shared physical context and (2) the shared social context.

During a face-to-face interaction the context of conversation includes objects, people and the setting of the place. The communicators know the location of these objects and they have an input of the visual field and an understanding of the physical setting. On the other hand, in a teleconferencing situation, the physical setting is virtual, not real. A communicator has no knowledge what objects and people are present with the addressee. Further, the communicator does not know what is seen by the other people. The use of deictic expression "What is this" is very easy and common in a face-to-face conversation but not so easy in a teleconferencing. Making a similar expression in teleconferencing means that the communicator has ascertained that the object is not only visible to the addressee, but he is also attending to it.

Schober (1993) pointed out another problem with the **shared physical context** between the addresser and the addressee in face-to-face conversation versus teleconferencing. In a face-to-face conversation, an object on the right side of the addressee is on the left side of the addresser. However, in teleconferencing the preference in window placement may alter the position of the addressee and can cause confusion among the participants in their conversation when they refer to the same object.

The second issue concerning the shared social context has deeper implications than the shared physical context. It is well known that eye gaze, gesture and clothing are important in perspective taking (Fussell & Benimoff, 1995). Video images do not display vividly social information as much as face-to-face information does. Fiske and Taylor (1991) have shown how we categorize information about others based on gender, ethnicity, and age factors. This categorization process is supported by physical features like facial characteristics, clothing, and so on. In the absence of clear display of such attributes, the range and extent of communication in teleconferencing may alter.

Commenting on this issue, Fussell and Benimoff (1995) wrote:

> Thus key issues for future development of telecommunications products and services are the identification of the information most useful for correctly categorizing others and the development of products that transmit this information. Electronic meeting systems should provide more than icon-sized bit map displays of each participant. Iconified images do not convey the full richness of social information that is present in face-to-face conversation. Images may be so small that users cannot detect the social information contained in them; they also may not be up-to-date, given that some systems allow users to supply a single picture of themselves, which they use in every situation. Systems in which users have the capability to transmit stored, scanned images themselves, plus some identifying information such as name and title, are an improvement; nevertheless, unless real-time video is present, important sources of information about others, particularly their engagement and interest in the meeting itself, will be lacking (p. 239-240).

BOX 6.5

A field experiment on the use of videoconferencing technology for job interviews

One of the most valid ways of selecting prospective employees has been through the interview. However, with globalization and the presence of offices at diverse geographical locations, it is becoming imperative to think of ways by which time, energy and money can be saved by the organization. Information technology has come to the rescue and has been followed by a spate of methods that do not require the physical presence of the candidate in front of the interviewer. One such method is videoconferencing.

The question however remains as to whether the videoconferenced interview can yield results as valid and reliable as those obtained through the traditional interview. Chapman and Rowe (2001) conducted a field study in this reference. A sample of 25 interviewers (aged 26 to 58 years) evaluated 92 real job applicants (mean age 21 years) who were randomly assigned to either a face-to-face interview condition or a desktop videoconferencing interview condition. Analyzing the evaluations obtained from the two conditions indicated that there was a bias in favor of the videoconference applicants vis-à-vis the face-to-face applicants, clearly pointing to the need to be aware of such biases as might creep in to the hiring process when communication technologies are used.

The results could also depend on attitudes to videoconferencing. Subjects who had a preliminary positive attitude towards the desk top system not only evaluated it positively after use but were also able to use it more efficiently (Townsend & co-workers, 2001).

Other issues in videoconferencing involve **turn taking** and **grounding of meaning.** It is commonly known that when two people communicate, any long delay is considered as awkward. When ABC or NBC news anchors like Peter Jennings or Tom Brokaw interview people located at far away places, any delay in their communication is generally attributed to a mechanical failure or some difficulty in comprehending the message. Research shows that when people communicate, they depend on **two types of cues** in their interaction: **linguistic** and **paralinguistic**. The linguistic functions refer to the **meaning of sentences.** The paralinguistic functions refer to the **characteristics of intonation** and other related issues such as failing intonation at the end of declarative sentences. Such cues are important in telephone conversation and guide turn taking (Rutter, 1987). In videoconferencing, deictic gestures (for example, pointing to a particular person in lieu of their name) can cause confusion and further distort interaction in communication. Future research in improving videoconferencing cannot ignore the significance of devices that can improve turn coordination. This is a clear example to show why technocrats depend on research in social psychology that describes the limits of technology. Given the high cost of videoconferencing, any ease of coordination in communication will be helpful to all the communicating parties.

Grounding of meaning: Understanding that a common ground has been established for communication

Grounding of meaning refers to an understanding that a common ground is established for communication (Fussell & Benimoff, 1995). Feedback from back-channel responses and conversational interactions provide meaning to the communication. In a typical talk show, eye gaze and facial expressions of members of the audience provide valuable information in interpreting the ongoing communication. When people in the audience say "I see" or "wow" and make expressions such as head nods or looks of puzzlement, it enriches the whole process of communication. Is it possible to display such back channel responses and conversational interactions in videoconferencing? Given the existing technology, it is not possible to do so. Moreover, we know that in face-to-face conversation, we can select what we want to hear and attend, but in the videoconferencing situation, it is the technical producer who filters information for us. Realizing the significance of gaze, gesture and other factors in communication, more research is needed to address the issues in communication based on technology.

There is yet another way social psychologists can help technologists. Several types of training materials are very complex and need to be performed as a team. There are a number of complex skills in aviation and other industries that require learning very complex material and coordinating high performance activities with other operators. Under such conditions, a considerable amount of time is spent in discussing how to master a complex task. In the chapter on education, a discussion of facilitating effects of cooperative tasks was presented. While the beneficial effects of cooperative learning are known from several conventional studies of social psychology, recent experiments in the learning of complex skills in a group setting are not only helping the technologists to improve their training material but also enabling social psychologists in understanding what contributes to the beneficial effects in a group setting. In a recent study, Prislin and co-workers (1996) used the Space Fortress (SF), a video-game-like research tool, which puts complex processing demands, such as, high work demands, prioritization, dynamic attention allocation, and complex coordination of perceptual and motor skills. They found that when subjects were allowed to have a group discussion, their performance was facilitated. In addition, they noted that social comparisons (comparing scores) and motivation (level of interest and eagerness to perform a task) were also related to the participant's performance. The analysis of an interaction between social comparison and motivation factors revealed that the social comparison dimension influenced participants in the low and average motivation groups but not in the highly motivated group. Based on these results, Prislin and co-workers argued that the complex learning representative of industrial tasks can be facilitated by group discussion. However, such beneficial effects of learning complex tasks are also related to several factors: gender of trainees, level of evaluation and comparison, schedules of practice and screening of participants.

Processing demands: What was learned and how was it learned

In short, rather than simply studying the comparative effects of cooperative and competitive learning, future research in social psychology should focus on the **processing demands** of a task. That is, **what was learned** and **how was it learned.** With the increasing use of technology, many tasks are becoming highly complex, and the interaction of social comparison and motivation involved in learning complex tasks may or may not be conducive to all that is learned in a cooperative classroom or in an industrial training program. Driskell and Salas (1991) argued that complex technologies have paradoxical effects. Such technologies may enhance operator capabilities but also increase potential for catastrophic circumstances. In a study on the effects of workload on team performance in a complex task situation, Urban, Weaver, Bowers and Rhodenizer (1996) showed that time pressure significantly degraded performance. They recommended that under such task conditions, training interventions will be most effective when initiated at the beginning of a program.

The success of technology in promoting **informal communication** will depend upon several factors. **First,** we must acknowledge the significance of human factors in the operation of a system. The precision of perception involving judgment, size of faces and objects, and other related factors are critical variables in promoting informal communications, if they are to remain informal in a true sense. **Second,** the behavioral cost is a critical factor in the use of such informal communication. Unless the system is not brought to the user, the success of technology will remain doubtful. **Third,** people are also concerned about the privacy of their conversations. The use of technology involves an electronic medium over which the two communicating people have no control. According to Kraut *et al.* (1990) many users may worry about the "subtleties of etiquette and the protocols that govern social interactions" (p. 196).

THE LIMITS OF SOCIAL PSYCHOLOGY OF TECHNOLOGY

Social and industrial psychologists have been criticized for overemphasizing the human side of an enterprise while ignoring the role of technology (Turnage, 1990; Majchrzak & Davis, 1990). A place of work involves workers, machines, and other attributes. In an organization, the optimal functioning of both the machines and the workers are important and both should support each other. Based on the problems of coalmine workers in Britain and the textile workers of India, the Tavistock Institute of Human Relations presented the concept of socio-technical systems to describe how social and technical aspects interact in an organization. While the technical aspect transforms inputs into outputs, the social aspect fulfills the needs of people. Unfortunately, social psychologists have often failed to broaden their focus to take into account the concerns of emerging technology, and they have followed a unidirectional approach in viewing the problems of a socio-technical system. According to Majchrzak and Davis (1990):

> Social psychologists have traditionally limited their research attention to individual and group behavior, leaving a serious examination of technological factors to the computer scientist or engineer. We have argued that such a limited perspective unnecessarily constraints the impact of social psychology (p. 61).

There are several ways in which social psychologists can remove this **barrier. First**, they need to appreciate the perspectives offered by the technologists. Given a suitable opportunity, they should step in the shoes of a technologist and view a human issue in the context of technology, and then pose a question, "Is there a conflict between people and machine?" A practical way to come to terms is that both technocrats and social psychologists should cross-train in each other's field to develop an appreciation of their common problems. **Second**, American social psychologists need to learn something from their fellow European social psychologists who are actively engaged in studying the relationship between socio-psychological factors and technology.

Finally, while the potential benefits of automation are known, its failures should be seen in a proper perspective. A good example is the complaint of many airline pilots who receive false signals when the plane flies too close to the ground. When should we attribute an error to the human operator or to the machine is one question that is constantly debated in scrutinizing the accidents. The interface of people and technology may show several dimensions of insignificance to the public but they are of a great personal value to the individual worker (for example, loss of control). Another offshoot of such studies would be to ascertain ways in which psychological research might contribute in making technology and its products environmentally benign (Nickerson, 2003). It seems that a warm handshake of technology with social psychology will take several years. With the rapid changes in technology, social psychology has no choice but to move along rapidly.

Donald A. Norman (1995), a stalwart of modern cognitive psychology, predicted at least **four major trends** in relation to behavior and technology:

- **An increase in the availability of "digital information," information encoded electronically in a form that is readily stored, transmitted and displayed......**
- **Widespread availability of high speed communication links reaching into every home, and even to every person via various forms of wired, optical and wireless transmission, including direct satellite transmission, cable and fiber optic lines to everywhere, and advances in compression technology that dramatically reduce the amount of information required to reproduce text, sound and pictures.**
- **Continually more computational devices, smaller and less expensive than ever before.....**
- **The ability to experience three dimensional sight and sound coupled to a person's own body position and movements. To be used for conferencing, for exploring new places, whether real or imagined. For educators, designers, explorers or just for entertainment** (p. 250-251).

Less than a decade after the publication of his article, all of the above have become a reality. But, the mere introduction of the technology is not enough. They would have to be matched to the person and to the society for whom the technology has been created. And it is here that the role of social psychology would become most crucial. Or, as Gordon H. Bower (1995) writing a chapter on "Empowering people through friendly technology: psychology in the twenty first century," wrote:

> I believe that technological innovations of the coming century will greatly expand the power of individuals to control their environment, to control themselves and guide their children, and thereby to better direct their own destiny. ......It is my contention that psychologists will play a pivotal role in helping design such technologies to be "user friendly" in fieldtesting their efficacy, and in refining the technological designs until they achieve a proper fit to the capabilities and talents of individual users (p. 18).

Summary

The rapid changes caused by technology are affecting us in our personal lives and at work. While the use of computers and other technical devices have caused stress and phobia in some people, others have made their transition smoothly. There are several other ways in which technology has affected us too. The chapter focused on the role of technology in work at offices and at manufacturing plants and how it has deskilled workers, eliminated middle managers and caused reorganization of workplaces.

The chapter also discussed the contribution of technology to health, especially in the realms of dissemination of health information, reproductive medicine and mental health.

Technology has also changed our ways to communicate with others. Can videoconferencing replace face-to-face meetings? What will be the nature of perspective-taking in teleconferencing? The applications of technology are compelling social psychologists to explore these issues.

Finally, this chapter cautions social psychologists that if they do not coordinate fast enough with the current changes in technology, it will be too late for them to catch up to the upcoming changes. One solution is to cross train in the areas of social psychology and technology.

Suggestions for Further Reading

1. Warschauer, M. (2003). *Technology and Social Inclusion: Rethinking the Digital Divide.* Cambridge: MIT.
2. Riva, G. & Galimberti, C. (Eds) (2001). *Towards Cyberpsychology: Mind, Cognition and Society in the Internet Age.* Amsterdam: IOS.
3. Bower, G.H. (1995). Empowering people through friendly technology: Psychology in the twenty-first century. In R.L. Solso and D.W. Massaro (Eds). *The Science of the Mind: 2001 and Beyond.* NY: Oxford University Press.

Some Key Terms

CAD
CIM
Cyber sickness
Cyberspace
Digital divide
Ergonomics
e-therapy
Failed impulse control
Grounding of meaning
High tech-high touch
Infotainment
Perspective-taking
Processing demands
Techno-centered people
Tele-commuting
Technological fix
Technophobia
Technostress
Telemedicine
The Big Five
Virtual debate

SOCIAL PSYCHOLOGY OF THE ENVIRONMENT

7

Chapter Outline

- An introduction to social psychology of the environment
  - The cross-cultural perspective on concern for environment
- Energy conservation
  - A useful tip to gas and electric companies: Efforts by Aronson and co-workers
- Water conservation
- Litter control
- Recycling
  - A model of consumer composting behavior
  - Curbside recycling programs
- Environmental stressors
  - Noise
  - Heat
- Population, space and built environments
  - Personal space
  - Cross-cultural perspective on personal space
  - Urban planning and residential environments
  - Natural environment
- Problems in maintaining pro-environmental behavior and its remedy
- Emerging issues for the application of social psychology
  - Social psychology of capsule habitats
  - Ecopsychology

AN INTRODUCTION TO SOCIAL PSYCHOLOGY OF THE ENVIRONMENT

Environmental psychology, erstwhile known as an offshoot of social psychology, has now gained its independent identity and is regarded as an interdisciplinary area of psychology that deals with the interaction between people and their environment. Generally speaking, we come across two types of environments: physical and social. When social environment influences us, we undoubtedly consider it as a legitimate area of study of social psychology (chapter 1). On the other hand, the influence of the physical environment constitutes the domain of environmental psychology.

Environmental psychology: Study of the interaction between people and their environments

Because physical environment is also an aspect of the social environment, the question that has often caused confusion in the study of social and environmental psychology is: What part of physical environment remains "physical"? At a conceptual level, human-made environments such as buildings are considered as examples of physical environments. At the methodological level, environmental psychology borrows heavily not only from social psychology but also from cognitive psychology, developmental psychology, health psychology and community psychology, at the one end, and geography, anthropology, architecture, engineering, and ecology, at the other end. The intellectual boundaries of environmental psychology have now become complex and multidisciplinary. Stokols (2000) identified the ways in which the physical-social environment affects almost all aspects of life: health, work, interpersonal relationships, personal well being and social cohesion. Typically, environmental psychology attempts to explore: how crowding, work environment, temperature and personal space influence people? What is the role of the environment in causing stress? How do people develop cognitive maps? And so on. In *The Handbook of Environmental Psychology*, Gifford (2002) outlines how environmental psychology does not simply consider problems, but also develops interventions to tackle those problems. Many of the areas focused upon by Gifford have direct implications for social psychology.

Stokols (1995) has identified **six major trends** in environmental psychology that have bearings on several areas of psychology. These six areas have considerable significance for social psychology as well. **First,** development of constructs and methods for the purpose of analyzing the relationship between environment and behavior have broadened social psychological perspectives. As you will see in this chapter, social psychology now deals with molar issues such as crowding, ecological perspective, and large-scale physical settings, in addition to micro level conventional topics such as cognition, learning, and perception.

Second, the study of environmental perception, attitudes and decision making has led to the growth of cross-paradigm research. For example, it has been shown how psychological concepts have been used by geographers and urban planners in understanding the mental maps of urban dwellers (Downs, 1970).

Third, the early influence of social psychology dominated situationist theories in environmental psychology by showing how environmental conditions predicted behavior changes. In other words, the relationship between situation and behavior was conceived as unidirectional. With the emergence of transactional theories, it has been demonstrated how the relationship between environment and behavior becomes reciprocal or bidirectional. Individuals respond to the environment and then restructure it, if they have the means to do so.

Fourth, with the emergence of transactional approaches, a new area of relationship between social psychology and environmental psychology was born: group-environment transactions. Issues like fear of crime, traffic congestion, graffiti, pollution, and resource shortages are related to the community at large. For example, Milgram and Jodelet (1976) wrote, "The perception of city is a social fact and as such, needs to be studied in its collective as well as its individual aspect" (p. 108). How do you perceive the Harlem and the Watts areas?

Fifth, both social and environmental psychology are actively involved in community problem solving, for example, people's reaction to environmental hazards and energy consumption. Together, they are trying to make an impact on public policy.

And **finally**, with the increase in the international scope of environmental psychology, new social psychological dimensions have emerged. Most psychologists outside Northern America feel that the social behavior aspect of psychology, as presented by North American psychologists, is extremely limited and narrow (see chapter 1, comments by Levy-Leboyer). When the Secretary-General of an Earth Summit conference (*Newsweek*, June 1, 1992) wanted an inspirational document for a child's bedroom so that children become aware of environmental problems, a delegate from the Third World remarked that most children in the Third World did not have bedrooms! Cross-cultural and cross-national experiences have benefited both social and environmental psychology in areas ranging from personal space preference of Americans to low hypertension and less obesity among Mabaan tribe members in Sudan.

The cross-cultural perspective on concern for environment

Noted environmental psychologist Levy-Leboyer and co-workers (1996) made a five-nation analysis of attitudes and behavior towards the environment. On the basis of a study of 742 teachers and engineers from five countries, namely, France, Germany, Italy, Portugal and the UK, they concluded that there were wide differences between the groups, not only on objective knowledge about environmental issues, but also in terms of **pro-environmental attitudes and behavior.** Concern for the environment has also been assessed in other countries. A survey on South African respondents has been reported by van Staden and co-workers (2002). The respondents were most concerned about poverty, litter and solid waste, air and water pollution. Also, underlying their concern for the 13 environmental issues, on which their opinion was elicited, was a single factor that can be called "**general global environmental concern.**" There were also differences in terms of cultural groups, education, and to some extent to gender and age. A similar general factor, that is, attitudes towards safety and risk issues, was seen to explain environmental concern and environmental behavior among Norwegian subjects (Iverson & Rundmo, 2002).

Pro-environmental attitudes: Positive attitudes towards protection of the environment and environmental resources

Pro-environmental behavior: Action that has positive effects for the environment

What can social psychology do to promote pro-environmental attitudes? Is changing attitudes enough for environmental concerns? What interventions will succeed in a community for not only changing attitudes but also for participating in pro-environmental programs? Millions of dollars are spent in the State of California alone to promote energy conservation but the results are not very encouraging. The reason: Even if attitudes are pro-environmental, behavior may not necessarily be so. Think for a moment about your own position. If someone asks you, "will you like to waste water or energy?" Your answer will be, "No," but if you examine your own behavior, you will notice that you often leave the faucet open while shaving. However, if you felt that the wasting of water would cause immediate problems to you, your attitude could be different. This has been seen by all of us in times of water shortage. Scientific evidence for such a direct implication factor has also been provided. People are more concerned about the environment and its impact on the community when they feel that they will have to bear the brunt of it. Thus, people were more concerned about an oil spill and its impact when it was felt that their immediate built environment would be affected than when it was to impact natural environments (Levi & co-workers, 2001).

While theories of social psychology have done well in accounting for the relationship between environment and behavior in simple forms, for example, unidirectional approaches, there have been enormous problems in developing a theoretical perspective to bridge the gap between attitudes and behavior, that is, will people behave in a predictable manner after contemplating a change in their attitude? A significant portion of this chapter will address this issue with respect to energy conservation, littering, and recycling. Other issues highlighting the contribution of social psychology are directly related to the physical environment, that is, heat, noise and space, etc.

ENERGY CONSERVATION

The consumption of energy in the U.S. is the highest in the world. It is also estimated that this consumption rate can be easily cut down by at least 50% without causing any significant financial burden (Williams & Ross, 1980), and yet most Americans are indifferent to advertisements and other persuasive attempts to save not only the resources of the community but also their own money. While we have made considerable inroads in our understanding of issues such as recycling behavior, there is lesser attention to the understanding of energy and water conservation issues (Vining & Ebreo, 2002).

Among the attempts that have been made to understand the dynamics of such behavior is that by Stern and Oskamp (1987). According to them, there are at least **5 major research traditions** regarding the management of scarce environmental resources:

- **The social psychological study of attitudes regarding pro-ecology behavior.**
- **The social psychological study of changes in attitudes towards the management of energy resources.**
- **Applied behavior analyses on methods of modifying environmentally destructive behavior and promoting more constructive habits.**
- **Studies on social factors affecting the diffusion of novel ideas and innovative practices regarding the conservation of resources.**
- **Evaluation research using cost-benefit analysis to understand the impact of governmental programs.**

The attitude model: Behavior will change with attitude change

According to Costanzo and co-workers (1986), two **social psychological models** have been used to encourage people to conserve energy: the attitude model and the rational economic model (REM). The **attitude model** stipulates that behavior will change following favorable changes in attitudes in favor of conservation. Obviously, this model implies that attitudes can change behavior. There are several problems with this type of assumption. Heberlein and Black (1976) reported that general pro-environmental attitudes are not related to specific pro-environmental behavior. For instance, not all automobile drivers who held pro-environmental beliefs purchased lead-free gas in the early seventies. Herberlein and Black studied the relationship between pro-environmental beliefs and gasoline consumption at four levels:

- **General pro-environmental attitudes.**
- **Attitudes concerning air pollution.**
- **Beliefs regarding lead-free gas.**
- **Personal obligation to use lead-free gas.**

The relationship between attitudes and behavior was found to be inconsistent for the first three conditions but specific behavior for using lead-free gas and specific attitudes for pollution caused by gasoline were highly related to each other. As the battery-powered automobiles have just started arriving in the market, one may expect a similar scenario for the relationship between one's preference for using battery-powered cars and specific attitudes for pollution caused by gasoline.

Commenting on the nature of the relationship between attitudes and behavior on energy conservation, Costanzo and co-workers, (1986) remarked: "At the level of attitudes, there is every indication that the potential for energy conservation is extremely high. For example, our regional survey indicates that there is a prevalent belief that the energy crisis is serious and worsening—roughly 85% of the respondents regard the energy crisis as serious, and over half (54.5%) believe it will worsen. Given these high levels of concern, one might expect conservation behavior to be widespread. However, we failed to uncover any clear relationship between energy-related attitudes and conservation behavior" (p. 521-522).

The second model, called the **rational economic model** (REM), was developed because of the following two reasons. First, the above stated attitude model was unsuccessful in changing behavior at a micro level. And second, it was assumed that people would follow behavior that is economically beneficial. In other words, if tax credits and rebates are offered or punishment such as fines is imposed, people are likely to behave in a way that tends to maximize their gain.

Rational economic model: People change only when it is economically beneficial to do so

The rational-economic model has also been criticized for its failure to bridge the gap between attitudes and behavior (Dennis & co-workers, 1990). First, the model fails to take into account cognitive and social factors that operate in a situation. People show inelasticity in their behavior. For example, even though drivers were punished financially for driving over 55 mph limit, a step that was taken to save gas, the driving behavior of many drivers did not change as they continued to drive at high speeds. Second, data showing cost-efficiency of energy saving programs are often questioned or considered exaggerated. People generally prefer an analysis based on common sense, for instance, information provided by neighbors or friends. Third, programs based on REM failed "to take into account how individuals perceive and react to them" (p. 1110, *ibid*). Most programs fail to connect with people.

Given the inability of existing models to explain why people with pro-environmental beliefs fail to translate these beliefs to their behavior, that is, the goal of consequence, Costanzo and co-workers (1986) presented a social psychological view of energy conservation behavior (Fig. 7.1) in which the attitude and the REM models have been integrated. To begin with, Costanzo and co-workers proposed that pro-conservation behavior consists of **psychological** and **positional variables.** Psychological variables refer to the information processing mechanism that consists of perception of information, evaluation of information, understanding of information, and retention of information. Informational interventions are important and their impact has also been shown by Staats, van Leeuwen and Wit (2000). Both short-term (over 4 week periods) and long-term improvements (after 1 year) were seen.

Socio-psychological model: Pro-conservation behavior is a function of both psychological and positional variables

Figure 7.1: Psychological and social factors in energy conservation behavior (adapted from Constanzo, *et al.*, 1986).

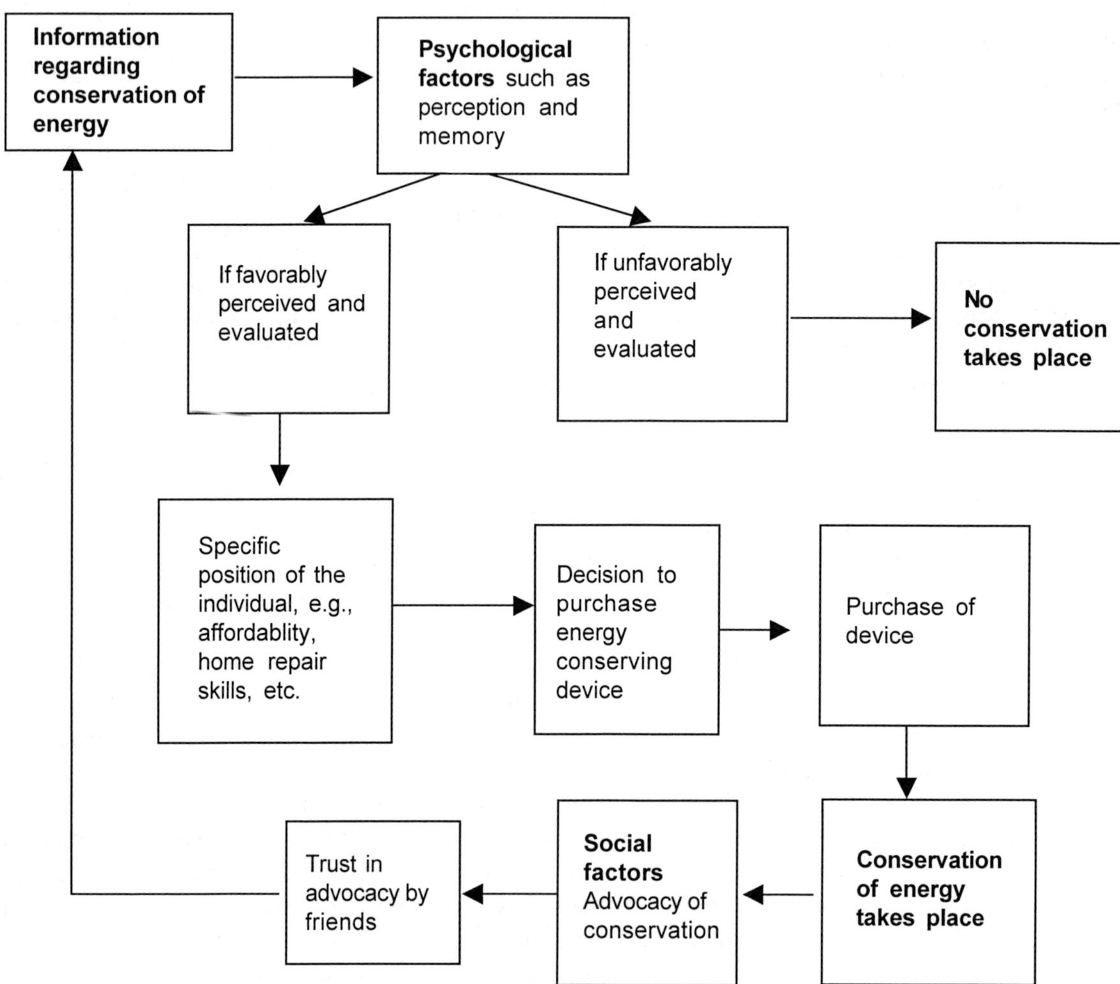

Positional variables refer to the situation of the decision maker. A situation may encourage or discourage an individual to adopt pro-environmental behavior. Disposable income, home ownership, home repair skills, and ownership of home technologies are important positional variables that will determine whether a person is likely to show pro-environmental behavior.

According to Costanzo and co-workers (*ibid*), information would be perceived if it is vivid, concrete and personalized. They have cited an example showing how people would trust the advice of a neighbor to buy a car more than to rely on a report published in the *Consumer Report*. Ironically, the *Consumer Report* gives information based on reports given by hundreds of people and yet one single report by a neighbor is considered more important (Nisbett & co-workers, 1976). Kahneman and Tversky (1979) reported that people are less impressed by any promise of gain than the threat of loss. In other words, if energy programs focus more on informing people how much they are losing, then people will act favorably than when people are told what they will gain.

After receiving information, people tend to evaluate it. In the first place, they look at the source of the message, that is, who is delivering the message. Obviously, if the source is not trustworthy, they would discard the information. In a study conducted in the New York state, it was found that consumers trusted instructions from the Public Service Commission but when the same instructions were sent by the utility company, they found them less credible (Craig & MacCann, 1978). The fact that a utility company has an interest in business makes people cautious in trusting their information.

The psychological variables concerning **understanding and remembering information** play an important part in energy conservation behavior. REM proposes that people make rational decisions through **cost-benefit analyses**. They do not always follow "expert" judgment but instead rely on "folk" judgment. In doing so, they make costly errors, especially when decisions are based on non-economic factors, for example, comfort, status, etc. People retain simple information better and use it first because it is convenient. Vague messages are forgotten quickly. In a study of 34 primary school children's understanding of energy waste (Kruger & Summers, 2000), it was found that these children had good prior awareness of some behavior that helped them to conserve energy, but their thinking was guided more by intuition than by scientific knowledge. It was also shown that this scientific knowledge could be instilled in the children, not only by specialist teachers of science but also by ordinary practitioners and could yet be very effective, if their subject and teaching knowledge were first enhanced by appropriate training. It is thus clear that what seems more important is not the knowledge of waste management but being trained to impart such knowledge to children in an effective manner.

Walton (1975) has delineated three social psychological propositions that may be used for the better acceptance of innovative practices. These are:

- The understanding of a new idea is enhanced if it is illustrated in a concrete fashion for the recipient and experienced by him/her. Thus, if the recipient is made to visit a site where such experiments are already in progress the idea is more likely to be accepted. Talking about water-harvesting projects in the developing countries, villagers are much more likely to start a water harvesting project in their own village after they have seen it in successful operation somewhere.
- A new set of ideas is more likely to be internalized and owned if the ideas are thought by the recipient first and are labeled by him/her or for him/her subsequently. Therefore, if after seeing a water-harvesting project, the villager is left to sort things out and thereafter if s/he comes out with the idea of its adoption in his/her own village, the project is more likely to be accepted.
- Presented with new ideas based on social psychological principles, people will act on them or not depending on their face validity rather than on empirical findings. The villager will be more likely to take action regarding the water-harvesting project if it seems to be running successfully, rather than if he is provided with data regarding its success.

On the basis of the above propositions Walton developed a model to explain the sources of influence on the design of a successful innovative practice.

Among **positional variables** in energy saving, affordability and ability to maintain operation are crucial variables. People who can afford and are highly motivated to use a battery-operated car may hesitate to buy this type of car because they are unsure of how to maintain the batteries, etc. Even the City of Santa Monica officials were not sure of how the battery-operated buses would perform. In December 1996, they decided to buy only three buses to try on an experimental basis. Given the situation, the General Motors Company had advertised (December, 1996) that it would be most easy to maintain their maiden battery-operated car.

Figure 7.2: Sources of influence on the design of an innovative practice (adapted from Walton, 1975).

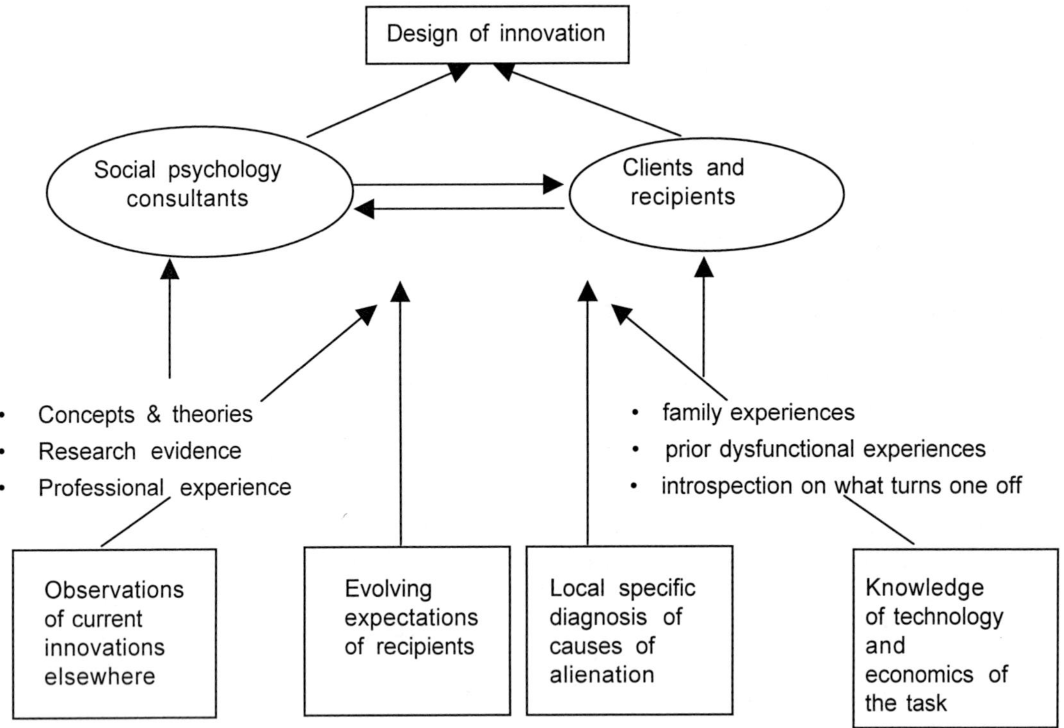

Dennis and co-workers (1990) analyzed studies on energy-saving information in three categories: antecedent, contingent, and feedback. **First, antecedent information** arrives before energy-saving behavior takes place. For instance, if you are shopping for a fuel efficient car, you look at the sticker showing "Miles Per Gallon." **Second,** contingent information is a reward given at the time of behavior. It is a consequence of the consumer's activity. If a company offers you 100 gallons of gas for free, because you decide to buy a car that gives great mileage per gallon, it is an example of a **contingent reward. Third, feedback** refers to information that comes after the use of an energy efficient device. For example, when you compare gas consumption at 55 mph and 80 mph, you get a feedback for fuel economy.

Becker and Seligman (1978) employed the feedback method for reducing electrical consumption in air-conditioning. Using a device that signaled outside temperature whenever it was below 68 degree F, the researcher noticed a decrease of 15% in energy use.

Brandon and Lewis (1999) have investigated the effect of feedback conditions, environment attitude and socio-demographic variables on energy consumption in the UK. Participants received feedback in various forms, with the maximum effect being seen when computers provided tips on saving energy. Moreover, this effect was more marked for people with pro-environmental attitudes. Results indicate that income and demographic factors predicted historic energy consumption but not current changes. In another study, in Canada (Berger, 1997), SES and demographic factors were found to be important antecedents to pro-environmental behavior. Feedback and goal setting were studied in energy conservation behavior in the Netherlands. Both self-set and assigned goals in combination with energy feedback produced over 21% savings as compared to the control group (McCalley & Midden, 2002).

In addition to energy saving information, several other psychological factors play an important part in changing energy consumption behavior. Based on some empirical work, it has been shown how (1) method of data presentation to consumers, (2) type of media channel and (3) acceptance of innovation play an important role in inducing people to save energy.

Studies on data presentation to consumers have benefited from the findings in cognitive psychology. Tversky and Kahneman (1981) demonstrated that people work harder to save a loss of $100 than to earn an additional $100. In material terms, there is no difference but not so in the psychological sense. Similarly, people will drive several miles to save $5 for an item costing $20 but they will not do so if the item costs $450. In both cases, there is an equal saving of $5. Here are some lessons from consumer behavior. If data are presented differently than what a consumer is accustomed to, there are chances that he/she will not change his/her behavior. As stated earlier, if consumers are told that they will lose a significant amount of money in the absence of an energy-saving device, they are more likely to adopt it, as compared to a situation in which they are made aware of their saving from the new device.

Pro-environmental behavior is influenced by **interactive media channels** significantly more than non-interactive media channels. People who use information provided by government departments prefer advice over mere supply of listings (Dennis & associates, 1990). It has also been found that social networking helps promote conservation. Publications like *Conservation Update* help customers develop their network. Leading departmental stores provide pro-environmental information on their computer terminals and help their customers in interacting with the right agency. A common example is that of stickers on the refrigerators giving information regarding their efficiency and addresses of relevant agencies.

Making people buy an environmentally useful gadget is a difficult task. Darley (1978) found in New Jersey that it was relatively easy for an innovator to convince friends and co-workers to use energy-efficient material but it wasn't easy with people in general in the same community. Again, good social networking and focus groups have been found to be successful in the adoption of innovations.

A common problem with energy conservation is that energy consumption is invisible and the results indicating large financial loss are not known immediately. For example, few consumers know that electric consumption for lighting accounts for less than 10% of their bill and are unaware of the relative cost involved in refrigeration, water-heating and air-conditioning. Dennis and co-workers (1990) concluded that economic incentives have failed to induce consumers to conserve energy because they could not understand the programs. Consider the following example: If you buy your groceries without knowing the price of individual items, you will know only the total amount of your purchase. Because you know the price of each grocery item, you remain careful in what you buy. People do not get this type of information in their energy bill, that is, what they paid for using energy for lighting, refrigerating, cooking, etc.

A useful tip to gas and electric companies: Efforts by Aronson and co-workers

Aronson and co-workers (Aronson and Gonzales, 1990; Gonzales, Aronson and Costanzo, 1988) were approached for energy conservation in the state of California where utility companies offer suggestions to customers to reduce energy conservation, but very few customers actually acted upon their recommendations. Aronson and co-workers focused on three issues to motivate customers to conserve energy.

First, homeowners must know the consequences of wasting energy. Most inspectors who provided this information to homeowners after their inspection work were mechanical in their description. For instance, a small crack under the door was not important to a homeowner but the same information was made vivid in the following way: "Look at the cracks around that door! It may not seem like much to you, but if you were to add up all the cracks around and under each of these doors, you would have the equivalent of a hole the size and circumference of a basketball" (Aronson, 1990, p. 128).

Second, Aronson and his co-workers emphasized that homeowners should be made aware of the cost of energy waste, not the rewards. As stated earlier, people will drive a long distance to save five dollars but they will not work to gain five dollars. In other words, people seem to act when they expect a loss rather than when they expect gain. Typically, the homeowners were told in this study that they would be carrying a hole in their pocket if they did not act.

Third, a foot-in-the-door technique was used. This technique shows that people generally accept requests of a larger magnitude after they had approved a smaller request. Using the same idea, the homeowners were asked to do their homework, for example, use the ladder, go over the roof, inspect the structure, and so on.

According to Aronson and co-workers, the above intervention program was successful because 61% homeowners followed the recommendations in sharp contrast to 39% only with the conventional method.

McMakin, Malone and Lundgren (2002), found that residents at two US military installations were motivated to conserve energy even without the use of financial incentives. The survey indicated that individuals were motivated by:

- **The desire to do the right thing.**
- **Set good examples for their children.**
- **Have comfortable homes.**

For sustained influence, the respondents recommended continued awareness and educational programs, incentives and disincentives. The above study has important implications for situations where users are not billed for individual energy use, for example, in dorms for students.

WATER CONSERVATION

As in the case of energy conservation, the need for water conservation has been felt for quite some time, especially at the time of drought in California in the 1990s. Although everyone seems to favor the conservation of water, people are apathetic in their behavior. It is an example of "apple-pie and motherhood" issue but not everyone practices it (Dickerson & co-workers, 1992).

Dissonance theory is most useful to explain water conservation attitudes and behavior

The **dissonance theory** (see chapter 1) proposes that people find themselves in a difficult situation when they hold opposite views, for example, when we believe that smoking causes cancer and yet we continue to smoke. When such a state of dissonance leads to an unpleasant state, individuals tend to reduce it by attitude or behavior changes. In doing so, people evaluate their self-concept, that is, whether they are doing what they preach. In other words, a dissonance situation can lead to self-appraisal leading to feelings of hypocrisy. In a clever experiment, Dickerson and co-workers (1992) first made their subjects "mindful" that they had been wasting water while showering and subsequently requested them to make a "public commitment" urging other people not to waste water. The study revealed that those subjects who faced a dissonance-arousing situation with this type of manipulation by the experimenters took shorter showers in comparison to subjects in a condition without any commitment (control group).

BOX 7.1

Water and energy conservation by hotel guests

It has generally been observed that people are less apt to conserve water and energy in public places than at home. The explanation normally given is that in public places, people fail to perceive direct negative effects, such as cost or shortage. At the same time it is clear that the hotel industry would definitely benefit if it could be provided certain scientifically tested strategies for reducing wastage of water and energy by its occupants.

A study by Agruse (1997) attempted to test this hypothesis in certain hotels in Texas. Data were collected from four classes of hotels: luxury, up-scale, mid-range, and economy from three Texas cities, namely, College Station, Houston and San Antonio. There were a total of fourteen hotels participating in the study.

Surprisingly, the results showed that, in general, individuals are more likely to practice water and energy conservation in a hotel than at home. There were, though, some specified groups that showed the opposite trend. At the same time there was clear support for the Fishbein model regarding behavioral intentions. As predicted by the model, the behavioral intentions of the participants were influenced to a greater degree by the perceived consequences of their behavior than by the perception of expectations of significant others. Thus perceived norms regarding behavior were not as important as perceived consequences.

Based on these findings, the hotel industry could develop strategies to develop greater water and energy conservation behavior among its customers.

Water conservation behavior can also be conceptualized as a **social dilemma** (Van Vugt, 2002), that is, a conflict between the short term self-interest of users and the long-term collective interest of the user community. The self-interest versus community perspective was studied by Van Vugt (2001) in the UK. Findings show that individuals maximized the self interest factors with the fixed tariff being associated with greater use than when there was a variable tariff, when there was a weak identification with the community. However, when people were made to develop a strong attachment with the community, people started showing self-restraint in their use and abuse of water.

While effective methods for water conservation in the UK depended on attachment to, and identification with the community, other factors have also been found to be important. In Jordan, for example, awareness of water conservation behavior by mandatory participation in ecological clubs at the school level led to an increase in participation among both students and their parents (Middlestadt & co-workers, 2001). An interesting piece of finding is from Mexico. On the basis of the structural model, Corral-Verdugo (2003) concluded that there is a significant relationship between people's tolerance to antisocial actions and their waste of water.

One of the major goals of environmental psychology is the search for **predictors** of responsible environmental behavior. We need to delineate both **personal characteristics** and **contextual features** facilitating pro-environmental behavior. In the past few decades, a vast amount of information has been obtained regarding potential predictors. These can be categorized as:

- **Psychological variables: environmental knowledge, pro-ecological attitudes, beliefs, notions, environmental skills and some personality traits.**
- **Situational variables: convenience of behavior, devices for conservation and norms for conservation.**

Demographic characteristics: age, gender, educational level and income.

A recent attempt to summarize the above classes of variables is through the concept of **Pro-Environmental Competency** (PEC) (Corral-Verdugo, 2002). While pro-environmental skills are important for such a competency, the need for conservation (environmental perceptions, beliefs, motives, and values) also has to be present to shape this competency. Requirements are socially constructed but they have to be individually grasped. Environmental goals and norms may be set up by the society, but the individual must perceive them and develop the necessary attitude and motivation for the behavior to occur. In a study by Corral-Verdugo (2002), in Mexico, such correlations were obtained between pro-environmental skills and pro-environmental requirements, showing the viability of the concept of PEC.

Pro-environmental competency PEC: Dependent upon pro-environmental skills and a positive attitude towards need for conservation

LITTER CONTROL

The USA is #1 in producing garbage. It is estimated that the cost of cleaning approximately seven million tons of litter is approximately one billion dollars. Litter does not simply involve money; it also causes health problems and the depletion of resources. People say, "Keep America beautiful" but you can see filthy conditions in inner cities or at parks and beaches.

Again, we notice a gap between what we say and what we do. Littering has become a social dilemma.

Attempts to remind people (for example, "Don't litter") were found to be counter-productive. Generally speaking, people do not like to be told what they should do. Weyant (1986) argued that if a "Don't litter here" sign involves a fine, the chances are that people will litter at that spot. Applying Brehm's (1966) reactance theory, Weyant contended that when a threat is posed to people, "they react in a manner that re-establishes their freedom" (p. 89).

Given the fact that people do not behave in a responsible manner, what can social psychology do to change the behavior of people? Earlier work by Schwartz (1970) indicated that customarily approved behavior called **norms**, are activated under certain conditions. If a company is dumping waste to save money and is disregarding laws, the other company is likely to do the same to remain competitive. In other words, people adopt the following attitude: If others are not caring about the environment, why should we? Schwartz proposed that until people are not aware of consequences of their action and do not take personal responsibility, it would be difficult to activate a pro-environmental norm.

Cialdini and co-workers (Cialdini, Kallgren & Reno, 1991; Cialdini, Reno & Kallgren, 1990; Reno, Cialdini & Kallgren, 1993) explored how injunctive and descriptive norms influence littering behavior. **Injunctive norms** are socially approved behavior, that is, what others approve. For example, we know that it is wrong to litter in a public area. **Descriptive norms** are our knowledge of what others are doing, irrespective of approval by others. For example, we observe how other people are behaving in order to decide our own behavior in a similar situation. Social psychological research has shown how understanding of both norms can help reduce littering.

Injunctive norms: Socially approved behavior

Descriptive norms: Knowledge of what others are doing

Let us first examine the descriptive norm which primarily involves a focus on how others are behaving. An ideal situation in the environment will be to find no litter at all. Unfortunately, this ideal situation has an exception. If an environment is totally clean, there are chances that some litter will accumulate. On the other hand, if there is only one piece of litter that sticks out like a sore thumb, the chances are that people will not litter at all. After stuffing the mailboxes with handbills, Cialdini and co-workers (1990) studied the behavior of college students at the time of picking their mail under the following three conditions:

Condition 1. Clean mailroom, no litter.

Condition 2. A piece of watermelon on the floor.

Condition 3. A piece of watermelon plus a lot of trash on the floor.

As predicted, littering was lowest when only one piece of litter was on the ground (Condition 2). In other words, a single violation of a norm makes people conscious that no other person has littered. As a result, they follow the behavior pattern of other people, that is, a descriptive norm has been activated in this situation.

Did you observe what people do when they find a handbill on the windshield of their car in a parking lot? If the handbill was not of interest to them, they would probably throw it out. Now, what would happen if people are made conscious that littering was bad (injunctive norm) before they reach their car? Cialdini and colleagues (*ibid*) have demonstrated that presenting a model behavior (for example, throwing a fast-food bag in the trash bin) shortly before subjects reached their car in a parking lot activated the injunctive norm, that is, fewer people tossed the handbill on the ground—less littering! There seems to be a lot of wisdom in the old saying: One small virtue gives birth to several virtues. Researches in social psychology show that such a small virtue will guide behavior if it is perceived, evaluated and recalled (information processing) in a timely manner.

I (Kool) recall a very interesting experience during a symposium I organized at my university in 1992. Before the presentation of participating speakers, I asked them if they would need a VCR, overhead projector or any other material during their presentation. I received one weird request from a very senior professor affiliated to a well known university: a few trash-filled bins and discarded newspapers. I was surprised as well as amused at his request. After the delegates had emptied the lecture hall for a short coffee break, the professor littered our lecture hall with garbage and discarded newspapers. Upon return to the lecture hall with the participating delegates, I was mad at what he had done but kept my cool as a decent host. The professor was enjoying my embarrassment with a smile. Soon after we settled in our seats, he got up and started picking up the litter. Seeing him cleaning the hall, a few attendees also got up and started helping him. Within seconds, many more people got up and started helping him! During his lecture, he commented: "Psychologists should not only conduct experiments but also demonstrate how their findings apply in everyday life." Needless to say, we learned from him how a good model can activate a norm for pro-environmental behavior. He did not spare me either and advised me in his lecture: learn to apply your work in real life.

At the same time, it appears that such "bystander effects" are observed for some acts of littering and not for others. In a study on the effect of the presence of others on people's reactions to norm violations on littering (Chekroun & Brauer, 2002), it was found that the presence of others inhibits people's tendency to communicate their disapproval to the deviant to a greater extent if the personal implication is low (that is, to an individual who draws graffiti in a shopping center) than when it is high (that is, to an individual throwing a plastic bottle in the bushes of a park).

RECYCLING

We discard a lot of stuff that can be re-used: aluminum cans, glass bottles, newspapers, and plastic material. If we reuse these materials, well over 70% energy required to manufacture these materials is likely to be saved. If we do not use these materials, we will need land to dispose of garbage. Additionally, non-use of these materials will deplete our natural resources. In other words, there are compelling arguments in favor of recycling but the problem is: most of us are indifferent to recycling.

What psychological theories and techniques can be used to induce people to engage in recycling of materials? Arbuthnut and co-researchers (1976-77; described in Weyant, 1986, p. 94) used the **foot-in-the-door technique** to engage people in recycling aluminum cans. The investigators first made a simple request to (1) save aluminum cans for one week; (2) write a letter to government officials to expand recycling program; and (3) respond to a survey concerning environmental protection. These requests required very little effort on the part of the participants. Comparison groups consisted of those subjects who participated in none or few request/s sessions. Observation of recycling behavior of subjects was conducted up to 18 months and the results showed that with the increase in the number of requests from zero to four, there was an increase in the percentage of people recycling the materials. Similarly, Werner and co-researchers (2002) observed that signs that validated student's complaints that aluminum can recycling was inconvenient, but persuaded them to recycle anyway. It led to a sustained behavioral change. The effects of such persuasion could be further enhanced by using a physically attractive persuader (Koestner & co-workers, 2001).

What motivates the subjects to engage in recycling? As stated earlier, REM has not been useful because people respond to financial incentives until they are offered. Participation in a program based on financial rewards leads subjects to believe that they have joined the program because of extrinsic reasons. According to self-perception theory (Bem, 1972), when people engage freely in a behavior, they tend to infer the causes of their behavior. In other words, we learn about ourselves when we participate and behave. Once subjects agree to small requests like writing pro-environmental letters, etc., they begin to realize the consequences of their own behavior. "In a sense," writes Weyant (1986), "we learn what kind of people we are by taking note of what we do" (p. 94).

A study by Witmer and Geller (1976) is a classic example demonstrating why financial incentives fail to maintain recycling behavior. In their study on dormitory residents, students were invited to participate under three conditions:

1. Prompt condition: students urged to recycle paper; contacted by flyers.
2. Raffle Contingency condition: one raffle ticket given for every pound of paper collected.
3. Contest condition: two dorms were paired and the one that collected highest amount of paper received $15 for its treasury.

Messages were given to residents under the above three conditions: Contingency, Contest and Prompt. As expected, the results showed that the collection of paper was highest in Raffle Contingency condition, followed by the Contest condition, and with no effect in the Prompt condition. However, recycling behavior returned soon to the baseline immediately after the distribution of the raffle ticket was withdrawn. An interesting finding of this study was that those students who resided closest to the collection center showed greatest participation.

Oskamp (1995) designed a study on recycling behavior to compare the effect of **five different interventions**: individual feedback, group feedback (neighborhood performance), information concerning procedures and incentives, a plea to recycle, and a control group (no intervention). The results of the study showed that the effects of feedback were most significant for both individual and group conditions. Overall, the frequency of recycling increased by 7% and the total amount of recyclables by 21%. The gain in the information and plea only condition were 4% and 13% respectively. In short, people respond better when they are given a feedback concerning their recycling behavior.

In another study by Schultz and Oskamp (1996), an attempt was made to see whether effort required by the behavior could explain the disparity between a positive attitude towards the environment and the actual pro-environmental behavior. The results of three experiments on undergraduates indicated a strong positive relationship between environmental concern and recycling behavior, but only under a high effort condition. Thus, when students who manifested high environmental concern were asked to participate in a drop-off recycling program, they readily complied, but when they were asked to participate in a curbside recycling program, their level of participation decreased. The first recycling program required greater effort than the latter.

According to Thogersen (1996), the **Subjective Expected Utility** (SEU) model has been popular in explaining attitudes towards recycling. This model is based on the assumption that when we get a chance to maximize our private use of things, we initiate an action. In order to increase the frequency and intensity of an environmentally beneficial behavior, we should increase benefits or add benefits to the existing benefits. On the other hand, a social psychological analysis has interpreted recycling behavior as a prosocial behavior. Schwartz (1977) contended that the moral decision to recycle involves three components: welfare of others, perceived responsibility, and evaluation of the act—good or bad. Such a view explores two options in the recycling behavior: denial of consequences, and denial of personal responsibility. From the available research evidence, it is clear that the denial of personal responsibility does not change the relationship between attitudes and behavior (Pieters, 1989). In other words, although people feel moral responsibility for recycling, they do not measure the consequences of their behavior. Thogersen (1996) further argued that when economic incentives were reframed to augment recycling, the feelings of obligation to recycle diminished. In short, the moral obligation to recycle restricts the usefulness of the SEU model in designing an intervention program. To engage people in recycling will involve an internalization process leading to the formation of personal norms. Studies of "recycle for cash" or other incentives show that such recycling behavior is independent of attitudes and norms (Oskamp & co-workers,1991).

Figure 7.3: An integrated waste management model (adapted from Taylor and Todd, 1997).

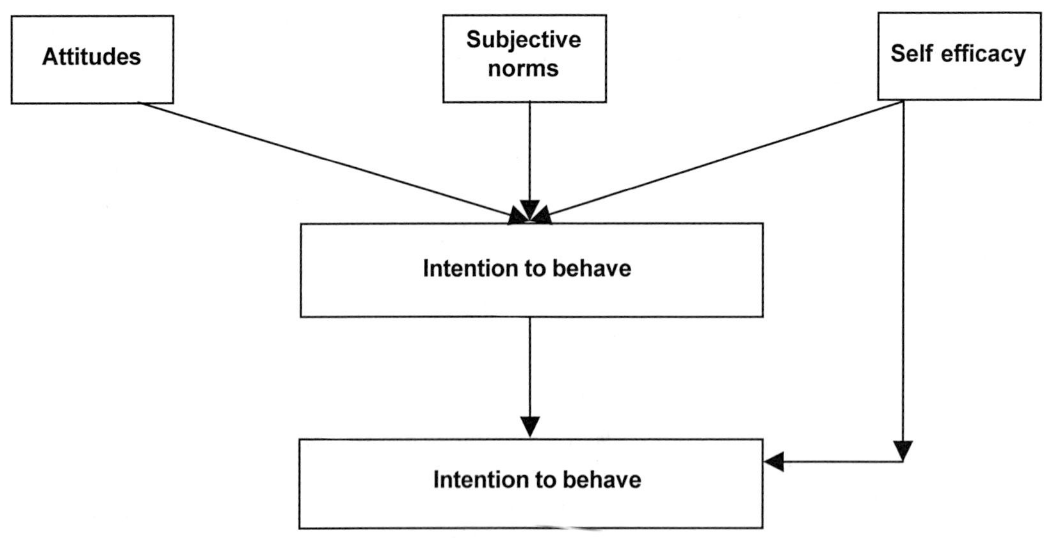

A model of consumer composting behavior

Taylor and Todd (1997) developed a model of waste management based on consumers' waste disposal behaviors. It is well known that consumers do not spontaneously engage in post-consumption behaviors such as recycling, reducing garbage and composting. The incentives for waste management do not work uniformly and it is not easy to market such programs. Moreover, the psychological explanations to account for environmental behavior have been found to be inadequate.

Subjective norms: Direct or indirect pressure from others to act in a specified manner

Taylor and Todd (*ibid*) compared three models in understanding post-consumption consumer behavior: (a) **a theory of reasoned action** (TRA); (b) **an environmental belief-behavior model** (EBB), and (c) **an integrated waste management** model. The theory of reasoned action (TRA) explains attitude-behavior relationship in the context of behavioral intentions and subjective norms. According to this theory, when people begin to think how they should behave, the best predictor of their behavior is their intention (Ajzen & Fishbein, 1980). However, people do not act in isolation; they are also conscious of subjective norms in a situation. For example, I am very serious in my efforts to organize a blood collection campaign and my attitudes are strongly tied to my behavior. However, if the people around me are not serious and do not show up for the blood donation, my involvement in this campaign will be affected by the attitude and behavior of other people. Subjective norms are direct or indirect pressures from other people to engage in a behavior or not.

The second model to test environmental behavior is the environment belief-behavior (EBB). This is a loosely knit model based on empirical research in the field of environmental behavior. The most significant aspect of this model is the perceived benefits of environmental behavior (Granzin & Olson, 1991; Pieters, 1991). If people perceive personal benefits such as the saving of money or the protecting of the environment, they are likely to engage in pro-environmental behaviors. However, the degree of knowledge and difficulty to perform pro-environmental behaviors are also major factors in determining if one can engage in such behaviors. For example, I want to save the environment but owing to my ignorance I may be using environmentally hazardous material, or else I may not know how to dispose of such material.

The third model used by Taylor and Todd was an integrated waste management model that combined the strengths of both TRA and EBB (Figure 7.3). In order to develop this model, Taylor and Todd relied on the extension of the TRA that includes the factor of perceived behavior control, that is, one's ability to perform behavior of interest (Ajzen, 1991). According to Taylor and Todd, "specifically, this model introduces intention as a mediator between attitude, subjective norm, perceived behavior control and behavior; it also suggests that attitude, subjective norm, and perceived behavioral control act as mediators between environmental beliefs and behavior intention" (p 602-603).

The above three models were tested in a study of consumer composting behavior. The data was collected on a sample of 1400 subjects who responded to a survey and completed a two-week diary of their composting behavior. The results of this study showed that although TRA has a strong theoretical base, its applications were poor in predicting pro-environmental behavior. Thogersen (1996) concluded that the TRA showed a weak relationship between attitudes and behavior related to recycling. The EBB model could not account for the complexity of variables but performed well within the limited conditions. When both TRA and EBB were combined to form the integrated waste management model, the clusters of attitude, subjective norm and perceived behavioral control were found to be related to behavioral intention, that is, one's commitment to indulge in pro-environmental behavior. A major strength of this model is that it relies on perceived behavioral control. This explains why consumer composting behavior is not voluntary but also requires knowledge, skills and resources in engaging in pro-environmental behaviors. These factors are positively supported by one's ability to perform tasks (self efficacy) and facilitating social conditions (compatibility) in maintaining one's pro-environmental behavior.

Another test of the **Fishbein-Ajzen model** and the **Schwartz model** was performed by Davies, Foxall and Pallister (2002) with reference to a curbside recycling program in the UK. These authors, too, concluded that cognitive variables, especially intention, failed to predict actual behavior and that a more elaborate integrated model of recycling was required.

BOX 7.2

New, Newer and Newest Recycling Problems

With the advance of technology, new materials are being manufactured, and so are new problems for disposing of or recycling the materials. Here is a report from the *Los Angeles Times* (Section D), dated December 18, 1996:

Last May, Paramount Pictures ordered a whopping 4,500 prints of its Great Summer Hope, "Mission Impossible," in what was to one of the widest theatrical openings ever. Months later, after a strong theatrical showing, the movie has moved into the video stores, but about 1,500 of those movie prints remain in warehouses across the country.

"Weighing about 50 pounds apiece, the prints are made of triacetate film stock and emulsions containing chromium, barium and silver."

"How to dispose of such film is a rising problem for the movie industry."

"In total, the industry generates about 15,500 tons of motion picture film annually, according to executives of Eastman Kodak, the industry's dominant supplier."

NOTE. Kodak has managed to reuse 25% of its film material at a Tennessee facility. The Director of Health, Safety and Environment for Kodak has conceded that it was difficult to recycle more film prints owing to economic and technical reasons.

Curbside recycling programs

Urban solid waste disposal is a growing problem across the globe. Existing landfills are running short of space, new waste processing facilities are increasingly difficult to develop. The most promising solutions for the above seem to be waste reduction and recycling with considerable emphasis being given to curbside recycling programs.

One of the **earliest curbside programs** was that developed in the city of Austin, Texas, USA. This facility came into existence over 20 years ago, and has been emulated by many other such programs. A survey was conducted on 1758 randomly selected customers of the city of Austin Solid Waste Services. The study concluded that concern for the environment and the belief that recycling reduces the amount of material sent to landfills was more important than household size or friend's and neighbor's recycling behavior (Davis, 2001).

Recycling has also been studied in the **cross national context.** A study across 15 countries of the European Union (Guerin, Crete & Mercier, 2001) investigating into the role of individual and contextual variables concluded that the greater the extent to which activists participate nationally in environmental organizations, the more the population is likely to participate in programs of waste recycling. This variable alone explained 45% of the total variance in recycling behavior. In another study by Yi (2000), factors shaping household waste generation and recycling behavior were assessed across three countries—Great Britain, Italy and the Netherlands. Findings included the dominance of belief and attitudinal factors over socio-demographic characteristics as the key determinant along with a strong sensitivity to the convenience factor. Thus the findings provide support for the Fishbein and Azjen's TRA model. However, when attempts were made to examine the TRA across four cultural groups, (Latino, European American, Asian and Filipino) in San Francisco, Gamba (2000), noted no difference across the cultural groups. Little support was obtained for the theory, with only 5% variance being accounted for by attitudes and subjective norms regarding curbside recycling. Convenience once again emerged as an important indicator. Little support was also obtained in another study in the UK for the TRA (Davies, Foxall & Pallister, 2002). Convenience frequently emerged as an important variable in recycling behavior, especially for curbside recycling programs (Domina & Koch, 2001; Ewing, 2001; Berger, 1997). Werner and co-workers (2002) observed that persuasion was more important than convenience in some cases.

ENVIRONMENTAL STRESSORS

We are grateful to nature for our existence. In our effort to adjust with the changes in nature or to improve the quality of our lives, the human race has learnt techniques to coexist with nature from time immemorial. During scorching heat, human beings used caves or the shade of a dense tree. Things changed dramatically with the advancement of technology. For example, to keep ourselves warm in winter, we use electricity generated by nuclear reactors, or to keep ourselves cool in summer, we use air-conditioning. And we began to alter the environment. Person-made changes have never been more threatening than what we see now in the 21st century. The alarming rate at which we are using chemical fertilizers and pesticides and burning various types of fuel has a serious impact on the properties of nature—water, air and soil. The rate at which animal, bird and sea life is disappearing and new diseases are cropping up is testimony that the present human race is writing for its future generation. The mechanical devices are not only affecting the natural environment but are also damaging our sensory, mental and motor abilities. After studying the lives of a group of tribal people in Sudan, the Mabaan, Samuel Rosen and co-researchers (1962) concluded that the members of this tribe had better hearing, less obesity, and rare hypertension (high blood pressure) than people in the US. The daily chores of a tribal person are so intense that they do not require a family fitness center in their village for the purpose of keeping their muscles tight or to worry about their weight.

There is an increasing evidence for a strong relationship between **environmental characteristics and mental health** (*Nation*, 2000); that some social environments may be "**toxic**" in that they may have greater negative impact on people who are vulnerable because of poor resources (*Nation*, 2000); and that they may increase risk of relapse among schizophrenics (Kennedy, 2001). We will refer to this issue again in a later part of this chapter.

The **effects of environmental stressors** has been studied in the global perspective across a variety of groups, for example, women, people in old age, children, factory workers, skilled workers, etc. A study in Italy (Magnavita, 2000) focused on how the outbreak of Mass Psychogenic Illness (MPI, a condition of high stress coupled with high level of conflict between job and home chores) could be prevented among women workers by workplace improvement. So great can be the impact of environmental stressors that a factor analysis of nine sources of stress among Chinese off-shore workers in the UK, concluded that the most important factor was the "Physical environment of the workplace" preceding factors such as "Safety," "Interface between job and family/social life" and "career and achievement." The authors (Wong, Chen, Yu, Lin & Cooper, 2002) concluded that perceived sources of stress in the Chinese was different from those found for other off-shore workers in the UK, indicating the relevance of socio-cultural factors.

Noise

Research on noise in the environment has consistently shown at least two adverse effects. **First**, those who are exposed to work places with loud noise suffer a hearing loss of approximately 10%. Residents near airports are also exposed to noise of roaring engines of several jet planes that fly over their houses. The Mabaans of Sudan had no such problems because their environment was quiet.

The **second** adverse effect of noise is related to annoyance and aggression. Whereas noise, say a rock concert, may be pleasant for some people, others may find it irritable and annoying. Further, irritation and annoyance are mediating variables that may lead to aggressive behavior. Research has shown that predictability and controllability of noise are related to tolerance and aggression (Glass & Singer, 1972; Geen & McCowen, 1984). When people were given an opportunity to control noise (for example, they have a switch to disconnect noise) in an experiment, they tolerated it easily without even using the control device (Glass & Singer, 1972). In other words, when people become aware that they have the means to control noise, they feel relatively less irritated by it. In another study (Geen & McCowen, 1984), low physiological arousal as measured by blood pressure was recorded when the subjects knew that they had control over noise. On the other hand, when noise was present at regular intervals such that it was predictable but subjects had means to control it, subjects showed aggression in aroused conditions.

There is compelling evidence from research that suggests that **controllability of noise** has a mitigating effect on aggression and contributes to lowered physiological arousal. Unpredictable noise may lead to lower level of frustration. Commenting on the role of noise, Bechtel and Churchman (2002) remarked that unwanted, uncontrollable and unpredictable had adverse consequences on health and well being.

Susan Staples (1996) remarked that although "....exposure to environmental noise has consistently been related to impairments in learning and performance, and noise has been implicated as a factor in stress-related health effects such as blood pressure increase. ....American psychology has yet to bring its methodological sophistication and broad, well developed theoretical frameworks fully to bear on the understanding of noise effects" (p. 148). Staples argued that the results of laboratory studies do not explain accurately the response of people in the community. Moreover, "annoyance with community noise does not habituate" (*ibid*, p.144), unlike what happens in most laboratory tasks. The acceptable levels of noise identified by the government agencies as "quiet" are considered four to eight times higher by the members of the public. Health related problems may not be caused by noise *per se*, but they may be related to subjective reactions to noise. According to Staples (*ibid*), psychological factors alone account for over half of the variance in reaction to noise. Psychological findings based on perceived control do not promise broad applications in the study of harmful effect of noise.

Heat

We have been hearing about "the greenhouse effect" or "global warming" for quite some time, albeit the scientific reasoning for such effects has been questioned. From a behavioral science perspective, our interest lies in examining the effect of hot weather on the behavior of people. Archival research has consistently shown that the rate of crime increases during summer (Carlsmith & Anderson, 1979) and that a linear relationship between temperature and crime rates was obviously present in the data analyzed for metropolitan cities.

Laboratory studies by Baron (1972) showed that annoyed subjects delivered significantly higher level of shocks in high temperature conditions as compared to relatively mild conditions. Although Baron's work was criticized in later studies, alternative explanations based on mediating effects of priming and negative feelings have been offered. Rule & co-workers (1987) contended that heat might cause negative feelings and aggressive thoughts were likely to be triggered under aversive conditions. Laboratory research had not shown any consistent relationship between heat and aggression because anger and escape during measurement of heat effects tended to confound the results of the studies (Anderson & Anderson, 1988).

Kenrick and MacFarlane (1986) conducted an interesting study on drivers in automobiles without air-conditioning. When a confederate riding in a car did not move after the signal turned green, the frequency and duration of horn-honking of the driver behind the confederate was found to increase with the increase in ambient temperature. Geen (1990) criticized the above study on the ground that the behavior of the honking driver was merely instrumental (not aggression), that is, to draw the attention of the driver ahead him/her. Irrespective of the merit of Kenrick and MacFarlane's study or Geen's criticism, it is generally concluded that high temperatures lead to aversive conditions, negative feelings and possibly aggression, and that behavior tends to vary under such conditions.

In an extensive review on temperature and aggression paradox, Anderson (1998) argued that heat may lead to increasing aggression on the one hand, but it may also deplete people of energy and alertness on the other hand. Therefore, he examined specifically **three effects of heat**: first, the **subjective perception** of subjects; second, **physiological effects** caused by the heat; and third, **performance of subjects** during heat. Unless results from studies in all these three areas are unanimous, according to Anderson, the temperature-aggression relationship would remain suspect. Referring to the state of hostility as related to the temperatures,

Anderson concluded, "In general, participants in our studies report the least hostility at about 75-78 degree F. Cold temperatures in the 57-60 degree F range yield higher state hostility ratings than comfortable temperatures, and about the same as 93-96 degree F" (p. 284). Potkanowicz and co-workers (2003) also showed how low temperatures could be as deleterious as high temperatures. Further, they argued that these effects might be moderated by the age factor, with older people manifesting greater problematic behavior than their younger counterparts.

POPULATION, SPACE AND BUILT ENVIRONMENTS

It is estimated that approximately 250 thousand children are born everyday and at this rate the population of the world will be doubled within 30 years. Obviously, increased population will have an impact on the resources available on earth—food, housing, land, and so on. The scarcity of land is so intense that it has begun to affect even the terminal part of our existence. To avoid expensive burial ground, people have started opting for burial towers where bodies are placed in a vertical order.

It is well known that overcrowding causes stress. Hard evidence supporting this belief emerged from the studies on animals. Christian (1963), a biologist, discovered that deer population on Chesapeake Bay reduced substantially not due to food shortage but because of stress resulting from overcrowding. In his carefully controlled experiments on rats, Calhoun (1962) observed that the population of rats grew very well but it did not exceed beyond two hundred. With the increase in population, fighting increased, sex behavior altered, territories became uncertain, and infant care poor. Studies on humans also show that overcrowding causes stress and alters behavior. Students in overcrowded college dormitories and off-campus apartments (long corridor and common bathroom and lounge) were more socially withdrawn than their counterparts in less crowded dormitories/apartments (Baum & Valins, 1977 & 1979; Lepore, Evans & Schneider, 1991).

The aversive effects of **crowding** need to be clearly understood. Sometimes we like overcrowded situations, for example, the cheering crowd in a football field, Pasadena Rose Parade on New Year's day, and so on. On the other hand, we feel "crowded" in a small room with two people only.

Population density: Neutral term referring to the no. of people in a given space

Population density is a neutral term that refers to the number of people in a given space. Density and crowding are not identical. The difference between **social and spatial** forms of density is important in understanding the nature of overcrowding. Experiences of social density tend to change as we change the number of people in a fixed space, for example, increasing the number of people from 20 to 50 in a 30 × 30 room. People in a town sometimes complain when influx from outsiders increase but the residential area remains static. Spatial density refers to a fixed number of people but the area may be varied from small to large. When we move from a smaller to a larger room but the number of guests remains the same in a party, spatial density changes but not social density. The two types of density may lead to differential effects on behavior (Altman, 1978). At the same time, the effects of spatial density may vary in developed and developing countries, and across different cultural settings and socio-economic strata. Another distinction has been made between

Spatial density: A fixed number of people but the area may be varied from small to large

inside and outside density (Jain, 1987). A large number of people inside a small dwelling may be perceived as high inside density. A large number of people living in the neighborhood is, however, high outside density.

Social density: Comparison of different sized groups in the same amount of space

The effects of overcrowding are substantial on both children and adults. Saegert (1982) concluded that children from overcrowded areas showed significantly more behavior problems at school than children from less crowded neighborhoods. Evans and co-workers (1998) also confirmed that chronic residential crowding is associated with behavior difficulties at school, poor academic achievement and poor parent-child relationships among 10-12 year olds living in urban India. Rodin (1976) found a high degree of helplessness among children belonging to crowded homes in a low income housing project.

As mentioned earlier, crowding tends to increase the arousal level of people and its effects can be negative, for example, high blood pressure, loss of control and low intimacy. Milgram (1970) reported that crowding may lead to sensory overload, that is, "inability of a system to process inputs from the environment because there are too many inputs for the system to cope up with, or because successive inputs come so fast that Input A cannot be processed when Input B is presented" (p. 1462). Under such conditions, people may prefer to withdraw or "shut down." In short, Milgram contended that the effects of overcrowding may deform daily lives by affecting:

- **Role performance, for example, no help to an injured pedestrian.**
- **Social norms, for example, aloofness.**
- **Cognitive processes, for example, selective replies/responses.**
- **Competition, for example, rush for a seat in a subway.**

Does crowding always lead to negative behavioral effects? It does not seem so. Various models have been proposed to specify the antecedents and consequences of the feeling of crowding (Stokols, 1976). The attribution model is social psychology's contribution to the understanding of the effects of crowding. It is our attributions that determine whether we perceive crowding or not. When we start attributing personal space encroachment to density, then only is crowding experienced (Worchel & Yohai, 1976).

Crowding has also been seen to affect **prosocial behavior**, with greater density producing lesser amounts of helping (Brickman & co-workers, 1973). This was documented even earlier in the famous experiment on bystander intervention (Darley & Latane, 1968). Aggression, too, has been seen to be a function of crowding. The equivocal results that have been obtained, however, suggest the role of moderator variables, which has later been validated by research on both children and adults. Interestingly, the gender differences in aggression due to crowding were found related to the size of the room. Males rated themselves more aggressive than females in small rooms. In large rooms, the results were the opposite (Stokols & co-workers, 1973). Other moderator variables include goal-blocking (Sundstrom, 1975), loss of control (Paulus & Mathews, 1980) and scarcity of valued resources (Rohe, 1982). All of the above findings indicate that effects of crowding do not depend on density *per se* but on the **perception of density**, and are therefore in line with the **attributions** people make during the overcrowding. When the impact of population density (as in cities) was compared across two locations in France, that is, in Paris and another small provincial town, it became clear that Parisians were significantly less civil than their provincial counterparts, and that, high density conditions reduced civility in both settings. The behavior being studied was the simple act of holding the door open for entrants behind them in departmental stores (Moser & Corroyer, 2001).

As we witness greater longevity, the problems of the aged are becoming important. This has led to a new discipline: environmental gerontology.

Personal space

Personal space refers to the area around the body of a person. If another person intrudes around it, it may cause discomfort. How close another person should come before he can cause discomfort is not defined; the boundary is very subjective. Generally speaking, personal space is the preferred distance that people want to maintain between themselves and those near them. Invasion of personal space may cause feelings of discomfort and lead people to move out of the place. Why do people become uncomfortable in a crowded elevator? Why do they want to get out at the earliest in a crowded elevator?

Personal space: The physical area around the body of the person

Personal space is affected by several factors: **age, cultural factors, sex, social status**, etc. Compared to Anglo-Americans, Hispanic Americans maintain closer distances in their interactions. In some cultures, it is a taboo to touch a female. The American army was told not to touch or stare at females in Saudi Arab, something quite common in the U.S. during social occasions. Hall (1963) presented a four-way division of personal space of Americans:

- **Intimate distance: 0 to 1½ feet: close family member.**
- **Personal distance: 1½ to 4 feet: friends.**
- **Social distance: 4 to 12 feet: business transactions.**
- **Public distance: more than 12 feet: formal public speaker.**

A few interesting conclusions based on personal space studies are reported below:

- **Standing in an elevator: first four people tend to occupy four corners; a female's personal space is often violated earlier than a male's; and females prefer to move away from a staring male.**
- **Personal space needs of children increase as they grow older.**
- **Females use smaller interaction distances than men.**
- **People maintain greater distance with high status people.**
- **Use of common rest arm in airplane seats: men use three times more than women.**
- **Side-by-side seating: females sit closer to people they like.**
- **Face-to-face seating: men sit closer to people they like.**
- **Optimum level of distance: people prefer not-too-close, not-too-far type of approach in first encounters like dating. People reciprocate when they want to increase intimacy.**
- **Personal seating arrangement preference.**

BOX 7.3

Women's visual privacy in traditional and modern neighborhoods in Damascus (Al-Kodmany, 2000)

The author conducted face-to-face interviews with 100 women (aged 18-40 years) at home in each of two middle class residential neighborhoods (one traditional and the other modern) in Damascus. The focus was on three aspects:

- **Extent of desire for visual privacy from outsiders.**
- **Satisfaction with achieved visual privacy in their homes.**
- **Preferences for specific architectural and urban design elements that affect their visual privacy.**

Results indicated that for women in both neighborhoods, the desire for visual privacy from outsiders is very high and important. Women view all home spaces, both indoor and outdoor as private and feel uncomfortable if outsiders view them in these spaces. Women tended to prefer traditional to modern homes, since they afforded greater privacy. Design elements studied included windows, curtains, doors, rooms, balconies, courtyards and fences.

Cross-cultural perspective on personal space

Little (1968) asked people from **five countries** to indicate how close two persons should be when having conversations. Greatest proximity was favored by the Greeks, followed by the Italians, Americans, Swedes, and the Scots, in that order. The degree of closeness permitted can also be taken as an **index of liking**. Arab, Indian and Pakistani students were the groups that sat closest together and they also rated their friendship most highly (Watson, 1970). Another setting in which the amount of proximity allowed to others is important, is during **negotiations**. While negotiating, Graham (1985) found the Brazilian negotiators looked and touched each other more than did the Americans or the Japanese. When strangers were studied in settings that did not ordinarily require conversation, for example, the **doctor's clinic**, Indonesians were likely to choose seats near strangers of the same sex, while Australians chose seats that separated them maximally (Noesjirwan, 1977). Students from South Africa preferred to keep greater distance from strangers than students from America.

These differences are not just of academic interest but have important implications for life. As soon as someone visits another country, they need to adapt their behavior to local norms if they want to give the desired impression. Collett (1971), for example, reported of a program in which English people were trained to stand closer to Arabs, make more eye contact, touch and smile more than they did at home.

These findings have even greater implications for the **expatriate manager**, that is, the manager who is working in a foreign country but has a local workforce. Thus there is an abundance of research on the problems of such managers (for example, Black & Gregerson, 1991; Furnham, 1990; Kidder, 1991). Hammer (1987) concluded that **three skills** were necessary for cross cultural living. **Firstly**, the person must have an intrapsychic focus and the ability to tolerate and manage the stress arising from relocation to novel physical and social environments. **Secondly,** the person should be capable of establishing and nurturing relationships with strangers from different cultures. And **lastly,** effective communication is important.

Cultural differences are also seen with respect to **built-up spaces**. In **individualist cultures**, homes tend to be clearly demarcated: doors, gardens, gates indicate a small "home" area. In **collectivist cultures**, physical boundaries may be clearly marked or may be permeable (Altman & Gauvain, 1981), though a certain set of rules do prevail even in such cultures so as to preserve privacy (Gudykunst, Ting-Toomey & Chua, 1988).

There has also been work on the effects of maintaining physical distance in some Asian countries. Jain (1993) assessed the feeling of crowding and **Comfortable Interpersonal Distance** (IPD) as reported by 480 husband-wife pairs equally drawn from four levels of density and three income groups. The results indicated that density differences were observed for familiar persons but not for strangers, and that the preferred IPD was greater in high density than in the low density areas. There were also differences due to income levels. Low income subjects preferred greater IPD compared to the middle and high income subjects. Gender differences were also noticeable, with men preferring less IPD for strangers than women, though the two sexes did not differ in their IPD for familiar persons. Ruback and co-workers (2003) summarizes many of the findings on crowding in south Asia.

Urban planning and residential environments

Environmental gerontology: The modification and optimization of space for the aged

For the first time in the history of the American Psychological Association a mini-convention was organized mainly due to the efforts of Dorothy Cantor, President of the APA Convention, 1996. She argued effectively that although psychologists have expertise in four areas of city life—family, school, community and the workplace, they have not used their knowledge and skills to uplift urban life. During the same mini-convention, Anthony Marsella (as reported by Sara Martin, *APA Monitor*, October, 1996) pointed out that by the end of the present century, approximately half of the people in this world will be residing in cities and within 25 years, the number of city dwellers will increase by 44%, that is, the population will increase to 8.3 billion. According to him, mental health problems of city-dwellers at risk include groups of youth, disabled, elderly, women, refugees and homeless. Certain occupational groups like taxi drivers and small store owners/workers in inner cities also face high risk at their work. Another speaker at the mini-convention, James Garbarino, introduced the term "**social toxicity**" to refer to deterioration in children's social environment (as reported by Martin & Murray, *APA Monitor*, 1996). We referred to this concept in an earlier section too and defined it as those social environments that may have a larger impact on vulnerable residents, for example, people with fewer resources (*Nation*, 2000).

Indeed, even by the year 2002, things remained very much the same. Lawrence (2002) argued that healthy residential environments have not been a high priority for environmental psychologists, despite the fact that a combination of urban design, land use patterns and transportation systems can help create healthier communities (Handy *et al.*, 2002); good urban design can aid spatial cognition (Devlin, 2001) and prevent crime (Taylor, 2002).

People develop positive and affective association with their residential environments. This bond is referred to as **topohilia.** At least in evolutionary terms, this tendency has its advantages: safety and the avoidance of dangerous exploration. It has been noted that when people live at a place for a significant time, they develop a feeling of control and dominance, that is, prior residence effect. Research studies indicate that people resist in signing documents at their own residence (Harris & McAndrew, 1986) and show increased dominance in conversation in their rooms (Taylor & Lanni, 1981). McAndrew (1993, p. 208-209) has reported that attachment to place can be measured. This sense of spatial identity is even more crucial in poor ethnic immigrant communities and is counter-productive for movement to new urban areas and new conditions of social life, even when desirable or necessary (Fried, 2000).

Topohilia: The tendency to develop positive association with their residential environment

According to Altman and Low (1992), **place attachment** is a positive emotional bond that grows between individuals and their environment. Such bonds are reflected in people's behavioral, affective and cognitive expressions. Attachment to a place grows through one's immediate experience in the physical environment of the place. When people move from one city to another or from one country to another, both the old and the new places have implications for one's attachment. Despite crowding and noise, a number of people living in the most congested cities like New York, Tokyo and Mexico City have developed a great deal of liking and affinity with their place.

An important question has been "**whether planners can create community.**" Hillier (2002) has examined this issue in the context of Western Australia urban design and focuses on how place attachment relates to a sense of community. The connection between public space and a sense of community was empirically examined by Talen (2000), and she concluded that newer suburban neighborhoods fare better than the more traditional neighborhoods.

Churchman and Mitrani (1997) conducted a study of those immigrants in Israel who had moved from the Soviet Union. They reported **three kinds of psychological consequences in migration**: satisfaction from the move, changes in social contacts and lifestyle, and, changes in psychological well being. According to them, if immigrants perceive the new environment to be different, it should not be taken to mean that they would not attach with the new environment. What matters in such cases is the direction of preference; if one does not attach to the new place, the preference for the old place may continue. One of the best examples of work on migration has been done by Feldman and Rosenthal (1990). In a study on Chinese high school students residing in two western nations, they found that cultural adaptation was very slow and that the rate of change varied with dimensions of behavior: parental behavior changed more slowly than that of their offspring.

Why are people **attracted to cities**? One important reason is economic opportunity. Additionally, a city provides enormous opportunities that are not available elsewhere: variety, eventfulness, choice and stimulation (Milgram, 1970, p. 1461). On the negative side, city-dwellers endure pollution, noise, traffic jams, loss of natural environment, and crime. While cities are growing rapidly in the world, so are problems of human concern, especially relating to physical and mental health of city-dwellers. Our passion for urban living and its downside are creating a unique ambivalence that is divided into optimism versus hopelessness, community action versus inaction, and helpfulness versus helplessness. Not surprisingly, city-dwellers are less satisfied than those living in small towns (Fischer, 1982).

What can social psychology do to improve life in urban environments? Most psychologists during the mini-convention of APA, 1996, on city life agreed that saving children and mental health should be the top priority. For this purpose, social psychologists should begin to identify people-at-risk in a city. It is important to understand that the profile of every city and the culture in which it is rooted is different. Social networking and empowerment are driving forces that lead to social change. The task of social psychology is to incorporate social context of a city and its culture in its research and arm itself with scientific data and conclusions to sustain social networking and empowerment.

It is equally necessary to take the **socio-cultural backdrop** into consideration. Gupte (1984 cf. Sinha, 1984), for example, surveyed many cities around the world, and concluded that, "in this crowded earth of ours, there is not just one population problem but many...population programs and policies must be tailored to suit a particular country, its culture and specific needs and conditions" (p. 319). As Sinha (1984) remarked, "development is primarily and ultimately related to the eco-cultural and social context of the country".

The current conditions in public housing in cities like Chicago, Los Angeles, St. Louis and New York City are unsafe and unhealthy. The magnitude of the problem is increasing and worsening everyday. Social psychological research has helped to improve public housing conditions in several ways. First, it is recommended that high-rise buildings be avoided in future construction. Second, the building should not have any pockets of isolated area. The Pruitt-Igoe complex in St. Louis, now dismantled, is a classic example of such poor construction. Third, a small cluster of houses for residents in an area is better than having a large number of houses without visible boundaries and opportunity for the residents to share responsibility in the neighborhood. Fourth, the concept of functional distance should be carefully used in designing buildings. This refers to the likelihood of people coming in contact with each other. Finally, by clearly identifying and marking pathways and boundaries, conflict and aggression can be reduced (Goldstein, 1986).

Natural environment

The impact of the natural environment is well known. Cowie (2002) remarked, "Natural environments often generate experiences that combine great emotional and moral power–charged experiences....and landscapes have the power to be invested with an emotional and moral charge where other stimuli may not." The restorative properties of viewing nature from the window have been documented by Kaplan (2001) especially in terms of satisfaction and well being. Effects of "greenness" have also been seen for cognitive functioning, especially for children from poor urban environments (Wells, 2000), and for pre-primary school children in Scandinavia, Fjortoft (2001) found that natural environment stimulates learning in general and motor development in particular. It can even lend to better attentional functioning (Faber & Taylor, 2002) and has been used for children with attention deficits and hyperactive deficits as restorative therapy.

Whitehouse (2000) reported of a healing garden and its impact on coping with stress in a children's hospital (see Box 7.4):

BOX 7.4

Healing gardens

Whitehouse reports of an innovative intervention in a children's hospital. The major goals of the research were as follows:

- **To look into the process of emotional healing using a healing garden in not only the patients of the hospital but also their families and the hospital staff.**
- **To identify any barriers that were preventing the use of the healing garden.**
- **To assess the satisfaction of the users of this garden as a healing tool.**

What was the design of the research? A multi-method design was used. This included post-occupancy evaluation, observations, surveys and in-depth qualitative interviews.

The major results? Firstly what was the reaction of the participants? The participants reported that they used the healing garden and other outdoor natural spaces as an escape from hospital stress. They also reported mood changes that could be specifically attributed to the effect of natural aspects such as greenery and running water.

Secondly, the interviews revealed that:

Natural environments, that offer maximal opportunity for multisensory stimulation to all those in the hospital, whether they be patients, their families or the hospital staff, are beneficial because the environment counteracts the cognitive demands of the hospital.

We need wider theories that can explain not only the impact of visual sensations from the natural environment but also stimuli from other senses.

Gardens in hospitals may serve as more basic issues and needs.

While healthy children may sometimes want more interactive things that a child can do, the chronically ill are very appreciative of the refuge provided by the garden and prefer familiar objects and plants that they can associate with the home.

The findings also pointed out that the garden was not being used as much or as effectively as was intended.

What were the learnings? Recommendations could be developed on the basis of the findings regarding the ways in which hospital healing gardens should be planned, designed and built.

PROBLEMS IN MAINTAINING PRO-ENVIRONMENTAL BEHAVIOR AND ITS REMEDY

Why do people fail to **maintain their pro-environmental behaviors**? When a community organizes a campaign for recycling, we enthusiastically contribute to it as good citizens for a few days but very soon we tend to slide back to our old habits. Consider the additional work we have to perform if we contribute to recycling-sorting aluminum cans, bottles, newspapers and so on separately everyday without any immediate rewards. If immediate consequences of an act are not visible, people, by and large, become indifferent and revert to old habits. According to Platt (1973) when people contribute to a social cause, they do not get immediate rewards. On the contrary, such behaviors bring negative consequences, for example, no material rewards, extra work and so on. In his theory of social trap, Platt contended that when people act in their own interest they tend to get some benefit, at least temporarily. It is well known that many industries had dumped their waste on land and in rivers in the 1950s and 1960s to save money and risked the lives of people who lived in their vicinity. At present, the worst sources of pollution in the USA are the organizations that are linked to the Department of Defense. In other words, when individuals or organizations maximize their immediate interests and ignore their social responsibilities, other people suffer. According to Platt, when immediate rewards overpower us, we tend to indulge in self-destructive behavior as well. What happens to us when we overeat our favorite ice-cream or consume additional cigarettes or alcohol under social pressure?

Platt suggested several techniques to support beneficial behaviors and to control detrimental behaviors. First, we should increase the rewards for beneficial behaviors. Second, any delay between detrimental behavior and penalty must be reduced because people get time to escape punishment. Third, there should be an increase in the control of government over illegal behaviors.

A serious problem with Platt's view is that it overlooks individual differences and fails to account for the cognitive pressures that are associated with the behavior. Our failure to maintain pro-environmental behavior is attributed to the way the reinforcements were offered in the past. When neither positive consequences for pro-environmental behavior are offered nor are negative consequences inflicted for the failure to maintain a safe environment, people continue to maintain their current behavior.

It seems that research on the apathy of people towards environmental issues has moved a long way and it is important that we begin to focus on the technique that will bring effective results. Several behavioral interventions have been used to alter detrimental environmental behaviors, including information campaigns, prompts (brief signals like "please do not litter"), incentives based on rewards (money, etc.) and modelling. In our discussion of water conservation, litter control and recycling most of these interventions were reported.

To **remove public apathy** towards environmental issues, community participation is also important. Wiesenfeld and Sanchez (2002) outlined the ways in which community participation was encouraged and made effective in Latin America. Describing how the state's approach had traditionally been to sideline the public point of view, the authors further showed how the governmental attitude has changed, now allowing the community members to not only state their needs and values regarding environmental issues but to also participate in the decision making process. In another study conducted in Venezuela, the authors (Wiesenfeld & Giuliani, 2002) concluded that while the community space was a salient part of the lives of the community members, there was a lack of awareness regarding the conservation of natural resources in the community. This latter could be one of the reasons for apathy among community members towards issues of environmental significance.

Taking a lead from Geller's (1990) work on behavior change techniques concerning environmental issues, Dwyer and co-workers (1993) presented 18 behavior interventions, 10 antecedent conditions and 8 consequence conditions, to preserve the environment (Figure 7.4). The antecedent interventions were divided into four groups: passive-individual, passive-group, active-individual, and active-group. The consequence conditions were divided into two groups: individual and group.

Figure 7.4: A taxonomy of interventions for producing pro-environmental behavior (adapted from Dwyer *et al.*, 1993).

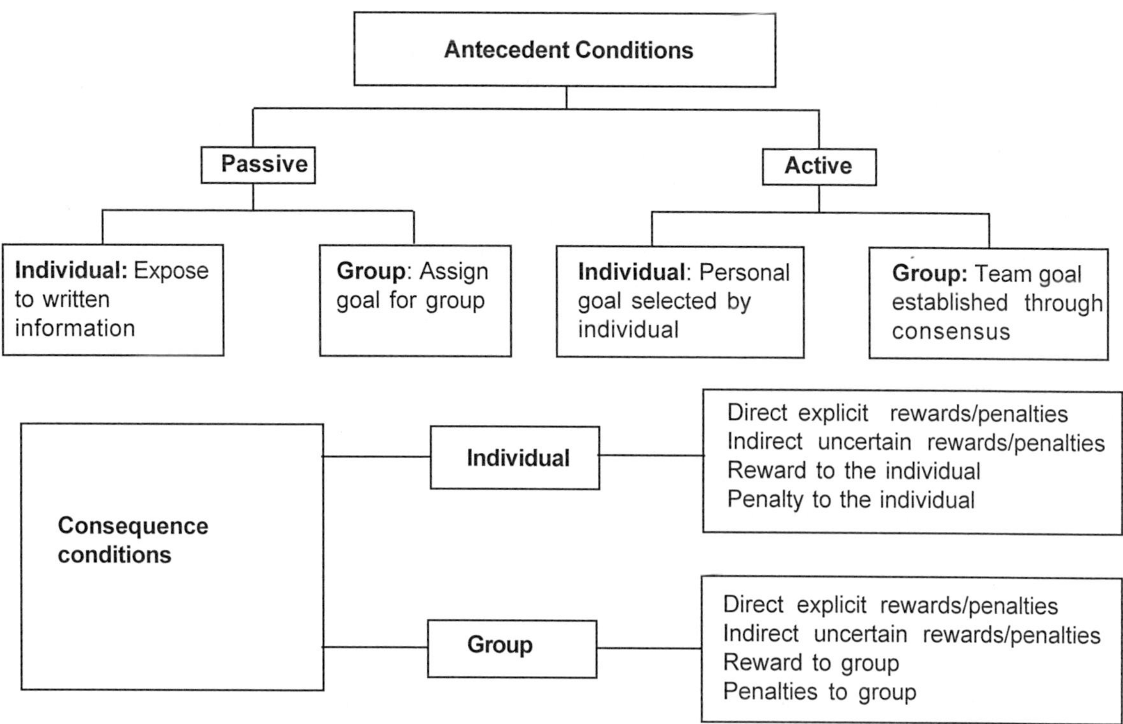

In a subsequent study by Porter, Leeming and Dwyer (1995) the effectiveness of interventions based on the above techniques was examined and they concluded that active antecedent conditions (for example, written commitment), goal setting and modelling increased the level of pro-environmental behavior. On the other hand, written prompts were least effective.

There has been some concern about the success of behavioral interventions (Kazdin, 1994). As applied to pro-environmental behaviors, this technique needs to be linked with the concept of "behavioral marketing" (Porter & co-workers, 1995). Because not all individuals and communities respond to pro-environmental interventions equally well, some are more influenced by advertisements than others who prefer active participation, a very important task of social psychologists is to collaborate with experts in marketing to target potential consumers who will respond to a particular intervention better than they do to others. If such interventions are tailored to fit the needs of individuals and communities, the chances of success of an intervention will increase and it may lead to a long-term behavior change. In the chapter on consumer behavior in this book, the reader will find how social psychologists can forge a relationship with marketing researchers to develop a plan of altruistic marketing, that is, how to reduce disturbed or disturbing consumer behavior. After all, psychologists have a long history in social marketing. For example, they have been helping marketing researchers to identify and develop products to facilitate the education of children with special needs. The preservation of our environment is a behavioral problem and the sooner we learn to preserve it, the sooner and the more beneficial will be the results for all of us who have inherited this earth.

Another reason for the relatively poor contribution of social psychology to environmental issues is the way in which people perceive different disciplines. People with technical backgrounds often see environmental issues as being a set of engineering problems and of consumer's motives as primarily financial. What is not taken into consideration are the various behavioral, social and institutional factors so important for the success of any intervention. Further social psychology is often viewed as a **soft science** in contrast to the **hard boiled** approach favored by technologists and policy makers (Oskamp & Stern, 1996). However, ignoring behavioral and social issues in environmental policy has important costs. When ignored, policies fail and it is only then that the policy makers are surprised. Belatedly, social psychologists are called in. It would be much better to introduce social psychologists for the prevention of social problems at the beginning, rather than trying to use them for cure purposes only at the end.

EMERGING ISSUES FOR THE APPLICATION OF SOCIAL PSYCHOLOGY

Social psychology of capsule habitats

The 21st century has brought in its wake new frontiers for not only work but also play. Thus we have Antarctic tourism and there are also plans of space tourism (Wickman, 1996). Such environments, hardly ever thought of before, offer unique opportunities for the application of and research in social psychology.

Two such environments are of special interest: ICE, that is, **Isolated Confined Environments,** and EUE, or, **Extreme and Unusual Environments** (Suedfeld, 1987). Prisons, mining and logging camps, habitats of hermits, transoceanic vessels, space ships and control areas of missile silos are some examples of non-EUE ICE. We also have ICE which comes within the rubric of EUEs, for example, deserts, unpopulated islands, mountain peaks and capsules, all of which involve extreme and unusual physical conditions.

Of greater interest to the social scientist is the **social milieu** in such remote environments. Typically they are composed of groups far removed from their natural social networks, with excursions into the surrounding environment being very rare, uncomfortable and dangerous. What is even more interesting is that, be it people in the Polar regions, space, underwater vessels or expeditions into remote mountainous areas, their problems show great similarity (Ursin & co-workers, 1991). Thus social monotony and its disruptive effects have been reported in Antarctica (Smith, 1969), in submarines (Sandal & co-workers, 1999) and in the Soviet space program (Bluth & Helppie, 1986).

Conflict is another common complaint. So great is its effect when you are bound within close quarters and unable to exit from it, that Admiral Byrd (1938) decided to go alone one winter in the Antarctica rather than watch a companion whose very way of chewing food was infuriating! In fact most of the conflicts were caused by extremely trivial matters (Palinkas, 1990). This is one area where Social Psychology has stepped in—some national space programs emphasized the selection of an entire group rather than individuals (Santy, 1994). Others have focused on cooperative training (Kass & co-workers, 1995). Even then, some foreign visitors in Russian and American space vehicles have experienced feelings of marginalisation (Kanas, 1997).

In such environments, people are removed from their customary social group: **self evaluation and self esteem suffers** and **role expectations** become confused. As new role expectations are worked out and micro-cultures develop, there are chances of stress (Harrison & co-workers, 1991). Incompatible roles may lead to further conflicts (Suedfeld, 1995). The intensity and range of **communication** are also affected. Depth of **self disclosure** may increase but maybe regretted later (Altman & Haythorn,1967), rumors may circulate freely (Cornelius, 1991), and there may be general effects of isolation on communication.

While most people can understand the **psychosocial stressors** associated with such capsule environments, few are aware that there is the other side of the coin too. Seligman (1998) laid considerable emphasis on positive capsule psychology, that is, the **salutogenic effects** of the experience. Despite all the stressors, the vast majority show little psychiatric symptomatology (for example, Peri, 1999). Rather, people have been seen to come back with more tolerance and affection for others and higher self-confidence (Suedfeld, 1998).

The above analyses provide excellent scope for the social psychologist. The areas of concern could be highly varied, ranging from interpersonal issues to the development of countermeasures (Holland & Curtiss, 1998). Thus scientists should look at the issue of crew composition—whether the type of crew which is best for performance would also be the one which is best in terms of emotional adaptation? Are the same variables optimal for both? Holland and co-workers also pointed to the training needs of crews, especially training in group dynamics, leadership, and discipline maintenance. Other pertinent issues relate to controlling and maintaining discipline; how do capsule micro cultures develop; and what makes them different from each other even in similar environments? And, what is the best way to help the family adjust to the voyager's departure? Countermeasure development could be centered on interpersonally-oriented selection, team-oriented training modules and the reduction of capsule-ground conflict. Certain organizational issues could also be addressed. Social psychologists would do well to look at the effects of flight duration, the sharing of knowledge, attitudes of crew-members, and, the requirements for effective management.

Bechtel (2002) analyzed the lessons learned from the **US expeditions to the Mars**. He noted that expeditions to the Mars were different from other space missions. So much so that earlier learning did not apply. Some of the areas considered salient by Bechtel are:

- **"Windows" in space.**
- **Weightlessness and its effects.**
- **Maximizing the positive aspects of staying in an isolated confined environment (ICE) by keeping occupants busy with useful work.**
- **Perception of "them" *v.* "us" relation between astronauts and control operators.**
- **Mixed sex groups and biological sex considerations in space.**
- **Environment habitability design.**
- **Recreation.**

Ecopsychology

In the past, environmental action consisted of scaring and shaming those who over-consume or did not recycle, which proved to be quite ineffective. **Ecopsychology**, in contrast, attempts to create positive and affirming motivations, derived from a bond of love and loyalty to nature (Bayland, 1995). People always desire to be part of a group. Humans are now trying to satisfy that need through violence, obsessive work, indulgence in sex or food and use of drugs. Howard Clinebell (1996) suggested a satisfying alternative to these futile attempts at fulfilment by identifying the problem as "alienation from nature" (p. 12). He believed that the alienation must be healed with nature. Theodore Roszac (1995) argued that human ignorance led to the feelings of isolation. Additionally, humans must realize the extent to which they are influenced by their environment(s), and must also realize they have the power to influence it. Humans need to be in-touch with the nature around them. In short, ecopsychology seeks to find underlying motivations for our bad environmental habits (Miller, 1994). The reader may find such analyses resembling positive psychology.

Ecopsychology could be seen as a sub-field of environmental psychology, although this would probably be resisted by many people in both fields. Donald Williams (1997) wrote that ecopsychology helps us to understand the psychodynamics of our relationship to the environment. In this definition the medical metaphor is gone, but the belief in the unconscious and the psychodynamic model is highlighted.

Eco-psychology: Interface between ecology and psychology

Brendan Hill (1999) wrote, "Ecopsychology is a term recently coined to describe the interface between ecology and psychology. It encompasses the human (and arguably, the non-human) psychological relationship with nature, in both directions." While the field has been slowly developing as an intellectual endeavor, some psychologists have been directly addressing the practicalities of the human-nature relationship. In the 20 years before the appearance of Roszak's book (Roszak, 1992), behavioral researchers published more than 100 experimental papers on how to change people's environmental behavior (Dwyer & co-workers, 1993). At the same time, sociologists and social psychologists were exploring the human-nature relationship using the tools of social and behavioral sciences (Stern, 1992). Rather than developing a theoretical ecopsychology, these researchers applied existing theories to problems of environmentally significant behavior (Winter, 1997).

In short, ecopsychology can be seen as spanning a range of questions from ecology through religion, anthropology, sociology, and political economy, to the psychology of individuals. The concerns of ecopsychology are the role of our actions in the global ecological crisis and the effects of our ecology (including the crisis) on our psychology. Out of this may come answers to the practical questions of how to change our actions in relation to more-than-human nature and how to change our experience of nature. One focus of ecopsychology has been on experiential learning aimed at helping people form a spiritual and emotional connection to the ecological systems of which they are a part. This has included wilderness experiences (Greenway, 1995; Harper, 1995), Internet courses and workshops with experiential exercises on how to reconnect with nature (Cohen, 1997), deep ecology workshops for groups (Macy & Brown, 1998) participation in environmental activist groups (O'Conner, 1995), and habitat restoration work (Shapiro, 1995).

A second focus for ecopsychology, which it shares with deep ecology, has been an emphasis on small group, community, and face-to-face contact as a way to change ecologically significant behavior and establish healthier relationships. Because of this emphasis on individual or local community change, behavioral psychology (Dwyer & co-workers, 1993) and popular education (Freire, 1990) seem to be consistent with other ecopsychological approaches.

Will mainstream psychology notice the environment? Will behavioral work go beyond recycling and carpooling to some of the core behaviors in the consumer society? Is ecopsychology useful? These and other issues seem to be worth exploring in future research in applied social psychology.

Summary

This chapter deals with the applications of social psychology as related to the environmental issues. In the context of popular theoretical models, such as the TRA, issues concerning energy conservation, water conservation, litter control and recyling were discussed. With reference to impact of physical environment on human habitat, the effects of noise, heat, personal spacing, and population were discussed. Finally, emerging issues like ecopsychology were also presented. Taken altogether, the major focus of the chapter revolved around the indifference of people in taking action on their environmental concerns while keeping their attitudes intact.

Suggestions for Further Reading

Suedfeld, P. & Steel, D.G. (2000). The environmental psychology of capsule environments. *Annual Review of Psychology*, 51, 227-253.

Bechtel, R.B. & Churchman, A. (Eds) (2002). *Handbook of Environmental Psychology*. NY: Wiley

Levy-Leboyer, C., Bonnes, M., Chase, J., *et al.* (1996). Determinants of pro-environmental behaviors: A five-country comparison. *European Psychologist*, 1, 123-129.

Some Key Terms

Attitude model
Descriptive norms
Dissonance theory
Ecopsychology
Environmental gerontology
Environmental psychology
Injunctive norms
Personal space
Population density
Pro-environmental attitudes
Pro-environmental behavior
Pro-environmental competency
Rational economic model
Social density
Social psychological model
Spatial density
Subjective norms
Topohilia

SOCIAL PSYCHOLOGY OF CONSUMER BEHAVIOR

8

Chapter Outline

- An introduction to social psychology of consumer behavior
- Advertising
- Persuasion
  - Cognitive factors
  - Affective factors
  - Compliance techniques
  - Use of gifts as a marketing tool
  - Cross-cultural aspects of gifting
- The Effect of television on consumer behavior
  - Perceived reality
  - Correlational studies
  - Cross-lagged correlational studies
  - Experimental research
  - Field studies
- New perspectives in consumer behavior research
  - Social marketing
  - Cause related marketing (CRM)
  - Consumer behavior in the cross-cultural perspective
  - e-commerce
  - Web advertising
- Limits to the application of social psychology to consumer behavior

AN INTRODUCTION TO SOCIAL PSYCHOLOGY OF CONSUMER BEHAVIOR

When people have money and a desire to acquire things, excessive buying may take place. Through advertisements and other persuasive techniques, we may be induced to buy things we would not have bought otherwise. Additionally, exposure to various lifestyles on television may prompt us to acquire goods to maintain or to raise our standards of living. Not surprisingly, the sale of Ford's Bronco—a van ostensibly used in a crime—skyrocketed during the national broadcast of superstar O.J. Simpson's trial in Los Angeles, USA, in 1994-95. Excessive consumption of goods can also cause adverse effects: smoking may lead to cancer; Nintendo games may delay children's homework; or violent films may cause an increase in aggression. This chapter deals with several intended and unintended effects of advertisements, compliance techniques and television in shaping the consumption behavior of people.

A significantly large amount of time in the life of an individual is centered on issues relating to health and money. If we eat reasonably well—neither too little nor too much—we can expect physical fitness and fewer health problems. The same applies to the money we earn. What would happen to us if we deprive ourselves by not spending money for some of our essential needs? Or, what would happen if we act like a "showboat spender" who happens to spend money to gain popularity? Are we not worried about our financial fitness? In the past few years, several scholars have focused attention on the psychology of money and have published useful books (for example, Dittmar's (1992), *The Social Psychology of Material Possessions;* Paul Wachtel's (1983), *The Poverty of Affluence: A Psychological Portrait of the American Way of Life;* Barry Schwartz's (1994), *The Costs of Living: How Market Freedom Erodes the Best Things in Life*; and Tim Kasser's (2002), *The High Price of Materialism.*

Are people different in their concerns for financial fitness? A number of psychologists believe that attitudes toward money are learned from parents just as any other form of acquired behavior (See Box 8.1). Belk (1982) reported that the significance of material objects is recognized by the age of five or six years and fully understood by the age of 10-11 years. Cheryl Fellows (as cited by Scott Sleek, 1995) even went to the extent of positing that individuals develop a unique "money personality." Whether individuals develop a unique money personality or not, the development of such an attitude toward money is linked to life experience and personality. This is further clarified by Falicov (2001), who studied the meaning of money with reference to different cultural groups. He concluded that money has a different meaning for Roman Catholic, working-class Latino, (that is, Mexicans, Cubans, etc.), and White, middle class Protestant Anglo-Americans. He explained the differences on the basis of the cultural dimension of individualism-collectivism; the focus on family rituals; spending on gifts, favors and interest free loans; culture; money and social class as tied to cash and credit economies; the cultural balance between work and leisure; religious beliefs, locus of control and obligations towards self and others; and, traditional and egalitarian marital roles. Taken together, these factors influence perceptions, attitudes and uses of money in different cultural and ethnic groups.

In fact, the choice of goods in the present day market has increased to such an extent that almost all of us have difficulty deciding which product would be the most durable and useful. And, in our pursuit to determine what to buy, we sacrifice enormous amounts of time and resources. For an average consumer, this exercise becomes a headache. On the other hand, there are consumers who get intimidated by sales-people and timidly buy what is presented to them. Do such people need assertiveness training?

In the above paragraphs, we reported some aspects of consumer behavior in which social psychology has shown a keen interest. For our purposes, **consumer behavior** is defined as "the acquisition, consumption, and disposition of goods, services, time, and ideas" (Jacoby, 1975, p. 979). In almost similar terms, Weyant (1986) defines consumer behavior as "the way people choose to use their personal resources,

Consumer behavior: The way people choose to use their personal resources, particularly money and leisure time

BOX 8.1

Money personality (based on a report by Scott Sleek, 1995)

Different mindsets

Gottfurcht divides the psychology of money into prosperity-thinking and poverty-thinking. Prosperity thinkers typically take more responsibility over money matters and are more optimistic about their financial status. Poverty thinkers avoid responsibility for their finances and usually feel that money is too scarce.

People develop their attitudes about money based on how their parents handled it. Children who receive no allowance or have it taken away as punishment, or who received no parental guidance on money management are likely to have trouble handling their money when they mature, he said.

In his workshops, Gottfurcht helps people understand their feelings about money and learn to discipline themselves financially while developing prosperity-thinking. They are encouraged to take 'baby steps' to change, such as researching higher paying jobs or seeking new investment opportunities. And they learn to drop many poverty-thinking behaviors, which can range from self-deprivation to becoming recklessly in debt.

Personal style

People's financial state usually reflects their psychological makeup and history, said Florida psychologist Cheryl Fellows, Ph.D., who is writing a book on the psychology of money.

"Each individual develops a unique 'money personality' based on family of origin, life experience and personality style, Fellows said. "This 'money personality' drives behavior in career, relationships, investing and general lifestyle.

The personality type includes the gambler, who takes undue risks with money; the miser, who is frugal to the point of self-deprivation; and the showboat spender, who spends money lavishly to gain attention. Each type of personality needs to strike a balance, learning that "money is important but not the be-all, end-all," she said.

Enhancing self esteem is a crucial way to help patients learn to handle their money when they are self-confident and skilled at dealing with people in the marketplace, she said."

particularly money and leisure time" (p. 141). While these definitions of consumer behavior are very broad, there is no denial that as consumers, we are influenced by both commercial and noncommercial stimuli, a subject with which social psychology has and should have legitimate concerns. We all know that with increase in material possessions, the socio-economic status of an individual in the hierarchy of society tends to elevate. Exchange of gifts is not only related to status, power and influence, but it also becomes a skillful game of the exchange of materials. According to Levy (1959), products can serve two **symbolic functions. First,** they may become symbolic of one's attitudes, values and personal orientations. In other words, they may show **expressive significance** of materials by attaching self-referent meanings. **Second,** material possessions indicate social affiliation and position, that is, they are symbolic of **categorical significance.** If I want to contribute to maintaining a clean

Expressive significance: When possessions show self-referent meaning

environment and therefore buy an electric car, it indicates my personal attitude and values (expressive significance). On the other hand, if I buy an electric car to maintain my affiliation with the environmental group to which I am affiliated, it will indicate a categorical significance. In many cases, both expressive and categorical significances become consonant, that is, I believe in a clean environment and I am also looking for a social forum to express my views collectively.

Categorical significance: When possessions show social referent meaning

Several scholars believe that material symbols are helpful in establishing one's identity (Dittmar, 1992; Wickland & Gollwitzer, 1982). While early research on the relationship between personality traits and buying consumer goods was inconclusive, recent research linking a consumer's self-image with a product has thrown a new light on the understanding of consumer behavior (Kasser, 2002; Myers, 2000). For example, in order to lure buyers, advertisers try to bring congruity between object-perception and self-perception. Advertisers rely on an image, something that is symbolic of the qualities of an object and of the individual who is using it. In order to be effective, market research analysts target gender and then match the product and its benefits as perceived by the buyer (Whipple & Courtney, 1985). A beautiful, slender female in a low seat car advertisement is congruent but not one in a high seat truck advertised as being "Like a rock."

Braun and Wickland (1989) showed that a compensatory relationship exists between lack of skills and ability and the possession of material symbols. For instance, law students felt a greater need for overt display (cars, clothing and so on) than those already practicing law. In addition, the researchers also noticed that compared to senior students, first year college students bought more university related attire and gadgets. Wickland and Gollwitzer (1982) proposed that when people are in doubt about their identity, they tend to buy relevant material symbols to enhance their identity as well as their affiliation with others. Material symbols lead to symbolic self-completion. In their study, Wickland and Gollwitzer (*ibid*) found that students who were not among the best in a business program made greater use of overt symbols of success (for example, expensive business suits, briefcases, etc.) than those expecting a solid career in the future. Such symbolic self-completion is also extended to our daily lives in many ways. For example, our unconditional love for pets and taking responsibility for their care is a fulfilment of our commitment that nurtures our own identity.

Does the presence and opinion of others cause a dramatic effect on consumer behavior? Several early researchers borrowed social psychological research findings and applied them directly to investigate consumer behavior. For example, Venkatesan (1966) designed a study based on **Asch's** research on **social conformity**. You may recall that Asch was interested in learning from his subjects, which one of the three lines was equal to an independent fourth line. When several confederates deliberately selected an unequal line to match the fourth line, the subject also showed a tendency to agree with their decision. The task in Venkatesan's study was the selection of business garments that were identical but were viewed differently by confederates. The results of this study showed that even though all the garments were identical, the subjects selected the garment that was the choice of most of the members of the confederate group. Post-experimental interviews indicated that the subjects changed their decisions because of the preference of other members in the group. Bagozzi and co-workers (2002) examined in depth the extent to which **theories of social psychology** could be applied to consumer behavior, especially in the context of **information processing** and **social cognitive communication processes, attitude models, emotion, social identity theory and action theory.**

ADVERTISING

The bottom line of any business is the volume of sales of a product or service. It is implied that people will not buy unless they have information that a product exists. Business organizations use a wide variety of methods to give information about their products to potential customers and lure them to buy these products. The most popular and common way to achieve this goal is to advertise products in various ways so that, at the minimum, people recognize the product. In order to make their advertisement effective, companies rely on several techniques: associate a product with a celebrity or music, use humor, enhance memory by arousing emotions (for example, "Proudly made in the USA"), etc.

At present, the advertisement business in the USA generates well over 70 billion dollars annually and will continue to increase as new ways of selling products on the information super highway emerge. It is interesting to point out that while no one can actually estimate what effect advertisements have had or will have on the sales of a product or service, there is almost a relentless faith among members of the business community that they would go nowhere without advertising their products. While a few businesses might have succeeded without advertising, their numbers and sales figures are certainly significantly lower than those of their competitors.

Research using the **split cable market test** showed the effect of advertisement by keeping track of people who buy advertised goods. In this method, consumers who had seen the advertisement and bought the advertised material are compared with a control group that had not seen the advertisement. Based on hundreds of split cable market tests, Abraham and Lodish (1990) concluded that the advertisements were particularly helpful for a new product: an average 21% increase in the sales of new products occurred with effective advertising.

Split cable market test: Method of studying effect of advertising on sales

The effect of advertisements on **gift buying and gift giving** provides us with additional insight. According to Mortelmans and Damen (2001), there are various occasions calling for gifts over the year. Some of the common ones are Christmas Day, Valentine's Day, Easter, etc. The authors note a transition. With each passing year, the commercial pressure through advertisements has been found to start earlier than the year preceding it. A research project was started in 1999 in Antwerp, Belgium to look into the effects of the burgeoning media pressure on 730 males and females between the ages 17-92 years. The results of this project provided evidence regarding the ways in which people react to such pressure through advertising in terms of their buying behavior.

The data obtained from the **household scanner panel** (a record prepared on the basis of each item purchased by a customer) also offer several unique ways to understand consumer behavior. According to Gupta, Chintagunta, Kaul and Wittinik (1996), this method helps us to understand **brand-switching behavior** over time. It also helps in monitoring **new brand performance** after it has been advertised. Lastly, this method informs us about the **stockpiling behavior** of consumers. Because household scanner data may not be representative of the population, any effect of advertising based on this technique should be accepted with caution.

Household scanner panel: Record prepared on the basis of each purchase by customer

Psychographics: Used for advertising to people having common characteristics

Another marketing technique that is based on psychological similarities of people is called "**psychographics.**" It is used for creating and advertising products to influence a group of people sharing some common characteristics. A number of researches looking into the psychographic characteristics of consumers and customers have been conducted. Wunderink (2002), interested in the psychographic characteristics of adults who give donations to charitable organizations, found that those subjects who were more likely to give donations were older, more educated, and were more likely to donate by bank transfer or through a pre-payment arrangement. The tobacco industry has been known for its use of psychographics for the promotion of its products. Ling and Glantz (2002) contended that physicians and public health professionals should also use such psychographic approaches to design tobacco control interventions. If tobacco use can be promoted through learning more about the psychographic characteristics of users and non-users, the authors argue that medical and public health professionals should be able to use the same or similar data to target their interventions for tobacco control. The authors suggested that in their efforts to counter tobacco marketing, the campaigns should include people of all ages, with a special focus on young adults, rather than simply concentrating on teenagers and children.

Subliminal messages: The flashing of messages for durations so short that they cannot be accurately perceived

Given the evidence that advertisement is helpful, the question arises: What makes advertisement more effective? A technique that has been used for the past three decades to influence consumers is based on **subliminal messages.** It consists of flashing messages on a screen so rapidly that the words cannot be consciously perceived. It is believed that under such conditions of delivery, the recipient would develop a sudden urge for the product. When Vicary publicly used this technique in the 1950s to promote Coca Cola, there was an increase in the sales of this beverage by approximately 18%. In addition to such **subliminal visual messages, subliminal auditory messages** have been developed to help people control their weight, smoking habits and self-esteem. Are subliminal messages effective? What is their specific influence? These issues have been debated for a long time and, in fact, several studies have yielded no effect at all (Greenwald, Spangenberg, Pratkanis & Eskenazi, 1991). It is almost certain that subliminal messages are ineffective in everyday life and they are no better than a visit to an astrologer. Contrary to such conclusions based mostly on field research, subliminal messages have been found to be effective in laboratory conditions. For example, Bargh and Pietromonaco (1982) found that subliminally presented words affected the proneness of a subject's mind in interpreting hostile or neutral conditions. Those subjects who were presented hostile words that were not consciously perceived interpreted subsequent neutral conditions as hostile. In other words, subliminal information has the potential to prepare a subject's mind in a given direction and influence the following incoming neutral information. Neuberg (1989) conducted a study to find out if watching competitive words would increase the likelihood of the display of competitive behavior among subjects who were placed in a Prisoner's Dilemma game, a situation in which a subject can play cooperatively or competitively to maximize his/her gain individually or collectively. Neuberg concluded that subliminally presented competitive words affected subjects who were predisposed to competition but such words had no effect on subjects who were participating in a cooperative spirit.

Based on available research on the psychological effects of subliminal presentation of material, Aronson and his co-workers (1994) concluded that advertisements influence our behavior without using subliminal messages. In addition, they are also of the view that advertisements reinforce cultural stereotypes by linking desirable cultural images with an object. For instance, look at cigarette advertisements of Marlboro linked to the macho Marlboro Man or Budweiser advertisements with young, pretty girls in bikinis at the beach. Gender stereotypes (for example, men are doers and women are observers) reinforce the imagery of consumers. Subtle non-verbal and non-emotional cues are used to depict a passive but expressive female or an aggressive but non-emotional male. While such advertisements are not subliminal, they tend to have a significant influence on our behavior. One way in which TV advertisement could become subliminal is when viewers engage in **zapping** (that is, channel switching). While non-zappers recalled more brand advertised than zappers, those recalled by the zappers were advertisements placed towards the end of the commercial break (Tse & Lee, 2001).

Zapping: Channel switching on the TV

In short, while it is not possible to accurately measure the impact of advertisement and subliminal messages on consumer behavior, there is no doubt that both influence viewers. Experts in marketing use sales data obtained from different sources to promote their products through carefully designed advertisements. The success or failure of their efforts depends on a complex set of factors—economic, social, political level of competition, etc.

PERSUASION

The purpose of advertising is to persuade an individual to buy a product. Most researches conducted during 1950s and 1960s on attitude change were based on the **information processing approach** to explain how people could be persuaded to buy a new product. There are **three key elements** in this approach: **source, message and audience**. The main idea behind this approach was to analyze, "**Who says what to whom.**" Accordingly, the research work on attitudes was geared to the prestige and credibility of the source, the type of message used in communication, and the characteristics of recipient.

Taken together, a framework of persuasion was prepared to show the circumstances in which attitude change was possible (Hovland, Janis & Kelly, 1953). In general, such studies yielded several interesting findings:

- **An expert will be more persuasive than a non-expert.**
- **Low self-esteem individuals will be more easily persuaded than those with high self esteem.**
- **Attractive communicators will be more effective than unattractive ones.**
- **A two-sided communication will be advantageous when a communicator's view is contrary to that of a recipient.**
- **Those who speak rapidly are more successful than those who speak slowly, that is, fast-talking salespersons and politicians are more persuasive than their counterparts.**

This is a partial list of several applications that resulted from earlier research on persuasion.

As applied to consumer psychology, a general approach to the study of consumer behavior consists of an analysis of the following **three** components:

- **Consumer Input (for example, economic and market situation).**
- **Intervening Variables (for example, attended material and preferences).**
- **Consumer Output (Consumer search, choices, and evaluation).**

The information processing approach to persuasion lost its impact in the 1970s when researchers began to focus on the nature of cognitive processes that caused change in the attitudes. In other words, the issue shifted from "Who says what to whom" to "**What was in one's mind that caused change in his/her attitude?**" This shift in research was brought about by many studies on persuasion (Garbarino & Edell, 1997; Richins, 1997; Petty & Cacioppo, 1986; Mandler, 1982). A brief description of cognitive and affective factors as applied to persuasion follows.

Cognitive factors

When people are exposed to a persuasive argument or advertisement, they can think about it either carefully or lightly. In addition to their ways of thinking (carefully or lightly), some other relevant thoughts also emerge to determine the nature of attitude change in an individual. Having this approach in mind, Petty and Cacioppo (1986) sought to determine those conditions in which an individual would carefully evaluate a situation (for example, buying an expensive gift, a car and so on). Under such conditions people spend a lot of their time examining the cost of an item, comparing it with several other options, and feel highly involved and motivated. When they act in this manner, they use the **central route** to evaluate a message. On the other hand, a **peripheral route** will involve little mental work or motivation to compare items. If a teenager says that he wants to buy a pair of Nike shoes just because it is used by Michael Jordon, he would be taking a peripheral route. This type of routing is also based on mental shortcuts, called heuristics (Chaiken, 1987), that is, when **personal involvement is low**. For example, if the same boy says that he would buy Nike shoes because most athlete's wear that brand, it will be a case of **heuristics** in the decision making process of the teenager.

Central route to persuasion: Use of rational thinking before being persuaded

Peripheral route to persuasion: Where personal involvement is low; based on heuristics

The above view used to explain persuasion is derived from the **Elaboration Likelihood Model (ELM)** that predicts the conditions under which a recipient of a message will (or will not) elaborate to evaluate the arguments presented to him/her (Petty & Cacioppo, 1986). The core components in the elaboration process are the ability and motivation levels of an individual. It is important to note that the dichotomy between central and peripheral routes is not as tight as it appears, for the motivation level of an individual can increase or sharpen with changes in circumstances. For example, the same boy who took a peripheral route in the motivational processing could also begin to realize that Nike makes durable and attractive shoes in comparison to other competitors, and thereby take a central route. Petty and Cacioppo (1996) concluded that consumer behavior changes made through taking the central route are "**more persistent, resistant to counter persuasion, and predictive of behavior**" (p. 2). They believe that the distinction between central and peripheral routes is useful in designing effective and long-term persuasion treatments and interventions.

Elaboration Likelihood Model: Model of persuasion predicting conditions under which recipient will elaborate on arguments presented to him

As applied to consumer behavior, people are likely to use a **central route** when they make **important and large purchases** (for example, a car or a home). A **peripheral route** is likely to be used when people buy items that are **frequently purchased** (for example, shampoo or toothpaste). This latter type of behavior can be very easily changed by altering the mood of a customer by presenting a celebrity or a beautiful model along with the advertised product.

Fishbein and Ajzen's (1980) **Theory of Reasoned Action** (TRA) was discussed in the chapter on environment. This theory predicts that if an intention guides the attitude of an individual, a specific behavior will occur. As discussed earlier, the theory has two core assumptions: **attitudes** and **subjective norms**. While attitudes are evaluative feelings about behavior, subjective norms are our beliefs concerning how others expect us to behave. An executive may not want to buy an expensive car in the belief that the value of his investment would depreciate. But the executive would feel peer pressure to buy an expensive car to maintain normative standards. When one's attitude and subjective norm are identical, it is easy to persuade an individual to buy a product. Fishbein and Ajzen's theory has been successfully applied in predicting voluntary consumer behavior (Singh, Leong, Tan & Wong, 1995; Beatty & Kable, 1988; Warshaw, 1980). Unfortunately, this theory has not been very successful in predicting behavior that is not voluntary. Further, the effectiveness of subjective norms in predicting behavior has been questioned. For example, Thompson, Haziris and Alekos (1994) were unable to find the effect of a subjective norm on the purchase of olive oil that is used for health reasons.

In order to cover the deficiency in their theory, Fishbein and Ajzen (1980) added one more component to their theory, that is, **perceived behavior control**. It means that in addition to the attitudes and subjective norms, we should also measure an individual's perceived ability to perform behavior of interest. While their theory is undoubtedly the best one available to account for the gap between attitudes and behavior, work on consumer behavior has given it somewhat mixed support. Using Fishbein and Ajzen's theory in understanding the determinants on consumer composting behavior, Taylor and Todd (1997) argued that an integrative model consisting of several components of attitudes (personal relative advantages, societal relative advantages and complexity), subjective norms (internal and external), perceived behavioral control (self-efficacy and compatibility), and intentions would be more effective in determining the relationship between attitudes and behavior than the theory of reasoned action (Please see the chapter on environment).

Recent research on the TRA also provides some insights regarding its efficacy in predicting consumer behavior. While Fishbein and Ajzen's multi-attribute attitude model and theory of reasoned action received great attention during the 1970s and the 1980s, the Elaboration Likelihood Model (Petty *et al.*, 1986) and the related dual process models are accepted to a greater extent (Friestad & Wright, 1995). According to Simonson and his colleagues (2001), research on persuasion in the context of consumer behavior can be divided into the **'hot'** and the **'cold'** aspects. Whereas the cold aspect focuses on the **role of beliefs** in the formation of attitudes and other related aspects of information processing regarding consumer decisions, the hot aspect looks into the **role of affect** and mood, arousal, regret, peripheral persuasion and the hedonic aspects of consumption and self-expressive motives for brand preference (for example, emotions). It is contended here that the research on consumer behavior is focusing more on the hot aspects with a decline of research on the cold aspects.

Affective factors

According to Mandler (1982), people have limited cognitive resources and therefore tend to use them judiciously. When people are overloaded with information they tend to **categorize information**, and the **mental effort** in developing a schema may cause arousal and elicit an emotional response. He proposed that information regarding a product may influence us in two ways. **First,** information concerning the object can cause an emotional reaction. For instance, I find the smell of garlic unpleasant. **Second,** the act of processing of information regarding an object itself can generate affective consequences. If a physician convinces me that garlic would be useful for my health, I may evaluate this information and form a schema but in doing so I may develop incongruity between the stimulus (garlic) and my knowledge concerning the usefulness of garlic (schema). When this incongruity between the stimulus and schema increases, the affect becomes increasingly negative. A positive or negative evaluation of the stimulus (garlic) will depend upon the effort involved in resolving the incongruity.

Mandler's theory has been successfully applied in several studies on consumer behavior. For instance, Peracchio and Tybout (1996) found that when attributes of a new product are moderately incongruent, the new product is evaluated more favorably as compared to the situation in which the attributes are either congruent or extremely incongruent. For example, they reported that a high-preservative soft drink or an all-natural, sweet carbonated beverage was judged less favorably than an all-natural soft drink (taste unknown). Given the implications of Mandler's theory, it is argued that a stimulus that conforms to expectation—congruity caused by the all-natural, sweet carbonated beverage—will not be arousing except that it will cause a mild positive response. On the other hand, if moderate incongruity is caused by an all-natural drink, it will lead to cognitive elaboration and arousal. Peracchio and Tybout (*ibid*) concluded, "a new product is evaluated more favorably when its attributes are moderately incongruent with a product category than when its attributes are either congruent or extremely incongruent with the schema" (p. 177).

There has been considerable debate among marketing psychologists regarding the context in which an advertisement should be presented to the audience. Should the introduction of a new product be presented when Princess Diana's funeral procession was shown on television? What effect does **programming context** have on the encoding of information about the new product? Using several pleasant and unpleasant scenarios, Meyers-Levy and Tybout (1997) attempted to determine the encoding effect of the context in which information was given to the subjects. Their results suggested that encoding depends on the appropriateness of the context's effect and the availability of cognitive resources. A lack of meaningful connection between the context and the target information was also related to the encoding process.

West, Brown and Hoch (1996) focused on another dimension of consumer behavior: **consumption vocabulary**. According to them, the stable preference of objects depends to a large extent upon consumer vocabulary that helps people to identify product features and simplify preference-related thoughts. They found that in the absence of a suitable vocabulary,

Consumption vocabulary: Words used to identify product features

consumers required considerable experience to make their decisions. In many cases, the preference of consumers could not develop at all.

Does the consumption of goods lead to **emotional responses**? Think about your excitement at the time you bought your first car or received a surprise gift from your parents during Christmas. There are many affective, including emotional, responses that are attached to consumption of goods. In order to measure such responses, Mehrabian and Russell (1974) developed a scale known as the **Pleasure-Arousal-Dominance (PAD) scale.** This scale was used in marketing research for over two decades to assess emotional responses to some types of products. Batra and Holbrook (1990) published a scale that measures 12 types of affective responses to advertising. More recently, Richins (1997) prepared a measure, the **Consumption Emotion Test (CET),** to assess the range of emotions consumers most frequently experience in consumption situations. These emotional expressions are: anger, discontent, worry, sadness, fear, shame, loneliness, romantic love, love, peacefulness, contentment, optimism, joy, excitement, surprise, and others (including guilt). It should be noted that this list of emotions is not related to or derived from the theoretical research conducted in social psychology that measures eight primary emotions; instead, Richins (1997) measured emotions in a wide range of consumption situations.

The argument in support of exploring emotions differently in consumption situation is that **consumption emotions are different** in character than those experienced in interpersonal relationships. Human beings express a very complex set of emotions, especially when the display of emotions is not very intense. Generally speaking, **consumption emotions are mild** and not expressed in the form of extreme anger or love. Using a narrow set of emotions as used in the traditional social psychological research may conceal considerable information and limit the implications of consumer research. For instance, Richins (1997) and Petty and Caccioppo (1996) have acknowledged that the traditional bipolar scales (e.g., good/bad; bored/relaxed) used to measure emotional responses have been ineffective in consumer research. Further, Richins argued that while emotional response is vicarious, indirectly experienced, and dramatic in case of an advertised product, it is confined to an actual product in a study of consumer behavior. No wonder—viewers pay attention to handsome males and beautiful females in the advertisement and can afford to ignore the actual product. This does not happen in a study of consumer emotion because the product has been used by the consumer.

The relationship between consumer behavior and advertisement is very complex. Brown and Stayman (1992) reported **two** effects of advertisement in their **dual-mediation model. First,** when claims about a product in the advertisement are ignored by the viewers, they operate at a **peripheral level** by relating their attitude toward an advertisement with the advertised product.

The **second** effect is indirect. It involves **motivation**, that is, to carefully examine the claims made in the advertisement, by using a **central route**. Fishbein and Ajzen's **theory of reasoned action** is helpful in explaining behavior in this situation because it accounts for the gap between attitudes and behavior. Unfortunately, this second effect produces weak results and, therefore, it is advised to mix the advantages of both central and peripheral routes in changing consumer behavior.

An interesting phenomenon in advertising is that the effects of a popular advertisement do not last long (Chattopadhyaya & Nedungadi, 1992). Popular advertisements can even draw our attention away from the advertised product.

Compliance techniques

Experimental work in social psychology in the past two decades has led to at least two techniques that have powerful applications in influencing consumer behavior: foot-in-the-door and door-in-the-face.

Foot-in-the-door: Make a small request followed by larger one only after the respondent has complied

The **foot-in-the-door technique** involves making a purposefully small request first and then presenting a very large request. The idea is that after making a very demanding small request, an individual, who accepts a small request, will subsequently also accept the large request. In our daily lives, we notice that we give donations in small amounts in the beginning but the contributions increase over a period of time. Why? According to Freedman and Fraser (1966), compliance with a small request leads an individual to self-perceive his/her role in a cause. While most Californians rejected a huge "Drive Carefully" sign in their front yards, a large number of subjects agreed to display a small label "Be a safe driver" in their car window. The same participants later agreed to display the large "Drive carefully" sign in their front yard.

In another study, Pliner, Hart, Kohl and Saari (1974) reported that 46% of Toronto residents were willing to contribute to the Cancer Society directly, but the number doubled when they were requested a day in advance to wear a pin advertising the fund raising event. Greenwald and collaborators (1987) asked subjects during the 1984 presidential election, "Do you expect that you will vote or not?" The actual voting rate turned out to be 41% higher among those who had said yes, compared to those who had not been asked this question.

Low-ball technique: First quote a low price and then add on other costs

A variation of this technique is known as **low-ball technique** (Cialdini, Cacioppo, Bassett & Miller, 1978). In this technique, a customer is first asked to participate in a task that is harmless or without any profit motive (for example, provide information on a car or listen to a tape). Once the customer agreed to this initial request, the chances of agreeing to a subsequent higher level request also increased. Car sales-persons often use this technique by quoting a very low price and persuading the customer to fill out the sales form. After a customer enters information on the form, the salesperson starts listing the cost of options and increases the price of car. This technique involves a momentum of compliance during which an individual makes a commitment. In addition to salespeople, politicians, military leaders, and dating couples often use this technique to take advantage of a situation. Box 8.2 describes how a scholar in the field of consumer psychology became a victim of this technique used by a Hare Krishna solicitor.

The question that arises in the first place is: Why do people agree to a small request? Because people want to maintain their self-image, they agree to a small request that they justify in terms of serving the community, or some other good cause. By agreeing to a small request, individuals begin to feel that their self-image is maintained. Once people find themselves in a comfort zone, it is easy to persuade them to accept a larger request. For example, if you ask your neighbor to donate $1 for American Cancer Society, the neighbor is

BOX 8.2

When a researcher studying foot-in-the-door also becomes a victim

"Returning from an interview for a job I had to change planes at Chicago's O'Hare Airport. Dashing through the terminal, I suddenly was confronted by an attractive woman dressed in weird clothing. She pressed a flower in my hand and said, "This is a gift for you!" After waiting for a moment to let her feigned benevolence soak in, she then asked for a donation for her religious group. Of course, I immediately reached for my billfold, succumbing to her duplicity.

After getting my ticket for the plane and waiting for it to arrive, I thought back on the experience. With the flower's fragrance still in my nose, I realized that I had been duped by the norm of reciprocity. What was worse, the week before I had just completed a study investigating its use. I was humbled—a researcher supposedly possessing a fundamental understanding of the principle had been taken in." John C. Mowen (1989) (p. 208).

likely to contribute to this worthy cause and feel good about contributing. Following successful action on this first request, one will be more likely to succeed in the second larger request. In short, once a strong positive self-image is established, use of the foot-in-the-door technique makes individuals show a long-term compliance behavior.

The other technique, called **door-in-the-face**, involves making an unreasonably large request first and then presenting a reasonably moderate request. For example, if you ask a person to buy a number of magazines at a time, most people will refuse, as if slamming the door in your face. Later, if you approach them with a few very selective deals, the same people will agree to buy. In other words, this technique allows people to shut the door owing to the very nature of the large request which is opposite to the foot-in-the-door technique.

Door-in-the-face: Make a large request first and then after refusal make a smaller, more reasonable request

The door-in-the-face technique works because people have a tendency to reciprocate when others change. In other words, when a sales-person changes his position from a very extreme one to a moderate one, we feel obligated to respond. The flat refusal in the first place now changes into a willingness to consider a reasonable offer. Cialdini and co-workers (1975) found that when college students were requested to escort adolescents from a detention center on a trip, only 17% consented. However, after rejecting a large request, approximately half the students agreed to escort the same adolescents for the trip.

Fig. 8.1: Procedures involved in the foot-in-the-door and door-in-the-face techniques.

THE DOOR-IN-THE-FACE

Large request → then moderate request → moderate request alone

THE FOOT-IN-THE-DOOR

Small request → then moderate request → moderate request alone

Note: → Indicates the direction of increased compliance. Remember, respondent's behavior and issues of committment are critical variables in employing these procedures.

Reciprocity norm: The tendency to reciprocate someone else's good behavior

An explanation for the success of the above technique is the **norm of reciprocity**. It means that as a matter of social norm we respond to a positive behavior from another by taking a reciprocal action. This norm becomes so habitual in our lives that we start acting mindlessly on it. Kunz and Woolcott (1976) reported that people reciprocated by sending Christmas cards to complete strangers who had sent them cards after their names had been drawn randomly from a telephone directory. Your experience in a grocery store may be similar. After tasting a sample of a food product, you spontaneously feel like buying it, although you may not use it for a long time. Not surprisingly, grocery stores found an increase in their sales after offering free samples to their customers (Packard, 1957). When people taste a product, it may increase its salience value and if people really like the quality of this product, they will be motivated to buy it.

Use of gifts as a marketing tool

The use of gifts as a marketing tool has been related to the norm of reciprocity. Strohmetz and co-workers (2002) found that when diners in a restaurant received a small piece of candy along with the check, they tended to give a bigger tip to the servers as compared to those diners who did not receive any candy. Moreover, the amount of the tip was seen to increase as the amount of the candy increased. Such results have also been obtained by the giving of free coupons by tobacco companies (MacFaden & co-workers, 2001). Similar are the effects of business gifting. Beltramini (2000) reports data to show that the intention for continued repurchase by corporate customer increased if they received a gift from the selling company. One of the common strategies to lure physicians to prescribe their products is the giving of gifts to both the practitioner and his family by pharmaceutical companies. The strategy has been found to be so effective that ethical concerns have been raised against such gifting practices (Tenery, 2000; McKinney & co-workers, 2000; Vollmann 2000).

Cross-cultural aspects of gifting

A number of researches clarify that the concept of gifting as well as the nature of the gifts varies from culture to culture. There are pronounced differences even within the same country. An interesting finding is that the in-store information search strategy varies with the culture (Laroche, Saad, Kim & Browne, 2000). When 115 English speaking subjects were compared with 213 French speaking subjects in Quebec, Canada, in their purchase of a Christmas gift, there were distinct patterns of in-store search behavior with reference to three factors, that is, of displays, brand and sales clerk assistance. It was also found that the English-speaking subjects had a more complex search strategy than the French speaking. The spending on gifts is also found to vary along the individual-collectivist dimension, as seen from the comparison between Roman Catholic, working class Latino and White middle class people (Falicov, 2001).

An even more potent example of how the concept of gifting varies across cultures was cited by Joy (2001). The data collected through interviews in Hong Kong shows that the Chinese culture discourages the concept of reciprocity and the very act of gifting for building relationships is not looked upon very kindly. This idea is in keeping with the Confucian ideal of encouraging self restraint and discouraging selfishness. That Chinese people differ from Westerners in their gift acceptance and offering behavior has also been reported by Hua (2000).

THE EFFECT OF TELEVISION ON CONSUMER BEHAVIOR

Consider the following facts about the role of television in everyday life of USA:

- 1945: A question in the Gallup poll was, "Do you know what television is"? Now we ask, "how many television sets do you have in your household"?
- At present 98.3% of households in the USA have television (*Los Angeles Times*, October 26, 1996): 9% in 1955; 65% in 1955; 93% in 1965. Federal Trade Commission, USA.
- A high school graduate (1997) who scored 1600 (maximum score) on the SAT said that she did not have a television at home. It was surprising.
- Two-thirds of Americans view television during their dinner. 60% kids watching televion at 10 AM Saturday morning.
- More than 50% of children would rather watch television than spend time with their parents.
- A number of TV programs that were popular in USA are becoming popular in well over 100 countries.
- On average, children watch TV for more than five hours a day; and a TV set is on for approximately seven hours a day.
- Western television programs are immensely popular in the East but not *vice versa.*
- In USA, 97% homes have a VCR; 90% have a CD player; and 9% have video games or other electronic gadgets (Bushman & Anderson, 2001).

How does **exposure to television** relate to consumer behavior? In the popular literature of social psychology, two explanations shed light on the issue. **First**, exposure to television programs involves paying attention to people, objects, and events presented in the programs. When the attended information is retained and subsequently motivates people to buy similar things, or behave in the ways portrayed in the television programs, the influence of television on a consumer becomes evident. Bandura's **social learning theory** explains how a behavior is modelled after watching and retaining contents of a program. The **second** explanation accounting for the influence of television relates to **priming effects**. Priming involves activation of a thought process at an implicit level. Displaying materials on various television programs can stimulate ideas about buying a particular object. Television programs often prime such ideas and initiate associations that are connected to materials presented in serials, movies, comedies, etc.

Priming: Activation of a thought process at the implicit level

While the reader may expect a separate chapter on the influence of television in this book, we decided to present this topic in the present chapter for the following three reasons. **First,** the presence of television in any contemporary home is like having a sofa, a computer, or any other common consumer product. Imagine what a visiting friend would think about you if he finds out that you do not possess a television in your home. The presence of television represents our mainstreaming in society and the channels we select to watch become symbolic of our identity.

Displacement effect: Taking time away from crucial tasks

Second, watching television can take significant time away from crucial tasks, including the use of things. This phenomenon is known as the **displacement effect.** Those who watch television regularly and for a long time are likely to have less time available to perform other activities. For instance, Parker (1963) reported a drop in the circulation of library books after television was introduced in the 1950s. Children who watch more television programs have less time for their homework (Keith & co-workers, 1986). A study of a Canadian town where television was introduced for the first time showed that the superior reading skills of children in Grades 2 and 3 declined and became similar to those of children who were already exposed to television in the previous years (Corteen & Williams, 1986). Television also affects children's daydreaming and creativity. Valkenburg and Van der Voort (1994) reported that while viewing television increased the frequency of daydreaming among children, the effects of television-viewing were adverse on their creativity.

Third, the content of television programs can cause unintended effects. Just as cigarettes can cause adverse effect on health, viewing high doses of violent programs can lead to an increase in violent behavior. Although television networks neither force us to watch violent programs nor do they tell us to follow displayed violent examples in dealing with people, one of the most adverse, unintended effect of watching violent programs on television is the increase in violence. Based on the available data, Centerwall (1989) found that there was a significant increase in the murder rates in the United States, Canada and South Africa after television was introduced in these countries.

Owing to our passion for the electronic box, called TV, the *US News & World Report* began an article on "Sex and Violence on TV" in this way: 'The family hour is gone' (September 11, 1995, p. 62). Given the above exposure to television, we can expect a significant impact of its programs on the behavior of viewers. Contrary to this simple belief, there is considerable debate over the real impact of television on our behavior. Like the controversy on the effect of subliminal exposure, the results of field and laboratory studies are at odds: while field studies question the impact of television on our behavior, evidence from a number of laboratory studies suggest how television shapes our behavior.

Research on the impact of television on behavior has been conducted most widely in the context of violence. Gerbner (1972) conducted the most systematic study in the 1960s to show how the frequency of violent episodes and prime-time are important in determining the extent of violence in a program and its impact on the viewers. He noticed that the programs designed for children had three times more violence than those shown for adults. His work at the School of Communications at the University of Pennsylvania led many other investigators to examine the relationship between television and violence methodically.

Perceived reality

If you ask tenth graders, "Are characters on television and in the real world alike?" you may get a mixed response but a majority of first graders may find TV and real life people alike (Lyle & Hoffman, 1972). Children, especially from the lower socio-economic strata, find violence more enjoyable and acceptable to watch than their upper strata counterparts (Greenberg & Gorden, 1972). A recent study on Generation Y college students revealed the ways in which students perceive characters in the real world and those in advertisements. Wolburg and Pokrywczynski (2001) found that gender and a variety of personality traits affect both the perceived value of the advertisements as a source of information and the relevance of the depictions in the media. Respondents rated depictions in the movies and in TV serials better than the depictions in the advertisements. This shows that media planners and marketing strategists need to be extremely careful while trying to communicate with this elusive group.

Correlational studies

Studies in which a relationship between increase in media violence and violent behavior has been established are called **correlational studies**. In a study by McIntyre and Teevan (1972) a violence rating was assigned to each program that the subjects watched. The subjects were also rated on their deviant behavior. The researchers found a significant positive correlation between the viewing of television violence and aggressive behavior. Dominick and Greenberg (1972) found that among children, approval of violence and willingness to use violence were correlated with their exposure to violence on television.

There is a serious flaw in correlational studies. Such studies do not tell us about the cause-effect relationship between the two variables. The process-oriented correlational studies attempt to minimize this deficiency by partialing out the impact of a third variable that may contaminate the strength of the correlation between the X and the Y variables. For example, if we find a significant positive relationship between television violence (variable X) and aggressive behavior of a child (variable Y), it may not be due to the relationship between these two variables alone, because a third variable (for example, parental encouragement to violence) may confound this relationship. Unless the effect of this third variable is subtracted, the real nature of the relationship between television violence and aggressive behavior will be questionable. In a study by McLeod and co-workers (1972), the relationship between violence viewing and adolescent aggression was found significant after partialing out the effects of parental attitudes, parental punishment, and other factors.

Another problem in correlational studies is that we do not know if X caused Y or Y caused X, that is, what is the direction of relationship between the two variables. To solve this problem, Chaffee and McLeod (1971) created two rival hypotheses (process analysis):

Hypothesis 1: Television violence increases aggressive behavior.

Hypothesis 2: Aggressive people watch violent TV programs.

By proposing such alternate explanations, we can find out how much individuals learned from television violence (Hypothesis 1) and what preference they already had for watching violent programs owing to their predisposition to violence (Hypothesis 2). In their study, Chaffee and McLeod found support for Hypothesis 1, that is, watching television violence is related to learning aggressive behavior. On the other hand, they did not find support for Hypothesis 2 (See Box 8.3).

BOX 8.3

Two hypotheses concerning television and violence

To support Hypothesis 1, you may ask the following questions:

- **Violent TV programs show me how to get back at people who make me angry.**
- **Sometimes I copy things I see people do on violent shows.**
- **Some programs give me ideas on how to get away with something without being caught.**

To support Hypothesis 2, you find out how many subjects score high on violence and if they also score high on television violence viewing.

Cross-lagged correlational studies

Lefkowitz, Eron, Walder and Huesmann (1972) used a **cross-lagged method** to show how preference of television violence among third grade children was positively and significantly correlated with aggressiveness 10 years later ($r = .31$). In this longitudinal study, the relationship between two variables, A1 (television violence) and B1 (aggressiveness), was measured when children were studying in the third grade. Ten years later the same children were again tested on the same variables, that is, now named A2 and B2. The magnitude of correlation between A1-B2 > B1-A2 showed that the television violence was a predictor for increased aggression among children (Fig. 8.3). Although cross-lagged studies do not exactly show a cause-effect relationship, they are viewed as nearly demonstrating such a relationship owing to their effectiveness in relating independent and dependent variables.

Fig. 8.2: An illustration of the cross-lagged correlation method.

- A1 = TV violence (grade 3)
- B1 = Aggression (grade 3)
- A2 = TV violence (10 years later)
- B2 = Aggression (10 years later)

Unfortunately, there is a long list of mediating variables that confound the relationship between media violence and individual aggression. Parental aggression, permissive attitudes in a family, and cultural beliefs are significant variables in determining the nature of aggression. The stimulation provided by television programs can interact with several social factors, and therefore the exact effects of the influence of television violence are not easy to determine. Summarizing their views on the complex relationship between television violence and human aggression, Baron and Richardson (1994) wrote, "....while existing evidence does indeed suggest that the high level of violence prevalent in current television and movie offerings probably contributes, along with other variables, to the occurrence of some aggressive encounters, care must be taken to avoid overstating or overemphasizing the importance of this relationship (p. 115).

Experimental research

Experimental studies directly show the effects of television violence on aggressive behavior. Experiments conducted by Bandura & co-workers (1963), set the trend for experimental research in this area (see chapter 1) and a number of significant experiments followed in the

1970s. Drabman and Thomas (1974) found that after watching a violent movie, children took longer to request adult intervention in a conflict compared to a control group having no such exposure. In another study, Leifer and Roberts (1972) created a response hierarchy of aggression (physical, verbal and non-violent alternatives). They asked children to respond to pictures, for example, "Hit them or leave them?" "Hit them or call them 'stupid'?" and so on. Leifer and Roberts concluded that the amount of aggression was related to the prior exposure to violence. For instance, television violence may increase the likelihood of aggressive behavior from the sixth probable response to the second one.

Field studies

Studies conducted by Huesmann, Lagerspetz and Eron (1984) in the USA and Finland showed that viewing television had a cumulative effect on aggression of children, that is, the more they watched, the more aggressive they became. Joy, Kimball and Zabrack (1986) got a chance to analyze the effects of television in a new situation in a Canadian town where there was no television until 1974. After the television was introduced in this town, aggressive behavior of children increased significantly as compared to the two other matched towns in the study. Another study of a novice television community on St. Helena Island revealed that boys appeared to have watched more violent acts than girls. Moreover, the boys tended to show more antisocial behavior than the girls after the television had been introduced in the community (Gunter, Charlton, Coles & Panting, 2000).

Huesmann and co-workers (1984, 1986) extended the Leikowitz and co-workers study (reported earlier in the context of cross-lagged correlation) and found that the same 8-year-old children who had acquired aggressive behavior displayed significantly higher antisocial behavior 22 years later, that is, at the age of 30 years. Huesmann and co-workers (1986) concluded: aggressive habits seem to be learned early in life, and once established, are resistant to change and predictive of serious adult antisocial behavior. If a child's observation of media violence promotes the learning of aggressive habits, it can have harmful lifelong consequences. Consistent with this theory, early television habits are, in fact, correlated with adult criminality (pp. 129-130).

For a detailed review of work on the influence of television on aggression, the reader is referred to Donnerstein, Slaby and Eron (1994) and Oskamp (1988). The purpose of reporting some selective correlational, experimental and field studies in this chapter is to inform the reader how in a very systematic way, social psychological research has attempted to relate television violence to aggressive behavior. On the other hand, a few psychologists (for example, Jonathan Freedman, 1984) opined that substantial evidence concerning the relationship between television violence and aggressive behavior in natural settings is lacking or unconvincing. In 1968, the National Commission on the Causes and Prevention of Violence in the USA held its hearings and concluded that "....it is reasonable to believe that a constant diet of violent behavior on television has an adverse effect on human character and attitudes." Since then there has been an organized effort by the popular TV networks to exploit the limitations of laboratory and field studies showing that such a relationship, in fact, exists. This situation is not unique to TV violence and aggressive behavior; a similar situation exists in regard to the relationship between advertising and consumption of tobacco. When the sale of Camel cigarettes was sagging and it was labeled as a brand for older people, the Joe Camel

BOX 8.4

Sex and violence on television

"Hollywood isn't convinced that media mayhem inspires the real thing. When I was little, I went to the movies every week and saw violent cartoons and two or three Westerns in which the entire Sioux nation was massacred by the cavalry, recalls Steven Bocho, creator of NYPD Blue. I never had a question that what I was watching was make-believe, because I was raised by a family that gave me a moral compass."

"On the other side of the debate stand 1,000 plus studies establishing links between TV violence and the way people behave in real life. In a 1970 study at Pennsylvania State University, psychologist Aletha Huston and a co-worker regularly showed a cartoon of fist-flying superheroes to one group of 4-year old and bland fare to another. Among kids in both groups known to be above average in aggressive behavior, those who saw the action heroes were more likely to hit and throw things after watching. Nor do the effects of TV violence fade after childhood. Psychologist Leonard Eron of the University of Michigan's Institute of Social Research has tracked 650 New York children from 1960 to the present, looking at viewing habits and behavior. Those who watched the most violent television as youngsters grew up to engage in the most aggressive behavior as adults, from spouse abuse to drunk driving."

The flaw in Bocho's argument, Eron says, is that not all homes have a moral compass. Besides no one's saying that all violence is inspired by television. One estimate based on an analysis of 275 studies by George Comstock, Newhouse professor of public communication at Syracuse University, is that perhaps 10% of antisocial and illegal acts can be linked to TV. "But wouldn't it be great if we could reduce the occurrence of violence in this nation by 10%?", asks Eron.

(Excerpts from a report in *US News & World Report*, September 11, 1995).

advertisement was especially targeted to the younger teenage population in order to boost sales. Within a few years, the consumption of this brand increased from 3% to 13% among adolescents (*ABC*, evening news with Peter Jennings, July 10, 1997). What does all this tell us? When money and power take precedence, as in the case of the powerful TV and tobacco industry, politicians and community leaders ignore researchers who are mostly confined to work in their laboratories. Had the Attorney General of the State of Mississippi, USA, not sued the tobacco companies for endangering the health of millions of people, individual lawsuits, like isolated researches, would not have restricted the free ride of tobacco tycoons. Without the active participation by researchers in their community issues, social sciences and medical research is likely to have little impact on public policy.

In their research work, Donnerstein, Slaby and Eron (1994) identified the following four effects of television violence:

- **An *aggressor effect* of increased meanness, aggression, and even violence toward others.**
- **A *victim effect* of increased fearfulness, mistrust or "mean world syndrome," and self-protective behavior (such as carrying a gun, which ironically increases one's risk of becoming a victim of violence).**

- **A *bystander effect* of increased desensitization, callousness, and behavioral apathy toward other victims of violence.**
- **An *appetite effect* of increased self-initiated behavior to further expose oneself to violent material (p. 240).**

They have also identified several **myths** (for example, television violence has a catharsis effect of actually reducing violence among viewers, etc.) that are misguiding the American public concerning the effects of television violence on an individual's aggression.

Donnerstein, Slaby and Eron (1994) have also pointed out that the effects of media are not always negative. Viewing **prosocial behavior** in television programming can be positive in the following **two** ways. **First**, exposure to prosocial behavior may increase helpful behavior toward others. And **second**, observing prosocial behavior may decease violence toward others.

BOX 8.5

What TV savvy parents can do to help their kids

1. A TV set is a stranger in your home. If you do not interrupt it, it will play sex and violence all day long.
2. Ask children to write down how long they watched TV and what they remember. Limit TV viewing for two hours per day.
3. Parents should watch TV with their children and discuss controversial issues with them.
4. Parents should be choosy in the selection of programs for children. Just as you do not pick the very first book you see in the library, in the same way do not select the very first program while channel-surfing.
5. You should say "no" if you do not approve a program. For example, tell your child that he should not watch, Married.... With Children" because you do not like the way kids and parents talk to each other.
6. Immunization from all bad programs is impossible. Write to TV station and newspapers and make your objections known. Children should participate in this effort.

Adapted from *US News & World Report*, September, 1995.

While the effect of television may not be so extensive in regard to adult behavior, a consistent dose of violence on television programs is most likely to have severe adverse effects on children. In his testimony to US Senate Judiciary Committee's Subcommittee hearing on the role of television, Eron (1993) pointed out that if a child watched television two to four hours per day, that same young person would have watched 8,000 murders and more than 1,00,000 episodes of violence upon leaving elementary school. Upon entering adulthood, a teenager would have been exposed to 2,00,000 acts of violence. Eron concluded that among all those who watch television, children are most susceptible to the effects of violence.

Wilson and her colleagues (2002) report the findings of another analysis of TV programs broadcast in the Los Angeles area for the period October, 1995 through June, 1996. Results show that the programs for children contained more violence than other types of programming. Nearly 70% of children's shows contained physical aggression, whereas only 60% of non-children shows contained some physical aggression. A typical hour of children's programming contained 14 episodes of violence as compared to only five during non-children programs. With such concentrated exposure to violence on TV, we can expect drastic effects. Results show that when high school students from Romania were divided into two groups, one viewing a violent program and the other a non-violent report, the former showed a very pessimistic mood and also perceived the world more negatively than those who did not watch the violent program (Pintea & Buss, 2002). A metaanalytical review of studies reported during the year 2000 revealed that exposure to violent video games not only increases physiological arousal and aggression related thoughts and feelings, but also decreased prosocial behavior (Anderson & Bushman, 2001).

Huesmann (1993) concluded that there are at least **three ways** in which children would show **strong influence of violence on television. First,** children imitate others and very often such imitation is indiscriminate. **Second,** media violence desensitizes people to the extent that their own views become less salient. And **third,** frequent exposure to violence makes children more accepting of violence as a solution to a problem. According to Huesmann, the most adverse effect of violence is seen when a model is rewarded after perpetrating violence.

In a very revealing article, Bushman and Anderson (2001) argued that media are mainly responsible for underplaying the impact of our scientific knowledge. According to them, much in the same way the powerful industrialists of tobacco industry suppressed the harmful effects of smoking, the tycoons in media industry are presenting counter claims, albeit pseudo scientific, to negate the adverse effects of media violence. With poor resources, social scientists are unable to air their views that the wealthy media owners can easily afford. It is unfortunate that the joint statement based on research findings of over 1000 studies by six major professional societies, including the APA, stating the causal relationship between media violence aggression have not been duly publicized to educate the public at large (*ibid*).

NEW PERSPECTIVES IN CONSUMER BEHAVIOR RESEARCH

Researchers in the area of psychology and marketing have not been united in their study of consumer behavior. Marketing researchers have criticized social psychology for its narrow approach based on laboratory experiments that are conducted mostly on college students (Wells, 1993). Such a reliance on college students and on unrealistic environments contributes to the bias in the formation of a psychological theory. On the contrary, marketing researchers follow a pragmatic approach that may not be necessarily driven by a conceptual framework. As already discussed in this chapter, several measures of consumption emotion have not been based on any popular theory in social psychology. Yet, they are objective and consistent measures of affective responses. We therefore suggest that any effort by social psychologists to enhance the effectiveness of an intervention program will have to involve a compromise between theory driven and data-oriented research. After all is said and done, the theory-driven research will have to be tested in some form in the real world. A pertinent question here is: Should social psychologists scale down their efforts in laboratory research to accommodate marketing scientists? Commenting on this situation, Nisbett (1990) wrote, "Euclid has more to do with curing disease than any physician who lived between Galen and Pascal. This is because geometry made possible the science of optics, which made possible the invention of the microscope, which made possible the germ theory of disease" (p. 1081). To sum up, the cogency of applied research will always prosper at the hands of theory-driven research and *vice versa*.

Petty and Cacioppo (1996) have contended that both social psychologists and marketing scientists should work together for common goals and that such an effort will bring them close in their research endeavors as well. They suggested that both should vigorously study altruistic marketing, an area that can benefit from both disciplines—psychology and marketing. Altruistic marketing, according to them, involves the study of disturbed or disturbing consumer behavior and attempts to develop effective treatment interventions for consumers facing adversity. Through altruistic marketing, it is possible to deal with a wide variety of social problems, ranging from the use of seat belts to condoms, and from consumption of cigarettes to alcohol.

Social marketing

Social marketing or altruistic marketing: The marketing of interventions to overcome disturbed or disturbing consumer

Social marketing (SM), or **marketing for altruistic** rather than for commercial purposes, has been embraced in a big way by both not-for-profit and profit–making organizations. While the former need it for bringing in donations and services, the latter use it as one more strategy to get to the heart of the customer. Musham and Trettin (2002) discuss the underlying assumptions and arguments in support of social marketing. **Firstly,** social marketing is ethically superior to commercial marketing because it works for the welfare of the society. **Secondly**, since efforts to instill health behavior, etc. by education and by providing information fail to be effective, such programs have to be 'sold' to the public. **Thirdly**, social marketing has been effective in bringing about long-term health behavior changes, where traditional public health services and public education had failed.

'Team Nutrition' (TN) is a US Department of Agriculture initiative to change children's eating habits through social marketing. It gives us an insight into how a social marketing program may be implemented. TN was a multi-channel nutrition intervention program, based on developing supportive relationships between school-teachers, administrators, local media, food professionals and other community partners. There was widespread acclaim of the program. It also clarified the management issues involved in devising and implementing any such program, especially the importance of forging links between the school, food specialists and external community agents (Levine & co-workers, 2002). A corporate SM program for recruiting future participants to a national level weight loss program has been described by Black and co-workers (2002). The role social psychology can play in devising such SM programs is delineated in Box 8.6.

SM is especially suited for promoting causes related to the prevention of the spread of **AIDS.** Yap and co-workers (2002) describe the assessment of a **needle social marketing intervention** among drug users in **China**. The evaluation brought to the fore important information regarding the particular drug user groups that need to be targeted. Their risk behavior, barriers, motives and possible messages and products need to be studied to promote a successful and acceptable intervention. SM has also been effectively used for **marketing tuberculosis prevention programs** among foreign-born **Vietnamese** (Houston, 2002), and for the development of an **information service for cancer patients** of **Northern Ireland** (Manning & Quigley, 2002). When campaigns were carried out in **Singapore** to study attitudes towards **genetically modified (GM) food**, it showed that the respondents' attitudes varied by gender

BOX 8.6

Applied social psychology in action: Factors determining alumni donations to their alma mater

One way in which social psychology can be of service to society is by conducting research on issues of societal concern. An example would be the research conducted by Teich (2002) for determining the factors underlying donations to institutes of learning.

It is common knowledge that most institutes of higher learning are not able to meet their expenses solely on the basis of the tuition fees collected from students. In this context, private institutes are harder pressed than their governmental counterparts. Coming often to their rescue are alumni who are willing to give donations to their alma mater in recognition of what they had got from the institute. It was keeping this in mind that the investigation described below was conducted.

Purpose: The express purpose of the investigation was to look into the factors that might affect alumni donations.

Sample: 129 alumni who had graduated from either of two participating institutes of higher learning from metropolitan New York, USA.

Theoretical underpinnings: The factors selected for investigation were based on the Fishbein and Ajzen Theory of Reasoned Action, with one modification. The modification was the inclusion of a hitherto unconsidered factor, that of affinity.

Procedure: On the basis of the above theory, duly modified, a questionnaire was constructed. It was pilot tested on 15 respondents, after which it was administered to the sample.

Results: The statistical analysis clarified that the Fishbein and Ajzen Theory of Reasoned Action can be used to understand alumni donations to their alma mater. Affinity as well as the antecedent factors had high Pearson's correlations significant at the .01 level, and the addition of the affinity variable increased the variance accounted for.

The implication of the study is that a donation campaign based on the theory of reasoned action would go a long way in making the campaign a success.

(women showing greater concern than men); by education (those with postgraduate education were the least concerned about the ethical and the health aspect and were ready to buy GM food if the consumer benefits were listed by the company; by marital status, with married people being less concerned about health issues; and by food habits, with vegetarians being more concerned than the non-vegetarians about the ethical aspects (Subrahmanyan & Cheng, 2000).

Another use of SM has been to understand the dynamics of **donation to charities behavior.** In the **Netherlands**, it was found that those people who are likely to donate more were older, more educated and more likely to donate through bank transfer. The **motives for donation** included the following: they had a positive attitude towards the organization because of the good work that it was doing, because it made them feel good, and also because it made them feel personally involved (Wunderink, 2002). Helping behavior examined in Australia has yielded similar results (Polonsky, Shelley & Voola, 2002). The usefulness of

psychographics in SM is viewed through the results of a survey conducted to study the use of a cancer information service in Northern Ireland. Women were more likely to use the service than men, as also relatives and friends as compared to patients themselves (Manning & Quigley, 2002).

When we analyze the findings of SM, we notice that the data are in line with the general **theories of altruism.** One theory often used to explain altruistic behavior has been the **social exchange theory.** There is empirical data for SM studies too in support of the social exchange theory. Thomas and Worrel (2002) studied voluntary help provided in three rural villages, one each in India, Botswana and the Philippines. The findings suggest that individuals provide assistance only if the assistance costs are outweighed by the benefits accruing from helping. The expectations of loans and quasi credit in return for the assistance affected the degree of assistance given by the individuals. The findings have great practical utility because it reveals how a simple strategy (for example, gifting) works.

People were found to be more likely to donate to charities that correlated with their personal self image (Polonsky & co-workers, 2002). In fact, it has been suggested that the **social identity explanations** in social psychology can help considerably to the understanding of consumer behavior (Reed, 2002). Marketing based on **social norms**, too, was also found successful as evidenced by the study of mass media campaigns for the reduction of high risk drinking among college students. Campaigns that attempted to correct misperceptions regarding campus-drinking norms were to a certain extent more effective. Further, the social norms approach coupled with information and greater advocacy would tend to increase the efficacy of the program (DeJong, 2002).

Cause related marketing (CRM)

A concept similar to social marketing is that of **cause related marketing (CRM)** used by both commercial and charitable organizations to promote certain causes, such as the fight against polio, control of blindness, etc. CRM operates by taking a particular cause piggy back on its original product. Thus, there are companies that say that every time you make a purchase of a product of the company, they will donate $1, say, to the Helpage organization.

Cause related marketing: When a commercial organization backs a cause primarily for marketing its own product

An examination of the effect of CRM on consumer attitudes deserves mention. Basil (2002) has concluded on the basis of three laboratory experiments that organizations towards which consumer attitudes are positive stand to gain from CRM. Secondly, the effect of CRM depends on whether the organization's image is perceived as fitting to the cause it is promoting. When consumer attitudes are imbalanced (that is, the attitude towards the organization and that towards the cause are opposite to each other) consumers tend to attain balance between the two. The nature of the attitude change that occurs depends on the pre-existing attitude valence towards the alliance partner, while change in the views towards the alliance relationship depends on pre-existing attitudes towards the company promoting the cause.

Consumer behavior in the cross-cultural perspective

Can we transport categories defined in one culture and use them to understand consumer behavior in another? Venkatesh (1995) believed that it was difficult. For example, **'modernism'** may have one meaning in the US but a totally different connotation in India. Thus, the role and significance of TV may be perceived differently in the two countries. The same may be said of the telephone or even the scooter. In Italy, it is a sign of elegant feminism; in the UK, a symbol for the youth; in India, it is a utilitarian family transport. Or, think of categories even within the US. Modernism may denote certain types of behavior in mainstream Americans but its correlates could vary for the first generation American immigrant. Thus, there is a growing realization that the new immigrant especially from Latin America and Asia is unlikely to assimilate in the mainstream American culture to the extent that the early immigrants did. Rather than referring to America as a melting pot, we may have to think of it more as a tossed salad (Hegeman, 1991). For the marketing practitioner, this population comprising the new immigrants has opened up new vistas: the consumption patterns of the new immigrant are sufficiently different and their numbers are large enough not to be regarded as marginal populations.

Ethno-consumerism: A conceptual framework to examine consumer behavior using constructs from within the culture

So, to understand the consumer who is a new immigrant, one must first understand their cultural underpinning. One of the first such studies was conducted by Hirschman (1981) of Jewish consumption patterns, followed by Penaloza (1994) and Zmud and Arce (1992) on Hispanics, Jain and Costa (1991); and by Joy and Dholakia (1991) on Asian Indian immigrants.

In contrast, we have cross-cultural consumer behavior, that is, **comparative consumerism**. Examples include studies on affluent Asian cultures, for example, Japan, (Anderson & Wadkins, 1991), Korea (Ko & Gentry, 1991), Hong Kong (Tse, Belk & Zhou, 1991); developing Asian cultures, for example, India (Venkatesh, 1994); developing African cultures (Belk, 1988) and emerging European markets (Ger, Belk and Lasere, 1993). The general theme in all of the above is how these different cultures are adopting Western style consumeristic tendencies while trying to retain their traditional value systems.

Comparative consumerism: The study of consumer behavior across cultures

As already discussed in this chapter, persuasion and social influence are pervasive issues in consumer behavior. In view of the important role played by cultural factors in persuasion and other forms of social influence, we as social psychologists should be able to define attitude change within the framework of culture. Reviewing research of the last ten years, Wood (2000) noted that such an inclusion of cultural factors in the domain of attitude literature remained an almost neglected aspect.

What would be the **effect of social class** on **cultural consumption**? Is class influential in cases where gender and race also significantly affect cultural tastes? Are there cross-national variations in these relationships? These are the questions that intrigued Katz-Gerro (2002) who then carried out a cross-national study in five countries (Italy, Israel, Germany, Sweden and the USA). The rationale behind choosing these countries was that they could all be classed as post industrial societies. The results revealed that despite such commonalities there were clear class differences, especially with reference to high-brow cultural consumption (for example, regarding dance, music, theatre, art, etc.). It was interesting to note that class correlated with consumption in different ways in the countries studied. The dividing line for consuming high-brow culture was located at the top end of class structure in Israel, the USA and Sweden, but located at the bottom of the class structure was Italy and Germany. Gender, race and religion also emerged as important variables.

BOX 8.7

Auto companies in India face cultural quirks (*The Economic Times*, May 17, 2002)

The quaint ways in which culture challenges the marketer of all categories of products are exemplified below:

- **The tractor industry: although the international trend is for the sloping nose of the tractor because it offers better visibility, it is a sure "no-no" as far as Indian farmers are concerned. The reason, anything that's nose down is akin to rubbing your nose in the dirt.**
- **While colors such as blue and red are in demand, no Indian farmer will touch a black chassis, because black is considered inauspicious.**
- **Ask car manufacturers in India and they say that three aspects are important:**
    - **All car makers must design their cars in a way that makes getting in and out of the vehicle easy, especially for those women who wear a sari (the traditional dress of Indian women).**
    - **Because of larger Indian families, space is very important, especially boot space.**
    - **As compared to their Western counterparts, many of the cars in India are driven by chauffeurs, so rear seat comfort is very important.**

These are some of the points that Ford worked on when it was designing its new model, Ikon, for the Indian market (Sen Gupta, 2002).

e-commerce

The **World Wide Web** is seeing an unparalleled yearly growth in both developed and developing countries. Alongside, we see a shift towards **e-commerce**. With greater market penetration and an increasing awareness of e-shopping, consumer behavior is undergoing a sea change. Even older people have started using the Internet (Trocchia & Janda, 2000). Shopping seems to have become easier than consuming. Hanapi and Kump (2003) have therefore developed the idea that future shopping behavior will see an increase in customers whose lack of time for consumption will force them to collect the products they purchase for later consumption. Other aspects that might undergo differences are e-satisfaction and e-loyalty. Empirical data accumulated over the last decade, with indications that the relationship between e-satisfaction and e-loyalty is moderated by both consumers' individual level factors (for example, aspirations) and the firms' business level factors like seasonal variations (Anderson & Srinivasan, 2003).

Eventually, countries with mature economies, for example, the USA and Japan, would show similarities in Internet adoption and people would know how to fulfil their needs most economically and efficiently (LaFerle, Edwards & Miguno, 2002).

Web advertising

In a very interesting study on the effect of **web advertising** on Hispanics, it was found that factors such as the attention people paid to web advertising, the frequency of 'clicks' and the frequency of exits were a function of the web user's beliefs, attitudes and demographic factors (Korgaonkar, Silverblatt & O'Leary, 2001). Do people just have a look at the web-based advertisement or are people adopting online shopping? Siu and Cheng (2001) concluded that people use a complex set of factors in their consumer behavior including, but not limited to, economic gains, availability, compatibility, venturesomeness and leadership on technological products.

Cyber space advertising has also been compared to advertising through other media. A study by Brackett and Carr (2001) on students found that students found web advertising to be irritating, annoying and an insult to people's intelligence. However, the students also predicted that web advertising would overtake advertising through TV in the future. Comparisons have also been made to determine product characteristics that are most influential in the choice of Internet advertising.

Lynch and his colleagues (2001) attempted to isolate the factors that drive **purchase intention** and **loyalty in e-commerce**, across different regions of the world. Subjects were surveyed concerning their opinions on the websites that they had visited in shopping for products in different categories. Questions included ratings of purchase intention, loyalty to website, affect and trust of the site. Actual shopping tasks by 299 respondents indicate that site quality, trust and positive affect are critical in explaining both purchase intention and loyalty to the site. Moreover, the impact of these factors varies across regions and highlights the need to tailor websites according to each world region and the product being offered.

LIMITS TO THE APPLICATION OF SOCIAL PSYCHOLOGY TO CONSUMER BEHAVIOR

In the chapter on the social psychology of environment, we presented a detailed description of how we waste our resources. If we do not change the intensity with which we consume materials, our behavior will deplete our natural resources in the near future. We are already facing problems regarding the dumping of waste—ships carrying waste from one state had to return to their original place because no state was willing to accept the garbage of another state. The euphoria caused by the upswing in stocks traded at the Wall Street and the ratings of J.D. Power have had a profound influence on consumers. Conversely, are there popular companies or organizations that also warn us of the consequences of excessive consumption? Unfortunately, the answer is pessimistic.

The virtues of simplicity are mostly discussed in religious places but hardly practiced even there. If you examine closely, our Gods and their residence have also become more fashionable and high-tech in the past few decades. Excessive consumption and waste display our financial strength and ability to move to a higher class. In our quest to achieve social ascendancy, we continue to use and abuse materials in unreasonable proportions and forget that we also owe something to other people and to Mother Earth. Ten years after drafting the *Declaration of Independence,* Thomas Jefferson remarked, "This world abounds indeed with misery; to lighten its burden, we must divide it with one another."

What kind of partnership will emerge between the consumer and the producer is not known but the fact is that the sooner it emerges, the greater will be its advantages in the near future. Altruistic marketing is one dimension of such an effort. The other important dimensions are, harmful effects of deceptive advertisements, promotion of dangerous products, and the exploitation of children. One example of how social psychology can have a meaningful partnership with consumer psychology is a study published in the British Medical Journal. The investigation carried out on 629 adolescents aged between 15 and 16 years of age attempted to clarify whether there was any link between the awareness and involvement with tobacco marketing and the smoking behavior of the people. The results suggested that awareness of and involvement with tobacco marketing were both significantly associated (p, 0.001) with smoking behavior. Teenagers were found to be aware of and participating in many forms of tobacco marketing (MacFadyen, Hastings & MacKintosh, 2001). If we consider the social psychological aspect of such participation, we would know that people adhere to their public statements and behave, by and large, accordingly. The reason for such behavior is that if the person does not do so, there will be considerable cognitive dissonance. Behaving in line with one's public proclamations tends to reduce such dissonance. Thus, while we are trying to run campaigns against smoking, and the majority of them are targeting young people, the efficacy of such campaigns would certainly be undermined by the active participation of the target group in tobacco promotion.

Social psychological research is also needed to address various issues related to consumer protection. In order to be effective, social psychology, in the first place, must learn to align its approaches to study behavior with the upcoming trends in other social sciences. It is time for the rat housed in the Skinner box to move out and press the lever of other social sciences to make a coordinated effort to advocate that we need to change our consumer behavior or be prepared to leave an unpleasant legacy for future generations.

Social psychology has important lessons to learn from its sister social sciences in research on consumer behavior. Unlike social psychologists, many social scientists have taken a broad view to determine the role of television in the construction of consumer reality. O'Guinn and Shrum (1997) have presented television as an agent of consumer socialization. They have argued that social scientists, including social psychologists, should focus on how television has transformed our perceptions and beliefs of social world, and not just attitudes and beliefs that are caused by advertised products or programs. In this role, O'Guinn and Shrum have identified five features of television. First, television is ubiquitous. From a scientific novelty during World War II, it has emerged as a common item, like a sofa, in the family room. Second, it has an invisible effect, similar to that of the food we eat. In other words, it has become a part of our existence. Third, it supplies private moments, images and stories of those people whom we have not met. Such experiences carry us far from the narrow range of environment in which we live. Fourth, television creates social reality that is vastly different from objective reality. For example, episodes of violence appear ten times more on television than in real social life. The conception about social problems based on census data or surveys is also different than the images provided by television programs. And lastly, television changes our outlook for consumption of goods. Viewers watch with keen interest what members of other social strata possess and how they consume. There seems to be a link between exposure to television and consumer cultivation.

In their concluding remarks, O'Guinn and Shrum wrote: "Our extensive use of and reliance on television allows us to believe we know how others, with whom we may rarely have significant direct contact, live and consume. What we think other people possess and consume and how widespread we believe those objects of consumption (and the affluence it implies) to be are of undisputed significance in social theory" (p. 290).

Social scientists have proposed that television constructs a social reality that is different from objective reality. According to the cultivation hypothesis (Gerbner, *et al.*, 1994), people learn through television programs about details of the culture to which they belong. Such programs often distort social reality and present an image that corresponds with the events depicted on the television. As mentioned earlier, television programs portray violence ten times more often than what we observe in our real lives. Young children, especially those under the age of five years, fail to distinguish between reality and fiction. Moreover, by casting men and women in traditional roles simultaneously, the programs on television may create a stereotypic image of gender. Signorielli and Lears (1992) found that the increase in the duration of television-viewing by young children was positively related to a strong stereotype concerning gender role.

In short, television's influence begins quite early in life, and a child is exposed to two realities—the objective world and a world presented by television. While the reality of the objective world is interactive, active and exploratory in nature, the reality created by television is passive and restrictive. The former is governed by the natural laws of life but the latter exists in the form of artifacts. In what ways the two realities interact in the mind of a child and influence her cognitive growth should form an important area of research in the near future.

Let's now view the prospects of **consumerism**? Often despised as self indulgent, consumers are frequently motivated by altruism and their needs to express their identity, to build relationships, and to obtain fulfilment and even to find a substitute for religion. Consumer power will grow and brands will be under pressure from rising customer expectations. Online shopping would most likely transform consumer behavior, especially driven by cost saving and convenience. Will retailers protect their traditional channels or go online because they are afraid not to? In this regard, creating consumer trust will be the foremost priority (Moynagh & Worsley, 2002).

Catterall and co-workers (2002) believed that the marketer of tomorrow will have to focus on consumers in the virtual world. Virtual communities will be formed and the marketer may well need a new ethnography to define this 'ethnic' group. Shopping over the web differs from physical store shopping in the amount and form of planning. Internet shoppers show better planning and less susceptibility to marketing activities (Dahlen & Lange, 2002). Marketing for Internet shoppers will have to deal with customers across various geographies, each characterized by its own idiosyncratic features. Since online shopping is still in its infancy in many developing countries as compared to the mature markets of the US, the two populations may require a different marketing mix for effectiveness (Lightner & co-workers, 2002). Before a company can envision what it will sell online and how it will do there should be an understanding of attitudes and behavior of its prospective customers (Teo, 2002) that vary from culture to culture (Teo, 2002).

And last, but not the least, what will be the impact of globalization on the consumer of tomorrow? Will there be greater similarity among customers from different cultures or will the cultural divide become stronger? While only time will tell the future course, some idea can be obtained from the writings of various thinkers and researchers in consumer psychology. Are consumers around the globe becoming more similar in terms of their consumer tendencies? Keillor, D'Amico and Horton (2001) interviewed 129 US respondents, 111 French respondents and 131 Malaysian respondents over a three-month period. Statistical analyses of the data revealed that national identity, consumer ethnocentrism and social identity bias emerged as key variables in consumer choices.

The noted social scientist Geert Hofstede, whose pioneering work on dimensions of cross-cultural differences is well known, believed that despite converging technology and the disappearing income differences across countries, we would not see a greater homogeneity of consumer behavior. In the hallmark issue of the *Journal of Retailing, Special Issue: Retailing in the 21-super (ST) century*, Hofstede and co-workers wrote:

> Rather consumer behavior will become more heterogeneous because of cultural differences. As consumer incomes converge across countries, the manifestation of value differences will become stronger. This phenomenon makes it extremely important to understand values of national cultures and their impact on consumer behavior. Retailing strategies for one country cannot be extended to other countries without adaptation as value differences become stronger (De Mooij & Hofstede, 2002).

In short, consumer behavior is a very complex subject and tangible research conclusions are not easy. Therefore any prediction based on social psychological principles is contingent upon a complex set of variables that vary both at the individual and societal levels as also in their interaction.

Summary

This chapter began with the analysis of individuals as consumers. Based on their personalities and childhood experiences, individuals learn to spend their money in different ways. Advertisement is a powerful source to persuade people to buy a product. While the exact impact of advertisement on consumer behavior is not known, it has been shown, especially with techniques like the split cable market test, that the role of advertisement in luring customers to buy a product is substantial.

Research on subliminal messages and compliance methods show that psychological techniques, consciously or subconsciously, influence consumer behavior. The role of two social psychological techniques (foot-in-the-door and door-in-the-face) was presented to show how behavior can be changed by making simple requests. Recent researches on cognitive and affective factors suggest that the levels of processing of information and its associated affective component are critical in changing consumer behavior. In this context, implications of the elaboration likelihood model and the theory of reasoned action were examined to show how social psychological research is helpful in explaining consumer behavior.

The remaining part of the chapter was concerned with the intended and unintended influence of television on our behavior. While on the one hand, television programs model and prompt behavior of people in acquiring things, on the other hand, watching violent programs may also lead to violent behavior. To address this issue, a number of research approaches were examined to illustrate how our understanding of the relationship between television violence and violent behavior has matured in the past two decades. Finally, we discussed a few upcoming areas of consumer behavior, including altruistic marketing, e-commerce and e-advertising, to show how social psychologists can work closely with experts in other disciplines to study disturbed consumers and develop intervention programs for them.

Suggestions for Further Reading

Simonson, I., Carmon, Z., Dhar, R. & co-workers (2001). Consumer research: In search of identity. *Annual Review of Psychology*, 52, 249-275.

Lynch, P.D., Kent, R.J. & co-workers (2001). The global Internet shopper: Evidence for shopping tasks in 12 countries. *Journal of Advertising Research*, 41, 15-23.

Brackett, L.K. & Carr, B.N.Jr (2001). Cyberspace advertising versus other media: Consumer versus mature student attitudes. *Journal of Advertising Research*, 41, 23-32.

Some Key Terms

Altruistic marketing
Categorical significance
Cause related marketing
Central route to persuasion
Comparative consumerism
Consumer behavior
Consumption vocabulary
Displacement effect
Door-in-the-face
Elaborative likelihood model
Ethnoconsumerism
Expressive significance
Foot-in-the-door
Household scanner panel
Low ball technique
Peripheral route to persuasion
Priming
Psychographics
Reciprocity norm
Social marketing
Split cable market test
Subliminal messages

SOCIAL PSYCHOLOGY OF AGGRESSION AND NON-VIOLENCE

9

Chapter Outline

- An introduction to social psychology of aggression and non-violence
  - Forms of aggression
  - Models of aggression and non-aggression
- The cross-cultural context of aggression
  - Reaction to insults
  - Expressing and suppressing aggression
- Causes and control of aggression
  - Learning alternate responses
  - Relaxation training
  - Catharsis
  - Contingency management training
  - Inducing incompatible responses
- Social psychology and conflict management
  - Role of culture in conflict management
  - Role of gender in conflict management
  - Role of social identity in conflict management
- The relationship between justice and violence
  - The perception of justice across cultures
  - The four faces of justice
- Justice and violence at work
  - Organizational change and the perception of justice
  - Workplace behavior and the perception of justice
- Tools for conflict management
  - Mediation
  - Integrative negotiation
  - Antecedents of integrative negotiation
  - Cross-cultural dimensions of negotiation
- Conflict and violence among teenagers
  - Some recent data on aggression and violence among children and youth
  - The contribution of psychologists to the understanding of youth violence

  - Antecedent factors of youth violence
  - Road rage
- Going beyond the individual: The psychology of peace
  - Defining non-violence
  - Terrorism and peace psychology
  - Attributions
- Psychological obstacles to peace
- Social psychological theories in the promotion of peace
  - The self-fulfilling prophecy
  - Prospect theory
  - GRIT
- Promoting cultures of peace and non-violence: Interventions for peace
  - Use of behavioral journalism to reduce moral disengagement (McAlister & co-workers, 2000)

AN INTRODUCTION TO SOCIAL PSYCHOLOGY OF AGGRESSION AND NON-VIOLENCE

They are not following dharma who resort to violence to achieve their purpose.

— Buddha

When psychologists use the word **aggression**, it refers to assaultive conduct. In general, it refers to **a tendency to inflict harm to another person**. Geen (1990) defines aggression as "the delivery of noxious stimulation to another person with the intent of harming that person, and in the expectation that the aversive stimulus will reach its destination" (p. 8). The opposite of aggression, non-aggression or non-violence, has been used interchangeably in this chapter to identify behavior that promotes peace, resolves conflicts and inhibits aggression.

Forms of aggression

Hostile aggression: Aggression due to feelings: hate

Two forms of such aggressive behavior are commonly described in the psychological literature: hostile and instrumental. **Hostile aggression** refers to feelings of revenge and hate shown by an individual. It is accompanied by a pattern of distinct autonomic activity, such as high blood pressure, and is mediated by bitterness and hate that may lead to explosive behavior. Among violent people "this potential may be undercontrolled, meaning that such persons allow themselves to attack or retaliate under circumstances where the rest of us would sulk, complain or retreat" (Toch, 1992, p. 2). **Instrumental aggression**, on the other hand, is motivated by a desire to obtain a reward rather than to injure another person. A bandit who wants money from the woman at the bank's teller is more interested in having the loot than on inflicting injury to her. Unlike hostile aggression, in instrumental aggression the aggressor has no desire to make the victim suffer. There are several other ways in which different forms of aggression have been analyzed (Table 9.1): **reactive-proactive**, **direct-indirect**, **active-passive**, and **verbal-physical** (Buss, 1961).

Instrumental aggression: Aggression motivated by a desire to obtain a reward

TABLE 9.1

A typology of human aggressive behaviors (*Source*: Buss, 1961)

	Active Direct Aggression	Active Indirect Aggression	Passive Direct Aggression	Passive Indirect Aggression
Physical Aggression	Hitting the victim	Playing practical jokes on victim	Staging a sit-in	Refusing to do something
Verbal Aggression	Using insults to hurt the victim	Engaging in gossip about the victim	Refusing to speak	Refusing permission

According to Toch (1992), people use violence when they believe that its use is justified. Even members of a fighting gang are peaceful when they are separated from other gang members. Criminals in the street become model prisoners in prison. Once taken out of the context, people show an enormous capacity to change. Bandura's (1979) work showed that aggression was the result of prior experiences and imitation, and it was maintained because it made sense to the individuals. Anticipated consequences of violence play a key role in sustaining violent behavior. While both hostile aggression and instrumental aggression are different—the former dealing with affective components, and the latter with obtaining the reinforcer—they are also similar in that both forms are influenced by the characteristics of the individual and the situations he or she is in.

There appears to be a fairly large **socio-cultural influence** on the manifestation of the two forms of aggressive behavior. For example, **Colombians** report more instrumental aggression than **Spaniards**, who, in turn, report more expressive representations of aggressive behavior. Gender too is important with males of both cultures reporting significantly more instrumental attributions, while females reported more expressive attributions to aggression (Andreu & co-workers, 2002). Similarly, Ramirez and co-workers (2001) also found males of both **Spanish** and **Japanese** student groups reporting more instrumental aggression and females more instrumental aggression. At the same time there was a cultural difference too, with the Spanish as a whole reporting a greater tendency toward expressive attributions than their Japanese counterparts. The mean violence score is also found to be greater for males than for females (Smith & co-workers, 2001). This type of **gender difference** can partly be explained on the basis of differences on arousal. A recent metaanalysis of emotional arousal and gender differences in aggression supported the idea that males are more easily aroused than females, and that males also have greater problems in regulating their arousal level than females (Knight & co-workers, 2002). These two factors taken together could well account for the seen gender differences in level of violence. Seeing such differences in the expression of aggression, it is imperative that they be considered while devising prevention programs for the control of aggressive behavior.

Models of aggression and non-aggression

A psychological analysis of violent and non-violent individuals should allow predictions regarding their behavior in various situations. In his model of aggression, **Goldstein** (1986) emphasized the significance of **long-term** and **situational factors** in shaping the behavior of individuals. In the **first** category he included long-term factors that are norm-based, referring to the **beliefs** of individuals, and developed on the basis of selective reinforcements from the society. A typical example of a long-term factor facilitating aggressive behavior is war. However, the same individual also learns not to aggress in a church, which is an example of a long-term factor for non-aggressive behavior. In the **second** category, Goldstein included situational factors associated with aggression and non-aggression. According to him, the presence of weapons increases the probability of aggression, while the presence of police officers reduces the probability of aggression. In other words, psychologists can easily manipulate conditions to show how situational and long-term factors can determine the nature and extent of aggressive and non-aggressive behavior of individuals.

Long-term factors: Norms based on selective reinforcement from society

Situational factors: Dependent on the situation at hand

TABLE 9.2

Long- and short-term factors in aggression and non-aggression
(*Source*: Goldstein, 1986)

	Long-term factors	Short-term factors
Aggression	Norm-based (war)	Decrease inhibition (alcohol)
Non-aggression	Norm-based (belief/religion)	Increase inhibition (pressure of police/parents

Note:To aggress or not to aggress will depend on the relative strength of the two tendencies.

Kool (1993) presented a **three-dimensional model of aggression** consisting of **aggression, morality** and **power** components. According to him, those high on aggression, low on moral components, and high on self-oriented power would represent the violent dimension as compared to the non-violent dimension that is characterized by low aggression, high morality and shared power orientation. His research also showed that non-violent individuals scored high on self-actualization and were willing to blame themselves more than their violent counterparts.

The study of the interaction of personality and situational factors shows how violent behavior erupts in one case but not in the other. Megangee (1966) noticed that violent people differed in terms of their **levels of inhibition** against aggression. Those with strong defenses and inhibition against aggression tended to store their tensions even at the abnormally high levels, but given an appropriate stimulus, they displayed intense aggression proportionate to their built-up tension. Such **over-controlled aggressors** usually do not have a long history of criminal record and in many cases they are charged for their first offense. In contrast, **under-controlled aggressors** have a short fuse. They are easily provoked and show frequent problems. Employing a unique approach, consisting of recent parolees interviewing such individuals, Toch (1992) presented a typology of violent men and women who became violent for different reasons (Table 9.3).

TABLE 9.3

Typology of violent men and women (*Source*: Toch, 1992)

Type	Description
Self-image promoters	Fear that they are worthless and unimportant, attempt to convince others that they are actually fearless and tough.
Self-image defenders	Attempt to defend their self-image against a largely imaginary slur from others.
Self-indulgers	Believe that others exist to serve their needs, react with anger when they refuse to do so.
Rep defenders	Aggress against others because it is their assigned social role to do so (for example, gang leaders).
Bulliers and sadists	Enjoy harming others, select targets weaker than themselves or arrange conditions so that they have an unfair advantage.
Self-defenders	Aggress out of fear that if they do not strike first, they will be victimized by others.

THE CROSS-CULTURAL CONTEXT OF AGGRESSION

The murder rate is currently seven times higher in the **US** than in **Britain**, and in **South Africa** it is 35 times higher. There also seems reason to posit that aggression is channelised in different ways in different cultures (Smith & Bond, 1993). Landau (1984) had hypothesized that murder rates would rise with higher stress, higher rates of inflation and falling social support systems across **thirteen countries**. The hypothesis was supported in all the countries except **Japan**, where he found a higher suicide rate rather than a higher murder rate.

Reaction to insults

Research on differences on power distance across cultures suggests that strong criticism from one's boss would be judged as less aggressive in a high power culture than in a low power culture. Bond and co-workers (1985 cf. Smith & Bond, 1993) attempted to verify this idea among students from cultures known to differ on power distance. A comparison of students in **Hong Kong** and the **US** revealed that in comparison to the Americans the reactions of the Chinese to insults from the boss were much more dependent upon who was receiving the insult. The Chinese often labeled in-group insults as scoldings, saw institutional insults as legitimate and saw less reason to dislike the person.

Expressing and suppressing aggression

Research on cultural norms for expressing aggression indicates considerable differences between societies (Leyens & Franczec, 1984 cf. Smith & Bond, 1993). For example, **Greeks** were found to be more aggressive than **Indians**. However, Rabbie (1982) reported in a study based on subjects in Holland that only those Greeks that were more sure of themselves were more aggressive than the Indians. While aggression is necessary for the survival of human beings, its expression has been encouraged or discouraged unevenly in cultures and with situations. Sen (1981) demonstrated through her experiments how people with beliefs in non-violence minimized their shock delivery in a Milgram type of experiment.

CAUSES AND CONTROL OF AGGRESSION

Given the magnitude of violence in our society, a question that is frequently raised is: what is the contribution of social psychology in understanding the causes of aggression and its control? This question has been answered in **two** ways. **First,** social psychologists have made an attempt to apply the general principles of psychology (for example, reinforcement or social learning theories) to show how aggression can be controlled. This approach is limited to the modification of behavior and its control without necessarily focusing on changing the environment or its components. We all know that it is easier to change an individual than to modify a situation. It is easier to arrest a murderer than to eliminate all those conditions that instigate bloodshed in a community.

The premise of the **second** approach is based on the assumption that control of aggression does not mean the elimination of aggression or promotion of non-aggression. The potential for aggression may still exist if adequate steps are not taken to foster non-aggressive factors. Containing a conflict does not mean resolving a conflict. The impetus to this approach stems from the work of peace psychologists who believe that peace-keeping is not the same as peace-making, much in the same way as a cure does not mean the prevention of a disease (Wagner, 1993; Kimmel, 1985). This latter approach is molar in nature and used especially for resolving conflicts between communities or countries. Commenting on the differences between the two approaches, Kool (1993) wrote, "It should be borne in mind that the nature of the

BOX 9.1

Understanding the incidence of violence against women

One of the first steps to the control of violence would be to evaluate its incidence, the major victim categories and the types of violence being commonly witnessed. Women form one major class of victims. A global overview of violence against women shows that because of the sensitivity of the subject, this type of violence is almost always under-reported. Nevertheless, the prevalence of violence suggests that globally millions of women are experiencing violence or living with its consequences.

Some of the most common forms of violence against women are as follows: intimate partner violence; sexual abuse by non-intimate partners; trafficking, forced prostitution, exploitation of labor, and debt bondage of women and girls; physical and sexual violence against prostitutes; sex selective abortion, female infanticide, and the deliberate neglect of girls; and rape in war (Watts & Zimmerman, 2002).

The same article also attempts to pinpoint the major perpetrators and potential perpetrators of violence against women. These could be spouses and partners, parents, other family members, neighbors, and men in positions of influence and power. Probably, the most important factor to consider is that in the vast majority of these cases, we do not always see violence against women as isolated incidence. There could also be a long-term trend of violence with the violence often continuing for decades together.

psychology of non-violence should not be misconstrued as an inverted mirror image of the psychology of violence. Just as truce does not mean the end of all war, keeping peace does not mean making peace. The sources for promoting violence and non-violence have different roots and conditions" (p. 21).

A person who is found guilty and put into prison is expected to accept responsibility for his action. In general, **prison sentences** serve several purposes. **A retributive purpose** is to punish criminals for their misdeeds. A **rehabilitative purpose** is to minimize the likelihood of its reoccurrence. And a **protective purpose** is to separate criminals from the law-abiding citizens so that the social order does not break down. A psychological analysis shows that prison sentences often fail to accomplish the very purposes for which they are intended. First of all, in most cases of criminal violence, the culprit is either not punished, or receives nominal punishment, or sentenced after a long delay. According to Goldstein (1986), "the longer the delay between aggression and its punishment, the less effective is the punishment in retarding aggressive behavior" (p. 147). It is well known from operant learning procedures that punishment received immediately after an undesirable act has a stronger inhibitory effect than when it is farther removed from the time of the origin of such behavior. In other words, the impact of the prison sentence weakens with the increase in delay in administering the punishment. According to social learning theory, when other potential criminals watch this happen very often in society, they learn that they can also escape punishment after committing a crime.

Can punishment be an effective deterrent to aggression? Not always. Studies show that when schools start having a **zero tolerance policy**, that is, a policy of not accepting any kind of misbehavior, no matter how small, or for what reason, it leads to greater violence (Casella, 2003). In fact, it was suggested that restorative justice procedures (detailed in the chapter on law) is a better strategy for the prevention of violence than extremely restrictive policies. Secondly, the famous "frustration-aggression hypothesis" states that frustration is the cause of aggression, and that the inhibition of aggression would depend upon the amount of punishment anticipated in a situation (Dollard & co-workers, 1939). Unfortunately, research evidence suggested that not all aggression is caused by frustration (Geen, 1990). People suffer from a wide variety of frustrations and each frustration does not necessarily lead to aggression. However, research evidence also suggests that if frustration causes anger, then people may not be able to anticipate the consequences of their aggressive act. When soldiers at war witness lynching of their fellow citizens, they often engage in unprecedented brutal retaliation in anger (Baron & Richardson, 1994). Laboratory experiments, in which an accomplice of the experimenter frustrates and arouses the shock controlling subject, show abnormal increases in aggression—even leading to death of the victim had those shocks been actually administered (Milgram, 1974).

Control of aggression is possible through many techniques. A description of a few selected techniques follows.

Learning alternate responses

People are generally unaware of the alternatives to violence. When confronted with an instigating situation, they pick up the most dominant response available in their repertoire. Provocations from others also lead to the formation of attributions concerning the intentions behind the action of their adversaries. We constantly judge the actions of other people, especially those who pose a threat to us. Under such conditions a typical response will be *"a tit for a tat."* When we developed a measure of non-violence (Kool & Sen, 1984), we asked college students about what would they prefer to do under various conditions (Table 9.4).

TABLE 9.4

Sample items from the non-violence test (*Source*: Kool & Sen, 1984)

1. The more I think of how bad someone's bad actions or thoughts are:
   (a) The more I try to understand how to get along with that person.
   (b) The more I get irritated and want to tell that person off.
2. When a stranger hurts me I believe:
   (a) Forgive and forget is the best policy.
   (b) A tooth for a tooth an eye for an eye is the best policy.
3. If someone breaks something that belongs to me:
   (a) I will probably become enraged.
   (b) I understand that accidents happen.

Not surprisingly, for item 3 many students selected option "a" for their response. Several students attributed not only careless but also rude behavior to the driver. After prompting students to offer as many alternatives as possible to deal with this situation, we noticed that the support for option "a" dropped considerably. From our discussion with the students it emerged that option "a" was the instantaneous response, whereas option "b" would have been time-consuming. Most **non-violent forms** of action require **logical analysis, self-control** and **persuasion** in comparison to a violent response that is not only instantaneous but also harmful. In a recent study, Kool and co-workers (2001) showed that the NVT items discriminated those who tend to morally include or exclude people.

The NVT showed a strong negative correlation (–.51) with the Buss-Durkee Scale of Aggression and its subscales. The NVT was also negatively correlated (–.44) with a test of Machiavellianism (Christie & Geis, 1970) and its subscales (Kool & Keyes, 1990). While Buddhists and Quakers scored on an average, 31.8 out of a maximum score of 36 on this scale, the average score for violent youths was under 20. The NVT has been used in several countries and has successfully identified those who have strong inhibitions against aggressive behavior.

Novaco (1975) concluded that anger is sustained by self-statements that are related to provoking situations. He developed a self instructional approach to manage anger and his intervention program consisted of three stages:

- **Cognitive preparation.**
- **Skill acquisition.**
- **Application training.**

Beginning with the first stage of cognitive preparation, the subjects are taught both positive and negative consequences of anger related cognitive, behavioral and physiological functions. In the skill acquisition stage they learn alternative patterns of behavior to deal with the anger inducing conditions. Table 9.5 describes sample items from the anger management training program.

TABLE 9.5

Sample items from anger management: Self-instructional training (*Source*: Novaco, 1975)

1. Preparing for provocation
   This is going to upset me but I know how to deal with it.
   I can work out a plan to handle it.
2. Impact and confrontation
   Stay calm. Just continue to relax.
   As long as I keep my cool, I'm in control.
3. Coping with arousal
   Getting upset won't help.
   It's just not worth it to get so angry.
4. Reflecting on the provocation
   (a) When conflict is unresolved.
       Try to shake it off. Don't let it interfere with your job.
   (b) When conflict is resolved, or coping is successful
       I handled that one pretty well. It worked.

Relaxation training

According to Goldstein (1989), "Relaxation training is the systematic application of **tension-sensitizing** and **tension-release** procedures in order to achieve a state of deep relaxation" (p. 51). It begins with tension enhancing and relaxation enhancing behaviors. After selecting an appropriate venue and going through the enhancing/relaxation cycle, a client is geared toward relaxation only condition, a stage in which tension-sensitizing is deleted. In the final phase, the client indulges in deeper relaxation. For example, she is asked to imagine a scene that is good and relaxing.

Catharsis

Catharsis: Process by which we can channelise our anger to socially acceptable forms of behavior

Aristotle recommended that people should watch tragic plays to release their negative feelings. Taking a clue from his views, Freud (1933) believed that if people were not allowed to express their feelings of hostility, their anger would accumulate over a period of time and the energy would find an outlet in the form of some mental illness or express itself in an act of extreme violence. Brill, in the USA, advocated Freud's ideas and advised his patients to watch prizefights periodically to purge their anger (Bushman & Anderson, 2001). In order to avoid such an undesirable condition, he recommended that such behavior should be allowed expression in socially approved conditions. In other words, expression of aggression in some acceptable form will reduce the occurrence of its expression in some harmful way, that is, catharsis will take place.

Unfortunately, several scholars (Bandura 1965; Berkowitz, 1993) have presented contrary evidence to show that engaging in aggression might in fact increase, not decrease, the level of aggression. Russell (1983), a sports psychologist, observed that the level of hostility increased among spectators as the game progressed and their negative feelings lasted for several hours after the game had ended. Geen (1990) reported a number of studies that show that rather than reducing its level, continued aggression tended to increase the intensity of the aggression. While the final verdict on catharsis theory has not been reached, the overwhelming evidence points out that the effects of catharsis are not uniform, and that those who have agreed or disagreed with its effects have ignored the personality orientation of individuals who experience catharsis in an anger-inducing condition. In her effort to resolve this issue, Sen (1993) selected high and low scoring subjects on the NVT (Kool & Sen, 1984) and tested them under a **Milgram type** of experimental situation in which a subject administered shocks to a confederate. Both violent and non-violent subjects in this study were provoked, and in one condition they had to wait before they could get a chance to deliver shocks to the confederate, but in another condition they were given the opportunity to shock a strange subject before they punished the confederate. Sen concluded that,

> First, the high scoring non-violent subjects delivered a significantly lower amount of shock than their violent counterparts. Second, the subjects in both groups gave higher shocks in the wait-annoyed condition as compared to those in the shock-annoyed condition. The most interesting feature of this study was the significant interaction effect for the violent and non-violent individuals under wait and shock conditions while they were annoyed or non-annoyed. The results showed that violent subjects grew more violent when they were annoyed than when they got a chance to express it (catharsis). A similar effect was noticed in the non-violent subjects but the magnitude of this effect was lower than that of the violent subjects (p. 159).

BOX 9.2

An opposite view: The constructive role of aggression, anger and jealousy

Are aggression and anger negative in all situations? Some researches examine these concepts in terms of coping strategies and affirm their positive role in adjusting to the problems in life. Fromm's (1941) benign or altruistic aggression that is shown to correct the behavior of an individual is a positive expression of behavior with a negative label. For example parents sometimes administer mild to severe physical punishment to improve the behavior of their children. In her book, *Anger: The misunderstood emotion*, Carol Travis (1989) presented a positive face of emotion of anger as well. It is argued that while the destructive role of anger is well known, its positive impact is less understood. Angry responses of individuals sometimes equip them with better sense of control, optimism and empowerment than those who show fear responses in coping up with the problems in life. Quoting studies by Tafrate and co-workers (2002), and other scholars, Tori DeAngelis (2003), in the *APA Monitor*, mentioned that there is support for positive long-term effects of anger episodes among people. Buss (1999), based on an evolutionary explanation, contended that jealousy is another emotion that was misunderstood, but it serves several important functions that are necessary for survival.

The results of this study clearly show that the opportunity to express one's aggression does not mechanically either reduce or increase the level of subsequent aggression. Instead, a complex set of intervening variables, including orientation to violence or non-violence, personality, and social learning, may account for the increase or decrease of subsequent aggression. In addition, recent researches show that aggression and anger should not be considered negative in all situations.

Contingency management training

Contingency management training is based on the **manipulation of rewards and punishments** to change behavior. In this method, a segment of behavior is treated positively or negatively on a contingency basis. That is, a desirable behavior is rewarded (or punished) after it is displayed. The procedure involves strategies for increasing the frequency of desirable behavior and decreasing the occurrence of undesirable behavior. For example, in order to control the disruptive behavior of a student in a classroom, we need to know how the behavior interfered with the learning process, what caused tension in the classroom, how classroom decorum was disturbed, and so on. Through systematic recording and observation, the child is taught to avoid the undesirable behavior and its consequences. In the final phase of the training, the child learns about positive reinforcers in relation to material social activity and token domains. In promoting desirable behavior, several **guidelines** are followed. **First,** the reinforcement must be presented as agreed. **Second,** the reinforcement must be consistent and immediate. **Third,** approximations to the desirable behavior should be adequately rewarded. And fourth, rewards should not be offered mechanically.

Contingency management training: Use of positive or negative reinforcements to control aggressive behavior

Using the principles of instrumental conditioning, the Social Learning Center of The Oregon Research Institute has adopted a behavior modification approach to deal with the children having behavioral problems and their parents. The focus of this institute is to improve the parental management skills concerning problem children. Its goal is to train parents to become effective fathers and mothers.

Inducing incompatible responses

If feelings incompatible to anger are induced, will it reduce aggression? We know that human beings are capable of conducting two tasks at a time, even though such tasks may be at times incompatible. Reading a technical book and daydreaming are not unusual. The antagonistic system within human beings, known as the **Yin and Yang** by the Chinese for a long time, indicates our capability to perform complex and incompatible tasks.

Yin and Yang: Antagonistic forces within us

Research has shown that by making subjects **empathize with the victim,** aggression can be reduced. Empathy is "an emotional response similar to that experienced by a victim" (Baron & Richardson, 1994, p. 344). Such an act involves compassion for another person's distress. In a series of studies, Batson (1991) has demonstrated that aggression is reduced after generating empathy among people. His subjects had watched a videotape in which a victim received shocks and was upset. However, when the subjects came to know that it was not the shocks but the traumatic experience of shocks during the

Inducing incompatible responses: Making people empathize with the victim to reduce aggression

childhood that was bothering the victim, a number of subjects volunteered to serve in place of the victim and offered to receive shocks on behalf of the victim.

In another study, Baron (1976) found that the **horn-honking behavior** of motorist reduced after they watched that a man on crutches was crossing the street. In the absence of this man, 90% people honked at the car drivers in front of them because they did not move after the light had turned green. However, creating empathy has little effect if the aggressor felt that there was a justification in harming the victim. Instead of helping people in distress, aggressors enjoyed the pain cues of victim. Military personnel are known to dehumanize their victims. For example, the American soldiers often called Asians "gooks," an expression that dehumanized them and brought rationalization to their acts of brutality.

Some people believe that **humor** can provide a cathartic effect and reduce aggressive behavior. According to Freud (1960/1905), humor will reduce some of the potential energy that is likely to be used in aggression. Again, there is a limit to the use of humor as an incompatible response to eliminate aggression. Research has shown that humor can backfire and increase the level of aggression (Zillman 1983; Berkowitz, 1970). Baron and Ball (1974) suggested that humor of a silly nature would reduce aggression but hostile humor would increase aggression.

SOCIAL PSYCHOLOGY AND CONFLICT MANAGEMENT

Not all adverse situations lead to aggression and violence. When people perceive an incompatibility between their own goals and those of others, negative psychological processes, such as mistrust and deliberate deception, can begin. A married couple seeking divorce is a typical example of such a conflict. Such couples often begin by indulging in **zero-sum thinking**, in which the other has to lose in order for one party to win. Under such adverse conditions, even a harmless proposal offered by either party is perceived as being selfish and threatening. According to Keashey and Fisher (1990, 1996), the elements of a conflict involve resources and subjective elements. While resources consist of material things, such as money, the latter category, subjective elements, is social psychological in nature, for it refers to perception, communication and attributions in a situation.

Morton Deutsch (1973) analyzed the nature of **perception, communication and attributions** in the context of **cooperation and competition** in a situation (please refer to Chapter 1). He proposed, firstly, that cooperative situations would help in building a constructive resolution to a problem. For example, a perception of cooperation would make people sensitive to similarities in a conflict situation, but in the case of competition among the members, it would lead to the perception of differences. Second, with respect to attitudes, more trust and help would be generated in a cooperative situation than in a competitive situation. And third, the nature of communication would also be different in cooperative and competitive situations. As opposed to a competitive situation, the cooperative situation would be highly open and respectful.

An important issue in a conflict resolution is **the perspective** of the involved members or parties. Research studies show that such perspectives may vary with respect to several factors. Three perspectives—culture, gender and professional identity—will be illustrated in terms of the resolution of conflicts.

Role of culture in conflict management

In the discussion concerning mental health issues, the role of a culture was highlighted, and later a distinction was made between two dimensions on which cultures differ—**collectivism and individualism** (please refer to the chapter on mental health). In the resolution of conflicts, a culture's orientation cannot be ignored. Because collectivism emphasizes harmony between one's own goals with the goals of the group, the willingness of a member to sacrifice one's personal interest will be high in comparison to a member who is affiliated to an individualistic culture. Leung (1987) found that the **collectivists** showed a strong tendency to avoid a conflict within their own group, but they did not hesitate to litigate with the members of the out-group. When universal (**etic**) and culture specific (**emic**) construals of conflict were examined across the **US and Japan**, it was clear that while there are universal aspects, the same conflict episode could be differently construed in the two cultures. The collectivistic Japanese perceived conflicts as being more compromise focused than their individualistic American counterparts (Gelfand & co-workers, 2001). In a wider study, that is, on subjects from four countries (**China, Germany, Japan and the US**), Oetzel and Ting-Toomey (2003) concluded that the individualistic/collectivistic dimension created important differences in the ways in which interpersonal conflicts were viewed and resolved.

Role of gender in conflict management

Men and women perceive distribution of justice differently. In the distribution of rewards, women veer away from an equitable distribution and prefer equal distribution. Whereas men show preference for payments based on productivity, women prefer equality (Stake, 1983). In other words, an effort to resolve a conflict will involve sensitivity to the gender variable because men and women have differing orientations to the distribution of rewards.

Role of social identity in conflict management

Finally, the identity of a person is a critical variable in a conflict resolution task. Roth and Shepard (1989) found that identity based on one's affiliation to a profession was critical in the interpretation of a conflict. For example, whereas law students believed that a party could win in a conflict, industrial relations students recommended a trade-off for the same conflict. Additionally, those studying clinical psychology viewed the same conflict between parties as a matter of interaction and relationship. Whose viewpoint is correct? A close look at conflict theories reveals that virtually all theories have considered **social identity** as an influence in the course and outcome of conflict (Opotow, 2003). Resolving a conflict is not an easy task, but it can be made relatively easier if the participants are made aware of the terms and conditions of a situation openly and honestly.

THE RELATIONSHIP BETWEEN JUSTICE AND VIOLENCE

The perception of justice across cultures

There has been an unending debate regarding what principles should determine parameters for "just," "fair" or "proper" behavior. Does morality or justice consist of:

- Obeying secular laws.
- Treating people equally.

- **Abiding by supernatural dictates, or,**
- **Displaying compassion.**

Piaget (1948) contended that "all morality consists in a system of rules, and the essence of all morality is to be sought for in the respect which the individual acquires for these rules." Thus people who break the rules need to be punished, or that there should be an unconditional application of the law enforcement principle (for example, in certain Islamic countries, there is the strict imposition of traditional Islamic punishments even in the 1990s (Williams, 1996). In contrast, in US law, decisions regarding blame of murder is dependent on the circumstances and the law differentiates between the legal categories of first and second degree murder, man slaughter, etc.

Treating people equally is the principle reflected in the work of Kohlberg (1976) who asserted that true justice consists of honoring universal rights for all people (that is, equal justice). Thus simply obeying laws does not lead to justice if these laws do not afford equal treatment to all people. While Kohlberg's perspective, based on males samples only, was focused in the principle of equity, Gilligan (1982) noted that a woman's concept of morality "centers around the understanding of responsibility and relationships, just as the male conception of morality as fairness ties moral development to the understanding of rights and rules" (p. 19). Gilligan concluded that females prefer caring and compassion over justice in contrast to men who prefer principles of justice and equity. Therefore, fairness is a matter of gender perspective.

The four faces of justice

Justice and feelings related to it do not constitute a unitary concept. Our feelings of injustice may stem from a variety of reasons. These may include, firstly, what is the treatment being meted to us and secondly, how it is being done. Sometimes, we may have been treated unfairly but we do not cast aspersions on the person from whom the treatment is coming only because of the extremely polite way in which the person has done it. We see at least **four perspectives** to justice orientation:

> **Four forms of justice:** Distributive, procedural, interactional, and informational

- **Distributive justice: amount of resources distributed.**
- **Procedural justice: procedure adopted to allocate resources.**
- **Interactional justice: perception of fairness.**
- **Informational justice: access to information in seeking justice.**

JUSTICE AND VIOLENCE AT WORK

Unfortunately, over the past two decades, the incidence of violence has increased dramatically at both places. Bachman (1994) reported that between 1987 and 1992, 1.7 million days of work were lost due to violence at the place of work in USA. Further, on average, 15 people are murdered at workplaces each week.

If we are to construct a profile of a disgruntled worker who is at risk to commit violence, **contextual (workplace)** and **personal factors** will predict **workplace violence** (Figure 9.1, Barling, 1996). Among **workplace factors**, the employees' perception of fairness (perceived justice), job conditions, and a punitive style of supervision are significant contributors to workplace violence. Barling considered electronic monitoring of work an important factor in causing violence because through this procedure the pace of work of an employee can be monitored. Thus, electronic monitoring not only leads to invasion of privacy, but also provides greater managerial control. Obviously, the worker under such surveillance finds himself under stress and strain. Among the **personal factors,** excessive use of alcohol, loss of self-esteem, and history of aggression are cited as critical in Barling's model. These personal factors tend to interact with the workplace factors to determine the level of violence at work.

Figure 9.1: Predictors of workplace violence (adapted from Barling, 1996).

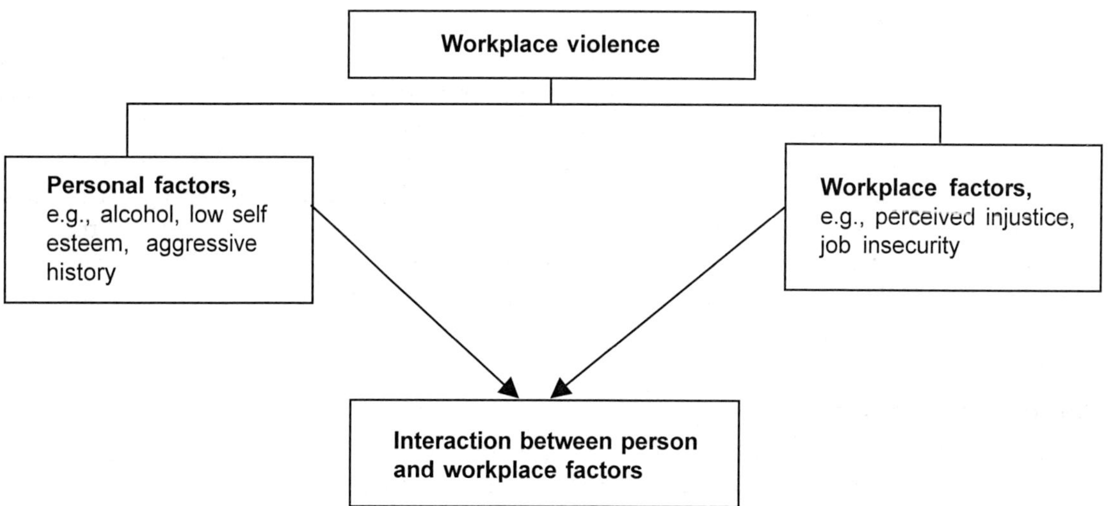

Distributive justice: The amount of resources being distributed

Folger and Baron (1996) used Buss's typology of aggression (Table 9.1) and applied it to illustrate workplace aggression (Table 9.6). They believed that several forms of aggression at the workplace could be very subtle. According to them, people perceive injustice in terms of not just what they get relative to others (**distributive justice**), but also how they get it (**procedural justice**). In principle, they believed that the connection between perceived injustice, frustration, and violence made sense, but the relationship between these variables is complex. In addition to the formal processes of distributive and procedural justice, a critical component in the perception of fairness is interpersonal justice. "**Interpersonal justice,**" writes Folger and Baron, "refers not to formal procedures but to the actions of people who implement those procedures and how those people conduct themselves" (p. 76). For example, if the attitude of administrators towards their employees is not good, even substantial rewards will be perceived as being unfair. Recent research has added a fourth dimension to justice, that is, **informational justice.** Informational justice is perceived when employees feel inequity in the availability of information crucial for them to do their work.

Procedural justice: The formal procedures for distribution

When **layoffs** occur, employees often perceive the action of their employer as being inequitable. They may feel that they are the victims of the unjust discretionary decisions of their employers. If we apply the concept of **distributive injustice** to this situation, an employee

TABLE 9.6

Categories of workplace violence (*Source*: Buss, 1961 and Folger & Baron, 1996)

Direct Aggression	Indirect Aggression
ACTIVE—	—PHYSICAL
Homicide	Theft
Assault	Defacing property
Interrupting others	Hiding needed resources
Obscene gestures	Sabotage
PASSIVE—	—PHYSICAL
Intentional slowdown	Coming late for meetings
Refusing to provide resources	Delaying work
Leaving when target person comes	Causing others to delay action
ACTIVE —	—VERBAL
Threats	Spreading rumors
Sexual harassment	Whistle blowing
Insults	Talking behind
Unfair performance appraisal	Target back
PASSIVE—	—VERBAL
Failure to return phone call	Failure to pass information
Not talking to target person	Failure to deny false rumors
Refusing target person's request	Failure to defend target

will be more concerned when he loses his job individually than collectively, as in a layoff situation. On the other hand, **procedural injustice** is hard to establish because employers are entitled to conduct layoffs. If employee viewpoints and personal biases of administrators are ignored, a perception of procedural injustice may emerge. However, the feeling of injustice is also determined by **cultural factors.** Murphy-Berman and his colleagues (1984 cf. Smith & Bond, 1993) examined in-group allocation of bonus on pay-cuts in India and the US, according to three criteria: equality, equity and need. In a collectivist country such as India, effects of needs for allocation of bonus or of lower pay cuts were emphasized to a greater extent than among Americans. Whether equity, equality or need will be considered more justifiable seems to a conjoint function of both the nature of the group and the nature of the culture. Studies show that when the in-group is to be considered, equality and need are more important than equity; but when the distribution is to be made to an out-group, equity is more important. However, this effect is more pronounced for collectivistic cultures as compared to the individualistic cultures (Leung & Bond, 1984).

Interpersonal injustice will take place if managers ignore simple courtesies, distance themselves from the employees, and change interpersonal demeanor. Any layoff is an emotional situation, and it should be handled with sympathy, compassion and honesty. Folger and Baron (1996) have recommended a set of distributive, procedural and interpersonal justice actions to prevent workplace violence (Table 9.7).

Interpersonal justice: Dependent on interpersonal behavior of distributor

TABLE 9.7

Actions to prevent workplace violence (*Sources*: Folger & Baron, 1996)

Distributive justice actions:
Layoffs and firings, for example, do not raise chief executive officer's pay when downsizing
Performance appraisal, for example, develop criteria on the basis of job analysis
Procedural justice actions:
Layoffs and firing, for example, use employee input where possible
Performance appraisal, for example, clarify standards in advance
Interpersonal justice actions:
Layoffs and firing, for example, explain sincerely and treat with dignity
Performance appraisal, for example, same as for layoffs and firing

Informational justice: Equitable availability of information

Each of the above-mentioned forms of justice translate into specific work related outcomes, such as commitment, job satisfaction, layoff, theft and organization citizenship behavior (OCB), as seen for an employee group in Chile (Mladinic & Isla, 2002). However, we also see additive effects of distributive and procedural justice, suggesting therefore that if injustice is perceived regarding both these aspects, the consequences would be much greater than if only one form of injustice is being perceived (Hauenstein & co-workers, 2001).

Organizational change and the perception of justice

One organizational aspect causing considerable **stress** is that of **organizational change** and the consequent threat of layoff. One common reason for the stress is the feeling or even the fear of inequity regarding the consequences of the change. It has been found that if the employees perceive both **distributive and procedural justice** regarding the change, stress is reduced (Brotheridge, 2003). While the latter was based on a study in Canada, the same has been found for Korean workers too. Chang (2002) observed that if the workers were given training regarding the appraisal system to be used for determining the layoff decisions, the employees perceived a high level of distributive justice and organizational commitment also remained at a high level. **Trust** is another important factor in determining the effects of proposed organizational change. While there seems to be little relationship between distributive justice and trust, there does exist a distinct relationship between interpersonal justice and trust regarding the effects of the proposed change, as seen in a study on British employees (Saunders & Thornhill, 2003). Therefore it does seem important for managers to focus on their patterns of communication with the employees. However, Janssen (2004) noted that in the Netherlands, innovative behavior produced stress only when both distributive and procedural justice was low.

Workplace behavior and the perception of justice

Perception of injustice has been an important predictor for workplace aggression, with procedural injustice being perceived as most unjust and thereby leading to more aggression than either distributive or interactional injustice (Kennedy, Homant & Homant, 2004). Another aspect is coping with both family and work and this often causes considerable stress. The ability to cope with such stress has been found related to procedural injustice (Judge & Colquitt, 2004). Further, procedural justice affects team performance too. Sinclair (2003) found that teams exposed to procedural justice were more cooperative than those who were not.

Justice sensitivity: An individual level factor deciding perception of unfairness

But why is it that two people may undergo the same treatment at work and yet, one may remain quite satisfied while the other may exhibit a strong sense of injustice? Fetchenhauer and Huang (2004) posit a variable called **justice sensitivity**. As found in a study by these researchers in the Netherlands, the higher the score of respondents to the justice sensitivity scale, the greater is the feeling of injustice. On the flip side, the higher their score on the scale, the more the respondents based their decisions on equality. So not only does the variable help determine reactions of individuals to unfair situations, but it also determines the choice of principles of equality or equity across individuals.

Some of the other aspects of work that have been found related to justice are the effects of flexible benefit plans (Cole & Flint, 2004), sabotage at the workplace (Ambrose, Seabright & Schwinke, 2002), with distributive, procedural and interactive justice having an additive effect on the severity of the sabotage. Justice perceptions have even been found to impact customers' reactions to various company policies (Humphrey & co-workers, 2004).

BOX 9.3

Prevention of violence at the workplace

Kinney (1995) designed a violence prevention program for identifying warning signs that predict violence. He called for an analysis of anchors in the life of an individual. Anchors are stabilizing forces that refer to one's personal characteristics and life circumstances, such as secure family, religious life, friendships, and economic security. He disagreed with those who believe that workplace violence is an instant decision of an employee.

Hardee Food Systems Inc. has implemented a practical program for the prevention of violence that is unique. The company addresses both internal and external threats to violence (Nicoletti & Spooner, 1996). The program consists of an extensive pre-employment screening of applicants, training of managers and handling threats. A 24-hour hotline, available for the reporting of safety concerns, is handled by a task force.

TOOLS FOR CONFLICT MANAGEMENT

Mediation

Mediation: Face to face interaction between the adversaries in the presence of a mediator

Mediation has emerged as an effective tool for the resolution of conflicts (Lewicki, Weiss & Lewin, 1992). Mediation involves a **face-to-face interaction** between the adversaries in the presence of a mediator. The process of mediation consists of the utilization of both formal and informal procedures in which the individuals or the parties establish preliminary contact and then show their willingness according to the terms mutually agreed upon with the mediator.

Kresel and Pruitt (1989) reported that the success rate of settlement by mediation was approximately 60%. More recently, Holaday (2002) emphasized the need for the study of developmental factors in the mediation process. For example, with variation in age and roles, the strategy adopted for mediation needed adjustment.

Integrative negotiation

Only recently has there been any attempt to study negotiation in a systematic fashion. One can posit a number of reasons due to which the scientific study of so important a phenomenon has remained neglected. Johnson and Johnson (2003) delineate four reasons for this neglect. These are:

- **Lack of conceptual clarity about the nature of integrative negotiation.**
- **Lack of a theoretical framework for the scientific study of integrative negotiation.**
- **Lack of a formal procedure for research on integrative negotiation.**
- **Limitations of existing research.**

Regarding the nature of integrative negotiation, one must say that people in the management sciences were the first to realize the limitations of traditional negotiation techniques and therefore sought newer ways to deal with organizational conflict. Recent empirical data too suggested that there could be an alternative to the traditional form of negotiation that generally leaves a feeling of loss to both parties. One of the methods that emerged was none other than that of integrative negotiation. Drawing on findings and theories of social psychology, management scientists drew up new ground rules for more effective results through negotiation (Kelly, 1975). Going a step further, the **Harvard Negotiation Project** (Fisher & Ury, 1983) developed a new form of negotiation called **principled negotiation**, based on four simple principles:

- **People: separate the people from the problem.**
- **Interests: focus on interests, not positions.**
- **Options: generate a variety of possibilities before deciding what to do.**
- **Criteria: insist that the result be based on some objective standard.**

Principled negotiation: Based on people, interests, options and criteria

Thus, there is a paradigm shift when we compare principled negotiation with either the hard or the soft forms of negotiation. Whereas, in the former, the two parties regard each other as adversaries, and in the latter they are friends, in the principled approach, the two parties are problem solvers. The ultimate aim is to resolve the conflict in such a way that the pie is expanded and a win-win situation is created for both parties. Moreover, since the final negotiated agreement is decided upon by the participants themselves and not by a third party, the commitment to the solution is also high.

Antecedents of integrative negotiation

It has been seen that integrative negotiation is more likely to take place under certain circumstances. These include a wide variety of **individual, group** and **situational variables.** One individual variable is the effect of **alcohol.** People under the influence of alcohol are seen to engage in not only more aggressive negotiation but also to commit more mistakes and arrive at less integrative negotiations (Schweitzer & Gomberg, 2001). Another individual variable is

motivation. Individuals who are prosocially motivated are more likely to work towards integrative negotiation than those who are egoistically motivated (Beersma & De Dreu, 2002). However, this study, based on subjects in the Netherlands, also clarified that the motivational variable interacted with other contextual variables such as task structure and decision rule. When the groups were formed in such a way that there was no commonality of interest among the parties, that is, groups in which there was an asymmetrical task structure, they engaged in not only more distributive and less integrative behavior, but also reached lower joint outcomes and experienced less positive group climate. This was specially so when the members were egoistically motivated (and not prosocially motivated) and were operating under the unanimity rule for decision making (as contrasted to the majority rule).

Group variables: When one party perceives the other as having a more distributive reputation the chances of integrative negotiation become less, even though there may be no truth in the reputation of the other party (Tinsley & co-workers, 2002). This effect becomes even more pronounced when we focus on how stereotype activation affects negotiations. When masculine traits are primed, that is, when participants are told explicitly that people with masculine traits are better at negotiation, distributive bargaining is more likely. However, when told that people with feminine traits are better negotiators, then more integrative solutions are reached (Kray *et al.* 2004). Besides the ways in which the two parties perceive each other, the actual nature of the two parties can also be a critical factor. In a Norwegian study, cooperative dyads got more integrative results than individualistic dyads (Schei & Rognes, 2003).

Contextual variables: One contextual factor is that of **time pressure**, with greater time pressure producing the greater use of heuristics and less integrative solutions (De Dreu, 2003). Another factor is the **number of issues** over which the two parties can negotiate. It has generally been believed that raising the number of issues over which people can negotiate increases the chances of an integrative negotiation. While this may be true, the effect of increasing the number of issues on the post negotiation satisfaction may not be positive. As we increase the number of issues, the two parties start engaging in what has been called **counterfactual thinking.** In other words, rather than being satisfied with the solution, they start thinking of the other possibilities that led to increase in the level of post negotiation dissatisfaction (Naquin, 2003).

Logrolling has been identified as significant variable in the resolution of conflicts. It refers to one party making initial concessions on low priority issues to be able to bargain for greater benefits at a later stage and on issues of higher priority. A study in Israel by Moran and Ritov (2002) analyzed how logrolling can be beneficial. It yielded not only benefits for the party that initiated the logrolling but also higher combined results for both the parties involved. Coincidentally, another study from Israel clarified how teams can be made to engage in integrative negotiation. When teams with clear learning goals, high learning values and team discussion were compared to those with performance goals, low learning values and no team discussion it was found that the former showed greater transfer of learning over a period of time (Bereby-Meyer & co-workers, 2004). It is only coincidental that both the studies chosen for discussion are from Israel, but such conclusions must be tested across cultures.

BOX 9.4

A negotiation role play exercise: How to teach people the techniques and the advantages of integrative negotiation

A common and extremely effective technique for changing behavior is role playing. Each participant in a role play exercise is provided a particular role to enact. They are also told to use certain principles to guide their behavior in that particular role. As they enact the role along the given guidelines, they experience, firsthand, many of the advantages that their new behavior has to offer.

Proksch, Ross and Estness (2002) developed an exercise in integrative negotiation using role play. The details are as follows: Based on newspaper articles and interviews with elected officials, a six day negotiation simulation was developed. The participants assumed the roles of either the Richland Town Board or the River City Mayor's Office and the goal was to resolve a conflict between the two governments.

What was the conflict? Several homeowners in the unincorporated town of Richland have had their wells fail and had asked to annex into River City. Richland officials want to stop such annexations and instead purchased water from River City. River City officials want to annex as much of Richland as possible and prevent it from incorporating.

What was the goal of the exercise? Both sides were provided with common information as well as with confidential information. Using their information, they had to negotiate over several days, seeking an agreement that addressed each side's interests and concerns.

What was the end result? As the participants enacted their role, they became aware of the advantages of integrative negotiation.

Cross-cultural dimensions of negotiation

It seems natural to expect greater use of integrative negotiation in **collectivistic cultures** than in **individualistic cultures**. Harnett and Cummings and co-workers (1980) found that whereas buyers from the **US, Finland, Spain, France and Belgium** all used their bargaining power to extract maximum profit, buyers from collectivist **Thailand and Japan** were more inclined to share profit equally between the buyer and the seller because they expected that this would benefit long-term relations between them. Trubisky, Ting-Toomey and Lin (1991) studied conflict resolution among **American** and **Taiwanese** students. The latter preferred an avoiding, integrating and compromising style, whereas the former preferred a dominating style.

But what happens **when cultures collide**? That is, suppose we pitted negotiators from two opposite types of culture against each other, how would the two behave? We pointed out in the above section that the reputation of the other party determines the nature of the negotiator's behavior. Some insight can be obtained from those findings. Specifically, Adair and co-workers (2001) studied negotiator behavior when one party was **American** and the other **Japanese.** In other words, one party came from an individualistic culture and the other from a collectivistic culture. They noted that the US negotiators exchanged information more directly and avoided influence when negotiating either with other Americans or with people of Japanese origin. Japanese people on the other hand modified their behavior, depending on whom they were negotiating with. When the other party was from their own culture, they conveyed information in an indirect way and also used influence tactics. However, when negotiating with Americans, they conformed to the American norms for negotiation. Thus, not only do people from collectivistic cultures behave differently from those from individualistic cultures but are also able to modify their behavior according to the situation. This latter can also be inferred from the general characteristics of people from collectivistic cultures.

Cultural frame shifting: The ability to shift between two culturally incompatible responses

One explanation for such modification of behavior is given by Benet-Martinez, Leu, Lee and Morris (2002). They proposed the concept of **cultural frame shifting**, that is, the ability to shift between two culturally based interpretative responses. This ability is moderated by the perceived compatibility between the two cultural orientations, or through **bicultural identity integration (BII)**. They describe three studies in which Chinese American bicultural people who perceived high BII responded in culturally appropriate ways. When they were exposed to Chinese primes, they made external attributions but when they were given American primes, they made internal attributions. However, those Chinese Americans who displayed low BII exhibited a reverse priming effect: no matter what type of prime they were given, they always tended to respond even more strongly with external attributions.

Bicultural identity integration: Perceived compatibility between the two cultural orientations

CONFLICT AND VIOLENCE AMONG TEENAGERS

Although figures from the Department of Justice in 1997 show that the overall crime rate is down, the homicide rate between 1984 and 1994, according to the *US News & World Report* (March 25, 1996), has tripled, and it has not gone down substantially in 1997. In fact, the same report, *Teenage Time Bombs*, claims that the arrest rates for the 10-17 year old juveniles have overtaken the arrest rates for the adults by a substantially high numbers. A US Department of Justice report of 1992 showed that since 1980, there had been a 79% increase in the number of juveniles (10-17 years) committing murder with guns (Berkowitz, 1994). The murder of three teenagers during the prayer time in a school in Kentucky (December, 1997) shocked, but not surprised, the nation.

Some recent data on aggression and violence among children and youth

Though the violent crime rates for the US dropped and reached its lowest ever levels in the year 2000, alarming trends still exist (Amodei & Scott, 2002). Some of the trends cited by Amodei and Scott have been given below:

- Victimization rates for teens and young adults are at their highest ever (USDOJ, 2000; NCIPC, 2001).
- Most homicide victims are young. In 1999, 12% of the homicide victims were under 18 years of age, and 63% were under 35 years of age (USDOJ, 2000).
- Homicide ranks as the second leading cause of deaths for the 15-24 years age group (NCIPC, 2001).
- Most teen offenders operate in gangs and the cause for most murders is gang related, that is, due to inter-gang rivalries (USDOJ, 2000).

- **Students carry 2,70,000 guns to school every day (APA, 2000).**
- **2,53,000 violent crimes occurred on school campuses in the year 1998 alone (USDOJ, 2000).**

The contribution of psychologists to the understanding of youth violence

The problem of youth violence, both as perpetrators and as victims of violence, is so pervasive, that even academicians and researchers are perturbed by it, and, the last couple of years have seen the publication of at least six new books on youth violence and aggression (reviewed by Smith & co-workers, 2003). Besides the early theories of frustration leading to aggression and the social learning theories, there has since then been an emphasis on understanding the issue from the social-cultural point of view. Amodei and Scott (2002) provide a very useful review of the theories. One of these is the **social information processing model** developed by Dodge and his colleagues (1980, 1986). According to this model, aggressive children show cognitive deficits and a hostile attribution bias, as compared to their non-aggressive counterparts. Thus aggressive children are found to attend to fewer environmental cues and to interpret the behavior of their peers as being more hostile than is actually the case (Dodge, 1980). They are also more likely to choose passive or aggressive responses to conflict (Dodge, 1986). Armed with this information interventions have been designed wherein attempts are made to enhance aggressive children's social information processing skills.

Social information processing model: Cognitive deficits in the processing of socially relevant information

Another model is the **cognitive script model** (Huesmann & Huesmann, cf, Amodei & Scott, 2002), according to which aggressive behavior is largely due to the child's learning of faulty scripts or programs in early childhood. The consistent retrieval of these aggressive scripts by the aggressive child leads to the consistent use of aggressive behavior. Interventions derived from this model focus on altering children's scripts and/or their normative beliefs regarding aggression. (Pepler & Slaby, 1996).

Cognitive script model: The learning of faulty ways of responding in early childhood

Developmental theories have also been posited (Loeber & Hay, 1997) to explain violence of younger population. Children can manifest an escalation in behavior culminating in violence in two different ways. Youth, who manifest the long-term escalation pattern, show a gradual development of violence that takes place over many years and begins with less serious forms of aggression. In contrast, there are those individuals who manifest a short-term escalation pattern but no gradual escalation over time. There are generally more of the former type than of the latter. As noted by Pepler and Slaby, (1996), interventions based on this model target less severe, but nonetheless problematic behavior before they escalate to more serious forms of violence.

Developmental theories: Focus on the development of aggression over time

Another model important for its role in devising interventions is the **social interactional model** (Patterson, 1986), which emphasizes the importance of different contexts for social learning at different stages of development. The model suggests that the focus of an effective intervention will depend on the child's stage of development. Thus during early childhood, the focus should be

Social interactional model: Child learns aggression from differing contexts at differing ages

more on parents, while during late childhood the focus should be on the peer group, that is, the primary agency of socialization at a particular developmental stage.

Antecedent factors of youth violence

Research indicates that there are a large number of individual and contextual factors that can cause or precipitate violent behavior among youth. These antecedents can be grouped as:

- **Individual factors.**
- **Family factors.**
- **Peer and school factors.**
- **Environmental and community factors.**
- **Cultural factors.**

While a detailed description of the effects of each of these factors would be beyond the scope of this book, we will describe some recent findings. **Individual factors** include a generally difficult temperament, which when coupled with other family and/or environmental factors have been found associated with violence (Kingston & Prior, 1995). While individual factors are important, the effect of these on violent behavior is moderated by social variables, (Hannon & co-workers, 2001). Among the **family** related factors found important are parental neglect, parental reinforcement of aggressive behavior, and harsh physical punishment during childhood (data reviewed by Amodei & Scott, 2002). The literature also supports a connection between children's witnessing of violence either at home or on the media and actual violent behavior shown by the child (Wilson & co-workers, 2002; Pintea & Bus, 2002; Johnson & co-workers, 2002; Anderson & Bushman, 2001).

It is estimated that approximately 2,000 gangs exist in 35 major cities. Their membership is increasing and the age profile of the gangs is currently 9-30 years of age, compared to 12-31 years in the 1970s. The cohesive nature of recruitment of the members and the conformity pressures by the gang leaders make these groups highly efficient and dangerous in displaying violence. According to Goldstein and Soriano (1994), a major task of social psychology is to understand how such gangs are formed and maintained. The success of an intervention program to control violence by gang members will depend on our understanding of their operations. Kazdin (1994) proposed that at least three types of interventions—early parent/ family, school based, and community based—should be developed to control any type of youth violence.

Johnson and Johnson (1997) are well known for their work on training children and adults in conflict resolution skills. In fact, their book, *Teaching Students to be Peacemakers,* is widely used for developing negotiation skills. The Non-violence and Children Program and the children's Creative Response to Conflict Program have developed several techniques and include books to train children in conflict resolution and non-violence. Judson (1984) described several exercises for children on sharing activities, understanding rules, and resisting affirmation (for further examples, see the chapter on education).

Do teenagers, especially those in their early teens, understand, and show sensitivity to, negotiations in resolving conflicts? What do they prefer in negotiations? Unfortunately, research in social psychology is meager and fails to arrive at any firm conclusion. Dudley,

Johnson and Johnson (1996) conducted a comprehensive study to investigate the preference of 176 students (grades 6 through 9) in a negotiation situation. They placed the children in a conflict situation and then gave them a choice to negotiate in either a distributive or an integrative way. In the distributive way, children could win by maximizing their gain at the cost of the other person. In the integrative way, they sought a mutually acceptable agreement that maximizes mutual benefits. The independent variable in their study was training in conflict resolution and peer mediation procedures as follows:

> Cooperative procedures including procedural learning, role playing, drill/review exercises, and small group discussions were used to teach (a) the nature of conflict, (b) how to engage in integrative negotiations, and (c) how to mediate schoolmates' conflicts. The negotiation procedure consisted of six steps (describing what you want, describing how you feel, explaining your reasons underlying your wants and feelings, reversing perspectives, inventing at least three optional agreements for mutual gain, and reaching an integrative agreement). The mediation procedure consisted of four steps (ending hostilities, ensuring commitment to mediation, facilitating negotiations, and formalizing the agreement). (Dudley, Johnson & Johnson, 1996, p. 2043).

Two dependent measures were used in this study. **First,** the researchers noted which participants engaged in integrative or distributive negotiations. **Second,** the participants were asked to write down the words they associated with the conflict. That is, the researchers wanted to know the attitudes toward conflict. The results showed that over 90% of participants preferred the distributive way. They mostly used negative words to describe their view of the conflict. However, an encouraging finding of this study was that after receiving training in resolving conflict, the participants became more positive.

Whether a child will prefer a violent or a non-violent way to resolve conflicts with peers is also dependent on whether the child has been a habitual witness of violence or not. When the use of a violent or peaceful strategy was compared across children who have been either witness or non-witness of violence, the results revealed that the strategy used depended on not only the differences between witness and non-witness, but also on gender, type of conflict and other individual difference factors (Ballif-Spanvill & co-workers, 2003). This shows that conflict resolution by children is not as simple as it appears. In short, such studies indicate that while training in the resolution of conflicts is helpful and yields positive effects, such factors also need to be considered.

Previous research on the development of **children's concept of distributive justice** has not been able to shed light on the child's ability to consider the characteristics of the recipients when making a judgment regarding fair sharing, with preschool children generally applying principles of equality (equal sharing to each individual person) when making decisions for the fair sharing of materials, regardless of the characteristics of the recipients. Wong and Nunes (2003) investigated into the extent to which preschool children would share toys equally across situations or on the basis of the characteristics of the recipients. The study also observed whether each member in a group would be counted as one unit for allocation across situations. Interestingly, the children's understanding of the concept of distributive justice is demonstrated by the children's ability to view situations differently based on the characteristics of the recipients. This elucidates the idea that even preschool children can and do take contextual information into account when making distributive justice decisions. Studying the development of the concept of distributive justice principles among Brazilian adolescents and children, Dell'Aglio and Hutz (2001) found that distributive justice follows a path of development analogous to that of Piagetian cognitive development. The study on children of differing ages revealed that the process is marked by three stages: the first stage, characterized by the use of authority (among 5-6 year olds), the next stage characterized by the use of equality (among 9-10 year olds) and the last stage, by the use of equity (among 13-14 year olds).

Road rage

Road rage: Anger on the road

With the ever-increasing incidence of aggression while behind the wheel among youth, a topic of current interest is the phenomenon of road rage. To understand road rage, we need to know what impels motorists to feel anger and then to express that anger in some form of aggression. The feeling of anger on the road could be due to the actions of other drivers. However, there is ample empirical evidence and anecdotal experience that not every person who has to face irrational behavior of other drivers on the road engages in aggressive behavior. What produces the difference between people who engage in aggressive driving and those who maintain their cool? A recent study provides some insight. Data was obtained on 109 college students who were compared on their **motivational orientations**, that is, whether they tended towards a **controlled orientation** or an **autonomy orientation**. By controlled orientation, the authors were referring to the regulation of behavior according to contingencies and pressure, whereas the autonomy orientation meant the regulation of behavior according to interest and choice. The results revealed that, firstly, the controlled orientation was associated with feeling more driving anger as a result of other driver's actions; secondly, the controlled orientation was associated with more aggressive driving behavior and more traffic citations; thirdly, the relationship between controlled orientation and aggressive driving was mediated by driving anger; and lastly, self esteem and social anxiety did not account for the results on motivational orientations. In other words it can be concluded that the controlled motivational orientation leads to more aggressive driving than the autonomy orientation (Knee & co-workers, 2001).

Another factor leading to road rage could be **personality**. Significant differences have been obtained on driving behavior, the Type A Behavior Pattern, attitudes and beliefs. However, those who engaged in aggressive driving were not seen to be significantly different from their non-aggressive counterparts, on the Big Five Personality factors of agreeableness, conscientiousness and neuroticism (Miles & Johnson, 2003).

In a very innovative study, 88 female and 51 male undergraduate psychology students completed a 40 item self-presentation style inventory and a 20 item road rage survey. These participants were then videotaped while walking into a room and introducing themselves to a confederate. The self-presentation style inventory categorized the participants in terms of three **self-presentation styles**, that is, the intimidation style, the ingratiation style and the exemplification style. Aggressive driving behavior correlated positively with the self-presentation style of intimidation and negatively with the self-presentation styles of ingratiation and exemplification. When the non-verbal behavior of these participants was analyzed on the basis of the videotape, the ways in which the three self-presentation styles were manifested became clear. The videotape revealed that intimidation and self-promotion styles were associated with no hesitation before sitting down, intimidation was further associated with focusing on the target, while exemplification was associated with initiating a handshake (Bassett & co-workers, 2002).

There is some empirical work that enables us to understand road rage in the **cross-cultural context.** A study in Sydney, Australia, clarified that road rage was perceived as a response to the stresses of urban living: not only to driving on crowded roads but also to the pressures of a competitive work environment and a lack of time. Further, gender and social class differences were noted in the ways in which subjects described their emotional responses to driving frustrations (Lupton, 2002). That there may not be cultural differences in the reasons for aggressive driving is clarified through a postal survey of over 2500 drivers from Britain, Finland and the Netherlands. The same type of behavior on the road was found to provoke anger and aggression in the three countries, with traffic density playing an important role in the precipitation of anger (Parker & co-workers, 2002).

GOING BEYOND THE INDIVIDUAL: THE PSYCHOLOGY OF PEACE

The formation of Division 48, Peace Psychology by the American Psychological Association in 1990 is a landmark in the history of American Psychology. Ironically, a Division of Military Psychology was created a long time ago. As it was mentioned earlier in this chapter, control of aggression does not necessarily mean elimination of aggression or the promotion of non-aggression; it may simply indicate a temporary absence of aggression as if it is a time-out situation or a truce after a war.

There are several **reasons for the slow growth of psychological studies on peace** and non-violence. **First,** psychologists prefer to use the word "aggression" over "violence" because aggression is usually described in the context of individual behavior, whereas violence is commonly used in an institutional or group context. According to Groebel and Hinde (1989), this difference in approach has led to a failure of the significant contributions so far to our understanding of major policy issues in controlling violence in our society. **Second,** psychologists have also neglected their rich heritage in the field of non-violence, an area in which they might have contributed very significantly. For instance, the work of William James on memory and emotion was explored in depth by psychologists, but his contribution in the field of non-violence remained largely unknown. Despite current ignorance about his work, according to Professor Lynd (1966) of Yale University, the contribution of William James in the area of non-violence was second only to Thoreau's. Tolman, Guthrie, Osgood, Maslow, May, Kohlberg and Erikson are other prominent psychologists who made significant contributions to the field of psychology of non-violence during the past five decades, but their work on peace and non-violence rarely figured in mainstream psychology (Kool, 1990, 1993).

The **third** reason for the slow growth of peace and non-violence studies is our extraordinary concern with the issues of aggression in our society. Issues on non-violence were certainly not our priority. For instance we ignored Thoreau's work. Through Dr. Martin Luther King it came back to the USA after Tolstoy in Russia and Gandhi in South Africa and India who refined Thoreau's technique of civil disobedience (Kool, 1990). Another example of neglect by scholars on issues of non-aggression is provided by Montagu (1976). He mentioned that scholars acquainted with non-aggressive tribes seemed uninterested in contributing an article to his book *Learning Non-aggression*.

A historical landmark in the field of aggression was created when a group of social scientists met in Seville, Spain and issued a joint statement, known as the Seville Statement (dated May 16, 1986), that we did not inherit a tendency to make a war. In 1994, the official publication of the American Psychological Association published three articles reporting the statement itself (The Seville Statement on Violence, 1994), the criticism of the statement (Beroldi, 1994), and its rebuttal (Scott & Ginsberg, 1994).

Defining non-violence

While psychologists are still debating on an acceptable definition of behavior that promotes peace and non-violence, Jeffrey Goldstein and Pawel Mlicki (1996) cited Herman's (1993) views: "Non-violence is both an attitude and a course of action that leads both an individual and a group of people to resist tyranny and injustice other than by physical force, and to build a community of caring by the reconciliation of adversaries. It also has a positive meaning as people strive to remove the causes of violent conflict, both human and environmental" (p. 269). As stated earlier, non-violence is not simply the absence of violence; it embodies presence of certain traits and behaviors. For instance, a factor analysis of Kool and Sen's Non-violence Test revealed that self-control, anti-punitiveness, forebearance, and inequity of justice constitute the psychological components of a non-violent person (Kool & Keyes, 1990).

Non-violence: Attitude and course of action that leads people to resist injustice by means other than the use of aggression

What should be the **task of peace psychology**? According to Miall (2002), peace psychologists have at least two tasks set out for them:

- **To explore into the nature of conflict and its forms.**
- **To explore pathways that promise less violent future directions.**

Cairns and Lewis (2003) too point to the role that psychology can play in ending **war** and promoting peace. There are at least three areas wherein psychology can make fruitful contributions:

- **Conflict resolution.**
- **Ending cycles of revenge post-conflict.**
- **Promoting world peace.**

Terrorism and peace psychology

Peace psychology has much to offer by way of analyzing the causes, prevention and impact of terrorism. Although terror and terrorists had always been a part of human suffering, the so called 9/11 brutal act has changed the thinking of the civilized world. In this context, Wagner (2002) is of the view that one of the most important contributions of peace psychology to the understanding of the event is the recognition that extreme acts do not occur in a vacuum. Experienced social injustice is the antecedent factor. Further, in a recent American Psychological Association publication, Pyszczynski, Greebay and Solomon (2002) presented their **terror management theory**. It stated that

Terror management theory: When people feel threatened and have the facts for continued violence, they blame and attack the culprit

when people feel threatened and are motivated to support their belief system by the facts that promote security, they begin to blame and attack those responsible for causing insecurity. The authors believed that because the culprits responsible for 9/11 were still at large and further attacks not being ruled out, the insecurity continues to exist and a backlash is nothing but a natural response.

A major task of applied social psychology now is to help people manage in the face of terrorism. The cost in terms of human suffering is enormous. Imagine what our life will be if we keep on worrying everyday how safely are we going to reach our office, take an airplane ride to visit our relatives, and so on. Keeping in mind the urgent need to address this issue, the **American Psychological Association** constituted a **task force, Response to Terrorism,** consisting of 15 psychologists. With the change in the world order after 9/11, the committee emphasized the need for training in resiliency, especially for children, and prepared material for the training of professionals in this field. In short, the tasks involved were: how to deal with trauma, tools for resilience, and bringing in the participation of community (*APA Monitor*, 2004, p. 34).

To be duly effective, peace psychologists need a concerted effort, bringing into its fold, psychologists from all parts of the globe. Thus Leung (2003) is of the opinion that Asian Peace Psychology too can make a relevant contribution. Theoretically, it can contribute by identifying novel peace and conflict phenomena in Asia; on the applied side, it can help develop insights for formulating strategies for the attainment of peace specific to the Asian context, and in general, for other parts of the world as well. For example, Montiel (2003) has identified the various forms of violence seen in Asia and has also provided strategies for the promotion of peace specifically suitable to the Asian context. She has described how, in Asia, direct violence takes the form of intrastate intermediate-sized armed conflicts. Structural violence, on the other hand, is associated with foreign invasions and authoritarian regimes, chronic poverty, and cultural heterogeneity of non-immigrant groups marked by asymmetric power relations. Montiel is of the view that because of the above nature of social conflict in Asia, peace psychologists working in this region should have a particular focus: they need to emphasize active non-violent political transformation, heal protracted-war traumas, encourage beliefs supporting economic democratization, create social voice and identity, and so engage in a culture-sensitive political peace-making process. Caspary (2003) has similarly shown us how religion can bring peace to the Middle East.

For a serious counteraction to the present global crisis, attempts have first to be made to diagnose the problems, and only thereafter should the focus be on interventions (Schmuck, 2003).

Attributions

Do we tend to rationalize violence? Yes, we certainly do, through the use of **attributions.** The attributions people make are very interesting and involve the same errors of attribution so commonly exhibited in other domains of behavior. As Sanderson and Darley (2002) put it, "I am moral but you are deterred": individuals tend to believe that they obey laws and exhibit moral behavior because of internal values. Others, in contrast, obey laws and exhibit moral behavior only due to the fear of punishment.

Terrorists often justify their action and attribute a moral dimension to their violence. Young Palestinians have sacrificed their lives for the cause of freedom and establishment of their independent state.

Another such attribution is **moral disengagement**. This refers to a set of aggressive responses to inter-group conflict in which people excuse violence by dehumanizing victims and providing moral justifications for the suffering that they inflict (Bandura, Barbaranelli, Caprara & Pastorelli, 1996). Stereotyping and tendencies toward victim-blaming and dehumanization are obviously connected to negative inter-group attitudes, but another crucial process is the invocation of a moral "right" to respond aggressively to threats of certain kinds.

Moral disengagement: People excuse violence by providing moral justifications

Using the Peace Test Scale, moral disengagement was measured among medical university and secondary school students in 21 nations (Grussendorf & co-workers, 2002). The results showed that moral disengagement is a significant predictor of opinions about specific threats. Interestingly, the mean scale scores for the students were significantly related to the national levels of spending on defense in each of the nations surveyed. Even 10 year old subjects understand about war and peace, as seen from interviews of Filipino children (Oppenheimer & Kuipers, 2003). Thus if peace is to take hold, peace educators must focus on re-education, centering on the individual, especially his attribution and Locus of Control (Nasser & co-workers, 2002).

PSYCHOLOGICAL OBSTACLES TO PEACE

An important way to promote peace in a community or between nations is to understand the psychological obstacles to peace. Borrowing from recent social psychological research on schema, Wessells (1993) noted that when the Cold War was depicted as heroic (for example, as a struggle between Good versus Evil) several obstacles to peace emerged. He reported three categories of obstacles that need to be removed to promote peace (Table 9.8). First, the

TABLE 9.8

Cognitive, affective and social obstacles to peace (*Source*: Wessels, 1993)

Cognitive obstacles:
- Attribution biases
- Selective attention and memory
- Ideological rigidity
- Compartmentalized thinking

Affective obstacles:
- Hostility
- Distrust
- Desire for power
- Hopelessness

Social obstacles:
- Group thinking
- Blaming and scapegoating
- Excessive obedience and conformity
- Legitimation of violence

cognitive barriers often cause distortion of the Third World countries and enemies. Second, the affective factors, such as fear concerning survival, may drive us in favor of stockpiling of arms and neglect peace-building. And third, the social obstacles may cause mistrust between the two parties. For example, creating images of the enemy and using it in the propaganda increases hostility between groups. In his empirical research work, Mann (1993) has shown how people rate appropriateness of tactics used in war. For example, when invaders used highly violent force against non-violent defenders, his subjects rated their tactics as most inappropriate, but when the invader was their own country, that is, the USA, the same tactics were treated leniently. Obviously, our concept of the use of excessive force is deeply affected by the group with which we are affiliated.

SOCIAL PSYCHOLOGICAL THEORIES IN THE PROMOTION OF PEACE

Nagata (1993) concluded that the appropriateness of moral behavior is judged by one's own sense of a community. Those who are excluded from the community are subjected to different moral values and rules. The panic and hysteria following Pearl Harbor and the internment of people of Japanese origin during the WW II are clear examples of **moral exclusion** (Nagata, 1993). Why were Germans in the USA not subjected to the same treatment? Because the people of German origin had assimilated into the mainstream culture and families, they were accepted as a part of moral community of the Caucasian Americans. Along the same lines, is the data on bystander intervention. Bystanders are more likely to help victims who are perceived as being members of the in-group rather than those who are considered as out-group. Even with the perpetrators of the crime, the bystanders are influential only when the perpetrator considers them as being in-group (Levine & co-workers, 2002). The works of Mann, Nagata and others showed that rules of war and moral considerations are highly prejudiced when one's own group is involved in judging violence. So pervasive is this prejudice that a group can start a war against another simply to preserve a single identity for the community. An observation and analysis of the periodic conflicts between Greeks and Turks in Cyprus reveals that the underlying intent of the unofficial militias is to maintain a distinct single identity within the community: "the idea is to wipe out all memory of the other group, to obliterate its traces, to rewrite the past and present" (Loisoz, 1988, p. 646).

Moral exclusion: Justification for not including people

The self-fulfilling prophecy

Morton Deutsch (1986), a prominent researcher in the field of conflict resolution, showed how the **self-fulfilling prophecy** explains pathology of behavior. According to him, if the leaders of two countries believed that war was likely and either side increased its military strength, the other side would naturally justify its initial approach. "The dynamics of arms race," writes Deutsch, "have the inherent quality of folie a' deux, wherein the self-fulfilling prophecies mutually reinforce one another. As a result, both sides are right to think that the other is provocative, dangerous, and malevolent. Each side, however, is blind to how its own policies have contributed to the development of the other's hostility" (p. 140).

Prospect theory

Prospect theory provides a good example to illustrate the applications of psychological findings from an individual level to a group setting. Originally, this theory was developed to explain individual choices but gradually it has been extended to decision making in international relations and mediation (Milburn and Isaac, 1995). Prospect theory begins with the analysis of the way individuals make their choices and weigh certainty or uncertainty of outcomes. Deutsch (1986) showed how the basic tenets of rationality was violated by policymakers and caused increased hostility between the two adversaries. According to Deutsch, "....people undervalue outcomes that are merely probable in comparison with outcomes that are obtainable with certainty. This "certainty effect" means that a gambler facing the prospect of a sure loss of a smaller amount if he or she stops now and an uncertain loss of a larger amount if he or she continues to gamble is apt to choose to take the risk of increasing his or her losses" (p. 141).

Prospect theory: Analysis of how individuals make their choices

GRIT

Osgood's (1962) theory of **Graduated and Reciprocated Initiatives in Tension Reduction**, commonly known as **GRIT**, suggested that if a few unambiguous peaceful gestures are made by a nation, an adversary is likely to reciprocate and the degree of mistrust and suspicion between the parties will reduce.

GRIT: Developed by Osgood, as a technique for conflict resolution between nations

Work in the area of conflict resolution has advanced considerably since Osgood proposed his pioneering theory. Pilisuk (1997) has reported that there are **two models** that are widely used in resolving conflicts: the **collaborative behavior model** and the **ideological reconciliation model**. The collaborative model encourages cooperative activity and illustrates a case in which it is applied. It is founded on the premise of Sherif and Sherif's Robber's Cave experiment using the concept of a superordinate goal which illustrates that members of an opposite group can help other group members if higher levels of goal are created in a situation. The ideological reconciliation model focuses on those issues that separate the two parties and use a process of continuous dialogue to reduce the ideological gap. Focusing on the controversial issue of abortion, Pilisuk used both methods to present a real life attempt to unite the two opposite groups. According to him, if the two groups work together on a superordinate goal and enter into hypothetical dialogues without necessarily changing their beliefs, there is a fairly good chance that the tension between the two groups would be reduced.

Collaborative model: Conflict resolution based on cooperative activity

It is encouraging to note that the efforts made by social psychologists in reducing conflict have been successful both at the local and international levels. Kelman (1986, 1993) has been actively involved in resolving conflict in the Middle East and has conducted several workshops on conflict resolution to train policy-makers. Lumsden and Wolfe (1996) have proposed a model workshop for tackling conflicts. They believe that diplomacy has become a part of the mainstream approach in solving disputes and therefore a problem solving approach should focus on various psycho-social dimensions of conflict. Kimmel (1995) has focused on a user-friendly approach and cultural understanding in developing a practical model of peace. Schwebel (1993) has focused on a historical perspective to analyze the role of psycho-social factors in peace movement. In short, research on the psychology of peace and its applications have ranged from experiments to case studies, and now social psychologists have a stronger empirical base to address local and global issues than ever before.

PROMOTING CULTURES OF PEACE AND NON-VIOLENCE: INTERVENTIONS FOR PEACE

One of the most effective starting points would be the school, where the child not only spends a considerable proportion of his waking hours, but is also substantially influenced by both teachers and peers. It has therefore been advocated that we promote cultures of peace and non-violence in schools. Malley, Beck and Adorno (2001) describe a framework that could be useful. According to Malley and co-workers, the post industrial era requires schools to take on new functions, especially in terms of inculcating values regarding a sense of community and useful citizenship. This requires a shift to a new ecological paradigm that should have the following foci:

- **Emphasizing the primacy of human relationships as the medium of learning.**
- **Cultivating contexts that bring out the best of human qualities.**
- **Creating communities that emphasize the development of the whole student.**
- **Emphasizing cooperation over competition.**
- **Valuing individual differences.**

Since such an extensive redesign of schools may not always be feasible, we need to also concentrate on strategies that can be used within the existing school system. Mattiani (2001) describes the **Peace Power! Project.** This is a set of concrete practical tools that can be flexibly combined to suit local school tastes and needs. Seeing the complexity of the situation, Gerstein & co-workers, (2003) point out that counseling psychologists have a very important role to play in promoting cultures of peace.

For peace at the community level too, several ideas have been advanced. Cultural change would be at the core of these strategies. Staub (2003) lists some ways to foster peace at the community level. These include:

- **The healing of past wounds.**
- **The creation of constructive ideologies.**
- **The creation of supportive communities.**
- **Reconciliation.**
- **The creation of shared collective memory.**
- **Education to promote peace.**
- **The development of inclusive caring in children.**

Specific **interventions** for promoting peace and building cultures of peace can be categorized into those for **school going children**, those for **young adults** at the university and college level, and those for **the community** at large. One such program is the **Peace Builders** intervention described by Flannery & co-workers (2003). This is a universal school based violence prevention program that attempts to alter the school by teaching both students and staff, simple rules and activities for improving the child's social competence. In one such initiative, eight matched schools (N > 4000, grades K-5) were randomly assigned to either of two conditions; immediate intervention and intervention after one year. The results reveal that even after one year the participating children maintained the gains made in terms of reduction of aggressive behavior and increase in prosocial behavior and other social competencies. Similar interventions include **RIPP (Responding in Peaceful and Positive ways)**, through the use of which 7th grade students were found to have fewer disciplinary code violations for violent offences. The authors also found that those most likely to benefit were students with higher pretest rates of problem behavior, including violent behavior, non-physical aggression and delinquent behavior (Farrell & co-workers, 2003). Building on the contents of the RIPP program is the **GREAT (Guiding Response Expectations for Adolescents for Today and Tomorrow)** initiative for schools and families. The program focuses on changing school norms. It consists of twenty 40 minute lessons taught by trained facilitator on a weekly basis during the school hours (Meyer & co-workers, 2004). Similar to the above is the **EHV program** for 4th and 5th grade students. Developed in Auton, England, it consisted of attempts to inculcate five core values: truth, love, peace, right conduct and non-violence. Testing its efficacy on 36 4th and 5th grade children in Istanbul, Turkey, Kulaksizoglu and Dilmac (2003) reported that the children showed a marked improvement in their moral maturity level.

One example of a **community level intervention** is the **Heritage Project**, described by Thompson and co-workers (2003). This program had as its goal, the inculcation of peace and social justice among school children, pre-service and in-service teachers, parents and other members of the community in USA.

War and peace can also be integrated into the **school curriculum**. Ediger (2003) shows us how. The author is of the view that democracy as an ideal should be emphasized in schools and in the society and concludes by listing **six ideals** that might foster peace. These are:

- **Respecting others by avoiding uncaring criticism, hateful words, physical attacks and self destructive behavior.**
- **Communicating clearly to solve problems.**
- **Listening to others and considering the feelings of others.**
- **Forgiving and apologizing and forgetting grudges.**
- **Respecting nature, including animal life.**
- **Being courageous, including challenging all forms of violence.**

However, whether they are students or even teachers, those who want to enter the area of counseling for cultures of peace would require mentoring. This new work arena may cause considerable role confusion, basically because the counselor has to move from a 'direct service' function to individuals to an 'indirect service' function involving often the community at large. Moeschberger and co-workers (2003) teach such students and professional counselors how to be successful in their endeavor.

We end this chapter by describing in detail how one program was initiated and carried out successfully in two Texas schools.

Use of behavioral journalism to reduce moral disengagement (McAlister & co-workers, 2000)

One communication technique that has been useful for healthy behavior change is termed behavioral journalism. The method is based on actual stories of behavioral change emanating from the audience itself. We can compare it to a very popular TV talk show, *The Oprah Show*. The psychological process utilized is that of peer modeling (McAlister, 1995), who reported success of the method in smoking cessation, cancer screening, and increased condom use, as demonstrated in community experiments in Finland and the United States.

What is the *modus operandi*? The technique primarily is based on the use of inexpensive publicity and production techniques and by organizing interpersonal contact and distribution of print materials by volunteers through existing community networks.

A recent application: A quasi-experimental research project was carried out among ninth-grade students in two Houston, Texas, schools to investigate whether students' behavioral journalism can change attitudes related to intergroup hostility.

One section of the survey contained questions about attitudes toward violence. Three questions were selected to measure moral disengagement and willingness to use violence in provocative situations. These were adapted from items and concepts studied by Cohen and Nisbett (1994, cf. McAlister *et al.*, 2000) in research on U.S. regional culture that associates violence in the South with beliefs about threat response and the use of firearms:

- **If someone hits you, you should hit them back.**
- **A person has the right to kill if it is necessary to defend their home or property.**
- **Carrying a weapon can make me safer.**

The program was conducted from December 1996 to May 1997, during which four behavioral journalism newsletters were distributed and read aloud in sessions led by a multicultural team of "Students for Peace" from the University of Texas School of Public Health. Each month the newsletters contained four to eight students' stories (at least two stories featuring Hispanic students' Spanish-language stories) about how they learned to overcome prejudice and increase tolerance for other ethnic groups. The fourth newsletter featured stories about students who rejected processes of moral disengagement.

Following the behavioral journalism procedure, each story explicitly focused on attitudes measured in the student surveys that were presumed to influence behavior. Peer models were interviewed to obtain statements corresponding to positive responses to the questions about intergroup attitudes, rights to retaliation, and use of deadly force. The procedures were so simple that they could be easily duplicated by volunteers in other schools. The popularity of the program can be gauged from the number of students, and even teachers, who expressed strong interest in the newsletters and class presentations, and to be models in the newsletters.

Publicity was obtained by releasing data from the baseline survey in the program school and a similar survey of Houston adults that was conducted in January, 1997, by telephone over the television media and press conferences.

What were the results? The campaign evidently was effective in promoting moral engagement by changing beliefs about the acceptability of violence. In line with earlier research, the changes came mainly from among those with the most aggressive attitudes. The reduced intentions for intergroup hostility among students at Sharpstown High School suggests that the cognitive effects were sufficient to achieve 50% reduction in the likelihood of discriminatory behaviors.

Summary

This chapter is divided into three parts. After describing the nature of aggression and its types, the first part focused on the control of aggression. A review of techniques to control aggression, such as self-instructional methods, relaxation training, catharsis and contingency management, was presented. Kool and Sen's (1984) measure of non-violence was also described.

In the second part of the chapter, issues concerning conflict management were discussed. A major attention was devoted to the workplace violence and its control. Subsequently, the problems concerning management of violence among young children and teenagers were also described. The role of social psychologists in the promotion of peace and non-violence was presented in the last part of this chapter. It was emphasized that the psychology of peace and non-violence is not an inverted mirror image of the psychology of violence.

Suggestions for Further Reading

LaFreniere, P., Masataka, N., Butvskaya, M. and co-workers (2002). Cross-cultural analysis of social competence and behavior problems in preschoolers. *Early Education & Development*, 13, 201-219.

Kool V.K. (Ed), (1993). *Non-violence: Social and Psychological Issues*. N.Y: University Press of America.

Kool, V.K. (Ed), (1990). *Perspectives in Non-violence*. NY: Springer-Verlag.

Mayton, D. (2001). Non-violence within cultures of peace: a means and ends. *Peace and Conflict: Journal of Peace Psychology*, 7, 143-155.

Some Key Terms

Bicultural identity integration
Catharsis
Cognitive script model
Collaborative model
Contingency management training
Cultural frame shifting
Developmental theories
Distributional justice
Four faces of justice
GRIT
Hostile aggression
Inducing incompatible responses
Informational justice
Instrumental aggression
Integrative negotiation
Interpersonal justice
Justice sensitivity
Long-term factors
Mediation
Moral disengagement
Moral exclusion
Non-violence
Principled negotiation
Procedural justice
Prospect theory
Reconciliation model
Relaxation training
Road rage
Self instructional method
Situational factors
Social information processing model
Yin and Yang

SOCIAL PSYCHOLOGY OF EDUCATION

10

Chapter Outline

- An introduction to social psychology of education
- Socialization in the school
- The cross-cultural aspect of education
  - Attitudes towards knowledge and learning
- The teacher: Attitudes and behavior
  - The Pygmalion effect
- Social learning in the school
  - Attitudes and expectations of students
  - Student control of teacher behavior
- Social psychology and the classroom
  - On changing the traditional classroom
- Social psychology and the process of classroom instruction
- Social psychology, child development and education: The case of Head Start
- Violence in the school
  - Preventing violence through social competence training
  - Conflict management in the school
  - Implementation of a conflict management program in school
- Social psychology of stress in students
  - Causes of stress among students
  - Stress in immigrant and international students
  - Coping strategies used by students
  - Stress and early life experiences
  - Stress and individual factors
  - Interventions for stress among students
- Social psychology of special education
  - Inclusionary education
  - Goals of inclusionary education
  - Developing a new nomenclature
  - Changing attitudes

- Interventions for attitude change
- Impact of inclusion

- Social psychological implications of E-learning

AN INTRODUCTION TO SOCIAL PSYCHOLOGY OF EDUCATION

Social psychology bears a very special relationship to the behavior of students in school. Generally speaking, schools are the first formal place outside the family where a child shows how his/her cognitive abilities are related to achievement and adjustment. While this relationship was not considered so important forty years ago, when a school dropout could move out and still make a comfortable living, there is an increasing pressure on school kids now to learn modern technical skills so as to survive in a highly competitive world.

Schools do not simply teach the children more knowledge. Schools teach children to think about the world in different ways; it can influence the child's moral value orientation (Minuchin & Shapiro, 1983); and, it has a major influence on the ways in which children organize their thoughts and cognitions (Rogoff, 1981). The concerns of the school go far beyond knowledge enhancement. It is equally concerned with disciplining the child; providing motivational inputs and fulfilling various social needs such as the need for achievement, the need for affiliation and the need for power. Each of these aims can be furthered by the systematic application of social psychology theory and research. This chapter will focus on the above issues and how social psychology can help in providing more effective education.

SOCIALIZATION IN THE SCHOOL

While no one contradicts that the **school is a vital socializing agent**, it is important to keep in mind that it exerts its influence not independently, but in interaction with other salient agencies such as the family and the peer group. An understanding of the social psychology of education entails an analysis of the place of the school in the entire social system. We therefore need to conceptualize the school from the **systems** point of view, that is, to understand the ways in which the school is interdependent and interrelated to the other vital subsystems of the society. Some of these other subsystems are the home, the neighborhood, and the church (or other religious institutes). It also becomes clear that student behavior is only partly determined by factors **intrinsic to the school**. What occurs with the child **outside the school** is an equally important antecedent. The school may thus be viewed as a well-knit conglomeration of at least three clusters:

> **The systems approach to school:** School as subsystem of the larger social system

- **The school (its size, facilities, organization, policies, etc.).**
- **The teacher (gender, age, ability, skill, personality, socio-cultural background, etc.).**
- **The peer group (its size, gender, morale, acceptance of the child, etc.).**

Together, these three clusters determine the emergent group dynamics faced by the child. It is these factors, vis-à-vis the out of school factors, that will determine how pervasive the effect of the school will be.

Figure 10.1: The school as a set of subsystems.

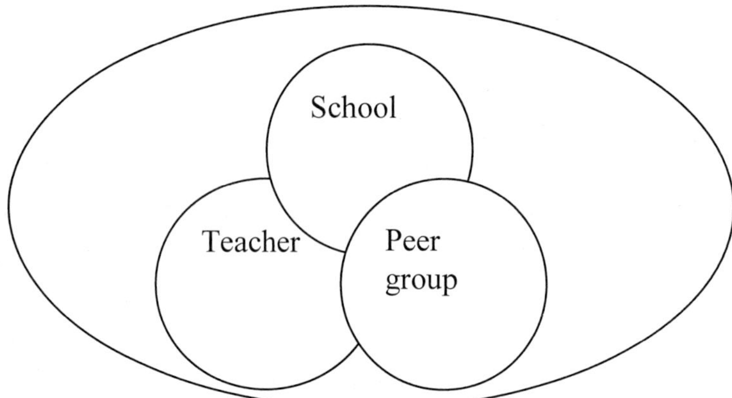

An important example of the interaction of the school with other social subsystems is provided by the **research on memory and cognitive learning.** Kurtz and co-workers (1988) obtained a dual confirmation of the relationship between parental and teacher attributions and beliefs on the one hand and child performance on the other. In a cross-cultural investigation, it was seen that adult attributions and beliefs regarding success and failure paralleled between country differences in strategy usage and attributional beliefs of the children. Thus, the researchers concluded that strategy training programs operate against a background of apparently strong messages from teachers and parents, both implicitly and explicitly. As a result, cognitive and meta-cognitive developments seem firmly embedded in **cultural values** and **expectations.** When solving of simple arithmetic problems by non-Chinese Canadian was compared with that by Chinese students educated in Canada and those educated in Asia, the results showed that the Chinese educated in Asia performed better than either of the two other groups. On further analysis, it was clear that the differences were not due to differences in formal education. Rather, the better performing group tended to use less of procedural strategies and better retrieval strategies than the students in the other two groups. Moreover, these differences were clearly cultural in origin (Campbell & Xue, 2001). Similar cultural influences have been observed for the memorization of words (Endo, 1988) and the retrieval of words by bilinguals (Kroll & Curley, 1988). The well known **Sapir-Whorf hypothesis** regarding culture playing a key role in language development has also been well corroborated by empirical findings (Hoosain & Salili, 1988; Naveh-Benjamin & Ayres, 1986).

Sapir-Whorf hypothesis: Culture determines language

It has also been seen that the **size** and **organization** of the school has important implications for the nature of facilities offered, and these, in turn, affect the role of the school in transmitting social and cultural values (Gump, 1980).

While both the school and the family act as primary agents of socialization, their *modus operandi* differs vastly. The **school differs from the family** as a socializing agent in at least **four** different ways:

- **It is more impersonal.**
- **It provides shorter periods of interaction.**

- **The adults often differ from one another and from the parents.**
- **It focuses on recurring and public evaluation (Hetherington & Parke, 1986).**

Teachers play a very important role in the lives of children the world over. However, there are both qualitative and quantitative cross-country differences in the impact of the school. Through a cross-national study (Chen & co-workers, 2003), it has been clarified that from among the non-parental adults, it is the teacher who plays the most important role in the life of the child. At the same time, when children in China were compared to their American counterparts, it was seen that the teacher is perceived as a more important socializing agent by the former than by the latter.

Seeing the very pervasive impact of the school, it is only natural that the school be able to **inculcate civic values** among their students. The International Association for the Evaluation of Educational Achievement conducted a Civic Education Study on 90,000, 14 year old students from 28 countries. The conclusion reached was that training in civic values is most effective when the school not only provides explicit training in these values but also ensures an open classroom climate for the discussion of civic issues and a participative school culture in general (Torney-Purta, 2002).

The extent to which the school will impact the students will also depend on certain **personal characteristics** of the students. One such characteristic is the child's attitude towards school, or what has been termed "**disposition to school education.**" This attitude constellation consists of a number of specific aspects, for example, attitudes to school, motivation to achieve, beliefs about personal control over learning and external constraints on learning (Kobal, 2003). To see whether there are national differences in "disposition to school education," 193 Slovenian high school students were compared to 207 British high school students. The data indicated that the latter are characterized by a more positive attitude to school than the former (Kobal, 2003).

Disposition to school education: Attitudes towards school and education

THE CROSS-CULTURAL ASPECT OF EDUCATION

Is there a cross cultural aspect to education? That is, does education have to be imparted in a culturally appropriate manner or, are there universal principles? There is at least some research evidence to show that while there may be some universally applicable principles (since we are all offspring of Homo Sapiens, irrespective of our cultural background) there are other aspects that are clearly culture specific.

Attitudes towards knowledge and learning

One of the first pieces of evidence regarding **culture specificity in learning** came from the findings that Asian children do better at school than their Western counterparts, and, that this difference becomes heightened for subjects such as mathematics and science (Harmon & co-workers, 1997 cf. Lueng, 2002). The results of the Third International Mathematics and Science Study also found that students from Hong Kong, Japan, Korea and Singapore outperformed their counterparts from the Western countries. This was despite the fact that students in these four countries displayed not only a relatively negative attitude towards mathematics, but also lacked confidence in doing mathematics (Lueng, 2002). Further, there was nothing that the students from these four countries had in common to explain their superior performance. This "**learning gap**" (as Stevenson & Stigler, 1992 have called it) has been explained in various ways. While some have attributed it to higher IQ among the Asians (Hernstein & Murray, 1994), others have held the view that the difference is due to higher achievement motivation (Tweed & Lehman, 2002), higher expectations of the Asian parents (Stevenson & Stigler, 1992) and even greater effort on the part of the Asian students (Stevenson & Lee, 1990).

Learning gap: Gap between potential to learn and actual learning

Recent analyses (for example, Li, 2002) have, however, explained the difference as being due to the difference in the very **attitudes to learning**. It is argued that East Asian cultures emphasize a **Confucian approach to learning,** while the Western cultures are more in favor of the **Socratic approach** (Tweed & Lehman, 2002). While the former is characterized by "effortful, pragmatic, and respectful learning; behavioral reform; and the acquisition of essential knowledge" (Gurung, 2003, p 145), the latter is "exemplified by questioning one's own beliefs, evaluating others' knowledge, having high esteem for self generated knowledge, and focusing on error to evoke doubt" (Gurung, 2003, p. 145). Or, as Li (2003) concluded:

Socratic approach: Based on a neutral body of knowledge that the student will master, depending on his internal capabilities

> In sum, European American middle and upper-middle class members basically view learning as a process by which individuals' minds acquire what is out there. Knowledge exists as a more or less neutral body that individuals' minds can acquire. The conceptual focus is on the distinction between this neutrally existing knowledge body and the internal characteristics of the individual that enable the person to acquire it...clearly, although learning is an important part of the lives of the US participants studied, it does not seem to evoke their passionate effect or to be intimately connected to their emotional, spiritual or moral lives (p. 261).

So, in a typical learning situation at school, Li is of the view that there are a set of **internal cognitive characteristics** which when coupled with **motivational characteristics** induce learning to take place.

> In contrast, the Chinese regard knowledge as something that is indispensable to their personal lives. This view is also consistent with the age-old Confucian understanding of learning. Knowledge accordingly includes not only the externally existing body but also social and moral knowing. ...Individuals also seek learning to cultivate themselves as a whole in the moral domain toward "self perfection" ...As a result, knowledge is not something that Chinese lives can do without but something that they must have (Li, 2003, p. 261).

Confucian approach: Based on a passion to learn, even irrespective of one's capabilities

In an article, with a very telling title "A cultural model of learning: Chinese heat and mind for wanting to learn," Li (2002) gives us further insight into the Confucian attitude to learning. It is differences such as these that probably best explain the superior performance of East Asian students even in subjects that they do not like or are not very confident about. They put in additional labor because of their passion to excel in all areas of learning, giving them an edge over their Western counterparts. Kool and Mishra (2003) have used the differences between the Socratic and the Confucian models to explain how the teaching of psychology varies in Indian and American universities.

Gurung (2003) preferred to think of these two styles of learning as two ends of a **continuum**, with students from different cultures often using both styles at times. Gurung gives the example of American students who are normally not interested in general education courses (Huba & Freed, 2000) and prefer to pay attention to courses that will enable them to get a good job. Such a pragmatic view of education is a major Confucian emphasis but students from the West also manifest it. He also points out that a combination of the two styles would probably provide a more complete education to students the world over.

Magolda (1992) proposed **five** different **styles of learning:**

- **Absolute knowers: who acquire information from authorities by listening or by active questioning and responding to authority.**
- **Transitional knowers: who understand knowledge through the uncertainty shown by others, or by being forced to think.**
- **Independent knowers: who feel free to decide on the basis of their own opinions.**
- **Contextual knowers: who construct knowledge by judging the evidence, the views of others and their own views.**

Most scholars believe that such typologies may provide educators with practical suggestions for enhancing education to a greater extent than the Confucian-Socratic dichotomy.

THE TEACHER: ATTITUDES AND BEHAVIOR

The Pygmalion effect

Do teachers form expectations concerning behavior and achievement of students and tend to overestimate or underestimate their performance? Unfortunately, several empirical studies demonstrate the relationship between teacher expectation and evaluation of students. Studies on **physical attractiveness** of students have consistently shown that teachers tend to overestimate the cognitive abilities of physically attractive students. Clifford and Walster (1973) found a strong positive correlation between intelligence and physical attractiveness of children. Even students' clothing and their abilities as rated by their teachers showed a fairly high degree of correlation (Babad, Inbar & Rosenthal, 1982).

> **Pygmalion effect:** Changes taking place in the student due to expectations of others

Rosenthal (1976) is well known for his research on the **expectancy effect**. According to him, if people have an expectation for certain behavior, the probability of the occurrence of that behavior increases. As discussed earlier, this type of expectancy is referred to as the **self-fulfilling prophecy**, or the **Pygmalion effect**.

In a well known study by Rosenthal and Jacobson (1968) a test was administered in the classroom of elementary school children and the teachers were informed that the scores of a few students were outstanding. Actually, the scores of these students were in no way different from the scores of other average students. When the researchers assessed the performance of students at the end of the year, the performance of those average students who had been identified as "**bloomers**" actually improved. Teachers confirmed that these students really performed very well. How did this happen? Babad, Bernieri and Rosenthal (1991) investigated the cause of this effect by videotaping teachers while they talked to their students. In earlier studies (Harris & Rosenthal, 1986 & 1985; Cooper, 1983) too, attempts had been made to delineate the factors that contributed to this effect.

To sum up, the researchers concluded that a number of factors were responsible for the improvement in performance. **First,** the teachers were paying more attention to those who bloomed than to the other students. **Second,** the "bloomers" received a lot of encouragement. **Third,** teachers actually taught them more difficult material. **Fourth,** the "bloomers" were called more frequently and treated with respect. The overall impact of this treatment was that the "bloomers" felt more motivated and worked harder to live up to the expectations of their teacher. Surprisingly, most teachers were unaware of how they had influenced their students through their smile and nods. In fact, the results of the Babad and co-workers (1991) study clarified that those who viewed the tape showing teachers' facial expression and voice clearly recognized how much a teacher liked his/her student. It was also clear from the tapes that teachers tend to teach more difficult material to their "bright" students, put questions to them more frequently, and allow them more time to answer questions. In other words, the net effect of teachers' behavior under these conditions emerges as a self-fulfilling prophecy. Kieren and Gold (2000) concluded that this Pygmalion effect commonly took place in a wide variety of educational and work settings. Rosenthal (2002) called this type of effect "**covert communication**" and concluded that we see it not only in schools but in every place—the court room, the psychological research laboratory, the office and the hospital.

The above findings have very significant implications for children who are identified as **"disadvantaged" or slow learners**. Should we expect that the performance of such children would be affected because of the low expectations of teachers? Fortunately, Rosenthal (1991) concluded that teacher expectation effect was not found in all cases; only 4 out of 10 studies showed such an effect. In other words, while this effect can be helpful or harmful, depending on the nature of expectation of a teacher, there is a limit to what this effect can do to a student. It most certainly cannot make a bright student appear dull or *vice versa*. It has a limited effect and, if used properly, it can enhance the growth of a student.

SOCIAL LEARNING IN THE SCHOOL

While operant conditioning principles have been used as far back as in 610 AD (O'Leary & O'Leary, 1977), there is sufficient evidence to show that reinforcement may not always be necessary and that under certain circumstances it may even prove counter-productive (Lepper, 1981). Thus, whether operant reinforcement principles should or should not be used will depend on the **intrinsic nature of the material** to be learnt, **the students** and the **social situation** in which the learning is to take place. Activities that are intrinsically interesting may lose their appeal, if rewards become associated with them. Tokens should be used only when the activities are by themselves unappealing. In fact there are occasions when social learning principles prove much more efficacious and economical. The success of the Sesame Street TV program would vouch for that (Ball & Bogatz, 1972).

Operant conditioning principles: Use of positive and negative reinforcers for modifying behavior

BOX 10.1

Social learning in action: The effects of Sesame Street

Much has been said and done regarding the negative effects of TV violence on children. But how about its positive effects? Can children learn new intellectual skills from watching TV? It was to answer this question that a program named Sesame Street was introduced to American children in the late 1960s. The show aimed at improving the cognitive skills of pre-schoolers so as to make them mentally ready for schooling. Since only two out of every five children were found to attend pre-school, the program hoped to bring the educational message to a large proportion of children who normally have no pre-school education. The show used puppet characters Cookie monster, Ernie and Bert and their companions to catch the interest of the small children. However, woven into the serial, was a well-defined set of educational goals.

A study by Ball and Bogatz (1972) showed that the serial definitely achieved its aim. Using a four-group design, based on how often the children watched the program, the evaluation study revealed that children who watched Sesame Street showed marked improvements on a variety of cognitive skills. Of greater importance is the fact that the improvements increased with the amount of viewing of the program. The learning context also did not seem to matter, with the children watching the program at home or at school showing the same amount of gains. Finally the results were not restricted to the middle class; disadvantaged children who watched the program also showed the improvements. Another interesting finding: reading skills too improved, though it was not one of the skills specifically taught on Sesame Street!

How did the learning take place? Were the children being subjected to an interactive learning program? Was it an example of an online, learning program? Were children being specifically taught the academic skills? No, it was none of these. By the simple use of clever attention holding tactics and watching the puppet characters learn, the children picked up the skills. These results leave little doubt that children learn by observation and that TV can be an important educational tool.

Seeing the success of the Sesame Street, other countries have introduced similar programs. A program devised in Israel, entitled "**Rechov Sumsum/Shara's Simsim**" was specifically formulated to counter negative stereotypes of Palestinian children regarding Arabs and Jews. The program operates by building a peer-oriented context that introduces children to the everyday lives of people from different cultures. A pre-post test study by Cole and his colleagues (2002) demonstrated the efficacy of the program in the reduction of negative stereotypes. The exposure to the program also led to an increase in the use of prosocial justifications for conflict resolution by the children.

Almost half a century since the Sesame Street program was first aired, psychologists have come together to assess the worldwide impact of the program. A special issue of the journal, *Early Education & Development* (Vol, 13, 2002) focused on the **Sesame Workshop model.** Cole (2002) analyzed how the Sesame Workshop model created effective educational media in the United States, S. Africa, Egypt and China.

Attitudes and expectations o students

Do students learn more and behave differently when they expect their teacher to be exceptionally talented and interesting? In their studies, Feldman and co-workers demonstrated that students learned more and perceived their teacher to be competent and interesting when they were told in advance that their teacher was outstanding (Feldman & Proshaska, 1979; Feldman & Theiss, 1982). Further research by Jamieson (1987) showed that those students who receive positive information about their teacher tended to pay more attention to the lecture. This effect escalated to the teacher also, who, in turn, gave superior grades to the students and found them enthusiastic about the course material. Students also tend to form **first impressions** of teachers much as teachers form impressions of students. Ambady and Rosenthal (1993) attempted to study the extent to which thin slices of non-verbal behavior and physical attractiveness could predict teacher evaluations by students. The study clarified that video clips as short as 6-15 seconds each were long enough to predict the ways in which the students evaluated their teachers. In other words, students based their evaluations of the teachers on the basis of extremely short first impressions and did not change them even after a whole semester.

Student control o teac er e a ior

By applying the principles of **operant learning** used by teachers, children have been taught to **modify their teachers' behavior**. In one California class, 12-15 year old were taught to reward positive teacher behavior by smiling and making eye contact and sitting straight (Gray & co-workers, 1974). These findings were also confirmed by Bates (1975). In short, the attitudes and behavior of both teachers and students tend to influence each other. The impact of teachers on students is as important as the impact of students on their teachers.

The effect of teachers on their students and the students' impact on teachers can be minimized if they are **forewarned about the expectations** they have for the other. For instance, Snyder (1992) found out that self-fulfilling prophecies were noticed in certain experimental tasks but not in others. In one study, he created two tasks for his subjects. In one task he asked them to find out if the person talking to them over the phone was obese or not. The goal in the other task was "to get along well" with the person with whom they were conversing. The results of his study clearly showed that the self-fulfilling prophecy occurred when the experimental goal was to determine the kind of person the woman was (obese or not). In other words, when men expected women to be obese, their attitude changed. So did the attitude of women who was conversing with the man. However, no such effect was visible when the subjects simply conversed without any goal of diagnosing the other person.

From the result of the above-cited study by Snyder, it is clear that people tend to confirm their erroneous beliefs in their interaction with others. **Social expectations** lead us to behave in a particular way and may lead to behavioral confirmation if we attempt to confirm such expectations. Beliefs regarding bright or dull students, race, disability and character may become self-confirming if we construct social reality based on our expectations. Fortunately, as stated earlier, forewarning people about their erroneous expectation tends to mitigate any harmful effect.

SOCIAL PSYCHOLOGY AND THE CLASSROOM

A typical classroom in an American school involves individual work and very little interaction with fellow students. While students deal with their teacher directly, their interaction with fellow students remains a matter of their own choice. By and large, an American school is competitive in nature. From their grades to giving answers to questions put to them by their teacher, students try to demonstrate that they have superior skills than their competitors. In this type of **competitive setting**, one can identify the individual merit and motivation of a student in a classroom but for a weak student, this type of situation may lead to considerable discouragement and frustration. Kim's study (1990) of the Hawaiian children is a good example to show the effects of cooperative and competitive settings on them. Many children in the schools of Hawaii were found to be at a low level of academic achievement but whenever there was something that required attention, they demonstrated initiative and high performance. In other words, in a competitive individualistic classroom setting they performed poorly but as they worked together and made a group effort, their performance improved dramatically. Given the vast difference between competitive and cooperative settings, Kim worked closely with the teachers for the purpose of not assigning specific tasks to students. The students managed their schedule of work by dividing it among themselves into small groups. The net effect was dramatic. The achievement scores of students improved remarkably. However, this effect was lost no sooner did the very same students return to their regular classrooms.

Individualistic cultures promote competition. "Individualists," writes Triandis (1994), "think of themselves as autonomous, independent of groups and believe that it is okay to do what they want to do,...." (p. 4). On the other hand, in **collectivist cultures**, people are concerned about behaving appropriately and keeping their goals subordinate to the group. As a result, the consistency in the behavior of people in collective cultures is less apparent than those in the individualistic cultures. Imagine a classroom having a collection of students from individualistic (the Anglos) and collective cultures (the Latinos)—a scenario that is common these days in the schools of California. If we keep the method of instruction inflexible in such classrooms, the evil effects of competition will be in no way less visible as we find in an economy based on competition without any control.

On changing the traditional classroom

After the Supreme Court, USA, decision in the case of Brown *v*. Board of Education of Topeka (1954), the historical practice of keeping white and black students in separate schools was legally nullified but the attitudes and behavior of teachers and students in particular and the community in general needed change to cope with the new situation. Given the privileged status of schools where white students studied, a competitive classroom was definitely not the solution for the **desegregation** of schools. One of the issues raised during the court deliberations was that the self concept of black students was poor. There was optimism at that time in the sense that white students would accept black students in the same school. Several social scientists (Stephan, 1978; Allport, 1954) anticipated this type of change but the actual results brought disappointment.

Taylor and Moghaddam (1994) point to research that shows that simply forming desegregated schools may not be enough to promote positive inter-group relations, because inter-group contact may not be as prevalent as believed. A more effective desegregation process that has been advocated by school scientists, is the use of **cooperative learning situations** (Slavin & Madden, 1994). The term cooperative learning is used to refer to any instructional process where small groups of students work together to maximize each other's learning (Johnson & Johnson, 1994). Also known as **peer tutoring**, the concept has received widespread attention as a means of enhancing efficiency, of both the tutor and the tutee (Allen & Feldman, 1976). One of the main reasons for its success is the developmental similarity between the learner and the teacher and the ability of the peer teacher to appreciate the difficulties being faced by the learner.

Cooperative learning: An instructional process where small groups of students work to maximize each other's learning

Aronson and his associates (1978) attempted to find out a solution of the problem with what we now know as the **jigsaw technique**. The procedure involved creating a small group by dividing a class into groups of five or six students each. The students selected one part of a lesson that they practiced thoroughly and taught to the other members of a group. The main idea in this type of teamwork is to involve everyone to master a part of a lesson and then learn the whole lesson collectively. No matter how bright a student was he/she had to depend on fellow students to understand the parts of a lesson he/she was not assigned. In other words, the puzzle of learning a lesson will not be solved unless a student joins a **collective and cooperative endeavor of learning.**

Jigsaw technique: Creating a small groups of students who help each other to learn

The above technique yielded positive results with fifth grade students in which teachers volunteered to test the success of cooperative learning (Blaney & co-workers, 1977). The results were particularly encouraging as they showed enhanced self esteem of the participating students and their liking for each other. Bridgemann (1981), Gonzalez (1979) and others have also shown how the jigsaw technique is superior to traditional methods of instruction in enhancing **positive interracial attitudes, empathy** and **academic scores** of minority students. In subsequent studies, Aronson and associates (1983) applied their technique for mainstreaming **handicapped children** in regular classrooms. The basic idea of the jigsaw technique was found to work in any setting if the work involved interaction among the students to achieve the common goals. The outcome of this approach led to greater mutual attraction, self esteem and achievement in comparison to traditional methods of classroom learning.

deVries and Slavin (1978) used the cooperative learning approach in the form of peer tutoring. In their method of **Teams-Game-Tournament (TGT)** the teachers in the classroom created several teams and each team consisted of 4-5 members. Initially, the teacher introduced a topic and then instructed students in each group to help each other to learn the material. After one week, teams competed with each other. A bright student of a group faced a bright student of another group; a slow learner faced a slow learner of another group, and so on. In other words, this approach encouraged cooperation as well as competition to seek out the best in all types of students.

Except for the fact that the team approach fosters competition between groups, both the jigsaw technique and the team approach lay emphasis on cooperation among the students to achieve goals. Both approaches are based on two popular social psychological findings. The jigsaw technique sought inspiration from **Gordon Allport's work** (1954) on prejudice in which he identified three factors in reducing prejudice: **common goals, equal status,** and **sanction by authorities.** The team approach was inspired by **Sherif and Sherif's** (1953) research on **super-ordinate goals.** They demonstrated how higher level goals could lead to cooperation and minimize undesirable effects of competition.

Overall, the results indicate that cooperative learning can have positive effects on student achievement, self esteem and inter-group relations. Some **long-term gains** have been noted by Stevens & Slavin, (1995). After two years, students in the cooperative classrooms had significant higher achievement in reading, vocabulary, reading comprehension, language expression and mathematical computation. Moreover, the gains were consistent across normal, gifted and disabled children.

Hoping that greater use of cooperative goal structure in which a student will be allowed to achieve a goal only after all the students had completed their target would increase cooperation among students, Johnson and Johnson (1975) presented a flexible program of cooperative learning. They believe that given the structure of the traditional classroom, there is bound to be competition and the students are likely to suffer in some way. They designed their program with emphasis on the knowing of the resources of each other, having small groups, encouraging division of labor, and developing positive attitudes.

In their book, *Joining Together*, Johnson and Johnson (1997) have focused on issues of **group dynamics** in promoting cooperative endeavors. Borrowing from Lewin's concept of **force field analysis** in which a problem is considered as a balance between forces operating in opposite directions, they proposed, "The implementation of cooperative learning within a school may be seen as a balance between **forces helping teachers** implement cooperative learning and **restraining teachers** from using cooperative learning. The use of cooperative learning is promoted by the teachers' awareness that it will increase student achievement, higher level reasoning, social skills, self esteem, and social support. The use of cooperative learning is restrained by teachers habitually using other instructional procedures, not being willing to commit the time to learn how to use cooperative learning, inherent fear of change, lack of willingness to revise their standard lessons, and incomplete understanding of what cooperative learning is...." (p. 271, Johnson & Johnson, 1997). In order to implement cooperative learning, they suggested that helping and restraining forces that operate in a system should be analyzed as follows (Fig 10.2):

Figure 10.2: Use of force field analysis for developing cooperative forms of learning. (*Source:* Johnson & Johnson, 1997)

Helping Forces	Restraining Forces
increases in achievement	habit of *status quo*
higher level of reasoning	time needed to learn how
improved social skills	fear of change
increased self esteem	time to revise lessons
more social support	lack of understanding
liking for school	teacher isolation

– No Use   Current Level of Use   + Skilled Use

While cooperative learning is an ideal goal, the bottom line in any classroom is the **motivational level** of students. Without motivation, even the best known students are unable to perform satisfactorily. While McClleland's pioneering (1961) work on achievement was applied fruitfully in the area of industrial psychology a long time ago, its implications in the classroom setting remained in low profile for a long time. What should a social psychologist do to enhance the **achievement motivation** of a student? Following the guidelines from **McClleland's training program** for enhancing achievement motivation, Kolb (1965) worked with high school children who were underachievers. In the first place, the participants learned the characteristics of high achievers. When they participated in various games, they were asked to imagine the characteristics of high achievers and apply them in their game settings. In doing so, they relied on personal responsibility, took moderate risk, and conceived ideas to improve their output. The purpose of this study was to help students to identify with high achievers.

In his widely known studies, deCharms (1972, 1976) developed a personal training program for teachers with the contention that teachers should focus on internal motivation of students. He believed that teachers should provide opportunities to students to perceive themselves as **causal agents**, that is, **"Origins,"** and not merely as **"pawns."** In a three year study, deCharms found that those teachers assigned randomly in a personal causation training program scored higher in terms of their students' achievement motivation and realistic goal setting.

SOCIAL PSYCHOLOGY AND THE PROCESS OF CLASSROOM INSTRUCTION

Because of the multidimensional nature of programs in classrooms, linking teacher behavior to student achievement has remained controversial for a long time. According to Brophy (1986), research on the teacher's effect on students is well over five decades old but no clear results are being evidenced. Brophy suggested that there is a problem in separating the **teacher's effect** from the **teacher's effectiveness.** While issues of teacher effects are concerned with teachers' effect on students, teachers' effectiveness highlights "success in producing achievement gain.... What constitutes teacher effectiveness is a matter of definition, and most definitions include students' affective and personal development in addition to their curriculum mastery" (Brophy, 1986, p. 1069). The teacher effects, as distinct from teacher effectiveness, are known as process-product or process outcome research that focus on causal relationships between teachers' performance and student achievement. Strictly in this sense, according to Brophy (1986, p. 1070), **teachers' effects** can be measured using the following criteria:

- **"Amount learned is related to opportunity to learn, whether measured in pages of curriculum covered or percentage of test items taught...."**
- **"....teachers emphasize instruction as basic to their role...."**
- **"Such teachers are seen as businesslike and task oriented...."**
- **"....little time is spent getting organized or dealing with misconduct."**
- **"....success rates are especially desirable when students must work independently for extended periods without teacher supervision."**
- **"students achieve more in classes where they spend most of their time being taught or supervised by their teachers rather than working on their own or not working at all."**

The above approach is a **product-centered approach** without any significant human concern. Should a teacher ignore cultural ability, socio-economic and affective components in classrooms? What about the **role of praise** and other **incentives** in the classroom? Are there qualitative issues that need to be examined and addressed? Again, Brophy (*ibid*) provides some clear answers to measure teacher effects. First of all, issues like praise and other incentives must be dealt with, with caution. "One should not automatically construe," writes Brophy, "teacher praise as reinforcement" (p. 1072). He felt that praise would be more useful with dependent or anxious students than those who are confident. Public praise of students can be intrusive and distracting. In other words, judging teacher effectiveness through measures like praise may cause a lot of problems.

A study of teacher effects is not insensitive to cognitive and affective differences between students. For example, in order to accommodate low-achieving students, teachers need to provide more structure to them than to those who are high-achieving. It may mean a slower pace of instruction, a greater amount of feedback, an increased redundancy, and more reviews to low-achieving students. One social psychological factor that correlates with teacher effect is socio-economic status (SES). The following quote from Brophy illustrates this point:

> High-SES students are likely to be confident, eager to participate, and responsive to challenge. They want respect and require feedback but usually do not need frequent encouragement or praise. They thrive in an environment that is academically stimulating and somewhat demanding. Low-SES students are more likely to require warmth and support in addition to good instruction and to need more encouragement for their efforts and praise for their success.

SOCIAL PSYCHOLOGY, CHILD DEVELOPMENT AND EDUCATION: THE CASE OF HEAD START

The **Head Start program** in the USA was conceived during President Lyndon Johnson's War on Poverty in 1960s. It was noticed that among poor people, 50 per cent were children, mostly under 12 years in age. A significant number of these children were not ready for enrollment into kindergarten or the first grade. A need to develop a massive intervention program was felt so as to provide educational and developmental services to preschool children belonging to low-income families. To achieve this goal, the Head Start program was offered with **six components:**

- **Education at pre-school level.**
- **Physical health examination.**
- **Nutrition.**
- **Mental health services.**
- **Parental involvement.**
- **Social services.**

Commenting on the growth of Head Start program, Senator Nancy Kassenbaum (1994) wrote, "It has grown from providing a few hours of service to 5,00,000 children for six to eight weeks in the summer of 1965 to the 1,370 Head Start grantees (over 36,000 classrooms) providing comprehensive services for 7,21,000 children lasting at least a half day for 128 days a year. Federal appropriations for the program have increased from $96.4 million to 2.8 billion. More than 13 million children have been served by the Head Start Program since it began" (pp. 123-124).

Not surprisingly, Senator Kassenbaum further observed, "Few federal programs have been the subject of as much research and evaluation as the Head Start program. In 1985, the Head Start Synthesis and Utilization Project brought together over 200 different evaluations and research projects involving Head Start...." (p. 124, *ibid*). The program has grown substantially to accommodate changes that have taken place at the family and community levels. After enjoying unprecedented popularity for a number of years, the overoptimism for the program has begun to fade.

A **major goal of the program** was to prepare children to enter schools by improving their cognitive skills. Obviously, at the psychological level, it was expected that the **intelligence scores of children would rise** if the Head Start program offered them opportunities for enriched environment. This assumption was based on the belief that IQ scores would increase dramatically after children were exposed to improvised environment.

The success of the Perry Pre-school program demonstrated the great success of the Head Start program. In this program 123 Black children were divided into experimental and control groups. Their IQ scores ranged from 70 to 85 points. Children between 3-4 years of age received enriched cognitive instruction for one or two years. At the end of the program, pre-school children scored on an average, 11 points higher in IQ tests as compared to their counterparts in the control group. Based on such early results and success of the Head Start program, an expectation of at least 10 points gain in the IQ scores was targeted by the managers of the program (Zigler & Styfco, 1994). Unfortunately, the dramatic effect of early gains in IQ scores of children faded away within a few years. Note that a major setback to the success of the most elaborate program for child development came from no other source than the evaluations based on psychological measurements.

According to Zigler and Styfco (1994), "Head Start is probably the most extensively evaluated social program in American history..." (p. 129) and it could not tell us that "a year or two of early intervention can guarantee a high school diploma or end of poverty" (p. 127, *ibid*). In other words, how do we determine the worth of Head Start if it fails to accomplish a major psychological goal? Social psychologists have learned, albeit late, that the success of a program is judged not by a psychological yardstick alone. Programs are administered in communities and their success should not be tied to levels of statistical significance alone. Even if the target of a ten points gain in IQ fell short of its intended goal, the Head Start children improved their readiness for school. Additionally, parents learned how to stimulate their present and future children. Such unintended effects are valuable and they are discovered as evaluation research and social psychology seek to identify areas of practical importance.

VIOLENCE IN THE SCHOOL

We turn now to the **prevention of violence** within the school. Recent incidence of violence in American schools have drawn the attention of several psychologists (Mulvey & Cauffman, 2001). Schultz and Schultz (1996) found that in a large high school in Southern California,

6% of the students reported bringing a gun to school at least once in a year. Given these alarming statistics, what can social psychology do to reduce violence in general and specifically in schools? According to Mulvey and Cauffman (2001), you might be frustrated to know that it would not be easy to get clear answers. When people ask questions about raging violence at schools like Columbine, Padukah and elsewhere and why the problems of such magnitude were not detected earlier, we wonder if we had known before the incidence what to look for and where. It is easy to seek answers as a hindsight. Because of the publicity given to such gory violence in schools, we became overwhelmingly concerned, but the truth is that the National Crime Survey revealed that the rate of victimization in schools has remained steadily unchanged between 1989 through 1995 (Mulvey & Cauffman, 2001).

BOX 10.2

Bullying at school

A common form of aggression that escalates into several other problems in schools is bullying. The Webster's dictionary defines bully as a mean person. So, what we find with children who indulge in bullying behavior:

According to Norwegian psychologist, Olweus (1993), by the age 24, 60% had one conviction; and 40% had three or more convictions (Bullying at School: What we know and what we can do).

Summarizing the proceedings of the APA Convention, 2004, deAngelis (2004) wrote:

- **It is a common myth that bullying is associated with low self-esteem; instead it may create more confidence.**
- **A common treatment may backfire as it may escalate.**
- **In conflict resolution sessions, the victim may feel re-victimized.**
- **School administrators should consider changing norms as an effective solution.**

Preventing violence through social competence training

Social competence training: Interventions aimed at improving social skills of a person

Social competence training is a broad term used to denote interventions that are based on the assumption that people resort to violence when they lack the skills necessary to manage conflicts with others. Therefore, if a child learns how to assert needs, to express anger without hurting others, and to respond to the anger of others without violence, he or she will be less likely to use violence.

Does social skill training work? Some integrative reviews, for example, that by Johnson and Johnson (1996) and a metaanalysis, for example, by Beelman, Pfingsten and Losel (1994) show that these programs are successful in producing better adjustment and more positive social behavior. Another program, ACHIEVE (Knoff & Batsche, 1995), that focused on the conflict management skills of teachers rather than that of students, has been able to produce reduction in student disobedience, fighting, abusive behavior, and disrespectfulness, with gains lasting over a three year period. However, one has to accept the fact that the gains are dependent on the type of student, school atmosphere, skills of students and the skills of the teachers.

BOX 10.3

Social competence training in schools

There are many ways in which such skills are taught (Guerra and co-workers, 1994), and the programs differ in their emphasis on behavioral techniques, cognitive or social techniques. The common core of most of the interventions, for example, H.A.W.K. (High Achievement, Wisdom and Knowledge) and B.U.I.L.D. (Broader Urban Involvement and Leadership Development) and S.A.V.E. (Students Against Violence Everywhere) is apparently to reduce the frequency of violent behavior (Prothrow-Stith & Weissman, 1991).

The basic procedures used are:

- **Monitoring: students are taught to observe their own thoughts, feelings and behaviors.**
- **Modelling: students observe non-violent responses to a variety of provoking situations such as failure of responding to anger.**
- **Conflict resolution: students are taught to recognize the early signs of a conflict and how to avoid escalation.**
- **Role playing: students act out responses to a hypothetical conflict situation while others watch and evaluate.**
- **Peer mediation: students are trained to mediate and negotiate the successful resolution of conflicts.**

Conflict management in the school

Since conflicts are natural and inevitable, skills are required to constructively manage these situations. For the same reason, it is necessary that they be introduced as early as possible in the life of the child. From the early works of Sherif and Sherif on team building and conflict management using the children's camps, it has become increasingly clear that the school is an ideal place where such training can be imparted. In their earlier work, Johnson and Johnson (1989) integrated social psychological theory, research and practice and presented a hallmark of a truly applied social psychological approach to conflict management.

According to Deutsch (1994), **three** broad sets of skills are necessary for the development of **constructive approaches to conflict resolution**. These are the skills involved in:

- **Establishing a cooperative, problem solving relationship with the other person.**
- **Developing a creative process for expanding the option necessary for resolving the conflict.**
- **Taking an outsider or analytical perspective to the conflict.**

Implementation of a conflict management program in school

A typical program for implementing a **conflict management program** consists of several stages (See Johnson & Johnson, 1997; 1994). Students are assigned to groups of four and then divided into pairs. Each pair is to research and present to the other pair their assigned position on the topic. The group must reach a consensus on the topic, and present a group report on which the students are evaluated. What are the students told to do? **Firstly**, they must be critical of ideas, not people. **Secondly**, they must focus on the best possible solution and not on winning. **Thirdly**, they have to encourage every one to participate. **Fourthly**, they are told to listen to everyone's ideas, even if they do not agree. **Fifthly**, they must try to understand both sides of the issue. Lastly, they are encouraged to change their mind if the arguments are convincing. Once the controversy is completed, there is a group processing of the experience with an emphasis on the skills involved in this constructive process.

The next step is **negotiation** and **peer mediation**. Essentially students are taught how to develop agreements to their conflicts so as to obtain a win-win solution. The procedure is as follows:

- **State what you want.**
- **State how you feel.**
- **State the reasons for your wants and feelings.**
- **Summarize your understandings of what the other person wants, how the other person feels and the reasons underlying both.**
- **Invent three optional plans for resolving the conflict.**
- **Choose one and shake hands.**

The preliminary evidence for their programs on children's conflict resolution behavior is promising (Johnson, Johnson Dudley & Acikgoz, 1994). In sum, based on an understanding of the social psychological processes involved in constructive and destructive conflict management, one can develop programs even for children. Such training has an impact not only on the handling of a specific dispute but also on the quality of relationships and personal achievements.

As we mentioned earlier, the issue of school violence is not easy to address. In their research, Mulvey and Cauffman (2001) contended that there are **three ways** in which the problems of school violence could be understood and also dealt with. An effective source of understanding the school violence is the children who are aware of the problem. However, in this regard false positives can do more harm than good. Second, children should develop a sense of belongingness and schools should do a lot more to promote it. And third, children should feel a positive connection with the school. Their commitment to the school is related to their belief in fairness that they form in interacting with the students, teachers and administrators. If a school remains active with respect to the above approaches, the incidence of violence could be minimized but may not be fully mitigated. There are societal issues that are broader than a school that operates as a subculture within the larger context of a community.

SOCIAL PSYCHOLOGY OF STRESS IN STUDENTS

Causes of stress among students

Issues concerning stress were addressed in the two chapters on health. In her book, *Stress in Life and at Work*, Agrawal (2001) reported that stress would be a major concern during the 21st century and its health consequences and economic cost would increase. With regard to children, Weissberg, Kumpfer and Seligman (2001) opined that the problem would be extremely serious. Dual career parents, divorce, single parenting, change in quality of interaction in family and other variables have changed the conditions in which children are being raised. They contended that one out of five children and adolescents experience mental health problems in a year that needed professional help but 75% to 80% never receive any help. Among 14 to 17 year old adolescents, 30% are at high risk; 35% at medium risk; and 35% with no involvement but need support.

Through their survey, Kouzma and Kennedy (2004) identified the following principal stressors:

- Examinations and their outcomes.
- Too much to do.
- Worry over future.
- Making choices about career.
- Studying for examinations.
- Amount to learn.
- Need to do well imposed by others.
- Self-imposed need to do well.

BOX 10.4

Stress among college students—1,100 suicides among college students: *Newsweek*, August 23, 2004

- American College Health Association reported that 40% students felt depressed and felt dysfunctional at least once in a year; 30% were suffering from anxiety or depression. Harvard University newspaper, Crimson, reported that an overwhelming majority of college students are suffering from mental health problems.
- Four New York University Students fell to death from high-rise buildings.
- MIT is recruiting emotionally resilient students.
- Wellness! hotline is used in many colleges.

Alexander Astin (1997), Director of Higher Education Research Institute at the University of California, Los Angeles, also studied the stress levels of college freshman and found that although the confidence level of college students had increased, the high cost of education, grades, and competition were causing greater stress among them than ever before. According to him, emotional health has become a serious threat for the students in the class of 2000. Paradoxically, with high confidence comes high self esteem but with greater capability, it seems that most students are becoming Type-A personalities, that is, with a greater drive but with more risk to health too. Students seem to be over-committing themselves, stretching themselves beyond their limits.

Astin's survey also showed that female college "freshmen" now are showing more frequent depression than those a decade ago, that is, 1/8 now against 1/10 a decade ago. There is a change among male college freshmen as well, that is, from 6% a decade ago to 7.4% at present. Cigarette smoking has also increased probably due to stress.

Some respite in stress is coming through grade inflation. In comparison to 1969 when A averages were only 12.5%, 31.5% reported earning A in their high school. Again, it is an additional incentive to become competitive and be Type A. Volunteerism has increased substantially not because students have become more altruistic but because it increases chances of getting a job or admission in a program. Yet, Astin's survey also showed that female college freshmen now are showing more frequent depression than those a decade ago, that is, 1/8 now against 1/10 a decade ago. There is a change among male college freshman as well, that is, from 6% a decade ago to 7.4% at present.

Similar findings have been reported in Singapore where **examinations** are a **common source of stress** (Parker & co-workers, 2003). However, only some children manifested its negative impacts. Those children whose parents were extremely compliant as far as examination results are considered and were monitoring them regularly were stressed by examination results. In other words, it is the **parental anxiety** that is causing **spillover effects** on the children. Such spillover effects were also noticeable in a study on the parents of children in the Head Start program; it was found that those parents who had an unmet need for mental health services tended to report more problem behavior among their offspring (Razzino & co-workers, 2003). When freshman athletes in Greece were researched upon, it was again clear that academic and social stressors along with the factor of poor coping mechanisms caused low academic grades among these athletes. These low grades further exacerbated the stress in a cyclical manner, the end result being that the athletes were not able to excel in either sports or academics (Papanikolaou & co-workers, 2003).

Stress in immigrant and international students

With the doors of universities the world over becoming more and more in favor of attracting students from different parts of the globe, we are seeing an ever increasing trend of people studying in a foreign country. While studying abroad provides both academic and social advantages to the students, it does not come without a cost. The major cost is the **acculturation shock**. Some recent literature from around the world shows how stressful studying abroad can be. There are a large number of **Asian students** studying in **American universities**. Some of the stressors reported by Asian women were the American university life itself, homesickness, language problems and academic/social stressors (Carr & co-workers, 2003). Chen and co-workers (2002) also reported that **East Asian students** felt considerably stressed in the US. There has been research on immigrant students to other countries too. In a study, both **Yugoslavian and Chinese** students in **Australia** were compared on adjustment patterns, and both showed stress but there were clear differences between the two groups. The Yugoslavians manifested greater integration with the Australian culture and norms than the Chinese, though variables such as age, gender and length of stay were also important (Sonderegger & Barrett, 2004). We discussed the concept of Bicultural Identity Integration in the chapter on aggression, and how people who show greater BII are able to alternate between differing cultural norms.

Coping strategies used by students

An important factor that emerges from the study of **coping processes** among students is that students from different cultural backgrounds tend to use differing ways of coping. When American students were compared with Spanish college students, there were mean differences in the level of stress, but not only also in differences in the coping process being employed (Connor-Smith & co-workers, 2004). Some of these differences could be mediated by the nature of the **self construals** being used by the students from differing cultures. It has been generally seen, that people from **collectivist cultures** exhibit a more **interdependent self construal** while those from **individualistic cultures** exhibit greater **independence in their self construal**. These differences in interdependent and independent self construals have been found to moderate the nature of the coping process. Those with an independent self construal used more primary control processes of coping while those with an interdependent self construal use more of secondary coping processes (Lam & Zane, 2004). Even in the same culture, **gifted children** tended to possess superior coping strategies: they tended to use problem-solving coping to a greater extent than the nongifted (Preuss & Dubow, 2004). Moreover, the nature of the coping used tends to determine the type of outcome for the student. When the relationship between coping strategy and outcomes of stressors was studied among Navajo adolescents, control and engagement types of coping led to less depression than the involuntary disengagement type of coping (Wadsworth & co-workers, 2004). In other words, **coping** among students seems to be a function of both **cultural and individual variables**. This would have important implications for any intervention program being designed to improve the coping with stress by the youth.

Stress and early life experiences

So important is the effect of early life experiences that McEwen (2003) concluded that children coming from what he calls **"risky families"** (that is, families characterized by aggression, lack of warmth and under/over regulation) were characterized by specific disorders in later life. Among **Turkish** immigrant children too, those children who were not living with both parents, or there had been a serious illness, death or remarriage in the family reported more emotional and behavioral problems (Murad & co-workers, 2004). Similar were the conclusions by Kinyanda and co-workers (2004) for youth in **Uganda**: those who attempted deliberate self harm were more likely to have disturbed interpersonal relationships, to come from poorer home backgrounds and to be experiencing loneliness. In contrast, junior high school students with positive life satisfaction were less likely to develop symptoms of stress in later life (Suldo & Huebner, 2004). Even among pre-schoolers in **Spain**, family influences were reported as the cause of somatic symptoms (Domenech-Llaberia & co-workers, 2004). So whether it is in the highly developed countries, the developing countries or the underdeveloped countries, families play an important role in creating or exacerbating stress among children and youth.

Stress and individual factors

There are some individual factors, too, that go a long way in causing stress to the student. One of these is **personality**. While people coming from one type of culture would have problems acculturating to another type of culture (for example, a person from a collectivist culture moving into an individualist culture and *vice versa*), there were problems for people even in their natural culture. Scott and co-workers (2004) discussed the problems of students with a strong **individualist personality** even in an individualist culture. Based on a study of 276 students attending an Australian university, they found that those who were very high on individualism had their own problems. These idiocentric youth were found to have less satisfying social support networks, lower intentions of seeking help from friends or family members and to be less skilled in managing self and others' emotions. Consequently, they suffered from higher levels of hopelessness and suicide ideation.

Another person variable was seen to be **anger,** which along with **resentment and anxiety,** was found to mediate the effects of interpersonal strain on violence and delinquency in **China** (Bao & co-workers, 2004). Age and gender differences are also noticeable. Stress in five to ten year olds in **Germany** (N = 1699) varied as a function of age, gender, grade and illness, with stress symptoms increasing with age, and grade. Also, girls were more stressful than the boys (Lohaus & co-workers, 2004).

Interventions for stress among students

No intervention can be designed without **systematic assessment** of the phenomenon and its antecedents. For a long time, the lack of scales specifically constructed for use with children and youth was prominent by its absence. The past few years have seen a considerable improvement with the **construction of many new scales** in different parts of the world. To name just a few, we have a scale constructed for Japanese children (Takata & Sakata, 2004); a Dutch translation of the Rothbert scale for children 3-7 years of age (Van den Bergh & co-workers, 2003); and a scale used for a comparative study of children in the US and Turkey (Sefa & Solmaz, 2003).

While there are innumerable ways for reducing stress, how should a program for students be designed? One way in which social psychology can help is by providing insights regarding the major causes of stress among students. Once we know what these causes are, we can design programs that would help mitigate the effects of these causes.

One **major cause** is **acculturation stress** among foreign students and students from other minority communities. Keeping the specific needs of immigrant and foreign students in mind is an important task for any educational institute that has a multi-cultural student population. It has generally been noticed that students from other countries are not able to take advantage of the counseling services available in the American universities because they are based on American values. Carr and co-workers (2003) describe how one American university overcame this problem. They started a women-counseling center for Asian students in the US. This center provided a **culturally sensitive environment** where women could meet and socialize with other Asian women, and talk about the issues that concerned them. It was noted that such group treatment methods were more effective than individual counseling sessions. Similarly, Jones (2004) describes an 8-week psycho-educational program **group intervention** for building psycho-social competence and the consequent reduction of stress among Black women in a US college. One cause of stress among foreign students is the lack of **social support systems.** The International Students Office was found to provide one more channel for social support (Chen & co-workers, 2002).

SOCIAL PSYCHOLOGY OF SPECIAL EDUCATION

Inclusionary education

Special education is not just about imparting education to children with special needs. It has also to take into consideration what will be the impact of schooling on the life and personality of such children. This is where insights from social psychology can be of use.

For decades together, in fact for centuries, children with special needs were educated in special schools catering to the special needs of these students. The general findings were that though the children became academically able, they were at a great social disadvantage because they did not know how to interact with people in the world at large. Bowlby (1980) advocated that institutionalization has a number of psychological drawbacks. Children brought up in homes and institutions, segregated from the rest of the world developed into what he called "affectionless creatures" unable to develop bonds of attachment even as adults. Another finding has been that people who were not mentally or physically challenged developed stereotypical conceptions regarding challenged people, with discrimination and a lack of understanding as the end result. One way of overcoming these negative consequences of segregated education and living was to mainstream children with special needs into the general schools. Greater contact with people with disabilities would also go a long way in the reduction of stereotypical images normally held by those who are not challenged. It would also help **reduce the stigma** attached to mental and physical disabilities. This was what started the idea of what today is better known as **inclusionary education.**

Goals of inclusionary education

According to Resman (2003), the **primary goal** is to educate people how to respect **peaceful cohabitation.** It also aims at the development of certain **core values** such as **understanding, tolerance and mutual respect.** While it has been comparatively easy to take policy decisions regarding inclusion at schools, implementing these policies has not been without problems. One major problem is whether every child who has a special need can and should be integrated into a normal school. Another problem is whether the teachers and the other pupils will accept the child with special needs. And last but not the least is the problem of funding and finding extra resources for inclusion of special needs children into the mainstream.

Developing a new nomenclature

One of the first steps towards inclusion was the attempt to remove the stigma attached to mental and physical disabilities. This was primarily achieved by developing a whole new system of terms; that is, the removal of terms considered disparaging to more neutral terms. We therefore started talking of people with disability and not disabled people. Then there was another shift: referring to them as people with special needs, and finally to calling them mentally and physically challenged. Similar was the change in names given to different classes of mental retardation. We have come a long way from the times in which the mentally retarded were referred to as the idiot savant, today differentiating between them only on the basis of severity (the severely, moderately and mildly mentally retarded). This trend is similar to the efforts in mitigating racial prejudices, for example, instead of saying colored people, we say, people of color.

Changing attitudes

The set of people that need to be first prepared to accept inclusion are the policy makers in the schools, that is, the **school principals and administrators.** So important has this become that **scales** have been constructed to measure the attitudes of school administrators towards inclusion. One such scale has been constructed for use in Australia, and has been found to be sufficiently reliable and valid (Bailey, 2004). In the Arab world too it has been found important to determine the attitude of educators and administrators towards people with disabilities, before working out the via media for inclusionary education. In a recent study (Alghazo & co-workers, 2003), both educators and administrators were found to have an overall negative attitude, for which corrective measures needed to be devised. Barriers to inclusion exist in other countries too: for example, in Vietnam (Villa & co-workers, 2003), Slovakia (Bronisova & Ucen, 2002), Russia (Agran, 2003), Hong Kong (Poon-McBrayer, 2003), etc. A large amount of literature on how to make inclusionary education more successful also implies that negative attitudes exist in other countries too and it apparently cuts across cultural barriers. Even in Russia, the majority of the respondents in a survey were knowledgeable about inclusionary practices in the US and Western Europe. While they were supportive of the idea, they also felt that segregated education was probably more beneficial for children with special needs (Agran, 2003). Similarly, when Moberg (2003) compared teachers in Zambia with those in Finland, he found that the factorial structure of attitudes towards inclusionary education (obtained through factor analysis) was the same in both the countries. Four factors were isolated, that is, social justice, meeting special needs of students with severe disabilities, teachers' competence, and quality of education for non-disabled students. At the same time, while the attitudes of the Zambian teachers were more critical, the Finnish teachers too perceived inclusion as leading to problems and the majority preferred segregated education.

Why do teachers and pupils tend to have **negative attitudes towards mainstreaming**? There are a number of reasons. One important reason is that the child with special needs requires special attention which detracts from the amount of attention that the teacher is able to give to those children who do not have special needs. This is especially so when children with learning and other intellectual problems are included in schools for non-special needs students. An example for the above is the findings of Engelbrecht and co-workers (2003) that in S. Africa the inclusion of pupils with intellectual deficits produces **more stress among teachers** than that due to children with physical problems. Another survey on teachers in Hong Kong revealed that there is a hierarchy of preference among teachers towards special children: those with learning disorders pose more challenges than the physically disabled (Pearson & co-workers, 2003). Type and severity of disability affected the preferred educational setting and there were clear differences in this regard between teacher respondents from two countries as diverse as Zambia and Finland (Moberg, 2003). There is a very plausible reason for the fear of having to teach children with intellectual deficits. General findings in the area of special education show that such children require a teacher not only with a different set of qualifications but also with a different type of temperament, characterized with greater patience and tolerance.

While teachers and their attitudes are crucial for the success of any inclusionary program, no less important is the **attitude of the parents** and that of **other pupils**. Thus, the decision to start such a program should be taken only after full preparation. Not only has this been found true for Slovenia (Resman, 2003), but also for Denmark (Nielsen, 2003). When parents of typically developing children were interviewed in Greece regarding how they would react if children with special needs were included in the same school, it was clear that the parents were generally positively oriented, with those who had had greater contact with special children being more positive towards inclusion (Tafa & Manolitsis, 2003).

BOX 10.5

Inclusionary practices in a few developing countries

Costa Rica (Stough, 2003): while special education has been there in the country for 60 years, it is only in the last five years that we see major paradigm shifts considered as the first step towards inclusion. Firstly, the Department of Special Education has developed a pragmatic educational classification system that describes the level of modifications required by students with disabilities, rather than one that is driven by their diagnostic label. Secondly, four educational service models have been developed to extend special education expertise. These are consulting teachers, educational assistance teams, itinerant teams, and resource centers, through which the country will be able to provide a more equitable distribution of special education professionals throughout the country.

China (McCabe, 2003): there has been considerable reform in special education as of 1978. Since that time, there have been efforts to include children with disabilities in general education classrooms. There has also been considerable initiative on the part of the government with national projects and local examples of children with disabilities, including children with autism, being included in public schools and educated in general education classrooms.

Vietnam (Villa & co-workers, 2003): it has been more than a decade since inclusionary practices were begun in Vietnam. The Ministry of Education and Training implemented a number of inclusion projects at the national level.

Meyer (2003) has attempted to extrapolate from the above studies on Vietnam, China and Costa Rica to provide some general guidelines regarding the greater efficacy of the delivery of education. She points out that we should read these articles through a different perspective, that is, to draw insights regarding how to deal with people the world over, including those without disabilities.

Interventions for attitude change

What are some of the methods that have been singled out for **change in attitudes** towards inclusion? What should be the components requiring attention? MacPherson-Court and co-workers (2003) carried out a survey on teacher trainees to assess necessary modifications and additions to the teacher training curriculum. Some of the aspects that the respondents felt strongly about were **classroom management, instructional planning** and **behavior management and collaboration skill.** Over and above, the general methods used for any type of attitude change, some very specific techniques have also been developed. For example, Campbell, Gilmore and Cuskally (2003) describe a technique that had been successfully used in **Australia.** They combined **structured field work** experiences with **information** based instruction to change attitudes of student teachers towards children with **Down's syndrome.** The student teachers at the end of a one semester unit were seen to have more knowledge about Down's syndrome. Further there was a clear change in attitudes. The participants became more positive towards the inclusion of children with Down's syndrome, towards children with disability in general and they also had greater ease in interacting with people with disabilities. Another innovative technique is **interactional ethnography**: the process of engaging in structured conversations and the analysis of the effects of that conversation on the change in attitudes (Cutter & co-workers, 2002).

Other pupils of the school also need to be educated regarding the needs of special children. This helps them to accept such children in the classroom and also to develop more **positive attitudes** towards them. Flem and co-workers (2004) give us a very interesting account of inclusive education in practice. This is the account of how one teacher managed to include special children in a normal classroom in Norway. The main themes that she worked on were the **cognitive learning process**, the **social learning process** and the **collaborative process**. Buysse (2003) describes how teachers in one school helped **inculcate friendships** among students and so change their attitudes towards children with special needs. Besides the teacher, schools that employ teacher assistants would find these assistants to be very helpful in making inclusion a success. Hill (2003) describes how teaching assistants were able to help in a Canadian school.

BOX 10.6

The role of individual teachers in inclusion at school

Doyle (2003) describes how the attempts of one single teacher can change the entire social climate of the school. This article describes how establishing a nurture group in a challenging infant school had a profound effect on the development of the school as a whole. Since May, 2000, the nurture group has been the hub of an evolutionary process, which the author was able to experience at first hand as the nurture group teacher. Under her guidance, all mainstream classrooms became increasingly nurturing and the impact of the nurture group practices became entrenched in the policies and practices of the whole school. This has had a significant, positive impact for a number of the most vulnerable pupils with social, emotional and behavioral difficulties and their mainstream peers. The mainstream application of these principles supported the school's evolution from special measures in 1997 to its current position, representing good value for money and was very effective in helping pupils with special educational needs.

Impact of inclusion

We have been focusing on how teachers, parents and other children react to inclusion. But what about its effects on the children who are being included? Do they stand to gain? To assess the **self concept and self esteem of children with special needs** after being integrated into a regular school, 97 students with special needs, from a school in **Spain**, served as the sample. Using a **sociometric analysis**, the results indicated that the special needs students have a **positive self concept** although it was significantly lower than that of their counterparts, especially on the social and academic dimensions. In addition, the study highlighted the **interrelationship between peer group perception and the self concept in the special needs students**. The authors pointed out that while school integration is a necessary condition for facilitating social integration and for the improvement of their self concept, it was not in itself always sufficient for optimization of both these aspects of socio-affective development

(Cambra & Silvestra, 2003). One way to enhance social skills and self esteem among students who are deficient on this aspect has been outlined by Ikeya and co-workers (2003). A **peer support program** was developed in **Japan,** based on experiences drawn from **games and role playing.** Third and sixth graders took part in an eight hour program after which it was found that there was a significant increase in self evaluation, self esteem and social skill scores. The implementation of such programs is not without problems. Onodera and co-workers (2003) analyzed some of the problems faced by schools that want to implement a program for the development of personal relationship skills in Japan.

What should be the long-term goal of special education? According to some special educators, for example, Renzaglia and his colleagues (2003), it should be to promote a lifetime of inclusion. Rather than working at just inclusionary practices in school, we need to focus on how to include people with mental and physical challenges in every aspect of life. We therefore work on integrating such individuals into society and not just in school. This requires firstly, the establishment of the concept of normalization as the philosophical basis for inclusion. We then need to establish principles and conditions that will foster normalization throughout the lifespan. Lastly, we need to think of normalization as a continuum along which all people, regardless of disability level, can successfully move up to more inclusive environments (Renzaglia & co-workers, 2003).

SOCIAL PSYCHOLOGICAL IMPLICATIONS OF E-LEARNING

The effects of technology in general and effects of computers and automation were discussed in particular in the chapter on technology. In this section we will focus on the 21st century classroom and its psycho-social dynamics. Now we have online teaching, online examinations, and online universities. No wonder, we have come a long way from the Skinnerian concept of programmed learning. With the advent of portable telephones, mobiles, computers, modems, faxes and other forms of digital media, new avenues are opening up for

BOX 10.7
Computers in Schools

Nine out of ten schools in the UK are now online, as compared to just over 1 in 10 in 1996. There is now one computer for roughly 8 pupils in secondary schools and one for every 12 in primary schools. Teachers in one British school can log on in each classroom, project their work onto screens and take the same computer home at the end of the day to prepare the next days lessons. The result—the school has been able to build up a huge bank of model lessons that can be re-used, updated or given to students who have missed classes. Research carried out in Durham reveals that computers enable pupils to access learning in a more efficient way than books or even educational TV (Brace, 2001). Moving to higher education, a large number of professional colleges and renowned universities are offering courses on-line, the idea being to enable people to access learning modules and take examinations from their homes and at their convenience rather than enroll for regular classroom teaching. Managerial training too has moved with the times. The well known "in-basket" game (developed by AT&T now has an e-mail version developed by Cubiks, on the basis that the latter provides a truer reflection of modern business practice (*TOI*, May 21, 2001).

students. How will they use these new media will determine in part the kinds of problems that may arise. Kiesler, Siegel and Mcguire (1984) first brought this issue to psychology's attention almost two decades ago, but social psychologists were slow to assess the impact of e-media.

The computer is fast becoming a second communication system for many people in our rapidly changing society. In fact, children the world over are not only becoming computer literate but more tech savvy than even their teachers. This is only one of the many issues that need to be addressed. Effective incorporation of computer revolution in instruction is an area to which the psychologist can contribute substantially (Schofield, 1995).

While everyone, from governments to educators and trainers and even parents, realize the convenience of electronically enabled learning, one has to think of the physical and **psychological costs** attached. Adults and children alike are found to be suffering from **tendinitis,** often so severe that people thereafter have trouble filling in even half page forms or turn the doorknobs of rooms. A recent study by the National Research Council's Institute of Medicine estimates that US business loses at least $45 billion each year in compensation costs, lost wages and productivity because of **musculo-skeletal problems** caused by overuse of the computer. At Cornell University, Allen Hedge studied children's postures as they use the PCs. About 1/2 to 2/3 of middle and high school children report some **pain or discomfort** after using the machine. **Hand blisters** and injuries have been noted in children due to moving the joystick too rapidly in Nintendo-type games. In Austria too, when students who used laptops were compared to those who don't, it was found that the former suffered from **physical discomfort** in the arms (Trimmel & co-workers, 2004). However, the same researchers also found that though there were costs involved, there was also an important upside to the use of laptops by the students. They had better spatial skills and were higher on competitive skills, participation, learning interest, motivation and pressure to perform.

These physical problems due to prolonged computer use are just the tip of the proverbial iceberg. The **psycho-social impacts** of e-learning are even greater. Confined to their homes or individual work stations, the **role of the peer group** is diminished. Traditionally, time spent with the peer group increases with the age of the child. As a result, time spent with adults decreases. Such interaction serves several important social functions. Play serves in developing competence of children by facilitating cognitive development and gaining mastery over the environment. Secondly, it provides critical opportunities to acquire social competencies (Hartup, 1983). And finally, it provides opportunity for emotional development (Singer, 1977). As the child grows older, peers serve at least three purposes: as reinforcers, as models and for social comparison purposes (Hetherington & Parke, 1986). Unfortunately, such interactive opportunities are narrowing more than ever before in the growth of children. As discussed in the chapter on technology, e-communication has even changed the adults lives.

Summary

The chapter began with social psychological issues that are related to socialization of children in school and the role the teacher plays in influencing the behavior of children. Social psychological factors such as the self-fulfilling prophecy, attitudes, cooperative learning, and stress were presented. A brief description of violence in schools was also presented and the material in this chapter supplemented the chapter on aggression and non-violence. The next part of the chapter referred to the issues related to the social psychology of special education. Finally, the impact of e-education was also examined in the context of learning in school.

Suggestions for Further Reading

Li, J. (2003). US and Chinese cultural beliefs about learning. *Journal of Educational Psychology,* 95, 258-267.

Rosenthal, R. (2002). Covert communication in classrooms, clinics, courtrooms and cubicles. *American Psychologist*, 57, 839-849.

Torney-Purta, J. (2002). The school's role in developing civic engagement: A study of adolescents in 28 countries. *Applied Developmental Science*, 6, 203-212.

Some Key Terms

Academic controversy
Confucian approach
Cooperative learning
Disposition to school education
E-learning
Inclusionary education
Jigsaw technique
Mainstreaming
Operant conditioning principles
Peer tutoring
Pygmalion effect
Sapir-Whorf hypothesis
Social competence training
Socratic approach
Systems approach to education

REFERENCES

Abbot, N.C., Harkness, E.F., Stevinson, C., Marshall, F.P., Conn, D.A. & Ernst, E. (2001). Spiritual healing as a therapy for chronic pain: A randomized clinical trial. *Pain,* 91, 79-89.

Abraham, M.M. & Lodish, L.M. (1990, May/June). Getting the most out of advertising and promotion. *Harvard Business Review,* 50-60.

Abramson, L.Y., Seligman, M.E. & Teasdale, J.D. (1978). Learned helplessness in humans: An attributional analysis. *The Journal of Abnormal Psychology*, 87, 49-74.

Adair, W.L., Okumura, T. & Brett, J.M. (2001). Negotiation behavior when cultures collide: The United States and Japan. *Journal of Applied Psychology*, 86, 371-385.

Adams, J.S. (1965). Inequity in social exchange. In L. Berkowitz (Ed.), *Advances in Experimental Social Psychology,* 2. New York: Academic Press.

Adler, T. (1991, December). *American Psychological Association Monitor.*

Adorno, T.W., Frankel-Brunswick, E., Levinson, D.J. & Sanford, R.W. (1950). *The Authoritarian Personality*. New York: Harper Press.

Agran, M. & Boykov, D. (2003). A preliminary survey of professional and student opinion of special education practice in contemporary Russia. *Research & Practice for Persons with Severe Disabilities*, 28, 91-100.

Agrawal, R. (1999). Should individuals with visual impairment be stressful: Some theoretical and empirical answers. In D.M. Pestonjee, U. Pareek & R. Agrawal (Eds.), *Studies in Stress and its Management*. New Delhi: Oxford-IBH, 199-218.

Agrawal, R. (2001). *Stress in Life and at Work*. New Delhi: Response Books.

Agruse, J.F. (1997). An exploratory study of the social and psychological factors affecting water and energy consumption by hotel guests. *Dissertation Abstracts International, Section A: Humanities and Social Sciences*, 57, 594.

Ahmadi, J. & Yazdanfar, F. (2002). Substance use among Iranian university students. *International Journal of Drug Policy,* 13, 507-508.

Ahmed, S.M. (2001). Differing health and health seeking behavior: Ethnic minorities of the Chittagong Hill Tracts, Bangladesh. *Asia-Pacific Journal of Public Health*, 13, 100-108.

Ahuvia, A.C. (2002). Individualism/collectivism and cultures of happiness: A theoretical conjecture on the relationship between consumption, culture and subjective well being at the national level. *Journal of Happiness Studies*, 3, 23-36.

Ai, A.L., Peterson, C. & Huang, B. (2003). The effect of religious spiritual coping on positive attitudes of adult Muslim refugees from Kosovo and Bosnia. *International Journal for the Psychology of Religion*, 13, 29-47.

Ajzen, I. & Fishbein, M. (1980). *Understanding Attitudes and Predicting Social Behavior.* Englewood Cliffs, NJ: Prentice-Hall.

Ajzen, I. (1991). The theory of planned behavior. *Organizational Behavior and Human Decision Processes*, 50, 179-211.

Al-Adawi, S., Dorvio, A.S.S., Burke, D.T., Moosa, S. & Al-Bahlani, S. (2002). A survey of anorexia nervosa using the Arabic version of the EAT-26 and "gold standard" interviews among Omani adolescents. *Eating and Weight Disorders,* 7, 304-311.

Alghazo, E.M., Dodeen, H. & Algaryouti, I.A. (2003). Attitudes of pre-service teachers towards persons with disabilities: Predicting for the success of inclusion. *College Student Journal*, 37, 515-522.

Al-Kodmany, K. (2000). Women's visual privacy in traditional and modern neighbourhoods in Damascus. *Journal of Architectural and Planning Research*, 17, 283-303.

Allen, V.L. & Feldman, R.S. (1976). *Children as Teachers: Theory and Research on Tutoring.* New York: Academic Press.

Allport, F.M. (1924). *Social Psychology*. Boston: Houghton Mifflin.

Allport, G. (1954). *The Nature of Prejudice*. Reading MA: Addison Wesley.

Allport, G.W. & Ross, J.M. (1967). Personal religious orientation and prejudice. *Journal of Personality and Social Psychology*, 5, 432-443.

Allport, G.W. (1960). *Personality and Social Encounters*. Boston: Beacon Press.

Allport, G.W. (1966). The religious context of prejudice. *Journal of the Scientific Study of Religion*, 5, 447-457.

Altemeyer, B. (2003). Why do religious fundamentalists tend to be prejudiced? *International Journal for the Psychology of Religion*, 13, 17-28.

Altman, I. & Haythorn, W.W. (1967). The ecology of isolated groups. *Behavioral Science,* 32, 169-182.

Altman, I. & Low, S. (Eds.)(1992). *Place Attachment*. New York: Plenum.

Altman, I. & Gauvain, M. (1981). A cross-cultural dialectic analysis of homes. In L. Liben, A. Patterson & N. Newcombe (Eds.), *Spatial Representation of Behavior across the Life Span*. New York: Academic.

Amaro, H. (1995). Love, sex and power. *American Psychologist*, 6, 437-447.

Ambady, N. & Rosenthal, R. (1993). Half a minute: Predicting teacher evaluations from thin slices of non-verbal behavior and teacher attractiveness. *Journal of Personality and Social Psychology*, 64, 431-441.

Ambrose, M.L., Seabright, M.A. & Schminke, M. (2002). Sabotage in the workplace: The role of organizational injustice. *Organizational Behavior & Human Decision Processes.* 89, 947-965

Amodei, N. & Scott, A.A. (2002). Psychologists' contribution to the prevention of youth violence. *The Social Science Journal*, 39, 511-526.

Anderson, B. (1989). Temperature and aggression: Ubiquitous effects of heat on occurrence of human violence. *Psychological Bulletin,* 166, 74-96.

Anderson, B., Kiecolt-Glaser, J. & Glaser, R. (1996). A behavioral model of cancer stress and disease course. *American Psychologist*, 5, 389-404.

Anderson, C.A. & Anderson, K.B. (1988). Temperature and aggression: Paradox, controversy, and a (fairly) clear picture. In R.S. Geen & E. Donnerstein (Eds.), *Human Aggression Theories, research and implications for social policy*. San Diego: Academic Press.

Anderson, C.A. & Bushman, B.J. (2001). Effects of violent video games on aggressive behavior, aggressive cognition, aggressive affect, physiological arousal, and prosocial behavior: A meta-analytic review of the scientific literature. *Psychological Science*. 12, 353-359.

Anderson, J., Bricout, J.C. & West, M.D. (2001). Telecommuting: Meeting the needs of businesses and employees with disabilities. *Journal of Vocational Rehabilitation*. 16, 97-104.

Anderson, L. & Wadkins, M. (1991). Japan: A culture of consumption? In R.H. Holman & M.R. Solomon(Eds.), *Advances in Consumer Research* (Vol 18, 129-134). Provo: Association for Consumer Research.

Anderson, R.E. & Srinivasan, S.S. (2003). E-satisfaction and E-loyalty: A contingency framework. *Psychology and Marketing*, 20, 123-138.

Andreu, J.M., Arango-Lasprilla, J.C.; Gonzalez, E., Castrillon, D., Valencia, O.L., Porras, J., Ortiz, P.A., Mejia, W., & Osorio, M.I. (2002). Diferencias culturales y de genero en la representacion social de la agresion: Comparacion entre estudiantes espanoles y colombianos. Cultural and gender differences in the social representation of aggression: A comparison of Spanish and Colombian students. *Advances en Psicologia Clinica Latinoamericana,* 20, 93-100.

Anthony, L.M., Clarke, M.C. & Anderson, S.J. (2000). Technophobia and personality subtypes in a sample of South African university students. *Computers in Human Behavior,* 16, 31-44.

Argote, L., Goodman, P.S. & Schkade, D. (1983). The human side of robotics: How workers react to robots. *Sloan Management Review*, 24, 31 41.

Argyris, M. (1975). Dangers in applying results from experimental social psychology. *American Psychologist*, 30, 468-475.

Aronson, E. & Gonzales, M. (1990). The social psychology of energy conservation. In J. Edwards (Ed.), *Social Influence Processes and Prevention*. New York: Plenum.

Aronson, E. & Yates, S. (1983). Cooperation in the classroom. In H.H. Blumberg, A.P. Hare, V. Kent, & M.F. Davies (Eds.), *Small Groups and Social Interaction*. New York: Wiley Press.

Aronson, E. (1990). Applying social psychology to desegregation and energy conservation. *Journal of Personality and Social Psychology Bulletin*, 16, 118-132.

Aronson, E., Stephen, C., Sikes, J., Blaney, N. & Snapp, M. (1978). *The Jigsaw Classroom*. Beverly Hills: Sage.

Aronson, E., Wilson, T.D. & Akert, R.M. (1994). *Social Psychology*. New York: Harper Collins College Publishers.

Asch, S.E. (1955). Opinions and social pressure. *Scientific American*, November, 31-35.

Ashing, K.T., Padilla, G., Tejero, J.& Kagawa-Singer, M. (2003). Understanding the breast cancer experience of Asian American women. *Psycho-Oncology*, 12, 38-58.

Astin, A.W. (1997). *31st Annual Survey*, UCLA Higher Education Research Institute Report, Los Angeles, CA.

Au, A.K. & Enderwick, P. (2000). A cognitive model on attitude towards technology adoption. *Journal of Managerial Psychology*, 15, 266-282.

Awofeso, N. (2003). Implementing smoking cessation programs in prison settings. *Addiction Research and Theory*, 11, 119-130.

Azar, B. (2002). Helping older adults get on the technology bandwagon. *Monitor on Psychology,* March, 28-29.

Babad, E.Y., Bern, F. & Rosenthal, R. (1991). Students or judges of teachers' verbal and non-verbal behavior. *American Education Research Journal*, 28, 211-234.

Babad, E.Y., Inbar, J. & Rosenthal, R. (1982). Teacher's judgement of student's potential as a function of education. *Psychological Bulletin*, 85, 217-238.

Bachman, R. (1994, July). *Violence and Theft in the Workplace.* Crime data brief: National crime vicitimization survey. Washington DC: Bureau of Justice Statistics; US Dept of Justice.

Bagozzi, R.P., Guerhan-Cnli, Z. & Priester, J.R. (2002). *The Social Psychology of Consumer Behavior*. Buckingham: Open University Press.

Bahrick, H.P. (1984). Memory for people. In J.E. Harris, & P.E. Morris (Eds.), *Everyday Memory, Actions, and Absent-mindedness*. Orlando: Academic Press.

Bailey, J. (2004). The validation of a scale to measure school principals' attitudes toward the inclusion of students with disabilities in regular schools. *Australian Psychologist*, 39, 76-87.

Bakker, M.J., Mullen, P.D., de Vries, H. & van Breukelen, G. (2003). Feasibility of implementation of a Dutch smoking cessation and relapse prevention protocol for pregnant women. *Patient Education and Counseling*, 49, 35-43.

Ball, S. & Bogatz, J. (1972). Summative research of Sesame Street: Implications for the study of preschool children. In A.D. Pick (Ed.), *Minnesota Symposia on Child Psychology,* 6. Minneapolis: University of Minnesota Press.

Ballif-Spanvill, B., Clayton, C.J. & Hendrix, S.B. (2003). Gender, types of conflict, and individual differences in the use of violent and peaceful strategies among children who have and have not witnessed interparental violence. *American Journal of Orthopsychiatry,* 73, 141-153.

Bandura, A. (1965). Influence of models' reinforcement contigencies on the acquisition of imitative responses. *Journal of Personality and Social Psychology*, 1, 589-595.

Bandura, A. (1977). *Social Learning Theory*. Englewood Cliffs NJ: Prentice-Hall.

Bandura, A. (1979). The social learning perspective: Mechanisms of aggression. In H. Toch (Ed.), *Psychology of Crime and Criminal Justice*. New York: Rinehart & Winston.

Bandura, A. (1986). *Social Foundations of Thought and Action: A Social-Cognitive Theory*. Englewood Cliffs: Prentice-Hall.

Bandura, A. (2003). On the psycho-social impact and mechanisms of spiritual modeling. cf., Powell, L.H. Shahabi, L. & Thoresen, C.E. (2003).

Bandura, A., Barbaranelli, C., Caprara, G.V. & Pastorelli, C. (1996). Mechanisms of moral disengagement in the exercise of moral agency. *Journal of Personality and Social Psychology*, 71, 364-374.

Bandura, A., Blanchard, E.B. & Ritter, B. (1969). Relative efficacy of desensitization and modeling approaches for inducing behavioral, affective, and attitudinal changes. *Journal of Personality and Social Psychology,* 13, 173-199.

Bandura, A., Grusee, J.E. & Menlove, F.L. (1967). Vicarious extinction and avoidance behaviors. *Journal of Personality and Social Psychology*, 5, 16-23.

Bandura, A. & Menlove, F.L. (1968). Factors determining vicarious extinction of avoidance behavior through symbolic modeling. *Journal of Personality and Social Psychology*, 8, 99-108.

Bandura, A., Ross, D. & Ross, S.A. (1963). Imitation of film mediated aggressive models. *Journal of Abnormal and Social Psychology*, 66, 3-11.

Bandura, A., Ross, D. & Ross, S.A. (1961). Transmission of aggression through imitation of aggressive models. *Journal of Abnormal Social Psychology*, 63, 575-582.

Bao, W., Haas, A., & Pi, Y. (2004). Life strain, negative emotions, and delinquency: An empirical test of general strain theory in the People's Republic of China. *International Journal of Offender Therapy & Comparative Criminology*, 48, 281-297.

Bargh, J.A. & Pietromonaco, P. (1982). Automatic information processing and social perception: The influence of trait information presented outside of conscious awareness on impression information. *Journal of Professional Social Psychology*, 43, 437-449.

Barling, J. (1996). The prediction, experience and consequence of workplace violence. In G.R. Vandenbos & E.Q. Bulatao (Eds.), *Violence on the Job: Indentifying Rights and Developing Strategies*. Washington DC: American Psychological Association.

Baron, R.A. (1972). Aggression as a function of ambient temperature and prior anger arousal. *Journal of Personality and Social Psychology*, 21, 183-189.

Baron, R.A. & Ball, R.L. (1974). The aggression inhibiting-influence of non-hostile humor. *Journal of Experimental Social Psychology,* 10, 23-33.

Baron, R.A. & Bell, P.A. (1973). Effects of heightened sexual arousal on physical aggression. *Proceedings of the American Psychological Association's 81st Annual Convention*, 171-172.

Baron, R.A. & Bell, P.A. (1975). Aggression and heat: Mediating effects of prior provocation and exposure to an aggressive model. *Journal of Personality and Social Psychology,* 31, 825-832.

Baron, R.A. (1976). The reduction of human aggression: A field study of the influence of incompatible reaction. *Journal of Applied Social Psychology*, 6, 260-274.

Baron, R.A., Richardson, D.R. (1994). *Human Aggression*. New York: Plenum.

Bartol, C.R. & Bartol, A.M. (1994). *Psychology and Law*. Pacific Grove CA: Brooks/Cole.

Basil, D.Z. (2002). Cause related marketing and consumer attitudes: The effects of balance and fit on cognitive processing. *Dissertation Abstracts International, Section A: Humanities and Social Sciences*, 63 (2A), 671.

Bassett, J.F., Cate, K.L., Dabbs, & J.M., Jr. (2002). Individual differences in self-presentation style: Driving an automobile and meeting a stranger. *Self & Identity*, 1, 281-288.

Bates, J.E. (1975). Effects of a child's imitation versus non-imitation on adult's verbal and non-verbal positivity. *Journal of Personality and Social Psychology*, 31, 840-851.

Batra, R. & Holbrook, M.B. (1990). Developing a typology of affective responses to advertising. *Psychology and Marketing*, 7, 11-25.

Batson, C.D. & Gray, R.A. (1981). Religious orientation and helping behavior: Responding to one's own or the victims needs? *Journal of Personality and Social Psychology*, 40, 511-520.

Batson, C.D. & Ventis, W.L. (1982). *The Religious Experience: A Social Psychological Perspective*. New York: Oxford University Press.

Batson, C.D. (1990). Good samaritans or priests and Levites: Using William James as a guide in the study of prosocial motivation. *Personality and Social Psychology Bulletin*, 16, 758-768.

Batson, C.D. (1991). *The Altruism Question: Toward Social Psychological Answer*. Hillsdale, NJ: Earlbaum.

Batson, C.D., Feink, C.H., Schoenrade, P.A., Fultz, J. & Pych, V. (1986). Religious orientation and overt verses covert racial prejudice. *Journal of Personality and Social Psychology*, 50, 175-181.

Batson, C.D., Schoenrade, P. & Ventis, W.L. (1993). *Religion and the Individual: A Social Psychological Perspective*. New York: Oxford University Press.

Baum, A. (1990). Stress, intrusive imagery and chronic distress. *Health Psychology*, 9, 653-675.

Baum, A. & Greenburg, N. E. (1991). Gender, stress and health. *Health Psychology*, 10 (2), 80-85.

Baum, A. & Valins, S. (1977). *Architecture and Social Behavior: Psychological Studies in Social Density*. Hillsdale, NY: Erlbaum.

Baum, A. & Valins, S. (1979). Architectural mediation of structural density and control: Crowding and the regulation of social control. In L. Berkowitz (Ed.), *Advances in Experimental Social Psychology* (vol. 2). New York: Academic Press.

Baumeister, R.F. (1991). *Meanings of Life*. New York: Guilford.

Baumgartner, F. (2002). The effect of hardiness in the choice of coping strategies in stressful situations. *Studia Psychologica*, 44, 69-75.

Baumrind, D.A. (1964). Some thoughts on ethics of research: After reading Milgram's behavioral study of obedience. *American Psychologist*, 19, 19-26.

Bayland Productions (Producer). (1995). *Ecopsychology: Restoring the Earth, Healing the Self* [Videotape]. Palo Alto, CA: Foundation for Global Community.

Beasley, M., Thompson, T. & Davidson, J. (2003). Resilience in responses to life stress: The effects of coping style and cognitive hardiness. *Personality & Individual Differences*, 34, 77-95.

Beatty, S.E. & Kable, I.R. (1988). Alternative hierarchies of the attitude behavior relationship: The impact of brand commitment and habit. *Journal of the Academy of Marketing Science*, 16, 1-10.

Bechtel, R.B. & Churchman, A. (Eds.) (2002). *Handbook of Environmental Psychology*. NewYork: Wiley.

Bechtel, R.B. (2002). On to Mars! In R.B. Bechtel & A Churchman (Eds.), *Handbook of Environmental Psychology*, 676-685. NewYork: Wiley.

Becker L.J. & Seligman, C. (1978). Reducing air-conditioning waste by signaling it is cool outside. *Journal of Personality and Social Psychology Bulletin,* 4, 412-415.

Bedau, H. & M. Radelet (1987). Miscarriages of justice in potentially capital cases. *Stanford Law Review,* 40, 21-179.

Beelman, A., Pfingston, U. & Losel, F. (1994). Effects of training social competence in children: A meta-analysis of recent evaluation studies. *Journal of Clinical Child Psychology*, 23, 260-271.

Beersma, B. & De Dreu, C.K.W. (2002). Integrative and distributive negotiation in small groups: Effects of task structure, decision rule, and social motive. *Organizational Behavior & Human Decision Processes*, 87, 227-252.

Behrman, B.W. & Davey, S.L. (2001). Eyewitness identification in actual criminal cases: An archival analysis. *Law & Human Behavior*, 25, 475-491.

Bekker, M.H.J. & Boselie, K.A.H.M. (2002). Gender and stress: Is gender role stress? A re-examination of the relationship between feminine gender role stress and eating disorders. *Stress and Health: Journal of the International Society for the Investigation of Stress*, 18, 141-149.

Belk, R.W. (1982). Acquiring, processing and collecting: Fundamental processes in consumer behavior. In R.F. Bush & S.D. Hunt (Eds.), *Marketing Theory: Philosophy of Science Perspectives*. Chicago: American Marketing Association.

Belk, R.W. (1988). Third world consumer culture. In E. Kumeu & A.F. Firat (Eds.), *Marketing and Development: Towards Broader Dimensions*, 103-127, Greenwich: JAI.

Beltramini, R.F. (2000). Exploring the effectiveness of business gifts: Replication and extension. *Journal of Advertising*, 29, 75-78.

Bem, D.J. (1972). Self-perception theory. In L. Berkowitz (Ed.), *Advances in Applied Social Psychology*, 6, 1-62. New York: Academic Press.

Benet-Martinez, V. & Karakitapoglu-Ayguen, Z. (2003). The interplay of cultural syndromes and personality in predicting life satisfaction: Comparing Asian Americans and European Americans. *Journal of Cross Cultural Psychology*, 34, 38-60.

Benet-Martinez, V., Leu, J., Lee, F. & Morris, M.W. (2002). Negotiating biculturalism: Cultural frame switching in biculturals with oppositional versus compatible cultural identities. *Journal of Cross-Cultural Psychology*, 33, 492-516.

Benor, D.J. (2002). Spiritual healing. In S. Scott (Ed.), *Handbook of Complementary and Alternative Therapies in Mental Health*, 249-268. San Diego: Academic.

Benson, P.L., Dehoritz, J., Garman, L., Hanson, E., Hochascwender, M., Lebold, C., Roh, R. & Sullivan, J. (1980). Interpersonal correlates of non-spontaneous helping behavior. *Journal of Social Psychology*, 110, 87-95.

Ben-Zur, H. (2003). Happy adolescents: The link between subjective well being, internal resources and parental factors. *Journal of Youth and Adolescence*, 32, 67-79.

Bereby-Meyer, Y., Moran, S. & Unger-Aviram, E. (2004). When performance goals deter performance: Transfer of skills in integrative negotiations. *Organizational Behavior & Human Decision Processes*, 93, 142-154.

Berg, G.E., Fonss, N., Reed, A.J. & VandeCreek, L. (1995). The impact of religious faith and practice on patients suffering from a major affective disorder: A cost analysis. *Journal of Pastoral Care*, 49, 359-363.

Berger, I.E. (1997). The demographies of recycling and the structure of environmental behavior. *Environment and Behavior*, 29, 515-531.

Berk, L.S., Tan, S.A., Fry, W.F., Napier, B.J., Lee, J.W., Hubbard, R.W., Lewis, J.E. & Eby, J.C. (1989). Neuroendocrine and stress hormone changes during mirthful laughter. *American Journal of the Medical Sciences*, 298, 390-396.

Berkman, L. & Syme, S.L. (1979). Social networks, host resistance, and mortality: A nine-year follow-up of Alameda County residents. *American Journal of Epidemiology*, 109, 186-204.

Berkowitz, L. (1965). Some aspects of observed aggression. *Journal of Personality and Social Psychology*, 2, 359-369.

Berkowitz, L. (1970). Aggressive humor as a stimulus to aggressive response. *Journal of Personality and Social Psychology*, 16, 710-717.

Berkowitz, L. (1993). *Aggression*. New York: McGraw Hill.

Berkowitz, L. (1994). Guns and youth. In L. D. Eron; J.H. Gentry & P. Schlegel (Eds.), *Reason to Hope: A psychological Perspective on Violence and Youth*. Washington DC: American Psychological Association.

Berkowitz, L. & Lepage, A. (1967). Weapons as aggression eliciting stimuli. *Journal of Personality and Social Psychology*, 7, 202-207.

Beroldi, G. (1994). Critique of the Seville statement on violence. *American Psychologist*, 49, 847-848

Berth, H., Dinkel, A. & Balck, F. (2002). Health through gene tests? Acceptance of and concerns about genetic testing in a German representative sample. *Zeitschrift fur Gesundheitpsychologie*, 10, 97-107.

Black, D.R., Blue, C.L., Coster, D.C. & Chrysler, L.M. (2002). Corporate social marketing: Message design to recruit program participants. *American Journal of Health Behavior*, 26, 188-189

Black, J.S. & Gregerson, H.B. (1991). When Yankee comes home: Factors related to expat and spouse repatriation. *Journal of Business Studies*, 22, 671-694.

Blaney, N., Stephen, C., Rosenfield, R., Aronson, E. & Sikes, J. (1977). Interdependence in the classroom: A field study. *Journal of Education Psychology*, 69, 121-128.

Blank, S., Zadik, Z., Katz, I., Mahazri, Y., Toker, I. & Barak, I. (2002). The emergence and treatment of anorexia and bulimia nervosa. A comprehensive and practical model. *International Journal of Adolescent Medicine and Health,* 14, 257-260.

Bluth, B.J. & Helppie, M. (1986). *Soviet Space Stations as Analogs* (2nd Ed.). NASA Grant NAGW-659.

Bock D.L. & Warren, N.C. (1972). Religious beliefs as a factor in obedience to destructive commands. *Review of Religious Research*, 13, 185-191.

Borchard, E. (1932). *Convicting the Innocent*. Garden City, NY: Doubleday.

Borgida, E. & Brekke, N. (1985). Psychological research on rape trials. In A. Burgess (Ed.), *Research Handbook on Rape and Sexual Assault.* New York: Garland Press.

Bourhis, R.Y., Roth, S. & MacQueen, G. (1989). Communication in a hospital setting: A survey of medical and everyday language use among patients, nurses and doctors. *Social Science and Medicine*, 28, 339-346.

Bowe, F.G. (2001). The deaf and hard of hearing Americans' instant messaging and e-mail use. *American Annals of the Deaf,* 147, 6-10.

Bowen, D.J., Sinal, R., Eng, E., Crystal, S. & Burke, W. (2003). Jewish identity and intentions to obtain breast cancer screening. *Cultural Diversity and Ethnic Minority Psychology*, 9, 79-87.

Bowen, R.C. & D'Arcy, C. (2003). Response of patients with panic disorder and symptoms of hypomania to cognitive behavior therapy for panic. *Bipolar Disorders,* 5, 144-149.

Bower, G.H. (1995). Empowering people through friendly technology: Psychology in the twenty-first century. In R.L. Solso & D.W. Massaro (Eds.), *The Science of the Mind: 2001 and Beyond*. New York: Oxford University Press.

Bowlby, J. (1980). Loss, sadness and depression. *Attachment and Loss,* Vol III. London: Basic Books.

Brace, A. (2001). Are IT-ignorant teachers failing the next generation? *The Times of India*, New Delhi, 21st May.

Bracket, L.K. & Carr, B.N. Jr. (2001). Cyberspace advertising vs other media: Consumer vs mature student attitudes. *Journal of Advertising Research*, 41, 23-32.

Brandon, D. (2001). Ordinary spirituality for helping professionals. *Ethical Human Sciences and Services*, 3, 189-195.

Brandon, G. & Lewis, A. (1999). Reducing household energy consumption: A qualitative and quantitative field study. *Journal of Environmental Psychology*, 19, 75-85.

Braun, O.L. & Wickland, R.A. (1989). Psychological antecedents of conspicuous consumption. *Journal of Economic Psychology*, 10, 161-187.

Breault, K.D. & Barkey, K. (1982). A comparative analysis of Durkheim's theory of egoistic suicide. *Sociological Quarterly*, 23, 321-331.

Brehm, J.C. (1966). *A Theory of Psychological Reactance*. New York: Academic Press.

Bridgemann, D. L. (1981). Enhanced role taking through cooperative interdependence: A field study. *Child Development*, 52, 1231-1238.

Britt, T.W., Adler, A.B. & Bartone, P.T. (2001). Deriving benefits from stressful events: The role of engagement in meaningful work and hardiness. *Journal of Occupational Health Psychology*, 6, 53-63.

Brod, C. (1988). *Technostress: Human Cost of Computer Revolution*. Reading, MA: Addison-Wesley.

Broidy, L.M., Nagin, D.S.; Tremblay, R.E. & Bates, J.E. (2003). Developmental Trajectories of Childhood Disruptive Behaviors and Adolescent Delinquency: A Six-Site, Cross-National Study. *Developmental Psychology*, 39, 222-245.

Bronišová, S. & Ucen, I. (2002). Postoje ziakov ucitel'ov a rodicov k inkluzívnemu vzdelávaniu. *Psychologia a Patopsychologia Dietata*, 37, 345-350.

Brooks-Gunn, J. Boyer, C.B. & Mein, K. (1985). Behavior research and intervention strategies. *American Psychologist*, 11.

Brooks-Gunn, J. Boyer, C.B. & Mein, K. (1988). Preventing HIV infection and AIDS in children and adolescents: Behavioral research and intervention strategies. *American Psychologist*, 11, 958-964.

Brophy, J. (1986). Teacher influences on student achievement. *American Psychologist*, 41, 1069-1077.

Brotheridge, C.M. (2003). The Role of Fairness in Mediating the Effects of Voice and Justification on Stress and Other Outcomes in a Climate of Organizational Change. *International Journal of Stress Management*, 10, 253-268.

Brown, K.S., Cameron, R., Madill, C., Payne, M.E., Filsinger, S., Manske, S.R. & Best, J.A. (2002). Outcome evaluation of a high school smoking reduction intevention based on extracurricular activities. *Preventive Medicine,* 35, 506-510.

Brown, K.W. & Ryan, R.M. (2003). The benefits of being present: Mindfulness and its role in psychological well being. *Journal of Personality and Social Psychology*, 84, 822-848.

Brown, L., Macintyre, K. & Trujillo, L. (2003). Interventions to reduce HIV/AIDS stigma: What have we learned? *AIDS Education and Prevention*, 15, 49-69.

Brown, R. (1965). *Social Psychology*. New York: Free Press.

Brown, R. (2001). Australian indigenous mental health. Australian and New Zealand *Journal of Mental Health Nursing*, 10, 33-41.

Brown, S.P. & Stayman, D.M. (1992). Antecedents and consequences of attitude toward the ad: A meta-analysis. *Journal of Consumer Research*, 19, 34-51.

Brown, W.S. (2002). Psychoneuroimmunology and western religious traditions. In H.G. Koenig and H.J. Cohen (Eds.). *The Link between Religion and Health: Psychoimmunology and the Faith Factor*, 262-274. London. Oxford University Press.

Brownell, K.D. & Rodin, J.L. (1994). The dieting maelstrom. *American Psychologist*, 9, 781-791.

Brudnoy, D. (1996, December 2). I have learned to hope. *Newsweek*, 74.

Brundtland, D. (2001). World health day celebrations, Mathari National Mental Hospital, Nairobi, Kenya, 4th April.

Bryant, F.B., Edwards, J., Tindale, R.S., Posvac, L. & Heath, L. (1992). *Methodological Issues in Applied Social Psychology*. New York: Plenum.

Buchanan, G.M. & Seligman, M.E.P. (1995). *Explanatory Style*. Hillsdale: Erlbaum.

Buckhout, R. (1974). Eyewitness Testimony. *Scientific American*, 231, 23-31.

Bulik, C., Sullivan, P.F. & Kendler, K.S. (2003). Genetic and environmental contributions to obesity binge eating. *International Journal of Eating Disorders*, 33, 293-298.

Burman, B. & Margolin, G. (1992). Analysis of the association between marital relationships and health problems: An interactional perspective. *Psychological Bulletin*, 112, 39-63.

Burrage, J. & Demi, A. (2003). Buddy programs for people infected with HIV. *JANAC: Journal of the Association of Nurses in AIDS Care*, 14, 52-62.

Burt, M.R. (1980). Cultural myths and supports for rape. *Journal of Personality and Social Psychology*, 38, 217-230.

Bushman, B.J. & Anderson, C.A. (2001). Media violence and the American public: Scientific facts and the media misinformation. *American Psychologist*, 56, 477-489.

Buss, A.H. (1961). *The Psychology of Aggression*. New York: Widen.

Buss, D.M. (1999). *Evolutionary Psychology: The New Science of the Mind*. Boston: Allyn & Bacon.

Bussing, R., Zima, B.T., Gary, F.A. & Garvan, C.W. (2002). Use of complementary and alternative medicine for symptoms of attention deficit hyperactivity disorder. *Psychiatric Services*, 53, 1096-1102.

Buysse, V., Goldman, B.D. & Skinner, M.L. (2003). Friendship formation in inclusive early childhood classrooms: What is the teacher's role? *Early Childhood Research Quarterly*, 18, 485-501.

Byrd, R.E. (1938). *Alone*. New York: Ace.

Byrne, D. (1971). *The Attraction Paradigm*. New York: Academic Press.

Cacioppo, J.T. & Brandon, M.E. (2002). Religious involvement and health: Complex determinism. *Psychological Inquiry*, 13, 204-206.

Cairns, E. & Lewis, C. A. (2003). Empowering peace. *Psychologist*. 16, 142-143.

Calhoun, J.B. (1962). Population density and social psychology. *Scientific American*, 206, 139-168.

Calhoun, L.G., Cann, A., Tedeschi, R.G. & McMillan, J. (2000). A correlational test of the relationship between post-traumatic growth, religion and cognitive processing. *Journal of Traumatic Stress*, 13, 521-527.

Cambra, C. & Silvestre, N. (2003). Students with special educational needs in the inclusive classroom: Social integration and self-concept. *European Journal of Special Needs Education*, 18, 197-208.

Campbell, J., Gilmore, L. & Cuskelly, M. (2003). Changing student teachers' attitudes towards disability and inclusion. *Journal of Intellectual & Developmental Disability*, 28, 369-379.

Campbell, J.I.D. & Xue, Q. (2001). Cognitive arithmetic across cultures. *Journal of Experimental Psychology: General*, 130, 299-315.

Campell, F.A. & Ramey, C.T. (1994). Effects of early intervention on intellectual and academic achievements: A follow-up study of children from low income families. *Child Development*, 65, 684-698.

Canadian Press (2004). Suicides in Japan hit record last year: Report. 23rd July.

Canales, M.K. & Geller, B.M. (2003). Surviving breast cancer: The role of complementary therapies. *Family and Community Health*, 26, 11-24.

Canning, H. & Mayer, J. (1966). Obesity: Its effect on college acceptance. *New England Journal of Medicine*, 275, 1172-1174.

Carlsmith, J.M. & Anderson, C.A. (1979). Ambiant temperature and the occurence of collective violence: A new analysis. *Journal of Personality and Social Psychology*, 37, 337-344.

Carr, J.L., Koyama, M. & Thiagarajan, M. (2003). A women's support group for Asian international students. *Journal of American College Health*, 52, 131-134.

Carrieri, M.P., Chesney, M.A., Spire, L.A., Sobel, A., Lepeu, G., Moatti, J.P., Boirot, C., Bouhnik, A.D., Cassuto, J.P., Dellamonica, P., Dujardin, P., Duran, S., Gallais, H., Gastaut, J.A., Lepeu, G., Marimoutou, C., Mechali, D., Moreau, J., Negre, M., Obadia, Y., Poizot-Martin, I., Pradier, C., Rey, D., Rouzioux, C., Tremolieres, F. & Vlahov, D. (2003). Failure to maintain adherence to HAART in a cohort of French HIV-positve injecting drug users. *International Journal of Behavioral Medicine*, 10, 1-14.

Casella, R. (2003). Zero tolerance policy in schools: Rationale, consequences, and alternatives. *Teachers College Record*, 105, 872-892.

Caspary, W.R. (2003). Holy war, holy peace: How religion can bring peace to the Middle East. *Political Psychology*, 24, 415-417.

Cassell, E.J. (2002). Compassion. In C.R. Snyder & J. Shane (Eds.), *Handbook of Positive Psychology*. London: Oxford University Press, 434-445.

Castenuovo, G., Gaggioli, A. & Riva, G. (2001). Cyberpsychology meets clinical psychology: The emergence of e-therapy in mental health care. In G. Riva & C. Galimberti (Eds.), *Towards Cyberpsychology: Mind, Cognition and Society in the Internet Age*. Amsterdam: Netherland Antilles: IOS Press, 229-252.

Catterall, M. & Maclaran, P. (2002). Researching consumers in virtual worlds: A cyberspace odyssey. *Journal of Consumer Behavior,* 1, 228-237.

Ceci, S.J. & Bruck, M. (1995). *Jeopardy in the Courtroom: A Scientific Analysis of Children's Testimony*. Washington D.C.: American Psychological Association Press.

Ceci, S.J. (1994). Cognitive and social functions in children's testimony. In J. Blackman, W.F. Casio, S.J. Ceci, G.B. Melton & M.D. Miller (Eds.), *Psychology in Litigation and Legislation*. Washington DC: American Psychological Association Press.

Center for Disease Control Report (1979).

Center for Disease Control Report (1994).

Centerwall, B.S. (1989). Exposure to television as a risk factor for violence. *American Journal of Epidemiology*, 129, 643-652.

Chaffee, S.H. & Mcleod, J.M. (1971). Adolescents, parents and television violence. Paper presented at American Psychological Association, Washington DC.

Chaiken, S. (1987). The heuristic model of persuasion. In M.P. Zanna, J.M. Olson & C.P. Herman (Eds.), *Social Influence: The Ontario Symposium,* Vol 5. Hillsdale: Earlbaum.

Chan, D.W. (2003). Hardiness and its role in the stress-burnout relationship among prospective Chinese teachers in Hong Kong. *Teaching & Teacher Education*, 19, 381-395.

Chandler, W.V. (1988). Smoking epidemic widens: Smoking rates rise sharply in the developing world while they decline in the west. *World Watch*, 1, 39-40.

Chang, E. (2002). Distributive justice and organizational commitment revisited: Moderation by layoff in the case of Korean employees. *Human Resource Management*, 41, 261-270.

Chang, L., McBride-Chang, C., Stewart, S.S. & Au, E. (2003). Life satisfaction, self-concept and family relations in Chinese adolescents and children. *International Journal of Behavioral Development,* 27, 182-189.

Chapman, D.S. & Rowe, P.M. (2001).The impact of video-conference technology, interview structure, and interviewer gender on interviewer evaluations in the employment interview: A field experiment. *Journal of Occupational and Organizational Psychology*, 74, 279-298.

Chapman, J.J. & Chapman, J.P. (1967). Genesis of popular but erroneous psychodiagnostic observations. *Journal of Abnormal Psychology*, 72, 193-204.

Chapman, L.J. (1967). Illusory correlation in observational reports. *Journal of Verbal Learning and Verbal Behavior,* 6, 151-155.

Chattopadhaya, A. & Nedungadi, P. (1992). Does attitude toward ad endure? The moderating effect of attention and delay. *Journal of Consumer Research*, 19, 26-32.

Chavda, D. (2002). We're having a tough time staying in senses, to pharmacist's delight. *The Economic Times,* New Delhi: 17th May.

Chee, D.S. (2002). The gold elixir: The circular path of the Tao (Carl Jung, Chang Po-Tuan). *Dissertation Abstracts International: Section B: The Sciences and Engineering* , 62, 5956.

Chekroun, P. & Brauer, M. (2002). The bystander effect and social control behavior: The effect of the presence of others on people's reactions to norm violations. *European Journal of Social Psychology*, 32, 853-866.

Chen, C., Greenberger, E., Farruggia, S., Bush, K. & Dong, Q. (2003). Beyond parents and peers: The role of important non-parental adults (VIPS) in adolescent development in China and the United States. *Psychology in the Schools*, 40, 35-50.

Chen, E., Touyz, S.W., Beumont, P.J.V., Fairburn, C.G., Griffiths, R., Butow, P., Russell, J., Schotte, D.E., Gertler, R. & Basten, C. (2003). Comparison of group and individual cognitive-behavioral therapy for patient with bulimia nervosa. *International Journal of Eating Disorders*, 33, 241-254.

Chen, H., Mallinckrodt, B. & Mobley, M. (2002). Attachment patterns of East Asian international students and sources of perceived social support as moderators of the impact of U.S. racism and cultural distress. *Asian Journal of Counselling*, 9, 27-48.

Chen, H., Sullivan, H.J. & Savenye, W.C. (2002). Perspectives on the future of computer use in China. *Educational Technology Research & Development*, 50, 92-101.

Chifunyise, T., Benoy, H. & Mukibi, B. (2002). An impact evaluation of student-teacher training in HIV/AIDS education in Zimbabwe. *Evaluation and Program Planning*, 25, 377-385.

Chowdhury, A., Sen, P., Ghosh, K.K. & Mukherjee, A. (2002). HIV/AIDS-KAB study: Report from Calcutta prison. *International Medical Journal*, 9, 199-203.

Christian, J.J. (1963). The pathology of over-population. *Military Medicine*, 128, 571-603.

Christianson, S. (1992) Emotional stress and memory: A critical review. *Psychological Bulletin,* 112, 2, 84-309.

Christie, R. & Geis, F.L. (1970). *Studies in Machiavellianism*. New York: Academic Press.

Churchman, A. & Mitrani, M. (1997). The role of physical environment in culture shock. *Environment and Behavio*r, 29-31, 64-86.

Cialdini, R.B., Cacioppo J.T., Bassett, R. & Miller, J.A. (1978). Low-ball procedure for producing compliance: Commitment then cost. *Journal of Personality and Social Psychology*, 36, 463-476.

Cialdini, R.B., Reno, R.R., & Kallgren, C.A. (1991). A focus theory of normative conduct: Recycling the concept of norms to reduce littering in public places. *Journal of Personality and Social Psychology*, 58, 1015-1026.

Cialdini, R.B., Vincent, J.E., Lewis, S.K., Catalan, J., Wheeler, D. & Danby, B.L. (1975). Reciprocal concessions procedure for indulging compliance: The door-in-the-face technique. *Journal of Personality and Social Psychology*, 31, 206-215.

Cincinatti Children's Hospital & Medical Center. (2000). *Children's testimony in sexual abuse cases studied.* May 8th.

Clay, R.A. (1996, August). *American Psychological Association Monitor.*

Clifford, M. & Walsler, E. (1973). The effect of physical attractiveness on teacher expectation. *Sociology of Education,* 46, 248.

Clinebell, H. (1996). *Ecotherapy: Healing ourselves, healing the Earth*. Minneapolis: Fortress Press.

Clough, A.R., Guyula, T., Yunupingu, M. & Burn, C.B. (2002). Diversity of substance use in eastern Arnhem Land (Australia): Patterns and recent changes. *Drug and Alcohol Review*, 21, 349-356.

Coe, C.L. (1999). Psychosocial factors and psychoneuroimmunology within a lifespan perspective. In D.P. Keating & C. Hertzman (Eds.), *Developmental Health and Wealth of Nations: Social, Biological and Educational Dynamics*, 201-219. New York: Guilford.

Coffin, P.O. (2002). Marketing harm reduction: A historical narrative of the International Harm Reduction Development Program. *International Journal of Drug Policy*, 13, 209-220.

Cohen, D. & Nisbett, R.E. (1994). Self-protection and the culture of honor: Explaining Southern violence. *Personality and Social Psychology Bulletin*, 20, 551-567.

Cohen, M.J. (1997). *Reconnecting with Nature: Finding wellness through restoring your bond with the Earth*. Corvallis, OR: Ecopress.

Cohen, S. & Mckay, G. (1984). Social support, stress and the buffer hypothesis: A theoretical analysis. In A. Baum, S.E. Taylor, & J.E. Snyder (Eds.), *Handbook of Psychology and Health: Social Psychological Aspect of Health*, 4, Hillsdale: Earlbaum.

Cohen, S. Tyrrell, D.A. & Smith, A.P. (1993). Negative life events, perceived stress, negative affect and susceptability to common cold. *Journal of Personality and Social Psychology*, 64, 131-140.

Cohen, S. & Williamson, T.M. (1991). Stress and infectious disease in humans. *Psychological Bulletin*, 109, 5-24.

Cohn, E.S. & Swift, M.B. (1992). Physical distance and AIDS: Too close for comfort? *Journal of Applied Social Psychology*, 22, 1442-1452.

Colahan, M. & Robinson, P.H. (2002). Multi-family groups in the treatment of young adults with eating disorders. *Journal of Family Therapy*, 24, 17-30.

Cole, C.C. (2002). Learning from Moshe, Hu Hu Zhu and Khokha: Insights into the global application of the formative research component of the Sesame Workshop Model. *Early Education and Development*, 13, 355-362.

Cole, C.F., Arafat, C., Tidhar, C.,Wafa, Z., Fox, N.A., Killen, M., Ardila-Rey, A., Leavitt, L.A., Lewis, A., Harmon, M., Smith, T.A., Martin, M.O., Kelly, D.L., Beaton, A.E. & Mullis, I.V.S. (1997). Performance assessment in IEA's third international mathemetics and science study. Chestnut Hill: Boston College, TIMMS International Study Center.

Cole, N.D. & Flint, D.H. (2004). Perceptions of distributive and procedural justice in employee benefits: Flexible versus traditional benefit plans. *Journal of Managerial Psychology*, 19, 19-40.

Collett, M.E. & Kovera, M.B. (2003). The effects of British and American trial procedures on the quality of juror decision-making. *Law & Human Behavior*, 27, 403-422.

Collett, P. (1971). On training Englishmen in the non-verbal behavior of Arabs. *International Journal of Psychology*, 6, 209-215.

Collins, R., Lincoln, R. & Frank, M.G. (2002). The effect of rapport in forensic interviewing. *Psychiatry, Psychology and Law,* 9, 69-78.

Connor-Smith, J.K. & Calvete, E. (2004). Cross-cultural equivalence of coping and involuntary responses to stress in Spain and the United States. *Anxiety, Stress & Coping: An International Journal*, 17, 163-185.

Contractor, N.S., Fulk, J., Monge, P.R. & Singhal, A. (1986). Cultural assumptions that influence the implementation of communication technologies. *Vikalpa,* 11, 287-299.

Coob, S. (1976) Social support as a mediator of life stress. *Psychosomatic Medicine*, 38, 300-316.

Cooper, H.M. (1983). The Pygmalion grows up: A model for teacher expectation, communication and performance influence. *Review of Education Research*, 49, 389-410.

Cornelius, P.E. (1991). Life in Antarctica. In A.A. Harrison, Y.A. Clearwater, & C.P. McKay (Eds.), *From Antarctica to Outer Space: Life in Isolation and Confinement,* 1-6. New York: Springer Verlag.

Corral-Verdugo, V. (2002). A structural model of pro-environmetal competency. *Environment and Behavior*, 34, 531-549.

Corral-Verdugo, V., Frias-Arnenta, M. & Gonzalez-Lomeli, D. (2003). On the relationship between antisocial and anti-environmental behaviors: An empirical study. *Population and Environment*, 24, 273-286.

Corteen, R.S. & Williams, T.M. (1986). Television and reading skills. In T.M. Williams (Eds.), *The Impact of Television: A Natural Experiment in Three Communities*. New York: The Academic Press.

Costanzo, M. Archer, D. Aronson, E. & Pettigrew, T. (1986). Energy conservation behavior. *American Psychologist*, 5, 521-528.

Couch, J.V. & Sigler, J.N. (2002). Gender of an expert witness and the jury verdict. *Psychological Record*, 52, 281-287.

Coughlin, E.K. (1996, May 16). A market perspective on religion. *Chronicle of Higher Education*, A12.

Cowie, R. (2002). Charged experiences of natural environments. *Current Psychology*: developmental, learning, personality, social, 21, 133-143.

Craig, C.S. & MacCann, J.M. (1978). Assessing communication effects on energy conservation. *Journal of Consumer Research*, 5, 82-88.

Crandel, C.S., Preisler, J.J., & Aussprung, J. (1992). Measuring life stress events in the lives of college students: The undergraduate stress questionnaire. *Journal of Behavioral Medicine*, 15, 627-662.

Crespin, T.R. & Austin, J.T. (2002). Computer technology applications in industrial and organizational psychology. *Cyber Psychology and Behavior, Special Issue: Internet and the Workplace*, 5, 279-303.

Cross, J.F., Cross, J., & Daly, J. (1971). Sex, race, age and beauty as factors in recognition of faces. *Perception and Psychophysics*, 10, 393-396.

Cross, T.L. (2003). Culture as a resource for mental health. *Cultural Diversity and Ethnic Minority Psychology*, 9, 354-359.

Crowther, J.H., Kichler, J.C., Shewood, N.E. & Kuhnert, M.E. (2002). The role of familial factors in bulimia nervosa: Eating disorders. *The Journal of Treatment and Prevention*, 10, 141-151.

Cummings, J.A. & Bonks, C.J. (2002). Facilitating interaction among students and faculty via web-based conferencing sytems. *Journal of Technology in Human Services*, 20, 245-265.

Currie, S.R., Nesbitt, K., Wood, C. & Lawson, A. (2003). Survey of smoking cessation services in Canadian addiction programs. *Journal of Substance Abuse Treatment*, 24, 59-65.

Cutter, J., Palincsar, A.S. & Magnusson, S. J. (2002). Supporting inclusion through case-based vignette conversations. *Learning Disabilities Research & Practice*, 17, 186-200.

D'Onofrio, C.N., Moskowitz, J.M. & Braverman, M.T. (2002). Curtailing tobacco use among youth: Evaluation of Project 4-Health. *Health Education and Behavior*, 29, 656-682.

Dafok, G.A. & Taylor, S.E. (1990). Victim's perception of social support: What is helpful from whom? *Journal of Personality and Social Psychology*, 58, 80-89.

Dahlen, M. & Lange, F. (2002). Real consumers in the virtual store. *Scandinavian Journal of Management*, 18, 341-363.

Dainik Jagaran (2004).

Dale, P.S., Loftus, E.F. & Rathbun, L. (1978). The influence of the form of the question on the eyewitness testimony of school children. *Journal of Psycholinguistic Research*, 7, 269-277.

Darley, J.M. & Batson, C.D. (1973). "From Jerusalem to Jericho": A study of situational and dispositional variables in helping behavior. *Journal of Personality and Social Psychology*, 27, 100-108.

Darley, J.M. (1978). Energy conservation as innovation and their diffusion. *Energy and Building*, 1, 339-343.

Davies, J., Foxall, G.R. & Palister, J. (2002). Beyond the intention-behavior mythology: An integrated model of recycling. *Marketing Theory*, 2, 29-114.

Davio, R.L. (2001). Influences and motivations on curbside recycling participation. *Dissertations Abstracts International: Section B: the Sciences and Engineering*, 62, 1292.

Davis, C., Williams, P., Redman, S., White, K. & King, E. (2003). Assessing the practical and psychosocial needs of rural women with early breast cancer in Australia. *Social Work in Health Care*, 36, 25-36.

Davis, S.L. & Bottoms, B.L. (2002). Effects of social support on children's eyewitness reports: A test of the underlying mechanism. *Law and Human Behavior*, 26, 185-215.

Dawes, R.M. (1994). *House of Cards: Psychology and Psychiatry built on Myth*. New York: Free Press.

DeAngelis, T. (1993, August). It's baaack: Television violence, concern for kid viewers. *American Psychological Association Monitor*, 16.

DeAngelis, T. (1995). Improving the quality of life for the seriously ill. *American Psychological Association Monitor*, 10, 19.

DeAngelis, T. (1995). The threat of AIDS isn't spurring safer sex. *American Psychologist Association Monitor*, 9, 43.

DeAngelis, T. (1995, March) *American Psychologist Association Monitor*.

DeAngelis, T. (1996, October). Seligman: Optimism can be vaccinated. *American Psychological Association Monitor*, 33.

DeAngelis, T. (2003). Where anger's a plus. *APA Monitor*, 34-3, 44-45.

DeAngelis, T. (2004). Bullying. *APA Monitor*, 2, 42

De Dreu, C.K.W. (2003). Time pressure and closing of the mind in negotiation. *Organizational Behavior & Human Decision Processes*, 91, 280-295

De La Fuente, L., De La Fuente, E. Inmaculada & Garcia, J. (2003). Effects of pretrial juror bias, strength of evidence and deliberation process on juror decisions: New validity evidence of the Juror Bias Scale scores. *Psychology, Crime & Law*, 9, 197-209.

De Mooij, M. & Hofstede, G. (2002). Convergence and divergence in consumer behavior: Implications for international retailing. *Journal of Retailing*, Special Issue, 78, 61-69.

Decaire, M. (2001). Applicability and ethnicity of behavioral lie detection. *Forensic Psychology*, September 1.

Decaire, M. (2002). Effective expert and factual witness behavior: A guideline. *Forensic Psychology*, January 10.

deCharms, S.R. (1972). Personal causation training the schools. *Journal of Applied Social Psychology*, 2, 95-113.

deCharms, S.R. (1976). *Enhancing Motivation: Change in the Classroom*. New York: Irvington.

DeJong, W. (2002). The role of mass media campaigns in reducing high risk drinking among college students. *Journal of Studies on Alcohol*, 14, 182-192.

Delfabbro, P. & Thrupp, L. (2003). The social determinants of youth gambling in South Australian adolescents. *Journal of Adolescence*, 26, 313-330.

Dell'Aglio, D.D. & Hutz, C.S. (2001). Padrões evolutivos na utilização dos princípios de justiça distributiva em crianças e adolescentes no sul do Brasil. *Psicologia: Reflexao e Critica*, 14, 97-106.

Delnevo, C.D., Pevzner, E.S., Steinberg, M.B., Warren, C.W. & Slade, J. (2002). Cigar use in New Jersey among adolescents and adults. *American Journal of Public Health*, 92, 943-945.

DeMarco, R. & Johnsen, C. (2003). Taking action in communities: Women living with HIV/AIDS lead the way. *Journal of Community Health Nursing*, 20, 51-62.

Dennis, M.L., Soderstrom, E.J., Koncinski, S. & Cavannaugh, B. (1990). Effective dissemination of energy related information: Applying social psychology and evaluation research. *American Psychologist*, 10, 1109-1117.

Deutsch, M. (1973). *The Resolution of Conflict*. New Haven CT: Yale University Press.

Deutsch, M. (1985). *Distributive Justice: A Social Psychological Perspective*. New Haven: Yale University Press.

Deutsch, M. (1986). Strategies for inducing cooperation. In R.K. White (Ed.), *Psychology and the Prevention of Nuclear War*. New York: New York University Press.

Deutsch, M. (1994). Constructive conflict resolution: Principles, training and research. *Journal of Social Issues*, 50, 13-32.

Devlin, A.S. (2001). *Mind and Maze: Spatial Cognition and Environmental Behavior*. Westport: Praeger.

deVries, D.L., & Slavin, R.E. (1978). Team games: Tournament review of ten classroom experiments. *Journal of Research and Development in Education*, 12, 28-38.

Dickerson, C., Thibodeau, R., Aronson, E. & Miller, D. (1992). Using cognitive dissonance to encourage water conservation. *The Journal of Social Psychology*, 22, 841-854.

Diener, E. & Diener, M. (1995). Cross-cultural correlates of life satisfaction and self esteem. *Journal of Personality and Social Psychology*, 68, 653-663.

Diener, E. (2000). Subjective well being: The science of happiness and a proposal for a national index. *American Psychologist*, 55, 34-43.

Diener, E., Lucas, R.E. & Oishi, S. (2002). Subjective well being: The science of happiness and life satisfaction. In C.R. Snyder & J. Shane (Eds.), *Handbook of Positive Psychology*, 463-473. London: Oxford University Press.

Diener, E., Oishi, S. & Lucas, R.E. (2003). Personality, culture and subjective well being: emotional and cognitive evaluations of life. *Annual Review of Psychology*, 54, 403-425.

Dimeteo, M.R. & DiNicola, D.D. (1982). *Achieving Patient Compliance*. New York: Pergamon.

Dimeteo, M.R. (1985). Physician-patient communication: Promoting a positive health care setting. In J.C. Rosen, & L.J. Solomon (Eds.), *Prevention in Health Psychology*. Hanover, NH: University of New England Press.

Dingfelder, S.F. (2003). Tibetan Buddhism and research psychology: A match made in Nirvana. *Monitor on Psychology*, 34, 46-48.

Dion, K.K. Berscheid, E. & Walsten, E. (1972). What is beautiful is good. *Journal of Personality and Social Psychology*, 24, 285-290.

Dishion, T.J. McCord, J. & Poulin, F. (1999). When interventions harm: Peer groups and problem behavior. *American Psychologist*, 54, 755-764.

Dittes, J.E. (1969). Psychology of religion. In G. Lindsey & E. Aronson (Eds.), *Handbook of Social Psychology VI*. Cambridge, MA: Addison-Wesley.

Dittmar, L. (1992). *The Social Psychology of Material Possessions*. New York: St. Martin.

Doan, B. & Gray, R.E. (1992). The heroic patient. A critical analysis of the relationship between illusion and mental health. *Canadian Journal of Behavioral Science*, 24, 253-266.

Dodge, K.A. (1980). Social cognition and children's aggressive behavior. *Child Development*, 51, 162–170.

Dodge, K.A. (1986). A social information-processing model of social competence in children. In M. Perlmutter (Ed.), *Minnesota Symposium on Child Psychology,* 18, 77–125. Hillsdale, NJ: Erlbaum.

Dolbier, C.l., Cocke, R.R., Leiferman, J.A., Steinhardt, M.A., Schapiro, S.J. Nehete, R.R., Perlman, J.E. & Sastry, J. (2001). Differences in functional immune responses of high vs low hardy healthy individuals. *Journal of Behavioral Medicine*, 24, 219-229.

Dollard, J., Doob, L.W., Miller, N.E., Mowrer, O.H. & Sears, R.R. (1939). *Frustration and Aggression*. New Haven, CT: Yale University Press.

Domènech-Llaberia, E., Jané, C., Canals, J., Ballespí, S.; Esparó, G. & Garralda, E. (2004). Parental reports of somatic symptoms in preschool children: Prevalence and associations in a Spanish sample. *Journal of the American Academy of Child & Adolescent Psychiatry,* 43, 598-604.

Domina, T. & Koch, K. (2002). Convenience and frequency of recycling: Implications for including textiles in curbside recycling programs. *Environment and Behavior*, 34, 216-238.

Dommick, J.R. & Greensburg, B.S. (1972). Attitude of violence: The interaction of television exposure, family attitudes and social class. In G.A. Comstock, & E.A. Rubinstein (Eds.), *Television and Social Behavior*, Vol. III.

Donohue, M.J. (1985). Intrinsic and extrinsic religiousness: Review and meta-analysis. *Journal of Personality and Social Psychology,* 48, 400-419.

Downing, J.D., Bekaquaptewa, D.J., Vargas, P.T., & Brock. T.C. (1995). "Behavior technologies" Caricature of Social Psychology. *American Psychologist*, 50, 3, 175-176.

Downs, R.M. (1970). The cognitive structure of an urban shopping center. *Environment and Behavior*, 2, 13-39.

Doyle, R. (2003). Developing the nurturing school: Spreading nurture group principles and practices into mainstream classrooms. *Emotional & Behavioural Difficulties*, 8, 252-266.

Drabman, R.S. & Thomas, M.H. (1974). Does media violence increase children's tolerance of real life aggression? *Developmental Psychology*, 10, 418-421.

Driskell, J.E. & Salas, E. (1991). Group decision making under stress. *Journal of Applied Psychology*, 76, 473-478.

Dudley, B.S. Johnson, D.W. & Johnson, R.T. (1996). Conflict resolution training and middle school students integrative negotiation behavior. *Journal of Applied Social Psychology,* 26, 2038-2052.

Duncan-Schetter, C., Feinstein, L.G., Taylor, S.E. & Falke, R.L. (1992). Patterns of coping with cancer. *Health Psychology*, 11, 79-87.

Duriez, B., Luyten, P., Snauwaert, B. & Hutsebaut, D. (2002). The importance of religiosity and values in predicting political attitudes: Evidence for the continuing importance of religiosity in Flanders(Belgium). *Mental Health, Religion and Culture*, 5, 35-51.

Durkheim, E. (1887). *Suicide*. New York: Free Press (1986).

Dweck, C.S., Chiu, C.Y. & Hong, Y.I. (1995). Implicit theories and their role in judgments and reactions: A world from two perspectives. *Psychological Inquiry*, 6, 267-285.

Dwyer, W.O., Leeming, F.C., Cobern, M.K., Porter, B.E. & Jackson, J.M. (1993). Critical review of behavioral interventions to preserve the environment: Research since 1980. *Environment and Behavior*, 25, 275-321.

Edell, J. & Burke, M.C. (1987). The power of feelings in understanding advertising effects. *Journal of Consumer Behavior*, 14, 421-433.

Ediger, M. (2003). War and peace in the curriculum. *Journal of Instructional Psychology*, 30, 288-293.

Edwards, A.C. (2003). Response to the spiritual intelligence debate: Are some conceptual distinctions needed here? *International Journal for the Psychology of Religion*, 13, 49-52.

Efran, M.C. (1974). The effect of physical appearance on a judgment of guilt, interpersonal attraction and the severity of recommended punishment in a simulated jury trial. *Journal of Research in Personality*, 8, 45-54.

Egeth, M.E. (1993). What do we not know about eyewitness identification? *American Psychologist*, 48, 5, 577-580.

Eidelson, R.J. & Eidelson, J.I. (2003). Dangerous ideas: Five beliefs that propel groups toward conflict. *American Psychologist*, 58-63, 182-192.

Eivors, A., Button, E., Warner, S. & Turner, K. (2003). Understanding the experience of dropout from treatment for anorexia nervosa. *European Eating Disorders Review*, 11, 90-107.

Ellis, A. (1962). *Reason and Emotion in Psychotherapy*. Secaucus, NJ: Citadel.

Ellison, C.G. & Levin, J.S. (1998). The religion-health connection: Evidence, theory and future directions. *Health Education and Behavior*, 25, 700-720.

Elsensohn, S. (2002). Dreams and shamans. *Analytiche Psychologie*, 33, 254-265.

Emmons, R.A. & Shelton, C.M. (2002). Gratitude and the science of positive psychology. In C.R. Snyder, & J. Shane (Eds.), *Handbook of Positive Psychology*, 459-471. London: Oxford University Press.

Emmons, R.A., Cheung, C. & Tehrani, K. (1998). Assessing spirituality through personal goals: Implications for research on religion and subjective well being. *Social Indicators Research*, 45, 391-422.

Endo, Y. (1988). The role of motoric aspect of representation: Spontaneous writing like behavior in Japanese. In M.M. Gruneberg, P.E. Morris & R.N. Sykes (Eds.), *Practical Aspects of Memory: Current Research and Issues,* 459-464. Chichester: Wiley.

Engelbrecht, P., Oswald, M., Swart, E. & Eloff, I. (2003). Including learners with intellectual disabilities: Stressful for teachers? *International Journal of Disability, Development & Education*. 50, 293-308.

Erickson, E. (1969). *Gandhi's Truth*. New York: W.W. Norton.

Erickson, E. (1986). Evolutionary and developmental considerations. In L. Grinswon (Ed.), *The Long Darkness: Psychological and Moral Perspectives on Nuclear Winter*. New Haven: Yale University Press.

Eron, L.D. (1993, August). Cited by T. DeAngelis in *American Psychological Association Monitor*, 16.

Eron, L.D., Gentry, J. & Schlegel, P. (Eds.) (1994). *Reason to Hope*. Washington, D.C.: American Psychological Association.

Estape, T., Estape, J., Grau, J.J. & Ferrer, C. (2003). Cancer knowledge among Spanish women participating in literacy schemes. *Psycho-Oncology*, 12, 194-197.

Ettlie, J.E. (1986). Facing the factory of future. In D.D. Davis (Ed.), *Managing Technological Innovation: Organizational Strategies for Implementing Advanced Manufacturing Technologies*. San Francisco: Jossey. Boss.

Evans, G.W., Lepore, S.J., Shejwal, B.R. & Palsane, M.N. (1998). Chronic residential crowding and children's well being: An ecological perspective. *Child Development*, 69, 1514-1523.

Evans, R.F. (1976). Smoking in children. Developing a solid psychological study of deterrence. *Preventive Medicine,* 5, 122-127.

Evans, T.M. (2003). Juvenile competency to stand trial: Problems and pitfalls. *American Journal of Forensic Psychology,* 21, 5-18.

Evers, K.E., Bishop, C.H., Gerhan, L.S., & Weisse, C.S. (1997). AIDS education effectivness as a function of sexual orientation and HIV stalling. *Journal of Applied Social Psychology*, 27, 902-914.

Ewing, G. (2001). Altruistic, egoistic and normative effects on curbside recycling. *Environment and Behavior*, 33, 733-764.

Exline, J.J. (2002). The picture is getting clearer, but is the scope too limited? Three overlooked questions in the psychology of religion. *Psychological Inquiry*, 13, 245-247.

Exline, J.J., Yalk, A.M. & Sanderson, W.C. (2000). Guilt, discord and alienation: The role of religious strain in depression and suicidality. *Journal of Clinical Psychology*, 56, 1481-1496.

Faber Taylor. A.J. (2002). Children, attention and nature: Evidence from AD/HD and poor urban populations. *Dissertations Abstracts International: Section B, the Sciences and Engineering*, 62, 3827.

Fago, D.P. (2003). Evaluation and Treatment of Neurodevelopmental Deficits in Sexually Aggressive Children and Adolescents. *Professional Psychology: Research and Practice*, 34, 248-257.

Falicov, C.J. (2001). The cultural meanings of money: The case of Latinos and Anglo-Americans. *American Behavioral Scientist*, 45, 313-328.

Farrell, A.D., Meyer, A.L., Sullivan, T.N. & Kung, E.M. (2003). Evaluation of the responding in peaceful and positive ways (RIPP) seventh grade violence prevention curriculum. *Journal of Child & Family Studies*, 12, 101-120

Fassino, S., Abbate-Daga, G., Amianto, F., Leombruni, P., Boggio, S. & Rovera, G.G. (2002). Temperament and character profile of eating disorders: A controlled study with the temperament and character inventory. *International Journal of Eating Disorders*, 32, 412-425.

Faulkner, J.E. & Dejong, G.F. (1966). Religiosity in SD: An empirical analysis. *Social Forces,* 45, 246-254.

Feagin, J.R. (1964). Prejudice and religious types: A focused study of Southern fundamentalists. *Journal for the Scientific Study of Religion,* 4, 3-13.

Feigenbaum, E.A. & McCorduck, P. (1983). *The Fifth Generation: Artificial Intelligence and Johan's Computer Challenge to the World.* Reading MA: Addison-Welsey.

Feldman, R. (Ed.) (1987). *Social Psychological Applications to Education.* Cambridge: Cambridge Universtiy

Feldman, R.S. & Proshaska, T. (1979). The student as pygmalion: Effect of student expectation on the teacher. *Journal of Educational Psychology*, 71, 485-493.

Feldman, R.S. & Theiss, A.J. (1982). The teacher and student as Pygmalions: Joint effect of teacher and student expectations. *Journal of Educational Psychology*, 74, 217-223.

Fernandez-Ballesteros, R. (2002). Social support and quality of life among older people in Spain. *Journal of Social Issues*, 58, 645-659.

Festinger, L. (1957). *A Theory of Cognitive Dissonance.* Evanston, IL: Row Peterson.

Festinger, L., Schachter, S. & Beck, K. (1950). *Social Pressures in Informal Groups.* Stanford, CA.: University of Stanford Press.

Fetchenhauer, D. & Huang, X. (2004). Justice sensitivity and distributive decisions in experimental games. *Personality & Individual Differences*, 36, 1015-1029.

Fiala, W.E., Bjorck, J.P. & Gorsuch, R.L. (2002). The religious support scale: Construction, validation and cross validation. *American Journal of Community Psychology*, 30, 761-786.

Fischer, C.S. (1982). *To Dwell among Friends: Personal Networking in Town and City.* Chicago: University of Chicago Press.

Fishbein, M. & Ajzen, L. (1974). *Belief, Attitude, Intention and Behavior: An Introduction to Theory and Research.* Reading, PA: Addison-Wesley.

Fishbein, M. & Azjen, I. (1980). Predictions and understanding of consumer behavior: Attitude behavior correspondence. In I. Azjen & M. Fishbein (Eds.), *Understanding Attitudes and Predicting Social Behavior*. Englewood Cliffs, NJ: Prentice-Hall.

Fisher, R. & Ury, W. (1983). *Getting to Yes.* New York: Penguin Books.

Fiske, S.L., Bersoff, D.N., Borgida, E., Deaux, K. & Heilman, M.E. (1991). Social science research on trial: Use of sex stereotyping research in Price vs Waterhouse vs Hopkins. *American Psychologist*, 46, 10, 1049-1060.

Fiske, S.T. & Taylor, S.E. (1991). *Social Cognition.* New York: McGraw-Hill.

Fitchett, G., Rybarczyk, B.D., DeMarco, G.A. & Nicholas, J.J. (1999). The role of religion in medical rehabilitation outcomes. *Rehabilitation Psychology*, 44, 1-22.

Fjortoft, I. (2001). The natural environment as a playground for children: The impact of outdoor play activities in pre-primary school children. *Early Childhood Education Journal*, 29, 111-117.

Flannery, D.J., Vazsonyi, A.T., Liau, A.K., Shenyang, P.K.E., Atha, H.W. & Embry, W. (2003). Initial behavior outcomes for the Peace-builders universal school-based violence prevention program. *Developmental Psychology*, 39, 292-308.

Flem, A., Moen, T. & Gudmundsdottir, S. (2004). Towards inclusive schools: A study of inclusive education in practice. *European Journal of Special Needs Education*, 19, 85-98.

Fleshner, M., Watkins, L.R., Lockwood, L.L., Grahn, R.E., *et al.* (1993). Blockade of the hypothalamic-pituitary-adrenal response to stress by intraventricular injection of dexamethasone: A method for studying the stress-induced peripheral effects of glucocorticoids. *Psychoneuroendocrinology,* 18, 251-263.

Flisher, A.J., Parry, C.D.H., Evans, J., Muller, M. & Lombard, C. (2003). Substance use by adolescents in Cape Town: Prevalence correlates. *Journal of Adolescent Health*, 32, 58-65.

Flora, J.A. & Thoreson, C.E.(1988). Reducing the risk of AIDS in adolescents. *American Psychologist*, 11, 965-970.

Fogel, J., Albert, S.M., Scnabel, F., Ditkoff, B.A. & Neugut, A.L. (2003). Racial/ethnic differences and potential psychological benefits in the use of the Internet by women with breast cancer. *Psycho-Oncology*, 12, 107-117.

Foley, L.A. & Pigott, M.A. (2002). Race, self-presentation and reverse discrimination in jury decisions. *American Journal of Forensic Psychology*, 20, 37-52.

Folger, R. & Baron, R.A. (1996). Violence and hostility at work: A model of reaction to perceived justice. In G.R. Vandenbos & E.Q. Bulatao (Eds.), *Violence on the Job: Identifying Rights and Developing Strategies.* Washington DC : American Psychological Association.

Forbus, K.D. & Feltovich, P.J. (2001). *Smart Machines in Education: The Coming Revolution in Educational Technology*. Cambridge: MIT Press.

Forest, O.S. (2000). *Dreaming the Council Ways: True Native Teachings from the Red Lodge.* York Beach: Samuel Weiser.

Freedman, J.L. (1984). Effect of television violence on aggressiveness. *Psychological Bulletin*, 96, 227-246.

Freedman, J.L. & Fraser, S.C. (1966). Compliance without pressure: The foot-in-the-door technique. *Journal of Personality and Social Psychology*, 4, 195-202.

Freeman, L.W. (1998). Effects of a comprehensive psychoneuroimmunological program on asthma symptoms and mood states in adult asthmatic patients. *Dissertation Abstracts International: Section B: The Sciences and Engineering,* 58(11-B), 6221.

Freire, M. (1975). Cultural action for freedom. *Harvard Educational Monograph*, 1.

Freire, P. (1990). *Pedagogy of the Oppressed.* New York: Continuum.

Freud, S. (1913). *Totem and Taboo.* London: Hogarth Press.

Freud, S. (1933). *New Introductory on Psychoanalysis*. New York: Norton.

Freud, S. (1960/1905). *Jokes and their Reactions?* New York: Norton. Translated from original work.

Fried, M. (2000). Continuities and discontinuities of place. *Journal of Environmental Psychology*, 20, 193-205.

Friedrichs, R.W. (1959). Christians and residential exclusion: An empirical study of a Northern dilemna. *Journal of Social Issues*, 15, 14-23.

Friestad, M. & Wright, P. (1995). Persuasion knowledge: Lay people's and researchers' beliefs about the psychology of advertising. *Journal of Consumer Research*, 22, 62-74.

Froggett, L. (2001). From rights to recognition: Mental health and spiritual healing among older Pakistanis. *Psychoanalytic Studies*, 3, 177-186.

Fromm, E. (1938). *Escape from Freedom.*

Funder, D.C. (2002). Why study religion? *Psychological Inquiry*, 13, 213-214.

Furnham, A. (1990). Expatriate stress: The problems of living abroad. In S. Fisher & C.L. Cooper (Eds.), *On the Move: The Psychology of Change and Transition.* Chichester: Wiley.

Fussell, S.R. & Beinhoff, L. (1995). Social and cognitive process in interpersonal communication: Implications for advanced telecommunications technologies. *Human Factors*, 37-2, 228-250.

Galimberti, C. & Riva, G. (2001). Actors, artifacts and interactions: Outline for a social psychology of cyberspace. In G. Riva & C. Galimberti (Eds.), *Towards Cyberpsychology: Mind, Cognition and Society in the Internet Age.* Amsterdam: Netherland Antilles: IOS Press, 229-252.

Galton, F. (1869). *Hereditary Genius: An Inquiring into Laws and Consequences.* London: MacMillan.

Gamba, R.J. (2000). A cross-cultural study of attitudes and behaviors regarding curbside recycling. *Dissertation Abstracts International Section B: The Sciences and Engineering*, 61, 2270.

Garbarino, E.L. & Edell, J.A. (1997). Cognitive effort, affect and choice. *The Journal of Consumer Behavior*, 24, 147-169.

Gardner, H. (1993). *Multiple Intelligences.* New York: Basic Books.

Garrioch, L. & Brimacombe (nee Luus), C.A.E. (2001). Lineup administrators' expectations: Their impact on eyewitness confidence. *Law & Human Behavior*, 25, 299-314.

Gartner, J. Lansen, D.B. & Allen, G.D. (1991). Religious commitment and mental health: A review of empirical literature. *Journal of Psychology and Theology*, 19, 6-25.

Geen, R.G. & McCowen, E.J. (1984). Effects of noise and attack on aggression and physical arousal. *Motivation and Emotion*, 8, 231-241.

Geen, R.G. (1990). *Human Aggression.* Pacific Grove, CA.: Brooks/Cole.

Gelfand, M.J., Nishii, L.H., Holcombe, K.M., Dyer, N., Ohbuchi, K. & Fukuno, M. (2001). Cultural influences on cognitive representations of conflict: Interpretations of conflict episodes in the United States and Japan. *Journal of Applied Psychology*, 86, 1059-1074.

Geller, E.S. (1990). Behavioral analysis and environmental preservation: Where have all the flowers gone? *Journal of Applied Behavioral Analysis*, 23, 269-273.

Ger, G., Belk, R.W. & Lasere, D.N. (1993). The development of consumer desires in marketising and developing economies: The case of Romania, Turkey. In L. McAlister & M.J. Rothschild (Eds.), *Advances in Consumer Research* (Vol. 20, 102-107), Provo: Association for Consumer Research.

Gerbner, A. (1972). Violence in television drama. Trends in symbolic functions. In G.A. Comstock & E.A. Rubinstein (Eds.), *Television and Social Behavior, Vol. I: Media Content and Control*. Washington DC: United States Government Printing Press.

Gerbner, G., Gross, L., Morgan, M. & Signorielli, N. (1994). Growing up with television: The cultivation perspective. In J. Bryant & D. Zillman (Eds.), *Media Effects: Advances in Theory and Research*. Hillsdale, NJ: Lawrence Erlbaum.

Gergen, K.J. (1973). Social psychology as history. *Journal of Personality and Social Psychology*, 26, 309-320.

Gergen, K.J. (1990). Social understanding and inscription of self. In J.W. Stigler, R.A. Shweder & G. Herdt. (Eds.), *Cultural Psychology*. Cambridge: Cambridge University Press, 569-606.

Gergen, K.J. (1999). *An Invitation to Social Construction*. London: Sage

Gergen, K.J. (2001). Psychological science in a postmodern context. *American Psychologist*, 56, 803-813.

Gerstein, L.H. & Moeschberger, S.L. (2003). Building cultures of peace: An urgent task for counseling professionals. *Journal of Counseling & Development*, 81, 115-119.

Gifford, R. (2002). Making a difference: Some ways environmental psychology has improved the world. In R.B.Bechtel & A Churchman (Eds.), *Handbook of Environmental Psychology*, 323-334. New York: Wiley.

Gilligan, C. (1982). *In a Different Voice*. Ca: Harvard University Press.

Glaser, R. & Kiecolt-Glaser, J.K. (Eds.) (1994). *Handbook of Human Stress and Immunity*. San Diego: Academic.

Glass, D.C., & Singer, J.E. (1972). *Urban Stress: Excerpts on Noise and Social Stressors*. New York: Academic Press.

Glock, C.Y. (1962). On the study of religious commiment. *Religious Education, Research Supplement*, 57 (4), S98-S110.

Godart, N.T., Flament, M.F., Curt, F., Perdereau, F., Lang, F., Venisse, J.L et al., (2003). Anxiety disorders in subjects seeking treatment for eating disorders: A DSM-IV controlled study. *Psychiatry Research*, 117, 245-258.

Goldinger, S.D., Kleider, H.M., Azuma, T. & Beike, D.R. (2003). Blaming the victim under memory load. *Psychological Science*, 14, 81-85.

Goldstein, A.P. (1989). *Aggressive Behavior: Assessment and Intervention*. New York: Pergamon Press.

Goldstein, A.P. & Soriano, F.I. (1994). Juvenile gangs. In L.D. Eron, J.H. Gentry & P. Schlegel (Eds.), *Reason to Hope: A Psychological Perspective on Violence and Youth.* Washington DC: American Psychological Association.

Goldstein, J. & Mlicki, P. (1996). Doing justice to non-violence. *Contemporary Psychology,* 41, 131-32.

Goldstein, J. (1986). *Aggression and Crimes of Violence.* New York: Oxford Press.

Gomes do Espirito, M.E. & Etheredge, G.D. (2003). HIV prevalence and sexual behavior of male clients of brothels. In Dakar, Senegal, *AIDS Care,* 15, 53-62.

Gomey, C. & Martin, B. (1993, June). Can women demand condom use? Gender and power in sex. Paper presented at the meeting of the *Ninth International Conference on AIDS*, Berlin, Germany.

Gonzalez, A. (1979). Classroom cooperation and ethnic balance. Unpublished doctoral dissertation. University of California at Santa Cruz.

Gonzales, M. Aronson, E. & Costanzo, M. (1988). Using social cognition and persuasion to promote energy conservation: A quasi-experiment. *Journal of Applied Social Psychology,* 18, 1049-1066.

Good, T.L. & Weinstein, R.S. (1986). Schools make a difference: Evidence, criticisms and new directions. *American Psychologist,* 41-10, 1090-1097.

Gore, S. (1978). The effect of social support in moderating the health consequnces of unemployment. *Journal of Health and Social Behavior*, 19, 157-165.

Graham, J.L. (1985). The influence of culture in the process of business negotiations: An exploratory study. *Journal of International Business Studies*, 16, 81-96.

Granzin, K.L. & Olson, J.E. (1991). Characterizing participants in activities protecting the environment: A focus on donating, recycling and conservation behaviors. *Journal of Public Policy and Marketing*, 10-2, 1-27.

Gray, F., Graubard, P.S. & Rosenberg, H. (1974). Little brother is changing you. *Psychology Today*, March, 42-46.

Greenberg, B.S. & Gordon, T.F. (1972). Children's perception of television violence: A prediction. In G.A. Comstock; E. A. Rubinstein & J.P. Murray (Eds.), *Television and Social Behavior*, Vol V. Washington DC: US Government Printing Office.

Greening, L., & Chandler, C.C. (1997). Why it can't happen to me: The base rate matters, but overestimating skill leads to underestimating risk. *Journal of Applied Social Psychology*, 27, 760-780.

Greenwald, A.G., Carnot, C.G., Beach, R. & Young, B. (1987). Increasing voting behavior by asking people if they expect to vote. *Journal of Applied Psychology*, 72, 315-318.

Greenwald, A.G., Spanenberg, E.R., Pratkauis, A.R. & Eskenazi, J. (1991). Double-blind tests of subliminal self-help audiotapes. *Psychological Science*, 2, 119-122.

Greenway, R. (1995). The wilderness effect and ecopsychology. In T. Roszak, M.E. Gomes, and A.D. Kanner (Eds.), *Ecopsychology: Restoring the Earth Healing the Mind.* San Francisco: Sierra Club Books.

Gregson, D. & Efran, J.S. (2002). *The Tao of Sobriety: Helping You to Recover from Alcohol and Drug Addiction.* New York: Thomas Dunne Books.

Griffith, W. & Jackson, T. (1973). Simulated jury decisions: The influence of jury defendent attitude similarity and dissimilarity. *Social Behavior and Personality*, 1, 1-7.

Griffiths, P.J. (2002). Psychoneuroimmunology and eastern religious traditions. In H.G. Koenig and H.J. Cohen (Eds.). *The Link between Religion and Health: Psychoimmunology and the Faith Factor*, 250-261. London: Oxford University Press.

Grigoroiu-Serbanescu, M., Magureanu, S., Milea, S., Dobrescu, L. & Marinescu, E. (2003). Modest familial aggregation of eating disorders in restrictive anorexia nervosa with adolescent onset in a Romanian sample. *European Child and Adolescent Psychiatry,* 12, i47-i53.

Grisso, T., Steinberg, L., Woolard, J., Cauffman, E., Scott, E., Graham, S., Lexcen, F., Reppucci, N.D. & Schwartz, R. Juveniles' competence to stand trial: A comparison of adolescents' and adults' capacities as trial defendants. *Law & Human Behavior*, 27, 333-363.

Groebel, J. & Hinde, R. (Eds.) (1989). *Aggression and War.* New York: Cambridge University Press.

Grusky, O., Liu, H. & Johnston, M. (2002). HIV/AIDS in China: 1990-2001. *AIDS and Behavior*, 6, 381-393.

Grussendorf, J., McAlister, A., Sandstrom, P., Udd, L.& Morrison, T.C. (2002). Resisting moral disengagement in support for war: Use of the "Peace Test" Scale among student groups in 2 groups. *Peace and Conflict: Journal of Peace Psychology*, 8, 73-84.

Gruzelier, J., Levy, J., Williams, J., & Henderson, D. (2001). Self-hypnosis in exam stress: Comparing immune and relaxation related imagery for influences on immunity, health and mood. *Contemporary Hypnosis*, 18, 73-86.

Guerin, D., Crete, J. & Mercer, J. (2001). A multilevel analysis of the determinants of recycling behavior in european countries. *Social Science Research,* 30, 195-218.

Guerra, N.G., Tolan, P. & Hammond, W.R. (1994). Prevention and treatment of adolescent violence. In L.D.Eron, J.H. Gentry and P. Schlegel (Eds.), *Reason to Hope: A Psychological Perspective on Violence and Youth*. Washington DC: American Psychological Association.

Gump, P.V. (1980). The school as a social situation. In M.R. Rozenweig & L.W. Porter (Eds.), *Annual Review of Psychology.* Palo Alto: Annual Reviews.

Gundykunst, W.B., Ting-Toomey, S. & Chua, E. (1988). *Culture and Interpersonal Communication*. Newbury Park: Sage.

Gupta, S., Chintaguta, P., Kaul, A. & Wittinik, D.R. (1996). Do household scanner data provide representative inferences from brand choices?: A comparison with store data. *The Journal of Marketing Research*, 33, 383-398.

Gurung, R.A.R. (2003). Comparing cultural and individual learning tendencies. *American Psychologist*, 58, 145-146.

Gutek, B.A. & Winter, S.J. (1990). Computer use, control over computers and job satisfaction. In S. Spacapan, & S. Oskamp (Eds.) *People's Reaction to Technology*. Newberry Park: Sage Publications.

Gutheil, T.G. & Hilliard, J.T. (2001). The treating psychiatrist thrust into the role of expert witness. *Psychiatric Services*, 52, 1526-1527.

Guttentag, M. (1977). Evolution and society. *Personality and Social Psychology Bulletin*, 3, 31-40.

Guttman, D. (1998). The psychoimmune system in later life: The problem of the late-onset disorders. In J. Lomranz (Ed.), *Handbook of Aging and Mental Health: An Integrative Approach*, 281-295. New York: Plenum.

Haddad, L.G. & Malak, M.Z. (2002). Smoking habits and attitudes towards smoking among university students in Jordan. *International Journal of Nursing Studies*, 39, 793-802.

Halim, S., Kaplan, H.B. & Pollack, M.S. (2000). Moderating effects of gender and vulnerability on the relationships between financial hardship, low education and immune response. *Stress Medicine*, 16, 167-177.

Hall, E.T. (1963). A system for the notation of proxemic behavior. *American Anthropologist*, 65, 1003-1026.

Hall, G.S. (1904). *Adolescence: Its Psychology, and its Relationships to Physiology, Anthropology, Sociology, Sex Drive, Religion and Education*. New York: Appleton.

Hall, T.J. & Edwards, K.J. (2002). The spiritual assessment inventory: A theistic model and measure for assessing spiritual development. *Journal for the Scientific Study of Religion*, 41, 341-357.

Hammer, M.R. (1987). Behavioral dimensions of intercultural effectiveness: A replication and extension. *International Journal of Intercultural Relations*, 31, 65-68.

Hanapi, H. & Kump, O. (2003). Collect now-consume later on: Innovative products in electronic commerce. *Decision Support Systems*, 34, 213-221.

Handelsman, M.M., Knapp, S. & Gottlieb, M.C. (2002). Positive ethics. In C.R. Snyder & J. Shane (Eds.), *Handbook of Positive Psychology*, 731- 744. London: Oxford University Press.

Handy, S.L., Boarnet, M.G., Ewing, R. & Killingsworth, R.E. (2002). How the built environment affects physical activity: Views from urban planning. *American Journal of Preventive Medicine*, 23, 64-73.

Haney, C. (1980). Psychology and legal change: On the limits of a factual jurisprudence. *Law and Human Behavior*, 4, 147-200.

Hannon, L., DeFronzo, J. & Prochnow, J. (2001). Moral commitment and the effects of social influences on violent delinquency. *Violence & Victims*, 16, 427-439.

Harkness, A.R., DeBono, K.G. & Borgida, E. (1985). Personal involvement and strategies for making contingency judgments: A stake in the dating game makes a difference. *Journal of Personality and Social Psychology*, 49, 22-32.

Harnett, D.L., Cummings, L.L. & Hughes, G.D. (1968). The influence of risk-taking propensity on bargaining behavior. *Behavioral Science*, 13, 91-101.

Harpaz, I. (2002). Advantages and disadvantages of telecommuting for the individual, organization and society. *Work Study: A Journal of Productivity Science*, 51, 74-80.

Harper, S. (1995). The way of wilderness. In T. Roszak, M.E. Gomes, and A.D. Kanner (Eds.) *Ecopsychology: Restoring the Earth Healing the Mind.* San Francisco: Sierra Club Books.

Harris, M. & Rosenthal, R. (1986). Four factors in the mediation of teacher expectancy effects. In R. Feldman (Ed.), *The Social Psychology of Education: Current Research and Theory*. New York: Cambridge University Press, 91-131.

Harris, P.B. & McAndrews, F.T. (1986). Territoriality and compliance: The influence of gender and location on willingness to sign petitions. *Journal of Social Psychology*, 126, 657-662.

Harrison, A.A., Clearwater, Y.A. & McKay, C.P. (1991). Introduction. In A.A. Harrison, Y.A. Clearwater, & C.P. McKay (Eds.), *From Antarctica to Outer Space: Life in Isolation and Confinement,* 1-6. New York: Springer Verlag.

Hartup, W.W. (1983). Peer relations. In P.H. Mussen (Ed.) *Handbook of Child Psychology*, Vol 4. New York: Wiley.

Hastie, R., Penrod, S.D. & Pennington, N. (1983). *Inside the Jury*. Cambridge, MA.: Harvard University Press.

Hauenstein, N.M.A.; McGonigle, T. & Flinder, S.W.A. (2001). Meta-analysis of the relationship between procedural justice and distributive justice: Implications for justice research. *Employee Responsibilities & Rights Journal*, 13, 39-56.

Hawkins, S.A. & Hastie, R. (1966). *The American Jury*. Boston: Little Brown.

Hayes, N.& Joseph, S. (2003). Big 5 correlates of three measures of subjective well being. *Personality and Individual Differences*, 34, 723-727.

Heath, L. (1992). *Issues in Applied Social Psychology*. New York: Plenum.

Hegeman, S. (1999). Shopping for identities: "A nation of nations" and the weak ethnicity of objects. *Public Culture*, 3, 71-92.

Heider, F. (1957). *The Psychology of Interpersonal Relations*. New York: Wiley.

Helms, M.M.& Raiszadeh, F.M.E. (2002). Virtual offices: Understanding and managing what you cannot see.*Work Study: A Journal of Productivity Science*. 51, 240-247.

Henerson, M.E., Morris, L.L. & Fitzgibbons, C.T. (1987). *How to Measure Attitudes*. Thousand Oaks CA: Sage Publishing.

Henry, J. (2003). Positive organizations. *Psychologist*, 16, 138-139.

Herbelein, T.A. & Black, J.S. (1976). Attitudinal specificity and the prediction of behavior in a field setting. *Journal of Personality and Social Psychology*, 33, 474-479.

Herberman, R.B. (2002). Stress, natural killer cells, and cancer. In H.G. Koenig and H.J.Cohen (Eds.). *The Link between Religion and Health: Psychoimmunology and the Faith Factor*, 69-83. London: Oxford University Press.

Herman, T. (1993). Exercises in non-violent action. In V.K. Kool (Ed.), *Non-violence: Social and Psychological Issues.* Lanham, MD: University of American Press.

Herrnstein, R.J., & Murray, C.L. (1994). *The Bell Curve*. New York: Free Press.

Hetherington, E.M. & Parke, R.D. (1986). *Child Psychology: A Contemporary Viewpoint*. New York: McGraw Hill.

Higgins, E.J., Rhodes, W.S. & Jones, C.R. (1977). Category accessibility and impression formation. *Journal of Experimental Social Psychology*, 12, 141-164.

Higgins, E.T., & Kruglanski, A.W. (1996). *Social Psychology: Handbook of Basic Principles*. New York: Guildford Press.

Hill, B. (1999). http://www.clan.com/environment/ecopsyweb/.

Hill, C. (2003). The role of instructional assistants in regular classrooms: Are they influencing inclusive practices? *Alberta Journal of Educational Research*, 49, 98-100.

Hill, E.J., Ferris, M. & Märtinson, V. (2003). Does it matter where you work? A comparison of how three work venues (traditional office, virtual office, and home office) influence aspects of work and personal/family life. *Journal of Vocational Behavior*, 63, 220-241.

Hill, P.C. & Pargament, K.I. (2003). Advances in the conceptualization and measurement of religion and spirituality. *American Psychologist*, 58, 64-74.

Hill, P.C., Pargament, K.I., Hood, R.W.Jr., McCullough, M.E., Swyers, J.P., Larson, D.B. & Zinnbauer, B.J. (2000). Conceptualizing religion and spirituality: Points of commonality; points of departure. *Journal for the Theory of Social Behavior,* 30, 51-77.

Hillier, J. (2002). Presumptive planning: From urban design to community creation in one move. In A.T. Fisher & C.C. Sonn et al. (Eds.), *Psychological Sense of Community: Research, Applications and Implications*, 43-67. New York: Kluwer Academic/Plenum.

Hiltunen, S.M.S. (2001). Seven stages of womanhood: A contemporary healing ritual from the Finnish mythology of the Kalevala. *Journal of Transpersonal Psychology*, 33, 113-129.

Hinz, T. & Pezdek, K. (2001). The effect of exposure to multiple lineups on face identification accuracy. *Law & Human Behavior*, 25, 185-198.

Hirschman, E. (1981). American jewish ethnicity: Its relationship to some selected aspects of consumer behavior. *Journal of Marketing,* 45, 102-110.

Hobbs, P. (2003). 'Is that what we're here about?': A lawyer's use of impression management in a closing argument at trial. *Discourse & Society*, 14, 273-290.

Hodges, J. & Angalet, B. (1968). The prime technical information source: The local work environment. *Human Factors*, 10-4, 425-430.

Hodgkinson, V.A. & Weitzman, M.S. (1992*). Giving and Volunteering in the United States.* Washington DC: Independent Sector.

Hofstede, G. (1980). *Culture's Consequences*. Beverly Hills: Sage.

Hoge, P.R. & Carroll, J.W. (1973). Religiosity and prejudice in Northern and Southern churches. *Journal of the Scientific Study of Religion,* 12, 181-187.

Holaday, L.C. (2002). Stage development theory: A natural framework for understanding the mediation process. *Negotiation Journal*, 18, 191-210.

Holland, A.W. & Curtis, K. (1998). Operational psychological countermeasures during the Lunar Mars Life Support test project. *Life Support Biosphere Science*, 5, 445-452.

Holland, K.D. & Holahan, C.K. (2003). The relation of social support and coping to positive adaptation to breast cancer. *Psychology and Health*, 18, 15-29.

Holmes, D. (1990). The evidence for repression: An examination of sixty years of research.

Holmes, T.M., & Rahe, R.H. (1967). The social readjustment rating scale. *Journal of Psychosomatic Research*, 11, 213-218.

Homans, G.C. (1974). *Social Behavior and its Elementary Forms*. New York: Harcourt, Brace & Jovanovich.

Hood, R.W. Jr. (1976). Mystical experience as related to present and anticipated future church participation. *Psychological Reports*, 39, 1127-36.

Hood, R.W. Jr. (1992). Sin and guilt in faith traditions: Issues for self-esteem. In J. Schumaker (Ed.), *Religion and Mental Health*. New York: Oxford University Press.

Hoosain, R. & Salili, F. (1988). Language differences, working memory and mathematical ability. In M.M. Gruneberg, P.E.Morris & R.N.Sykes (Eds.), *Practical Aspects of Memory: Current Research and Issues*, 512-517. Chichester: Wiley.

Houston, H.R. (2002). Marketing tuberculosis prevention programs to foreign born Vietnamese: The role of culture in the effective diffusion of public sector health care services. *Journal of Non-profit and Public Sector Marketing*, 10, 1-19.

Hovland, C.L. Janis, K.& Kelly, H.H. (1953). *Communication and Persuasion*. New Haven: Yale University Press.

Hua, Z. (2000). The sequential organisation of gift offering and acceptance in Chinese. *Journal of Pragmatics*, 32, 81-103.

Huba, M.E. & Freed, J.E. (2000). *Learner Centered Assessment on College Campuses: Shifting the Focus from Teaching to Learning*. Boston: Allyn & Bacon.

Huesmann, L.R. (1986). Psychological processes promoting the relationship between exposure to media violence and aggressive behavior by the viewer. *Journal of Social Issues*, 42, 125-139.

Huesmann, L.R. (1993, August). Cited by T. Angelis. It's baaack: Television violence, concern for kid viewers. *American Psychological Association Monitor*, 16.

Huesmann, L.R., Eron, L.D., Lefkowitz, M.M. & Walden, L. (1984). Stability of aggression over time and generations. *Developmental Psychology*, 20, 1120-1134.

Huesmann, L.R., Lagersbetz, K. & Eron, L.D. (1984). Intervening variables in the television violence-aggression relation: Evidence for two countries. *Developmental Psychology*, 20-5, 746-775.

Huff, C. Ronald, A. Rattner, & E. Sagarin (1996). *Convicted But Innocent*. Thousand Oaks, CA: Sage Publications

Huff, M. & Edwards, S. (2001). Using technology tools to enhance learning in social work diversity courses. *Journal of Technology in Human Services*, 18, 51-64.

Hughes-d'Aeth, A. (2002). Evaluation of HIV/AIDS peer education projects in Zambia. *Evaluation and Program Planning*, 25, 397-407.

Humphrey, S.E., Ellis, A.P.J., Conlon, D.E. & Tinsley, C H. (2004). Understanding customer reactions to brokered ultimatums: Applying negotiation and justice theory. *Journal of Applied Psychology*, 89, 466-482.

Hunt, M., Kouimtsidis, C., Reynolds, M., Lind, J. & Ghodse, H. (2003). Smoking among patients admitted to a general hospital: A missed opportunity for early intervention. *Drugs: Education, Prevention and Policy*, 10, 31-38.

Huston, A.C., Watkins, B.A., & Kunkel, D. (1989). Public policy and children's television. *American Psychologist*, 44, 424-433.

Idler, E.L. & Kasl, S.V. (1997). Religion among disabled and non-disabled persons: I. Cross-sectional patterns in health practices, social activities, and well-being. *Journals of Gerontology Series B: Psychological Sciences and Social Sciences*, 52, S294-S305.

Igreja, V. & Reidessed, P. (2002). Children's and adolescents' traumatic loss of their parents and their treatment by traditional healers in Mozambique. *Kinderanalyse,* 10, 253-262.

Ikeya, T. & Kasai, Makiko (2003). *Japanese Journal of Counseling Science,* 36, 206-220.

Ironson, G., Antoni, M.H., Schneiderman, N., Chesney, M.A., O'Cleirigh, C., Balbin, E., Greenwood, D., Lutgendorf, S., LaPerreire, A., Klimas, N. & Fletcher, M.A. (2002). Coping interventions for optimal disease management. In M.A.Chesney & M.H.Anthony (Eds.), *Innovative Approaches to Health Psychology: Prevention and Treatment Lessons from AIDS*, 167-195. Washington DC:American Psychological Association.

Ironson, G., Balbin, E. & Schneiderman, N. (2002). Health psychology and infectious diseases. In T.J. Boll & S.B. Bennett (Eds.), *Handbook of Clinical Health Psychology,* Vol 1, 5-36. Washington DC: American Psychological Association.

Ironson, G. & Schneiderman, N. (2002). Psychological factors, spirituality/ religiousness, and immune function in HIV/AIDS patients. In Koenig, H.G. & Cohen, H.J. (2002). *The Link between Religion and Health: Psychoneuroimmunology and the Faith Facto*r. 139-159. London: Oxford University Press.

Ironson, G., Solomon, G.F., Balbin, E.G., O'Cleirigh, C., George, M.A. & Kumar, M. (2002). The Ironson-Woods Spirituality/Religiousness Index is associated with long survival, health behaviors, less distress, and low cortisol in people with HIV/AIDS. *Annals of Behavioral Medicine,* 24, 34-48.

Iverson, H. & Rundmo, T. (2002). Environmental concern and environmental behavior among the Norwegian public. *Journal of Risk Research*, 5, 265-279.

J.M. Stoppard & McMullen, L.M. (Eds.). *Situating Sadness: Women and Depression in Social Context*. New York: New York University Press.

Jacobs, M.K., Christensen, A., Snibbe, J.R., Dolezal-Wood, S., Huber, A. & Polterok, A. (2001). A comparison of computer-based versus traditional individual psychotherapy. *Professional Psychology: Research and Practice*, 32, 92-96.

Jacobs, R.C. & Campbell, D.T. (1961). The perpetuation of an arbitrary tradition through several generations of a laboratory microculture. *Journal of Abnormal and Social Psychology*, 62, 649-658.

Jacoby, J. (1975). Consumer psychology as a social psychological sphere of action. *American Psychologist*, 30, 977-987.

Jaeger, B., Ruggiero, G.M., Edlund, B., Gomez-Peretta, C., Lang, F., Mohammadkhani, P., Sahleen-Veasey, C., Schomer, H. & Lamprecht, F. (2002). Body dissatisfaction and its interrelations with other risk factor for bulimia nervosa in 12 countries. *Psychotherapy and Psychosomatics*, 71, 54-61.

Jain, R. & Costa, J.A. (1991). Research progress report: Fragrance use in India. In J.A. Costa (Ed.), *Gender and Consumer Behavior,* 1, 77-84. Salt Lake City: University of Utah Press.

Jain, U. (1993). Concomitants of population density in India. *Journal of Social Psychology*, 133, 331-336.

James, W. (1902). *The Varieties of Religious Experience: A Study in Human Nature.* Cambridge: Harvard Universtiy Press (1985).

Jamieson, D.W., Lydon, J.E., Stewart, G & Zanna, M.P. (1987). Pygmalion revisited: New evidence for student expectancy effects in the classroom. *Journal of Educational Psychology,* 79, 461-466.

Janis, I.L. (1958). *Psychological Stress.* New York: Wiley.

Janis, I.L. & Mann, L. (1965). The effectiveness of emotive role playing in modifying smoking habits and attitudes. *Journal of Experimental Research in Personality*, 1, 84-90.

Janssen, O. (2004). How fairness perceptions make innovative behavior more or less stressful. *Journal of Organizational Behavior*. 25, 201-215.

Johansson, I. & Berteroe, C.M. (2003). Getting no respect: Barriers to mammography for a group of Swedish women. *Health Care for Women International*, 24, 8-17.

Johnson, D.W., & Johnson, R.T. (1975). *Learning Together and Alone.* Englewood Cliffs, NJ: Prentice-Hall.

Johnson, D.W. & Johnson, R.T. (1989). *Cooperation and Competition: Theory and Research.* Edina: Interaction Book Company.

Johnson, D.W., & Johnson, R.T. (1992). *Positive Interdependence: The Heart of Cooperative Learning.* Edina MN: Interaction Book Company.

Johnson, D.W. & Johnson, R.T. (1994). Cooperative learning in a culturally diverse classroom. In R. DeVillar, C. Faltis & J. Cummins. (Eds.), *Cultural Diversity in Schools.* New York: State University of New York Press, 57-74.

Johnson, D.W & Johnson, R.T. (1996). Conflict resolution and peer mediated programs in elementary and secondary schools: A review of research. Unpublished manuscript, University of Minnesota.

Johnson, D.W. & Johnson, R.T. (1997). *Joining Together. Group Theory and Group Skills.* Needham Heights, MA: Allyn & Bacon.

Johnson, D.W. & Johnson, R.T. (2003). Fieldtesting integrative negotiations. *Peace & Conflict: Journal of Peace Psychology*, 9, 39-68.

Johnson, D.W., Johnson, R.T., Dudley, B. & Acikgoz (1994). Effects of conflict resolution training on elementary school students. *Journal of Social Psychology*, 134, 803-817.

Johnson, P., Heimann, V. & O'Neill, K. (2001). The "wonderland" of virtual teams. *Journal of Workplace Learning*, 13, 24-30,

Johnson, R.M., Kotch, J.B., Catellier, D.J., Winsor, J.R., Dufort, V., Hunter, W., Amaya-Jackson, L. (2002). Adverse behavioral and emotional outcomes from child abuse and witnessed violence. *Child Maltreatment: Journal of the American Professional Society on the Abuse of Children*, 7, 179-186.

Jones, C.S. & Kaplan, M.F. (2003). The effects of racially stereotypical crimes on juror decision-making and information-processing strategies. *Basic & Applied Social Psychology*, 25, 1-13

Jones, L. (2002). Adolescent understandings of political violence and psychological well-being: A qualitative study from Bosnia Herzegovina. *Social Psychology and Medicine*, 55, 1351-1371.

Jones, L.V. (2004). Enhancing Psychosocial Competence among Black Women in College. *Social Work*, 49, 75-84.

Josephson, W.L. (1987). Television violence and children's aggression: Testing the priming social script and distribution predictions. *Journal of Personality and Social Psychology*, 53, 882-890.

Joy, A. (2001). Gift giving in Hong Kong and the continuum of social ties. *Journal of Consumer Research*, 28, 239-256.

Joy, A. & Dholakia, R.R. (1991). Remembrances of things past: The meaning of home possessions to Indian professionals in Canada. *Journal of Social Behavior and Personality*, 6, 385-402.

Joy, L.A., Kimball, M.M. & Zabrack, M.L. (1986). Television and children's aggressive behavior. In T.M. Williams (Ed.), *The Impact of Television: A Natural Experiment in Three Communities*. Orlando, Fl: Academic Press.

Judge, T.A. & Colquitt, J.A. (2004). Organizational justice and stress: The mediating role of work-family conflict. *Journal of Applied Psychology*, 89, 395-404.

Judson, S. (1964). *A Manual of Non-violence and Children*. Philadelphia, PA: New Society Publishers.

Kahn, R.L. & Antonucci, T.C. (1980). Convoys over the life course: Attachment, roles and social support. In P.B. Baltes and O.G. Brim, (Eds.), *Life Span Development and Behavior*. New York: Academic.

Kahnmann, D. & Tversky, A. (1979). Prospect theory: An analysis of decision under risk. *Econometrica*, 47, 263-291.

Kalichman, S.C. (2003). What are the legal aspects of AIDS? In S.C. Kalichman, *The Inside Story on AIDS*, 225-241. Washington DC: American Psychological Association.

Kalichman, S.C., Weinhardt, L., Benotsch, E. DiFonzo, K., Luke, W. & Austin, J. (2002). Internet access and internet use for health information among people living with HIV-AIDS. *Patient Education & Counseling*, 46, 109-116.

Kalvern, H. & Zeisel, H. (1966). *The American Jury*. Chicago: University of Chicago Press.

Kamali, A., Quigley, M., Nakiyingi, J., Kinsman, J., Kengeya-Kayondo, J., Gopal, R., Ojwiya, A., Hughes, P., Carpenter, L.M. & Whitworth, J. (2003). Syndromic management of sexually transmitted infections and behavior change interventions on transmission of HIV-1 in rural Uganda: A community randomized trial. *Lancet,* 361, 645-652.

Kaminer, W. (1996, October 13). The inner you. *The Los Angeles Times,* 13-22.

Kanas, N. (1997). Psychosocial value of space simulation for extended space flight. *Advances in Space Biological Medicine*, 6, 81-91.

Kanas, N. (2002). Group therapeutic approaches for people with eating problems. *International Journal of Group Psychotherapy*, 52, 589-593.

Kaplan, R. (2001). The nature of the view from home: Psychological benefits. *Environment and Behavior*, 33, 507-542.

Kaplan, R.M.C., & Toshima, M.T. (1990). Social relationship in chronic disease and disability. In I.G. Sarason, B.R. Sarason, C.G.R. Pierce (Eds.), *Social Support: An Interachismist Perspective.* New York: Wiley.

Kass, J., Kass, R., Sauraltidinov, I. (1995). Psychological considerations of man in space: Problems and solutions. *Acta Astronaut*, 36, 657-660.

Kassenbaum, N. (1994). Head Start: Only the best for America's children. *American Psychologist*, 49, 123-126.

Kassin, S.M., Ellsworth, P.C. & Smith, V.L. (1989). Testimony: A survey of experts. *American Psychologist*, 44, 8, 1089-1098.

Katz-Gerro, T. (2002). Highbrow cultural consumption and class distinction in Italy, Israel, W. Gremany, Sweden and USA. *Social Forces,* 81, 207-229.

Kaufman, G.D. (1981). *The Theological Imagination: Constructing a Concept of God.* Philadelphia: Westminister.

Kaye, H.L. (2002). Psychoneuroimmunology and religion: Implications for society and culture. In H.G. Koenig and H.J. Cohen (Eds.). *The Link between Religion and Health: Psychoimmunology and the Faith Factor*, 174-196. London: Oxford University Press.

Kazdin, A.E. (1993). Adolescent mental health. *American Psychologist*, 48, 127-161.

Kazdin, A.E. (1994). *Behavior Modification in Applied Settings*. Pacific Grove, CA: Brooks & Cole Publishing Co.

Kazdin, A.E. (1994). Intervention for aggressive and antisocial children. In L.D. Eron, J.H. Gentry & P. Schlegel (Eds.), *Reason to Hope: A Psychological Perspective on Violence and Youth.* Washington DC: American Psychological Association.

Keashey, L. & Fisher, R.J. (1990). Towards a contingency approach to third party intervention in regional conflict: A cypress illustration. *Interactive Journal*, 45, 424-453.

Keashey, L. & Fisher, R.J. (1996). A contingency perspective on conflict intervention: Theoretical and practical considerations. In J. Bercovitch (Ed.), *Resolving Interventional Conflict*. Boulder, CO: Lynne Richner Publishers.

Kebbell, M.R. (2000). The law concerning the conduct of lineups in England and Wales: How well does it satisfy the recommendations of the American psychology-law society. *Law and Human Behavior*, 24, 309-315.

Kedia, B.L. & Bhagat, R.S. (1988). Cultural constraints on transfer of technology across nations: Implications for research in international and comparative management. *Academy of Management Review*, 13, 559-571.

Kehoe-Schwartz, E., Scott, V. & Birman, B.F. (1994). Student mobility in the nation's elementary schoolds. *Education Considerations*, 22, 13-19.

Keisher, C.A. (1971). *The Psychology of Commitments. Experts linking Behavior to Attitudes*. New York: Academic Press.

Keith, T.Z., Reimers, T.M., Fehrmann, P.G., Pottebaum, S.M. & Aubey, L.W. (1986). Parental involvement, homework, and television time: Direct and indirect effects on high school achievement. *Journal of Educational Psychology*, 78, 373-380.

Kelder, S.H., Prokhorov, A., Barroso, C.S., Murray, N., Orpinas, P. & McCormic, L. (2003). Smoking differences among African, American, Hispanic and white middle school students in an urban setting. *Addictive Behaviors*, 28, 513-522.

Keller, S.E., Shifflet, S.C., Schliefer, S.J. & Bartlett, J.A. (1994). Stress, immunity and health. In Glaser, R. & Kiecolt-Glaser, J.K. (Eds.), (1994). *Handbook of Human Stress and Immunity*. San Diego: Academic.

Kelley, H.H. (1967). Attribution theory in social psychology. In D.L. Vine (Ed.), *Nebraska Symposium on Motivation*. Lincoln: University of Nebraska Press.

Kellog, R. & Baron, R.S. (1975). Attribution theory, insomnia and the reverse placebo effect. *Journal of Personality and Social Psychology*, 32, 231-236.

Kelly, J. (1975). *Organizational Behavior*. Homewood, Ill: Dorsey-Irwin.

Kelman, H. (1986). The interactional approach to conflict resolution. In R.K. White (Ed.), *Psychology and the Prevention of Nuclear War*. New York: New York University Press.

Kelman, H. (1993). Coalition across conflict lines: The interplay of conflicts within and between the Israeli and Palestinian communities. In S. Worchel, & J. Smithson (Eds.), *Conflict between People and Groups*. Chicago: Nelson-Hall.

Kendrick, D.T. & MacFarland, S.W. (1986). Ambient temperature and horn blowing: A field study of heat/aggression relationship. *Environment and Behavior*, 14, 94-102.

Kennedy, D.B., Homant, R.J. & Homant, M.R. (2004). Perception of injustice as a predictor of support for workplace aggression. *Journal of Business & Psychology*, 18, 323-336.

Kennedy, M.J.B. (2001). The effect of neighbourhood environments on schizophrenic relapse: A socio cultural perspective. *Dissertation Abstracts International, Section A: Humanities and Social Sciences*, 61, 4554.

Kenrick, D.T. & MacFarlane, S.W. (1986). Ambient temperature and horn honking: A field study of the heat/ aggression relationship. *Environment and Behavior*, 18, 179-191.

Kerr, B. & McAlister, J. (2000). Shamanic journey: An apprenticeship in spiritual intelligence. *Advanced Development*, 9, 45-55.

Kersting, K. (2003). Turning happiness into economic power. *Monitor on Psychology*, 34, 26-27.

Kersting, K. (2004). Custom tailored resilience. *APA Monitor*, 35-2, 34.

Kettunen, P. (2002). The function of confession: A study based on experiences. *Pastoral Psychology*, 51, 13-25.

Keyes, C.L., Shmotkin, D. & Ryff, C.D. (2002). Optimizing well being: The empirical encounter of two traditions. *Journal of Personality and Social Psychology*, 82, 1007-1022.

Kidder, L.H. (1991). Japanese returnees: Loose threads in a tight culture. Unpublished manuscript. Temple University.

Kiecolt-Glaser, J.F. & Glaser, R. (1992). PNI: Can psychological interventions modulate immunity. *Journal of Counseling and Clinical Psychology,* 60, 569-575.

Kiecolt-Glaser, J.K. & Glaser, R. (2002). Depression and immue function: Central pathways to morbidity and mortality. *Journal of Psychosomatic Research*, 53, 873-876.

Kiecolt-Glaser, J.K., Page, G.G., Marucha, P.T., MacCallum, R.C. & Glaser, R. (1998). Psychological influences on surgical recovery" perspectives from psychoneuroimmunology. *American Psychologist*, 53, 1209-1218.

Kiellor, B.D., D'Amico, M. & Horton, V. (2001). Global consumer tendencies. *Psychology and Marketing*, 18, 1-19.

Kieren, N.M. & Gold, M.A (2000). Pygmalion in the work organization: A meta-analysis. *Journal of Organizational Behavior*, 21, 913-928.

Kiesler, S., Siegel, J. & McGuire, T.W. (1984). Social psychological aspects of computer mediated communication. *American Psychologist,* 39, 1123-1134.

Kim, J.E. & Nesselroade, J.R. (2003). Relationships among social support, self concept and well being of older adults: A study of process using dynamic factor models. *International Journal of Behavioral Development*, 27, 49-63.

Kim, U. (1990). Indigenous psychology: Science and applications. In R. Brislin (Ed.), *Applied Cross Cultural.*

Kimmel, P.R. (1985). Learning about peace: Choices and the US Academy of Peace as seen from two different perspectives. *American Psychologist,* 40, 536-541.

Kimmel, P.R. (1995). Sustainability and cultural understanding: Peace psychology as public interest science. P & C: *Journal of Personality Psychology*, 1, 101-116.

King, P.E., Furrow, J.L. & Roth, N. (2002). The influence of families and peers on adolescent religiousness. *Journal of Psychology and Christianity*, 21, 109-120.

Kingston, L. & Prior, M. (1995). The development of patterns of stable, transient, and school-aged aggressive behavior in young children. *Journal of the American Academy of Child and Adolescent Psychiatry,* 34, 348–358.

Kinney, J.A. (1995). *Essentials of Managing Workplace Violence.* Charlotte, NC: Pinkerton Service Group.

Kinsey, A.L., Pomeroy, W.B., Martin, C.E. & Gebbard, P.H. (1953). *Sexual Behavior in the Human Female.* Philadelphia: Saunders.

Kinyanda, E., Hjelmeland, H. & Musisi, S. (2004). Deliberate self-harm as seen in Kampala, Uganda: A case-control study. *Social Psychiatry & Psychiatric Epidemiology*, 39, 318-325.

Kipnis, D. (1996). Accounting for the use of behavior technologies in social psychology. *American Psychologist,* 49, 165-172.

Kirby, D., Short, L., Collins, S.J., Rugg, D., Kolbe, L., Howard, M., Miller, B., Somerstein, F. & Zarbin, L. (1994). School based programs to reduce sexual risk behavior: A review of effectiveness. *Public Health Reports,* 109, 339-360.

Kirkpatrick, L.A. (1995). Attachment theory and religious experience. In R.W. Hood, Jr. (Ed.), *Handbook of Religious Experience,* 446-475. Birmingham: Religious Education Press.

Kirkpatrick, L.A., Kellas, S. & Shillito, D. (1993). Loneliness and perceptions of social support from God. Paper presented at the 101st Annual Convention of the American Psychological Association, Toronto, Canada.

Kleinman, A. (1988). *The Illness Narrative.* New York: Basic Books.

Kleinman, A. & Cohen, A. (1997). Psychiatry's global challenge. *Scientific American*, 3, 86-89.

Klump, K.L., Wonderlich, S., Lehoux, P., Lilenfeld, L.R.R. & Bulik, C.M. (2002). Does environment matter? A review of non-shared environment and eating disorders. *International Journal of Eating Disorders*, 31, 118-135.

Knee, C.R., Neighbors, C. & Vietor, N.A. (2001). Self-determination theory as a framework for understanding road rage. *Journal of Applied Social Psychology,* 31, 889-904.

Knight, G.P., Guthrie, I.K., Page, M.C. & Fabes, R.A. (2002). Emotional arousal and gender differences in aggression: A meta-analysis. *Aggressive Behavior,* 28, 366-393.

Knight, J.L., Guilamo, T.A. & Sanchez-Ross, M.G. (2001). Famous or infamous? The influence of celebrity status and race on perceptions of responsibility for rape. *Basic & Applied Social Psychology*, 183-190.

Knoff, H. & Batsche, G. (1995). Project ACHIEVE: Analyzing a school reform program for at-risk and underachieving students. *School Psychology Review*, 24, 579-603.

Knopf, C. (1982). *Proceedings of Probe Research Seminar of Voice Technology.* New Brunswick, NJ: Probe Research, Inc.

Ko, G. & Gentry, J.W. (1991). The development of the time orientation for use in cross-cultural research. In R.H. Holman & M.R. Solomon (Eds.), *Advances in Consumer Research,* 18, 135-142. Provo: Association for Consumer Research.

Kobal, D. (2003). Self concept and dispositions to school education: A comparative study of groups of Central and Western Europeans. *Studia Psychologica*, 45, 21-36.

Kobasa, S.C. (1979). Stressful life events, personality and health: An inquiring into hardiness. *Journal of Personality and Social Psychology,* 37, 1-11.

Kobasa, S.C. (1982). The hardy personality: Towards a social psychology of stress and health. In J. Suls, & G. Sanders (Eds.), *Social Psychology of Health and Illness*, Hillsdale: Earlbaum.

Koch, S. & Leary, D.E. (Eds.) (1985). *A Century of Psychology as a Science.* New York: McGraw Hill.

Koehler, S.P. & Willis, F.N. (1994). Traffic citations in relation to gender. *Journal of Social Psychology*, 24, 1919-1926.

Koenig, H.G. & Cohen, H.J. (2002). Psychological stress and autoimmune disease. In H.G. Koenig and H.J. Cohen (Eds.). *The Link between Religion and Health: Psychoimmunology and the Faith Factor*, 174-196. London: Oxford University Press.

Koenig, H.G. & Cohen, H.J. (2002). Psychosocial factors, immunology and wound healing. In Koenig, H.G. & Cohen, H.J. (2002). *The Link between Religion and Health: Psychoneuroimmunology and the Faith Factor,* 124-138. London: Oxford University Press.

Koenig, H.G. & Cohen, H.J. (2002). *The Link between Religion and Health: Psychoneuroimmunology and the Faith Factor*. London: Oxford University Press.

Koenig, H.G., McCulough, M.E., & Larson, D.B. (2001). *Handbook of Religion and Health.* New York: Oxford University Press.

Koenig, H.G., Pargament, K.I. & Nielsen, J. (1998). Religious coping and heath status in medically ill hospitalized older adults. *Journal of Nervous and Mental Disease*, 186, 513-521.

Koestner, R., Houlfort, N., Paquet, S. & Knight, C. (2001). On the risks of recycling because of guilt: An examination of the consequence of introjection. *Journal of Applied Social Psychology*, 31, 2545-2560.

Kohlberg, L. (1976). Moral stages and moralization: The cognitive developmental approach. In T. Lickona (Ed.), *Moral Development and Behavior*. NewYork: Holt.

Kolb, D.A. (1965). Achievement motivation training for under-achieving high school boys. *Journal of Personality and Social Psychology*, 2, 783-792.

Kool, V.K. (1983). Some variables related to authoritarianism in India. In V.K. Kool & J.J. Ray (Eds.), *Authoritarianism across Cultures*. Bombay, India: Himalaya Publishing House.

Kool, V.K. (1990). *Perspectives on Non-violence.* New York: Springer-Verlag.

Kool, V.K. (Ed.) (1993). *Non-violence: Social and psychological Issues.* Lanham MD: University Press of America.

Kool, V.K., Diaz, J., Brown, J. & Hama, H. (2002). Psychological research, non-violence and cultural orientation: An empirical analysis. *Regional Peace Studies Consortium Journal*, 55-74.

Kool, V.K. & Keyes, M.L. (1990). Explorations in the non-violent personality. In V.K. Kool (Ed.), *Perspectives on Non-violence.* New York: Springer-Verlag.

Kool, V.K. & Mishra, K. (2003). A comparative analysis of psychology teaching in India and the USA. Paper presented at the 17th Annual Conference on Teaching and Learning of Psychology, Navele Grande, New York, March.

Kool, V.K. & Sen, M. (1984). The non-violence test. In D.M. Pestonjee (Ed.), *Second Handbook of Psychological and Sociological Instruments,* 48-54. Ahmedabad: Indian Institute of Management.

Korgaonkar, P., Silverblatt, R. & O'Leary, B. (2001). Web advertising and Hispanics. *Journal of Consumer Marketing*, 18, 134-152.

Koropeckyj-Cox, T. (2002). Beyond parental status: Psychological well being in middle and old age. *Journal of Marriage and Family*, 64, 957-971.

Kouzma, N.M. & Kennedy, G.A. (2004). Self-reported sources of stress in senior high school students. *Psychological Reports*, 94, 314-316.

Kraus, A.S. & Lilienfield, A.M. (1959). Some epidemiological aspects of high mortality rates in the young widowed group. *Journal of Chronic Disease*, 10, 207-217.

Krause, N. (1998). Neighborhood deterioration, religious coping and changes in health during late life. *Gerontologist*, 38, 653-664.

Krause, N., Chatters, L.M., Meltzer, T. & Morgan, D.L. (2000). Negative interaction in the church: Insights from focus groups with older adults. *Review of Religious Practice*, 41, 510-533.

Krause, N., Herzog, A.R. & Baker, E. (1992). Providing support to others and well-being in later life. *Journals of Gerontology*, 47, 300-311.

Krauss, R.M. & Fussell, S.R. (1991). Perspective taking in communication: Representations of others knowledge in reference. *Social Cognition*, 9, 2-24.

Kraut, R.E., Fish, R.S., Root, R.W. & Chalfonte, B.L. (1990). Informal communication in organization: Form, function and technology. In S. Spacapan, & S. Oskamp (Eds.), *People's Reaction to Technology*. Newberry Park: Sage Publications.

Kray, L.J., Reb, J., Galinsky, A.D. & Thompson, L. (2004). Stereotype reactance at the bargaining table: The effect of stereotype activation and power on claiming and creating value. *Personality & Social Psychology Bulletin,* 30, 399-411.

Kresel, K. & Pruitt, G.L. (Eds.) (1989). *Mediation Research: The Process and Effectiveness of Third Party Intervention.* San Fransico, CA: Jossey-Bass.

Krippner, S. (2000). The epistemology and technologies of shamanic states of consciousness. *Journal of Consciousness Studies*, 7, 93-118.

Kroll, J.F. & Curley, J. (1988). Lexical memory in novice bilinguals: The role of concepts in retrieving second language words. In M.M. Gruneberg, P.E. Morris & R.N. Sykes (Eds.), *Practical Aspects of Memory: Current Research and Issues*, 389-395. Chichester: Wiley.

Kulaksizoglu, A. & Dilmac, B. (2003). Imparting education in human values to primary education students and testing it by implementing a Moral Maturity Scale. *Studia Psychological*, 45, 43-50.

Kunz, P.R. & Woolcott, M. (1976). Season's greetings: From my status to your's. *Social Science Research*, 5, 269-278.

Kurtz, B., Schneider, W., Carr, M., Bprkowski, J.G. & Turner, L.A. (1988). Sources of memory and metamemory development: Societal, parental and educational influences. In M.M. Gruneberg, P.E. Morris & R.N. Sykes (Eds.), *Practical Aspects of Memory: Current Research and Issues*, 537-542. Chichester: Wiley.

LaFreniere, P., Masataka, N., Butovskaya, M., Chen, Q., Dessen, M.A., Atwanger, K., Schreiner, S., Montirosso, R. & Frigerio, A. (2002). Cross-cultural analysis of social competence and behavior problems in pre-schoolers. *Early Education & Development*. 13, 201-219.

Lam, A.G., Zane, N. & Nolan, W.S. (2004). Ethnic Differences in Coping with Interpersonal Stressors: A Test of Self-Construals as Cultural Mediators. *Journal of Cross-Cultural Psychology*, 35, 446-459.

Lam, W.W.T. & Fielding, R. (2003). The evolving experience of illness for Chinese women with breast cancer: A qualititative study. *Psycho-Oncology*, 12, 127-140.

Lamb, D. (1995, November 5). Relighting the joy of smoking. *Los Angeles Times*.

Lambert, V.A., Lambert, C.E. Jr., Yamase, H. (2003). Psychological hardiness, workplace stress and related stress reduction strategies. *Nursing & Health Sciences*, 5, 181-184

Landau, S.E. (1984). Trends in violence and aggression: A cross-cultural analysis. *International Journal of Comparative Sociology*, 25, 133-158.

Lando, M. (1993). Formal quit smoking treatments. In C.T. Orleans, & J. Slade (Eds.), *Nicotine Addiction: Principles and Management*. New York: Oxford University Press.

Landrine, H. & Klonoft, E.A. (1992). Culture and health related schemas: A review and proposal for interdisciplinary integration. *Health Psychology*, 11, 267-276.

Landwehr, P.H., Bothwell, R.K., Jeanmard, M., Luque, L.R., Brown, R.L., III & Breaux, M. (2002). Racism in rape trials. *Journal of Social Psychology*, 142, 667-669.

Landy, D., & Aronson, E. (1969). The influence of character of the criminal and his victim on the decisions of simulated jurors. *Journal of Experimental Personality and Social Psychology*, 5, 141-152.

Lang, A., Goulet, C., Aita, M., Giguere, V., Lamarre, H., Perreault, E. (2001). Weathering the storm of perinatal bereavement via hardiness. *Death Studies*, 25, 497-512.

Langer, E. (2002). Well-being: Mindfulness versus positive evaluation. In C.R. Snyder & J. Shane (Eds.), *Handbook of Positive Psychology*, 214-230. London: Oxford University Press.

Langer, E.S., & Rodin, J. (1976). The effect of choice and enhanced personal responsivity for the aged: A field experiment in an institutional setting. *Journal of Personality and Social Psychology*, 34, 191-198.

Laroche, M., Saad, G., Kim, C. & Browne, E. (2000). A cross-cultural study on in-store information search strategies for a Christmas gift. *Journal of Business Research*, 49, 113-126.

Larson, D.B. & Larson, S.S. (2003). Spirituality's potential relevance to physical and emotional health: A brief review of quantitative research. *Journal of Psychology and Theology*, 13, 37-51

Larson, D.B., Pattison, E.M., Blazes, D.G., Omran, A.R. & Kaplan, B.H. (1986). Systematic analysis of research on religious variables in four major psychiatric journals: 1978-1982. *American Journal of Psychology*, 143, 329-334.

Latane, B. & Darley, J.M. (1970). *The Unresponsive Bystander: Why doesn't He Help?* Englewood-Cliffs: Prentice-Hall.

Latzer, Y., Hochdorf, Z., Bachar, E. & Canetti, L. (2002). Attachment style and family functioning as discriminating factors in eating disorders. *Contemporary Family Therapy: An International Journal*, 24, 581-599.

Lau, J.T.F. & Tsui, H.Y. (2002). Surveillance of HIV/AIDS-related attitudes and perceptions among the general public in Hong Kong from 1994 to 2000. *AIDS Education and Prevention*, 14, 419-431.

Lawrence, R.J. (2002). Healthy residential environments. In R.B. Bechtel & A. Churchman (Eds.), *Handbook of Environmental Psychology*, 394-412. NewYork: Wiley.

Lazarus, R.S. (1966). *Psychological Stress and the Coping Process*. New York: McGraw-Hill.

Le Ferle, C., Edwards, S.M. & Mizuno, Y. (2002). Internet diffusion in Japan: Cultural considerations. *Journal of Advertising Research*, 42, 65-79.

Lecci, L. & Myers, B. (2002). Examining the construct validity of the original and revised JBS: A cross-validation of sample and method. *Law & Human Behavior*, 26, 455-463.

Lee, J.J. (2002). Religion and college attendance: Change among students. *Review of Higher Education,* 25, 369-384.

Lee, M.M., Chang, J.S., Jacobs, B. & Wrensch, M.R. (2002). Complementary and alternative medicine among men with prostrate cancer in 4 ethnic populations. *American Journal of Public Health*, 92, 1606-1609.

Lee, S., Kwok, K., Liau, C. & Leung, T. (2002). Screening Chinese patients with eating disorders using the eating attitudes test in Hong Kong. *International Journal of Eating Disorders*, 32, 91-97.

Leeming, D. (2002). *Myth: A Biography of Belief*. London: Oxford University Press.

Leeper, M.R. & Gurtner, J. (1989). Children and computers: Approaching the twenty-first century. *American Psychologist*, 2, 170-178.

Lefcourt, H.M. & Thomas, S. (1998). Humor and stress revisited. In W. Ruch (Ed.), *The Sense of Humor: Explorations of a Personality Characteristic*, 179-202. Berlin: Walter de Gruyter.

Lefkowitz, M.M., Eron, L.D., Walden, L.D. & Heusmann, L.R. (1992). Television violence and child aggression: A follow-up study. In G.A. Comstock & E.A. Rubenstein (Eds.), *Television and Social Behavior*, Vol. III. Washington: US Government Printing Office.

Leichtman, M.D. & Ceci, S.J. (1995). The effects of stereotypes and suggestions on preschooler's reports. *Developmental Psychology*, 31, 568-578.

Leifer, A.D. & Roberts, D.F. (1972). Children's response to television violence. In J.P. Murray, E.A. Rubenstein & G.A. Comstock (Eds.), *Television and Social Behavior*, Vol. II. Washington: US Government Printing Office.

Leigh, B.C. & Stall, R. (1993). Substance use and risky sexual behavior for exposure to HIV: Issues in methodology, interpretation and prevention. *American Psychologist*, 10, 1023-1036.

Lepore, S.J., Evans, G.W. & Schneider, M.L. (1991). Dynamic role of social support in the link between chronic stress and psychological distress. *Journal of Personality and Social Psychology*, 61, 899-909.

Lepper, M.R. (1981). Intrinsic and extrinsic motivation in children: Detrimental effects of superfluous controls. In W.A. Collins (Ed.), *Minnesota Symposia on Child Psychology*, Vol 14. Hillsdale: Erlbaum.

Lerner, M.J. (1980). *The Belief on a Just World: A Fundamental Delusion*. New York: Plenum.

Leser, G., Richman, B.A. & Yung, F. (2003). The educational impact of Rechov SumSum/ Shara's SimSim: A Sesame Street television series to promote respect and understanding among children living in Israel, the West Bank and Gaza. *International Journal of Behavioral Development*, 27, 409-422.

Leuba, J.H. (1937). The making of a psychologist of religion. In V. Fern (Ed.), *Religion in Transition*. New York: McMillan.

Leung, F.K.S. (2002). Behind the high achievement of East Asian students. *Educational Research and Evaluation*, 8, 87-108.

Leung, K. (1987). Some determinants of reactions to procedural models of conflict resolution: A cross-national study. *Journal of Personality and Social Psychology*, 53, 898-908.

Leung, K. (2003). Asian peace psychology: What can it offer? *Peace & Conflict: Journal of Peace Psychology*, 9, 297-302.

Leung, K. & Bond, M.H. (1984). The impact of cultural collectivism on reward allocation. *Journal of Personality and Social Psychology*, 47, 793-804.

Levant, R.F., Tolan, P. & Dodgen, D. (2002). New directions in children's mental health policy: Psychology's role. *Professional Psychology: Research and Practice*, 33, 115-124.

Leventhal, H.& Cleary, P.D. (1980). The smoking problem: A review of research and theory in behavioral risk modification. *Psychological Bulletin*, 88, 370-405.

Levi, A.M. (2002). Up to forty: Lineup size, the modified sequential lineup, and the sequential lineup. *International Journal of Cognitive Technology*, 7, 39-46.

Levi, D., Kocher, S. & Aboud, R. (2001). Technological disasters in natural and built environments. *Environment and Behavior*, 33, 78-92.

Levine, E., Olander, C., Lefebvre, C., Cusick, P., Biesiadecki, L. & McGoldrick, D. (2002). The team nutrition pilot study: Lessons learnt from implementing a comprehensive school based intervention. *Journal of Nutrition Education and Behavior*, 34, 109-116.

Levine, M., Cassidy, C., Brazier, G. & Reicher, S. (2002). Self-categorization and bystander non-intervention: Two experimental studies. *Journal of Applied Social Psychology*, 32, 1452-1463.

Levy, S.J. (1959). Symbols for sale. *Harvard Business Review*, 37, 117-124.

Levy, S.M. (1990). Psychosocial risk fading and cancer progression: Mediating pathways linking behavior and disease. In K.D. Craig and S.M. Weis (Eds.), *Health Enhancement, Disease Prevention, and Early Intervention: Biobehavioral Perspectives*. New York: Springer.

Levy-Leboyer, C. (1988). Success and failure in applying psychology. *American Psychologist*, 10, 779-785.

Levy-Leboyer, C., Bonnes, M., Chase, J., Ferreira-Marques, J. et al., (1996). Determinants of pro-environmental behaviors: A five countries comparison. *European Psychologist*, 1, 123-129.

Lewicki, R.J., Weiss, S. E. & Lewin, D. (1992). Models of conflict resolution and third party intervention: A review and synthesis. *Journal of Organizational Behavior*, 13, 209-252.

Lewin, K. (1951). *Field Theory in Social Science*. Chicago: University of Chicago Press.

Lewis, C.E. (1966). Factors concerning the return of men to work with congestive heart failure. *Journal of Chronic Disease,* 19, 1192-1209.

Li, J. (2002). A cultural model of learning: Chinese "heart and mind for wanting to learn". *Journal of Cross-Cultural Psychology,* 33, 248-269

Li, J. (2003). The core of Confucian learning. *American Psychologist*, 58, 146-147

Lightner, N.J., Yenisey, M.M., Ozok, A.A. & Salvendy, G. (2002). *Behavior and Information Technology*, 21, 373-385.

Lindzey, G.A. & Aronson, E. (Eds.) (1969). *Handbook of Social Psychology,* Vol 5. Reading, MA: Addison-Wesley.

Ling, P.M. & Glantz, S.A. (2002). Using tobacco industry marketing research to design more effective tobacco control campaigns. *Journal of the American Medical Association*, 287, 2983-2989.

Lippa, R.A. (1994). *Introduction to Social Psychology*. Belmont CA: Brooks/Cole.

Little, K.B. (1968). Cultural variations in social schemata. *Journal of Personality and Social Psychology*, 10, 1-7.

Lock, J. (2002). Treating adolescents with eating disorders in the family context: Empirical theoretical considerations. *Child and Adolescent Psychiatric Clinics of North America*, 11, 331-342.

Loeber. R. & Hay, D. (1997). Key issues in the development of aggression and violence from childhood to early adulthood. *Annual Review of Psychology,* 48, 371–410.

Loewenthal, K.M., MacLeod, A.K. & Cinnirella, M. (2002). Are women more religious than men? Gender differences in religious activity among different religious groups in the UK. *Personality and Individual Differences*, 32, 133-139.

Loftus, E. (1979). *Eyewitness Testimony*. Cambridge, MA: Harvard University.

Loftus, E.F. (1991). Revolving questions in the psychological data. *American Psychologist*, 48, 10, 1046-1048.

Loftus, E.F. (1993). The reality of repressed memories. *American Psychologist*, 48, 5, 518-537.

Loftus, E.F. & Rosenwald, L.A. (1995). Recovered memories: Unearthing the past in court. *Journal of Psychiatry & Law,* 23, 349-361.

Loftus, E.F., Miller, D.G. & Bain, K.J. (1978) Semantic interpretation of verbal information into a visual memory. *Journal of Experimental Psychology: Human Learning and Memory*, 4, 19-31.

Loftus, E.F., Smith, K.D., Klinger, M.R. & Fielder, J. (1994). Memory and mismemory for health events. In J.M. Tanner (Ed.), *Questions about Questions*. New York: Russell Sage Foundation.

Lohaus, A., Beyer, A. & Klein-Hebling, J. (2004). Stresserleben und Stresssymptomatik bei Kindern und Jugendlichen. *Zeitschrift für Entwicklungspsychologie und Pädagogische Psychologie,* 36, 38-46.

Loisoz, P. (1988). Intercommunal killing in Cyprus. *Man,* 23, 639-653.

Lopez, S.J. & Snyder, C.R. (Eds.) (2003). *Positive Psychological Assessment: A Handbook of Models and Measures*. Washington DC: American Psychological Association.

Lord, C.G., Lopper, M.R. & Preston, E. (1984). Considering the opposite: A corrective stategy for social judgments. *Journal of Personality and Social Psychology*, 47, 1231-1243.

Lorenz, K. (1976). *On Aggression*. New York: Bantam Books.

Los Angeles Times (1996, December 27).

Los Angeles Times (1996, November 25). Shame and silence in Rexburg.

Lovallo. W.R. (1997). *Stress and Health*. Thousand Oaks: Sage.

Lundsen, M. & Wolfe, R. (1996). Evolution of the problem solving workshop: An introduction to social psychological approaches to conflict resolution. *P & C: Journal of Personality Psychology,* 2, 37-68.

Lupton, D. (2002). Road rage: Drivers' understandings and experiences. *Journal of Sociology,* 38, 275-290.

Lyle, J. & Hoffman, H.R. (1972). Children's use of television and the media. In E.A. Rubenstein, G.A. Comstock & J.P. Murray (Eds.), *Television in Day-to-day Life: Patterns of Use.* Washington: US Government Printing Office.

Lynch, P.D., Kent, R.J. & Srinivasan, S.S. (2001). The global internet shopper: Evidence for shopping tasks in 12 countries. *Journal of Advertising Research*, 41, 15-23.

Lynd, S. (Ed.) (1966). *Non-violence in America: A Documentary History.* New York: The Bobbs-Merrill Corp.

Ma, G.X., Shive, S., Legos, P. & Tan, Y. (2003). Ethnic diference in adolescent smoking behaviors, sources of tobacco, knowledge and attitudes toward restriction policies. *Addictive Behaviors*, 28, 249-268.

Mabala, R. & Allen, K.B. (2002). Participatory action research on HIV/AIDS through a popular theater approach in Tanzania. *Evaluation and Program Planning*, 25, 333-339.

MacFadyen, L., Hastings, G. & MacKintosh, A.M. (2001). Cross-sectional study of young people's awareness of and involvement with tobacco marketing. *British Medical Journal*, 322, 513-517.

Maciak, B.J., Moore, M.T., Leviton, L.C. & Guinan, M.E. (1998). Preventing Halloween arson in an urban setting: A model for multisectoral planning and community participation. *Health Education & Behavior*, 25, 194-211.

MacPherson-Court, L., McDonald, L. & Sobsey, D. (2003). Inclusive Education Survey: Meeting the Educational Needs of Preservice Teachers. *Developmental Disabilities Bulletin*. 31, 57-85.

Macy, J., & Brown, M.Y. (1998) *Coming Back to Life: Practices to Reconnect Our Lives, Our World*. Gabriola Island, BC: New Society Publishers.

Maddux, J.E. (2002). Stopping the "madness": Positive psychology and the deconstruction of the illness ideology and the DSM. In C.R.Snyder & J. Shane (Eds.), *Handbook of Positive Psychology*, 13-25. London: Oxford University Press.

Magid, B. (2002). *Ordinary Mind: Exploring the Common Ground of Zen and Psychotherapy*. Somerville: Wisdom.

Magnavita, N. (2000). Industrial mass psychogenic illness: The unfashionable diagnosis. *British Journal of Medical Psychology*, 73, 371-375.

Magolda, M.G.B. (1992). *Knowing and Reasoning in College: Gender Related Patterns in Students' Intellectual Development*. San Fransisco: Jossey Bass.

Mahoney, A.M., Pargament, K.I., Jewell, T., Swank, A.B., Scott, E., Emery, E. & Rye, M. (1999). Marriage and the spiritual realm: The role of proximal and distal religious constructs in marital functioning. *Journal of Family Psychology*, 13, 321-338.

Maier, S.F., Watkins, L.R. & Fleshner, M. (1996). Psychoneuroimmunology: The interface between behavior, brain and immunity. *American Psychologist*, 12, 1006-1117.

Majchrzak, A. (1988). *The Human Side of Factory Automation*. San Francsico: Jossey-Boss.

Majchrzak, A., Chang, T.C., Banfield, W., Eberts, R.E. & Salvendy, G. (1987). *Human Effects of Computer-aided Design*. London: Taylor and Francis.

Majchrzak, A. & Davis, D.D. (1990). The human side of flexible factory automation: Research and management practice. In S. Spacapan & S. Oskamp (Eds.), *People's Reaction to Technology*. Newberry Park: Sage Publications.

Malley, J., Beck, M. & Adorno, D. (2001). Building an ecology for non-violence in schools. *International Journal of Reality Therapy*, 21, 22-26.

Malpass, R.S. & Kravitz, D.A. (1969). Recognition for faces of own and other race. *Journal of Personality and Social Psychology*, 13, 330-334.

Mandler, G. (1982). The structure of value: Accounting for taste. In M.S. Clarke, & S.T. Fiske (Eds.), *Perception, Cognition and Development: Interactional Analysis.* Hillsdale: Earlbaum.

Mann, J. (1993). A social perspective of rules of war: A research strategy for studying civilian-based defense. In V. Kool (Ed.), *Non-violence: Social and Psychological Issues.* Lanham MD: University Press of America.

Manning, D.L. & Quigley, P. (2002). Understanding the needs of people using a cancer information service in Northern Ireland. *European Journal of Cancer Care*, 11, 139-142.

Markey, P.M.; Wells, S.M. & Markey, C.N. (2002). Social and personality psychology in the culture of cyberspace. In S.P. Serge (Ed.), *Advances in Psychology Research*, 9, 94-113. Huntingdon: Nova-Science Publishers.

Markus, H.R. & Kitiyama, S. (1991). Cultural variation in the self concept: Culture and self implications for cognition, emotion and motivation. *Psychological Review*, 98, 224-253.

Marler, P.L. & Hadaway, C.K. (2002). "Being religious" or "being spiritual" in America: A zero-sum proposition? *Journal for the Scientific Study of Religion*, 41, 289-300.

Marsella, A.J. (1980). Depressive experience and disorder across cultures. In H.C. Triandis & J. Draguns (Eds.), *Handbook of Cross Cultural Psychology, Psychopathology,* 6. Boston: Allyn and Bacon.

Marsland, A.L., Bachen, E.A., Cohen, S., Rabin, B. & Manuck, S.B. (2002). Stress, immune reactivity and susceptibility to infectious disease. *Physiology and Behavior*, 77, 711-716.

Martin, A.M., Kaplan, M.F. & Alamo, J.M. (2003). Discussion content and perception of deliberation in western European versus American juries. *Psychology, Crime & Law*, 9, 247-263.

Martin, S. & Murray, B. (1996). Social toxity undermines youngsters in inner cities. *American Psychological Association Monitor,* 10, 27.

Martin, S. (October, 1996). Modern cities can't cope with population increases. *American Psychological Association Monitor*, 10, 26.

Martin-Causey, T. (2002). Spirituality as a multicultural consideration: Implications for practice and training. *Dissertation Abstracts International, Section B: The Sciences and Engineering*, 62, 5972.

Maslow, A. (1954). *Motivation and Personality*. New York: Harper and Row.

Maslow, A. (1968). *Towards a Psychology of Being*. Princeton: Princeton University Press.

Maton, K.I. (1989). The stress-buffering role of spiritual support: Cross-sectional and prospective investigations. *Journal for the Scientific Study of Religion*, 28, 310-323.

Mattaini, M.A. (2001). Constructing cultures of non-violence: The Peace Power! strategy. *Education & Treatment of Children*, 24, 430-447.

Mattis, J.S. (2002). Religion and spirituality in the meaning-making and coping experiences of African-American women: A qualititaive analysis. *Psychology of Women Quarterly*, 26, 309-321.

McAliglin, A., Perry, C., Killian, J., Shinkard, L.A. & Malloby, N. (1980). Pilot study of smoking, alcohol and drug abuse prevention. *Journal of Public Health*, 70, 719-721.

McAlister, A.L., Ama, E., Barroso, C., Peters, R.J. & Kelder, S. (2000). Promoting tolerance and moral engagement through peer modeling. *Cultural Diversity and Ethnic Minority Psychology,* 6, 363-373.

McAndrew, F.T. (1992). *Environmental Psychology*. Pacific Grove Ca.: Brooks/Cole.

McCabe, H. (2003). The beginnings of inclusion in the People's Republic of China. *Research & Practice for Persons with Severe Disabilities,* 28, 16-22.

McCalley, L.T. & Midden, C.J.H. (2002). Energy conservation through product-integrated feedback: The roles of goal-setting and social orientation. *Journal of Economic Psychology,* 23, 589-603.

McClelland, D.C. (1961). *The Achieving Society*. Princeton: Van Nostrand.

McClleland, D.C., Atkinson, T.W., Clark, R.A. & Lowell, E.L. (1953). *The Achievement Motive*. New York: Appleton-Century-Crofts.

McCullough, M.E., Hoyt, W.T., Larson, D.B., Koenig, H.G. & Thoresen, C. (2000). Religious involvement and mortality: A meta-analytic review. *Health Psychology*, 19, 211-222.

McCullough, M.E. & Witvliet, C.V. (2002). The psychology of forgiveness. In C.R. Snyder & J. Shane (Eds.), *Handbook of Positive Psychology*, 446-458. London: Oxford University Press.

McDade, T.W. (2001). Lifestyle incongruity, social integration and immune function in Samoan adolescents. *Social Science and Medicine*, 53, 1351-1362.

McDermot, B.M., Batik, M., Roberts, L. & Gibbon, P. (2002). Parent and child report of family functioning in a clinical child and adolescent eating disorders sample. *Australian and New Zealand Journal of Psychiatry*, 36, 501-514.

McDougall, W. (1908). *Introduction to Social Psychology*. London: Methuen.

McEwen, B.S. (2003). Early life influences on life-long patterns of behavior and health. *Mental Retardation & Developmental Disabilities Research Reviews,* 9, 149-154.

McIntyre, J.J. & Teevan, J.J. (1972). Television violence and deviant behavior. In G.A. Comstock & E.A. Rubenstein (Eds.), *Television and Social Behavior*, Vol. III. Washington: US Government Printing Office.

McKinney, W.P. & Rich, E.C. (2000). Gifts to physicians from the pharmaceutical industry. *Journal of the American Medical Association*, 283, 2656-2657.

McKusick, L. (1988). The impact of AIDS on practitioner and client: Notes for the therapeutic relationship. *American Psychologist*, 11, 935-941.

McLeod, J.M., Atkin, C.K. & Chaffee, S.H. (1972). Adolescents, parents and television use: Adolescent self report measures from Maryland and Wisconsin sample. In G.A. Comstock, & E.A. Rubenstein (Eds.), *Television and Social Behavior,* Vol. III. Washington: US Government Printing Office.

McMakin, A.H., Malone, E. & Lundgren, R.E. (2002). Motivating residents to conserve energy without financial incentives. *Environment and Behavior*, 34, 848-863.

Meer, J.B.W. van der., Small, I.B., Crighton, E.J. & Ford, N. (2002). Perceived health and psychological well being in the Aral Sea area: Results from a survey in an area of slow environmental degradation. In, J.M. Havenaar, J.G. Cwikel et al. (Eds.), *Toxic Turmoil: Psychological and Societal Consequences of Ecological Disasters*, 163-182. New York: Kluwer Academic/Plenum.

Megangee, E.I. (1966). Undercontrolled and overcontrolled personality types in extreme antisocial aggression. *Psychological Monographs,* 80.

Mehrabian, A. & Russell, S. (1974). *An Approach to Environmental Psychology*. Cambridge: MIT Publishing.

Melton, G. (1992). Children as partners for justice: Next step for developmentalists. *Monographs for the Society for Research in Child Development*, 57, 153-159.

Meyer, A.L., Allison, K.W., Reese, L.E. & Gay, F.N. (2004). Choosing to be violence free in middle school: The student component of the GREAT schools and families program. *American Journal of Preventive Medicine*, 26, 20-28.

Meyer, L.H. (2003). Wanted: Internationally appropriate best practices. *Research & Practice for Persons with Severe Disabilities*, 28, 33-36.

Meyers-Levy, J. & Tybout, A.M. (1997). Context effects at encoding and judgment in consumption setting: The role of cognitive resources. *Journal of Consumer Research*, 24, 1-14.

Miall, H. (2002). Shaping a vision: The task of peace studies. *Peace & Conflict: Journal of Peace Psychology,* 8, 387-388

Middlestadt, S., Grieser, M., Hernandez, O., Tabaishat, K., Sanchack, J., Southwall, B. & Schwartz, R. (2001). Turning minds on and facets off: Water conservation education in Jordanian schools. *Journal of Environmental Education,* 32, 37-45.

Midgely, C. (1991). Teacher sense of efficacy and transition to middle level schools. *Middle School Journal*, 22, 10-14.

Milburn, T. & Isaac, P. (1995). Prospect theory: Implications for interactive mediation. *Peace and Conflict: Journal of Peace Psychology,* 1, 333-342.

Miles, D.E. & Johnson, G.L. (2003). Aggressive driving behaviors: Are there psychological and attitudinal predictors? *Transportation Research Part F: Traffic Psychology & Behaviour,* 6, 147-161.

Milgram, S. & Jodelet, D. (1976). Psychological maps of Paris. In H. M. Proshansky, W.M. Nelson & L.G. Rivlin (Eds.), *Environmental Psychology*, 2nd Edition, 104-124. New York: Holt, Rinehart and Winston.

Milgram, S. (1970). The experience of living in cities. *Science,* 167, 1461-1468.

Milgram, S. (1974). *Obedience to Authority*. New York: Harper Row.

Mill, J.E. (2003). Shrouded in secrecy: Breaking the news to HIV infection to Ghanian women. *Journal of Transcultural Nursing*, 14, 6-16.

Miller, D.P. (1994). The voice of the earth. *The Sun*, 220, 6-10.

Miller, G.E. & Cohen, S. (2001). Psychological interventions and the immue system: A meta-analytic review and critique. *Health Psychology*, 20, 47-63.

Minuchin, P.P. & Shapiro, E.K. (1983). The school as a context for social development. In P.H. Mussen (Ed.), *The Handbook of Child Psychology,* Vol 4, New York: Wiley.

Miyazaki, T., Ishikawa, T., Limori, H., Miki, A., Wenner, M., Fukunishi, I. & Kawamura, N. (2003). Relationship between perceived social support and immune function. *Stress and Health*, 19, 3-7.

Mladinic, A. & Isla, P. (2002). Justicia organizacional: Entendiendo la equidad en las organizaciones. Psykhe: *Revista de la Escuela de Psicología,* 11, 171-179.

Moberg, S. (2003). Education for all in the North and the South: Teachers' attitudes towards inclusive education in Finland and Zambia. *Education & Training in Developmental Disabilities*, 38, 417-428.

Moeschberger, Scott L. & Ordóñez, A. (2003). Working towards building cultures of peace: A primer for students and new professionals. *International Journal for the Advancement of Counselling*, 25, 317-323.

Moghaddam, F.M. (1998). *Social Psychology: Exploring Universals Across Cultures.* New York: Freeman.

Monahan, J. & Walker, L. (1988). *Social Science in Law: Cases and Materials.* New York: Westbury Foundation Press.

Monchuk, J. (2001). Canadian workers stressed out, less loyal to employers. Calgary: Canadian Press, Oct 23rd.

Montagu, A. (1976). *Learning Non-aggression: The Experience of Non-liberate Societies.* New York: Oxford University Press.

Montiel, C.J. (2003). Peace psychology in Asia. *Peace & Conflict: Journal of Peace Psychology,* 9, 297-302.

Moore, S.M. & Ohtsuka, K. (1999). The prediction of gambling behavior and problem gambling from attitudes and perceived norms. *Social Behavior and Personality*, 27, 455-466.

Moran, S. & Ritov, I. (2002). Initial perceptions in negotiations: Evaluation and response to 'logrolling' offers. *Journal of Behavioral Decision Making*, 15, 101-124.

Morin, S. (1988). AIDS: The challenge to psychology. *American Psychologist*, 11, 838-892.

Mortelmans, D. & Damen, S. (2001). Attitudes on commercialisation and anti-commercial reactions on gift-giving occasions in Belgium. *Journal of Consumer Behaviour*, 1, 156-173.

Moser, G. & Corroyer, D. (2001). Politeness in the urban environment: Is city life still synonymous with civility? *Environment and Behavior*, 33, 611-625.

Mowen, J.C. (1989). Consumer psychology. In W.L. Gregory, & W.J. Burrows (Eds.), *Introduction to Applied Psychology*. Glenview, IL: Scott Foresman and Company.

Moynagh, M. & Worsley, R. (2002). Tomorrow's consumer: The shifting balance of power. *Journal of Consumer Behavior*, 1, 293-301.

Mullany, L.C., Maung, C. & Beyrer, C. (2003). HIV/AIDS knowledge, attitudes and practices among Burmese migrant factory workers in Tak province, Thailand. *AIDS Care*, 15, 63-70.

Muller, W. (1999). *Sabbath: Restoring the Sacred Rhythm of Rest*. New York: Bantam Books.

Mulvey, E.P. & Cauffman, E. (2001). The inherent limits of predicting school violence. *American Psychologist*, 56, 797-802

Mundorf, N., Bryant, J. & Brownell, W. (1997). Aging and infotainment technologies: Cross-cultural perspectives. In H.S. Noor Al-Deen (Ed.), *Cross-cultural Communication and Aging in the United States*. Mahwah: Lawrence Erlbaum.

Munsterberg, H. (1908). *On the Witness Stand*. New York: Doubleday & Page.

Murad, S.D., Joung, I.M.A., Verhulst, F.C., Mackenbach, J.P., Crijnen, A.A.M. (2004). Determinants of self-reported emotional and behavioral problems in Turkish immigrant adolescents aged 11-18. *Social Psychiatry & Psychiatric Epidemiology*, 39, 196-207.

Murphy, H.B.M. (1982). Culture and schizophrenia. In A.R. Issa (Ed.), *Culture and Psychopathology*. Baltimore: Baltimore University Press.

Murphy-Berman, V., Berman, J.J., Singh, P., Pachauri, A. and Kumar, P. (1984). Factors affecting allocation to needy and meritorious recipients: A cross-cultural comparison. *Journal of Personality and Social Psychology*, 42, 1267-72.

Musham, C. & Trettin, L. (2002). Bringing health services to the poor through social marketing: Ethical issues. *Journal of Health Care for the Poor and Undeserved*, 13, 280-287.

Myers, D. (1996). *Social Psychology*. New York: McGraw-Hill.

Myers, D.G. (2000). *The American Paradox: Spiritual Hunger in an Age of Plenty*. New Haven, CT: Yale University Press.

Nagata, D. (1993). Moral exclusion and non-violence: The Japanese internment. In V.K. Kool (Ed.), *Non-violence: Social and Psychological Issues*. Lanham MD: University Press of America.

Nagata, T., Kawarada, Y., Ohshima, J., Iketani, T. & Kiriike, N. (2002). Drug use disorders in Japanese eating disorder patients. *Psychiatry Research*, 109, 181-191.

Nagata, T., Ohima, J., Wada, A., Yamada, H. & Iketani, T. (2003). Temperament and character of Japanese eating disorder patients. *Comprehensive Psychiatry*, 44, 142-145.

Naisbitt, J. (1982). *Megatrends: Ten New Directions Transforming our Lives*. New York: Warner.

Nandy, A. (1983). Adorno in India. In V.K. Kool & J.J. Ray (Eds.), *Authoritarianism across Cultures*. Bombay, India: Himalaya Publishing House.

Naquin, C.E. (2003). The agony of opportunity in negotiation: Number of negotiable issues, counterfactual thinking, and feelings of satisfaction. *Organizational Behavior & Human Decision Processes*, 91, 97-107.

Nasser, R. & Abouchedid, K. (2002). Attributions for the causes of peace and locus of control: Their relation in a country where there is conflict. *Current Research in Social Psychology,* 7, 94-113.

Nation, M., Cruoto, C., Wandersman, A., Kumpfer, K.L., Seybolt, D., Morrissey-Kane, E. & Davino, K. (2003). What works in prevention principles of effective prevention programs, *American Psychologist*, 58, No. 6/7, 449-456

Nation, M.A. (2000). Neighbourhoods and mental health: A test of the relationship between ecological variables and psychological health. *Dissertation Abstracts International, Section B: The Sciences and Engineering*, 60, 3574.

National Advisory Mental Health Council Report (1996). Basic behavioral science research for mental health. Excerpts in *American Psychologist*, 51, 5, 478-484.

National Institute of Mental Health (2001). The invisible disease: Depression, understanding new hope. Geneva: WHO.

Navaco, W. (1975). *Anger Control: The Development and Evolution of an Experimental Treatment.* Lexington, MA: Lexington.

Naveh-Benjamin, M. & Ayres, T.J. (1986). Digit span, reading rate and linguistic relativity. *The Quarterly Journal of Experimental Psychology*, 38, 739-751.

Neuberg, S.L. (1989). The goal of forming accurate impressions during social interactions: Attenuating the impact of negative expectancies. *The Journal of Social Psychology*, 56, 374-386.

Neuhauser, L. & Kreps, G.L. (2003). Rethinking communication in the E-health era. *Journal of Health Psychology*, 8, 7-23.

Newlin, M.H. & Wang, A.Y. (2002). Integrating technology and pedagogy: Web instruction and seven principles of undergraduate education. *Teaching of Psychology*, 29, 325-330.

Newsweek (1996, December 2). I have learned to cope, Brudnoy.

Newsweek, (1992, June 1).

Nickerson, R.S. (2003). *Psychology and Environmental Change*. Mahwah: Lawrence Erlbaum.

Nicoletti, J. & Spooner, K. (1996). Violence in the workplace: Response and intervention strategies. In G. R. Vandenbos & E.Q. Bulatao (Eds.), *Violence on the Job: Indentifying Rights and Developing Strategies.* Washington DC: American Psychological Association.

Nielsen, J.C. (2003). Den rummelige folkeskole: Psykologisk Paedagogisk Radgivning Monograf. *Mono*, 40, 17-23.

Nieva, V., Neuman, P.D. & Bottlick, G. (1990). Factory automation and production jobs: A longitudinal study. In S. Spacapan & S. Oskamp (Eds.), *People's Reaction to Technology.* Newberry Park: Sage Publication.

Nigg, C.R. (2003). Technology's influence on physical activity and exercise science: The present and the future. *Psychology of Sport & Exercise*, 4, 57-65.

Nisbett, R.E. (1990). The anti-creativity letters: Advice from a senior temper to a junior temper. *American Psychologist*, 45, 1078-82.

Nisbett, R.E., Borgida, E., Crandall, R. & Reed, H. (1976). Popular induction: Information is not necessarily informative. In J.S. Carroll & J.W. Payne (Eds.), *Cognition and Social Behavior*. Hillsdale, NJ: Erlbaum.

Nisbett, R.E., Fong, G.T., Lehman, D.R. & Cheng, P.W. (1987). Teaching reasoning. *Science*, 238, 625-631.

Noble, K.D. (2000). Spiritual intelligence: A new frame of mind. *Advanced Development*, 9, 1-29.

Noesjirwan, J. (1977). Contrasting cultural patterns of interpersonal closeness in doctors waiting rooms in Sydney and Djakarta. *Journal of Cross Cultural Psychology*, 8, 357-368.

Nora, K. & Imada, A. (1988) *Participatory Ergonomics*. Philadelphia: Taylor and Francis.

Norman, D.A. (1995). The future of the mind lies in technology. In R.L. Solso & D.W. Massaro (Eds.), *The Science of the Mind: 2001 and Beyond*. New York: Oxford University Press.

Nullis, C. (2001). WHO urges more attention to mental health problems. Associated Press, 4th October.

Nyoye, A. (2002). Hope healing communities in contemporary Africa. *Journal of Humanistic Psychology*, 42, 57-81.

O'Conner, R.D. (1969). Modification of social withdrawal through symbolic modeling. *Journal of Applied Behavior Analysis*, 2, 15-22.

O'Conner, T. (1995). Therapy for a dying planet. In T. Roszak, M.E. Gomes, and A.D. Kanner (Eds.) *Ecopsychology: Restoring the Earth Healing the Mind*. San Francisco: Sierra Club Books.

O'Guinn, T.C. & Shaun, L.J. (1997). The role of television in the construction of consumer reality. *Journal of Consumer Research*, 23, 278-294.

O'Laughlin, J., Makni, H., Tremblay, M., Lacroix, C., Gervais, A., Dery, V., Meshefedjian, G. & Paradis, G. (2001). Smoking cessation counseling practices of general practitioners in Montreal. *Preventive Medicine*, 33, 627-638.

O'Leary, K.D. & O'Leary, S.G. (Eds.) (1977). *Classroom Management*. New York: Pergamon.

Oener, B. (2000). Innovation and adaptation in a Turkish sample: A preliminary study. *Journal of Psychology*, 134, 671-676.

Oetzel, J.G. & Ting-Toomey, S. (2003). Face concerns in interpersonal conflict: A cross-cultural empirical test of the face negotiation theory. *Communication Research*, 30, 599-624.

Oliner, S.P. & Oliner, P.M. (1988). *The Altruistic Personality: Rescuers of Jews in Nazi Europe*. New York: Free Press.

Olweus, D. (1993). *Bullying at School: What We Know and What We Can Do*. London: Blackwell.

Oman, D. & Thoresen, C.E. (2002). "Does religion cause health?": Differing interpretations and diverse meanings. *Journal of Health Psychology*, 7, 365-380.

Oman, D., Thoresen, C.E. & McMahon, K. (1999). Volunteerism and mortality among the community-dwelling elderly. *Journal of Health Psychology*, 4, 301-306.

Onodera, M. & Kawamura, S. (2003). *Japanese Journal of Counseling Science,* 36, 272-281.

Opotow, S. (2003). Forging social identity and social conflict. *Peace & Conflict: Journal of Peace Psychology*, 9, 177-179.

Oppenheimer, L. & Kuipers, I. (2003). Filipino children's understanding of peace, war, and strategies to attain peace. *Peace & Conflict: Journal of Peace Psychology*. 9, 235-257.

Osgood, C.E. (1962). *An Alternative to War or Surrender*. Inbara, IL: University of Illinois Press.

Oskamp, S. (1995). Applying social psychology to avoid ecological disaster. *Journal of Social Issues*, 51-4, 217-239.

Oskamp, S. (Ed.) (1988). Television as a social issue: *Applied Social Psychology,* Annual Issue Vol. 8. Newbury Park, CA: Sage.

Oskamp, S., Harrington, M.J., Edwards, T.C., Sherwood, D.L., Okuda, S.M. & Swanson, D.C. (1991). Factors influencing household recycling behavior. *Environment and Behavior*, 23, 494-519.

Oswald, A.J. (2003). How much do external factors affect well being? *Psychologist*, 16, 140-141.

Ovadia, A. (1994). Reasoning patterns inhibiting school effectiveness: The case of the fallacy of bifunction. *Urban Review*, 26 (1), 35-40.

Packard, V. (1957). *The Hidden Persuaders*. New York: D. McKay.

Palinkas, L.A. (1990). Psychosocial effects of adjustment in Antarctica: Lessons for long duration space flight. *Journal of Space Crew*, 27, 471-177.

Papanikolaou, Z., Nikolaidis, D., Patsiaouras, A., Alexopoulos, P. (2003). Commentary: The freshman experience: high stress - low grades. *Athletic Insight: Online Journal of Sport Psychology,* 5 [np], http://www.athleticinsight.com/Vol5Iss4/Commentary.htm.

Pargament, K.I. (2002). The bitter and the sweet: An evaluation of the costs and benefits of religiousness. *Psychological Inquiry*, 13, 168-181.

Pargament, K.I., Kennell, J., Hathaway, W., Grevengoed, N., Newman, J. & Jones, W. (1988). Religion and the problem solving process: Three styles of coping. *Journal for the Scientific Study of Religion*, 27, 90-104.

Pargament, K.I., Koenig, H.G. & Perez, L.M. (2000). The many method of religious coping: Development and initial validation of the RCOPE. *Journal of Clinical Psychology*, 56, 519-543.

Pargament, K.I., Koenig, H.G., Tarakeshwar, N. & Hahn, J. (2001). Religious struggle as a predictor of mortality among medically ill elderly patients: A two year longitudinal study. *Archives of Internal Medicine,* 161, 1881-1885.

Parker, D., Lajunen, T. & Summala, H. (2002). Anger and aggression among drivers in three European countries. *Accident Analysis & Prevention,* 34, 229-235.

Parker, E.B. (1963). The effects of television on public library circulation. *Public Opinion Quarterly*, 27, 578-589.

Parker, G., Cai, Y., Tan, S., Dear, K., Henderson, A.S., Poh, G.T., Kwee, G.C. (2003). Examination stress in Singapore primary schoolchildren: How compliance by subjects can impact on study results. *Acta Psychiatrica Scandinavica,* 108, 239-243.

Parker, J.F. & Myers, A. (2001). Attempts to improve children's lineup identifications from sequential presentation lineups. *Journal of Applied Social Psychology*, 31, 796-815.

Patel, D.R., Pratt, H.D. & Greydanus, D.E. (2003). Treatment of adolescents with anorexia nervosa. *Journal of Adolescent Research*, 18, 244-260.

Patterson, G.R. (1986). Performance models for antisocial boys. *American Psychologist*, 41, 432–444.

Pattilo, M.M., Chesley, D., Castles, P. & Sutter, R. (2002). Faith community nursing: Parish nursing/Health Ministry Collaboration model in central Texas. *Family and Community Health*, 25, 41-51.

Patton, M.S. (1988). Suffering and damage in Catholic sexuality. *Journal of Religion and Health*, 27, 129-142.

Paulik, K. (2001). Hardiness, optimism, self-confidence and occupational stress among university teachers. *Studia Psychologica*, 43, 91-100.

Pavlov, I.P. (1927). *Conditioned Reflexes*. Winston: Oxford Press.

Payne, I.R., Bergin, A.E., Bielema, K.A. & Jenkins, P.H. (1991). Review of religion and mental health: Prevention and enhancement of psychosocial functioning. *Prevention in Human Services*, 2, 11-40.

Pearson, V., Lo, E, Chui, E. & Wong, D. (2003). A heart to learn and care? Teachers' responses toward special needs children in mainstream schools in Hong Kong. *Disability & Society*. 18, 489-508.

Peneloza, L. (1994). Atravesando fronteras/border crossing: A critical ethnographic study of migrant Mexicans. *Journal of Consumer Research*, 21, 32-54.

Pennington, N., & Hastie, R. (1986). Evidence evaluation in complex decision making. *Journal of Personality and Social Psychology,* 51, 242-258.

Pepitone, A. (1981). Lessons from the history of social psychology. *American Psychologist*, 9, 972-985.

Pepler, D.J. & Slaby, R.G. (1996). Theoretical and developmental perspectives on youth and violence. In L.D. Eron, J.H. Gentry, & P. Schlegel (Eds.), *Reason to Hope: A Psychosocial Perspective on Violence and Youth,* 27–58. Washington DC: American Psychological Association.

Peracchio, L.A. & Tybout, A.M. (1996). The moderating role of prior knowledge in schema based product evaluation. *Journal of Consumer Research*, 23, 177-192.

Percz, F. & Dabis, F. (2003). HIV prevention in Latin America: Reaching youth in Colombia. *AIDS Care*, 15, 77-87.

Peri, A., Scarlata, C., Barbarito, M. (1999). Preliminary studies on the psychological adjustment in the Italian Antarctic summer campaigns. *Environment and Behavior.*

Pescosolido, B. (1990). The social context of religious integration and suicide: Pursuing the network explanation. *Sociological Quarterly*, 31, 337-357.

Peters, P. & den Dulk, L. (2003). Cross cultural differences in managers' support for home based telework: A theoretical elaboration. *International Journal of Cross-Cultural Management*, 3, 329-346.

Peterson, C. (2000). The future of optimism. *American Psychologist*, 55, 44-55.

Petty, R.E. & Cacioppo, J.T. (1986). The effects of involvement on responses to argument validity: Central and reciprocal routes to persuasion. *Journal of Personality and Social Psychology*, 46, 69-81.

Petty, R.E. & Cacioppo, J.T. (1986). The elaboration likelihood model of persuasion. In L. Berkowitz (Ed.), *Advances in Experimental Social Psychology*, 19, 123-205. New York: Academic Press.

Petty, R.E. & Cacioppo, J.T. (1996). Addressing disturbing and disturbed consumer behavior: Is it necessary to change the way we conduct behavioral science? *The Journal of Marketing Research*, 33, 1-8.

Pfeifer, J.E. & Ogloff, J.R.P. (2003). Mock juror ratings of guilt in Canada: Modern racism and ethnic heritage. *Social Behavior & Personality,* 31, 301-312.

Piaget, J. (1948). *The Moral Judgement of the Child.* Glencoe: Free Press.

Pieters, R.G.M. (1989). *Attitude and Behavior in a Source Separation Program: A Garbology Approach.* Delft, Netherlands: Euburon.

Pieters, R.G.M. (1991). Changing garbage disposal patterns of consumers: Motivation, ability and performance. *Journal of Public Policy and Marketing*, 10 (2), 59-76.

Piko, B.F. (2002). Does knowledge count? Attitudes toward smoking among medical, nursing and pharmacy students in Hungary. *Journal of Community Health*: The publication for health promotion and disease prevention, 27, 269-276.

Pilisuk, M. (1997). Resolving idealogical clashes through dialogue: Abortion as a case study. *P & C: Journal of Personality Psychology,* 3, 135-148.

Pintea, S. & Bus, I. (2002). Efectele negative ale agresivitatii promovate de mass-media. Negative effects of mass-media aggression. *Cognitie Creier Comportament.* 6, 85-106.

Piot, P. (2002). In Aids Alert. *The Times of India*, New Delhi, 3rd July 2002.

Plante, T.G. & Sherman, A.C. (2001). *Faith and Health: Psychological Perspectives.* New York: Guilford.

Platt, J. (1973). Social traps. *American Psychologist*, 28, 641-651.

Pleck, J.H., Sonetien, F.L. & Ku, L. (1993). Masculine ideology: Its impact on adolescent males heterosexual relationships. *Journal of Social Issues*, 49 (31), 11-19.

Pliner, P., Hart, H., Kohl, J. & Saari, D.C. (1976). Compliance without pressure: Some further data on the foot-in-the-door technique. *Journal of Experimental Social Psychology*, 10, 17-22.

Polonski, M.J., Shelley, L. & Voola, R. (2002). An examination of helping behavior: Some evidence from Australia. *Journal of Non-profit and Pulic Sector Marketing,* 10, 67-82.

Poole, D.A. & Lindsay, D.S. (1995). Interviewing preschoolers: Effects of non-suggestive techniques, parental coaching and leading questions on reports of non-experienced events. *Journal of Experimental Child Psychology,* 60, 129-154.

Poole, D.A. & White, L.T. (1993). Two years later: The effects of question repetition and retention interval on the eyewitness testimony of children and adults. *Developmental Psychology*, 29, 844-853.

Poon-McBrayer, K.F. (2003). To integrate or not to integrate: Systemic dilemmas in Hong Kong. *Journal of Special Education,* 37, 249-256.

Popper, K. (1959). *Logic of Scientific Discovery*, 5, 66, 795-802. New York: Basic Books.

Porter, B.E., Leeming, F.C. & Dwyer, W.O. (1995). Solid waste recovery: A review of behavioral programs to increase recycling. *Environment and Behavior*, 27, 122-152.

Posvac, E.J. & Carey, R.G. (2003). *Program Evaluation: Methods and Case Studies*. Upper Saddle River: Prentice-Hall.

Posvac, E.J. & Carey, R.G. (1992). *Program Evaluation*. Englewood Cliffs, NJ: Prentice-Hall.

Potkanowicz, Edward S., Caine-Bish, Natalie, Otterstetter, Ronald, Glickman, Ellen L. (2003). Age Effects on Thermal, Metabolic, and Perceptual Responses to Acute Cold Exposure. *Aviation, Space, & Environmental Medicine*, 74, 1157-1162.

Potter, W.J. (1987). Does television viewing hinder academic achievement among adolescents? *Human Communications Research*, 14, 27-46.

Powell, L.H., Shahabi, L. & Thoresen, C.E. (2003). Religion and spirituality: Linkages to health. *American Psychologist*, 58, 36-52.

Preuss, L.J. & Dubow, E.F. (2004). A comparison between intellectually gifted and typical children in their coping responses to a school and a peer stressor. *Roeper Review*, 26, 105-111.

Prilleltensky, I. (1989). Psychology and status quo. *American Psychologist*, 5, 795-802.

Prince, R.& Geissle, P.W. (2001). Becoming "one who treats": A case of a Luo healer and her grandson in Western Kenya. *Anthropology and Education Quarterly*, 32, 447-471.

Prislin, R., Jordan, J.A., Worchel, S. W., Scinmer, F.T. & Shebilske, W.L. (1996). Effects of group disunion on aquisition of complex skills. *Human Factors*, 38-3, 404-416.

Pritchard, M.E. & Keenan, J.M. (2002). Does jury deliberation really improve jurors' memories? *Applied Cognitive Psychology*, 16, 589-601.

Priya, K.R. (2002). Suffering and healing among the survivors of Bhuj earthquake. *Psychological Studies*, 47, 106-112.

Prokop, C.K., Bradley, L.A., Burish, T.G., Anderson, K.O. & Fox, J.E. (1991). *Health Psychology: Clinical Methods and Research*, New York: MacMillan.

Proksch, B., Ross, W. & Estness, T. (2002). Negotiation role-play exercise: "Water, water, everywhere, but not a drop to drink:" the Richland-river. *International Journal of Conflict Management*, 13, 355-380.

Prothrow-Stith, D & Weissman, M. (1991). *Deadly Consequences: How Violence is Destroying our Teenage Population and a Plan to Begin Solving the Problem*. New York: Harper.

Pyszczynski, T., Greenberg, J. & Solomon, S. (2002). *In the Wake of 9/11*. Washington DC: American Psychological Association.

Rabbie, J., cf R. Jaap (1982). Is there a discontinuity or a reciprocity effect in cooperation and competition between individuals and groups? *European Journal of Social Psychology*, 28, 1998, 483-507.

Raghuram, R., Venkateswaran, A., Ramakrishna, J. & Weiss, M.G. (2002). Traditional community resources for mental health: A report of temple healing from India. *British Medical Journal*, 325, 38-40.

Rajan, I., Mishra, U.S. & Sarma, P.S. (2001). Health concerns among India's elderly. *International Journal of Aging and Human Development*, 53, 181-194.

Raleigh, N.C. (2002). Mildly depressed women live longer: A study. *Associated Press*, May.

Ramirez, J.M., Andreu, J.M. & Fujihara, T. (2001). Cultural and sex differences in aggression: A comparison between Japanese and Spanish students using two different inventories. *Aggressive Behavior*, 27, 313-322.

Rastam, M., Gillberg, C. & Wentz, E. (2003). Outcome of teenage-onset anorexia nervosa in a Swedish community-based sample. *European Child and Adolescent Psychiatry*, 12, i78-i90.

Rattner, A. (1983) *When Justice Goes Wrong: Convicting the Innocent*. Unpublished doctoral dissertation, Ohio State University.

Razzino, B.E., New, M., Lewin, A. & Joseph, J. (2003). Need for and Use of Mental Health Services among Parents of Children in the Head Start Program. *Psychiatric Services*, 55, 583-586.

Readers Digest (1996, March).

Reddy, K.S., Arora, M., Perry, C.L., Nair, B., Kohli, A., Lytle, L., Stigler, M. & Prabhakaran, D. (2002). Tobacco and alcohol use outcomes of a school based intervention in New Delhi. *American Journal of Health Behavior*, 26, 173-181.

Reed, A. II (2002). Social identity as a useful perspective for self concept based consumer research. *Psychology and Marketing*, 19, 235-266.

Reger, G.M. & Rogers, S.A. (2002). Diagnostic differences in religious coping among individuals with persistent mental illness. *Journal of Psychology and Christianity*, 21, 341-348.

Reinisch, T.M., Sanders, S.A. & Ziemba-Davis, M. (1988). The study of sexual behavior in relation to the transmission of human immunodeficency virus: Caveats and recommendations. *American Psychologist*, 11, 921-928.

Reno, R.R., Cialdini, R.B., & Kallgren, C.A. (1993). The transituational influence of social norms. *Journal of Personality and Social Psychology*, 64, 104-112.

Renzaglia, A., Karvonen, M., Drasgow, E. & Stoxen, C.C. (2003). Promoting a lifetime of inclusion. *Focus on Autism & Other Developmental Disabilities*, 18, 140-149.

Reppucci, N.D. (1984). The wisdom of Solomon: Issues in child custody determination. In N.D. Reppucci, I.A. Weithorn, E.P. Mulevy, & J. Monohan (Eds.), *Children, Mental Health and the Law*. Newbury Park: Sage Publishers.

Resman, M. (2003). Integrácia/Inklúzia medzi zámerom a uskutocnením. *Psychologia a Patopsychologia Dietata,* 38, 161-174.

Rice, P.L. (2000). Death in birth: The cultural construction of stillbirth, neonatal death and maternal death among Hmong women in Australia. *Omega: Journal of Death and Dying*, 41, 39-57.

Richins, M.L. (1997). Measuring emotions in the consumption experience. *Journal of Consumer Behavior*, 24, 127-146

Ridley, D.S. & Walther, B. (1995). *Creating Responsible Learners: The Role of a Positive Classroom Environment.* Washington DC: American Psychological Association.

Riedel, B.W., Robinson, L.A., Klesges, R.C. & McLain-Allen, B. (2002). What motivates adolescent smokers to make a quit attempt? *Drug and Alcohol Dependence*, 68, 167-174.

Riedel, B.W., Robinson, L.A., Klesges, R.C. & McLain-Allen, B. (2003). Ethnic differences in smoking withdrawal effects among adolescents. *Addictive Behaviors*, 28, 129-140.

Riva, G. & Galimberti, C. (Eds.). (2001). *Towards Cyberpsychology: Mind, Cognition and Society in the Internet Age*, 229-252. Amsterdam: Netherland Antilles: IOS Press.

Rivera, R. M. Baños, Arbona, C. Botella; Perpiña, C., Castellano, S.Q. (2001). Tratamiento mediante realidad virtual para la fobia a volar: un estudio de caso. *Clinica y Salud,* 12, 391-404.

Robb, A.S. & Dadson, M.J. (2002). Eating disorders in males. *Child and Adolescent Psychiatric Clinics of North America*, 11, 399-418.

Roberts, S., Black, C. & Todd, K. (2002). The living with cancer education programme: II evaluation of an Australian education and support programme for cancer patients and their family and friends. *European Journal of Cancer Care,* 11, 280-289.

Robinson, M.D. & Johnson, J.T. (1996). Recall memory, recognition memory, and the eyewitness confidence-accuracy correlation. *Journal of Applied Psychology*, 81, 587-594.

Rodin, J. (1976). Density, perceived choice and response in controllable and uncontrollable outcomes. *Journal of Experimental Social Psychology,* 12, 564-578.

Rodin, J. (1985). The applications of social psychology. In G. Lindzey, & E. Aronson (Eds.), *Handbook of Social Psychology,* 2. New York: Random House.

Rodin, M. (1992). The social construction of premenstrual syndrome. *Social Science and Medicine*, 35, 49-56.

Rogoff, B. (1981). Schooling and the development of cognitive skills. In H.C. Triandis & A. Heron (Eds.), *Handbook of Cross-Cultural Psychology: Developmental Psychology,* 4. Boston: Allyn & Bacon.

Roper, R. (1980). Jury size and verdict consistency: "The line has to be drawn somewhere?" *Law and Society Review,* 14, 977-995.

Roper, R. & Shewan, D. (2002). Compliance and eyewitness testimony: Do eyewitnesses comply with misleading "expert pressure" during investigative interviewing? *Legal and Criminological Psychology*, 7, 155-163.

Rosen, D.H. & Crouse, E.M. (2000). The Tao of wisdom: Integration of Taoism and the psychologies of Jung, Erikson and Maslow. In P. Young-Eisendrath & M.E. Miller (Eds.), *The Psychology of Mature Spirituality: Integrity, Wisdom and Transcendence*, 120-129. New York: Brunner-Routledge.

Rosen, S., Benjamin, M., Plestin, D., El-Mofty, A. & Satti, M. (1962). Prebycusis study of a relatively noise-free population in the Sudan. *Annals of Otology, Rhinology and Laryngology*, 71, 727-743.

Rosenhan, D.L. (1973). On being sane in insane places. *Science*, 179, 250-258.

Rosenthal, R. (1976). *Experimentation Effects in Behavioral Research*. New York: Irvington.

Rosenthal, R. (1991). Teacher expectancy effects: A brief update 25 years after the Pygmalion experiment. *Journal of Research in Education*, 1, 3-12.

Rosenthal, R. (2002). Covert communication in classrooms, clinics, courtrooms and cubicles. *American Psychologist*, 57, 839-849.

Rosenthal, R. & Jacobson, L. (1968). *Pygmalion in the Classroom*. New York: Holt and Winston.

Ross, D.F., Ceci, S.J., Dunning, D. & Toglia, M.P. (1994). Unconscious transference and mistaken identity: When a witness misidentifies a familiar but innocent person. *Journal of Applied Psychology*, 79, 918-930.

Rossell, C. (1990). *The Carrot on the Stick for School Segregation Policy: Magnet Schools or Forced Busing*. Philadelphia: Temple University Press.

Rossi, P.H. & Freeman, H.E. (1989). *Evaluation*. Newburry Park: Sage.

Rossi, P.H., Lipsey, M.W. & Freeeman, H.E. (2004). *Evaluation: A Systematic Approach*. Thousand Oaks, CA: Sage.

Roszak, T. (1992). *The Voice of the Earth*. New York: Simon & Schuster.

Roszak, T. (1995). *Ecopsychology: Restoring the Earth, Healing the Mind*. New York: Sierra Press.

Roth, J. & Sheppard, B.K. (1989). The framing of disputes: An empirical test. Paper presented at the European Conference of Psychology; Amsterdam, Holland.

Rotter, J.B. (1966). Generalized expectancies for internal verses external control of reinforcement. *Psychological Manuscripts, General and Applied*, 80, 1-609.

Ruback, R.B., Begum, H.A.; Tariq, N., Kamal, A. & Pandey, J. (2002). Reactions to environmental stressors: Gender differences in the slums of Dhaka and Islamabad. *Journal of Cross-Cultural Psychology*, 33, 100-119.

Ruble, D.N., Constango, P.E. & Higgins, E.T. (1992). Social psychological foundation of mental health. In D.N. Ruble, P.R. Constanzo & M.E. Oliveri (Eds.), *The Social Psychology of Mental Health*. New York: Guilford.

Ruiz, R.J. & Pearson, A.J. (1999). Psychoneuroimmunology and preterm birth: A holistic model for obstetrical nursing practice and research. *American Journal of Maternal/Child-Nursing*, 24, 230-236.

Rule, B.G., Taylor, B.R. & Dobbs, A.R. (1987). Priming effects of heat on aggressive thoughts. *Social Cognition,* 5, 131-143.

Russell, K.M., Swenson, M.M., Skelton, A.M.& Shedd-Steele, R. (2003). The meaning of health in mammography screening for African American women. *Health Care for Women International*, 24, 27-39.

Rutter, D. (1987). *Communicating by Telephone*. Oxford, UK: Pergamon Press.

Sabini, J. (1992). *Social Psychology*. New York: Norton Publishing.

Sabini, J. (1995). *Social Psychology*, 2nd Edition. New York: Norton Publishing.

Sadler, G.B., Takahashi, M. & Nguyen, T. (2003). Japanese American women: Behaviors and attitude toward breast cancer education and screening. *Health Care for Women International*, 24, 18-26.

Saeed, K., Gater, R., Hussain, A. & Mubbashar, M. (2000). The prevalence, classification and treatment of mental disorders of native faith healers in rural Pakistan. *Social Psychiatry and Psychiatric Epidemiology*, 35, 480-485.

Saegert, S. (1982). Environment and children's mental health. Residential density and low income children. In A. Baum, & J. Singer (Eds.), *Handbook of Psychology of Health,* 2. Hillsdale, NJ: Earlbaum.

Saks, M. J. (1977). *Jury Verdicts*. Lexington, MA: Lexington Books.

Saks, M.J. (1996). The role of research in implementing the U.N. Convention on the rights of the child. *American Psychologist*, 12, 1262-1266.

Salovey, P., Mayer, J.D. & Caruso, D. (2002). The positive psychology of emotional intelligence. In C.R. Snyder & J. Shane (Eds.), *Handbook of Positive Psychology*, 159-171. London: Oxford University Press.

Sandal, G.M., Endreson, I.M., Vaernes, R.J. & Ursin, H. (1999). Personality and coping strategies during submarine missions. *Military Psychology.*

Sanders, M.S. & McCormick, E.J. (1993). *Human Factors in Engineering and Design*. New York: McGraw Hill.

Sanderson, C.A. & Darley, J.M. (2002). "I am moral but you are deterred": Differential attributions of why people obey the law. *Journal of Applied Social Psychology*, 32, 375-405.

Santana, S., Rocha, N.P.T. (2002). Que oportunidade de trabalho para o cidadão incapacitado? *Analise Psicologica*, 20, 419-431.

Santisteban, D.A., Coatsworth, J.D., Perez-Vidal, A., Kurtines, W.M., Schwartz, J.J., La Perriere, A & Szapocznik, J. (2003). Efficacy of brief strategic family therapy in modifying hispanic adolescent behavior problems and substance use. *Journal of Family Psychology*, 17, 121-133.

Santy, P.A. (1994). *Choosing the Right Stuff: The Psychological Selection of Astronauts and Cosmonauts*. Westport CT: Praeger.

Saranson, S.B. (1981). *Psychology Misdirected*. New York; Free Press.

Saunders, M.N.K. & Thornhill, A. (2003). Organisational justice, trust and the management of change: An exploration. *Personnel Review*, 32, 360-375.

Saxe, L., Cross, T. & Silverman, N. (1988). Children's mental health. *American Psychologist*, 43, 800-807.

Saywitz, K., Goodman, G.S., Nichols, E. & Moan, S.F. (1991). Children's memories of a physical examination involving genital touch: Implications for reports of child sexual abuse. *Journal of Clinical and Consulting Psychology*, 59, 682-691.

Scarpa, A. (2003). Community violence exposure in young adults. *Trauma Violence & Abuse*, 4, 210-227.

Scarpa, A., Fikretoglu, D., Bowser, F., Hurley, J.D., Pappert, C.A., Romero, N., Van Voorhees, E. (2002). Community violence exposure in university students: A replication and extension. *Journal of Interpersonal Violence,* 17, 253-272.

Scarr, S. (1987, May). Twenty years of growing up. *Psychology Today*, 26.

Scattolon, Y. (2003). "I just went on....there was no feeling better, there was no feeling worse": Rural women's experiences of living with and managing "depression". In J.M. Stoppard. & L.M. McMullen (Eds.), *Situating Sadness: Women and Depression in Social Context,* 162-182. New York: New York University Press.

Schaaf, J.M, Alexander, K.W., Goodman, G.S., Ghetti, S., Edelstein, R.S. & Castelli, P. (2002). Children's eyewitness memory: True disclosures and false reports. In B.L. Bottoms., M.B. Kovera et al. (Eds.). *Children, Social Science and the Law*, 342-377. New York: Cambridge University Press.

Scheck, B., Neufeld, P. & Dwyer, J. (2001). *Actual Innocence: When Justice Goes Wrong and How to Make it Right*. NY: Penguin Books.

Schei, V. & Rognes, J.K. (2003). Knowing me, knowing you: Own orientation and information about the opponent's orientation in negotiation. *International Journal of Conflict Management,* 14, 43-59.

Scheier, M.F. & Carver, C.S. (1992). Effects of optimism on psychological and physical well being: The benefits of being optimistic. *Current Directions in Psychological Science*, 2, 26-30.

Schmidt, R.E. (2001). Experts stress need for long term mental health treatment. Washington: Associated Press, September 26.

Schmidt, U. (2003). Aetiology of eating disorders in the 21st century: New answers to old questions. *European Child and Adolescent Psychiatry*, 12, i30-i37.

Schmuck, P. (2003). The future of industrial civilization: Are there ways out of the global crisis? *Peace & Conflict: Journal of Peace Psychology*, 9, 181-183.

Schober, M.F. (1993). Spatial perspective taking in conversation. *Cognition*, 47, 1-24.

Schofield, J.W. (1995). *Computers and Classroom Culture*. New York: Cambridge University Press.

Schulteis, M.T. & Rizzo, A.A. (2001). The application of virtual reality technology in rehabilitation. *Rehabilitation Psychology*, 46, 296-311.

Schultz, D.P. & Schultz, S.E. (1996). *A History of Modern Psychology*. Fortworth, TX: Harcourt Brace.

Schultz, P.W. & Oskamp, S. (1996). Effort as a moderator of the attitude-behavior relationship: General environmental concern and recycling. *Social Psychological Quarterly*, 59, 375-383.

Schultz, R. (1976). Effects of control and predictability on the physical and psychological well-being of the institutionalized aged. *Journal of Personality and Social Psychology*, 33, 563-573.

Schumaker, J.F. (1992). Introduction. In J. Schumaker (Ed.), *Religion and Mental Health*. New York: Oxford University Press.

Schwartz, B. (1994). *The Costs of Living: How Market Freedom Erodes the Better Things in Life*. New York: W. W. Norton.

Schwartz, K. (2002). Exploring family dynamics: Eating attitudes and behaviors; a qualitative analysis of female children of Holocaust survivors. *Dissertation Abstracts International: Section B: The Sciences and Engineering*, 62(9B), 4236.

Schwartz, R. (1976). Effect of control and predictability on the physical and psyhological well-being of the institutionalized aged. *Journal of Personality and Social Psychology*, 33, 563-573.

Schwartz, S.H. (1970). Moral decision making and behavior. In J. Macauly & L. Berkowitz (Eds.), *Altruism and Helping Behavior*. New York: Academic Press.

Schwartz, S.H. (1977). Normative influence on altruism. In L. Berkowitz (Ed.), *Advances in Experimental Social Psychology*, 10. New York: Academic Press.

Schwebel, M. (1993). What makes the peace movement: Psychological factors in historical perspectives. In V.K. Kool (Ed.), *Non-violence: Social and psychological Issues*. Lanham MD: University Press of America.

Schweitzer, M.E. & Gomberg, L.E. (2001). The impact of alcohol on negotiator behavior: Experimental evidence. *Journal of Applied Social Psychology*, 31, 2095-2126.

Scott, G., Ciarrochi, J. & Deane, F.P. (2004). Disadvantages of being an individualist in an individualistic culture: Idiocentrism, emotional competence, stress, and mental health. *Australian Psychologist*, 39, 143-153.

Scott, J.P. & Ginsburg, B.E. (1994). The Seville statement on violence revisited. *American Psychologist*, 49, 849-850.

Sculer, D.B. (1990). Effects of family mobility on student achievement. *ERS Spectrum*, 6, 17-24.

Sefa, B. & Solmaz, B. (2003). Quick Trauma Assessment with Sefa Bulut Children—Post Traumatic Stress Disorder Screening Survey: After a Natural Disaster in Different Groups in Two Different Countries. *Tohoku Psychologica Folia*, 62, 13-23.

Seligman, M.E.P. (1975). *Helplessness: On Depression, Development and Death*. San Francisco: Freeman Press.

Seligman, M.E.P. (1998, October). What is the "good life"? *APA Monitor*, 29, 2.

Seligman, M.E.P. (2003). Positive psychology: Fundamental assumptions. *Psychologist*, 16, 126-127.

Seligman, M.E.P., Peterson, C., Kaslow, N.J., Tannenbaum, R.L., Alloy, L.B. & Abramson, L.Y. (1984). Attributional style and depressive symptoms among children. *Journal of Abnormal Psychology*, 93, 235-238.

Selye, H. (1956). *The Stress of Life*. New York: McGraw Hill.

Sen Gupta, N. (2002). A small boot that pinches Indians. New Delhi: *The Economic Times*, 17th May.

Sen, M. (1993). Non-violence: An emprical study in India. In V.K. Kool (Ed.), *Non-violence: Social and Psychological Issues*. Lanham MD: University Press of America.

Sensales, G. & Greenfield, P.M. (1995). Attitudes toward computers, science and technology: A cross-cultural comparison between students in Rome and Los Angeles. *Journal of Cross-Cultural Psychology*, 26, 229-242.

Shannon, S. (Ed) (2002). *Handbook of Complementary and Alternative Therapies in Mental Health*. San Diego: Academic.

Shapiro, A. & Taylor, M. (2002). Effects of a community based intervention program on the subjective well-being, institutionalization and mortality of low income elders. *Gerontologist*, 42, 334-341.

Shapiro, E. (1995). Restoring habitats, communities, and souls. In T. Roszak, M.E. Gomes, and A.D. Kanner (Eds.), *Ecopsychology: Restoring the Earth Healing the Mind*. San Francisco: Sierra Club Books.

Sharan, S. & Sharan, Y. (1976). *Small Group Teaching*. Englewood Cliffs NJ: Educational Technology.

Shaver, P., Lenauner, M. & Sadds, S. (1980). Religiousness, conversion, and subjective well-being: The healthy minded religion of modern American women. *American Journal of Psychiatry*, 137, 1563-1568.

Shedler, J., Mayman, M. & Manis, M. (1993). The illusion of mental health. *American Psychologist*, 48, 1117-1131.

Sherif, M. (1937). An experimental approach to the study of attitudes. *Sociometry*, 1, 90-98.

Sherif, M., & Sherif, C. (1953). *Groups in Harmony and Tension*. New York: Harper and Row.

Shiloh, S., Berkenstadt, N., Meiram, M., Bot-Miriam-Katz, N. & Goldman, B. (1997). Mediating effects of percieved control in coping with a death threat: The case of genetic counseling. *Journal of Applied Social Psychology*, 27, 1146-1174.

Shoemaker, D.J., South, D.R. & Love, T. (1973). Facial stereotyping deviant behavior and judgments of guilt or innocence. *Social Forces*, 51, 427-433.

Sicalides, E.I. (2002). Expressive and instrumental personality traits, racial identity attitudes, and physical appearance among White female undergraduate and graduate students. *Dissertation Abstracts International Section A: Humanities and Social Sciences*, 62, 4076.

Signorielli, L. & Lears, M. (1992). Children, television, and conceptions about chores: Attitudes and behaviors. *Sex Roles*, 27, 157-170.

Silver, M. (1995, September 11). Sex and violence on television. *US News and World Report*, 62-68.

Simonson, I., Carmon, Z., Dhar, R., Drolet, A. & Nowlis, S.M. (2001). Consumer research: In search of identity. *Annual Review of Psychology*, 52, 248-275.

Simpson, M.R. (2001). 'God healed me': Religious responses to events in the cancer trajectory of breast cancer survivors in central Appalachia. *Dissertation Abstracts International:Section B: The Sciences and Engineering*, 62, 2667.

Sinclair, A.L. (2003). The Effects of Justice and Cooperation on Team Effectiveness. *Small Group Research*, 34, 74-100.

Singer, J.L. (1977). Television, imaginative play and cognitive development: Some problems and possibilities. Paper presented at the Meeting of the American Psychological Association, San Francisco.

Singer, J.L. (1990). Repression and Dissociation: Implications for Personality, Theory, Psychopathology, and Health. Chicago: University of Chicago Press.

Singh, K., Leong, S.M., Tan, C.T. & Wong, K.C. (1995). A theory of reasoned action and action perspective of voting behavior: Model of empirical test. *Psychology and Marketing*, 12, 37-51.

Siu, N.Y. & Cheng, M.M. (2001). A study of the expected adoption of online shopping: The case of Hong Kong. *Journal of International Consumer Marketing*, 13, 87-106.

Skinner, B.F. (1938). *The Behavior of Organisms*. New York: Appleton Century.

Skinner, B.F. (1971). *Beyond Freedom and Dignity*. New York: Alfred Knopf.

Skinner, B.F. (1974). *About Behaviorism*. New York: Alfred A. Knopf.

Skinner, B.F. (1986). What is wrong with daily life in the western world. *American Psychologist*, 5, 568-574.

Skinner, B.F. (1987). Whatever happened to psychology as a science of behavior? *American Psychologist*, 42, 8, 780-786.

Slavin, R.E. & Madden, N. (1994). Pieces of the puzzle: The jigsaw method. In S. Sharan (Ed.), *Handbook of Cooperative Learning Methods*. Westport: Greenwood.

Sleek, S. (1995, July). Consumers can share the good life. *American Psychological Association Monitor,* 9-10.

Sleek, S. (1999). Many Eyewitnesses Identify Wrong Person. *APA Monitor*, 4.

Smith, P.B. & Bond, M.H. (1999). *Social Psychology across Cultures*. Needham Heights: Allyn and Bacon.

Smith, A.D., Sturza, M.L., Livsey, S.E., McCarthy, C. & Davidson, W.S. II (2003). Wither context: A review of recent publications regarding youth violence and aggression. *Journal of Adolescence*, 26, 381-384.

Smith, B.W., Pargament, K.I., Brant, C.R. & Oliver, J.M. (2000). Noah revisited: Religious coping by church members and the impact of the 1993 Midwest flood. *Journal of Community Psychology*, 28, 169-186.

Smith, J., Borchelt, M., Maier, H. & Jopp, D. (2002). Health and well being in the young old and oldest old. *Journal of Social Issues*, 58, 715-732.

Smith, M.J. (1988). Electronic performance monitoring of the workplace: Part of a new industrial revolution. *Human Factors*, 31-2. 1-3.

Smith, P.B. & Bond, M.H. (1993). *Social Psychology across Cultures*. New York: Harvester-Wheatsheaf.

Smith, S. (1969). Studies in small groups in confinement. In J.P. Zubek (Ed.), *Sensory Deprivation: 15 Years of Research*, 374-409. New York: Appleton-Century-Crofts.

Smith, S.C., Ellis, J.B. & Benson, T.A. (2001). Gender, gender roles and attitudes towards violence: Are viewpoints changing? *Social Behavior & Personality*, 29, 43-47.

Smith, V.L. (1991). Prototypes in the courtroom: Lay representatives of legal concepts. *Journal of Personality and Social Psychology*, 61, 857-872.

Snibbe, A.C. & Markus, H.R. (2002). The psychology of religion and the religion of psychology. *Psychological Inquiry*, 13, 229-234.

Snyder, M. (1992). Motivational foundations of behavioral confirmation. In M.P. Zanna (Ed.), *Advances in Experimental Social Psychology, 25*. San Diego: Academic Press.

Snyder, M. & Swann, W.B. (1978). Hypothesis testing procedures in social interaction. *Journal of Personality and Social Psychology*, 36, 1202-1212.

Solomon, G.F. (2002). The development and history of psychoneuroimmunology. In H.G. Koenig and H.J. Cohen (Eds.). *The Link between Religion and Health: Psychoimmunology and the Faith Factor*, 31-42. London: Oxford University Press.

Solomon, R.M. & Horn, J.M. (1986). Post-shooting traumatic reactions: A pilot study. In J.T. Reese & H.A. Goldstein (Eds.), *Psychological Services for Law Enforcement*. Washington DC: US Government Publishing Office.

Sonderegger, R. & Barrett, P.M. (2004). Patterns of cultural adjustment among young migrants to Australia. *Journal of Child & Family Studies,* 13, 341-356.

Song, C. (2001). Anxiety and the immune system: The modulation of benzodiazepines. *Stress and Health*, 17, 129-131.

Soskolne, V. & Shtarkshall, R.A. (2002). Migration and HIV prevention programmes: Linking structural factors, culture, and individual behavior—An Israeli experience. *Social Science and Medicine*, 55, 1297-1307.

Spacapan, S. & Oskamp, S. (Eds.) (1990). *People's Reaction to Technology*. Newberry Park: Sage Publications.

Sparks, K., Faragher, B. & Cooper, C.L. (2001). Well being and occupational health in the 21st century workplace. *Journal of Occupational & Organizational Psychology*, 74, 489-509.

Spiegel, D. & Fawzy, F.I. (2002). Psychosocial interventions and prognosis in cancer. In Koenig, H.G. & Cohen, H.J. (2002). *The Link between Religion and Health: Psychoneuroimmunology and the Faith Factor*, 84-100. London: Oxford University Press.

Spiegel, D., Bloom, J.R., Kraemer, H.C. & Gottheil, E. (1989). Effect of psychosocial treatment on survival of patients with meta-static breast cancer. *Lancet*, 2, 888-891.

Spilka, B., Hood, R.W. Jr. & Gorsuch, R.L. (1985). *The Psychology of Religion: An Empirical Approach*. Englewood Cliffs, NJ: Prentice-Hall.

Spirig, R. (2002). In invisibility and isolation: The experience of HIV-affected families in German-speaking Switzerland. *Qualitative Health Research,* 12, 1323-1337.

Sporer, S.L. (2001). The cross-race effect: Beyond recognition of faces in the laboratory. *Psychology, Public Policy, & Law,* 7, 170-200.

Srivastava, R (2002). Some cheer for gloomy juvenile homes. *The Times of India*. New Delhi, 8th July.

Staats, H., van Leeuwen, E. & Wit, A. (2000). A longitudinal study of informational interventions to save energy in an office building. *Journal of Applied Behavior Analysis*, 33, 101-104.

Stack, S. (1992). Religiosity, depression and suicide. In J. Schumaker (Ed.), *Religion and Mental Health*. New York: Oxford University Press.

Stake, J.E. (1983). Factors in reward distribution: Allocation, motive, gender, and Protestant ethics. *Journal of Personality and Social Psychology*, 44, 410-418.

Stamm, B.H. (2003). Bridging the rural-urban divide with telehealth and telemedicine. In B.H. Stamm (Ed.), *Rural Behavioral Health Care: An Interdisciplinary Guide,* 145-155.

Staples, S.L. (1996). Human response to environmental noise. *American Psychologist*, 2, 143-150.

Starbuck, E.D. (1937). Religion's use of me. In V. Fern (Ed.), *Religion in Transition*. New York: McMillan.

Staub, E. (2003). Notes on cultures of violence, cultures of caring and peace, and the fulfillment of basic human needs. *Political Psychology,* 24, 1-21.

Steffen, P.R., Hinderliter, A. L., Blumenthal, J. A. & Sherwood, A. (2001). Religious coping, ethnicity, and ambulatory blood pressure. *Psychosomatic Medicine*, 63, 523-530.

Steiner, H., Kwan, W., Shaffer, T.G., Walker, S., Miller, S., Sagar, A. & Lock, J. (2003). Risk and protective factors for juvenile eating disorders. *European Child and Adolescent Psychiatry*, 12, i38-i46.

Stephan, C. & Tuly, J.C. (1977). The influence of physical attractiveness of a plaintiff on the decision of simulated jurors. *Journal of Social Psychology*, 101, 149-150.

Stephan, W.G. (1978). School desegregation: An evaluation of predictions made in Brown v. Board of education. *Psychological Bulletin*, 85, 217-238.

Steptoe, A., Wardle, J., Cui, W., Baban, A., Glass, K., Polzer, K., Tsuda, A. & Vinck, J. (2002). An international comparison of tobacco smoking beliefs and risk awareness in university students from 23 countries. *Addiction,* 97, 1561-1571.

Stern, P.C. & Oskamp, S. (1987). Managing scarce environmental resources. In D. Stokols & I. Altman (Eds.), *Handbook of Environmentel Psychology*, 2, 1043-1088.

Stern, P.C. (1992). Psychological dimensions of global environmental change. *Annual Review of Psychology,* 43, 269-302.

Sternberg, R., Wagner, R.K. & Okargac, L. (1993). Preschool intelligence: The nature and role of tacit knowledge in work and at school. In H. Reese & J. Puckett (Eds.), *Advances in Lifespan Development*. Hillsdale, NJ: Earlbaum.

Sternberg, R., Wagner, R.K., Williams, W. & Horvath, J. (1995). *Testing commonsense. American Psychologist,* 11, 912-927.

Stevens, R. & Slavin, R. (1995). The cooperative elementary school: Effects on students' achievement, attitudes and social relations. *American Educational Research Journal*, 32, 321-351.

Stevenson, H.W. & Lee, S.Y. (1990). *Context of Achievement*. Monograph of the Society of Research in Child Development, 55, (1-2, serial no. 221).

Stevenson, H.W. & Stigler, J.W. (1992). *The Learning Gap*. New York: Simon & Schuster.

Stokols, D. (1995). The paradox of environmental psychology. *American Psychologist*, 10, 821-837.

Stokols, D. (2000). Theory development in environmental psychology: A prospective view. In S. Wapner & J.Demick. et al. (Eds.) *Theoretical Perspectives in Environment-Behavior Research,* 269-276. Dordrecht: Kluwer Academic.

Storms, M.D. & Nisbett, R.E. (1970). Insomnia and the attributions of process. *Journal of Personality and Social Psychology,* 16, 319-328.

Stough, L.M. (2003). Special Education and Severe Disabilities in Costa Rica: Developing Inclusion in a Developing Country. *Research & Practice for Persons with Severe Disabilities,* 28, 7-15.

Stowell, J.R., McGuire, L., Robles, T., Glaser, R., Kiecolt-Glaser, J.K. (2003). Psychoneuroimmunology. In A.M. Nezu, C. Maguth et al., (Eds.), *Handbook of Psychology: Health Psychology*, 9, 75-95. New York: Wiley.

Strawbridge, W.J., Cohen, R.D. & Shema, S.J. (2000). Comparative strength of association between religious attendance and survival. *International Journal of Psychiatry in Medicine*, 30, 299-308.

Strohmetz, D.B., Rind, B., Fisher, R. & Lynn, M. (2002). Sweetening the till: The use of candy to increase restaurant tipping. *Journal of Applied Social Psychology*, 32, 300-309.

Struckman-Johnson, D., & Struckman-Johnson, C. (1996). Can you say no to condoms. *Journal of Applied Social Psychology,* 26, 1068-1083.

Struve, J.K. (2001). The future of the church as a primary health place. *Journal of Religious Gerontology*, 13, 17-24.

Subrahmanyan, S. & Cheng, P.S. (2000). Perceptions and attitudes of Singaporeans toward genetically modified food. *Journal of Consumer Affairs*, 34, 269-290.

Sudfeld, P. & Ikard, F.F. (1974). The use of sensory deprevation in facilitating the reduction of cigarette smoking. *Journal of Consulting and Clinical Psychology*, 42, 888-895.

Suedfeld, P. (1987). Extreme and unusual environments. In D. Stokols & I. Altman (Eds.), *Handbook of Environmental Psychology*, 1, 863-886. New York: Wiley.

Suedfeld, P. (1990). Leadership and group behavior in ICE. Presented to Astronaut Candidate Class, Johnson Space Center, Houston.

Suedfeld, P. & Steele, D.G. (2000). The environmental psychology of capsule habitats. *Annual Review of Psychology*, 51, 227-253.

Suh, E.M. (2002). Culture, identity consistency and subjective well-being. *Journal of Personality and Social Psychology*, 83, 1378-1391.

Suhail, K. & Nisa, Z. (2002). Prevalence of eating disorders in Pakistan: Relationship with depression and body shape. *Eating and Weight Disorders*, 7, 131-138.

Suldo, S.M. & Huebner, E.S. (2004). Does life satisfaction moderate the effects of stressful life events on psychopathological behavior during adolescence? *School Psychology Quarterly*, 19, 93-105.

Sullivan, C.F. (2003). Gendered cybersupport: A thematic analysis of two online cancer support groups. *Journal of Health Psychology*, 8, 83-103.

Sun, Y. & Croyle, R.T. (1995). Level of health threat as a moderation of social comparison preferences. *Journal of Applied Social Psychology*, 25.

Sussman, S., Dent, C.W. & Stacy, A.W. (1996). The relation of pro-drug use myth with self-reported drug use among youth in high school. *Journal of Applied Social Psychology*, 26, 2014-2037.

Sutherland, R., Gross, J. & Hayne, H. (1996). Adult's understanding of young children's testimony. *Journal of Applied Psychology*, 81, 777-785.

Sweeney, L.T. & Haney, C. (1992). The influence of race on stereotyping: A meta-analytic review of experimental studies. *Science and the Law*, 10, 179-195.

Sweetening the till: The use of candy to increase restaurant tipping. *Journal of Applied Social Psychology*, 32, 300-309.

Szczupal, B. (2004). Rehabilitation through hypotherapy of children with various developmental problems. *Annuntiatus,* 17, 2.

Tacon, A.M. (2003). Meditation as a complementary therapy in cancer. *Family and Mental Health*, 26, 64-73.

Tafa, E. & Manolitsis, G. (2003). Attitudes of Greek parents of typically developing kindergarten children towards inclusive education. *European Journal of Special Needs Education*, 18, 155-171.

Takata, Y. & Sakata, Y. (2004). Development of a psychosomatic complaints scale for adolescents. *Psychiatry & Clinical Neurosciences*, 58, 3-7.

Talen, E. (2000). Measuring the public realm: A preliminary assessment of the link between public space and sense of community. *Journal of Architectural and Planning Research*, 17, 344-360.

Tambashe, B. Oleko, Speizer, Ilene S., Amouzou, Agbessi, Djangone, A.M. Rachelle (2003). Evaluation of the PSAMAO "Roulez Protégé" mass media campaign in Burkina Faso. *AIDS Education and Prevention,* 15, 33-48.

Tamney, J.B. (1992). Religion and self-actualization. In J. Schumaker (Ed.), *Religion and Mental Health*. New York: Oxford University Press.

Tangney, J.P. (2002). Humility. In C.R. Snyder & J. Shane (Eds.), *Handbook of Positive Psychology,* 411-419. London: Oxford University Press.

Tanner, L. (2002). Depression treatment in US soared over 10 year period. Chicago: Associated Press, 8th January.

Tarakeshwar, N., Swank, A.B., Pargament, K.I. & Mahoney, A. (2001). The sanctification of nature and theological conservatism: A study of opposite correlates of environmentalism. *Review of Religious Research,* 42, 387-404.

Tavris, C. (1989). *Anger: The Misunderstood Emotion*. Simon & Schuster.

Taylor, C.Z. (2002). Religious addiction: Obsession with spirituality. *Pastoral Psychology*, 50, 291-315.

Taylor, D.M. & Moghaddam, F.M. (1994). *Theories of Intergroup Relations: International Social Psychological Perspectives*. Westport: Praeger.

Taylor, R.B. (2002). Crime prevention through environmental design (CPTED): Yes, no, maybe, unknowable, and all of the above. In R.B. Bechtel & A. Churchman (Eds.), *Handbook of Environmental Psychology*, 413-426. New York: Wiley.

Taylor, R.B. & Lanni, J.C. (1981). Territorial dominance: The influence of residential advantage in triadic decision making. *Journal of Personality and Social Pscyhology*, 41, 909-915.

Taylor, R.J. & Chatters, L.M. (1988). Church members as a source of informal social support. *Review of Religious Research*, 30, 193-203.

Taylor, S. & Todd, P. (1997). Understanding the determinants of consumer composting behavior. *Journal of Applied Social Psychology*, 27, 602-628.

Taylor, S.E. (1989). *Positive Illusions: Creative Self Deception and the Healthy Mind*. New York: Basic Books.

Taylor, S.E. (1995). *Health Psychology*. New York: McGraw-Hill.

Taylor, S.E., Lichman, R.R., & Wood, J.V. (1984). Attribution beliefs about control and adjustment to breast cancer. *Journal of Personality and Social Psychology*, 46, 489-502.

Teich, I. (2002). A marketing perspective of donation attitudes and intentions: An analysis of selected factors which may impact alumni contributions. *Dissertation Abstracts International Section A: Humanities and Social Sciences*, 62 (7A), 2489.

Tenant, N. (2002). The future of cloning: On the possibility of serial immortality. In J.H. Fetzer (Ed.). *Consciousness Evolving*. Amsterdam: John Benjamins, 223-237.

Tenery, R.M., Jr. (2000). "Gifts to physicians from the pharmaceutical industry": Reply. *Journal of the American Medical Association*, 283, 2657-2658.

Teo, T.S.H. (2002). Attitudes toward online shopping and the internet. *Behavior and Information Technology*, 21, 259-271.

Terhune-Young, M. (2001). The personal mythology of a shaman/healer. *Dissertation Asbstracts International: Section B: The Sciences and Engineering*, 62, 2947.

The Seville statement on violence (1984). *American Psychologist,* 49, 845-846.

The Times of India (2001). The Rules of Engagement, *Ascent*, 1.

The Times of India (2001). Would you pass the e-mail test? New Delhi, 2nd May.

The Times of India (2002). Boys too are victims of eating disorders, says PGI doctor. New Delhi, 4th June.

The Times of India (2002). Buddhism's dialogue with science. New Delhi, 7th October.

The Times of India (2002). Credit remains a dirty word in Indian Psyche. New Delhi, 3rd July.

The Times of India (2002). Gadgets that can help find children. New Delhi, 3rd September.

The Times of India (2002). Some cheer for gloomy juvenile homes. New Delhi, 8th July.

The Times of India (2003). Youngest in class face stress. New Delhi, 30th August.

The Times of India (2003). Zen and the art of corporate productivity. New Delhi, 6th August.

The Times of India. UK Plans to create army of robot-soldiers by 2008. New Delhi, 2nd July, 2002.

The World Health Report. (2001). Mental health: New understanding, new hope. Geneva: WHO.

Thogersen, J. (1996). Recycling and morality. A critical review of the literature. *Environment and Behavior*, 28-4, 536-558.

Thomas, J.P. & Worrall, T. (2002). Gift giving, quasi-credit and reciprocity. *Rationality & Society,* 14, 308-352.

Thomas, R.M. (2001). *Folk Psychology across Cultures*. Thousand Oaks: Sage.

Thompson, C. et al. (1998) *Eyewitness Memory: Theoretical and Applied Perspectives*. Mahwah, NJ: Lawrence Erlbaum Associates.

Thompson, C.E., Murry, S.L., Harris, D., Annan, J.R. (2003). Healing inside and out: Promoting social justice and peace in a racially divided U.S. community. *International Journal for the Advancement of Counselling*, 25, 215-223.

Thompson, K.E., Hazinis, W. & Alekos, P.J. (1994). Attitudes and food choice behavior. *British Food Journal*, 96 (11), 9-13.

Thoresen, C.E. & Harris, A.H.S. (2002). Spirituality and health: What's the evidence and what's needed. *Annals of Behavioral Medicine*, 24, 3-13.

Thurstone, L.L. & Chave, E.J. (1929). *The Measurement of Attitudes*. Chicago: University of Chicago Press.

Thurstone, T.G. cf Bashaw, W.L. & Bashaw, C.T. (1988). Thelma Gwinn Thurstone: Career strategies and contributions to measurement. *Psychology of Women Quarterly*, 12, 341-356.

Tiger, L. (1979). *Optimism: The Biology of Hope*. New York: Simon & Schuster.

Tinsley, C.H., O'Connor, K.M. & Sullivan, B.A. (2002). Tough guys finish last: The perils of a distributive reputation. *Organizational Behavior & Human Decision Processes*, 88, 621-642.

Tix, A.P. & Frazier, P.A. (1998). The use of religious coping during stressful life events: Main effects, moderation and mediation. *Journal of Consulting and Clinical Psychology*, 66, 411-422.

Toch, H. (1992). *Violent Men*. Washington DC: American Psychological Association.

Tomes, H. (2003). Keeping mental health on the front burner. *Monitor on Psychology*, 34, 54.

Tornatzky, L.G. (1989). Technological change and the structure of work. In J. Hackman, L.W. Hoffman, R.H. Moos, S.H. Osipow, & L.G. Tornatzky (Eds.), *Psychology and Work: Productivity, Change and Employment*. Washington DC: American Psychological Association.

Torney-Purta, J. (2002). The school's role in developing civic engagement: A study of adolescents in twenty-eight countries. *Applied Developmental Science*, 6, 203-212.

Townsend, A.M., Demarie, S.M. & Hendrickson, A.R. (2001). Desktop video-conferencing in virtual workgroups: Anticipation, system evaluation and performance. *Information Systems Journal*, 11, 213-226.

Tozzi, F., Sullivan, P.F., Fera, J.L., McKenzie, J. & Bulik, C.M. (2003). Causes and recovery in anorexia nervosa: The patient's perspective. *International Journal of Eating Disorders*, 33, 243-154.

Triandis, H.C. (1994). *Culture and Social Behavior*. New York: McGraw-Hill.

Trimmel, M. & Bachmann, J. (2004). Cognitive, social, motivational and health aspects of students in laptop classrooms. *Journal of Computer Assisted Learning*, 20, 151-158.

Triplett, N. (1987). The dynomagenic factors in pace making competition. *American Journal of Psychology*, 9, 507-533.

Trocchia, P.J. & Janda, S. (2000). A phenomenological investigation of internet usage among older individuals. *Journal of Consumer Marketing*, 17, 605-616.

Trubisky, P. Ting-Toomey, S. & Lin, S. (1991). The influence of individualism, collectivism and self-monitoring on conflict styles. *International Journal of Intercultural Relations,* 15, 65-84.

Tse, A.C.B. & Lee, R.P.W. (2001). Zapping during commercial breaks. *Journal of Advertising Research*, 41, 25-29.

Tse, D.K. & Belk, R.W. & Zhou, N. (1991). Becoming a consumer society: A longitudinal analysis of print advertisements from Hong Kong, the people's Republic of China and Taiwan. *Journal of Consumer Research*, 15, 179-201.

Tukey, J. W. (1977). *Exploring Data Analysis*. Reading: Addison Wesley.

Turnage, J.J. (1990). The challenge of new workplace technology for psychology. *American Psychologist*, 2, 171-178.

Turner, N., Barling, J. & Zacharatos, A. (2002). Positive psychology at work. In C.R. Snyder & J. Shane (Eds.), *Handbook of Positive Psychology*, 715-728. London: Oxford University Press.

Turnipseed, D.L. (2003). Hardy personality: A potential link with organizational citizenship behavior. *Psychological Reports*, 93, 529-543.

Tversky, A. & Kahneman, D. (1974). Judgement under uncertainty: Heuristics and biases. *Science*, 185, 1124-1131.

Tversky, A. & Kahneman, D. (1981). The framing of decisions and the psychology of choice. *Science,* 211, 453-458.

Tweed, R.G. & Lehman, D.R. (2002). Learning considered within a cultural context: Confucian and Socratic approaches. *American Psychologist*, 57, 89-99.

Tyson, G.A. & Hubert, C.J. (2000). Australian adolescents' explanation of juvenile delinquency. *Journal of Psychology*, 52, 119-124.

Tyson, G.A. & Hubert, C.J. (2002). Cultural differences in adolescents' explanation of juvenile delinquency. *Journal of Cross-Cultural Psychology*, 33, 450-463.

Urban, J.M., Weaver, J.L., Bowens, C.A. & Rhodenizer, L. (1996). Effects of workload and performance: Implications for complex team decision making. *Human Factors*, 38-2, 300-310.

Ursin, H., Bergan, T., Collet, J., Endreson, I.M. et al. (1991). Psychobiological studies of individuals in small, isolated groups in the Antarctic and in space analogs. *Environment and Behavior*, 23, 766-781.

Valdes Diaz, M.& Arroyo Serrano, M.C. (2002). Coping strategies and anxiety: Preliminary survey on a sample of women with eating disorders. *Ansiedad y Estres*, 8, 49-58.

Valentine, T., Harris, N., Piera, A.C., Darling, S. (2003). Are police video identifications fair to African-Caribbean suspects? *Applied Cognitive Psychology*, 17, 459-476.

Valkenburg, P.M. & Van der Vroot, T.H.A. (1994). Influence of TV on daydreaming and creative imagination: A review of research. *Psychological Bulletin*, 116, 316-339.

Van den Bergh, B.R.H., Ackx, M. (2003). Een Nederlandse versie van Rothbarts 'Children's Behavior Questionnaire': Interne consistentie en driefactorenmodel van de subschalen. *Kind en Adolescent*, 24, 77-84.

Van Hemmert, D.A., Van de Vijver, F.J.R. & Poortinga, Y.H. (2002). The Beck Depression Inventory as a measure of subjective well-being: A cross-national study. *Journal of Happiness Studies*, 3, 257-286.

van Staden, F., Willers, V., Craffert, L., Marais, J., Fiedeldey, A., & Fiedeldey-Van Dijk, C. (2002). Concerns and reactions to environmental issues: South African respondent characteristics. *Reports from the Psychology Department, University of South Africa*, 42, 1-31.

Van Vugt, M. (2001). Community identification and moderating the impact of financial incentives in a natural social dilemma: Water conservation. *Personality and Social Psychology*, 27, 1440-1449.

Van Vugt, M. (2002). Central, individual or collective control? Social dilemma strategies for natural resource management. *American Behavioral Scientist*, 45, 783-800.

VandeCreek, L., Janus, M., Pennebaker, J.W. & Binau, B. (2002). Praying about difficult experiences as self disclosure to God. *International Journal for the Psychology of Religion*, 12, 29-39.

VandeCreek, L., Pargament, K.I., Belavich, T., Cowell, B. & Friedel, L. (1999). The unique benefits of religious support during cardiac bypass surgery. *Journal of Pastoral Care*, 53, 19-29.

VandenBos, G.R. & Bulatao, E.Q. (1996). *Violence on the Job*. Washington DC: American Psychological Association.

Venkatesan, M. (1966). The expected study of consumer behavior, conformity, and independence. *Journal of Marketing Research*, 3, 384-387.

Venkatesan, R. (2003). A holisitic way of doing business. *The Times of India*, New Delhi, 24th March.

Venkatesh, A. (1994). Gender identity in the Indian context: A socio-cultural construction of the female customer. In J.A. Costa (Ed.), *Gender issues and Consumer Behavior*, 42-62. Thousand Oaks: Sage.

Venkatesh, A. (1995). Ethnocentrism: A new paradigm to study cultural and cross-cultural consumer behavior. In J.A. Costa & G.J. Bamozy (Eds.), *Marketing in a Multicultural World*. Thousand Oaks: Sage, 26-67.

Vest, M.J., Tarnoff, K.A., Carr, J.C., Vest, J.M. & O'Brien, F.P. (2003). Factors influencing a manager's decision to discipline employees for refusal to work with an HIV/AIDS infected co-worker. *Employee Responsibilities and Rights Journal*, 15, 31-43.

Villa, R.A., van Tac, L., Muc, P.M., Ryan, S., Thuy, N.T.M., Weill, C. & Thousand, J.S. (2003). Inclusion in Vietnam: More than a decade of implementation. *Research & Practice for Persons with Severe Disabilities*, 28, 23-32.

Vining, J. & Ebreo, A. (2002). Emerging theoretical and methodological perspectives on conservation behavior. In R.B. Bechtel & A. Churchman (Eds.), *Handbook of Environmental Psychology*, 541-558. New York: Wiley.

Violanti, J.M. (1992). *Police Retirement: The Impact of Change*. Springfield, IL.: C.C. Thomas Publishers.

Violanti, J.M. (1996). *Violence toward Innocent: Police Suicide in the Workplace*. In G.R. VandenBos & E.Q. Bulatao (Eds.), *Violence on the Job*. Washington DC: American Psychological Association Publishers.

Visconti, E., Celentano, L.P., Marinaci, S., Scoppettuolo, G. & Tamburrini, E. (2002). Mother to child human immunodeficiency virus (HIV) transmission: What HIV infected women think. Our experience in Rome, Italy. *International Journal of STD and AIDS*, 13, 551-553.

Visser, A.P., Goodkin, K., Vingerhoets, A.J.J.M., Peters, A.A.W., Boon, M., Garssen, B., Fletcher, M.A. (2000). Cervical cancer: Psychosocial and psychoneuroimmunological issues. In K. Goodkin & A.P. Visser (Eds.), *Psychoneuroimmunology: Stress, Mental Disorders and Health*, 41-75. Washington DC: American Psychiatric Publishing Inc.

Vollmann, J. (2000). Gifts to physicians from the pharmaceutical industry. *Journal of the American Medical Association*, 283, 2656.

Vrij, A. (1998) "Psychological Factors in Eyewitness Testimony" In A. Memon, A. Vrij, and R. Bull, *Psychology and the Law: Truthfulness, Accuracy, and Credibility*. London: McGraw-Hill.

Vrij, A., Firmin, H.R. (2001). Beautiful thus innocent? The impact of defendants' and victims' physical attractiveness and participants' rape beliefs on impression formation in alleged rape cases. *International Review of Victimology*, 8, 245-255.

Wachtel, P. (1983). *The Poverty of Affluence: A Psychological Portrait of the American Way of Life*. New York: Free Press.

Wadsworth, M.E., Rieckmann, T., Benson, M.A., Compas, B.E. (2004). Coping and Responses to Stress in Navajo Adolescents: Psychometric Properties of the Responses to Stress Questionnaire. *Journal of Community Psychology*, 32, 391-411.

Wagner, R.V. (1993). The differential psychological effects of positive and negative approaches to praise. In V.K. Kool (Ed.*), Non-violence: Social and Psychological Issues*. Lanham MD: University Press of America.

Wagner, R.V. (2002). Peace and conflict's first response to September 11. *Peace & Conflict: Journal of Peace Psychology*, 8, 1-2.

Walberg, H.J., Schiller, D. & Haertel, G.D. (1979, November). The quiet revolution in experimental research. *Phi Delta Kappan,* 179-183.

Wallace, K.A., Bisconti, Toni L., & Bergeman, C.S. (2001). The mediational effect of hardiness on social support and optimal outcomes in later life. *Basic & Applied Social Psychology*, 23, 267-279.

Wallin, U. & Kronvall, P. (2002). Anorexia nervosa in teenagers: Change in family function after family therapy, at 2-year follow-up. *Nordic Journal of Psychiatry*, 56, 363-369.

Wallston, B.S., Alagna, S.W. & Devellis, B.M. (1983). Social support and physical health. *Health Psychology,* 2, 367-391.

Wallston, K.A., Wallston, B.S. & DeVellis, R. (1978). Development of the multidimensional health locus of control (MHLC) scales. *Health Education Monographs*, 6, 161-170.

Walters, G.D. (2001). The shaman effect in couselling clients with alcohol problems. *Alcoholism Treatment Quarterly*, 19, 31-43.

Walton, R.E. (1975). Using social psychology to create new plant culture. In M. Deutsch & H.A. Hornstein (Eds.) *Applying Social Psychology*. New Jersey: Erlbaum.

Wandersman, A. & Florin, P. (2003). Arson prevention. *American Psychologist*, 58, 441-448.

Wang, Q. & Lin, G. (2003). Sex exchange and HIV-related risk behaviors among female heroin users in China. *Journal of Drug Issues*, 33, 119-132.

Warschauer, M. (2003). *Technology and Social Inclusion: Rethinking the Digital Divide*. Cambridge: MIT Press.

Warshaw, P.R. (1980). A new model for predicting behavioral interactions: An alternative to Fishbein. *Journal of Marketing Research*, 17, 153-172.

Watkins, B. & Lask, B. (2002). Eating disorders in school-aged children. *Child and Adolescent Psychiatric Clinics of North America*, 11, 185-199.

Watson, O.M. (1985). *Proxemic Behavior: A Cross-Cultural Study*. The Hague: Mouton.

Watts, C. & Zimmerman, C. (2002). Violence against women: Global scope and magnitude. *Lancet*, 359 (9313), 1232-1237

Waysman, M., Schwarzwald, J., Solomon, Z. (2001). Hardiness: An examination of its relationship with positive and negative long-term changes following trauma. *Journal of Traumatic Stress*, 14, 531-548.

Weaver, A.J., Kline, A.E.; Samford, J.A., Lucas, L.A., Larson, D.B. & Gorsuch, R.L. (1998). Is religion taboo in psychology? A systematic analysis of research on religion in seven major American Psychological Association journals: 1991-1994. *Journal of Psychology and Christianity*, 17, 220-234.

Weibe, D.J. & Williams, P.G. (1992). Hardiness and health: A socio-physiological perspective on stress and adaptation. *Journal of Social and Clinical Psychology*, 11, 238-262.

Weil, M.M. & Rosen, L.D. (1995). The psychological impact of technology from a global perspctive: A study of technological sophistication and technophobia in university students from twenty-three countries. *Computers in Human Behavior*, 11, 95-133.

Weissberg, R.P., Kumpfer, K.L. & Seligman, M.E.P. (2003). Prevention that works for children and youth: An introduction. *American Psychologist*, 56, 425-432.

Weissberg, R.P., Walberg, H.J., O'Brien, M.U. & Kuster, C.B. (2003). *Long-term Trends in the Well-being of Children and Youth*. Washington DC: Child Welfare League of America Press.

Wells, C.V. & Kipnis, D. (2001). Trust, dependency and control in the contemporary organization. *Journal of Business & Psychology*, 15, 593-603.

Wells, G. (1987). Applied Eyewitness Testimony Research: System Variables and Estimator Variables, 139-56. In Wrightsman et al., *On the Witness Stand*. CA: Sage.

Wells, G.L. (1993). What do we know about eyewitness identification? *American Psychologist*, 48(5), 553-571.

Wells, G.L. & Luus, C.A.E. (1990). Police lineups as experiments: Social methodology as a framework for properly conducted lineups. *Personality and Social Psychology Bulletin*, 16, 106-117.

Wells, N.M. (2000). At home with nature: Effects of "greenness" on children's cognitive functioning. *Environment and Behavior*, 32, 775-795.

Wells, W.D. (1993). Discovery oriented consumer research. *Journal of Consumer Research*, 19, 489-504.

Werner, C.M., Stoll, R., Birch, P. & White, P.H. (2002). Clinical validation and cognitive elaboration: Signs that encourage sustained recycling. *Basic and Applied Social Psychology*, 24, 185-203.

Werner, N.E. & Silbereisen, R.K. Family relationship quality and contact with deviant peers as predictors of adolescent problem behaviors: The moderating role of gender. *Journal of Adolescent Research*, 18, 454-480.

Wessells, M. (1993). Psychological obstacles to peace. In V.K. Kool (Ed.*), Non-violence: Social and Psychological Issues.*

West, P.W., Brown, C.L. & Huch, S.J. (1996). Consumption vocabulary and preference formation. *Journal of Consumer Research*, 23, 120-135.

Wexler, J. (1985). Role styles of women police officers. *Sex Roles*, 12, 749-755.

Weyant, J. (1986). *Applied Social Psychology*. Oxford, England: Oxford University Press.

Whipple, T.W. & Courtney, A.K. (1985). Female role portrayals in advertising and communication effectiveness: A review. *Journal of Advertising*, 14, 4-8.

Whitehouse, S.L. (2000). Healing gardens and coping with stress at a children's hospital: A multimethod evaluation. *Dissertation Abstracts International*: *Section B*: *The Sciences and Engineering*, 60, 4259.

WHO (2001). *The World Health Report*. Mental health: New understanding, new hope. Geneva: WHO.

Wiborg, G. & Hanewinkel, R. (2002). Effectiveness of the "smoke free class competition" in delaying the onset of smoking in adolescence. *Preventive Medicine: An International Journal Devoted to Practice and Theory*, 35, 241-249.

Wickland, R.A. & Gollwitzer, P.M. (1982). *Symbolic Self-completion*. Hillsdale: Earlbaum.

Wickman, H. (1990). Human machine interaction in space flight. In S. Spacapan & S. Oskamp (Eds.), *People's Reaction to Technology*. Newberry Park: Sage Publication.

Wiesenfeld, E. & Giuliani, F. (2002). Sustainable development and identity in two Venezuelan communities. *Environment and Behavior*, 34, 81-96.

Wiesenfeld, E. & Sanchez, E. (2002). Sustained participation: A commuity based approach to addressing environmental problems. In R.B. Bechtel & A. Churchman (Eds.), *Handbook of Environmental Psychology*, 629-643. NewYork: Wiley.

Williams, D. (1997) http://www.cgjung.com/ecopsych.html

Williams, D.G., Weibe, D.J. & Smith, T.W. (1992). Coping processes as mediators between hardiness and health. *Journal of Behavioral Medicine*, 15, 237-255.

Williams, P. (1996). War without end. *Middle East*, 262, 5-6.

Williams, R.H. & Ross, M.H. (1980, March/ April). Drilling for oil and gas in our houses. *Technology Review*, 24-36.

Wills, T.A., Yaeger, A.M. & Sandy, J.M. (2003). Buffering effect of religiosity for adolescent substance use. *Psychology of Addictive Behaviors*, 17, 24-31.

Wilson, B.D.M., Hayes, E., Greene, G.J., Kelly, J.G. & Iscoe, I. (2003). Community psychology. In D.K. Freedman (Ed.), *Handbook of Psychology: History of Psychology*, 431-449. New York: Wiley.

Wilson, B.J., Smith, S.L., Potter, W. J., Kunkel, D., Linz, D., Colvin, C.M. & Donnerstein, E. (2002). Violence in children's television programming: Assessing the risks. *Journal of Communication*, 52, 5-35.

Wilson, G.D. (Ed.) (1973). *The Psychology of Conservatism*. London: Academic Press.

Winett, R.A. (1995). A framework for health promotion and disease prevention programs. *American Psychologist*, 50, 341-350.

Winter, D.D. (1996). *Ecological Psychology: Healing the Split between Planet and Self*. New York: Harper Collins.

Witmer, J.F. & Geller, E.S. (1976). Facilitating paper recycling: Effects of prompts, raffles and contests. *Journal of Applied Analysis of Behavior*, 9, 315-322.

Wolburg, J.M. & Pokrywczynski, J. (2001). A psychographic analysis of Generation Y college students. *Journal of Advertising Research*, 41, 33-52.

Wong, M.M.A. & Nunes, T. (2003). Hong Kong children's concept of distributive justice. *Early Child Development & Care*, 173, 119-129.

Wong, T.W, Chen, W., Yu, T., Lin, Y. & Cooper, C.L. (2002). Perceived sources of occupational stress among Chinese offshore oil installation workers. *Stress & Health*, 18, 217-226.

Wood, D. Bruner, J. & Ross, G. (1976). The role of tutoring in problem solving. *Journal of Child Psychiatry and Psychology*, 17, 89-100.

Wood, J.V. (1989). Theory and research concerning social comparisons of personal attributes. *Psychological Bulletin*, 106, 231-248.

Wood, W. (2000). Attitude change: Persuasion and social influence. *Annual Review of Psychology*, 51, 539-570.

World Health Organization (1979). Report. Geneva: WHO.

World Health Organization (1995). Special report. Geneva: WHO.

World Health Organization (2001). Special report. Geneva: 6th November.

World Values Study Group (1994). *World Values Survey*, 1981-1994 and 1990-1993 (computer file, ICPSR Version). Ann Arbor: Institute for Social Research.

Wright, D.B., Boyd, C.E. & Tredoux, C.G. (2001). A field study of own race bias in South Africa and England. *Psychology, Public Policy and Law*, 7, 119-133.

Wright, D.B. & Stroud, J.N. (2002). Age differences in lineup identification accuracy: People are better with their own age. *Law and Behavior*, 26, 641-654.

Wrightsman, C.S. (1991). *Psychology and the Legal System*. Belmont, CA.: Brooks/Cole Publishing.

Wuensch, K.L., Campbell, M.W., Kesler, F.C., Moore, C.H. (2002). Racial bias in decisions made by mock jurors evaluating a case of sexual harassment. *Journal of Social Psychology*, 142, 587-600.

Wulff, D.M. (1991). *Psychology of Religion.* New York: Wiley.

Wunderink; S.R. (2002). Individual financial donations to charities in the Netherlands: Why, how and how much? *Journal of Non-profit and Public Sector Marketing*, 10, 21-39.

Xu, L., Wang, X., Xie, Y. & Sun, Y. (2002). A comparative study on coping styles of male juvenile offenders. *Chinese Journal of Clinical Psychology*, 10, 313.

Yamatsuji, M., Yamashita, T., Arii, I., Taga, C., Tatara, N. & Fukui, K. (2003). Seasonal variations in eating disorder subtypes in Japan. *International Journal of Eating Disorders*, 33, 71-77.

Yap, L., Wu, Z., Liu, W., Ming, Z. & Liang, S. (2002). A rapid assessment and its implications for a needle social marketing intervention among injecting drug users in China. *International Journal of Drug Policy*, 13, 57-68.

Yep, G.A., Reece, S.T., & Negron, E.L. (2003). Culture and stigma in a bonafide group: Boundaries and context in a "Closed" support group for "Asian Americans" living with HIV infection. In L.R. Frey (Ed.), *Group Communication in Context: Studies of Bonafide Groups,* 2nd Ed., 157-180. Mahwah: Lawrence Erlbaum.

Yerkes, R. & Dodson, J. (1908) The relation of strength of stimulus to rapidity of habit-information. *Journal of Comparative Neurology and Psychology,* 18, 459-482.

Yi, Y. (2000). Social structural and social psychological factors affecting household level environment decision making: A three country comparison of determinants of household recycling behavior (Great Britain, Italy, Netherlands). *Dissertation Abstracts International Section A: Humanities and Social Sciences*, 60, 2707.

Yinger, J.M. (1969). A structural examination of religion. *Journal for the Scientific Study of Religion*, 8, 88-99.

Young, K. (1996, October). *American Psychological Association Monitor.*

Yuchtman-Yaar, E. & Gootlieb, A. (1985). Technological development and the meaning of work: A cross-cultural perspective. *Human Relations*, 38, 603-621.

Yuval, N., Guttmann-Steinmetz, S., Koenen, K., Levinovsky, L., Zakin, G. & Dekel, Rachel. Do attachment and hardiness relate to each other and to mental health in real-life stress. *Journal of Social & Personal Relationships*, 86, 844-858.

Zajonc, R.B. 91965). Social Facilitation. *Science,* 149, 269-274.

Zakin, G., Solomon, Z., Neria, Y. (2003). Hardiness, attachment style, and long-term psychological distress among Israeli POWs and combat veterans. *Personality* & *Individual Differences*, 34, 819-829.

Zamichow, N. (1996, October 26). Enjoying real life unplugged. *Los Angeles Times*, 1.

Zigler, E. & Styfco, S. (1994). Head Start: Criticisms in a constructive context. *American Psychologist*, 49, 127-132.

Zillman, D. (1969). *Emotional Arousal as a Factor in Communication Mediated Behavior.* Unpublished Doctoral Dissertation, University of Pennsylvania, Philadelphia.

Zillman, D. (1983) Disparagement humor. In P.E. McGhee & J.K. Goldstein (Eds.), *Handbook of Humor Research,* 1. New York: Springer-Verlag.

Zimbardo, P.G. (1969). The human choice: Individuation, reason, and order versus de-individuation, impulse, and choice. In W.J.A. Arnold & D. Levine (Eds.), *Nebraska Symposium on Motivation,* 17. Lincoln: University of Nebraska Press.

Zittel, K.M., Lawrence, S. & Wodarski, J.S. (2002). Biopsychosocial model of health and healing: Implications for health social work practice. *Journal of Human Behavior in the Social Environment*, 5, 19-33.

Zmud, J. & Arce, C. (1992). The ethnicity and consumption relationship. In J.F. Sherry & B. Sterthal (Eds.), *Advances in Consumer Research,* 19, 443-449. Provo: Association for Consumer Research.

Zuckerman, D.M., Kasl, S.V. & Ostfeld, A.M. (1984). Psychosocial predictors of mortality among the elderly poor: The role of religion, well-being, and social contacts. *American Journal of Epidemiology*, 119, 410-423.

NAME INDEX

SUBJECT INDEX